Communications in Computer and Information Science 1756

More information about this series at https://link.springer.com/bookseries/7899

Miguel Botto-Tobar ·
Marcelo Zambrano Vizuete ·
Sergio Montes León · Pablo Torres-Carrión ·
Benjamin Durakovic (Eds.)

Applied Technologies

4th International Conference, ICAT 2022
Quito, Ecuador, November 23–25, 2022
Revised Selected Papers, Part II

Springer

Editors
Miguel Botto-Tobar (iD)
Eindhoven University of Technology
Eindhoven, The Netherlands

Sergio Montes León (iD)
Universidad Rey Juan Carlos
Madrid, Spain

Benjamin Durakovic (iD)
International University of Sarajevo
Sarajevo, Bosnia and Herzegovina

Marcelo Zambrano Vizuete (iD)
Universidad Técnica del Norte
Ibarra, Ecuador

Pablo Torres-Carrión (iD)
Universidad Técnica Particular de Loja
Loja, Ecuador

ISSN 1865-0929 ISSN 1865-0937 (electronic)
Communications in Computer and Information Science
ISBN 978-3-031-24970-9 ISBN 978-3-031-24971-6 (eBook)
https://doi.org/10.1007/978-3-031-24971-6

This Springer imprint is published by the registered company Springer Nature Switzerland AG
The registered company address is: Gewerbestrasse 11, 6330 Cham, Switzerland

Preface

The Universidad de las Fuerzas Armadas ESPE in its 100th anniversary organized the International XVII Congress on Science and Technology and co-hosted the 4th International Conference on Applied Technologies (ICAT) in the main campus in Quito, Ecuador during November 23–25, 2022 and was organized in collaboration with GDEON. The ICAT series aims to bring together top researchers and practitioners working in different domains in the field of computer science to exchange their expertise and to discuss the perspectives of development and collaboration. The content of this volume is related to the following subjects:

- AT for Engineering Applications
- Electronics
- Knowledge Exploration in Life Sciences

ICAT 2022 received 415 submissions written in English by 1245 authors coming from 12 different countries. All these papers were peer-reviewed by the ICAT 2022 Program Committee consisting of 185 high-quality researchers. To ensure a high-quality and thoughtful review process, we assigned each paper at least three reviewers. Based on the peer reviews, 114 full papers were accepted, resulting in an 27% acceptance rate, which was within our goal of less than 40%.

We would like to express our sincere gratitude to the invited speakers for their inspirational talks, to the authors for submitting their work to this conference, and to the reviewers for sharing their experience during the selection process.

November 2022

Miguel Botto-Tobar
Marcelo Zambrano Vizuete
Sergio Montes León
Pablo Torres-Carrión
Benjamin Durakovic

Organization

General Chair

Miguel Botto-Tobar   Eindhoven University of Technology,
The Netherlands

Program Committee Chairs

Miguel Botto-Tobar   Eindhoven University of Technology,
The Netherlands

Marcelo Zambrano Vizuete   Universidad Técnica del Norte, Ecuador

Sergio Montes León   Universidad Rey Juan Carlos, Spain

Pablo Torres-Carrión   Universidad Técnica Particular de Loja, Ecuador

Benjamin Durakovic   International University of Sarajevo,
Bosnia and Herzegovina

Organizing Chairs

Miguel Botto-Tobar   Eindhoven University of Technology,
The Netherlands

Marcelo Zambrano Vizuete   Universidad Técnica del Norte, Ecuador

Sergio Montes León   Universidad Rey Juan Carlos, Spain

Pablo Torres-Carrión   Universidad Técnica Particular de Loja, Ecuador

Benjamin Durakovic   International University of Sarajevo,
Bosnia and Herzegovina

Steering Committee

Miguel Botto-Tobar   Eindhoven University of Technology,
The Netherlands

Angela Díaz Cadena   Universitat de Valencia, Spain

Program Committee

Andrea Bonci   Marche Polytechnic University, Italy

Ahmed Lateef Khalaf   Al-Mamoun University College, Iraq

Aiko Yamashita   Oslo Metropolitan University, Norway

Alejandro Donaire   Queensland University of Technology, Australia

Alejandro Ramos Nolazco	Instituto Tecnológico y de Estudios Superiores Monterrey, Mexico
Alex Cazañas	The University of Queensland, Australia
Alex Santamaria Philco	Universitat Politècnica de València, Spain
Alfonso Guijarro Rodriguez	University of Guayaquil, Ecuador
Allan Avendaño Sudario	Escuela Superior Politécnica del Litoral (ESPOL), Ecuador
Alexandra González Eras	Universidad Politécnica de Madrid, Spain
Ana Núñez Ávila	Universitat Politècnica de València, Spain
Ana Zambrano	Escuela Politécnica Nacional (EPN), Ecuador
Andres Carrera Rivera	University of Melbourne, Australia
Andres Cueva Costales	University of Melbourne, Australia
Andrés Robles Durazno	Edinburgh Napier University, UK
Andrés Vargas Gonzalez	Syracuse University, USA
Angel Cuenca Ortega	Universitat Politècnica de València, Spain
Ángela Díaz Cadena	Universitat de València, Spain
Angelo Trotta	University of Bologna, Italy
Antonio Gómez Exposito	University of Sevilla, Spain
Aras Can Onal	Tobb University Economics and Technology, Turkey
Arian Bahrami	University of Tehran, Iran
Benoît Macq	Université catholique de Louvain, Belgium
Benjamin Durakovic	International University of Sarajevo, Bosnia and Herzegovina
Bernhard Hitpass	Universidad Federico Santa María, Chile
Bin Lin	Università della Svizzera italiana (USI), Switzerland
Carlos Saavedra	Escuela Superior Politécnica del Litoral (ESPOL), Ecuador
Catriona Kennedy	University of Manchester, UK
César Ayabaca Sarria	Escuela Politécnica Nacional (EPN), Ecuador
Cesar Azurdia Meza	University of Chile, Chile
Christian León Paliz	Université de Neuchâtel, Switzerland
Chrysovalantou Ziogou	Chemical Process and Energy Resources Institute, Greece
Cristian Zambrano Vega	Universidad de Málaga, Spain, and Universidad Técnica Estatal de Quevedo, Ecuador
Cristiano Premebida	Loughborough University, ISR-UC, UK
Daniel Magües Martinez	Universidad Autónoma de Madrid, Spain
Danilo Jaramillo Hurtado	Universidad Politécnica de Madrid, Spain
Darío Piccirilli	Universidad Nacional de La Plata, Argentina
Darsana Josyula	Bowie State University, USA
David Benavides Cuevas	Universidad de Sevilla, Spain

David Blanes	Universitat Politècnica de València, Spain
David Ojeda	Universidad Técnica del Norte, Ecuador
David Rivera Espín	University of Melbourne, Australia
Denis Efimov	Inria, France
Diego Barragán Guerrero	Universidad Técnica Particular de Loja (UTPL), Ecuador
Diego Peluffo-Ordoñez	Yachay Tech, Ecuador
Dimitris Chrysostomou	Aalborg University, Denmark
Domingo Biel	Universitat Politècnica de Catalunya, Spain
Doris Macías Mendoza	Universitat Politècnica de València, Spain
Edison Espinoza	Universidad de las Fuerzas Armadas (ESPE), Ecuador
Edwin Rivas	Universidad Distrital de Colombia, Colombia
Ehsan Arabi	University of Michigan, USA
Emanuele Frontoni	Università Politecnica delle Marche, Italy
Emil Pricop	Petroleum-Gas University of Ploiesti, Romania
Erick Cuenca	Université catholique de Louvain, Belgium
Fabian Calero	University of Waterloo, Canada
Fan Yang	Tsinghua University, China
Fariza Nasaruddin	University of Malaya, Malaysia
Felipe Ebert	Universidade Federal de Pernambuco (UFPE), Brazil
Fernanda Molina Miranda	Universidad Politécnica de Madrid, Spain
Fernando Almeida	University of Campinas, Brazil
Fernando Flores Pulgar	Université de Lyon, France
Firas Raheem	University of Technology, Iraq
Francisco Calvente	Universitat Rovira i Virgili, Spain
Francisco Obando	Universidad del Cauca, Colombia
Franklin Parrales	University of Guayaquil, Ecuador
Freddy Flores Bahamonde	Universidad Técnica Federico Santa María, Chile
Gabriel Barros Gavilanes	INP Toulouse, France
Gabriel López Fonseca	Sheffield Hallam University, UK
Gema Rodriguez-Perez	LibreSoft, and Universidad Rey Juan Carlos, Spain
Ginger Saltos Bernal	Escuela Superior Politécnica del Litoral (ESPOL), Ecuador
Giovanni Pau	Kore University of Enna, Italy
Guilherme Avelino	Universidade Federal do Piauí (UFP), Brazil
Guilherme Pereira	Universidade Federal de Minas Gerais (UFMG), Brazil
Guillermo Pizarro Vásquez	Universidad Politécnica de Madrid, Spain
Gustavo Andrade Miranda	Universidad Politécnica de Madrid, Spain

Hernán Montes León	Universidad Rey Juan Carlos, Spain
Ibraheem Kasim	University of Baghdad, Iraq
Ilya Afanasyev	Innopolis University, Russia
Israel Pineda Arias	Chonbuk National University, South Korea
Jaime Meza	Université de Fribourg, Switzerland
Janneth Chicaiza Espinosa	Universidad Técnica Particular de Loja (UTPL), Ecuador
Javier Gonzalez-Huerta	Blekinge Institute of Technology, Sweden
Javier Monroy	University of Malaga, Spain
Javier Sebastian	University of Oviedo, Spain
Jawad K. Ali	University of Technology, Iraq
Jefferson Ribadeneira Ramírez	Escuela Superior Politécnica de Chimborazo, Ecuador
Jerwin Prabu	BRS, India
Jong Hyuk Park	Korea Institute of Science and Technology, South Korea
Jorge Charco Aguirre	Universitat Politècnica de València, Spain
Jorge Eterovic	Universidad Nacional de La Matanza, Argentina
Jorge Gómez Gómez	Universidad de Córdoba, Colombia
Juan Corrales	Institut Universitaire de France et SIGMA Clermont, France
Juan Romero Arguello	University of Manchester, UK
Julián Andrés Galindo	Université Grenoble Alpes, France
Julian Galindo	Inria, France
Julio Albuja Sánchez	James Cook University, Australia
Kelly Garces	Universidad de Los Andes, Colombia
Kester Quist-Aphetsi	Center for Research, Information, Technology and Advanced Computing, Ghana
Korkut Bekiroglu	SUNY Polytechnic Institute, USA
Kunde Yang	Northwestern Polytechnic University, China
Lina Ochoa	CWI, The Netherlands
Lohana Lema Moreira	Universidad de Especialidades Espíritu Santo (UEES), Ecuador
Lorena Guachi Guachi	Yachay Tech, Ecuador
Lorena Montoya Freire	Aalto University, Finland
Lorenzo Cevallos Torres	Universidad de Guayaquil, Ecuador
Luis Galárraga	Inria, France
Luis Martinez	Universitat Rovira i Virgili, Spain
Luis Urquiza-Aguiar	Escuela Politécnica Nacional (EPN), Ecuador
Maikel Leyva Vazquez	Universidad de Guayaquil, Ecuador
Manuel Sucunuta	Universidad Técnica Particular de Loja (UTPL), Ecuador
Marcela Ruiz	Utrecht University, The Netherlands

Patricia Ludeña González	Universidad Técnica Particular de Loja (UTPL), Ecuador
Paulo Batista	CIDEHUS.UÉ-Interdisciplinary Center for History, Cultures, and Societies of the University of Évora, Portugal
Paulo Chiliguano	Queen Mary University of London, UK
Pedro Neto	University of Coimbra, Portugal
Praveen Damacharla	Purdue University Northwest, USA
Priscila Cedillo	Universidad de Cuenca, Ecuador
Radu-Emil Precup	Politehnica University of Timisoara, Romania
Ramin Yousefi	Islamic Azad University, Iran
René Guamán Quinche	Universidad de los Paises Vascos, Spain
Ricardo Martins	University of Coimbra, Portugal
Richard Ramirez Anormaliza	Universitat Politècnica de Catalunya, Spain
Richard Rivera	IMDEA Software Institute, Spain
Richard Stern	Carnegie Mellon University, USA
Rijo Jackson Tom	SRM University, India
Roberto Murphy	University of Colorado Denver, USA
Roberto Sabatini	RMIT University, Australia
Rodolfo Alfredo Bertone	Universidad Nacional de La Plata, Argentina
Rodrigo Barba	Universidad Técnica Particular de Loja (UTPL), Ecuador
Rodrigo Saraguro Bravo	Universitat Politècnica de València, Spain
Ronald Barriga Díaz	Universidad de Guayaquil, Ecuador
Ronnie Guerra	Pontificia Universidad Católica del Perú, Perú
Ruben Rumipamba-Zambrano	Universitat Politecnica de Catalanya, Spain
Saeed Rafee Nekoo	Universidad de Sevilla, Spain
Saleh Mobayen	University of Zanjan, Iran
Samiha Fadloun	Université de Montpellier, France
Sergio Montes León	Universidad de las Fuerzas Armadas (ESPE), Ecuador
Stefanos Gritzalis	University of the Aegean, Greece
Syed Manzoor Qasim	King Abdulaziz City for Science and Technology, Saudi Arabia
Tatiana Mayorga	Universidad de las Fuerzas Armadas (ESPE), Ecuador
Tenreiro Machado	Polytechnic of Porto, Portugal
Thomas Sjögren	Swedish Defence Research Agency (FOI), Sweden
Tiago Curi	Federal University of Santa Catarina, Brazil
Tony T. Luo	A*STAR, Singapore
Trung Duong	Queen's University Belfast, UK
Vanessa Jurado Vite	Universidad Politécnica Salesiana, Ecuador

Waldo Orellana	Universitat de València, Spain
Washington Velasquez Vargas	Universidad Politécnica de Madrid, Spain
Wayne Staats	Sandia National Labs, USA
Willian Zamora	Universidad Laíca Eloy Alfaro de Manabí, Ecuador
Yessenia Cabrera Maldonado	University of Cuenca, Ecuador
Yerferson Torres Berru	Universidad de Salamanca, Spain and Instituto Tecnológico Loja, Ecuador
Zhanyu Ma	Beijing University of Posts and Telecommunications, China

Organizing Institutions

Sponsoring Institutions

Collaborators

Waldo Orellana
Washington Velasquez Vargas
Wayne Staats
Wilian Zamora

Yessenia Cabrera Maldonado
Yerisson Torres Berru

Zhanyu Ma

Universitat de Valencia, Spain
Universidad Politecnica de Madrid, Spain
Sandia National Labs, USA
Universidad Laica Eloy Alfaro de Manabi, Ecuador
University of Cuenca, Ecuador
Universidad de Salamanca, Spain and Instituto Tecnologico Loja, Ecuador
Beijing University of Posts and Telecommunications, China

Organizing Institutions

Sponsoring Institutions

Collaborators

Contents – Part II

Electronics

Knowledge Exploration in Life Sciences

AT for Engineering Applications

Experimental Study of Low Cycle Fatigue in Welded Reinforcing Steel Bars ASTM A706

Lenin Abatta-Jácome[✉], Carlos Naranjo-Guatemala, Daniel Naranjo-Torres, and Edison E. Haro

Departamento de Ciencias de la Energía y Mecánica, Universidad de las Fuerzas Armadas ESPE, PO BOX, 171-5-231B Sangolquí, Ecuador
{lrabatta,crnaranjo,ednaranjo3,eeharo}@espe.edu.ec

Abstract. ASTM A706 steel, used as concrete reinforcement in civil works, is often joined by overlapping or welding, this research addresses the welding joint, using the methodology proposed by AWS D1.4, static tests with an application of monotonic loads and low-cycle fatigue tests to evaluate the behavior of steel under extreme stress such as in a beam-column connection. The behavior of reinforcing steel bars of 14, 16, and 18 mm in diameter with and without welding was studied to compare the results. It is concluded that the smaller diameter bars present greater difficulty to be welded, reflecting an inadequate behavior when carrying out the destructive mechanical tests. Welded reinforcing steel bars with a larger diameter show good behavior in destructive mechanical tests, both static and cyclic, however, their use is not recommended in places of high demand since welding is directly related to compliance with the parameters of the AWS, welder, consumables, among other parameters that can affect the mechanical performance of the joint.

Keywords: Rebar · Reinforced bar · Low cycle fatigue · Weld

1 Introduction

The structural configuration has been satisfactorily studied and known; the behavior depends on the designer's ability to make earthquake-resistant designs and the materials used in the construction.

When a seismic event occurs, specific elements of the building must exhaust their capacity by bending, forming plastic hinges, dissipating energy, and producing low-cycle fatigue in the reinforcing steel, which is permanent deformation for each load cycle. Applied. According to (J.B. Mander 1994), during a seismic event, longitudinal reinforcing steel in reinforced structural concrete elements can be expected to experience large tensile and compressive strain reversals of typically one to five fully reversed amplitudes. The fracture of longitudinal reinforcing steel is due to low cycle fatigue, which is one of the prominent failure modes for bending members with or without low levels of axial loading. (J.B. Mander 1994), initially, it analyzes the static behavior of

A615 grade 40 steel, with a universal testing machine MTS 809.40 with a capacity of 250 kN, obtaining stress versus strain curves by applying a monotonic load. After obtaining the characteristic static curves, the experimental study of low-cycle fatigue with a sinusoidal load function and frequencies that ranged between 0.025 and 0.15 Hz was carried out, resulting in an average deformation rate (peak to peak) of 0.005/s for most tests. According to (Jeff 2000), who conducted a series of studies, at the University of New York, Buffalo, in his low-cycle fatigue experiment, used reinforcing bars according to the ASTM A615 grade 60.

According to (Apostolopoulos 2008), an experimental study, was carried out to evaluate the effects of the progressive accumulation of corrosion damage on the low-cycle fatigue behavior of S500s reinforcing steel bars. This experiment determined that low-cycle fatigue can satisfactorily simulate the load applied to steel reinforcement of concrete structures during seismic actions. Steel bar specimens were tested by removing the imperfections by filing, and the fatigue behavior of these specimens was compared with ordinary specimens that are widely used as concrete reinforcement. The low-cycle fatigue tests carried out indicated that the presence of protrusions considerably reduces performance under the action of cyclic loads.

A significant increase in the number of cycles to failure was also observed, as well as in the energy dissipated, while there was a reduction in the load capacity due to the decrease in section. The results indicate that the use of smooth steel bars could be considered for certain applications such as reinforced concrete frame areas, especially for structures located in seismically active areas. The material has a diameter analyzed has a nominal diameter of 12 mm. The free length of the sample between the jaws was set at six times the nominal diameter. No modification was made to the geometry of the steel bars to meet the standards for strain-controlled fatigue testing.

According to (Hawileth 2009), research work was carried out on the resistance to fatigue of low cycles in reinforcing steel bars BS 460B and B500B. It performs strain-controlled, constant-amplitude mechanical tests with a load application frequency of 0.05 Hz. The maximum applied axial strain amplitude ranges from 3 to 10%. Recording hysteresis loops and plastic amplitudes.

According to (Rocha 2014), the most critical parameter in this type of research is the clamping system of the specimen. Specimen exhaustion is related to the manufacturing process where imperfections are produced - defects that extend into the cross-section and cracks initiated by imperfections located very close to the base of the transverse ribs.

Kashani 2015, performed tension and compression testing, and the effect of inelastic buckling related to low-cycle fatigue exhaustion in reinforcing bars was investigated experimentally. The researcher performed 90 low-cycle fatigue tests on reinforcing bars with different buckling amplitudes and lengths.

The specimen includes thirty bars with a diameter of 12 mm, 16 mm, and smooth bars with a diameter of 12 mm. For each group of samples, three static tensile tests are carried out to evaluate the properties of the material. A universal testing machine was used, with hydraulic clamps of a capacity of 250 kN.

According to (Abatta 2016), who researched the behavior of reinforcing steel bars of Ecuadorian production, evaluated the behavior of the reinforcing steel bar applying loads exclusively to traction, plastically deforming for each applied load cycle, producing low-cycle fatigue.

Experimentation and numerical simulation carried out by (Pantazopoulos 2018) identified that, in reinforcing steel bars to which cyclic loads were applied, producing fatigue, several defects were associated with thermal and mechanical factors associated with the manufacture of the bar, which was observed under to the application of electron microscopy techniques and computational simulation.

Other investigations such as the one proposed by (Shwania 2019) associate the decrease in ductility of a steel-reinforced concrete structural member with the space between the welds of the reinforcing steel bars, as well as their diameter, determining a little ductility in smaller diameters.

Wire mesh reinforcements have also been studied, (Arroyo 2020), which analyzed the behavior of electro-welded steel mesh in structural walls, determining its performance in the face of seismic events, emphasizing ductility.

Researchers such as (Aldabagh 2021), analyzed the effects of low-cycle fatigue in reinforcing steel bars, considering plastic deformation in various amplitudes without machining the specimens, showing inelastic buckling in the compression loading process. However, recent research, such as the one proposed by (Luijters 2021), determined that a reinforcing steel bar embedded in concrete does not show a significant difference in fatigue resistance, applying numerical simulation techniques.

Several attempts have been made to improve the capacity of reinforcing steel bars such as the research proposed by (Li 2022) applying a metallic coating to the reinforcing steel bar, improving the fatigue capacity of steel bars and the reinforcement.

Mathematical models also have been made to predict the useful life of a reinforcing steel bar, this topic was addressed by (Gao 2022) who applied the formulation of Coffin and Manson. This experiment intended to determine the behavior and useful life of a bar that is subjected to cyclic loads producing fatigue.

The main objective of this research is to analyze, through experimental techniques, the behavior of welded reinforcing steel bars subjected to the action of cyclic loads, producing low cycle fatigue.

2 Methodology

Depending on the state of the art and considering that the three steel producers (yellow, red, white), guarantee the weldability of their products, the following types of test pieces are established in Fig. 1:

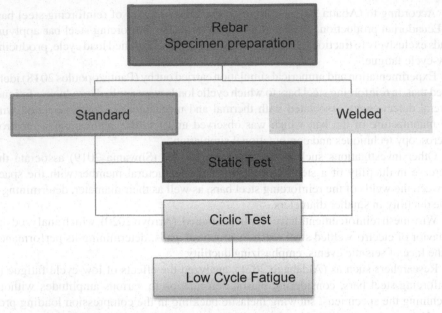

Fig. 1. Mechanical test.

A total of 126 static and cyclic tests of 3 different types of diameters (14, 16, and 18 mm) and three brands of specimen bars were carried out.

The static test was performed according to the Ecuadorian standard (INEN-0109 2009), with a load application time of around 120 s, easily programmable in the universal testing machine.

Based on similar experimentation performed before by other authors, it was established that low-cycle fatigue can be done by applying cyclic loads in traction-traction (Abatta 2016), assuming exhaustion due to the bending of simply reinforced concrete beams, which is adjusted to the technological availability.

For this investigation, a sinusoidal type function was used, which also was used by researchers (Mander 1994), (Kashani 2015) y (Abatta 2016), due to the uniformity of load application on the specimen, compared to the step function or others.

For the development of this research, a universal testing machine MTS 810 was used for programming both the frequency and the load function. The experimentation is carried out under force control, preventing the specimen from losing adherence. Determining a stress versus percentage elongation diagram, in which plastic deformation is evidenced for each applied load cycle.

The welding process was carried out based on the parameters defined by (AWS-D1.4 2005). The percentage of carbon equivalent calculated is 0.55, which is the maximum limit established by the standard (ASTM-A706 2016) and under these parameters, the SMAW process, and the 3/32" diameter bare E9018 were selected. The geometry proposed by the AWS is detailed in Table 1 and Fig. 2.

Table 1. CJP for reinforcing steel bars according to AWS (original AWS tables).

CJP Groove Weld Requirements for Direct Butt Joints (see 3.4)

Bar Axis Orientation	Optional Types of CJP Groove Weld	Optional Figure 3.2 Detail
Horizontal	Single-V	A
	Double-V	B
	Single-V with Split Pipe Backing	C[a]
Vertical	Single-Bevel	D
	Double-Bevel	E
	Single-Bevel with Split Pipe Backing	C[a]

[a] Bars shall be of equal diameter.

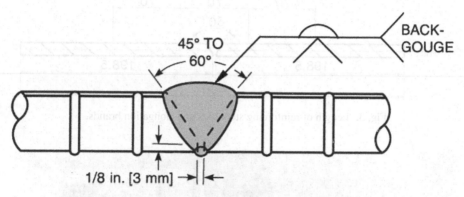

Fig. 2. Welding on reinforcing steel bars in horizontal position

The geometry of the reinforcing steel bars to be welded and the brands for measuring the elongation are detailed in Fig. 3.

The welding process was developed with qualified welders with multiple passes and cleaning between passes, Fig. 4.

Based on the carbon equivalent of 0.55% and for diameters up to 19 mm, it is not necessary to preheat or apply additional heat in the welding process between passes, Table 2.

The cyclic test was performed with a sinusoidal load function and a load application frequency of 1 Hz. Testing the specimens under the same stress state, exhausting their capacity in an average of 18 cycles, Fig. 5.

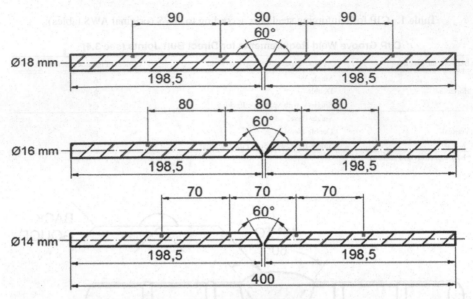

Fig. 3. Length of reinforcing steel bars and elongation brands.

Fig. 4. Welding process.

Table 2. Minimum preheat and inter-pass temperatures (original AWS tables).

Minimum Preheat and Interpass Temperatures[a, b] **(see 5.2.1)**

Carbon Equivalent (C.E.) Range, %[c, d]	Size of Reinforcing Bar	SMAW with Low-Hydrogen Electrodes, GMAW, or FCAW	
		Minimum Temperature	
		°F	°C
Up to 0.40	Up to 11 [36] inclusive	none[e]	none[e]
	14 and 18 [43 and 57]	50	10
Over 0.40 to 0.45 inclusive	Up to 11 [36] inclusive	none[e]	none[e]
	14 and 18 [43 and 57]	50	10
Over 0.45 to 0.55 inclusive	Up to 6 [19] inclusive	none[e]	none[e]
	7 to 11 [22 to 36]	50	10
	14 to 18 [43 to 57]	200	90
Over 0.55 to 0.65 inclusive	Up to 6 [19] inclusive	100	40
	7 to 11 [22 to 36]	200	90
	14 to 18 [43 to 57]	300	150
Over 0.65 to 0.75	Up to 6 [19] inclusive	300	150
	7 to 18 [22 to 57] inclusive	400	200
Over 0.75	Up to 6 [19] inclusive	300	150
	7 to 18 [22 to 57] inclusive	500	260

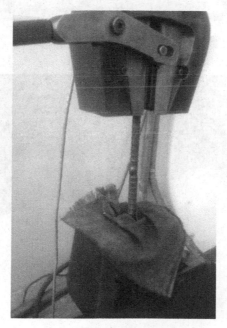

Fig. 5. Cyclic mechanical tests.

3 Results and Discussion

According to (Zolotorevski 1976) the structure of real metals and alloys and the distribution of their defects are not the same, even within the limits of the same sample. This behavior was observed due to the mechanical properties of the specimen structure and it was determined by the different defects found at several volumes of the specimen.

Figure 6, shows reinforcing steel bars that have exhausted their capacity due to the experimentation HAZ, while Fig. 7 shows welding defects.

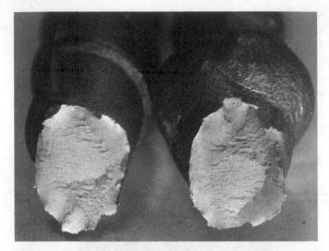

Fig. 6. HAZ failure.

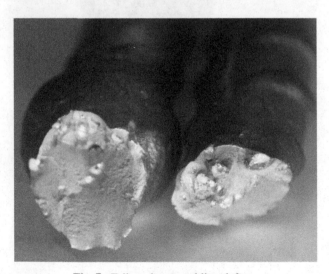

Fig. 7. Failure due to welding defects.

Results of Unwelded Specimens The results of the static mechanical tests of non-welded reinforcing steel bars are shown in Fig. 8, while in Fig. 9 the tests with the application of cyclic loads are shown.

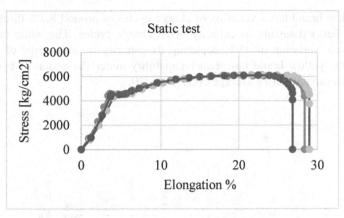

Fig. 8. Characteristic static test standard specimens.

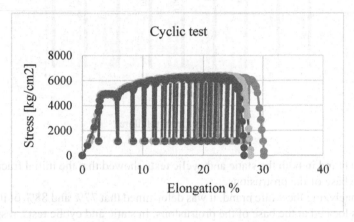

Fig. 9. Characteristic cyclic test standard specimens.

According to the results, the limit value for the minimum creep was 4284 kg/cm^2, and the maximum was 4935 kg/cm^2 related to the global standard specimens.

Elongation, a parameter controlled by standards (INEN-2167 2011) e (INEN-0109 2009), shows that the standard specimens have an elongation of 26% in both the static and cyclic tests.

The yellow brand presents, on average, a greater elongation with a value of 26%, while the greatest contraction is presented by the red brand with 53%.

With an average exhaustion capacity of 21, 17, and 15 cycles for the bars of 14, 16, and 18 mm in diameter, respectively. It is determined that to smallest the diameter, the greatest is the capacity of load cycles that the A706 reinforcement steel resists, under the same stress state.

The red brand specimen has the smallest variation of results with 6.3% along the commercial bar of 12 m, however, this brand is the one that resists the least number of load application cycles with an average of 17 cycles load.

The yellow brand has a variation of charge cycles of around 8.7% throughout the commercial bar, exhausting its capacity in 18 charge cycles. The white brand has a depletion cycle variation of 15%, depleting its capacity in an average of 18 cycles. Therefore, the yellow brand has greater capability under the action of cyclic loads, exhausting its capacity in 18 average cycles, Fig. 10.

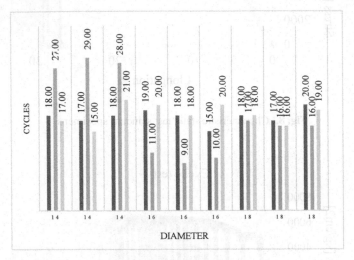

Fig. 10. Specimen failure

The red brand in both the static and cyclic tests showed that the initial fracture point starts at the base of the protrusions.

When analyzing the white brand, it was determined that 77% and 88% of its fracture initiation is located at the base of the protrusions, in static and cyclic tests, respectively.

Result of Welded Specimens The creep limit of 100% welded specimens satisfactorily complies with the provisions of the standard (INEN-2167 2011), while 96% of them comply with the ultimate tensile strength, Figs. 11a and 11b.

Two of the 54 welded specimens do not meet the ultimate tensile strength. 96% of the welded specimens satisfactorily comply with the standard (INEN-2167 2011). The welded specimens easily meet the resistance requirements, being suitable for use in designs that include reinforced concrete elements, prior to a check by non-destructive tests on welding, as it is shown in Fig. 10; however, the use of steel bars is not recommended for reinforcing steel welded in places of high demand.

On the other hand, although the welded specimens meet the mechanical resistance requirements, they are less ductile compared to the non-welded specimens.

The specimens with the smallest diameter are those with the least elongation, with 15%, 19%, and 23% corresponding to the average elongation for the bars of 14, 16, and 18 mm in diameter, respectively. Corroborating what was mentioned by the welder, who expressed difficulties in the process of welding thin specimens.

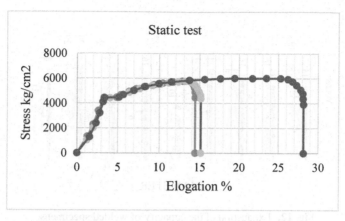

Fig. 11a. Characteristic static test of welded specimens

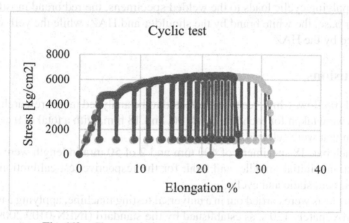

Fig. 11b. Characteristic cyclic test standard specimens

The obtained results meet the mechanical strength requirements. These welded elements are not suitable in places where the formation of a plastic hinge is expected due to the decrease in ductility compared to a standard test piece.

The exhaustion cycles are directly related to the capacity with the base material minus the ductility lost by the welding process, obtaining an average capacity exhaustion of 14 cycles per, that is, 23% less than the samples without weld, Fig. 12.

Unlike the unwelded specimens, these have two additional possibilities for their breakage, the first due to the HAZ (Heat Affected Zone), and the second, imperfections in the welding process.

The welded specimens of the red brand in the static test, continue to show a tendency to fracture at the base of the protrusions in 55% and the HAZ in 33%, the white brand presents breakage in 44% at the base of the highlights and 44% by the HAZ, the yellow brand is mostly affected by the HAZ in 44%.

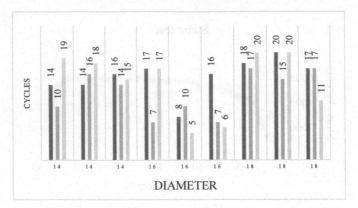

Fig. 12. Exhaustion of the capacity of welded specimens.

When applying cyclic loads to the welded specimens, the red brand mostly fails by the shoulder base, the white brand by the shoulder and HAZ, while the yellow brand is 56% affected by the HAZ.

4   Conclusions

Three brands (yellow, white, red) were selected to be analyzed in this research, of which 3 diameters were taken for each brand, 14, 16, and 18 mm, with a total of 9 commercial bars of 12 m that were selected.

From each bar, 18 specimens of 400 mm and 2 of 50 mm in length were extracted, in three sections, initial, middle, and final, for the respective test-calibration tests and official tests, both static and cyclic.

The static tests were carried out in a universal testing machine, applying a monotonic load in approximately 120 s, as established by the standard (INEN-0109 2009).

The standard test tubes of the three brands analyzed satisfactorily meet the requirements established by the standard (INEN-2167 2011). There is a variation of 0.6% of the mechanical properties in relation to standard specimens of commercial bar, it is due to imperfections - defects in the cross-section as it was established by (Rocha 2014).

The cyclical mechanical tests showed that the exhausting capacity of the samples had an average of 18 cycles, under a sinusoidal load function and frequency of application of 1 Hz load; it is similar to the vibration period of a 10-story building.

A descriptive statistical analysis was carried out to determine that the specimens of the red and white brands have a tendency to initiation and propagation fracture from the base of the protrusions since these do not comply with what is established in the standard (INEN-2167 2011), exceeding its dimensions depending on the diameter.

The variation in the mechanical behavior of the standard specimens under the action of dynamic cyclic loads is due to the protrusions and the process of forming the bars from the raw material.

70% of the specimens tested by destructive mechanical tests started their fracture at the base of the protrusion, confirming the study carried out by the researchers (Rocha 2014) and (Abatta 2016).

The yellow brand specimens, in the three diameters analyzed, presented similar results in the destructive test under the action of dynamic cyclic loads. These results showed a tendency in the separation of the hysteresis loops. Also, the yellow brand has a greater elongation than the red and white brands with 26%.

References

Abatta L., A. C.: Analysis of the Fracture of Steel Reinforcing Bars under Low Cycle. Recent Advances in Biology & Nanotechnology, 1–3 (2016)

Apostolopoulos: The effect of ribs on the mechanical behavior of corbared reinforcing steel bars S500s under low-cycle fatigue. Materials and Structures, 991–999 (2008)

Arroyo, O.: Seismic performance of mid-rise thin concrete wall buildings lightly reinforced with deformed bars or welded wire mesh. Engineering Structures (2020)

ASTM-A706: Especificación estándar para barras de acero de baja aleación deformadas para refuerzo de hormigón. American Society for Testing and Materials, 7 (2016)

AWS-D1.4: Structural Welding Code - Reinforcing Steel. American Welding Society, 1–84 (2005)

Brown Jeff, K.S.: Low Cycle Fatigue Behavior of Longitudinal Reinforcement in Reinforced Concrete Bridge Columns. Multidiplinary Center For Earthquake Engineering Research, University of Central Florida. ISSN 1520-295X, 1–108 (2000)

Gao, L.: Fatigue life prediction of HTRB630E steel bars based on modified coffin-manson model under pre-strain. Structures (2022)

Hawileth, A.O.: Low-cycle fatigue life behaviour of BS 460B and BS B500B steel reinforcing bars. Fatigue & Fracture of Engineering Materials & Structures, 397–407 (2009)

INEN-0109: Ensayo de tracción para materiales metálicos a temperatura ambiente. Instituto ecuatoriano de normalización, 1–43 (2009)

INEN-2167: VArilla de acero con resaltes, laminadas en caliente, soldables, microaleadas o termotratadas para hormigón. instituto ecuatoriano de normalización, 1 19 (2011)

J.B. Mander, F.P.: Low cycle fatigue behavior of reinforcing steel. ASCE , 453–468 (1994)

Kashani, B.M.: Influence of inelastic buckling on low-cycle fatigue degradation of reinforcing bars. Construction and Building Materials, 664–673 (2015)

Li, W.: Mechanical properties of HRB400E/316L stainless steel clad rebar under low-cycle fatigue. Structures (2022)

Luijters, I.: Fatigue strength of rebars embedded in concrete—A numerical approach. Engineering Fracture Mechanics (2021)

NEC-SE-DS: Peligro sísmico diseño sismo resistente. Ecuador: Norma Ecuatoriana de la Construcción (2015)

Pantazopoulos, G.: Fatigue failure analysis of a Ø14 B500C steel rebar: Metallurgical evaluation and numerical simulation. Engineering Failure Analysis (2018)

Rocha, M.: Fatigue Behaviour of Steel Reinforcement Bars at Very High Number of Cycles. Lausanne, Suisse: École Politechnique Fédérale de Lausanne (2014)

Saif Aldabagh, M.S.: Low-cycle fatigue performance of high-strength steel reinforcing bars considering the effect of inelastic buckling. Engineering Structures (2021)

Shwania, M.: Ductility of Concrete Members Reinforced with Welded Wire Reinforcement. Engineering Structures (2019)

Zolotorevski: Pruebas mecanicas y propiedades de los metales. Rusia: Mir Moscú (1976)

Spirometer with Automatic Disinfection

Nancy Guerrón[1]([✉]) [iD], Rodolfo Maestre[2] [iD], Andrés Bonilla[1], and Karen Toaquiza[1]

[1] Universidad de las Fuerzas Armadas ESPE, 171103 Sangolquí, Ecuador
neguerron@espe.edu.ec
[2] Universidad Politécnica de Sinaloa, 82199 Mazatlán, Sinaloa, Mexico

Abstract. Given the increase in lung diseases in recent years, a turbine spirometer with semi-automatic disinfection and remote monitoring was designed and built at the University of the Armed Forces ESPE. Validation tests were performed with ten users of internal medicine and outpatient clinic of the Hospital Andino in the city of Riobamba and the cooperation of a pulmonologist of the hospital. The spirometry data was compared with data produced by a commercial spirometer of similar characteristics; no significant differences were found between the two devices (t = 3.27). Laboratory tests showed that the ozone disinfection system applied eliminates bacteria that can incubate due to the reuse of the equipment's nozzle, which will allow a reduction in the cost of spirometry tests performed by the hospital on its patients.

Keyword: Spirometer · Disinfection systems · Lung diseases

1 Introduction

Given the worldwide increase in the number of respiratory conditions due to the presence of COVID 19 since December 2019, a number of accessible and easy-to-use measurement equipment and systems have been developed, focused on providing medical services remotely in various areas of study such as respiratory medicine.

Spirometry is a noninvasive medical test, mainly used for the diagnosis and follow-up of respiratory pathologies. This standardized test evaluates the mechanical properties of the respiratory system and identifies airflow obstructions [1]. The interpretation of spirometry is based on comparing the values produced by the patient with those that would theoretically correspond to a healthy individual with the same anthropometric characteristics [2].

The spirometry equipment called pneumotachograph, incorporate mathematical algorithms and use different types of sensors, such as pressure, piezoelectric, ultrasonic, wedge, turbine, or others, which provide data on the pressure difference according to the expiration of each individual. Once the physical signal has been interpreted, it will be converted into an electrical signal, to be analyzed digitally. In this study, the turbine pneumotachograph was chosen, which is described below.

A portable spirometer was developed to diagnose chronic obstructive pulmonary disease [3] and another to diagnose various lung diseases [4]. Diaz [5] developed a Portable Electronic Spirometer with Visualization on Mobile Device. Several low-cost

M. Botto-Tobar et al. (Eds.): ICAT 2022, CCIS 1756, pp. 16–31, 2023.
https://doi.org/10.1007/978-3-031-24971-6_2

turbine spirometers have been developed as metrological support [6] or for lung disease detection [7].Some spirometers use various control methods for data processing, such as Mazón's [8], where fuzzy control in the LabVIEW platform is used for data processing. Spirometers are also found that use the internet of things (IoMT) for the interconnection of various electronic devices and the online display of spirometric results [9]. In a recent study [10], a machine learning system was developed to obtain the lung age of a person by spirometry. In this study conducted with sixty-two patients [11], two spirometers were compared, one portable and the other desktop, obtaining similar readings; therefore, both types could be useful in the measurement of spirometric parameters in patients with obstructive respiratory diseases.

Spirometry tests present a high exposure to a risk of contagion for both patients and medical personnel, therefore, recommendations have been developed regarding the use of the spirometer to avoid Covid-19 contagion [12]. There are also recommendations on the requirements for conventional spirometers and portable equipment, as well as on hygiene and quality control measures for spirometers [2].

In a conventional spirometry test, the mouthpiece used by the patient must be sterilized or discarded after the test, implying an additional expense for public health institutions, so this study developed an automatic disinfection method that optimizes the use of the device and eliminates the possibility of contagion to other patients.

This study will design and test a digital turbine spirometer with a remote monitoring system using IoMT to evaluate pulmonary function in patients in the internal medicine and outpatient areas of the Andean Hospital in the city of Riobamba, Ecuador. This equipment will be equipped with an automatic disinfection system to prevent contagion.

1.1 Spirometric Variables

The main variables in forced spirometry are: Forced vital capacity (FVC), forced expiratory volume in the first second (FEV1), FEV_1/FVC ratio and peak expiratory flow (PEF) [2].

- FVC represents the maximum volume of air exhaled in a maximal forced expiratory maneuver, initiated after a maximal inspiratory maneuver;
- FEV1 is the amount of air that is moved in the first second of a forced exhalation;
- FEV_1/FVC is a rate, which relates the first two variables, so it is usually represented as a percentage (its nominal value in adults is >70%);
- PEF is the maximum amount of air that can be exhaled per second in a forced expiration. It represents the maximum peak flow obtained in a flow-volume curve (See Fig. 1) and occurs before 15% of the FVC has been expelled.

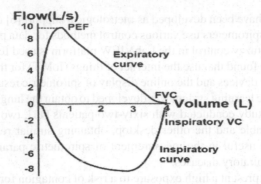

Fig. 1. Flow-volume curve. Available via license: Creative Commons Attribution-Noncommercial 4.0 International.

1.2 Turbine Pneumotachograph

The turbine pneumotachograph shown in Fig. 2 is designed to transform the exhaled air flow signal into an electrical signal capable of being manipulated by any electronic system; it consists of a shaft on which a propeller rotates thanks to the air flow. It is easy to implement, resistant to disturbances, accessible in price and dimensioning, for the work environment projected in this study. By means of a sensor, the rotation speed is measured and, based on these revolutions, the air flow is calculated, which when integrated, the expiratory volume is obtained [13].

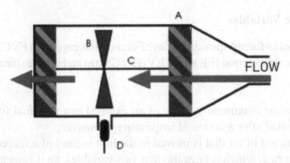

Fig. 2. Turbine pneumotachograph, where A represents the blades to direct the air flow, B: propeller and C: propeller shaft, D; optical sensor for speed measurement. Adapted from [13], page 39.

To calculate the flow velocity of exhaled air, the Eq. 1 is used:

$$vf = vh * ct \tag{1}$$

where:
vh = propeller speed
vf = air flow rate
ct = turbine constant

To calculate the airflow, Bernoulli's principle is used:

$$Q = Ac * vf$$

$$Q = \pi . r^2 . vf \tag{2}$$

where:

Q = Volumetric Flow

Ac = Circular nozzle area

Subsequently, the lung volume is calculated, using the same Bernoulli principle:

$$Q = \frac{\Delta V}{\Delta t} \quad \Delta V = Q . \Delta t$$

$$\int_{t1}^{t2} \Delta V = \int_{t1}^{t2} Q . \Delta t$$

$$V = \int_{t1}^{t2} Q . \Delta t \tag{3}$$

where:

Δt = Time variation

ΔV = Volume variation

Since the volumetric flow is updated at each sampling time interval, a straight line is defined (Eq. 4) passing through the points A = (x1, y1) corresponding to the initial volumetric flow at t1 and B = (x2, y2) corresponding to the final volumetric flow at t2.

$$y = \frac{y_2 - y_1}{x_2 - x_1}(x - x_1) + y_1$$

The integral with respect to time of this curve yields lung volume (Eq. 4)

$$V = \int_{t1}^{t2} y dx$$

$$V = \frac{m}{2} * \left[(t_2)^2 - (t_1)^2 \right] + [t_2 - t_1] * [y_1 - m * x_1] \tag{4}$$

1.3 Medical Equipment Disinfection Systems

These systems are very important for the prevention of infections associated with inappropriate disinfection of reusable objects. Among the disinfection alternatives are chemical agents, ultraviolet light, ultrasound, use of disposable material and water vapor [14–18]. The results of Orellana, et al. [19] show that ozone used for a period of time of 25 min is an excellent disinfectant, while after 30 min it acts as a sterilizer; in the analysis performed on 17 hand-pieces and 51 drills for dental use, it was observed that the number of colonies of 10 different types of bacteria decreases as the exposure time increases.

In 2020, Taran, et al. [20] in their research "Portable ozone sterilization device with mechanical and ultrasonic cleaning units for dentistry" developed a portable device for cleaning and sterilization of dental instruments with ozone at a concentration of 8.5 mg/l. As results, they obtained that after 10 min of exposure, Pseudomonas aeruginosa cells are completely eliminated, and after 20 min, the inactivation of Escherichia coli and Staphylococcus aurous bacteria occurs after 30 min of treatment.

For this research, ozone disinfection was chosen, which is a gas with high oxidizing power and an effective and safe solution for disinfecting hospitals and food industries [21]. Since it is a gas that spreads through each area of the equipment that needs to be sterilized, it does not have the capacity to damage the surfaces to which it is exposed, given that the ozone concentrations and the exposure time necessary to exterminate contaminating agents are very low and it does not leave residues that are harmful to humans [22].

2   Materials and Methods

There are three sections: Sect. 2.1 contains a description of the study participants; Sect. 2.2 contains the design of the spirometry system. Finally, Sect. 2.3 defines the study variables.

2.1   Participants

Ten adult patients from the Riobamba Hospital (see Table 1), including internal medicine and external consultation, participated in the validation of the prototype developed. The participants did not present pulmonary diseases at the time of the test.

Table 1. Anthropometric characteristics of the patients in this study

Patient	Age	Size (cm)	Weight (Kg)	Gender	Specialty
1	62	165	62	Male	External consultation
2	26	165	64	Male	External consultation
3	30	155	55	Female	External consultation
4	47	150	61	Female	External consultation
5	40	155	74	Female	External consultation
6	59	154	67	Female	Internal medicine
7	42	155	58	Female	Internal medicine
8	33	160	62	Male	Internal medicine
9	64	168	65	Male	Internal medicine
10	31	156	52	Male	Internal medicine

2.2 Spirometry System

2.2.1 CAD of the Pneumotachograph

SolidWorks software was used for the computer-aided design (CAD), which models in 3D each of the components that make up the spirometer. The mechanical structure of the pneumotachograph or case is intended to serve as the main support between the user performing the spirometry test and the sensor that will interpret the information. It was taken into consideration measures that allow a correct grip of the user, as well as a slight inclination in the profile of the case, which allows more slack in the wrist while the patient is using the device (See Fig. 3).

Optical sensors measure the speed of the turbine. The optical sensor consists of infrared emitter-receiver LEDs with 3mm encapsulation, which can be used to interpret the received signal and obtain the necessary data for the spirometry test.

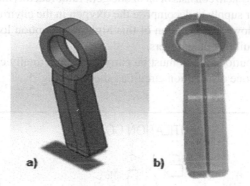

Fig. 3. a) CAD design; b) 3D printing on PLA

The sensors are placed in the pneumotachograph by means of a coupling (See Fig. 4) that allows the appropriate distribution of two pairs of sensors to monitor the behavior of the turbine propeller and determine the direction of rotation of the turbine, without the need to have direct contact or interfere with it during the spirometry test.

2.2.2 Disinfection System Design

The disinfection process lasts 30 min and is carried out as follows:

- From 0 to 10 min, a reactor is activated to generate the gas necessary for disinfection. A fan system is activated to ensure that the ozone reaches the inside of the equipment.

- From 11 to 20 min, the reactor is deactivated; the fans continue to run to ensure that the ozone disinfects all the equipment.

- From 21 to 30 min, a servomotor is activated to open the fans. The fans continue to run in order to help the ozone residue to escape so that the disinfection chamber can be ventilated.

At the end of the process, the fans stop running, the servo is deactivated to close the vents and the disinfection chamber can be used again.

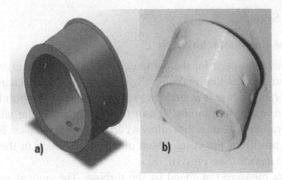

Fig. 4. a) CAD design; b) PLA 3D printing of the coupling

The disinfection system consists of an ozone generator reactor; model OZ10G, which requires 110 V power supply to decompose the oxygen in the environment (See Fig. 6). The power circuit allows manipulation of this high consumption load and is separated from the control circuit by optocouplers.

The ozone distribution system must be carried out in a totally closed environment, which requires an ozone distribution circuit as shown in Fig. 5.

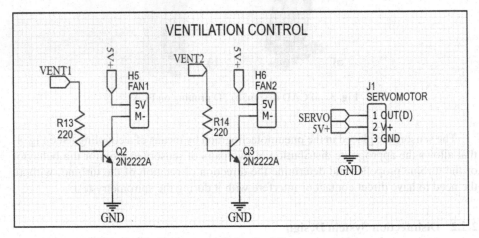

Fig. 5. Ventilation control circuit of the pneumotachograph

To automate this procedure, a system of fans (See Fig. 6) is implemented that open automatically by means of a rack and pinion system that act by means of a servomotor and two fans, which will be operating by means of an On-Off control as well as the ozone generator reactor.

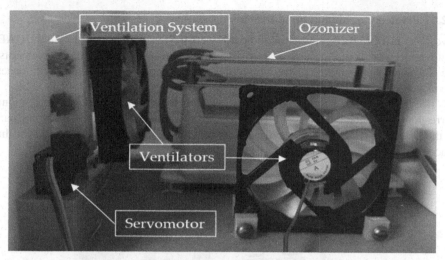

Fig. 6. Pneumotachograph disinfection chamber.

2.2.3 Conditioning and Data Acquisition System

The conditioning system allows the reading and interpretation of the signals provided by the sensors, minimizing noise and allowing a clean signal to pass through to the data acquisition card. The sensor signal is sent to a non-inverting amplifier, which is also used as an isolation circuit between the data acquisition card and the sensor (See Fig. 7).

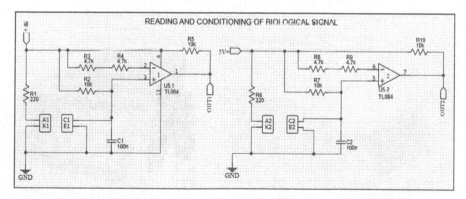

Fig. 7. Biological signal reading and conditioning.

For data acquisition, the ESP8266 NodeMCU card was used, due to its small size, low cost and because it facilitates connection to a Wifi network. The HMI screen chosen was the Nextion NX8048T050, because of its compatibility with the data card; it is also tactile and has its own software and libraries that facilitate programming. Nextion Editor was used to develop the graphical interface (HMI).

2.2.4   Printed Circuit and Final Design

Two 70 × 110 mm PCB printed circuit boards were designed, measures that fit the CAD that has been proposed in this research. The first board contains the control elements, the electronic cards and the connection to the power supply. The second board houses the electronic components.

The design of the base allows the prototype to work in two separate spaces, one corresponding to the circuitry and the other to the disinfection system. The front part of the prototype is used for displaying the HMI screen and the rear part is used for the placement of the vents (See Fig. 8).

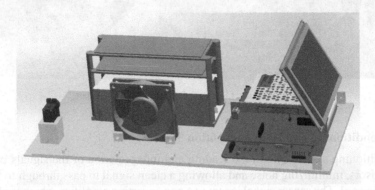

Fig. 8. CAD prototype of the spirometer base.

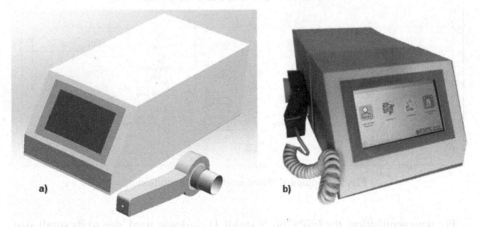

Fig. 9. Spirometer a) CAD final spirometer; b) Final 3D printed prototype.

Finally, a top cover was designed to isolate the entire disinfection system to avoid possible problems between the interaction of ozone and the circuitry, and at the same time to be easy to assemble with the rest of the parts. The parts are 3D printed with poly lactic acid (PLA), which is a long lasting, low cost material and its external porosity can be covered with acrylic paint. The final assembled prototype can be seen in Fig. 9.

2.2.5 Design of the User Interface

Figure 10 shows the structure of the local HMI which controls all the functions of the spirometer.

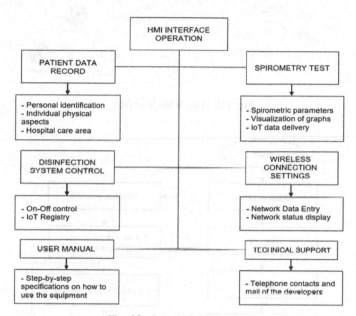

Fig. 10. Local HMI structure

The main HMI interface includes four sections: patient data logging, spirometry test, disinfection control and device settings and configuration.

Secondary interfaces are used for data verification and test start, another screen is used to configure the Wi-Fi network, for data communication via IoMT, so that a data log can be kept on a web page for each patient and thus be accessible from any device with internet connectivity. Another screen is used to review the test data, which can be viewed in graphical, textual or printed form. Finally, another screen was developed to control the disinfection system (See Fig. 11).

2.2.6 Remote Interface Design

To visualize patient information and spirometric results, a web page was designed in HTML and CSS in Visual Studio Code (See Fig. 12) and to establish communication between the ESP8266 NodeMCU, PHP language, PhpMyAdmin and Heidi SQL were used.

The results of the main page are shown in Fig. 13.

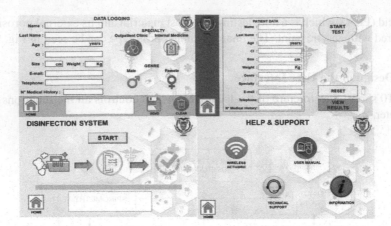

Fig. 11. Main HMI Interface

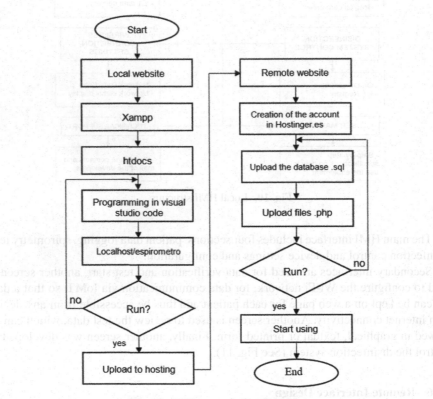

Fig. 12. WEB page design flowchart

Fig. 13. Main window of the WEB page

2.3 Study Variables

Table 2 summarizes the variables of this study.

2.3.1 Spirometric Variables

According to García-Río [2] the theoretical spirometric values are determined by a series of equations that depend on the anthropometric characteristics of the patients (sex, age, height, weight).

With the developed spirometer, the FVC, FEV1, PEF and FEV1/FVC values defined in Sect. 1.1 can be estimated. A weighted average low-pass digital filter is applied to the input data to remove noise and interference. The filtered output is stored in two different vectors, one for calculating volumetric flow and one for lung volume.

- FCV, obtained as the last value stored in the lung volume vector.
- FVE1, a sampling period accounting for a sum of 1000 ms is used with the volumetric flow vector.
- PEF is the largest value detected in the volumetric flow vector.
- FVC/FEV1 is the ratio of the FVC value to FVE1.

2.3.2 Disinfection System Variables

Before and after the disinfection process, samples were taken to determine the presence of pathogenic elements before and after each spirometry test. Sterile gloves, surgical mask and swabs, which are changed for each patient, are used to take the samples. These samples are analyzed by a laboratory specialized in microbiology, which performs a culture test to determine the presence or absence of microorganisms.

Table 2. Study Variables

Spirometric variables	Disinfection system variables
FCV, FVE1, PEF, FVC/FEV1	Microbiological analysis

3   Results

The tests performed with the prototype spirometer to ten outpatients and internal medicine patients at the Hospital Andino in the city of Riobamba were compared with a commercial spirometer MIR Spirobank Smart Spirometer available at the Hospital.

3.1   Spirometry Tests

The results of the spirometric tests are shown in Table 3.

Table 3. Results Spirometry tests

Patient	FVC (Lt)		FEV1 (Lt/s)		PEF(Lt)		FEV1/FVC (%)	
	P	C	P	C	P	C	P	C
1	4.08	4.22	3.28	3.2	7.32	7.01	73.9	76.7
2	4.59	4.6	4.07	3.89	9.01	8.58	81.11	84.71
3	3.54	3.41	3.02	2.9	6.18	6.1	86.38	85.31
4	3.05	2.93	2.48	2.39	5.46	5.43	82.86	81.61
5	2.97	2.86	2.68	2.56	5.24	5.05	85.73	89.51
6	2.91	2.82	2.30	2.24	5.28	5.31	78.86	79.87
7	3.41	3.26	2.78	2.67	5.82	5.8	83.60	82.22
8	4.15	4.17	3.63	3.48	8.22	7.86	78.63	80.23
9	4.04	3.89	3.1	3.01	7.16	7.53	73.82	77.49
10	3.62	3.45	3.06	2.92	6.19	6.11	85.95	84.98

Note: P represents data taken by the prototype and C data obtained by the commercial spirometer

The dependence of the four variables was evaluated with a two-tailed t-student test for 9 degrees of freedom, which was statistically non-significant (t = 3.27), compared to t = 2.26 established for a confidence margin of 95%. Consequently, the readings of the two spirometers are valid to evaluate the spirometric parameters. In addition, the difference in the reading of spirometric variables with the prototype designed is less than 4% compared to the commercial spirometer.

3.2   Disinfection System Results

Two samples were taken using sterile swabs. The first one is called "contaminated spirometer" and the second one is called "sterilized spirometer". The first sample is taken after the spirometry test, while the second sample is taken after applying the disinfection process to the equipment. The two samples are sent to a microbiological laboratory for analysis.

In the ten patients the laboratory tests performed after the disinfection process show that there is no bacterial growth. Therefore, the disinfection system works in 100% of the cases analyzed.

The following is an example of the analysis performed on a patient.

3.2.1 Contaminated Spirometer

Growing:

ISOLATED GERM: Streptococcus viridans are present.

ANTIBIOGRAM:

Amikacin: Susceptible.

Amoxa + AC Clavul: Sensitive.

Ampicillin + Sul: Susceptible.

Cephalexin: Sensitive.

Ceefoxitin: Susceptible.

Ciprofloxacin: Resistant.

Clindamycin: Resistant.

Erythromycin: Susceptible.

Oxacillin: Resistant.

Trimethoprim Sulfa: Susceptible.

3.2.2 Sterilized Spirometer

Growing:

ISOLATED GERM: No bacterial growth at 24 and 48 h of incubation.

4 Discussion

Breathing exposes the body to a number of pollutants, which could be the cause of a number of lung diseases, leading to requests for spirometry tests. The spirometry technique completed in the last 50 years of the 20th century involves standardized and rigorous processes approved by the European Respiratory Society (ERS) and the American Thoracic Society (ATS) to reach valid and diagnostic conclusions [23].

The equipment developed in this research work not only considered international standards but also auto-disinfection as an economical alternative to avoid contagion in the users of the equipment, at the end of the spirometric test.

Undoubtedly, this invention will concur in a future patent, since it reduces the cost of the test in public hospitals and makes it easier to obtain reliable data for the diagnosis performed by doctors in the hospital and whose results can be visualized from all healthcare settings, for their collaboration.

To standardize the treatment of spirometry-related data and enable information exchange, Salas [24] used the CDA R2 (Clinical Document Architecture, Release 2) standard of HL7 (Health Level Seven) version 3. In this work all the data provided by the spirometer can be visualized in a remote interface programmed in HTML, CSS and PHP whose communication with the data acquisition card is based on the HTTP protocol establishing an IoMT network connection; the system allows the use of security credentials to access patient information.

References

1. Torre-Bouscoulet, L., Villca-Alá, N., et al.: Sociedad Mexicana de Estudios sobre Tuberculosis y Enfermedades del Aparato Respiratorio. RE, Neumologia y cirugía de tórax. Unidad de Patología, Sanatorio de Huipulco (2016)
2. García-Río, F., Calle, M., Burgos, F., et al.: Spirometry. Arch. Bronconeumol. **49**, 388–401 (2013). https://doi.org/10.1016/J.ARBR.2013.07.007
3. Harun Al Rasyid, M.U., Kemalasari, S.M., Sukaridhoto, S.: Design and Development of Portable Spirometer. In: 2018 IEEE International Conference on Consumer Electronics-Taiwan (ICCE-TW), pp 1–2. IEEE (2018)
4. Ibrahim, S.N., Jusoh, A.Z., Malik, N.A., Mazalan, S.: Development of portable digital spirometer using NI sbRIO. In: 2017 IEEE 4th International Conference on Smart Instrumentation, Measurement and Application (ICSIMA), pp. 1–4. IEEE, Putrajaya (2017)
5. Gómez Chacon, A.F., Díaz Suarez, R.A., Pabon Castillo, V.A., Vera Medina, S.F.: Espirómetro electrónico portátil con visualización en dispositivo móvil. Sci. Tech. **24**, 154 (2019). https://doi.org/10.22517/23447214.18451
6. Sokol, Y.I., Tomashevsky, R.S., Kolisnyk, K.V.: Turbine spirometers metrological support. In: 2016 International Conference on Electronics and Information Technology (EIT), pp. 1–4. IEEE, Odessa (2016)
7. Sridevi, P., Kundu, P., Islam, T., et al.: A Low-cost Venturi Tube Spirometer for the Diagnosis of COPD. In: TENCON 2018 - 2018 IEEE Region 10 Conference. IEEE, Jeju, pp. 0723–0726 (2018)
8. Mazón A' RS' SE 'Ramírez, M, 'Cabrera A.: Medicion del volumen pulmonar utilizando control difuso en la plataforma labview. 2016 VII Congr. Nac. Tecnol. Apl. a Ciencias Salud, 1–8 (2016)
9. 'Mendoza, P., Ávila K., Vilora, C., Jabba, D.: Internet of Things and Home-Centered Health. Salud Uninorte **32**, 337–351 (2016)
10. Mukhopadhyay, S., Chen, Y., Morais, S., et al.: A Machine-Learning Model for Lung Age Forecasting by Analyzing Exhalations. (2022). https://doi.org/10.3390/s22031106
11. Boros, P.W., Maciejewski, A., Nowicki, M.M., Wesołowski, S.: PRACA ORYGINALNA Comparability of portable and desktop spirometry: a randomized, parallel assignment, open-label clinical trial (2022). https://doi.org/10.5603/ARM.a2022.0013
12. 'Ferreira, A.: Espirometría en tiempos de COVID-19. Rev Alerg e Inmunol Clínica 2020, pp. 1–3 (2020)
13. Mejía, G.: Diseño y desarrollo de un espirómetro de flujo de bajo costo. Universidad Nacional Autónoma de México (2010)
14. Desinfección de agua contaminada empleando ultrasonido de 1MHz. en presencia de nanofibras de Carbono (2007)
15. del Castillo, E.S., Pérez, A.R., Alfonso, G.D.: Nuevo sistema de desinfección de alto nivel por vapor fluente a baja temperatura. Enfermedades Infecc y Microbiol **22**, 31–38 (2002)
16. Estudio del diseño e implementación de un sistema de pruebas para desinfección de equipos de protección personal N95 mediante radiación ultravioleta. https://tesis.pucp.edu.pe/reposi torio/handle/20.500.12404/18111. Accessed 28 Sept 2022

17. De, I., Sistema De Evaluación, U.N., De, C., et al.: Implementación de un sistema de evaluación y capacitación de limpieza y desinfección de equipos biomédicos en los servicios de UCI y II del hospital universitario San José de Popayan (2021). https://doi.org/10.48713/10336_31558
18. De Medicina, F., Odontoloxía, E.: Desinfección con ozono de los conductos radiculares tratados endodóncicamente (2016)
19. Orellana, M., Gonzalez, J., Menchaca, E., et al.: El ozono como una alternativa para esterilizar piezas de mano y fresas en odontología. Rev. Latinoam. Ortod. y Odontopediatría (2010)
20. Taran, V., Garkusha, I., Gnidenko, Y., et al.: Portable ozone sterilization device with mechanical and ultrasonic cleaning units for dentistry. Rev. Sci. Instrum. **91**, 084105 (2020). https://doi.org/10.1063/1.5145279
21. Martínez, C.: La desinfección con ozono es un sistema eficaz, seguro y sostenible. In: Geriatricarea (2020). https://www.geriatricarea.com/2020/10/09/la-desinfeccion-con-ozono-es-un-sistema-eficaz-seguro-sostenible-y-economico/. Accessed 28 Sept 2022
22. Westover, C., Rahmatulloev, S., Danko, D., et al.: Ozone Treatment for Elimination of Bacteria in Medical Environments. bioRxiv (2018). https://doi.org/10.1101/420737
23. Vásquez, J., Pérez, R.: Manual de Espirometría, Tercera. Asociación Latinoamericana del Tórax, México (2018)
24. Salas, T., Rubies, C., Gallego, C., et al.: Requerimientos técnicos de los espirómetros en la estrategia para garantizar el acceso a una espirometría de calidad. Arch. Bronconeumol. **47**, 466–469 (2011). https://doi.org/10.1016/J.ARBRES.2011.06.005

Nonlinear Behavior of Steel Frames with Concentric and Eccentric Bracing

Brian Cagua(✉), Julia Pilatasig, Roberto Aguiar, and Cecibel Morales

Departamento de Ciencias de la Tierra y la Construcción, Universidad de las Fuerzas Armadas ESPE, 171103 Sangolqui, Ecuador
bjcagua@espe.edu.com

Abstract. The performance-based seismic design allows an understanding of the behavior of structures, relating damage limits and structural parameters to the capacity of the structures. These results provide tools to meet acceptable technical and economic objectives aimed at controlling the structural response and obtaining a given level of damage. This paper presents the seismic performance evaluation and compares the nonlinear behavior under monotonic loads of 27 structural typologies. These structures correspond to 4, 8, and 12-story steel moment frames, others with bracing configurations, such as chevron brace and multistory X-brace, and eccentrically braced frames. The analyses of this research are carried out using the CEINCI-LAB computer program, where new functions have been developed that, together with the OpenSees computer system, allow the execution of nonlinear analyses (Pushover) in a user-friendly interface. When evaluating the seismic performance level of the 27 typologies, under the established design conditions, it is determined that only 2 of the 27 structures (8 and 12 stories without bracing) suffer significant damage to their structural elements, however, they maintain a level of safety that will allow the structure to be functional after repairs or reinforcements. The remaining 25 typologies remain functional, so their operation can be recovered immediately.

Keywords: Steel frame · Steel bracing · Computer application CEINCI-LAB · OpenSees · Pushover

1 Introduction

The mechanisms of seismic energy release in Ecuador are mainly produced by two seismic sources, the first corresponds to subduction (inter- and intra-plate), and the second is due to the set of cortical (surface) faults [1]. The geographical characteristics of the area and its energy release are responsible for the main cases of severe damage and collapse of structures; proof of this is the 2016 Manabí-Ecuador earthquake [2]. A proper design of structures tries to obtain an adequate relationship between strength and stiffness concerning lateral loads, preventing the failure of the structure and controlling its deformations [3].

The current seismic-resistant design philosophy in Ecuador is based on a design methodology by capacity, which implies that energy dissipation is based on an adequate damage sequence in the elements to ensure the stability of the structure (in special moment frames this translates into damage concentrated first in beams and then in columns). This philosophy is changing to a performance-based design, so, seeking to satisfy a human need that meets certain qualitative attributes, intending to raise the level of protection so that the structure remains operational after a seismic event. Therefore, it is important to find techniques for energy dissipation, base isolation, and active control, to avoid major damage to the structure and achieve a low-cost repair. [4]. However, in Ecuador and some Latin American countries, these special systems are not accessible in all structures. Consequently, it is important to look for energy dissipation mechanisms in which the concentration of damage occurs in easily replaceable elements at low acquisition costs. Due to the growing trend of change in the seismic-resistant design philosophy, works such as [5–7], have explored the use of replaceable elements. These elements can be steel diagonals or link elements (in eccentric bracing).

This study determines the seismic behavior of 27 types of steel frames without diagonals, with concentric diagonals and eccentric diagonals, the latter with connecting elements of 3 different lengths and 2 types of diagonal connections. Seismic behavior is evaluated using capacity curves and the analysis of the damage mechanisms produced by the application of monotonic lateral loads, using nonlinear static analysis procedures. In addition, the seismic performance point for the design earthquake (475-year return period) is determined. The initial design of the frames will be presented employing methodologies recommended in the national standard NEC 15, considering linear static analysis and then the design will be verified utilizing non-linear static analysis. All this will be executed through of the CEINCI-LAB and OpenSees computational system functions.

2 Methodology

2.1 Description of the Geometry of the Analysis Frames

The analysis and design are performed for 4, 8, and 12-story steel structures with three spans and three different structural systems, following the procedures described in [8–10] and under the guidelines of the national and international standards such as NEC-15, ASCE/SEI 41-17, ANSI/AISC 341-16, AISC/SEI 360-16, AISC/SEI 358-16, ASCE 7–16. In the case of bracing systems, the bracing is located in the central span. The height between floors is 2.88 m, except for the first floor, which maintains a height of 3.60 m. The span width is 7 m for the central span and 5 m for the lateral spans (see Fig. 1). As indicated in [8], frames 1 and 2 have the same geometry; therefore, the lateral rigidity of each frame is the same. Consequently, it is possible to analyze each frame independently, considering the gravity loads a collaborating area of 6 m. For this study, the analysis of the frame corresponding to axis 1 is carried out.

Of the three types of the structural system considered for the analysis (see Table 1), the first corresponds to a special moment frame system with HBE-type columns and IPE-type beams. The second structural system consists of steel frames with concentric bracing in the shape of an inverted V and X bracing on different floors, formed by HBE-type columns, IPE-type beams, and HSS-type square tubular diagonals. The third structural system corresponds to steel frames with eccentric bracing and a central link

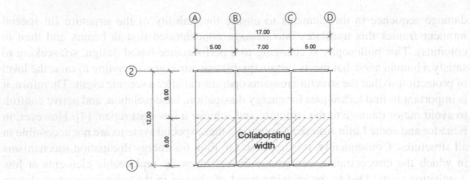

Fig. 1. Plan view of the structure.

Table 1. Typologies of analysis.

Type	Structural System	4-story	8-story	12-story
1	Steel frames			
2	Steel frames with concentric bracing in inverted V-bracing			
2	Steel frames with multistory X-bracing			
3	Steel frames with eccentric bracing			

element. Three lengths of the link element are considered, these correspond to 0.75, 1.25, and 1.75 m so that the link element has yielded in shear, in bending and combined shear, and only in bending. Connections in the diagonals are considered to work axially and subjected to combined flexure and axial.

2.2 Design Applying the NEC-15 Standard

Load States. The current Ecuadorian Construction Standard (NEC-15) recognizes three main load states: permanent loads, variable loads, and accidental loads. For design purposes, in the case of permanent loads, a value of 500 kgf/m^2 for the floor and 380 kgf/m^2 for the roof is considered; the former corresponds to the sum of the self-weight of the slab, masonry, weight of installations, ceiling, and subfloor. For use or variable loads, according to NEC-15 guidelines, a load of 250 kgf/m^2 for the floor and 100 kgf/m^2 for the roof is considered [11]. For the analysis of flat frames, equivalent load states are obtained considering a collaborating width of 6 m, having as a result the forces per unit length. All values are shown in the following Table 2.

Table 2. Load states for design.

Description	$\left[kgf/m^2 \right]$	$[T/m]$
Permanent floor load	500	3.00
Permanent roof load	380	2.10
Live floor load	250	1.50
Live load on the roof	100	0.60

Load Combinations. The design of elements according to the LRFD methodology is based on the increase of stresses with the application of factors to the different load states and their combination. In [11] seven load combinations are proposed for design, which are presented as follows (Table 3).

Where D corresponds to the permanent load or own weight; L to the live overload; E to the earthquake load; S to the snow load and W to the wind load.

Seismic Design Parameters. Seismic design parameters. Based on the shear wave velocity calculations performed in different soil studies carried out in the city of Quito, it has been concluded that in this area there are, for the most part, type D soils and in a few places, type C soils, although there also type E and F soils [12]. Therefore, for this study, it is assumed that the structures of analysis are implanted in Quito on a soil type D. Based on this consideration, the following table presents the parameters for the seismic design of the structures. The parameters are taken about [13] (Table 4).

Table 3. Load combinations for design.

Combination 1	1.4D
Combination 2	1.2D + 1.6L + 0.5max[L;S;R]
Combination 3	1.2D + 1.6max[L;S;R] + max[L;0.5W]
Combination 4	1.2D + 1.0W + L + max[L;S;R]
Combination 5	1.2D + 1.0E + L + 0.2S
Combination 6	0.9D + 1.0W
Combination 7	0.9D + 1.0E

Table 4. Seismic design parameters.

Parameter	Variable	Value	Observation
Zona Seismic	V	–	–
Acceleration factor in the area	Z	0.4	–
Tipo del perfil del suelo	D	–	–
Site factor Fa	Fa	1.2	–
Site factor Fd	Fd	1.19	–
Inelastic soil behavior factor	Fs	1.28	–
Factor	r	1	–
Spectral amplification relation	n	2.48	–
Acceleration in T = To	Sa_O [g]	1.19	$S_a = \eta Z F_a$
The period limit in T = To	T_O [s]	0.127	$T_o = 0.10 F_s \frac{F_d}{F_a}$
The period limit in T = Tc	T_C [s]	0.698	$T_c = 0.55 F_s \frac{F_d}{F_a}$
The period limit in T = T_L	T_L [s]	2.856	–

Figure 2 shows the design spectrum for the city of Quito, considering soil type D. The design elastic spectrum is shown in blue and the reduced inelastic spectrum with a factor R = 6 is shown in green. Although the National Standard allows the use of values higher than 6, it has been considered to use a value of R equal to 6 in a conservative way concerning lateral forces, meaning that higher forces will be used for the design of these structural systems.

2.3 Nonlinear Static Analysis

The Pushover analysis considers the nonlinear characteristics of the materials of the structure and carries it to collapse through the application of incremental lateral loads, with which the capacity curve that characterizes the structure can be obtained. The obtaining of the capacity curve and the plastic hinge formation sequence was performed

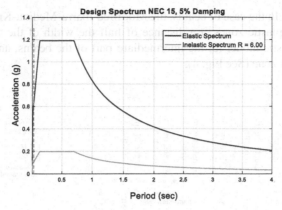

Fig. 2. Design spectrum for soil type D.

using the CEINCI-LAB computer system in conjunction with OpenSees. The functions developed for this purpose are described more specifically in the work of [14].

Among the options for modeling the nonlinearity of element material in OpenSees, there are the concentrated plasticity models and the distributed plasticity models. (See Fig. 3). Knowing that concentrated plasticity models are less complex and computationally less expensive, they are taken as a reference for the development of this analysis. The model consists of dividing each structural member and assigning plasticity zones, where damage is likely to be concentrated and, once its capacity is reached, plastic hinges will appear. These plastic hinges can be represented in terms of curvatures, rotations, or displacements according to the type of stresses to which they will be subjected [15].

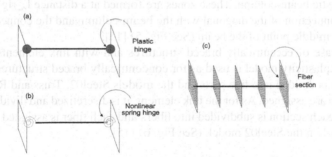

Fig. 3. Models of material nonlinearity. Source: [15]

For the development of Pushover analyses, the use of a lateral load pattern with the shape of the first mode of vibration and a concentrated plasticity model to represent the nonlinearity of the materials was considered. For this, each element is divided into five parts, two of them with a length of zero, which represent the zones of concentrated plasticity. In the case of columns, the Steel01 bilinear model has been used to simulate the nonlinear behavior, this zone is located at half the width of the beam from its centerline. An elastic model is used for the central zone of the column, and a rigid model for the connection zones. In the case of beams, the Modified Ibarra-Medina-Krawinkler model was used for the plastic zones at a distance of half the width of the column from its centerline, the elastic model for the intermediate part of the beams, and a rigid model for the connection zone (See Fig. 4).

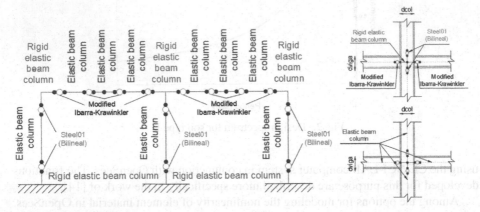

Fig. 4. Nonlinear analysis models for Pushover in OpenSees. Source: [15].

In the case of structures with concentric diagonals, it is useful to generate a node in the central span of the beam. For the modeling of the diagonals, a concentrated plasticity model is considered, therefore, the element is divided into five parts: rigid elements at the ends, followed by a hinge of zero length, and in the center an element with inelastic properties of armature type. Here three types of materials are identified, Steel02, Truss, and Rigid elastic beam-column. These zones are formed at a distance L_rig and are the same for a connection of the diagonal with the beam-column and the connection of the diagonal to a middle point of the beam (See Fig. 5) [15].

For the case of eccentrically braced structures and with link elements, the same concentrated plasticity model is used as for concentrically braced structures, meaning, each element is divided into five parts and the models Steel02, Truss and Rigid elastic beam-column are assigned. As for the link element, it is discretized and divided into sections, where each section is subdivided into fibers and each fiber is assigned a nonlinear property based on the Steel02 model. (See Fig. 6) [15].

2.4 Determination of the Seismic Performance Point Based on ASCE/SEI 41-17 Methodology

In this work, the ASCE/SEI 41-17 methodology is used, in which the coefficient method is used to modify the linear elastic response of an equivalent system of one degree of freedom, in that way estimate the maximum global displacement, also known as the target displacement (δ_t).

From the capacity curves of the Pushover analysis, an idealized Force-Displacement curve is determined from which the effective lateral rigidity of the structure (k_e) is obtained. Based on this parameter, the effective fundamental period (T_e), is calculated,

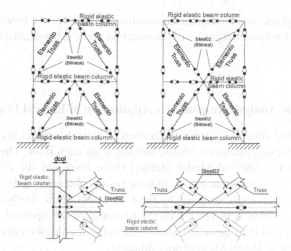

Fig. 5. Concentrated plasticity model of concentrically braced structures for Pushover. Source: [15]

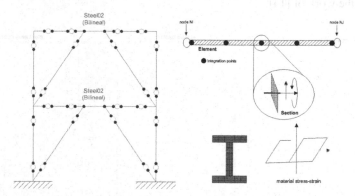

Fig. 6. Model of plasticity in structures with eccentric bracing and link elements for Pushover in OpenSees. Source: [15].

which when plotted in the seismic response spectrum allows obtaining the maximum response acceleration (S_a) corresponding to the equivalent oscillator. Equation (1) can be used to obtain the target displacement (δt) at which the performance point of the structure under study is found in its respective capacity curve [16].

$$\delta_t = C_o C_1 C_2 S_a \frac{T_e^2}{4\pi^2} g \tag{1}$$

where C_o is the coefficient that converts the spectral displacement of a one-degree-of-freedom system to elastic displacement at the top of a multiple-degree-of-freedom system; C_1 s the coefficient that relates the expected maximum inelastic displacement to the elastic displacement; C2 is the coefficient to represent the effects of pinched hysteresis shape, cyclic stiffness degradation, and strength decay on the maximum displacement; S_a

is the spectral response acceleration corresponding to the effective fundamental period; T_e is the effective fundamental period of the structure and g is the acceleration of gravity.

3   Results

3.1   Linear Static Analysis Response for Application of Lateral Loads

The response of the structures to the application of lateral loads is presented through graphs representing displacements, drifts, and shear on each floor. These results were determined using the Spectral Modal Method (blue line) and the Equivalent Static Method (red line). It is important to note that the results obtained by the Spectral Modal Method are lower than those obtained by the Equivalent Static Method. On the other hand, one of the controls is to verify that the response of the Spectral Modal Method is not less than 80% of the Equivalent Static Method. For analysis and comparison, the results of the Spectral Modal Method are evaluated.

The following graphic shows the results obtained for a 12-story structure with concentric diagonals in the form of an inverted V. The results of the 27 structures are better detailed in the work of [14].

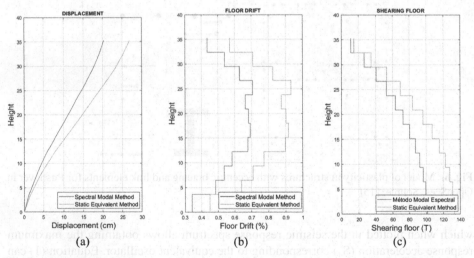

Fig. 7. Linear analysis response of 12-story steel structure with inverted V-shaped concentric bracing a) Maximum inelastic displacement, b) Inelastic floor drifts, c) Floor shear

3.2   Capacity Curves

The capacity curves resulting from the nonlinear static analysis (Pushover) are presented and, in general, it is evident that the displacement is greater according to the height of the structure. In Fig. 8, the capacity curves for 4, 8, and 12-story structures without bracing are shown. This analysis shows that in all three cases the structures have a residual

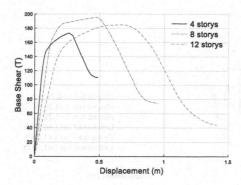

Fig. 8. Capacity curves of structures without bracing.

resistance after reaching their maximum capacity and that the 8-story structure has a higher capacity compared to the 4 and 12-story structures. (See Fig. 8).

The following figure shows the capacity curves for 4, 8, and 12-story structures with concentric inverted V bracing (Fig. 9a) and X in multiple stories (Fig. 9b). It is observed that the 12-story structure can resist approximately two times the shear force of the 4-story structure and that both the 8-story and 12-story structures have a residual strength after reaching their maximum capacity. It is also observed that structures with concentric bracing in inverted V and multi-story X bracing have similar behaviors in terms of capacity.

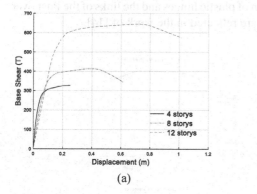

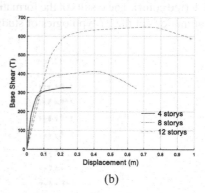

(a)   (b)

Fig. 9. Capacity curves of structures with concentric bracings a) Inverted V-shaped bracings, b) X-shaped bracings in multiple floors

The capacity curves for 12-story structures with eccentric bracing and hinged and embedded link elements of 0.75 m, 1.25 m, and 1.75 m length are shown below. (See Fig. 10). It is observed that the capacity of the structures does not have greater variation when modeling the hinged or embedded link, however, structures with shorter link elements present greater capacity than structures with longer link elements. Similar behavior is observed in the capacity of the 4 and 8-story structures. The capacity curves of these structures are better detailed in the work of [14].

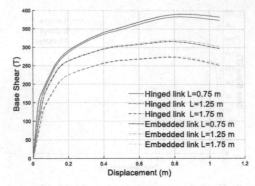

Fig. 10. Capacity curves of 12-story structure with eccentric bracing and 0.75 m, 1.25 m, and 1.75 m hinged-embedded link elements.

3.3 Failure Mechanisms

The functions created for this purpose allow visualizing graphically the formation of the plastic hinges up to the target displacement level and up to the ultimate displacement level of the structure. Other functions allow for visualization in an animated version of the Pushover of each structure with its capacity curve at different points, being of interest the maximum displacement point, and the target displacement point. (See Fig. 11). The formation of plastic hinges responds to the limit states of the elements, Immediately Occupational IO (green color), Life Safety LS (yellow color), and Collapse Prevention CP (red color). The results of the formation of plastic hinges and the links of the Pushover animations of the 27 typologies of study are reflected in the work of [14].

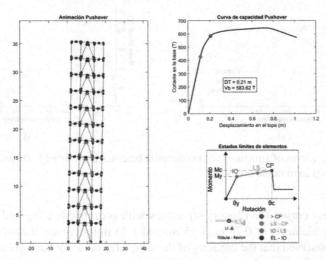

Fig. 11. Capacity curve in target displacement - SCBF V inverted 12 stories.

3.4 Performance Points

The following table shows the target displacement and performance level of the 27 study structures (Table 5).

Table 5. Seismic design parameters.

Type	Story_Spans	Story	Δ Target	Target Displacement			Performance level
			m	u	Ru	Ru*ρ*ΩE	
SMF	4P_3V	4	0.15	1.54	1.42	6.72	Functional
	8P_3V	8	0.33	1.94	1.80	7.43	Life Safety
	12P_3V	12	0.50	2.08	1.97	7.67	Life Safety
V inverted	4P_3V	4	0.03	0.79	0.86	7.60	Occupational
	8P_3V	8	0.12	1.39	1.30	7.54	Functional
	12P_3V	12	0.21	1.29	1.24	7.88	Functional
X	4P_3V	4	0.03	0.77	0.85	7.54	Occupational
	8P_3V	8	0.13	1.39	1.30	7.55	Functional
	12P_3V	12	0.17	0.97	0.97	6.31	Occupational
E_ART_L1	4P_3V	4	0.03	0.97	0.98	7.56	Occupational
	8P_3V	8	0.11	1.49	1.36	7.60	Functional
	12P_3V	12	0.24	2.21	1.95	7.69	Functional
E_ART_L2	4P_3V	4	0.05	1.21	1.15	7.18	Functional
	8P_3V	8	0.14	1.82	1.61	7.46	Functional
	12P_3V	12	0.26	2.49	2.17	7.55	Functional
E_ART_L3	4P_3V	4	0.06	1.39	1.28	6.87	Functional
	8P_3V	8	0.17	2.10	1.83	7.39	Functional
	12P_3V	12	0.29	2.60	2.28	7.53	Functional
E_EMP_L1	4P_3V	4	0.03	0.96	0.97	7.58	Occupational
	8P_3V	8	0.11	1.46	1.34	7.61	Functional
	12P_3V	12	0.24	2.17	1.92	7.71	Functional
E_EMP_L2	4P_3V	4	0.05	1.20	1.14	7.16	Functional
	8P_3V	8	0.13	1.80	1.60	7.46	Functional
	12P_3V	12	0.26	2.45	2.15	7.53	Functional
E_EMP_L3	4P_3V	4	0.06	1.39	1.27	6.86	Functional
	8P_3V	8	0.17	2.09	1.82	7.40	Functional
	12P_3V	12	0.29	2.58	2.27	7.53	Functional

4   Discussion of Results

After analyzing the performance level of the structures, it is evident that 20 of the 27 study typologies remain at a "Functional" performance level, which means that minimal damage to the structure is expected, and it remains in a suitable condition to continue functioning. In addition, 5 of the 27 analysis typologies are at an "Immediately Occupational" performance level, which means that there is no significant damage to the structure, therefore, the structural elements maintain their function and the structure can be used after minor repairs. Finally, 2 of the 27 typologies are at a "Life Safety" performance level, which means that the structural elements have suffered significant damage that has reduced their rigidity, however, the structure still maintains a level of safety for its occupants, although repairs or reinforcement are required to function. In general, the seismic performance level of unbraced structures is lower compared to braced structures. The critical cases among the parameters of this study are the 8 and 12-story structures, considered medium-height structures, however, the structures present behavior that allows taking actions and avoiding catastrophic losses at the moment of a seismic event, that is to say, their performance level is maintained in a "Life Safety" range.

The results of the linear static analysis performed under the NEC-15 guidelines, quantifiable mainly in displacements, drifts, and shear forces at each floor, show that floor drifts are significantly reduced in braced structures, therefore, a system with bracing is more efficient than a braced system without bracing. In addition, the floor drifts of a system with concentric bracing with inverted V-shaped diagonals and a system with concentric X-shaped bracing on multiple floors are similar, meaning that both systems provide similar stiffness to the structure. The same is the case with eccentrically braced structures, although the length of the link may define if the link yields in shear, flexure, or both, the behavior of eccentrically braced structures with hinged or embedded link elements, concerning floor drifts, is similar within this type of structural system. For this same system, it is found that there is an increase in the derivatives as the length of the link increases.

The capacity curves obtained as a result of the nonlinear static analysis (Pushover) show that the capacity of the structures with concentric and eccentric bracing is higher than the capacity of the structure without bracing. Also, in the case of structures with concentric bracing, regardless of the type of diagonal (inverted V or multi-story X), the capacity is similar in both cases. Finally, in the case of eccentrically braced structures, there is no significant variation in their capacity if the type of link connection (hinged or embedded) is evaluated; however, the capacity of the structure is higher with smaller link elements and is lower with larger link elements.

The failure mechanisms and the sequence of plastic hinge formation show that there is a higher concentration of hinges on the lower floors of the structures, independent of their number of floors or their structural configuration. Specifically, the formation of plastic hinges for moment-resisting frames is concentrated in the beams, for frames with centric bracing in the diagonals and for eccentric bracing, plastic hinges are mainly found in the connecting elements. This shows that all the designed structures conform to adequate performance levels and have acceptable collapse mechanisms from a structural perspective, meaning damage to beams, diagonals or linking elements, and floor columns.

The development of functions in the CEINCI-LAB Computational System and Open-Sees, presents an interface that allows the user to enter the values of profile dimensions and material properties, in addition to modifying the codes according to their requirements. Therefore, it is possible to include dimensional errors in the fabrication of structural elements or changes in the material properties, which in turn allows the execution of designs that are closer to reality.

References

1. Quinde, P., Reinoso, E.: Estudio de peligro sísmico de Ecuador y propuesta de espectros de diseño para la Ciudad de Cuenca. Ingeniería sísmica, (94), 1–26. México (2016)
2. Vanegas, J.: Estudios de las causas de demolición de edificios afectados por el sismo del 16 de abril del 2016 en Chone. UCSG, Guayaquil (2018)
3. Gándara, C.: Análisis comparativo de diseño por desempeño de dos estructuras de acero (PEM y PAE). UEES, Guayaquil (2019)
4. Soong, T., Spencer, B.: Supplemental energy dissipation: State of the art and state of the practice. Eng. Struct. **24**, 243–259 (2002)
5. Ramadan, T., Ghobarah, A.: Behavior of bolted link-column joints in eccentrically braced frames. Canadian Journal of Civil Engineering. Canada (1995)
6. Mansour, N., Christopoulos, C., Tremblay, R.: Experimental validation of replaceable shear links for eccentrically braced steel frames. J. Struct. Eng. **137**(10), 1141–1152, Canada (2011)
7. Dusicka, P., Lewis, G.: Investigation of Replaceable Sacrificial Steel Links. Earthquake Spectra, Canada (2010)
8. Cagua, B., Aguiar, R., Pilatasig, J.: Nuevas funciones de CEINCI-LAB para el análisis y diseño de pórticos de acero con arriostramientos excéntricos. Revista Internacional de Ingeniería de Estructuras **26**(2), 199–283 (2021)
9. Cagua, B., Aguiar, R., Pilatasig., J, Mora, D.: Acoplamiento de OpenSees con CEINCI-LAB para análisis estático no lineal. Primera parte: reforzamiento sísmico con diagonales de acero. Revista Internacional de Ingeniería de Estructuras **25**(3), 367–420 (2020)
10. Cagua, B., Aguiar, R., Pilatasig., J.: Nuevas Funciones de CEINCI-LAB para el análisis y diseño de pórticos de acero con arriostramientos concéntricos **26**(2), 199–284 (2021)
11. Dirección de Comunicación Social MIDUVI.: NEC Norma Ecuatoriana de la Construcción, Cargas (No Sísmicas). MIDUVI, Quito (2014)
12. Aguiar, R.: Microzonificación Sísmica de Quito. 2 ed. IPGH, Quito (2017)
13. Dirección de Comunicación Social MIDUVI.: NEC Norma Ecuatoriana de la Construcción, Peligro sísmico y diseño sismoresistente). MIDUVI, Quito (2014)
14. Pilatasig, J.: Comportamiento no lineal de pórticos de acero con diagonales concéntricas y excéntricas. UFA-ESPE, Quito (2021)
15. Aguiar, R., Cagua, B., Pilatasig, J.: Pushover con Acoplamiento de CEINCI-LAB y OpenSees. A.H. Barbat, Barcelona (2020)
16. American Society of Civil Engineers.: ASCE standard, ASCE/SEI 41-17, seismic evaluation and retrofit of existing buildings. American Society of Civil Engineers, Virginia (2017)
17. American Institute of Steel Construction.: ANSI/AISC 341-16 Seismic Provisions for Structural Steel Buildings. AISC, Chicago (2016)
18. American Institute of Steel Construction.: ANSI/AISC 360-16 Specification for Structural Steel Buildings. AISC, Chicago (2016)
19. American Institute of Steel Construction.: ANSI/AISC 358-16 Prequalified Connections for Special and Intermediate Steel Moment Frames for Seismic Applications. AISC, Chicago (2016)
20. American Society of Civil Engineers.: ASCE 7-16 Minimum Design Loads and Associated Criteria for Buildings and Other Structures. ASCE, Virginia (2016)

Tensile Strength PLA Reinforced with Perolera Pineapple Fiber Comparison, Based on the Reinforcement Fiber Direction

C. G. Cárdenas-Arias[1,2](✉), E. Zuza-Hernández[2], J. E. Quiroga-Méndez[3], and O. Lengerke-Perez[1]

[1] Design and Materials Research Group (DIMAT), Automation and Control Energy Systems Research Group (GISEAC), Electromechanical Engineering, Faculty of Natural Sciences and Engineering, Unidades Tecnológicas de Santander UTS, Calle de los Estudiantes No. 9-82, 680005 Bucaramanga, Colombia
ccardenas@correo.uts.edu.co

[2] Doctoral Program in Sustainable Materials and Process Engineering, Department of Sustainable Materials and Process Engineering, University of the Basque Country, UPV/EHU, Engineer Torres Quevedo Plaza, 1, 48013 Bilbao, Spain

[3] Energy and Materials Research Group, Mechanical Engineering School, Universidad Industrial de Santander, Calle 9 Carrera 27, Bucaramanga, Colombia

Abstract. The mechanical behavior of a reinforced polylactic material with perolera pineapple fiber study is presented in order to determine its potential as an alternative industrial input material. First, the necessary information about the lactic acid production with biodegradable materials and materials reinforced with natural fibers was collected; secondly, the procedure to be followed to generate the raw material with which the composite material was developed was defined. Thirdly, the material testing experimental design reinforced with perolera pineapple fiber was made; and finally, the stress tests were carried out on the already reinforced composite material to know its mechanical properties and determine its behavior. The results obtained allow a behavior comparison of tensile resistance of PLA and PLA reinforced with pineapple fiber.

Keywords: Pineapple fiber · PLA · Tensile strength · Biopolymer · Bio composite

1 Introduction

In recent years, the planet has experienced drastic changes due to the pollution generated by plastics and other elements made with products that have a slow degrading capacity, that is, they take time to decompose. Bags derived from plastic material take a degradation cycle of up to one hundred and fifty years and according to the United Nations (UN), five hundred billion bags are used each year [1]. Today, there is the possibility of acting on this crisis and starting to implement biodegradable materials, therefore, a commitment is expected to make good use of materials, resources or energies that are renewable, biodegradable or reusable in order to mitigate, eliminate or create new alternatives that help in the care of the environment.

Various studies have been carried out on the use of polymers and their incorporation with materials of organic origin that reduce environmental pollution, in recent years, for which inputs of plant origin have been taken into account [2] such as banana, pineapple and cocoa, among others, which can be used to generate materials that provide resistance similar to those of non-vegetable origin, presenting some points in favor of their use, such as, for example, they are biodegradable, they tend to break less, they are not toxic and they are less heavy [3].

Taking into account that Santander is one of Colombia departments that has a large production of perolera pineapple [4], this is considered a great opportunity to take advantage of tropical fruit leaf to incorporate it into the creation of a bio composite material, giving way to advances in the industry that are of benefit to the community.

There are two types of plants that produce natural fibers, primary and secondary; the primary ones are those that grow for their fiber content, such as cotton, and the secondary ones from which the fibers are extracted as a by-product, an example of these is the pineapple. In recent years, compounds reinforced with natural fibers have been studied, which have shown that they offer good mechanical performance, for this reason, they have focused on finding more of these renewable materials that are also eco-friendly [5].

Pineapple is one of the most produced tropical fruits worldwide, it is bromeliad family part originated in America, in tropical climate zones with relatively high temperatures between 20 and 34 °C and is surviving on land capable [6].

Pineapple leaves, the product to be used, grow between 30 and 100 cm long, an adult pineapple plant has a maximum of 80 leaves, its shape is elongated and ribbed [6].

The reinforcement can be carried out in different ways, one of these being the direction of the reinforcement with respect to the longitudinal axis. This paper presents a study on the tensile resistance comparison of material bio composite based on the pineapple fiber direction at along polymer.

2 Methodology

A PLA filament biopolymer with pineapple fiber reinforcement, obtained from the fruit leaf, was prepared. For this, an injection machine was used, where the PLA was melted and deposited in molds, where the fiber had been located in three directions with respect to the longitudinal axis, obtaining test tubes with long fibers located parallel to the axis, test tubes with short fiber located in a transverse to the axis and specimens with short fiber reinforcement in different random directions (Fig. 1).

2.1 Polylactic Acid PLA

Polylactic acid is an ecological thermoplastic polyester that originates from a fermentation process from natural resources such as cassava starch, wheat, corn, sugar cane, tapioca, among others; in this it differs from other industrial materials that are not biodegradable because they are generated from fossil fuels [7].

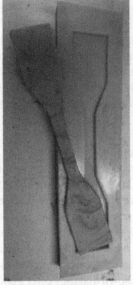

Fig. 1. Injector, mold and work product

Polylactic acid is generated from lactic acid, a natural raw material, obtained through fermentation. Lactic acid is a chiral compound that, depending on its origin, can be the D-isomer, the L-isomer or a DL mixture. Lactic acid polymerization can be controlled to certain molecular weights and different degrees of crystallinity by appropriate selection of reaction guidelines such as pressure, temperature, catalyst selection and reaction time. In turn, the level of crystallinity and the physical and mechanical characteristics of the raw material depend on the molecular weight and the isomer chosen to carry out the polymerization. While PLLA and PDLA are semi crystalline, PDLLA is amorphous [8].

This acid kind can be produced by chemical means, where two processes are generated, one is the acetaldehyde alteration with HCN 'hydrocyanic acid' with which acetonitrile is obtained, which can be hydrolyzed to lactic acid; the other way lactic acid producing is in the acetaldehyde high-pressure reaction with carbon monoxide and water together with sulfuric acid, which acts as a catalyst. Another obtaining method it comes from biotechnology. The lactic acid production originates from the substrate's fermentation rich in carbohydrates by bacteria or fungi and depends on the microorganism pattern used, the pH, the temperature, among others [9].

Initially, an attempt was made to develop polylactic from pineapple, a procedure that, when analyzing the literature, was found to be quite complex. A homemade method was tested, easy to develop, for which cornstarch, water, glycerin, vinegar and a heat source or reverberatory are required.

The procedure carried out was as follows: in a pot, the ingredients mentioned above were added one by one and stirred until a uniform mixture was left, followed by cooking over medium heat until it reached its boiling temperature, it is important not to stop beating for the necessary time in which a uniform gel-like consistency is achieved, this is so that the mixture does not stick to the pot bottom or the edges, during this step it is observed how little by little a mixture is formed gelatinous, at the end when the desired consistency was achieved, it was lowered from the heat and placed in the mold to let it cool.

When the material cooled, it was observed that its consistency was very low, basically creating a paste, which is why this product and this method were discarded (Fig. 2).

Fig. 2. PLA production from corn starch

It was proposed to make a more industrial procedure, which consists of polymerization from the lactide formation. For this, first the lactide had to be obtained and then a polymerization process for which the following reagents and equipment were needed: lactic acid, 60% sulfuric acid, stannous chloride, ethanol, heating plate and magnetic agitation and assembly to neutralize acid vapors.

To extract the lactide, the following procedure was followed:

The heating and magnetic stirring plate is prepared at 80 °C temperature with 300 rpm speed; apart in a container, 100 mL of lactic acid and 5 mL of 60% sulfuric acid were added, then this mixture was taken to iron to leave it there for 30 min.

After 30 min, the temperature was increased to 120 °C, 5 mL more of 60% sulfuric acid were added.

When it was two hours old, another 5 mL of 60% sulfuric acid was added and it was left heating for 3 to 5 h, noting the consistency that the mixture was taking (Fig. 3).

Fig. 3. Lactide formation process

Finally, 5 mL of 60% sulfuric acid was added and after 2 h the consistency obtained was analyzed, taking into account that if it is brown and viscous it means that lactide was obtained (Fig. 4).

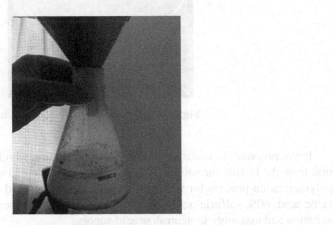

Fig. 4. Lactide produced

At the process end, PLA was obtained, but without the necessary characteristics, because it did not reach the required degree of hardness. Information was obtained that other additives and special equipment were needed to generate the different reactions that would add the expected hardness.

It was then decided to use the commercial PLA filament, used in 3D printers.

2.2 Reinforcement Fiber

The pineapple leaf fiber, being a natural material origin, its characteristics and compositions vary for many reasons, including: the species, the climate and the soil. Basically, pineapple leaf fiber is chemically composed of 70–82% Holocellulose, 5–12% lignin and 1.1% ash, however, these data may vary depending on the fibers age and the crop conditions [10].

The main chemical composition of fibers such as coir, banana, pineapple leaf, sisal, palmyra, hemp, etc., are cellulose and lignin that are analyzed in the Table. Natural fibers are made up of cellulose and lignin; These celluloses consist of many fibrils along the length that are associated with hydrogen bonding to provide strength and flexibility [11] (Fig. 5).

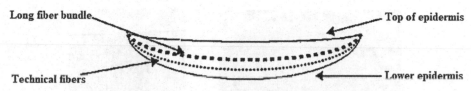

Fig. 5. Pineapple leaf cross section

The fiber extraction from the pineapple leaf by means of the ball mill is one of the best obtaining techniques, where a large quantity of elemental fibers is obtained due to its small diameter, but it has a high cost, which is a disadvantage for many farmers. The next method that provides a significant quantity is the blade mill, which is not as expensive and therefore may be more viable, the least suitable is the dry leaf milling, where a very low quality of pineapple leaf fiber is obtained [12].

When a better-quality fiber is required, it must be extracted by chemical methods since they have better functional properties with respect to the fiber obtained by the manual method, but it is a little more expensive and this process is also more delayed compared to the other methods mentioned.

Due to the industrial resource's situation, it was decided to obtain the fiber manually, based on the fact that the work objective is to make a comparison, for which this procedure is viable.

To obtain the reinforcing fiber, long pineapple leaves were taken, beaten with a mallet to soften them, combed with a fine-bristled steel wire brush and immersed in water for 20 min to remove the cellulose part. They were dried for 24 h in ambient air and then combed again until the desired material was obtained (Fig. 6).

Fig. 6. Process to obtain the reinforcing fiber

2.3 Specimen Molds

Normally injection molds consist of two parts, a female, which is the one that contains the cavity and another part that is normally called male, which is the movable part, and allows the casting to be extracted or removed.

Due to the work conditions, one-part molds were developed, where the reinforcement was deposited according to the need and the PLA was then forged.

Some silicone, aluminum and Teflon test tubes were made, respecting the ASTM D638-14 standard [13], for the specimen's dimensions (Fig. 7).

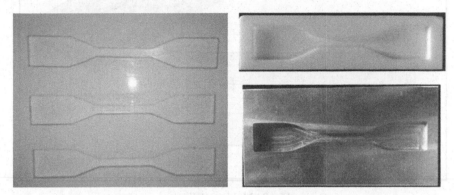

Fig. 7. Specimen molds

For the silicone molds, some cardboard specimens were made with a die, they were plastered and sanded, to leave them at the normalized dimension. Subsequently, the silicone was set and allowed to cool, to obtain the desired matrix (Fig. 8).

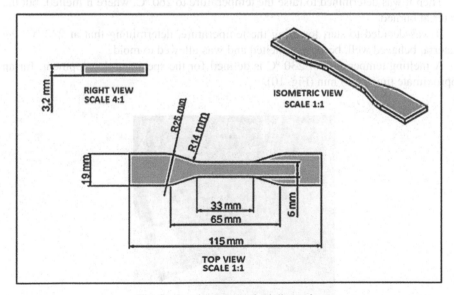

Fig. 8. Specimens standard dimension

To develop the molds in aluminum and Teflon, a CNC machining center was used. The CNC work involved developing the mold modeling in CAD software (Fig. 9).

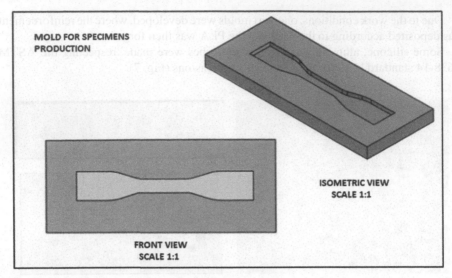

Fig. 9. Mold modeling

2.4 Specimens

Initially it was tried to melt at 150 °C, temperature at which the material melted, but it was not allowed to mold.

Then it was determined to raise the temperature to 260 °C, where it melted, but the material burned.

It was decided to start lowering the temperature, determining that at 230 °C, the material behaved well, because it melted and was allowed to mold.

A melting temperature of 230 °C is defined for the specimen development, for an approximate time of 13 min (Fig. 10).

Fig. 10. Specimen molding

The molds were prepared with the fiber located in the direction that it was desired to generate and test the specimen. Specimens were made with the fiber located longitudinally, transversely, randomly along the mold and without reinforcement, to have a reference point.

Five specimens were manufactured with each fiber direction, according to the recommendation of the experiments design. The fiber matrix ratio was 80–20 (Fig. 11).

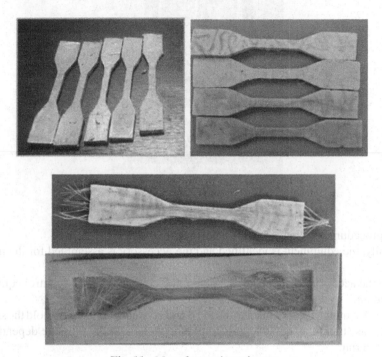

Fig. 11. Manufactured specimens

2.5 Tension Test

The tension tests were carried out under the ASTM D638-14 standard in the Industrial University of Santander laboratories. With these tests, force and axial displacement data were generated, which were used to calculate the stresses, prepare the graph of stress vs. strain and thereby evaluate the mechanical properties of the specimens.

The tensile test was carried out on an MTS BIONIX universal testing machine. The test purpose is to determine how much resistance the specimens have when subjected to tension, applying two forces located at the ends that deform said specimen until it breaks and thus obtain the stress vs. strain diagram (Fig. 12).

The parameters required by the machine were adjusted, such as: displacement speed: 3 mm/min, displacement direction depending on the test, which in this case would be tension and specimen dimensions, and the tests were carried out by breaking the specimens.

Fig. 12. MTS universal testing machine

The procedure is following:

Initially, the equipment is identified and the accessory is assembled for the traction test.

Once the accessory is mounted, the pump, the computer and the control equipment are turned on.

Proceed to mount the specimen in the MTS and activate the clamps to hold the sample. Keeping it as straight as possible, it is important to look at the pressure depending on the test material.

From the computer, the MTS is turned on and the pump pressure is increased, then the test program is opened and next to it the corresponding test, if necessary, it is modified giving the appropriate parameters such as displacement and speed.

The test is executed from the computer, once the test is finished, the specimen is removed, opening the jaws.

Test data is exported to a USB stick for further analysis.

At the test end, it was evident that the pressure is a determining test parameter, since it must be configured depending on the test material (Fig. 13).

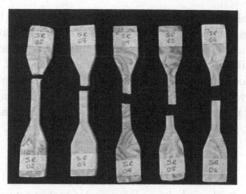

Fig. 13. Broken specimens in the test

3 Results

When carrying out the stress tests for each specimen under the NTC 595 [14] and ASTM 638-14 standards, the necessary data were obtained to calculations´ make, prepare the stress vs. strain graphs and study the specimens' mechanical behavior when stress was applied.

The tensile tests results are evidenced in the diagrams presented below, in which the stress values are on the "Y" axis and the strain values on the "X" axis.

The first tests were made to the PLA-only specimens to know their mechanical properties and that these data would serve to compare them with the reinforced specimens' results (Fig. 14).

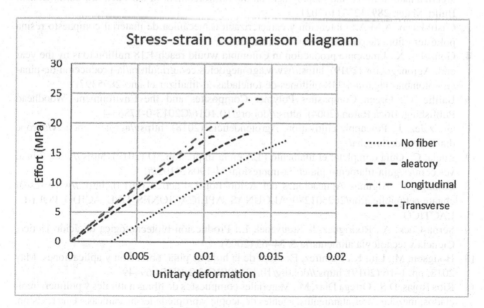

Fig. 14. Stress-strain comparison diagram

Based on the graph, it can be seen that there is no yield point, but that the material behavior produced has a fairly proportional relationship between stress and strain. It can also be commented that the reinforcement effectively influences the matrix, improving, in this case, the tensile strength, and that, according to the work objective, it can be shown that the fiber location direction with respect to the specimen longitudinal axis, it is important for achieve this increase in applied load capacity, causing different increases according to the fiber position, where the longitudinal position turned out to be the best reinforcement option.

4 Conclusions

The work objective was achieved, determining a relationship between the fiber position with respect to the specimen longitudinal axis, where it was found that the longitudinal direction is the one that contributes the most in tensile strength, followed closely by the random and finally the transverse direction.

It was also possible to determine that generating polylactic acid from natural sources, not petrochemicals, is not easy and that the required investment is high. A good study of return on capital must be done to develop these processes. This is going to make it difficult to replace plastic in the short term in all industrial applications.

References

1. Naciones Unidas: United Nations Environment Assembly Report of the United Nations Environment Program, pp. 1–5 (2019). https://undocs.org/pdf?symbol=es/a/74/25
2. Benzerara, M., Guihéneuf, S., Belouettar, R., Perrot, A.: Combined and synergic effect of algerian natural fibres and biopolymers on the reinforcement of extruded raw earth. Constr. Build. Mater. **289**, 123211 (2021)
3. Castiblanco, A.M.A.: Obtención y caracterización mecánica de material compuesto resina poliéster - fibra de piña, Universidad Libre (2017)
4. Gonzáles, X.: Pineapple production in Colombia would reach 1.18 million tons by the year end. Agronegocios (2019). https://www.agronegocios.co/agricultura/la-produccion-de-pina-en-colombia-llegaria-a-118-millones-de-toneladas-al-finalizar-el-ano-2895397
5. Baillie, C.: Green Composites Polymer Composites and the Environment. Woodhead Publishing, Boca Raton (2004). https://doi.org/10.1016/C2013-0-17863-4
6. González, J.: Pineapple cultivation. Agrotendencia (2018). https://agrotendencia.tv/agropedia/cultivo-de-la-pina/
7. Lucia, C.: Guía completa: el filamento PLA en la impresión 3D (2019). https://www.3dnatives.com/es/guia-filamento-pla-en-la-impresion-3d-190820192/#!
8. Zuluaga, F.: Algunas Aplicaciones del Ácido Poli-L-Láctico (2013). https://www.researchgate.net/publication/262501280_ALGUNAS_APLICACIONES_DEL_ACIDO_POLI-L-LACTICO
9. Serna-Cock, A., Rodriguez-de Stouvenel, L.: Producción biotecnológica de ácido láctico. Ciencia y tecnología alimentaria **5**, 54–65 (2005)
10. Hodgson, M., Liu, K., Ramírez, F.: Fibra de la hoja de piña, obtención y aplicaciones, May 2018, pp. 1–16 (2019). https://doi.org/10.13140/RG.2.2.18654.69449
11. Rios Rojas, D.S., Ortega Diaz, M.: Materiales compuestos de fibras naturales y polímero reciclados: mezclas, pretratamientos, agentes de acople y propiedades mecánicas - Una revision. CRAIUSTA (2021). http://hdl.handle.net/11634/33854

12. Kengkhetkit, N., Wongpreedee, T., Amornsakchai, T.: Pineapple leaf fiber: from waste to high-performance green reinforcement for plastics and rubbers. In: Kalia, S. (ed.) Lignocellulosic Composite Materials. SSPCM, pp. 271–291. Springer, Cham (2018). https://doi.org/10.1007/978-3-319-68696-7_6
13. A. S. for T. M. ASTM, ASTM D638 Standard Test Method for Tensile Properties of Plastics
14. N. T. C. NTC, NTC 595 Test method to determine the tensile properties of plastics, vol. 571 (2007)

Evaluation of Horizontal and Vertical Positions Obtained from an Unmanned Aircraft Vehicle Applied to Large Scale Cartography of Infrastructure Loss Due to the Earthquake of April 2016 in Ecuador

Juan Sani, Alfonso Tierra⊙, Theofilos Toulkeridis(✉) ⊙, and Oswaldo Padilla⊙

Universidad de las Fuerzas Armadas ESPE, Sangolquí, Ecuador
ttoulkeridis@espe.edu.ec

Abstract. The development technology of Unmanned Aircraft Vehicles (UAV) allows the improvement of new applications and it may be used to obtain geospatial information with high precision. In this study we present the evaluation of an ortho-mosaic and a digital surface model (DSM), which both have been generated from information received by UAV flights. The horizontal control points were obtained by precision positioning with GPS and they were referred at SIRGAS system, epoch 2014.0. The vertical points were obtained by spirit leveling referred at vertical datum "La Libertad" in Ecuador. These results indicate that it is possible to realize cartography scales 1:500 scales, and digital elevation model a 1:500 scales with contour line of 1 m. Such high resolution of the UAV has been used to evaluate the damage provoked by the 7.8 Mw earthquake, which occurred at the 16th of April 2016 in the coastal part of Ecuador. The quick application of the UAV and the generation of such images and data obtained, supported the rescue teams in the recovery of victims and helped to improve a fast evaluation and quantification of the collapses of the infrastructure.

Keywords: UAV · GPS · Spirit leveling · Ortho-mosaic · DSM · Ecuador

1 Introduction

The advancement and improvement of geospatial technologies enable the development of precise applications at lower cost compared to traditionally used methodologies [1]. Hereby, the introduction of the Unmanned Aircraft Systems (UAS) technology allows the advance of new applications fields because its high-resolution, data capture helps to improve previously less advanced or determined areas. Actually, with the technology of Unmanned Aircraft Vehicles (UAV) geospatial information of almost any terrain and even previously inaccessible areas is able to be generated after geospatial data were obtained. The geospatial information needs to be of high precision to be able to be used in engineering applications, requiring a strict evaluation of such data. UAV applications were widespread used [2–6] as they have allowed to determine real-time thermal data over fire hazards [7–9], to obtain an image for the generation of a highly accurate 3D model combined with photogrammetric processing [10], in the mitigation of systematic error in topographic models [11], in the disaster evaluation of collapsed buildings [12, 13]; in the mapping and monitoring of sand dunes and beaches [14], coastal environments [15], vegetation [16], biodiversity [17] and agriculture [18, 19], rangeland [20, 21] or even conflicts [22] as well as in the application in remote sensing in large scale (1:1000) topographic mapping [23]. UAV systems have also been variably used in geomatic applications [24] and in diverse landscapes such as rangeland environments [25] among many others [26–34].

At the present, UAV's are equipped with more sensitive cameras, being able to capture scenes and spots with a resolution of as low as a few centimeters, becoming an extremely useful and viable option for the generation of geospatial information at large scales [35–40]. In this respect, based on the mentioned with information obtained with an UAV allows to generate ortho-mosaics and digital elevation models for cartography purposes in large scales.

Therefore, the main objective of this work has been to evaluate both, horizontal and vertical positions, to large scales of the ortho-mosaic and Digital Surface Model (DSM) obtained from UAV flights, generated by means of photogrammetric techniques. To fulfill such purpose, we have evaluated the horizontal positions of the ortho-mosaic comparing them with the horizontal coordinates obtained from Global Positioning Systems (GPS) and additionally the vertical positions of the DSM comparing them with the height obtained from the spirit leveling. The second objective of this study has been to use such high resolution images and data to the quick evaluation of the damages provoked by a recent earthquake in Ecuador. On the 16th of April 2016, a Mw 7.8 earthquake impacted coastal Ecuador, being the most devastating registered in northern South America in this century so far. The UAV images and high resolution data were used with the purpose of an adequate recovery of some of the devasted zones.

2 Unmanned Aircraft Systems (UAS)

An UAS consists of a set of elements that allow the flight of an unmanned aircraft [41–43]. The elements involved in these systems will determine different types of UAS platforms [44]. Three main UAS components are commonly identified, namely the UAV, the ground control station and the communication data link [41]. They form different types of architectures of UAS [45, 46].

An Unmanned Aerial Vehicle (UAV) has the capacity of maintaining a sustained and controlled automatically by a flight plan. UAVs have been used in several applications, and different sensors have been incorporated in order to obtain more precise measurements. In this study we have used a UAV with photogrammetric purposes. This UAV photogrammetry may be understood as a new tool in measurement, that combines aerial and terrestrial photogrammetry. Additionally, this UAV benefit of being of lower costs, when compared with traditional methods and applications [47]. In this respect, TrimbleTM has created an UAS called "UX5 Aerial Imaging Solutions", allowing to receive large amounts of data covering several hectares in less than one hour in time. In addition, it enables the integration of processing software for specific details of UAVs, making so possible the generation of high-quality photogrammetric products [48–50].

3 Survey Area and UAV Flight Plan in the Test Phase

The study area was located at the Campus of the Universidad de las Fuerzas Armadas ESPE in Sangolquí (latitude = 0° 18′ 48″ S, longitude = 78° 26′ 37″ W and height = 2500 m approximately), in the central-northern highlands of Ecuador to be the surveyed area. In an outline map of the ESPE campus are eleven control points located, which were used in the photogrammetric process. In such points were determined horizontal and vertical coordinates. The horizontal coordinates were obtained using GPS positioning, with double frequency receiver, and referred at SIRGAS-Ecuador (SIstema de Referencia Geocéntrico para las AmericaS) Reference Frame at epoch 2014.0 aligned at International Terrestrial Reference Frame 2008 (ITRF08) [51]. It was used the static method relative with one hour of tracking and 30 s between epochs. The vertical coordinates in these points were obtained realizing the spirit leveling, with a closed leveling line of 8 mm\sqrt K (K in kilometers). These heights are referred as vertical datum "La Libertad" in coastal Ecuador.

The UAV model UX5 Trimble has been used for the execution of the flight plan in the presented study area. Flight parameters were defined for the image-taking, with a flying height at a middle ground of about 120 m, with a GSD of 3.8 cm, having both longitudinal and transverse overlapping of some 82% and flight duration time of 38 min. In order to complete the coverage of the surveyed area, following the set-up of the flight plan and mentioned parameters, we obtained a total of 893 photographs in 32 flight lines.

Hereby, the information on the coordinates of the centers of exposure for each photo and their values yaw, pitch, and roll were indicated as they are necessary for further internal guidance. With this information the photogrammetric block adjustment has been determined using the Trimble Business Center (TBC) software, generating ortho-mosaic and DSM models.

In order to evaluate the horizontal position of the ortho-mosaic obtained from the photogrammetric process, the GPS positioning of 70 distributed points in the study area have been performed, considering them as evaluation points. They were obtained their coordinates Universal Transverse Mercator (UTM), North (N) and East (E) in the SIRGAS, at epoch 2014.0 aligned at International Terrestrial Reference Frame 2008 (ITRF08) [51]. It was used the Fast Static method with 10 min of tracking, with double frequency receiver.

In order to evaluate the vertical position of the DSM, the spirit leveling of two lines has been realized. In the first line (L1) we obtained the height of 17 points, while in the second line (L2) a total of 19 points were obtained. These heights are referred to the vertical datum of Ecuador "La Libertad" and UTM plane coordinates (East, North) referred as SIRGAS were calculated from the GPS positioning.

4 Geodynamic Setting of the 16th of April 2016 Earthquake

Due to its geodynamic situation along the Pacific Rim, the coastal Ecuadorian is considered a high seismic hazard region, due to intense seismic activity, mainly caused by subduction of the oceanic Nazca plate and a presence of active faults that generate crustal and subduction earthquakes [52–60]. They involved human and materials losses, as they hit cities, besides considering that Ecuador is one of the most densely populated countries in South America [61–65]. The active continental margin and associated subduction zone between the oceanic Nazca Plate with the continental South American and Caribbean Plates, both separated by the Guayaquil-Caracas Mega Shear [66–68] give rise to tsunamis of tectonic as well submarine landslide origin [69–75].

From the known record of the last two centuries, the Ecuadorian shoreline has witnessed a dozen times strong earthquakes and marine quakes, some of which generated tsunamis by mainly local origins with various intensities one being of up to 8.8 Mw in 1906 [76–80], while evidences of paleo-tsunami deposits are scarce [81]. Other prominent examples of earthquakes with subsequent tsunamis along the Ecuador–Colombia subduction zone include tsunamis in 1942 (Mw 7.8), 1958 (Mw 7.7) and 1979 (Mw 8.2) within the 600-km long rupture area of the great 1906 event [82]. While the 1906 event caused the death of up to 1500 persons in Ecuador and Colombia with an unknown financial damage to the existing infrastructure, the 1979 tsunami killed in Colombia at least 807 persons and destroyed approximately 10,000 homes, knocking out electric power and telephone lines [74, 83].

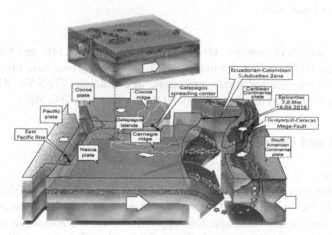

Fig. 1. Geodynamic setting of Ecuador, the Galapagos Islands and the Carnegie Ridge. Adapted from [84].

In the late afternoon of Saturday, at 18:58:36 (UTC-05:00) local time, a devastating earthquake with a magnitude of 7.8 Mw impacted coastal Ecuador [85–87]. The seismic event with an epicenter 29 km SSE of Muisne, Province of Esmeraldas (Figs. 1 and 2) occurred within a depth of 21 km, killing 663, filling tens of thousands in refugee camps and affecting some two million persons directly. In many aspects, the mentioned earthquake has many similarities with the earthquake of the 14th of May 1942. Nonetheless the resulting tsunami based on a triggered submarine landslide did not have any remark-able impact. The earthquake impacted a large part of a variety of coastal cities destroying a large proportion of some close-by villages and cities, including damages in Pedernales, Jama, Chone, Portoviejo among others (Fig. 2), in which lines of electricity transmis-sion, infrastructure of water supply, hospitals, schools, private and public buildings, main roads and highways have been severely affected or even completely destroyed. The costs of the damages of the mentioned infrastructure are summing up an approximate loss of some 3.3 billion USD [57, 88, 89].

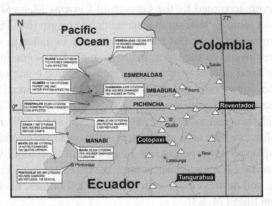

Fig. 2. Epicenter of the 7.8 Mw earthquake (red dot) and a selection of damages in the coastal area [86]. (Color figure online)

After the mainshock, almost 100 aftershocks between 3.8 Mw and 6.8 Mw were recorded by the USGS in Ecuador until July 14, last day until we have processed data; the epicenters were localized within a rectangle of coordinates [79.5 W - 81.5 W, 2 S - 1 N] reaching the highest magnitudes around the rupture zone [86, 90].

5   Results and Discussion

A)   Test phase
Based on the aerial photographs, which were obtained with the UAV-UX5 and the previously mentioned defined flight parameters in the test phase, the evaluation of the ortho-mosaic and DSM have been applied for both, horizontal and vertical coor-dinates respectively. The errors in the position point in planes coordinates (UTM) must be minor or equal a third of the scale. Therefore, this results that the errors of the scales 1:1000, 1:500, 1:250, 1:100; correspond to be less than 33.3 cm, 16.7 cm, 8.3 cm, and 3.3 cm, respectively. We calculated also the differences in the coordi-nates obtained for UTM between GPS and ortho mosaic. There, the differences in the point position east and north of the 70 identification points (IP; Fig. 5), are indi-cated and labeled as differences in the horizontal position (DIF_Hz). The arithmetic mean of the DIF_Hz has been 2.1 cm, with a standard deviation of 2.6 cm, and a maximum difference of 12.3 cm. Hereby, 75% are less than or equal to 3.3 cm; the

98% of IP are less than or equal to 8.3 cm, while 100% of the points have a difference minor to 16.7 cm. This means, it is possible and adequate to perform cartography with scale of 1:500 and 1:250 by using UAV. Additionally, these results indicate the possibility of being able to generate cartography at large scales ranging from 1: 500 to 1:5000, which may be used for general planning. The scale of 1:500 may be used for administration purposes, urban land as well as land use. Such data may even be used for certain projects that need cartography at scales of 1:250.

In the evaluation of the vertical coordinate, the error in height must be minor or equal to a fourth of the contour line, i.e., for scales 1:250 with intervals of 50 cm must be a vertical tolerance of 12.5 cm, while at a scale of 1:500 with contour lines of 1 m must be of 25 cm and at scales of 1:1000 with 1m contour lines, the error tolerance must be of 25 cm.

It has been demonstrated that the height values obtained with the spirit leveling, the heights obtained from DSM, as well as the height differences of the line 1 (L1) and line 2 (L2). The average difference has been of 3.2 cm, while the standard deviation reached 7.8 cm, with differences between −12.9 cm and 15.8 cm. According to the date, 80% of the points have a difference in the height between ±12.3 cm, while all of the points are between ±16 cm. This indicates that the heights obtained from DSM are compatible for contour line of 1m, which is used to scales of 1:500 and 1:1000.

James and Robson (2014) evaluated the Digital Elevation Model (DEM) for a UAV flight simulation using the VMS photogrammetric software and not including control points in the photogrammetric block adjustment. They got deformations to the order of 0.2 m in an approximate horizontal distance of 100 m, and one to two orders of magnitude in height. Unfortunately, They did not use checkpoints obtained in the field in order to detect the error in height of a given topographical model. In a further study [23], the checkpoints and horizontal check GPS has been used by the RTK (Real Time Kinematic) method, which is a less accurate method compared to the post-processed static and fast static methods as we have used. Hereby, the obtained errors in height in the different images were of about 0.73 m to 0.52 m, while the horizontal errors reached up to 0.24 m. Similar results were obtained by using UAV techniques, Terrestrial Laser Scanning (TLS) and (Global Navigation Systems) achieved by GNSS differences in distance with a RMS of 22 cm and vertically of about 20 cm vertical [15].

For mapping purposes the plane coordinates data of the ortho-mosaic need to be geo-referenced to a reference system, while the vertical need to be related to the datum height of the corresponding country. Therefore, the development and evaluation of both ortho-mosaic as well as the DSM, GPS precision data and geometric leveling have been used, with the aim that this will be geo-referenced to SIRGAS and the vertical datum.

B) Application in the disaster zone.
Shortly after the main earthquake of the 16th of April 2016, we moved towards a variety of devastated areas like Portoviejo, Chone, Bahia de Cadaquez, Calceta, San Vicente, Cojimies, Jama, Tarqui-Manta (Manabí) and Mompiche, Muisne, Pedernales (Esmeraldas), in order to apply the mentioned techniques with the high-resolution images and data. Due to the high amount of images and data we will

Fig. 3. Overview map of Portoviejo with the indication of the destruction. In Portoviejo, we have counted 92 completely destroyed buildings (red circles), 157 buildings partially collapsed (green circles) and 358 at risk to collapse (yellow circles) of a total of 70,428 buildings resulting to some 0.86% corresponding of destruction of the total. (Color figure online)

(a)   (b)

Fig. 4. a–b: Details of the high-resolution images of some of the destruction in Portoviejo.

Fig. 5. Above: Overview of a quarter of the city of Manta called Tarqui, where we counted destruction in 38,83% of the buildings.

(a)   (b)

Fig. 6. a: Left: The high-resolution image of the same city part. b: Right: An enlarged part of Fig. 6a demonstrating the details of the destruction of a building.

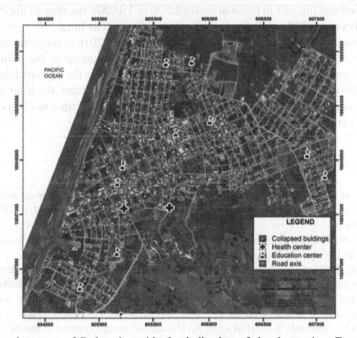

Fig. 7. Overview map of Pedernales with the indication of the destruction. From the 6018 buildings in total, 635 were destroyed in Pedernales, corresponding to a total loss of some 10,55%.

present only a few representative images and the evaluation of such. The percentage of destruction has been varied, due to different soil conditions, distance to the epicenter and degree of seismic resistance of the buildings and further infrastructure. The amount of destruction has been a result of a comparison of images prior the earthquake with the ones we obtained in April-May 2016. In case of the buildings, a numeric evaluation based on the UAV data resulted to the classification of complete or partial destructions as well as affects with some destruction (Figs. 3 and 4a–b). In some cases, we classified just between complete destruction and no to little affects (Figs. 5, 6a–b and 7). Thus, such data may support a fast response of governmental organizations like in other countries [91–93].

6 Conclusions

Based on the parameters defined in the flight planning and executed by the UAV-UX5, we may conclude the following:

The whole amount of the evaluation points has minor differences to 16.7 cm, being a third of the scale. This means, that the UAV is able to be used to determine geospatial data with compatible scales of 1:500. This scale may be used for administration purposes, urban land, land use and cadastral.

For the generation of digital elevation models, it is possible to obtain heights compatible with contours line of 1 m (used in scales 1:500 or 1:1000), because all the evaluation points are between ±25 cm, reflecting a fourth of the contour lines.

Such images of the UAV obtained on April and May of 2016 in the devastated zones of the Provinces of Manabí and Esmeraldas after the earthquake of the 16th of April 2016, have been an extraordinary support as a tool to determine the degree of destruction for the authorities and rescue organizations. Even more important, the high resolution images obtained by the UAV's supported also the recovery of victims and helped to save a high amount of lives after the earthquake.

References

1. Liu, X., et al.: An area-based position and attitude estimation for unmanned aerial vehicle navigation. Sci. China Technol. Sci. **58**(5), 916–926 (2015). https://doi.org/10.1007/s11431-015-5818-z
2. Nonami, K.: Prospect and recent research & development for civil use autonomous unmanned aircraft as UAV and MAV. J. Syst. Des. Dyn. **1**(2), 120–128 (2007)
3. Valavanis, K.P. (ed.): Advances in Unmanned Aerial Vehicles: State of the Art and the Road to Autonomy, vol. 33. Springer, Cham (2008). https://doi.org/10.1007/978-1-4020-6114-1
4. Cavoukian, A.: Privacy and drones: unmanned aerial vehicles. Information and Privacy Commissioner of Ontario, Canada, pp. 1–30 (2012)
5. Watts, A.C., Ambrosia, V.G., Hinkley, E.A.: Unmanned aircraft systems in remote sensing and scientific research: classification and considerations of use. Remote Sens. **4**(6), 1671–1692 (2012)
6. Finn, R.L., Wright, D.: Unmanned aircraft systems: surveillance, ethics and privacy in civil applications. Comput. Law Secur. Rev. **28**(2), 184–194 (2012)
7. Ambrosia, V., et al.: Demonstrating UAV-acquired real-time thermal data over fires. Photogramm. Eng. Remote. Sens. **69**(4), 391–402 (2003)
8. Pardo, J.A., Aguilar, W.G., Toulkeridis, T.: Wireless communication system for the transmission of thermal images from UAV. In: 2017 CHILEAN Conference on Electrical, Electronics Engineering, Information and Communication Technologies (CHILECON), pp. 1–5 (2017)

9. Reyes, D., et al.: Use of multitemporal indexes in the identification of forest fires–a case study of southern Chile. In: 2019 6th International Conference on eDemocracy and eGovernment, ICEDEG 2019, pp. 203–210 (2019)
10. Puschel, H., Saubier, M., Eisenbeiss, H.: A 3D model of castle Landerberg (CH) from combined photogrammetric processing of terrestrial and UAV-based images. In: The International archives of the Photogrammetry, Remote Sensing and Spatial Information Sciences, vol. XXXVII, Part B6B, pp. 93–98, Beijing, China (2008)
11. James, M., Robson, S.: Mitigating systematic error in topographic models derived from UAV and ground-based image networks. Earth Surface Processes Land Forms **39**(10), pp. 1413–1420 (2014)
12. Hua, C., Qi, J., Shang, H., Hu, W., Han, J.: Detection of collapsed buildings with the aerial images captured from UAV. Sci. China Inf. Sci. **58**, 32102 (2015). https://doi.org/10.1007/s11432-015-5341-7
13. Bai, Y., Adriano, B., Mas, E., Gokon, H., Koshimura, S.: Object-based building damage assessment methodology using only post event ALOS-2/PALSAR-2 dual Polarimetric SAR intensity images. J. Disaster Res. **12**(2), 259–271 (2017)
14. Gonçalves, J., Henriques, R.: UAV photogrammetry for topographic monitoring of coastal areas. ISPRS J. Photogrametric Remote Sens. **104**, 101–111 (2015). https://doi.org/10.1016/j.isprsjprs.2015.02.009
15. Mancini, F., Dubbini, M., Gattelli, M., Stecchi, F., Fabbri, S., Gabbianelli, G.: using unmanned aerial vehicles (UAV) for high-resolution reconstruction of topography: the structure from motion approach on coastal environments. Remote Sens. **5**(12), 6880–6898 (2013)
16. Berni, J.A., Zarco-Tejada, P.J., Suárez, L., Fereres, E.: Thermal and narrowband multispectral remote sensing for vegetation monitoring from an unmanned aerial vehicle. IEEE Trans. Geosci. Remote Sens. **47**(3), 722–738 (2009)
17. Getzin, S., Wiegand, K., Schöning, I.: Assessing biodiversity in forests using very high-resolution images and unmanned aerial vehicles. Methods Ecol. Evol. **3**(2), 397–404 (2012)
18. Herwitz, S.R., et al.: Imaging from an unmanned aerial vehicle: agricultural surveillance and decision support. Comput. Electron. Agric. **44**(1), 49–61 (2004)
19. Zhang, C., Kovacs, J.M.: The application of small unmanned aerial systems for precision agriculture: a review. Precision Agric. **13**(6), 693–712 (2012)
20. Laliberte, A.S., Goforth, M.A., Steele, C.M., Rango, A.: Multispectral remote sensing from unmanned aircraft: Image processing workflows and applications for range-land environments. Remote Sens. **3**(11), 2529–2551 (2011)
21. Laliberte, A.S., Herrick, J.E., Rango, A., Winters, C.: Acquisition, orthorectification, and object-based classification of unmanned aerial vehicle (UAV) imagery for range-land monitoring. Photogramm. Eng. Remote. Sens. **76**(6), 661–672 (2010)
22. Kreps, S., Kaag, J.: The use of unmanned aerial vehicles in contemporary conflict: a legal and ethical analysis. Polity **44**(2), 260–285 (2012)
23. Tianyun, X., Xiaocheng, T., Defang, Y., Yonghe, X., Hongliang, Y.: UAV remote sensing applications in large-scale mapping in the hilly region of Tibetan Plateau. Int. J. Control Autom. **8**(3), 279–286 (2015). https://doi.org/10.14257/ljca.2015.8.3.28
24. Remondino, F., Barazzetti, L., Nex, F., Scaioni, M., Sarazzi, D.: UAV photogrammetry for mapping and 3D modeling : current status and future perspectives. In: The International archives of the Photogrammetry, Remote Sensing and Spatial Information Sciences, vol. XXXVIII-1/C22. ISPRS, pp. 25–31, Zurich, Switzerland (2011)
25. Laliberte, A.S., Rango, A.: Texture and scale in object-based analysis of subdecimeter resolution unmanned aerial vehicle (UAV) imagery. IEEE Trans. Geosci. Remote Sens. **47**(3), 761–770 (2009)

26. Toulkeridis, T., Zach, I.: Wind directions of volcanic ash-charged clouds in Ecuador–implications for the public and flight safety. Geomatics Nat. Hazards Risks 8(2), 242–256 (2017)

27. Moncayo Cevallos, L.N., et al.: A NDVI analysis contrasting different spectrum data methodologies applied in pasture crops previous grazing–a case study from Ecuador. In: 2018 5th International Conference on eDemocracy and eGovernment, ICEDEG 2018, vol. 8372318, pp. 126–135 (2018)

28. Del Rocío Suango Sánchez, V., et al.: Use of geotechnologies and multicriteria evaluation in land use policy–the case of the urban area expansion of the city of Babahoyo, Ecuador. In: 2019 6th International Conference on eDemocracy and eGovernment, ICEDEG 2019, pp. 194–202 (2019)

29. Cepeda-Velastegui, M.V., López Estévez, M.J., Padilla-Almeida, O., Toulkeridis, T.: Determination of open pit mining zones through digital processing of multi-spectral images and PPI method–a case study of Southern Ecuador. In: 2019 6th International Conference on eDemocracy and eGovernment, ICEDEG 2019, pp. 188–193 (2019)

30. Zapata Vela, J., Galarza Vinueza, J., Yánez Toapanta, M., Toulkeridis, T., Ordoñez, E.: Determination of the natural plant coverage of the Eloy Alfaro Canton, NW Ecuador. In: 2020 7th International Conference on eDemocracy and eGovernment, ICEDEG 2020, pp. 174–181 (2020)

31. Guascal, E., Rojas, S., Kirby, E., Toulkeridis, T., Fuertes, W., Heredia, M.: Application of remote sensing techniques in the estimation of forest biomass of a recreation area by UAV and radar images in Ecuador. In: 2020 7th International Conference on eDemocracy and eGovernment, ICEDEG 2020, pp. 182–189 (2020)

32. Mora Villacís, M.G., Cañarte Ruiz, D.A., Kirby, E., Maiguashca Guzmán, J.A., Toulkeridis, T.: Index relationship of vegetation with the development of a Quinoa Crop (Chenopodium quinoa) in its first phenological stages in Central Ecuador based on GIS techniques. In: 2020 7th International Conference on eDemocracy and eGovernment, ICEDEG 2020, pp. 190–199 (2020)

33. Cañarte Ruiz, D.A., Mora Villacís, M.G., Kirby, E., Maiguashca Guzmán, J.A., Toulkeridis, T.: Correlation of NDVI obtained by different methodologies of spectral data collection in a commercial crop of Quinoa (Chenopodium quinoa) in Central Ecuador. In: 2020 7th International Conference on eDemocracy and eGovernment, ICEDEG 2020, pp. 207–214 (2020)

34. Viera-Torres, M., Sinde-González, I., Gil-Docampo, M., Bravo, V., Toulkeridis, T.: Generation of the base line in the early detection of bud rot and the red ring disease in oil palms by geospatial technologies. Remote Sens. 12(19), 3229 (2020)

35. Everaerts, J.: The use of unmanned aerial vehicles (UAVs) for remote sensing and mapping. Int. Arch. Photogramm. Remote. Sens. Spat. Inf. Sci. 37, 1187–1192 (2008)

36. Harwin, S., Lucieer, A.: Assessing the accuracy of georeferenced point clouds produced via multi-view stereopsis from unmanned aerial vehicle (UAV) imagery. Remote Sens. 4(6), 1573–1599 (2012)

37. Turner, D., Lucieer, A., Watson, C.: An automated technique for generating georectified mosaics from ultra-high resolution unmanned aerial vehicle (UAV) imagery, based on structure from motion (SfM) point clouds. Remote Sens. 4(5), 1392–1410 (2012)

38. Anderson, K., Gaston, K.J.: Lightweight unmanned aerial vehicles will revolutionize spatial ecology. Front. Ecol. Environ. 11(3), 138–146 (2013)

39. Zarco-Tejada, P.J., Diaz-Varela, R., Angileri, V., Loudjani, P.: Tree height quantification using very high resolution imagery acquired from an unmanned aerial vehicle (UAV) and automatic 3D photo-reconstruction methods. Eur. J. Agron. 55, 89–99 (2014)

40. Immerzeel, W.W., et al.: High-resolution monitoring of Himalayan glacier dynamics using unmanned aerial vehicles. Remote Sens. Environ. 150, 93–103 (2014)

41. Austin, R.: Unmanned aircraft systems: UAVS design, development and deployment, 54. John Wiley & Sons, New York (2011)
42. Stevens, B.L., Lewis, F.L., Johnson, E.N.: Aircraft Control and Simulation: Dynamics, Controls Design, and Autonomous Systems, 3rd edn. Wiley, New York (2015)
43. Marshall, D.M., Barnhart, R.K., Shappee, E., Most, M.T. (eds.): Introduction to Unmanned Aircraft Systems. CRC Press, Boca Raton (2015)
44. Watts, A.C., et al.: Small unmanned aircraft systems for low-altitude aerial surveys. J. Wildl. Manag. **74**(7), 1614–1619 (2010)
45. Colomina, I., Molina, P.: Unmanned aerial systems for photogrammetry and remote sensing: a review. ISPRS J. Photogramm. Remote Sens. **92**, 79–97 (2014)
46. Grimaccia, F., Aghaei, M., Mussetta, M., Leva, S., Quater, P.B.: Planning for PV plant performance monitoring by means of unmanned aerial systems (UAS). Int. J. Energy Environ. Eng. **6**(1), 47–54 (2014). https://doi.org/10.1007/s40095-014-0149-6
47. Eisenbeiss, H.: UAV photogrammetry in plant sciences and geology. In: 6th ARIDA Workshop on Innovations in 3D Measurement, Modeling and Visualization, Povo (Trento), Italy (2008c)
48. Cesetti, A., Frontoni, E., Mancini, A., Ascani, A., Zingaretti, P., Longhi, S.: A visual global positioning systems unmanned aerial vehicles used in photogrammetric applications. J. Intell. Robot. Syst. **61**, 157–168 (2011). https://doi.org/10.1007/s10846-010-9489-5
49. Gómez-Candón, D., De Castro, A.I., López-Granados, F.: Assessing the accuracy of mosaics from unmanned aerial vehicle (UAV) imagery for precision agriculture purposes in wheat. Precision Agric. **15**(1), 44–56 (2013). https://doi.org/10.1007/s11119-013-9335-4
50. Cosyn, P., Miller, R.: Trimble UX5 aerial imaging solutions: a new standard in accuracy, robustness and performance for photogrammetric aerial mapping. White Paper, Trimble, pp. 1–6, USA (2013)
51. Altamini, Z., Collilieux, X., Métivier, L.: ITRF08: an improved solution of the international terrestrial reference frame. J. Geodesy **85**(8), 457–473 (2011). https://doi.org/10.1007/s00 190-011-0444-4
52. Gusiakov, V.K.: Tsunami generation potential of different tsunamigenic regions in the Pacific. Mar. Geol. **215**(1–2), 3–9 (2005)
53. Pararas-Carayannis, G.: Potential of tsunami generation along the Colombia/Ecuador subduction margin and the Dolores-Guayaquil mega-thrust. Sci. Tsunami Haz. **31**(3), 209–230 (2012)
54. Rodriguez, F., et al.: The economic evaluation and significance of an early relocation versus complete destruction by a potential tsunami of a coastal city in Ecuador. Sci. Tsunami Haz. **35**(1), 18–35 (2016)
55. Parra, H., Benito, M.B., Gaspar-Escribano, J.M.: Seismic hazard assessment in continental Ecuador. Bull. Earthq. Eng. **14**(8), 2129–2159 (2016). https://doi.org/10.1007/s10518-016-9906-7
56. Toulkeridis, T.: The Evaluation of unexpected results of a seismic hazard applied to a modern hydroelectric center in central Ecuador. J. Struct. Eng. **43**(4), 373–380 (2016)
57. Toulkeridis, T., et al.: The 7.8 Mw Earthquake and Tsunami of the 16th April 2016 in Ecuador-Seismic evaluation, geological field survey and economic implications. Sci. Tsunami Haz. **36**, 197–242 (2017)
58. Chunga, K., Mulas, M., Alvarez, A., Galarza, J., Toulkeridis, T.: Characterization of seismogenetic crustal faults in the Gulf of Guayaquil. Ecuador. Andean Geology **46**(1), 66–81 (2019)
59. Chunga, K., Toulkeridis, T., Vera-Grunauer, X., Gutierrez, M., Cahuana, N., Alvarez, A.: A review of earthquakes and tsunami records and characterization of capable faults on the northwestern coast of Ecuador. Sci. Tsunami Haz. **36**, 100–127 (2017)
60. Aviles-Campoverde, D., et al.: NW Ecuador. Geosciences **11**, 20 (2016)

61. Rodríguez Espinosa, F., et al.: Economic evaluation of recovering a natural protection with concurrent relocation of the threatened public of tsunami hazards in central coastal Ecuador. Sci. Tsunami Haz. **36**, 293–306 (2017)
62. Rodriguez, F., et al.: J. Tsunami Soc. Int. **35**(1) (2016)
63. Rodriguez, F., Toulkeridis, T., Padilla, O., Mato, F.: Economic risk assessment of Cotopaxi volcano Ecuador in case of a future lahar emplacement. Nat. Hazards **85**(1), 605–618 (2017)
64. Navas, L., Caiza, P., Toulkeridis, T.: An evaluated comparison between the molecule and steel framing construction systems–implications for the seismic vulnerable Ecuador. Malaysian Construct. Res. J. **26**(3), 87–109 (2018)
65. Echegaray-Aveiga, R.C., Rodríguez, F., Toulkeridis, T., Echegaray-Avciga, R.D.: Effects of potential lahars of the Cotopaxi volcano on housing market prices. J. Appl. Volcanol. **9**, 1–11 (2019)
66. Kellogg, J.N., Vega, V.: Tectonic development of Panama, Costa Rica and the Colombian Andes: constraints from global positioning system geodetic studies and gravity. Geol. Soc. Am. Special Paper **295**, 75–90 (1995)
67. Egbue, O., Kellogg, J.: Pleistocene to Present North Andean "escape." Tectono-Phys. **489**, 248–257 (2010)
68. Gutscher, M.A., Malavieille, J.S.L., Collot, J.-Y.: Tectonic segmentation of the North Andean margin: impact of the Carnegie ridge collision. Earth Planet. Sci. Lett. **168**, 255–270 (1999)
69. Shepperd, G.L., Moberly, R.: Coastal structure of the continental margin, north-west Peru and southwest Ecuador. Geol. Soc. Am. Mem. **154**, 351–392 (1981)
70. Pontoise, B., Monfret, T.: Shallow seismogenic zone detected from an offshore-onshore temporary seismic network in the Esmeraldas area (Northern Ecuador). Geochem. Geophys. Geosyst. **5**(2) (2004)
71. Ratzov, G., Collot, J.Y., Sosson, M., Migeon, S.: Mass-transport deposits in the northern Ecuador subduction trench: result of frontal erosion over multiple seismic cycles. Earth Planet. Sci. Lett. **296**(1), 89–102 (2010)
72. Ratzov, G., et al.: Submarine landslides along the North Ecuador–South Colombia convergent margin: possible tectonic control. In: Lykousis, V., Sakellariou, D., Locat, J. (eds.) Submarine Mass Movements and Their Consequences. Advances in Natural and Technological Hazards Research, vol. 27, pp. 47–55. Springer, Cham (2007). https://doi.org/10.1007/978-1-4020-6512-5_6
73. Ioualalen, M., Ratzov, G., Collot, J.Y., Sanclemente, E.: The tsunami signature on a submerged promontory: the case study of the Atacames Promontory, Ecuador. Geophys. J. Int. **184**(2), 680–688 (2011)
74. Pararas-Carayannis, G.: The Earthquake and Tsunami of December 12, 1979, in Colombia. International Tsunami Information Center Report, Abstracted article in Tsunami Newsletter, vol. XIII, No. 1 (1980)
75. Toulkeridis, T., et al.: Contrasting results of potential tsunami hazards in Muisne, central coast of Ecuador. Sci. Tsunami Haz. **36**, 13–40 (2017)
76. Rudolph, E., Szirtes, S.: Das kolumbianische Erdbeben am 31 Januar 1906. Gerlands Beitr. z. Geophysik **2**, 132–275 (1911)
77. Kelleher, J.A.: Ruptures zones of large South American earthquakes and some predictions. J. Geophys. Res. **77**(11), 2087–2103 (1972)
78. Beck, S.L., Ruff, L.J.: The rupture process of the great 1979 Colombia earthquake: evidence for the asperity model. J. Geophys. Res. **89**, 9281–9291 (1984)
79. Kanamori, H., McNally, K.C.: Variable rupture mode of the subduction zone along the Ecuador-Colombia coast. Bull. Seismol. Soc. Am. **72**(4), 1241–1253 (1982)
80. Swenson, J.L., Beck, S.L.: Historical 1942 Ecuador and 1942 Peru subduction earthquakes, and earthquake cycles along Colombia-Ecuador and Peru subduction segments. Pure Appl. Geophys. **146**(1), 67–101 (1996)

81. Chunga, K., Toulkeridis, T.: First evidence of paleo-tsunami deposits of a major historic event in Ecuador. J. Tsunami Soc. Int. **33**, 55–69 (2014)
82. Collot, J.Y., et al.: Are rupture zone limits of great subduction earthquakes controlled by upper plate structures? Evidence from multichannel seismic reflection data acquired across the northern Ecuador–southwest Colombia margin. J. Geophys. Res. Solid Earth **109**(B11) (2004)
83. USGS (United States Geological Service): Historic Earthquakes, 1906 January 31st (2016a). http://earthquake.usgs.gov/earthquakes/world/events/1906_01_31.php
84. Toulkeridis: Volcanic Galápagos Volcánico. Ediecuatorial, Quito, Ecuador, p. 364 (2011)
85. Toulkeridis, T., Mato, F., Toulkeridis-Estrella, K., Perez Salinas, J.C., Tapia, S., Fuertes, W.: Real-time radioactive precursor of the April 16, 2016 Mw 7.8 earthquake and tsunami in Ecuador. Sci. Tsunami Haz. **37**, 34–48 (2018)
86. Toulkeridis, T., et al.: Two independent real-time precursors of the 7.8 Mw earthquake in Ecuador based on radioactive and geodetic processes—powerful tools for an early warning system. J. Geodyn. **126**, 12–22 (2019)
87. USGS (United States Geological Service): M7.8 – 29 km SSE of Muisne, Ecuador (2016b). http://earthquake.usgs.gov/earthquakes/eventpage/us20005j32#general
88. El Telegrafo (2016). http://www.eltelegrafo.com.ec/noticias/ecuador/3/manana-se-daran-a-conocer-cifras-oficiales-del-costo-del-terremoto
89. Yépez, V., Toledo, J., Toulkeridis, T.: The armed forces as a state institution in immediate response and its participation as an articulator in the risk management in Ecuador. Smart Innov. Syst. Technol. **181**, 545–554 (2020)
90. Mato, F., Toulkeridis, T.: An unsupervised K-means based clustering method for geophysical post-earthquake diagnosis. In: 2017 IEEE Symposium Series on Computational Intelligence (SSCI), pp. 1–8 (2018)
91. Hosokawa, M., Takanashi, K., Doshida, S., Endo, M., Jeong, B.: Development of the wide-area earthquake damage estimation system and mashup of disaster prevention information. J. Disaster Res. **12**(1), 118–130 (2017)
92. Koresawa, A.: Government's response to the Great East Japan earthquake and tsunami. J. Disaster Res. **7**, 517–527 (2012)
93. Takeuchi, K., Tanaka, S.: Recovery from catastrophe and building back better. J. Disaster Res. **11**(6), 1190–1201 (2016)

Masonry Reinforcement Using Cabuya Fiber and Perimetral Electro-Welded Mesh

H. Valdivieso(✉) ⓘD and P. Caiza ⓘD

Universidad de las Fuerzas Armadas ESPE, Sangolquí, Ecuador
hfvaldivieso@espe.edu.ec

Abstract. Ecuador is located in an earthquake prone zone and, therefore, has a seismic hazard that is considered latent, in other words, that always exists and that could be revealed at any moment. This premise leads to constructions that should have a particularly rigorous degree of structural safety and that, above all, should protect people's lives.

This paper develops a proposal for structural reinforcement of block masonry walls through the use of mortars with cabuya fiber. This aims to be an eco-friendly solution since it uses raw materials from the Andean area.

Two types of tests are carried out in order to verify the contribution of the cabuya fiber as structural reinforcement. The first type of test is executed with the reinforced mortars, which shows an improvement of 19.71% in compressive strength, compared to mortars without any type of reinforcement.

The second type of test was carried out on two reinforced concrete frames infilled with block masonry, where it is shown that the percentage of strength improvement against seismic loads in a masonry reinforced using electro-welded mesh and cabuya fiber is 78.46% compared to simple infilled frames. Horizontal displacements at the top of the frame are also reduced by 32.04%.

The results shows that the use of cabuya fibers and electro-welded mesh could be a different structural safety method, exploiting a ecofriendly resource that has been forgotten by farmers at the moment.

Keywords: Fiber reinforcement · Mortar · Compressive strength · Horizontal displacement

1 Introduction

This work shows experimental research on the possible constructive characteristics in Latin America, specifically Ecuador, of infill-masonry reinforcement in simple single-span frames. A method of structural reinforcement based on the improvement of the compressive behavior of the masonry through the use of natural fiber of cabuya and electro-welded mesh is proposed.

Ecuador has a high seismic risk, both because it is in an area of high seismic hazard, and because its main construction system, frames with low-quality infill masonry, has poor structural behavior in the event of earthquakes.

M. Botto-Tobar et al. (Eds.): ICAT 2022, CCIS 1756, pp. 74–88, 2023.
https://doi.org/10.1007/978-3-031-24971-6_6

Indeed, Ecuador has tectonic faults produced by the subduction of the Nazca plate under the South American continental plate, as well as important transverse faults (the western edge of the Northanden Block), and local surface faults, for example, in Quito, capital of Ecuador, where there is a fault system with an approximate length of 60 km [1].

Regarding the quality of building construction, it is worth mentioning that in Ecuador it is diverse and dynamic. However, informal construction actually predominates, for which a large part of the structures built annually do not have adequate permits. This type of constructions is based on the experience of unskilled labor and, do not comply with current regulations.

All these parameters directly influence the seismic risk of current buildings. Therefore, it is necessary to search for new structural strengthening methods that improve behavior against seismic loads. But not only this, knowing the importance and urgency of protecting the environment, the reinforcement methods must be eco-friendly.

Additionally, it is worth insisting that the National Institute of Statistics and Census (in Spanish, INEC) officially confirms on its "Ecuador in Figures" web page that there is a significant percentage of illegal constructions. For example, in 2020 around 24,764 buildings were built, of which 19,203 had construction permits, reflecting that there is a deficit of 5,561 (22.46%) illegal constructions, which is reflected in Fig. 1.

Fig. 1. Buildings with construction permits (in Spanish, "Permisos de construcción") vs total of buildings to be constructed (in Spanish, "Edificaciones a construir"), 2020 [2]

These figures indicate that in Ecuador there is a culture that does not prioritize structural safety and that places great emphasis on cost reduction.

Finally, considering the characteristics of construction in Ecuador, the natural fiber of cabuya was used as an eco-friendly structural reinforcement method, which can become an interesting proposal for structural reinforcement, economical and easy to apply, without the need for skilled labor supervision.

2   Materials and Method

2.1   Method

Previous making an analysis of the reinforced fibers method, it´s necessary to do a flowchart like a summary of the investigation. First, it's necessary to make a micro test mortar previous to apply this kind of methods in simple frames in scale 1:1 (Fig. 2).

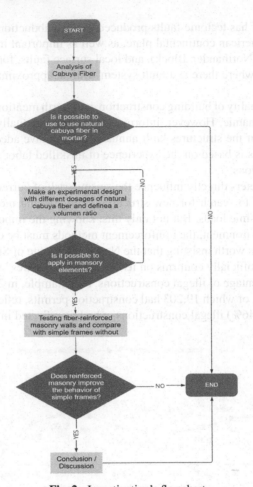

Fig. 2. Investigation's flowchart

2.2 Natural Fiber Description

The cabuya is a natural fiber, derived from the penca or fique, which is commonly found in the Andean moors in cold and high-altitude climates.

According to Pruna and others [3], the Ministry of Agriculture, Livestock, Aquaculture and Fisheries (MAGAP) indicates that 5400 tons of cabuya fiber were produced in Ecuador in 2008, whose production is estimated to have increased considerably since this material has been used in the development of the textile industry, at the moment, MAGAP does not have a record of cabuya fiber produces.

So, in these days natural fibers are not used in structural safety designs, because this kind of fiber are underutilized material and most uses are focused on decorative handicraft product. However, if we use at least 1% of the annual national production (54 tons) in structural reinforced process, it is possible to reinforce 540,000 homes with an average of 100 m^2 of masonry with reinforcement.

The newspaper "La Hora" said that cabuya fiber are ancestral natural fiber that have not been exploited with a business vision; on the contrary, these types of plants have been forgotten by field workers. So, this investigation tries to use the properties of the cabuya fiber as a different proposal to other types of structural safety methods.

If a structural safety program for housing is promoted at the national level, management systems could be used that allow, through strategic alliances, to generate mass production of optimal raw material to be used in the reinforcement of structures.

Through a process of extraction and drying of the fiber, a completely dry raw material can be obtained, in threads, which is commonly used in handicrafts as shown in Fig. 3.

Fig. 3. The raw cabuya fiber

In order to identify the mechanical properties, the study carried out by Llerena in 2019 was used, the results of which are as follows:

Table 1. Mechanical Properties of natural cabuya fiber [4]

Type of resistence	Value
Tensile strength	305.15 MPa
Elongation previous Fracture	4.96%
Modulus of elasticity	7.50 MPa
Density	1.30 g/cm³

As shown in Table 1, the fiber has a high tensile strength. However, it does not have a high elongation before falling apart.

The natural fiber of cabuya also tends to degrade considering that it is exposed to environmental conditions and microorganisms that cause deterioration over time;

according to Pinchao and others [5], the cabuya fiber is governed by the following linear equation B = 0.547t + 3.365, where "B" is biodegradation in percentage and "t" is time (expressed in days). Its average life span before total degradation is 182 days, as shown in Figs. 4 and 5.

Figure 5 shows in detail the degradation process of cabuya fiber over time, which shows that natural fiber without prior treatment tends to be easily biodegraded. As evidenced on day 64, the filaments are disintegrated and denote less quantity compared with day 8.

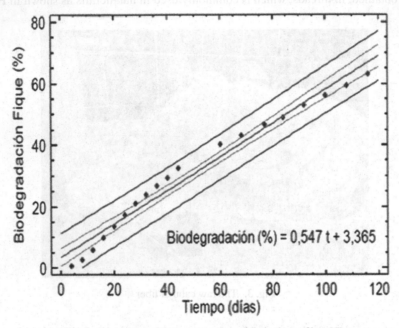

Fig. 4. Lineal degradation equation of the cabuya fiber [5]

For plaster, a mixture of natural fiber with Portland cement mortar is used. However, López and Pucha [6] indicate that the alkalinity of the cement accelerates the degradation of the filaments. Therefore, they recommend to immerse the fiber in resin prior to being used with the cement-sand mixture or, failing that, partially changing the Portland cement with puzzolanic cement.

2.3 Micro Tests of Reinforced Mortars

In order to determine the resistance of the fiber-reinforced mortar, compression tests were carried out on 50 × 50 × 50 mm cubes, according to the Ecuadorian INEN 488:2009 standard. For which prefabricated plasters were used, at a cement-sand ratio 1:4 that should determine a compressive strength of at least 7.5 MPa. This mortar was mixed with completely dry cabuya fibers, 20 mm. in length, as shown in Fig. 6.

In Ecuador, mortars with dosages of 1:6 and 1:4 are commonly used for plastering or binder mortars, considering that much of their strength will depend on the amount

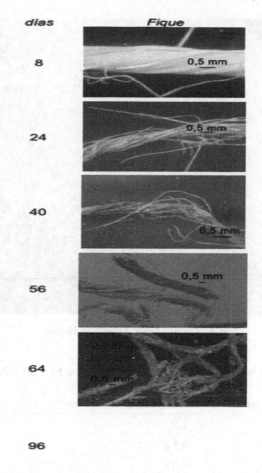

Fig. 5. Cabuya Fiber degradation process [5]

of water introduced into the mixture. An unreinforced mortar that had a compressive strength of 75 kg/cm^2 was obtained in this work.

Tests were carried out with different dosages of cabuya fiber, in order to determine the optimal percentage that should be mixed together with the mortar to reinforce it. A sample of 750 cm^3 of mortar was made for each type of dosage, considering that it is the volume necessary to carry out 6 compression tests on 50 × 50 × 50 mm cubes. Table 2 shows the protocol of the tested samples.

From each protocol, 6 samples were tested in total, at 3, 8 and 28 days, in order to know the behavior of the reinforced mortar. The following results, showed in Fig. 7, were obtained:

As shown in Fig. 7, six types of samples were tested, in order to know if the fibers of cabuya contribute to their behavior. Figure 7 shows that when reinforcing the mortar with natural fiber of cabuya in the proportion of 1g., the compressive behavior increases by 1.49 MPa. A result of 9.05 MPa of compressive strength was obtained, compared to

Fig. 6. Cabuya Fiber, Length = 20 mm.

Table 2. Weight of cabuya fiber on an INEN test $50 \times 50 \times 50$ mm

Test	Cabuya Fiber IN 750 cm^3
1	-
2	0.5 g
3	1.0 g
4	1.5 g
5	2.0 g

a sample without any type of reinforcement, where a result of 7.56 MPa was obtained. That is, 19.71% more strength at 28 days of maturity of the sample.

Figure 8 shows that the reinforced mortar is much more compact than an unreinforced mortar, the fibers having been distributed throughout the cement-sand dosage in a monolithic and uniform manner.

Once the optimum percentage of natural cabuya fiber (1 g/750 cm^3) has been obtained within a cement-sand mixture, the following volumetric relationship can be calculated:

$$X = 1333.33 \text{ g./cm}^3 \tag{1}$$

RESULTS OF PROTOCOL

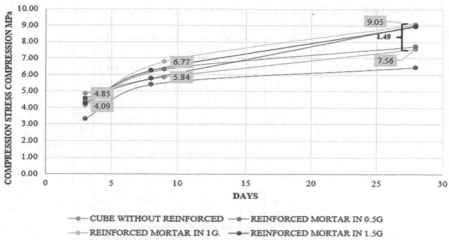

Fig. 7. Compression test results according to protocols

Fig. 8. Cabuya fiber in the mortar

2.4 Tests in Masonry Simple Walls

Two simple frames with infill masonry were tested. These tests are part of a larger research program on masonry infill reinforcement. For this reason, the same geometry of the frame published in the research project of Albuja D. and Pantoja J. [7] was used. The results of the lateral load test that these authors carried out on the unreinforced masonry wall will serve as comparison with the reinforcement model tested in this research project. The model proposed in this research project is as follows:

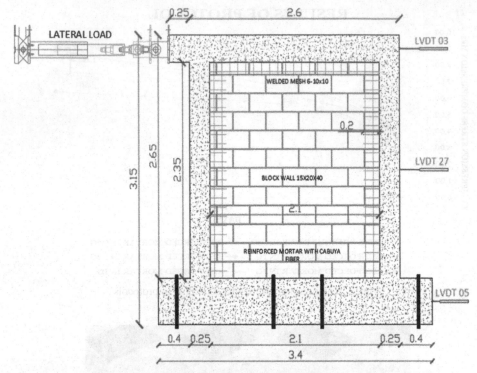

Fig. 9. Simple frame model tested

As shown in Fig. 9, the geometry of the test proposed in this research is based on a simple single-span frame, anchored to a reaction slab with 4 bolts, which simulates a fixed support. Additionally, lateral loads with a maximum of 30 tons are applied in the horizontal direction, thus simulating the seismic load applied to structures and buildings.

An electro-welded mesh 6 mm@10 cm was used. It was cut in strips 20 cm width and arranged near the perimeter formed by the reinforce concrete frame in order to absorb the strains generated in the nodes of the simple frame. The stresses resulting from the applied load are additionally dissipated by the fiber-reinforced mortar. For the construction of the full web masonry, a $15 \times 20 \times 40$ cm pressed block was used, as well as a 1 cm thick binder mortar.

The reinforced mortar for plastering had a dosage of 1,333.33 g/m^3 cabuya fiber, in a layer with a thickness of 24 mm, as can be better seen in Fig. 10.

The graph displacement vs lateral load in a frame without reinforcement, detailed by Albuja D. and Pantoja J. (2017), is shown in Fig. 11:

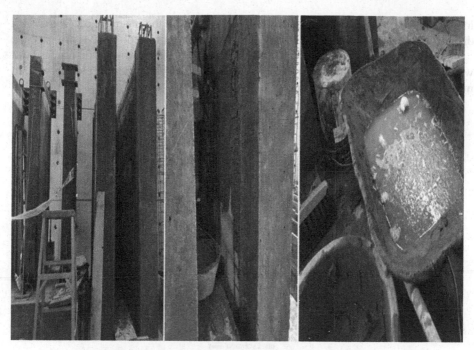

Fig. 10. Construction method of masonry reinforced walls

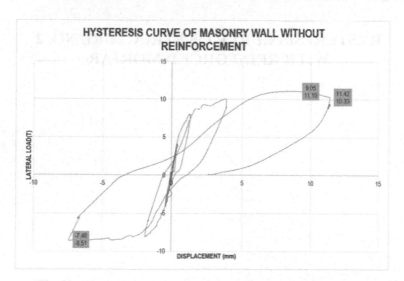

Fig. 11. Hysteresis diagram results in a wall without reinforcing [7]

Figure 11 reflects the dynamic behavior of the frame without reinforcement, where the horizontal seismic load was applied with negative and positive cycles. The results show a horizontal displacement of 9.05 mm after having applied a maximum horizontal load of 11.10 tons prior to failure of the frame itself. On the other hand, a maximum displacement of 11.42 mm was registered but with a lower load of 10.33 ton.

These results serve to compare them with those obtained in two tests on frames built with the same characteristics, but reinforced with natural cabuya fiber and electro-welded mesh in the aforementioned manner. The results are:

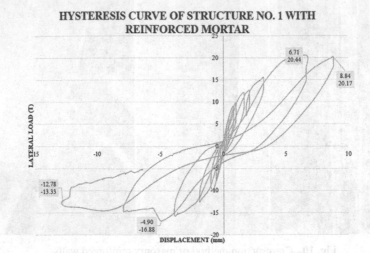

Fig. 12. Hysteresis diagram results in the structure No. 1 with reinforced mortar

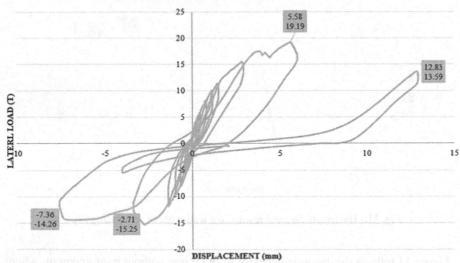

Fig. 13. Hysteresis diagram results in the structure No. 2 with reinforced mortar

As shown in Fig. 12, the system frame-reinforced masonry resists an applied load of 20.44 ton, which generates a maximum displacement of 6.71 mm. When analyzing the behavior of the frame after the application of the maximum load, it maintains toughness, even after reaching a strength of 20.17 ton with a horizontal displacement of 8.84 mm.

Figure 13 shows the results of frame No. 2, which resisted 19.19 ton with a horizontal displacement of 5.58 mm. In the same way than the previous test, it maintains considerable toughness before collapsing.

On average, it can be said that the system frame - masonry reinforced with cabuya fiber and electro-welded mesh improves its strength behavior by 78.46% (8.71 ton) and reduces horizontal displacement by 32.04% (2.9 mm.), allowing a safer construction from the structural point of view, as shown in Fig. 14:

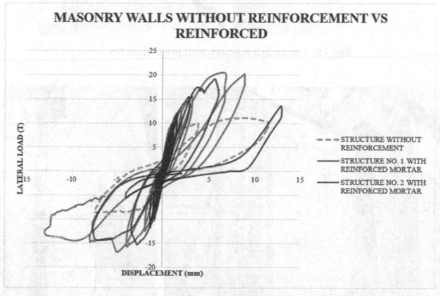

Fig. 14. Summary results between Structure with reinforced mortar vs not reinforced

In Figs. 15 and 16, the final results of the tests carried out on structural systems 1 and 2 are observed. It is determined that both systems failed first in the masonry, in the form of an X at 45°, due to diagonal tension. Within the plane of the masonry, the existence of micro cracks is also evident, which indicates that the natural fiber of cabuya absorbed and distributed stresses.

Fig. 15. Failure in a masonry wall in structure No. 1

Fig. 16. Failure in a masonry wall in structure No. 2

3   Discussion

In the first type of tests with the mortar cubes of $50 \times 50 \times 50$ mm, it is determined that the length of the cabuya fiber influence in the mortar strength. In the summary diagram in Fig. 7, it is shown also that increasing the percentage of cabuya fiber not necessarily improve the compression strength, but rather that it could get lower results than a prototype without reinforcement.

The alternative proposed for the reinforcement of structures at the masonry level shows strength levels higher than those obtained without reinforcement. Note also that, in order to reduce costs, only the perimeter of the masonry panel is reinforced with the steel mesh. It is confirmed that the mesh distributes stresses, avoiding concentrations, since there is micro cracking.

The distribution of stress and the resulting micro cracking is also possible due to the presence of the fiber of cabuya. Recognizing the possible degradation of the cabuya fiber, its protection by means of resins is proposed.

The test shows that cabuya fiber reduces the displacements of the structures No. 1 and 2 vs. structural systems without reinforcing.

The walls show failure forming an X in the masonry due to diagonal tension stresses. However, the masonry walls never fall apart.

4   Conclusions

The horizontal load tests, applied to the reinforced structural systems 1 and 2, show that the use of electro-welded mesh and mortars reinforced with fiber of cabuya, considerably improves the structural behavior.

For the reinforcement, materials from the area that are eco-friendly with the environment were used, as is the case of the natural fiber of cabuya. It is important to note that actually these materials are not exploited to improve the reinforcement and structural safety.

The cabuya fiber should be protected with resins. Despite this shortcoming, the natural cabuya fiber contributes considerably to the reinforcement of mortars, increasing their compressive strength capacity.

Finally, it is worth mentioning that, although it is true that the natural fiber of cabuya absorbs a percentage of the stress generated (product of the application of horizontal loads towards the frame), it is necessary to take into consideration that several tests could be generated to verify which is the optimal length for its use.

References

1. Parra, H., Benito, M., Gaspar, J., Fernández, A., Luna, M., Molina, X.: Estimación de la peligrosidad sísmica en Ecuador Continental. Universidad de las Fuerzas Armadas ESPE, Quito (2017)
2. INEC Ecuador en cifras. https://www.ecuadorencifras.gob.ec/documentos/web-inec/Estadi sticas_Economicas/Encuesta_Edificaciones/2020/3.%202020_ENED_Boletin_tecnico.pdf. Accessed 01 Oct 2021
3. Pruna, L., Velasco, F., Chachapoya. F., Paredes, C.: Elaboración de la fibra de cabuya en tejido plano como matriz de refuerzo para la construcción de un retrovisor. INGENIUS - Revista de Ciencia y Tecnología. **24**, 82 (2020)
4. Llerena, J.: Reforzamiento a cortante en paredes de ladrillo, bloque y adobe utilizando materiales compuestos FRCM de cabuya. UNACH Universidad Nacional de Chimborazo, Riobamba (2019)
5. Pinchao, Y., Osorio, O., Checa, O., Elizabeth, T.: Estudio sobre la Velocidad y Tiempo de Biodegradación Bajo Condiciones Controladas de Fibras Naturales de Fique (Furcraea andina) y Algodón (Gossypium barbadense). Información Tecnológica – Res. Gate. **30**(4), 63–64 (2019)

6. López, E., Pucha, Á.: Mejoramiento de la durabilidad de materiales compuestos FRCM reforzados con fibras de cabuya, evaluando las propiedades a tracción y adherencia. UNACH Universidad Nacional de Chimborazo, Riobamba (2017)
7. Albuja, D., Pantoja, J.: Estudio del Reforzamiento de la mampostería de Bloque de Hormigón con Malla Electrosoldada mediante ensayos destructivos, Escuela Politécnica Nacional, Quito (2017)

Evaluation of the Seismic Vulnerability of the Huachi Chico Parish in Ecuador

Fabiana Cunalata[1]($\boxtimes$) and Pablo Caiza[2]

[1] Programa de Maestría de Investigación en Ingeniería Civil Mención Estructuras, Universidad de las Fuerzas Armadas ESPE, Sangolquí, Ecuador
fecunalata@espe.edu.ec

[2] Departamento de Ciencias de la Tierra y Construcción, Universidad de las Fuerzas Armadas ESPE, Sangolquí, Ecuador
pecaiza1@espe.edu.ec

Abstract. The results of a study of seismic vulnerability in residential buildings of the Huachi Chico parish at the city of Ambato, in Ecuador are shown. Rapid visual screening of homes was carried out using the forms presented in the Ecuadorian Construction Standard (NEC), FEMA P-154 and the procedure developed by the Venezuelan Foundation for Seismological Research FUNVISIS in which indexes of vulnerability, risk and seismic prioritization are assigned. In addition, to explicitly determine the structural exposure, the methodology developed by the Global Earthquake Model Foundation (GEM foundation), within the framework of the South America Risk Assessment (SARA) project, was used. In total, 998 buildings were surveyed and compared with a cadastral data base that includes information on structures for residential use. The results obtained meet acceptance criteria, and therefore, it can be concluded that the parish presents a medium to high vulnerability, with the most frequent construction system being reinforced concrete frames infilled with masonry walls of 1 to 2 stories and 3 to 5 stories.

Keywords: Structural vulnerability · GEM · FEMA · NEC · FUNVISIS

1 Introduction

Much of the seismic activity in South America is produced by the subduction between the Nazca and Pacific plates, this being one of the most important reasons for the identification of Ecuador as a multi-natural hazard country. It is necessary to prevent possible damage to structures due to this seismic hazard and, among other aspects, improve the construction quality of buildings. The earthquake in April 16, 2016 in Pedernales, Ecuador, magnitude 7.8 Mw, that killed 670 people and had economic losses of up to 3.34 billion usd, also provided relevant data on buildings that collapsed or that reached a high damage level. Among the predominant observed characteristics are: constructions carried out without considering regulations, lack of control during construction, and poor forecast of structural damage [1].

Considering that earthquake occurrence is still beyond the control of science, it is important to improve the seismic behavior of the existing buildings. In this way, it will be possible to mitigate the losses that earthquakes could cause. Thus, seismic vulnerability studies are born in order to create mitigation plans for future disasters [2].

Huachi Chico constitutes one of the most representative parishes of the city of Ambato. It is the second largest urban district, with an area of 580,350 hectares. According to information from the municipal cadaster, Huachi Chico has a total of 7,484 land properties and 8,374 homes. It has also one of the highest concentration of population and has buildings of great importance classified within the categories of essential and special occupation structures, according to the Ecuadorian Construction Standard. The growth of its population in recent years has been remarkable. Being an area with a high degree of urban consolidation, its reshaping metropolitan process continues. Many people have chosen the sector to build their homes as independent houses, housing complexes or apartments buildings. Public, as well as educational institutions and shopping centers are also located in this area.

Four geological faults cross this parish: The Huachi Chico fault on the west side, the Ambato fault to the north, and two shorter faults in the center and south. See Fig. 1. Thus, the seismic hazard is really high. That is why the rapid structural evaluation against seismic risks is a necessary complement to assure the safety of the population.

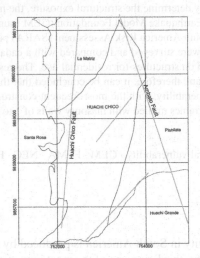

Fig. 1. Geological faults in Huachi Chico parish

This research seeks to evaluate the residential buildings of the Huachi Chico parish through a rapid visual screening considering the methodologies presented by the FEMA P-154 regulation, the Ecuadorian Construction Standard (NEC 2015) and the Venezuelan Foundation for Seismological Research FUNVISIS. In addition, using the methodology proposed by SARA (South America Risk Assessment), the GEM (Global Earthquake Model) taxonomy will be used to identify the frequent structural typologies in the study area.

2 Materials and Methods

To carry out the vulnerability study, the urban cadaster of the parish was considered, which indicated the existence of 8,374 buildings. From this total, a minimum sample of 947 buildings was determined.

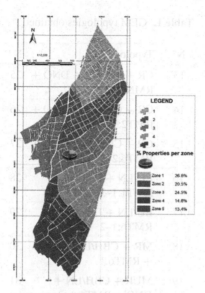

Fig. 2. Parish división into zones

To carry out the surveys, 7 undergraduate students from the Civil Engineering Department at Universidad de las Fuerzas Armadas ESPE participated, who collaborated with data processing and obtaining part of the results. The number of dwellings obtained in the sample, 947, were distributed throughout the parish, which was divided into 5 zones considering the main streets, as shown in Fig. 2.

The collection of information was carried out through field work in the 5 zones. In total, 998 buildings were checked. For each technical review, the FEMA, FUNVISIS, and NEC 2015 forms were used. The "IDCT do Survey" application and the Open Quake platform, tools created by GEM, were also used to obtain the taxonomy of the surveyed houses. For the FEMA form, the one corresponding to a very high seismic region was used. For FUNVISIS and NEC, the forms proposed by each method were considered.

In order to process the information obtained in the surveys, a database in Excel was used. This collects data from all three methodologies. For example, it shows the results of degree of vulnerability and prioritization indices for FUNVISIS. The GEM taxonomy obtained through the GEM "IDCT do survey" application and the web platform is also added to this database.

On the other hand, to validate the information collected in the field, a survey of the total existing properties in the parish was carried out using the Google Street View tool. With this, a new database was created on the 7,484 properties of the parish.

To determine the GEM taxonomies of the parish, the database with the houses surveyed in the field was used. Initially, a total of 56 structural typologies were established, which after filtering were reduced to 25. Finally, 36 typologies were obtained, considering those obtained in the surveys with the Google Street View tool. Look at Table 1 on the number of typologies and the acronyms used.

Table 1. GEM typologies obtained

N°	Typology	N°	Typology	N°	Typology
1	CR + CIP/LFINF + DUC + RMN:1–2	13	CR + CIP/LN + DNO + RMN:1–3	25	W + W99/LN + DNO + RMT6:1–2
2	CR + CIP/LFINF + DUC + RMN:3–5	14	CR + CIP/LN + DNO + RMT2:1–2	26	EU/LN + DNO + RMT7:2
3	CR + CIP/LFINF + DNO + RMT1:1–2	15	CR + CIP/LN + DNO + RMT6:2–4	27	MATO/LN + DNO + RMT6:1–2
4	CR + CIP/LFINF + DNO + RMT1:3–4	16	EU/LN + DNO + RMT1:1–3	28	MATO/LN + DUC + RMN:1–4
5	CR + CIP/LFINF + DNO + RMT2:1–2	17	EU/LN + DNO + RMT6:1–2	29	CR + CIP/LFINF + DNO + RMT7:1–4
6	CR + CIP/LFINF + DNO + RMT6:1–3	18	MR + CBH/LN + DNO + RMT6:1	30	CR + CIP/LFINF + DNO + RMT7:1–4
7	CR + CIP/LFINF + DUC + RMT1:1–2	19	MUR + CBH/LN + DNO + RMT6:1–3	31	S/LFINF + DNO + RMT7:1–2
8	CR + CIP/LFINF + DUC + RMT1:3–4	20	MUR + CBH/LN + DNO + RMT1:1–2	32	CR + CIP/LFM + DUC + RMN:1–2
9	CR + CIP/LFINF + DUC + RMT2:1–2	21	MUR + CLBRS/LN + DNO + RMT1:1–2	33	CR + CIP/LFM + DNO + RMT6:1–2
10	CR + CIP/LFINF + DUC + RMT2:3–4	22	MUR + CLBRS/LN + DNO + RMT6:2	34	W + W99/LN + DNO + RMT7:2
11	CR + CIP/LFINF + DUC + RMT6:1–2	23	S/LN + DNO + RMT6:1	35	CR + CIP/LFINF + DUC + RMN:6–10
12	CR + CIP/LFINF + DUC + RMT6:3–4	24	W + W99/LN + DNO + RMT1:1–2	36	CR + CIP/LFINF + DNO + RMT6:4–6

2.1 Generation of the Mapping Scheme

The mapping scheme identifies structural typologies within a georeferenced database. Thus, each building is assigned a structural typology according to the GEM taxonomy. In this work, with the database of all existing buildings in the parish, a GEM taxonomy was assigned considering: material and technology of the lateral load resistant system, lateral load resistant system, ductility, material of roof deck, and number of stories.

3 Results

The buildings surveyed are of residential and mixed use and will be compared with the information obtained through the Google Street View tool.

3.1 Results of Surveys Carried Out Through Direct Visual Inspection

Number of Stories. Figure 3 shows that most of the buildings have between one and two stories, corresponding to 63.8%, followed by structures with three to five structures with 35.9% and those with 6 to 10 stories with 0.3%.

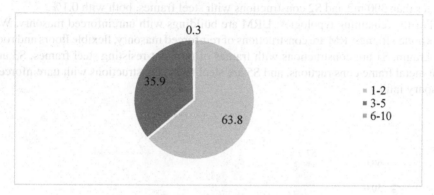

Fig. 3. Number of stories

Structural Typologies. Once the forms were completed, the most frequent structural typologies were obtained.

FUNVISIS. Figure 4 shows that the most frequent building typology are reinforced concrete frames filled with clay or concrete block walls with 66.9%, followed by reinforced concrete frames with a 22.3%, the least frequent typology being that of structural systems with load-bearing elements of confined masonry walls with a percentage of 0.1%.

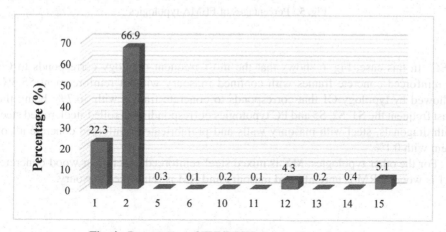

Fig. 4. Percentages of FUNVISIS structural typologies

In Fig. 4, the number 1 corresponds to reinforced concrete frames, 2: reinforced concrete frames filled with clay or concrete block walls, 5: steel frames, 6: steel frames with tubular shapes, 10: mixed systems of frames and masonry of low construction quality with a height of no more than 2 stories, 13 refers to the same typology as 12 with a height of more than two stories, 14: one-story bahareque dwellings, and 15: dwellings of precarious construction.

FEMA. In this case, Fig. 5 shows that the most frequent typology corresponds to C3 or reinforced concrete frames with non-reinforced masonry infill walls 57.9%, followed by typology C1 that corresponds to constructions with moment resistant concrete frames with 35.1%. The least frequent being W1A multi-storey wooden frames with an area greater than 300 m2 and S2 constructions with steel frames, both with 0.1%.

For the remaining typologies: URM are buildings with unreinforced masonry, W1 are wooden frames, RM are constructions of reinforced masonry, flexible floors and roof diaphragm, S1 are constructions with frames of moment-resisting steel frames, S3 are light metal frame constructions, and S5 are steel frame constructions with unreinforced masonry infill.

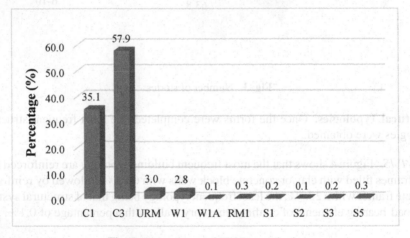

Fig. 5. Percentages of FEMA typologies

NEC. In this case, Fig. 6 shows that the most frequent typology corresponds to C3 or reinforced concrete frames with confined masonry without reinforcement 55.3%, followed by typology C1 that corresponds to concrete frames with 36.7%; being the least frequent the S1, S2, S5 and PC typologies corresponding to rolled steel, rolled steel with diagonals, steel with masonry walls and prefabricated reinforced concrete all of them with 0.1%.

For the other typologies: MX is mixed steel-reinforced concrete or wood-concrete, W1 is wood, URM is unreinforced masonry and RM is reinforced masonry.

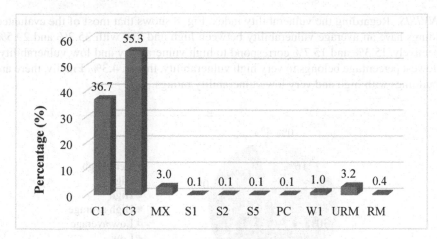

Fig. 6. Percentages of NEC typologies

GEM. In total, 56 structural typologies were found, which after a filtering process were reduced to 25. Therefore, Fig. 7 shows that the most frequent typology is the one that corresponds to reinforced concrete frames cast on site and filled with walls, with reinforced concrete slabs without additional coatings and 1 to 2 stories height, with 50.1%. Followed by the typology with the same characteristics but 3 to 5 stories height, with 27.6%. Finally, the least frequent typology is 2-story non-ductile wooden buildings without a lateral load-resistant system and with a metal sheet or asbestos roof.

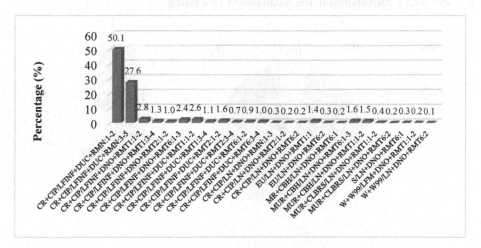

Fig. 7. Percentages of GEM typologies

Scores Once the indicated forms were applied, the final scores were calculated according to FEMA and NEC, as well as the vulnerability indices for FUNVISIS, among which the results for the vulnerability and risk indices will be shown.

FUNVISIS. Regarding the vulnerability index, Fig. 8 shows that most of the evaluated buildings have an average vulnerability between high and low with 35.2% and 29.5% respectively. 15.3% and 15.7% correspond to high vulnerability and low vulnerability; the lowest percentage belongs to very high vulnerability, that is, 4.3%. Finally, there are no buildings with high and very low vulnerability ratings.

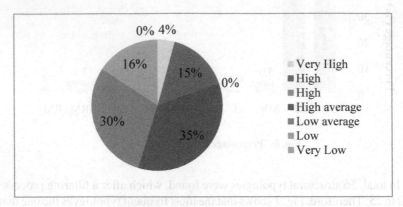

Fig. 8. Vulnerability index rating

For the risk index, Fig. 9 shows that most of the evaluated buildings have a high level corresponding to 53.7%, followed by a medium-high risk rating with a percentage of 23.6%. 14.9% of the buildings have a high risk and the lowest percentage presented is 3.4%, which corresponds to the medium-low risk rating.

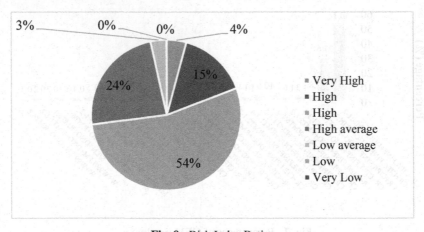

Fig. 9. Risk Index Rating

NEC. This methodology shows, see Fig. 10, that the majority of evaluated buildings have a high vulnerability with 67.5%; 4.9% of buildings have a medium vulnerability and 27.6% have a low degree of vulnerability.

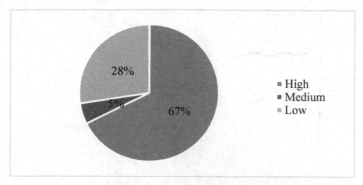

Fig. 10. Percentages of NEC Vulnerability

FEMA. Figure 11 shows that the majority of evaluated buildings have a high vulnerability with 67.5%; 4.9% of buildings have a medium vulnerability and 27.6% have a low degree of vulnerability.

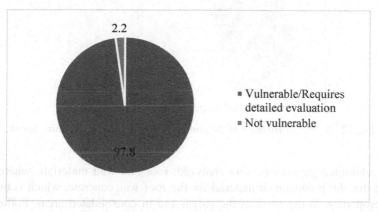

Fig. 11. Percentages of FEMA Vulnerability

3.2 Results of the Virtual Evaluations

To carry out the virtual surveys, the Google Street View tool was used and a new database was built with the 7484 properties that constitute the parish in order to verify the validity of the data collected in the field.

Number of Stories. It is observed that in the analyzed parish, buildings with 1 to 2 floors predominate with a percentage of 49.5%, a smaller percentage are buildings with 3 to 5 floors (13.9%) and a minimum percentage are structures with 6 to 10 floors (0.1%) which indicates that there are very few buildings in the parish with this number of floors. See Fig. 12.

Fig. 12. Spatial distribution of the number of stories in Huachi Chico parish

Two additional parameters were analyzed: roof and wall materials, where it was observed that the predominant material for the roof was concrete, which is used in a greater proportion in the north of the parish and in consolidated areas. Followed by metallic or asbestos sheets, which are observed, for the most part, in the southern part, where poorly planned houses were visualized in addition to being considered an area in process of urban consolidation. Another option used is the tile roof that is distributed evenly throughout the parish.

As for the wall material, the most used correspond to block and brick. A small number of buildings are made of earth walls that are presented in the north and south of the parish, corresponding to old houses.

Scores.
FUNVISIS. It can be seen that 14.4% of the buildings in the parish have a medium-high vulnerability and 21.1% a medium-low vulnerability. 19.3% show a low degree of vulnerability while percentages less than 2.2% and 6.3% belong to very high and high vulnerability, respectively. See Fig. 13.

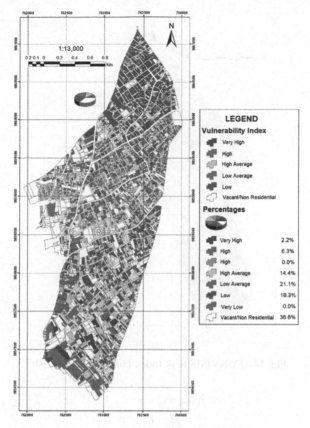

Fig. 13. FUNVISIS Vulnerability index Huachi Chico parish

For the risk index, Fig. 14 shows that the parish has a high risk level as it has the highest percentage, that is, 32.0%, followed by medium-high risk with 22.8%. Percentages less than 6.3% and 2.2% belong to high and very high risk levels, respectively. It can also be noted that the medium-high level of risk is distributed for the most part in zones 1 and 3. Few buildings in the zones in question present very high, and high risk levels; however, these levels are present in the central and southern areas of the parish, which may be due to poor construction planning, especially in the southern area.

NEC. It can be seen that the parish has a high degree of vulnerability with 62.6%, a small percentage of 0.8% has a medium level of vulnerability and no building with low vulnerability is recorded. Note that 36.6% corresponds to vacant or non-residential land. See Fig. 15.

FEMA. It can be seen that 63.4% of the buildings in the parish require a detailed evaluation. See Fig. 16.

GEM. It is important to point out that the predominant typology corresponds to reinforced concrete frames filled with cast-in-place masonry, ductile, with a concrete roof

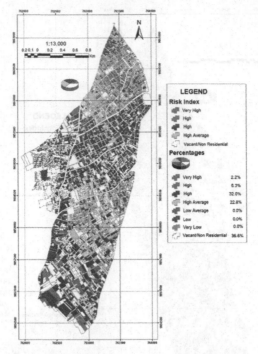

Fig. 14. FUNVISIS Risk Index Huachi Chico parish

Fig. 15. Spatial distribution of NEC vulnerability index Huachi Chico parish

Fig. 16. Spatial distribution of FEMA vulnerability index Huachi Chico parish

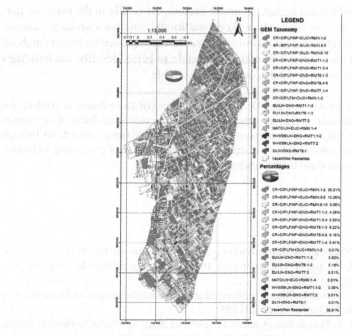

Fig. 17. Spatial distribution GEM taxonomy

without additional coating of 1 to 2 stories and 3 to 5 stories. Followed by cast-inplace reinforced concrete frames filled with non-ductile masonry covered with metal sheets or asbestos; small percentages are distributed in the rest of the typologies found. See Fig. 17.

4 Conclusions

To verify the validity of the information, a comparison was made between the field surveys and the visual surveys, finding that the same trend is maintained in each of the parameters analyzed. Therefore, it can be concluded that the results obtained are acceptable.

The analyzed parish presents a medium to high vulnerability, so it is important to think about reinforcement plans that allow improving the quality of existing constructions.

The frequent typology according to the three forms used and the GEM taxonomy is the reinforced concrete frame with masonry infill walls of 1 to 2 stories and 3 to 5 stories, which indicates that the residential buildings of parish buildings are of low and medium height.

This study shows the importance of carrying out a technical evaluation of seismic risk including procedures managed at an international level. GEM provides an easy way to bring together the most important characteristics of a building or group of buildings.

It is important to have an orderly construction control process and a review of buildings before, during and after construction, in order to verify compliance with regulations and have an orderly growth of cities.

Google Street View limited access to certain sectors, especially in the southern part of the parish, therefore, it is necessary to keep traditional databases updated because they serve as a point of reference for seismic risk studies. An updated cadastral database that includes relevant parameters will make it possible to better describe the buildings and thus complete and accurate databases will be available.

Acknowledgments. To the Autonomous Decentralized Municipal Government of Ambato for its collaboration with information regarding the cadaster and the geological faults of the canton. To the engineer José Poveda and the students of the University of the Universidad de las Fuerzas Armadas ESPE for their collaboration in carrying out the surveys, data processing, obtaining results and the contributions made to this Research Project.

References

1. Escuela Politécnica Nacional, GeoHazards Internacional, Municipio del Distrito Metropolitano de Quito, ORSTOM, Q., and OYO Corporation. Proyecto para el manejo del riesgo sísmico de Quito. TRAMA, Quito (1995)
2. Yépez, F., Barbat, A., Canas, J.: Riesgo, peligrosidad y vulnerabilidad sísmica de edificios de mampostería. España: Editor A.H Barbat (1995)
3. Gobierno Provincial de Tungurahua. Agenda Tungurahua desde la Visión Territorial. Tungurahua (2015–2017)

4. Aguilar, A.: Análisis de vulnerabilidad no estructural del Hospital de Solca de la ciudad de Ambato y sus consecuencias. Ambato, Tungurahua, Ecuador: IAEN Diplomado Superior en Gestión Integral de Riesgos y Desastres (2008)
5. GAD Municipalidad de Ambato: Actualización del Plan de Desarrollo y Ordenamiento Territorial. Ambato (2015)
6. Caballero, Á.: Determinación de la Vulnerabilidad Sísmica por medio del Método del Índice de Vulnerabilidad en las estructuras ubicadas en el Centro Histórico de la ciudad de Sincelejo, utilizando la tecnología del Sistema de Información Geográfica. Universidad del Norte, Sincelejo (2007)
7. Aguiar, R., Rivas, A.: Microzonificación Sísmica de Ambato. Instituto Panamericano de Geografía e Historia, Ecuador (2018)

Proposal for a Unique Cartographic Projection System for the Galapagos Islands in Order to Generate Cartography at Large Scales

Marco P. Luna(iD), Andrea Almeida(iD), Gabriela Cisneros(iD),
and Theofilos Toulkeridis$^{(\boxtimes)}$ (iD)

Departmento de Ciencias de la Tierra y Construcción, Universidad de las Fuerzas Armadas
ESPE, General Rumiñahui SN y Ambato, 171103 Sangolquí, Ecuador
ttoulkeridis@espe.edu.ec

Abstract. The conservation of Galapagos is a priority component in Ecuador's territorial planning and administration policy, because it is a world benchmark for biodiversity. It is also located in four different zones in the U.T.M representation (15 N, 15 S, 16 N, 16 S). In this sense, it is necessary to have a detailed and precise representation of this territory, which is why the lack of a single cartographic projection system that ensures minimal deformations and meets the precision required for large scales has been evidenced. The objective of the current study has been to define and validate a unique Local Cartographic Projection System for Galapagos in order to generate cartography at large scales, by calculating cartographic, geodetic and topographic parameters. Such investigation consisted of verifying several projections that due to their characteristics were better adapted to the study area. The four best ones were selected based on the calculation of the linear deformation modules, errors in distances and areas, which served to determine the planimetric precisions with which the best projection could be obtained to be used from scales 1:1000 to smaller. The Modified Gauss Krüger projection was selected using the Bessel ellipsoid (1841), obtaining precisions of less than 0.30 m, which corresponds to the parameters established by the Military Geographic Institute of Ecuador (IGM) to generate cartography at a scale of 1:1000.

Keywords: Projection geographic · Ellipsoid · Conformal projection · UTM · LTM · Galápagos

1 Introduction

Cartographic projection systems arise in response to the need to represent a territory based on a specific purpose that can be navigation, engineering, local or regional territorial planning, among others [1–3]. These allow to indicate part or all of the Earth's surface on a plane from a wide variety of scales. The design of map projections and the choice of corresponding parameters are generally done to minimize distortions in the ellipsoid-to-datum transformation for an area of interest [4]. In this sense, when applying a cartographic projection system, the presence of minimum or maximum deformations (distortions) will result, depending on the physical magnitude to be preserved, be it surface, distances or angles, since the selection of the magnitude to conserve will depend on the purpose of the map, considering that only one of the mentioned magnitudes can be conserved and not all at the same time.

Each projection has advantages and disadvantages, with the appropriate projection of a map depending on the scale and the purposes for which it will be used. Although there are a large number of map projections [5], some projections are suitable for application to small areas. Others are exclusive to mapping large extensions with an east-west direction, and some to map areas with a large extension with a north-south location [6]. In this way, several investigations have focused on analyzing, defining and validating new projection systems that are based on mathematical development through analytical and numerical methods [7].

It should be noted that the cartographic projection that is generally used worldwide is the Universal Transverse Mercator (UTM). However, this presents a series of appreciable deformations in the representations at larger scales, so in order to solve this problem, local cartographic projections have been developed that are adapted to the geographical conditions of each place. Such is the case of Mexico, which officially uses three projections, the Universal Transverse Mercator, used in topographic charts for medium and large scales, the Lambert Conformal Conic, adapted to the conditions of the country for its representation on small and large scales. Normal Mercator, used for maritime navigation purposes. The Korean peninsula uses the Gauss-Schreiber and Gauss-Krüger projections [8] and Colombia the Gauss-Krüger projection [9].

With all of the aforementioned, the problem arises in the representation of the Galapagos Islands, that by not having a single cartographic representation system, it has been decided to apply the conventional UTM projection system, which has certain drawbacks. This occurs because the area under study is located at the extremes of zones 15 and 16 and in the northern and southern hemispheres, generating four different UTM projection systems.

Therefore, in the current study, the definition and validation of a single Cartographic Projection System for the Galapagos Islands is proposed in order to generate large-scale cartography that covers the entire Island territory and ensures minimal deformations. Accuracies are determined by the graphic design, which is defined as that quantity, which, at the scale of the chart, corresponds to the minimum appreciable distance [10].

In order to accomplish such purpose, some projection systems that best adapt to the geographical location of the archipelago were selected, through a theoretical analysis of said projections, thus ensuring minimal deformations in their representation on the plane. From this, cartographic, geodetic and topographic parameters were defined, thus obtaining a unique projection system that will ensure integrated management of geo-information and compliance with the required precisions. In addition, it was decided to simplify and speed up the spatial analyzes to the maximum in order to enhance decision-making, avoiding the division of the archipelago into multiple geographical zones, which generate topological discontinuities of the information, as well as complications to carry out regional-type analyses.

2 Methodology

The methodology proposed in this research consisted of three stages, of which first has been the selection of projections for the area under study, followed by the development of a geodetic network for comparison and analysis, and finally the selection of the projection with minimum deformation.

2.1 Selection of Projections for the Study Area

For the first stage, representation characteristics of various projections were analyzed, such as orientation of the territory, extension of area, scale of representation, relief and its applications in regions with characteristics similar to the study area, thus determining which would be the most suitable for the Galapagos Islands. Whereas nine projections were selected, being Mercator projection, Equatorial Stereographic Projection, Oblique Stereographic Projection, Secant Cylindrical Projection, Universal Transverse Mercator Projection (UTM), Modified Gauss-Krüger Projection, Local Transverse Mercator Projection (LTM), Ejidal Projection and Oblique Mercator Projection. All these projections are conformal, since this feature imposes the condition that, at a point, the angles are conserved and the scale error is the same in all directions. These qualities are locally shape-preserving and make them particularly useful for calculations involving directions, azimuths, and distances. However, they are much more difficult to calculate and build [11]. The first selection was realized based on the deformation modulus of each projection (Table 1).

Next, several parameters of each of the projections were determined, such as the central meridian, parallel of origin and scale factor. The Gauss Kruger projection was modified by introducing a scale factor, selected through iterations and choosing the one that gave us the best results. The central meridians and parallels were also defined based on the parameters established in each projection. With these parameters, the linear deformation modules were calculated for a grid of 418 points distributed every 10 min in latitude and longitude within the study area. These results served to select four projections with minimal deformations from two conditions. The first consisted in obtaining the statistics of the linear deformation modules calculated for the grid. Central tendency statistics were determined, such as mean, standard deviation, minimum and maximum. Also, the calculation of the root-mean-square error (rmse) was considered.

For the second condition, it was analyzed that the linear deformation modules are within the limits established for scales 1:1000 and 1:5000, from the modeling of these, where the Military Geographic Institute (IGM) standard was used, which for 1:1000 scale the precision is 0.30 m and for 1:5000 a precision of 1.5 m is established [12]. From this the minimum and maximum linear strain moduli were determined. For this, it was determined that the precisions previously calculated would be the maximum admissible error in the deformations for distances that reach up to 10,000m, because the shape of the maps is trapezoidal, very approximately equal to that of a square 10,000m long.

Table 1. Linear deformation modules of the initially selected projections.

Projection	Linear deformation modules
Mercator	$L = \frac{\sqrt{1-e^2\sin^2\varphi}}{\cos\varphi}$
Equatorial Stereographic	$L = \frac{2\sqrt{\sin^2\chi\sin^2\Delta\lambda_1 + (\cos\chi + \cos\Delta\lambda_1)^2}}{(1+\cos\chi*\cos\Delta\lambda_1)^2}$
Oblique Stereographic	$L = \frac{2}{1+\sin\chi\sin\varphi_0 + \cos\chi_0\cos\chi\cos\Delta\lambda_1}$
Secant Cylindrical	$L = \frac{\cos\varphi_0*\sqrt{1-e^2*\sin^2\varphi}}{\cos\varphi*\sqrt{1-e^2*\sin^2\varphi_0}}$
U.T.M	$L = 0.9996*\left[1 + \frac{\Delta\lambda^2}{2}*\cos^2\varphi\left(1+\eta^2\right) + \frac{\Delta\lambda^4}{24}*\cos^4\varphi\left(5-4t^2\right)\right]$
Gauss-Krüger	$L = \left[1 + \frac{\Delta\lambda_1^2}{2}*\cos^2\varphi\left(1+\eta^2\right) + \frac{\Delta\lambda_1^4}{24}*\cos^4\varphi\left(5-4t^2\right)\right]$
L.T.M	$L = 1.00001113*\left[1 + \frac{\Delta\lambda_1^2}{2}*\cos^2\varphi\left(1+\eta^2\right) + \frac{\Delta\lambda_1^4}{24}*\cos^4\varphi\left(5-4t^2\right)\right]$
Ejidal	$L = \left[1 + \frac{\Delta\lambda_2^2}{2}*\cos^2\varphi\left(1+\eta^2\right) + \frac{\Delta\lambda_1^4}{24}*\cos^4\varphi\left(5-4t^2\right)\right]$
Oblique Mercator	$L = \frac{A*\cos(Bx/A)*\sin\theta'}{a*\cos\varphi*\cos(B*\Delta\lambda_1)}$

Subsequently, in order to know the behavior of the linear deformation modules and their compliance in each projection, the 418 points were interpolated using the IDW (Inverse Distance Weighting) method in the ArcGIS V.10.8 software.

2.2 Development of Geodetic Network for the Comparison of Projections

The network was configured with five vertices, of which three are part of the National GPS Network of Ecuador (RENAGE) and two to the stations of the Continuous Monitoring GNSS Network of Ecuador (REGME). RENAGE stations are BALT, ISAB and STCR, while those of the REGME are GLPS and ICEC. For the execution of the geodesic network in the Galapagos Islands, there were two receivers and the tracking time was 4 h for each session. The differential static positioning method was used to obtain millimetric precision in positioning [13]. To perform this phase, the Trimble Business Center (TBC) Software was used, in its version 2.5. The Project Configuration was established, where the Coordinate System, Calculations (Tolerance in Points), Baseline Processing (Solution Type, Frequency, Generate Residuals, Processing Interval, Quality and Satellites), Network Adjustment and Default Standard Errors (GNSS) were defined. The network is indicated in Fig. 1.

This network was linked to the REGME so that, in order to obtain an adequate adjustment, the GLPS and ICEC coordinates were obtained from the weekly solutions of the Geodetic Reference System for the Americas (SIRGAS), which are referred to the IGb14 framework. This reference frame is the one that was in force at the date of

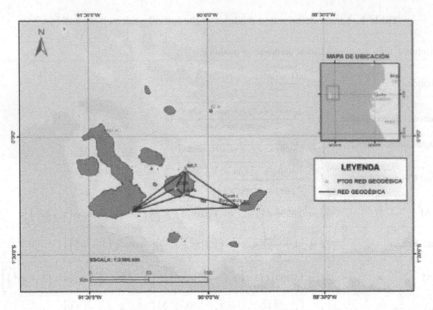

Fig. 1. Galapagos geodetic network.

data collection and because it is generated with an improved modeling of the non-linear movements of the stations, including the seasonal signals of the positions of the stations [14].

2.3   Analysis and Selection of the Projection with Minimum Deformation

In this phase, we worked with data taken in the field in order to determine linear and surface deformation modules, errors in distances and projected surfaces and their compliance for scales 1:1000 and 1:5000. While map projection parameters are typically selected to minimize ellipsoid-to-grid distortions for a region, in some cases it might be more convenient to study and minimize ground-to-grid distortions [4].

The distance between two points reduced to the ellipsoid, which will later be projected onto the plane, is a clearly defined magnitude that is measured along the geodesic line that passes through both ends. On the contrary, at a certain height, above or below the ellipsoid, the notion of horizontal distance becomes ambiguous. Thus, the horizontal distance can mean the projected distance on the local geodetic horizon of the first point or the horizon of the second point, or it can be defined for a species of average height, or with an alternative definition [14]. Whereas the distances to be verified were the distances projected to the mean horizon, but not the ellipsoidal distances, since the points measured in the field are at different altitudes and therefore are not on the ellipsoid. For this, the global Cartesian coordinates (X, Y, Z) were used, applying the Euclidean formula to obtain the distance D between the different vertices of the network.

$$D = \sqrt{(X_1 - X_2)^2 + (Y_1 - Y_2)^2 + (Z_1 - Z_2)^2} \tag{1}$$

For the reduction to the middle horizon, the following correction is used:

$$c = \frac{\Delta h^2}{2D} + \frac{\Delta h^4}{8D^3} \tag{2}$$

To finally have the distance to the middle horizon D1 [15].

$$D_1 = D + c \tag{3}$$

For the comparison of the areas, we proceeded to calculate the areas.

Of the five vertices of the network, all the possible distances between these vertices were compared, that is, 10 distances (C_2^5), likewise for the comparison of the areas, the areas of all the possible triangles of the network were made, which 10 also resulted (C_3^5). These were compared with the areas obtained from the Lambert equivalent projection (conserves the areas). Additionally, to determine which ellipsoid best fits the study area, it was calculated with the ellipsoids listed in Table 2.

Table 2. Some official ellipsoid in use throughout the world [16]

Name	Date	Equatorial Radius, a meters	Flattening f	Use
Everest	1830	6 377 276	1: 300,800	India
Bessel	1841	6 377 397	1: 299,150	Germany, Holland, Indonesia
Airy	1858	6 377 563	1: 299,330	Great Britain
Clarke	1858	6 378 294	1: 294,300	
Clarke	1866	6 378 206	1: 295,000	USA
Clarke	1880	6 378 249	1: 293,500	South Africa
Hayford	1909	6 378 388	1: 297,000	Internationally adopted
Krassovsky	1948	6 378 245	1: 298,300	Russia, Eastern Countries

To determine the errors presented in the distances, the difference between the ellipsoidal distances with the plane distances for the four selected projections was calculated. In turn, in order to have a better perception of these and considering the established tolerances of 0.3 m, the error made for every 10 km along the total distance of each pair of coordinates was adjusted, based on a rule of three simple, as indicated in Eq. (4).

$$error = \frac{|projected\_dist - ellipsoidal\_dist| * 10000}{ellipsoidal\_dist} \tag{4}$$

For the case of area errors, the absolute difference between the ellipsoidal areas and the projected areas was calculated.

3   Results and Discussion

From the interpolation of the 418 points taken in a 10'x10'grid, the four best projections were selected, being Secant Cylindrical, Local Transverse Mercator, Modified Gauss

Krüger and Equatorial Stereographic. The green color indicates the areas in which each projection presents the least linear deformations. Figures 2, 3, 4, and 5 illustrate the maps that indicate compliance with the precision of the projections for a scale of 1:5000. While in Figs. 6, 7, 8 and 9 instead the maps are presented in which the fulfillment of the precision of the projections for scale 1:1000 is evidenced.

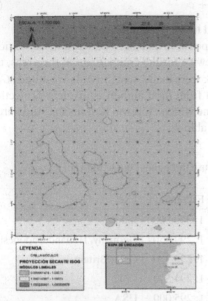

Fig. 2. Linear deformation modules for Cylindrical Secant at Scale 1:5000.

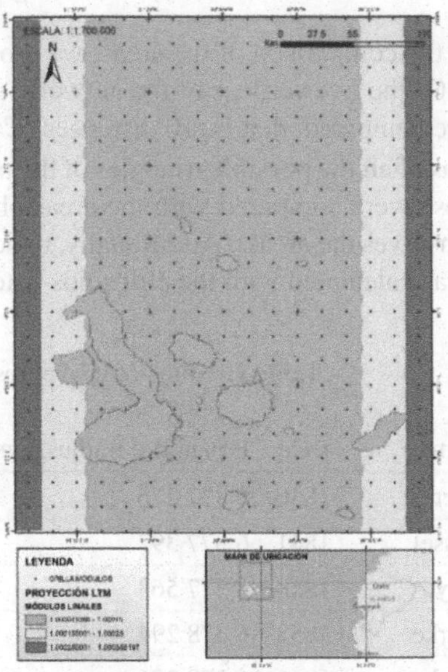

Fig. 3. Linear deformation modules for LTM at Scale 1:5000.

Table 3 lists the values of linear deformation obtained from the grid of equally spaced points. This table indicates which best statistics correspond to the projections selected above; In addition, these values assert that the UTM projection is not suitable for the Galapagos archipelago, since it reaches linear errors of up to 0.98 m/km, not being for large scales. [17] propose that the UTM projection is a commonly used projection for maps ranging in scale from 1:24,000 to 1:250,000.

For the comparison of distances and areas, we first proceeded to obtain the global coordinates (Latitude, longitude and ellipsoidal height) of the geodetic network, whose results are indicated in Table 4, the same ones that were transformed into global Cartesian coordinates (X, Y and Z).

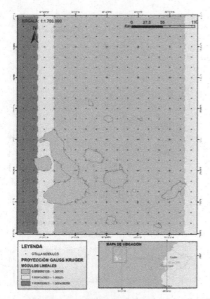

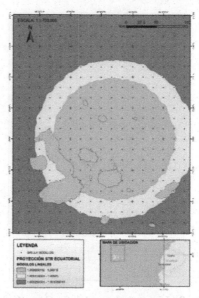

Fig. 4. Linear Strain Modules for Gauss-Krüger Modified at 1:5000 Scale.

Fig. 5. Linear deformation modules for Equatorial Stereographic at 1:5000 Scale

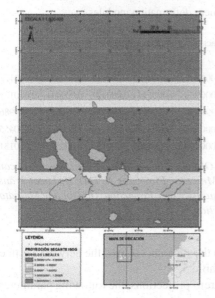

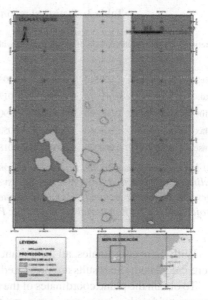

Fig. 6. Linear deformation modules for Cylindrical Secant at Scale 1:1000.

Fig. 7. Linear deformation modules for LTM at 1:1000 Scale.

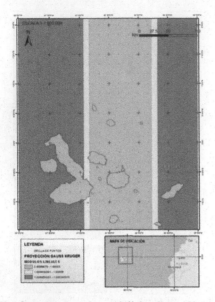

Fig. 8. Linear strain moduli for Gauss-Krüger **Fig. 9.** Linear deformation modules for
Modified to Scale 1:1000   Equatorial Stereographic at 1:1000 Scale

Table 3. Statistical report of linear deformation modules

Statistics	Linear strain moduli of the projections with respect to a grid of equally spaced points								
	a	b	c	d	e	f	g	h	i
Mean	1.000164	1.000310	1.000355	1.000080	1.000347	1.000139	1.000119	0.999707	1.000122
Std. Dev.	0.000171	0.000211	0.000268	0.000171	0.000358	0.000114	0.000127	0.000441	0.000134
Min	0.999985	1.000000	0.999831	0.999901	0.999753	1.000011	0.999985	0.998892	0.999986
Max	1.000590	1.001040	1.001051	1.000507	1.000981	1.000356	1.000426	1.000942	1.000455
rmse	0.000237	0.000375	0.000444	0.000189	0.000499	0.000180	0.000173	0.000529	0.000181

(a) Mercator Projection, (b) Ejidal Projection, (c) Oblique Stereographic Projection, (d) Secant Cylindrical Projection, (e) Universal Transverse Mercator Projection (UTM), (f) Local Transverse Mercator Projection (LTM), (g) Modified Gauss-Krüger Projection, (h) Oblique Mercator Projection and (i) Equatorial Stereographic Projection.

With these coordinates, all the distances to the mean horizon of the network vertices were calculated, the results are presented in Table 5.

To obtain the plane coordinates of the different projections, the following parameters were considered:

- Central meridian: 90° 30′ W
- Origin latitude: 0° 30′N
- False East: 200 000 m
- False North: 500 000 m

Table 4. Global geodetic network coordinates

ID	Latitude (Global)	Longitude	Height (meter)
BALT	S 0°25'53.41436''	W 90°17'00.29464''	14.0893
GLPS	S 0°44'34.79210''	W 90°18'13.19290''	1.7695
ICEC	S 0°54'26.41670''	W 89°36'14.22510''	51.5627
ISAB	S 0°57'27.76547''	W 90°57'55.68882''	−2.6417
STCR	S 0°39'06.13221''	W 90°24'27.66032''	412.7592

The scale factor for the LTM projection is 0.999995, while for the modified Gauss Krüger projection, several iterations were carried out in order to establish the most appropriate, the value being 1.00008. Table 6 shows the rmse values for each projection and corresponding ellipsoid.

Table 5. Distance between vertexes of the geodetic network.

Distances	D - Direct Distance (m)	D_1 - Distance to the mean horizon (m)
BALT - GLPS	34516.919	34516.917
BALT - ICEC	92133.158	92133.150
BALT - ISAB	95651.583	95651.582
BALT - STCR	28007.204	28004.366
GLPS - ICEC	79975.337	79975.321
GLPS - ISAB	77394.689	77394.689
GLPS - STCR	15367.187	15361.69
ICEC - ISAB	151642.865	151642.856
ICEC - STCR	93825.362	93824.667
ISAB - STCR	70711.226	70710.006

Table 6 indicates that the lowest mean square error corresponds to the Modified Gauss Krüger projection and the Bessel ellipsoid (1841) with an rmse value equal to 1.852. It should be noted that the Bessel geodetic datum is a Bessel spheroid originating in 1841 that is the reference ellipsoid, while WGS84 is the reference ellipsoid currently used for GPS satellites [18]. The highest values correspond to the secant cylindrical projections and the equatorial stereographic, these are well above the values obtained in the LTM and modified Gauss Krüger projections.

Table 7 lists that the lowest values committed when measuring a distance of 10,000 m also correspond to the LTM and modified Gauss Krüger projections, very far from these are the secant cylindrical projections and the equatorial stereographic.

Of the two best projections, the highest values correspond to the LTM projection using the Walbeck ellipsoid with a value of 1,517 m and the modified Gauss Krüger

Table 6. Root-mean error for different projections.

Elipsoides	LTM	Gauss Krüger	Cylindr. Secant	Equator Stereogr.
Walbeck 1819	5.166	5.781	130.676	131.218
Airy 1830	8.327	2.890	136.064	136.586
Everest 1830	7.282	2.072	133.703	134.233
Bessel 1841	4.991	1.852	134.691	135.217
Clarke 1858	7.041	11.491	142.939	143.438
Shubert 1859	3.521	13.607	144.774	145.267
Clarke 1866	3.930	9.700	141.570	142.073
Clarke 1880	5.676	9.928	141.948	142.450
Hayford 1909	4.843	12.489	143.179	143.678
Krassowsky 1940	3.054	11.661	142.353	142.855
GRS80 –WGS84	3.054	9.601	140.965	141.471

Table 7. Average errors made when measuring a distance of 10000 m.

Ellipsoids	LTM	Gauss Krüger	Cylindr. Secant	Equator. Stereogr.
Walbeck 1819	1.517	0.667	21.179	21.257
Airy 1830	0.727	0.266	22.085	22.135
Everest 1830	1.067	0.279	21.657	21.735
Bessel 1841	1,001	0.273	21.824	21.887
Clarke 1858	0.476	0.988	23.339	23.389
Shubert 1859	0.639	0.667	23.661	23.711
Clarke 1866	0.413	0.800	23.095	23.145
Clarke 1880	0.491	0.790	23.163	23.213
Hayford 1909	0.437	1.241	23.381	23.431
Krassowsky 1940	0.380	1.201	23.235	23.285
GRS80WGS84	0.274	0.942	22.987	23.037

projection with the Hayford ellipsoid. According to [18] these values represent the accuracy with which one is going to work and it is intimately linked to the graphics whose value is 0.2 mm. However, the IGM considers this value to be 0.3 mm, so that for a scale of 1:5000 the minimum appreciable distance is 1.5 m and for a scale of 1:1000 it is 0.3 m, because, as can be seen from the Using an ellipsoid that best fits the study area influences the accuracy of the projection. The projection that would meet this requirement would be the Gauss Krüger projection using the Airy, Everest, and Bessel ellipsoids with accuracies of 0.266, 0.279, and 0.273, respectively.

Therefore, the best statistics correspond to the Gauss Krüger projection whose parameters are the following:

- Projection: Gauss Krüger Modified
- Ellipsoid: Bessel (1841)
- Semi-major axis (a) = 6 377 3971
- Flattening (f) = 1/ 299.150
- Scale factor = 1.00008
- Central Meridian = 90° 30′ W
- Origin Latitude = 0° 30' N
- False East = 200 000
- False North = 500 000

For the analysis of the areas, the statistics do not favor any of the projections that were better in the comparison of distances, as indicated in Table 8.

Table 8. Root-mean-square error of the areas measured in km^2

Ellipsoids	LTM	Gauss Krüger	Cylindrical Secant	Equatorial Stereographic
Walbeck 1819	11,5831	11,2811	0,1567	0,2790
Airy 1830	11,7214	11,4193	0,1568	0,2790
Everest 1830	11,6619	11,3598	0,1567	0,2790
Bessel 1841	11,7276	11,4256	0,1568	0,2790
Clarke 1858	11,9293	11,6272	0,1569	0,2791
Shubert 1859	12,0193	11,7171	0,1569	0,2791
Clarke 1866	11,8992	11,5971	0,1569	0,2791
Clarke 1880	11,9617	11,6596	0,1569	0,2791
Hayford 1909	11,8177	11,5155	0,1568	0,2791
Krassowsky 1940	11,7610	11,4589	0,1568	0,2791
GRS80WGS84	11,7661	11,4640	0,1568	0,2791

These results indicate that the best projections for calculating the area are the secant cylindrical projections and the equatorial stereographic projections.

4 Conclusions

The interpolation of the linear deformation modules for different points within a study area is a first approximation to select those projections that meet the parameters established at a given scale.

The selection of the scale factor is also of great importance, which in our case was obtained through successive iterations with values from 0.9996 onwards, resulting in the value of 1.00008, which corresponds approximately to the average height of the terrain area, that is, this value will depend on the height of the terrain.

Similarly, the use of an ellipsoid that fits better to the study area improves the precision of the projection; The Bessel ellipsoid (1841) was chosen, with which values lower than 0.30 m were obtained, which correspond to the parameters established by the IGM of Ecuador to generate cartography at a 1:1000 scale. Finally, the projection that gave the best results was the Modified Gauss Krüger Projection, using the indicated parameters.

References

1. Mora, M.J.M., González, C.A.L., Hidalgo, D.A.E., Toulkeridis, T.: Determination of altitudes of the three main Ecuadorian summits through GNSS positioning. Geodesy Geodyn. **13**, 343–351 (2022)
2. Orejuela, I.P., González, C.L., Guerra, X.B., Mora, E.C., Toulkeridis, T.: Geoid undulation modeling through the Cokriging method–a case study of Guayaquil, Ecuador. Geodesy Geodyn. **12**(5), 356–367 (2021)
3. Luna, M.P., Staller, A., Toulkeridis, T., Parra, H.: Methodological approach for the estimation of a new velocity model for continental Ecuador. Open Geosci. **9**(1), 719–734 (2017)
4. Baselga, S.: Two conformal projections for constant-height surface to plane mapping. J. Surv. Eng. **147**(2), 06020004 (2021)
5. Snyder, J.P.: Map Projections--A Working Manual, vol. 1395. US Government Printing Office (1987)
6. Cosarca, O., Cosarca, C., Calin, A.: Projections and Reference Local Systems in Engineering Survey (2013). http://www.wseas.us/e-library/conferences/2013/Antalya/GENG/GENG-01. pdf
7. Panou, G., Korakitis, R.: Analytical and numerical methods of converting Cartesian to ellipsoidal coordinates. J. Geodetic Sci. **11**(1), 111–121 (2021)
8. Lee, H., Seo, W.: A comparative study of transverse cylindrical projection functions by a series of numerical simulations. J. Korean Soc. Surv. Geod. Photogramm. Cartogr. **31**(2), 121–134 (2013)
9. Niño, E.N.: Comparación de la nueva proyección cartográfica para Colombia-Origen Nacional-con las proyecciones Gauss-Krüger y cartesiana local. Mapping **201**, 4–14 (2020)
10. Dennis, M.L.: NOAA Special Publication NOS NGS 13 The State Plane Coordinate System (2018)
11. IGM. ESPECIFICACIONES TÉCNICAS GENERALES PARA LA REALIZACIÓN DE CARTOGRAFÍA TOPOGRÁFICA A CUALQUIER ESCALA. IGM, Quito (2006). http://www.igm.gob.ec/work/files/downloads/especcarto3.html
12. Seeber, G.: Satellite Geodesy. De Gruyter, Berlin New York (2008). https://doi.org/10.1515/9783110200089
13. Altamimi, Z., et al.: ITRF2014: a new release of the international terrestrial reference frame modeling nonlinear station motions. J. Geophys. Res. Solid Earth. **121**(8), 6109–6131 (2016)
14. Rollins, C.M., Meyer, T.H.: Four methods for low-distortion projections. J. Surv. Eng. **145**(4), 04019017 (2019)
15. Meyer, T.H.: Introduction to Geometrical and Physical Geodesy: Foundations of Geomatics. Esri Press (2018)

16. Banko, A., Banković, T., Pavasović, M., Đapo, A.: An all-in-one application for temporal coordinate transformation in geodesy and geoinformatics. ISPRS Int. J. Geo Inf. **9**(5), 323 (2020)
17. Bertici, R., et al.: Comparative analysis of Mercator and UTM map projections. Res. J. Agric. Sci. **46**(2), 1–8 (2014)
18. Gamboa, J.M.M.: Fundamentos para cartografía náutica. JM ediciones (2006)

Prioritization of a Micro-basin of the Daule River Sub-basin with Strong Erosional Problems and Their Effect to the Turbidity of the Water in the City of Guayaquil, Coastal Ecuador

Carlos Aníbal Gutiérrez-Caiza[1] and Theofilos Toulkeridis[2]([⊠])

[1] Grupo de Investigación de Recursos Hídricos y Acuáticos, Universidad Regional Amazónica Ikiam, Parroquia Muyuna, kilómetro 7 vía a Alto Tena, Tena 150101, Ecuador
[2] Departamento de Ciencias de la Tierra y Construcción, Universidad de las Fuerzas Armadas ESPE, General Rumiñahui SN y Ambato, Sangolquí 171103, Ecuador
ttoulkeridis@espe.edu.ec

Abstract. The drinking water intake of the city of Guayaquil is located on the Daule River, supplying 2.7 million inhabitants who are affected by the turbidity of the water, even leading INERGAGUA to suspend the service with high economic losses. Given this, water erosion and the effects of land use were calculated using the Universal Soil Loss Equation (USLE), estimating the Erosivity factor (R) through the Fournier climatic aggressiveness index. Mean monthly and annual rainfall data from 14 stations in the basin were used. The other variables such as soil erodibility factor (K), slope length and gradient (LS), coverage factor (C), use factor and soil management (P), were quantified with a mathematical analysis of the variables. Initially, the sub-basin was considered as a global model and then as a distributed model, subdividing it into 88 micro-basins, allowing a more accurate estimate of an average annual water erosion of 130.04 t/ha/year. To determine the type and level of erosion, the FAO scale was used, observing 14 micro-basins with erosion rates ranging from 154.3487 t/ha/year to 846.3418 t/ha/year, whose range of erosion goes from very severe to catastrophic, which results to the requirement of immediate intervention. Applying the sediment delivery factor (SDF), it was estimated that 5.12% of the total eroded, that is, 8,089 tons/ha/year reaches the river.

Keywords: Water erosion · Sediments · Sub-basin · Micro-basin · Level of erosion

1 Introduction

Erosion is the process of soil loss that occurs mainly due to the action of wind (wind erosion) and water (water erosion) [29]. Average erosion rates around the world have been estimated at 16 tons/ha/year [18]. This represents a loss of 0.9 to 0.95 mm of soil annually [31]. This rate of erosion is increasing due to the continuous expansion of the agricultural frontier (deforestation), overgrazing and urbanization [2]. Therefore, it is

M. Botto-Tobar et al. (Eds.): ICAT 2022, CCIS 1756, pp. 118–134, 2023.
https://doi.org/10.1007/978-3-031-24971-6_9

indicated that erosion should be considered as a global problem with environmental and social impacts [1, 29, 31]. In the world, 25% of the land used for agriculture is seriously degraded, reducing productivity [27, 37]. The most serious form of soil degradation is caused by erosion [41, 42].

About 50% of the Ecuadorian territory is affected by erosion processes and constitutes one of the main aspects of natural resource degradation [28]. Hereby, the degree of erosion in hydrographic sub-basins of the Ecuadorian highlands corresponds to 39.13% critical, 28.26% moderate, 26.09% potential and 2.1% normal, leading to loss of biodiversity, soil degradation, high sedimentation in reservoirs, riverbeds and floods [19, 30], indicate that water erosion in the sub-basins of the 24 de Mayo canton, Ecuador as: R. Grande with 6.49; R. Guineal with 6.4 and the Congo with 16.6 t/ha/year; exceed the tolerance established by the FAO (0.4–1.8 t/ha/year), which leads to agricultural soils losing their productive capacity. One of the widely used methods for estimating potential erosion is the Universal Soil Loss Equation (USLE) [3], which relates the most important elements of water erosion: precipitation, topography, vegetation and ground. Although other WEPP or EUROSEM erosion estimation models have been mentioned in the literature, the (USLE) method remains attractive due to its simplicity [8, 12], and the ease relative to your input data [3].

The EUPS-USLE method has the advantage that the erosivity index allows considering the differences in rainfall from one storm to another, or from one season to another, however in practice it is very difficult to have the data that allow estimating the erosivity index due to the scarcity and deficit of pluviographs in the hydrographic sub-basins, which has given rise to the search for other models that predict precipitation based on parameters provided by the meteorological network (pluviometry). For this research, the Fournier Aggressiveness Index (FDI) for the period (2000–2016) will be used, whose equation and arguments are detailed below.

Research conducted have let to appreciate the importance of evaluating water erosion at the sub-basin and micro-basin level, in order to infer what can happen in the event of a soil degradation trend. In this sense, the primary objective of the current study was to estimate water erosion with the Universal Soil Loss Equation (USLE) in the Daule River sub-basin at a global level and at a micro-basin level that allows locating the micro-basin or basins with the greatest affectation for its prioritization and immediate intervention, carrying out field studies in the selected micro-basins and using meteorological information from the National Institute of Meteorology and Hydrology (INAMHI) from 14 stations distributed in the Daule River sub-basin.

2 Methodology

2.1 Study Area

The current study was performed in the Daule River sub-basin, which is part of the Guayas River sub-basin with an area of 32,217.14 km^2 (Fig. 1). It is located between the coordinates 550150.750 E, 9844878.00 N; 667366.93 E, 9900379.00 N; 703261.625 E, 9972496.00 N; 599645.06 E, 9765610.00 N. This occurred at an average altitude of 10 m below sea level and 830 m above sea level in the highest part, comprising a total area of 11,567.08 km^2, of which 295 km^2 (2.55%) corresponds to the "Daule - Peripa" dam and the remaining 11,272.08 km^2 (97.45%) are composed of land in which different towns are settled and products of the area are grown (see Fig. 1).

Fig. 1. Geographical location of the Daule River sub-basin

A general reconnaissance of the sub-basin and micro-basins was conducted with the support of cartography and a navigator (GPS) that allowed observing its geomorphological, hydrological, edaphological and land use status. In order to estimate water erosion in the 88 micro-basins, the Universal Soil Loss Equation (USLE) was used, which form the Daule River sub-basin [49]. This method is widely used to determine laminar water erosion through five factors that are related to each other, being precipitation, soil erodibility, vegetation, topography and cultivation practices [23] (see Fig. 2).

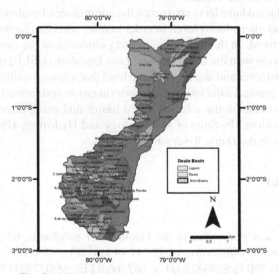

Fig. 2. Micro-basins of the Daule River sub-basin

Once the study area was defined, the USLE equation was applied as a direct parametric method. The USLE Equation [1] is a methodology that allows quantifying annual quantities of eroded soil per unit area that was proposed by [50].

$$A = RKLSCP \qquad (1)$$

where:

A = Annual average soil loss (t ha-1 year-1).

R = Rain erosivity factor (MJ mm ha -1 h - 1year-1).

K = Soil erodibility factor (t ha h ha-1 MJ-1 mm-1).

LS = Slope length and slope gradient (dimensionless). C = Factor dependent on coverage (dimensionless).

P = Soil use and management factor (dimensionless).

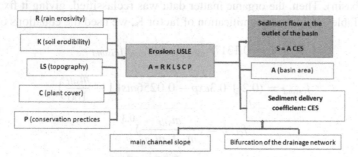

Fig. 3. Schematic summary of the methodology used in this work.

The methodological process used for the current study is illustrated in Fig. 3, beginning with the calculation of the parameters R, K, LS, C and P that allow obtaining the annual average soil loss A. Furthermore, we estimated the sediment delivery coefficient CES as a function of the slope of the main channel and the bifurcation coefficient, which multiplied by the area of the basin allows obtaining the percentage of sediment that reaches the main channel.

2.2 Calculation of the R-factor

The estimation of the erosive power of rainfall was estimated by applying the Fournier aggressiveness index (IdF) based on the pi²/P ratio, allowing the erosivity factors of rainfall to be obtained at each site of the Daule river sub-basin (Table 1).

$$IdF = \sum_{i=1}^{12} \frac{pi^2}{P} \qquad (2)$$

where:

IdF = Fournier index of the period,

p_i = maximum monthly precipitation of the period (mm),

P = total annual precipitation of the period (mm).

The data was obtained from 14 meteorological stations of the National Institute of Meteorology and Hydrology (INAMHI) that are distributed throughout the Daule River sub-basin. The study period comprises the years 1990–2018, within which the rainiest months in each of the stations and the corresponding annual precipitation were determined, and then equation [2] was applied.

2.3 Calculation of the K-factor

The erodability factor (K) describes the susceptibility of the soil to be eroded, as it is a function of the organic matter content, surface texture, structure and permeability of the soil. The Digital soil map of the world [20] was used, while the information on soil type and organic matter obtained was retrieved from the metadata catalog with a scale of 1:250,000. The map was cut only for the study area with the software of Arcgis (Daule River sub-basin). Then, the organic matter data was reclassified, giving it fixed values of MO% (Table 2). For the quantification of factor K, we used the equations of [47]:

$$K = 0.1317 f_{csand} \cdot f_{cl-si} \cdot f_{orgc} \cdot f_{hisand} \tag{3}$$

$$f_{csand} = (0.2 + 0.3exp - 0.0256ms\left(1 - \frac{m_{silt}}{100}\right) \tag{4}$$

$$f_{cl-si} = (\frac{m_{silt}}{m_c + m_{silt}})^{0.3} \tag{5}$$

$$f_{orgc} = 1 - \frac{0.25orgC}{orgC + exp[3.72 - 2.95orgC]} \tag{6}$$

$$f_{hisand} = 1 - \frac{0.70(1 - \frac{m_s}{100})}{(1 - \frac{ms}{100} + exp[-5.51 + 22.9(1 + \frac{ms}{100}]} \tag{7}$$

where:

fcsand = sand content, fcl-si = silt-clay content, forgc = organic carbon content, fhisand = sand content.

2.4 Calculation of the LS Factor

The LS factor estimates the effects of length and slope during sheet erosion [48]. For the calculation of LS [49] proposed the following equations:

$$L = \left(\frac{\lambda}{22.1}\right)^m \tag{8}$$

$$S = 65, 41Sen2\theta + 4, 56Sen\theta + 0, 065 \tag{9}$$

where:

L: Is the length factor of the slope (dimensionless), λ: Is the uniform length of the terrain (meters), m: Is the exponent whose value varies between 0.2 and 0.5 according to the value of the slope of the slope between < 1 and > 5%, S: It is the inclination

Table 1. Reclassification of the attributes of sand, silt-clay and organic matter percentages for the Daule River sub-basin based on the metadata and the technical memory of the information collection.

Soil sample	Sand % Top soil	Silt % Top soil	Clay % Top soil	OC % Top soil	F cuand	F ci-si	F orgc	Fhisand
BK	81.6	6.8	11.7	0.44	0.2	0.7406	0.9906	1.0
LC	64.3	12.2	23.5	0.63	0.2	0.7246	0.9777	1.0
ND	38.9	17.6	43.6	1.57	0.2	0.6880	0.8009	1.0
TH	41.0	41.3	17.7	7.03	0.2	0.8985	0.75	1.0
TV	64.5	26.2	9.3	1.4	02	0.9128	0.8303	1.0
VP	25.1	12.2	32.7	0.68	0.2	0.5801	0.9727	1.0

subfactor of the slope (dimensionless), θ: It is the angle of inclination of the uniform terrain in degrees. Based on the work of [26], they propose the following update for the USLE:

$$L = (\frac{\lambda}{22.13})^m \tag{10}$$

$$m = \frac{\beta}{1+\beta} \tag{11}$$

$$\beta = \frac{\frac{sin\theta}{0.0896}}{3(sin\theta)^{0.8} + 0.56} \tag{12}$$

$$S = 10.8sin\theta + 0.03 (For slopes < 9\%) \tag{13}$$

$$S = 16.8 \sin\theta - 0.5 (For slopes \geq 9\%) \tag{14}$$

$$S = 3(\sin\theta)0.8 + 0.56 (For \ \lambda < 4.5 \ m) \tag{15}$$

$$\lambda : slope \ length(m); \ \theta : slope \ angle \tag{16}$$

2.5 Calculation of Factor C

The vegetation factor represents the degree of protection that the vegetation cover offers to the soil, since it helps to stop soil erosion. For the calculation of this parameter there are tabulations, not equations [25, 49] proposed in their model values between 0 and 1 that will depend on the type of existing vegetation and its degree of coverage, for which they relied on field visits and assigned values based on [49] and by other authors like [17]. It is noteworthy to mention that the land cover data were obtained from the land use and cover map of SIGTIERRAS and the Ministry of the Environment, with a scale of 1:25,000.

Table 2. Coverage factor values (factor C) used in the study

Land use	Factor c	Land use	Factor c
Industrial or commercial areas	1,000	bare ground	1,000
Mainly agricultural land with natural vegetation	0,435	Bean (low dense)	0,450
natural grassland	0,130	Yucca	0,430
Forest scrub in transition	0,153	Carrot	0,690
Sheet of water	1,000	Cocoa	0,180
fruit trees	0,525	Corn-bean association	0,210
Areas with sparse vegetation	0,090	dense grass	0,005
Sugar cane	0,040	Soy (low dense)	0,460
Vegetables	0,040	Tobacco	0,545
citrus	0,375	Brown (shaded)	0,090
Vineyard	0,400	dense forest	0,001
Rice	0,190	bananas, bananas	0.250
Cereal	0,700	onion, spring onion	0,820
Fallow	0,400	Peanut	0,575
Corn	0,530	Brown(no shade)	0,180
almonds	0,540	cantaloupe	0,265
Wooded forest	0,010	nature forest	0,003
Arable land	0,450	Guadua	0,014
Permanently irrigated land	0,507	Pineapple	0,330
Mining extraction zone	1.000	Areas with sparse vegetation	0.900

2.6 Calculation of the P-Factor

It represents the relationship between the soil losses that take place under a certain soil conservation practice and the losses that occur in the same area without the existence of conservation practices. This parameter takes values between 0 and 1. The practices included in this term are: contour lines, strip crops (alternate crops on contours), and terraces [21]. During the field visits it was observed that there are no cultivation practices and rather practices that degrade and erode the soil (perpendicular grooves to the level caves on slopes) are observed, for which the P factor for the entire sub-basin is estimated 1.

2.7 Calculation of the Sediment Delivery Coefficient SDC

To determine the sediment delivery coefficient (SDC), the following equation has been applied [7]:

$$SDC = 36A^{-0.2} + \frac{2}{logP} + logbr \tag{17}$$

where: SDC = % of the total material mobilized in the sub-basin that leaves it,
   A = area of the sub-basin in km^2,
   P = slope of the main course expressed as so much per one,
   br = bifurcation coefficient of the hydrographic network. The latter was calculated according to the methodology described in [5], using the information from the river layer of the Military Geographic Institute (Scale 1:1,000,000), obtained through the IGM4 Geoportal. With equation [16] the bifurcation index is estimated.

$$\frac{\sum_{i=1}^{n-1} \frac{c_i}{c_{i+1}}(c_i+c_{i+1})}{\sum_{i=1}^{n-1} \llbracket (c_i\rrbracket +c_{i+1})} \tag{18}$$

where:
   n is the highest order of the channel of the sub-basin,
   C_i is the number of channels of order i, and.
   C_{i+1} is the number of channels of order i + 1.

3 Results

According to Table 3, R has a minimum value of 175.73 corresponding to the Valle de la Virgen station and a maximum value of 872.61 corresponding to the Murucubamba station. Isoerosivity values in the sub-basin range from 200 MJ*mm/ha*h*year to minimum values of 1200 MJ*mm/ha*h*year. Erosivities ranging from 400 MJ*mm/ha*h*year to 800 MJ*mm/ha*h*year occur at the head of the sub-basin, while in the lower part it varies between 400 MJ*mm/ha*h*year and 200 MJ*mm/ha*h*year (Factor R - Fig. 4).

The values of the erodibility index K vary from 0.014517 to 0.019968 and considering the distribution of the K isolines in the sub-basin, there is an average value of the sub-basin of K = 0.0172425 (Factor K - Fig. 5). The combined effect of slope and length of land exposed to sheet erosion and in LS rills varies between 0.02999 (5° to 12° slope), up to 346.826 (>70° slope), (LS Factor - Fig. 6).

Within the sub-basin there are around 35 crop species for which similar crops were associated, obtaining 20 land uses (Table 3). The values of C fluctuate between 0.001 (dense forest) to 1.00 (bare ground), (Factor C - Fig. 7). The P factor related to soil conservation practices was taken as a general value of 1, due to the fact that erroneous cultivation practices are observed throughout the sub-basin, such as furrows perpendicular to the contour lines throughout the sub-basin, favoring soil erosion.

Table 3. Values of R in each meteorological station located in the Daule River sub-basin

Code	Weather Station	R (MJ*mm/ha*h*year)
M-0249	Valle de La Virgen	175.73
M-0248	Dos Hermanas	629.89
M-0160	El Carmen	697.51
M-0161	Flavio Alfaro	300.06
M-1225	La Sierrilla	442.65
M-0623	Palmeras Unidas (Palmar)	484.60
M-1207	Nobol	462.84
M-1085	Plan América-Daule	291.22
M-0476	La Capilla-INAMHI	608.60
M-0171	Camposano # 2	410.63
M0475	Colimes de Balzar-INAMHI	604.06
M0166	Olmedo - Manabí	594.96
M0247	Murucubamba	872.61
M0786	Puerto Limón	490.99

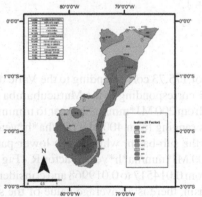 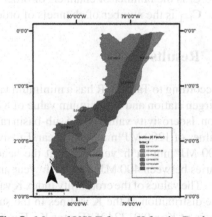

Fig. 4. Map of USLE factor R for the Daule River sub-basin

Fig. 5. Map of USLE factor K for the Daule River sub-basin

Figures 4, 5, 6 y 7 demonstrate the maps of the factors R, K. LS and C. They allow an impression of the way each of these factors has been obtained to finally multiply each other, with the factor P being the same a 1 and finally obtain the factor A that corresponds to the average annual soil loss (t ha-1 year-1) of the Daule River sub-basin.

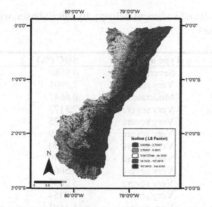 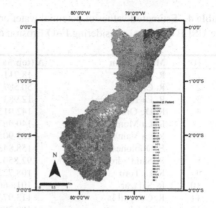

Fig. 6. Map of USLE factors LS for the Daule River sub-basin;

Fig. 7. Map of USLE factor C for the Daule River sub-basin

Taking the sub-basin as a global model, the total hydric erosion is 158.00 ton/ha/year and around 66.3% of the total area of the sub-basin is at a normal degree of erosion (0.5 t/ha/year), while 7.0 to 20.0% of the surface of the sub-basin is between light and moderate erosion (0.5–15 t/ha/year), 3.6% of the territory has severe erosion (15–20 t/ha/year) with losses of soil ranging from 15 to 20 t/ha/year, while 0.7 to 1.7% of the territory of the sub-basin corresponds to very severe to catastrophic erosion (50–200 t/ha/year) with soil losses ranging between 75 to 200 t/ha/year. All of this is occurring in the southwestern part of the sub-basin (Fig. 8).

Figure 8 indicates the distribution of hydric erosion in the Daule River sub-basin as a global model and the respective scales of the [20], observing a greater deterioration in the southwestern part of it. The calculation of the amount of eroded material in tons per hectare and per year was also estimated for the 88 micro-basins individually considering a semi-distributed model, obtaining a value of total water erosion in the sub-basin of 130.04 ton/ha/year. 13.64% of the hydric erosion corresponds to 12 micro-basins that have a catastrophic degree of erosion (>200 ton/ha/year), these being: R. Agua Fría, R. Chicompe, R. Guineal, E. Andrecillo, R.Tres Ríos, R. Los Limos, R. Calvo, E. Pescado, E. Boquerán, E. Don Pablo, R. Paján and E. Santa Lucía, they are located in the southwestern part of the Daule River subbasin.

Table 4. Estimated values of potential water erosion and sediment delivery by micro-basin, with the USLE equation, considering FAO Erosion classes

ID	Micro-basin	A (ton/ha/year)	Type of erosion	SDC (%)
1	R. Pupusa	18.711	Severe	0.9580
2	R. Cajones	50.587	Very severe	2.5901
3	R. La Esperanza	12.983	Moderate	0.6647
4	R. De Oro	142.915	Very severe	7.3173
5	R. La Morena	140.967	Very severe	7.2175
6	R. La Vaina	163.905	Very severe	8.3919
7	E. Doblones	158.848	Very severe	8.1330
8	R. San Pedro	92.850	Very severe	4.7540
9	R. El Toro	108.722	Very severe	5.5666
10	R. Salazar	101.666	Very severe	5.2053
11	R. Conguil 1	113.973	Very severe	5.8354
12	R. Calabozo	100.396	Very severe	5.1403
13	R.Peripa	13.478	Moderate	0.6901
14	R. Congoma	18.714	Severe	0.9582
15	R. Nila	11.559	Moderate	0.5919
16	R. Armadillo	52.981	Very severe	2.7127
17	R. Chaune	0.005	Regular	0.0003
18	R. Salapi Grande	0.156	Regular	0.0080
19	R. Salapi Chico	0.116	Regular	0.0060
20	Q. S.N.	53.153	Very severe	2.7214
21	R. Come y Paga	75.600	Very severe	3.8707
22	R. Solano	97.470	Very severe	4.9905
23	R. Tigre	192.375	Very severe	9.8496
24	E. Salto Grande	1.052	Mild	0.0539
25	E. Conguillo	3.125	Mild	0.1600
26	R. Congo	2.780	Mild	0.1424
27	R. Mata de Plátano	163.984	Very severe	8.3960
28	R. Cangagua	187.704	Very severe	9.6104
29	E. Saiba	47.9747	Severe	2.4563
30	R. Agua Fría	333.234	Catastrophic	17.0616
31	R. Chicompe	662.418	Catastrophic	33.9158
32	R. Guineal	812.592	Catastrophic	41.6047
33	E. Andrecillo	668.982	Catastrophic	34.2519
34	R.T res Ríos	691.891	Catastrophic	35.4248
35	R. Los Limos	533.744	Catastrophic	27.3277
36	R. Calvo	816.341	Catastrophic	41.7967
37	E. Pescado	610.945	Catastrophic	31.2804
38	E. Boquerán	739.932	Catastrophic	37.8845
39	E. Don Pablo	311.496	Catastrophic	15.9486
40	E. Perinao	0.5086	Mild	0.0260
41	R. Gramalotal	42.8728	Severe	2.1951
42	R. de Gamez	170.352	Very severe	8.7221
43	E.S.N.	152.207	Very severe	7.7930
44	R. Cascol	126.593	Very severe	6.4816
45	R.S.N.	92.7828	Very severe	4.7505
46	R. Paján	665.577	Catastrophic	34.0775
47	E. Santa Lucía	534.252	Catastrophic	27.3537
48	R. Hondo	195.372	Very severe	10.0030
49	R. Colimes	181.156	Very severe	9.2752
50	R. Chico	177.584	Very severe	9.0923
51	R.S.N.	123.109	Very severe	6.3032
52	E. Pricel	158.856	Very severe	8.1334
53	E. Las Cruces	31.0569	Severe	1.5901
54	E. Las Iguanas	83.505	Very severe	4.2755
55	R .Las Muras	164.920	Very severe	8.4439
56	E. El Tigre	0.758	Mild	0.0388

(*continued*)

Table 4. (*continued*)

ID	Micro-basin	A (ton/ha/year)	Type of erosion	SDC (%)
57	E. Mestancia	2.054	Mild	0.1052
58	R. Lascano	154.348	Very severe	7.9027
59	E.S.N.	3.680	Mild	0.1884
60	R. Sota	19.137	Severe	0.9798
61	E. El Guabito	1.428	Mild	0.0732
62	E. Sequel	0.940	Mild	0.0482
63	E. Pozo Hondo	1.239	Mild	0.0635
64	E. Jujanal	0.794	Mild	0.0407
65	E. Mesa	0.453	Regular	0.0232
66	E. El Mate	0.027	Regular	0.0014
67	E. Boca de Pancha	0.119	Regular	0.0061
68	E. La Fortuna	1.458	Mild	0.0746
69	E. Grande de Colorado	1.600	Mild	0.0819
70	E. Loco	0.820	Mild	0.0420
71	R. Cade	3.242	Mild	0.1660
72	E. de las Guineas	0.136	Regular	0.0070
73	E. Limón	0.895	Mild	0.0458
74	R. Villao	1.814	Mild	0.0929
75	E. de la Naranja	1.279	Mild	0.0655
76	R. Pricel	5.802	Moderate	0.2971
77	E. Bijama	1.435	Mild	0.0735
78	R. El Guabito	6.476	Moderate	0.3316
79	E. El Arenoso	1.464	Mild	0.0750
80	R. Jerusalén	0.030	Regular	0.0016
81	R. Bachillero	0.039	Regular	0.0020
82	R. de la Derecha	0.111	Regular	0.0057
83	E. del Limón	1.129	Mild	0.0578
84	R.S.N.	2.453	Mild	0.1256
85	R. Paco	1.986	Mild	0.1017
86	E.S.N.	0.882	Mild	0.0452
87	E. Petrillos	9.720	Moderate	0.4977
88	Drenajes Menores	4.756	Mild	0.2435

Some 32.95% of the micro-basins suffer from a very severe degree of erosion (50 ton/ha/year to 200 ton/ha/year) that are distributed in the western part of the sub-basin from the upper part to the lower part of it. Some 6.81% of micro-basins have severe to moderate erosion from 15 ton/ha/year to 20 ton/ha/year and 5 ton/ha/year to 15 ton/ha/year respectively, which are located in the southwest of the sub-basin. 28.40% have a light erosion of 0.5 ton/ha/year to 5 ton/ha/year and 11.36% have a normal erosion of 0.5 ton/ha/year (Fig. 9).

Of the total sediments of 130.04 ton/ha/year produced by the micro-basins, 6.66% reaches the main channel, that is, 8.66 ton/ha/year.

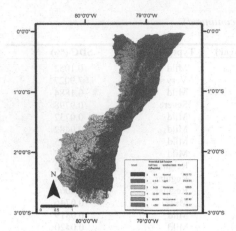

Fig. 8. Spatial distribution of predicted and actual soil loss rates in t ha − 1 yr − 1 and a spatially explicit assessment of the prediction accuracy of the Daule River sub-basin USLE

Fig. 9. Spatial distribution of predicted and actual soil loss rates in t ha^{-1} yr − ^{1} and a spatially explicit assessment of the prediction accuracy of the USLE for the Daule River microwatersheds.

4 Discussion

[49] proposed the USLE (Universal Soil Loss Equation), which has been the most widely accepted and used empirical erosion model to assess soil loss for more than 30 years. They also suggested obtaining the value of factor C and/or P, considering the proportion between tolerable erosion and potential erosion. By modeling changes in factors C and/or P, changes in coverage and management practices or pertinent mechanical practices that produce erosion below the tolerable level can be identified.

Water erosion produces irreversible changes in a hydrographic sub-basin. The specific degradation of the Daule River sub-basin estimated as a global model is 158.0 ton/ha/year and estimating at the level of micro-basins as a semi-distributed model it is 130.04 ton/ha/year, so the average erosion of the sub-basin is 144.0 ton/ha/year, which corresponds to a very severe erosion, according to the [20], this is due to the fact that most of the sub-basin is intervened, predominantly coffee, cocoa, banana and lemon crops. Cultivation practices are null, since furrows are observed perpendicular to the contour lines, favoring soil erosion. Water erosion in the twelve most degraded micro-basins such as: R. Agua Fría, R. Chicope, R. Guineal, E. Andrecillo, R.Tres Ríos, R. Los Limos, R. Calvo, E. Pescado, E. Boquerán, E. Don Pablo, R. Paján and E. Santa Lucía correspond to catastrophic erosion (> 200 ton/ha/year), they are located in the southwestern part of the Daule River sub-basin.

These results give the opportunity to those who develop plans for the management of natural resources, to project the changes and even model them and evaluate their impact before implementing them, as in the management and sustainable agricultural development [10], and the erosion risk assessment for watershed management [39].

The values of C in the 88 micro-watersheds fluctuate between 0.001 (dense forest) to 1.00 (bare soil) and the P factor is equal to 1 since there is no cultivation practice.

[49] Suggested obtaining the value of the C/P factor, considering the ratio between tolerable erosion and potential erosion. Through the modeling of changes in the C/P factors, changes in coverage and soil management practices that produce erosion below the permissible limits can be identified.

However, not all the material generated by the water erosion process reaches the drainage network, therefore, sediment production is defined as the volume that is transported to the main collectors. To estimate the sediments that reach the channel, the sediment delivery ratio (SDR) is used. It is defined as the capacity of the eroded soil that can be delivered to the outlet of a particular basin [51]. This depends on the main fluvial course (order of the rivers), being the steeper the slope, the greater the drag force, and also on the forks of the drainage network. Additionally, the greater the number of forks, the greater the transport capacity [34]. Therefore, the equation of [7].

Human activities alter the edaphological characteristics, which in turn modifies the hydraulic [46] and hydrological response of a basin [4]. There is a proportional relationship between urban coverage and land use. For the same rain event, the volume of runoff increases in impermeabilized areas. Therefore, poor soil management is a conditioning element of susceptibility to erosion [4].

A protected soil is less vulnerable to erosion. The plants provide mechanical support at the underground level and biophysical protection at the aerial level [4]. The combined effect of the slope and the length of the land exposed to sheet and rill erosion LS, varies between 0.02999 (5° to 12° slope), up to 346,826 (>70° slope) in the entire sub-basin of the river Daule. In soils with steep and long slopes, live barriers are the best guarantee to reduce the erosive action of runoff [22], recover the natural fertility of the soil and increase macro and microbiological diversity [33]. Among the main advantages of vegetation cover are improving the appearance of the land, the quality of the soil and the ecosystem in general, providing ecosystem services, reducing erosion, reducing the speed of surface runoff, increasing the infiltration of water into the soil, improve the quality, structure and mechanical resistance of the soil, such as providing stability, roughness and porosity to the soil through organic matter [4].

5 Conclusions

The annual loss of soil per hectare in the Daule River sub-basin ranges from 0.50 to 200 tons/ha/year, with an average value of 130.04 tons/ha/year. In the micro-watersheds with values less than 0.5 tons there is almost no soil loss, due to the vegetation cover that it presents, few agricultural activities and high content of organic matter resulting from the decomposition of plant material.

The most latent risk of water erosion is located predominantly in the southwestern and southern areas of the Daule River sub-basin, where there is strong human intervention and the rate of erosion in the sub-basin is greater than 200 tons/ha/year.

The micro-basins with catastrophic erosion are the most deteriorated and, therefore, with the greatest hydric erosion and sediment contribution, for which immediate intervention is required. Therefore, it is recommended to consider a manageable number of hectares of the micro-watershed that meets the manageability characteristics, which must be agreed upon with their owners.

Acknowledgments. This research is the partial result of the Water Erosion Study for the prioritization of a micro-basin of the Daule River sub-basin, responsible for the turbidity of the raw water collected for Guayaquil, developed for INTERAGUA, through CESA, AVSF, LIVELIHOODS, who allowed writing this article, my thanks to them.

References

1. Addis, H., Klik, A., Strohmeier, S.: Spatial variability of selected soil attributes under agricultural land use system in a mountainous watershed, Ethiopia. Int. J. Geosci. **6**, 605–613 (2015). https://doi.org/10.4236/ijg.2015.66047
2. Abdulkareem, J.H., et al.: Prediction of spatial soil loss impacted by long-term land-use/land-cover change in a tropical watershed. Geosci. Front. **10**, 389–403 (2019)
3. Alewell, C., et al.: Using the USLE: Chances, challenges and limitations of soil erosion modelling. Internat. Soil Water Conser, Res. **7**(3), 203–225 (2019)
4. Alvarado-García, V., Pérez-Gómez, G., Gastezzi-Arias, P.: Calidad del ecosistema urbano del río Torres, San José, Costa Rica: factores bióticos y abióticos. Cuadernos de Investigación UNED **12**(2), 527–542 (2020)
5. Andreazzini, M.J. et al.: Producción de sedimentos en una cuenca de Sierras Pampeanas, Córdoba, Argentina: Estimación para distintos escenarios (2014)
6. Aparicio, F.: Fundamentos de hidrología de superficie. Editorial Limusa S.A, México (2017)
7. Arnoldus, H.M.J.: Una aproximación del factor de lluvia en la ecuación universal de pérdida de suelo (1980)
8. Avendaño Salas, C., Sanz Montero, M.E., Cobo Rayán, R., Gómez Montaña, J.L.: Sediment yield at Spanish reservoirs and its relationships with the drainage basin area (1997)
9. Bagarello, V., Di Piazza, G.V., Ferro, V., Giordano, G.: Predicting unit plot soil loss in Sicily, south Italy. Hydrol. Process. **22**, 586–595 (2008). https://doi.org/10.1002/hyp.6621
10. Bagherzadeh, A.: Estimation of soil losses by USLE model using GIS at Mashhad plain, Northeast of Iran. Arab. J. Geosci. **7**(1), 211–220 (2012). https://doi.org/10.1007/s12517-012-0730-3
11. Bhan, S.K., Saha, S.K., Pande, L.M., Prasad, J.: Use of remote sensing and GIS technology in sustainable agriculture management and development. Indian Institute of Remote Sensing, NRSA. DEHRADUN, India. 10 pags (2000)
12. Benavidez, R., Jackson, B., Maxwell, D., Norton, K.: A review of the (Revised) Universal Soil Loss Equation ((R) USLE): with a view to increasing its global applicability and improving soil loss estimates. Hydrol. Earth Syst. Sci **22**, 6059–6086 (2018)
13. Cao, L., Zhang, K., Dai, H., Liang, Y.: Modeling Interrill Erosion on Unpaved Roads in the Loess Plateau of China. Land Degrad. Dev. **26**, 825–832 (2015)
14. Castro Mendoza, I., et al.: Áreas de conservación en subsubcuencas aportadoras del sistema hidroeléctrico Grijalva, México. RIHA La Habana **36**, 73–87 (2015)
15. Cortes Torres, H.G., et al.: Characterization of rainfall on erosion in Mexico using multivariate methods. Inst. Nac. de Invest. Forestales, Agrícolas y Pecuarias **3**, 115–138 (1992)
16. David, W.P.: Soil and water conservation planning: Polivy issues and reccomendations. J. Philippine Develop. **15**, 47–84 (1988)
17. Ddis, H.K., Klik, A.: Predicting the spatial distribution of soil erodibility factor using USLE nomograph in an agricultural watershed, Ethiopia. Inter. Soil Water Conserv. Res. **3**, 282–290 (2015). https://doi.org/10.1016/j.iswcr.2015.11.002
18. Delgado, F., Vásquez, I.: MIPACS. Modelo Índice de Productividad con aplicación a la conservación de suelos. Centro Interamericano de Desarrollo e Investigación Ambiental y Territorial (CIDIAT). Mérida-Venezuela. 14 p. (1997)

19. Den Biggelaar, C.. et al.: The Global Impact Of Soil Erosion On Productivity. I: Absolute and Relative Erosion-induced Yield Losses. Advances in Agronomy (2003)
20. Espinosa, P.: Caracterización por erosión de las subcuencas hidrográficas de la sierra ecuatoriana. Quito, Ecuador, primera edición. pp. 85–98 (1993)
21. FAO. Metodología provisional para la evaluación de la degradación de los suelos. Organización de las Naciones Unidas para la Agricultura y Alimentación. Roma (1980)
22. Ferrán Conill, A.: modelización de la erosión hídrica en los suelos. el enfoque de sistemas en las ctma. Didáctica Ambiental S.L. (2007) ISSN: 1698–5893
23. Hincapié, E., Ramírez, F.A.: Riesgo a la erosión en suelos de ladera de la zona cafetera. Centro Nacional de Investigaciones de Café (Cenicafé) (2013)
24. Lianes, E. et al.: Estimación de la erosión hídrica en los suelos de la microsubcuenca Tzalá, San Marcos, Guatemala, Agronomía Costarricense, pp. 217–235 (2009)
25. Mapa Mundial de Suelos. Roma, Italia: FAO: UNESCO. APA, ISO 690-2
26. Mancilla, G.: Erosión bajo cubiertas vegetales en la Cordillera de Nahuelbuta (VIII Región), p. 177. Forestal, Departamento de Silvicultura, Universidad de Chile, Tesis Ing (1995)
27. McCool, D.K., Foster, G.R., Weesies, G.A.: Slope length and steepness factors (LS), Chapter 4, pp. 101–141 in Renard et al.) (1997)
28. Navas, L., Caiza, P., Toulkeridis, T.: An evaluated comparison between the molecule and steel framing construction systems - Implications for the seismic vulnerable Ecuador. Malaysian Construct. Res. J. 26(3), 87–109 (2018)
29. Noni, G., Trujillo, G.: La erosión actual y potencial en Ecuador: Localización, manifestaciones y causas (1986)
30. Pimentel, D.: La erosión del suelo: una amenaza alimentaria y ambiental. Medio Ambiente, Desarrollo y Sostenibilidad 8, 119–137 (2006)
31. Palma, R., Pinargote, J., Lucy, G.: Técnicas de Manejo y Conservación de Suelos en Escenarios Cafetaleros en Zonas Susceptibles a Erosión. KillKana Técnica 3(1), 13–18 (2019)
32. Pham, V.A., et al.: New provincial records of skinks (Squamata: Scincidae) from northwestern Vietnam. Biodiversity Data Journal 3(e4284), 1–21 (2015)
33. Renard, K., et al.: Predicting soil erosion by water: a guide to conservation planning with the Revised Universal Soil Loss Equation (RUSLE) 65–1000 (1997)
34. San Román Rincón, A., Santana Cóccaro, J.: Identificando zonas con diferentes compactación subsuperficial en base al rendimiento de maíz e imágenes satelitales (2020)
35. Sánchez, Á., et al.: Productividad potencial del SAF cacao asociado con árboles forestales. Revista Iberoamericana de Bioeconomía y Cambio Climático 4(7), 862–877 (2018)
36. Salazar Yánez, N.A.: Restauración hidrológica-forestal en una subcuenca hidrográfica. Caso de estudio: Subcuenca del Estero Potrerillos (Provincia de Guayas). Escuela Politécnica Nacional, Quito, Ecuador (2016)
37. Sandoval-Erazo, W, et al.: Sedimentological study of the reservoir of the Manduriacu hydroelectric project, northern Ecuador. In: IOP Conference Series: Earth and Environmental Science, vol. 191(1), p. 012119. IOP Publishing (2018b)
38. Sandoval-Erazo, W., et al.: Velocity and time of concentration of a basin - a renewed approach applied in the Rio Grande Basin, Ecuador. In: IOP Conference Series: Earth and Environmental Science, vol. 191(1), p. 012117. IOP Publishing (2018a)
39. Pinargote-Chóez, Santos., de los, J.: Erosión hídrica en la subcuenca alta del rio Guineal, del cantón 24 de Mayo, Ecuador, No 3, Marzo 2021, pp. 1992–2004 (2021) ISSN: 2550 - 682X
40. Singh, G.R., Babu, R., Narain, P., Bhushan, L.S., Abrol, I.P.: Soil erosion rates in India. J. Soil Water Conserv. 41, 97–99 (1992)
41. Tan, Z., Leung, L.R., Li, H.Y., Tesfa, T.: Modeling sediment yield in land surface and earth system models: model comparison, development, and evaluation. J. Adv. Model. Earth Syst. 10, 2192–2213 (2018)

42. Tayupanta, J., Córdova, J.: Algunas alternativas agronómicas y mecánicas y mecánicos para evitar la pérdida de suelo. Estación Experimental Santa Catalina, INIAP. Publicación miscelánea N°. 54. Quito, Ecuador, p. 40 (1990)

43. Toulkeridis, T., Clauer, N., Kröner, A.: Chemical variations in clay minerals of the Archean Barberton Greenstone Belt (South Africa). Precambr. Res. **79**, 195–207 (1996)

44. Toulkeridis, T., Clauer, N., Kröner, A., Todt, W.: Mineralogy, geochemistry and isotopic dating of shales from the Barberton Greenstone Belt, South Africa: Provenance and tectonic implications. South African J. of Geol. **118**, 389–410 (2015)

45. Townsend-Small, A., et al.: Suspended sediments and organic matter in mountain headwaters of the Amazon River: Results from a 1-year time series study in the central Peruvian Andes. Geochim. Cosmochim. Acta **72**, 732–740 (2008)

46. Valencia, D.M.R., Nájera, J.D.C.Z.: Estudio de la respuesta hidrológica en la cuenca urbana de montaña San Luis-Palogrande. Revista UIS Ingenierías **17**(1), 115–126 (2018)

47. Viramontes, D., et al.: Variables de suelos determinantes del escurrimiento y la erosión en un sector de la Sierra Madre Occidental. Tecn. y ciencias del agua **21**(1), 73–83 (2006)

48. Williams, J.R., Berndt, H.D.: Sediment yield computed with universal equation. J. Hydrol. (Amsterdam) **98**, 2087–2098 (1972)

49. Wischmeier, W.H., Mannering, J.V.: Relation of Soil Properties to its Erodibility1. Soil Sci. Soc. Am. J. **33**, 131 (1969)

50. Wischmeier, W.H., Smith, D.D.: Rainfall energy and its relationship to soil loss. EOS Trans. Am. Geophys. Union **39**, 285–291 (1958)

51. Wischmeier, W.H., Smith, D.D.: Predicting Rainfall Erosion Losses - A Guide to Conservation Planning. Agriculture Handbook No. 537.Agriculture Science and Education Administration, Washington, District of ColumUSA (1978)

52. Wu, W.Q., et al.: Molecular doping enabled scalable blading of efficient hole-transport-layer-free perovskite solar cells. Nat. Commun. **9**(1), 1–8 (2018)

Water, Sanitation and Socioeconomic Situation in Two Communities in the Cayapas River, Ecuador

Angie Fernández Lorenzo[1](✉) , Zlata Dolores Borsic Laborde[1] ,
Darío Roberto Bolaños Guerrón[2] , Raúl Ricardo Fernández Concepción[3] ,
and Marco Antonio Hernández Arauz[1]

[1] Department of Economic, Administrative and Commercial Sciences, Universidad de las
Fuerzas Armadas-ESPE, Quito, Ecuador
aafernandez2@espe.edu.ec

[2] Department of Earth and Construction Sciences, Universidad de las Fuerzas Armadas-ESPE,
Quito, Ecuador

[3] Universidad de Pinar del Río, Pinar del Río, Cuba

Abstract. The current research was carried out under a descriptive survey approach, using 123 dwellings as the statistical population in the Loma Linda and
Zapallo Grande communities, both from the San José del Cayapas parish, on
the banks of the Cayapas River, Ecuador. Both communities are self-identifying
Chachi indigenous ethnic groups and the main access route is by canoe across the
river. They do not have access to drinking water. Their main source of supply is
the river and rainwater. They identify the quality of the water as a probable cause
of various diseases when drinking it without treatment. It was identified that the
main source of income is agriculture, which is used mainly for food, together with
unfavorable housing conditions, access to social security, and low participation in
social and political spaces. The statistical analysis defined relationships between
socioeconomic variables such as the number of families in the home, the number
of family members, level of participation in social and political spaces, economic
activities and destination of income in the way they dispose of solid waste, the
type of toilet and shower, the way they drink the water and diseases that affect
them.

Keywords: Water · Sanitation · Drinking water · Indigenous communities ·
Sources of supplies

1 Introduction

Water is the natural resource with the highest incidence in the economic and social life of
a country [1]. In this sense, on July 26, 2010, in session 64 of the United Nations General
Assembly, *"water and sanitation were declared a human right and nations parties were
urged to carry out strategies, actions and plans of action necessary to achieve access to
water and sanitation for all its citizens"* [2]. Accordingly, the need for states to develop

M. Botto-Tobar et al. (Eds.): ICAT 2022, CCIS 1756, pp. 135–147, 2023.
https://doi.org/10.1007/978-3-031-24971-6_10

public policies and provide the budgetary allocations required to fulfill that purpose is recognized.

According to data from CEPAL [3] and a study carried out by the Superior Politécnica del Litoral School [4], in Ecuador, there are areas where groundwater is the only accessible resource to supply populations or to irrigate crops. Particularly in basins deficient in surface resources, for which it constitutes the essential resource for food security and vital for the functioning of ecosystems; despite this, from 1983 to the present date, the national hydrogeological map has not been updated at a scale of 1:1'000000. Furthermore, there are no studies available to identify areas susceptible to water pollution and overexploitation. To establish water protection strategies, define and prioritize solutions, and maintain an adequate water monitoring and observation system. On the other hand, the inadequate use of water reveals various public health problems that afflict various areas of the national territory.

In this sense, the World Health Organization - WHO [5] points out that the efficient management of water supply, sanitation, and the management of water resources can boost countries' economic growth before it contributes to the reduction of pore reducing poverty and its availability or deficit; it depends on the development of the activities of the populations and before, the Millennium Development Goals aim to reduce the percentage of the world population that does not have sustainable access to "drinking water from an improved source of water supply located at the place of use, available when needed and that does not contain fecal contamination or priority chemical substances" [5]. Thus, if the water is of poor quality, it represents a threat to the sanitary conditions of the poorest population, and the costs of medical care to treat these types of conditions have a negative influence on the family economy of the poorest population. Which makes them a more vulnerable stratum with little chance of opting for a minimum degree of development.

1.1 Purpose of Research

This research aimed to establish the relationship between socioeconomic aspects regarding access to drinking water and sanitation. The study shows the socioeconomic analysis of problems of water supply and sanitation in the Loma Linda and Zapallo Grande communities, both from the San José del Cayapas town, on the banks of the Cayapas River.

2   Methodology

Case Study and Data Collection
Eloy Alfaro town is located in the northeast of the Esmeraldas province, which has an extension of about 15900 km2 and more than half a million inhabitants. Its capital, of the same name, has a population of 200000 inhabitants and is the home tone of the country's main ports, in addition to the Transandino Pipeline terminal. The foundation of this town dates from October 16, 1941. The San José del Cayapas town belonging to

this town has several communities located in the upper area of the Cayapas River, with River Supply and sanitation being among its main problems [6].

The research focused its application on two communities in this town, located along the Cayapas River in District 08D02. This district is a tropical region, with high humidity and rainfall, with temperatures ranging from 25 to 28 °C, or more, in the summer season (dry season). It is a forested territory with important biodiversity, both forestry and faunal. The Cayapas River crosses the town, being a navigable river in almost its entire journey, constituting the axis of the life of its inhabitants; in the area is the Cotacachi-Cayapas ecological reserve, a mangrove forest of great biodiversity in fauna and flora.

The social situation of the Esmeraldas province is a deed by the figures provided by the National Institute of Statistics and Census [7], which have not been updated subsequently:

- The poverty rate is 50%, which means that half of the population has perceptive incomes lower than the minimum cost of the basket of goods and services.
- The rate of homelessness or extreme poverty is 21%, higher than the national average of 13%.
- Chronic malnutrition is in 21% of children between 1 and 5 years old.
- Primary schooling is 92%.
- Full employment is 28%, underemployment is 68%, and unemployment is 7%.

Almost 55% of the population of the town Eloy Alfaro is self-identified as Afro-Ecuadorian and 13% as Chachi currently, there are approximately 11.000 individuals distributed in 50 communities, most of them on the banks of the Cayapas River. The Chachi population is located in the upper part of the river, while Afro-Ecuadorian communities predominate near Bourbon [7].

In general, the economy presents a weak dynamic about the capacity of the sector to generate synergy in the economic activities of the inhabitants of the area. Identifying that the productive activities that are currently carried out are not very diversified, on the contrary, most are extractive activities; that is there is no value and value-added to the production that is obtained. About crops are varied: bananas, citrus fruits, bananas, and cassava; livestock is focused on cattle rearing and industry. Thanks to the great forest wealth of the area, they are intensely dedicated to the timber industry [8]. This production contributes both to provincial domestic consumption and to the market of the provinces of Imbabura, Pichincha, and Tungurahua [9].

The problem incentivized by this research is the existence in the Eloy Alfaro town of a poor water supply network and a precarious sanitation system, in the absence of any advanced wastewater channeling or wastewater treatment system, marked by a high level of poverty and other socio-economic problems.

2.1 Testing Tools

A diagnostic questionnaire was designed on obtaining, managing, and consuming water, as well as other socioeconomic data of interest for research, based on the following observation instruments, previously validated by their authors:

1. Water Form of the National Survey of Employment, Unemployment, and Underemployment-ENEMDU [10].
2. Socio-economic test applied to vulnerable groups in the Rumiñahui town. Linking project with society "Promotion of the generation of sectoral policies through technical advice for updating and monitoring the baseline of priority groups in the Rumiñahui town" [11].
3. Test No. 1 with the home connection. Socio-economic survey [12].

The questions were adapted to the characteristics of the target population, previously descry, and they are shown in appendix A. Based on the existing census and georeferencing, the number of dwellings in each community was determined, and their selection was decided by census or sampling. In the case of the Loma Linda community which hat has a total of 36 homes, the survey was applied in 100% of the homes.

In the Zapallo Grande community with a total of 113 dwellings, a representative sample of 87 houses was defined, applying the formula of the simple estimation method for Random Unrestricted Sampling [13]. The parameters considered were level of significance ($\alpha = 0.05$); absolute error ($d = 0.05$); probability value ($P = 0.5$).

The selection of the 87 houses would guarantee the randomness and representativeness of the sample in the study. It was performed using the Random Number Table of Kendall and Babington [14] from the coding in the previous map.

Table 1 shows the data from surveys applied in both communities:

Table 1. Number of surveyed homes

Community	Number of surveyed homes
Loma Linda	36
Zapallo Grande	87
Total	**123**

Source: Research finding

To validate the diagnostic instrument, a pilot test was carried out on 10% of the selected dwellings in the sample, making the required adjustments.

After the definitive application of the questionnaire, Cronbach's Alpha (α) was calculated, resulting in a value of 0.70, demonstrating that the internal consistency of the scale used is adequate [15, 16].

The information analysis was performed applying descriptive statistics, specifically frequency tables and Pearson's Chi-square test; as well as inferential statistics through the correlation analysis of variables using Spearman's Rho coefficient, for data without normality. For the application of the Spearman test, the scale proposed by Sampieri, Fernández & Baptista [17] was used.

Microsoft Excel and SPSS v25 programs were used for information processing and analysis.

Study Sections and variables

As communities of interest for the study, from the seven presents in the town, the following were defined: Loma Linda and Zapallo Grande.

Loma Linda is located in the upper part of the Cayapas River to the buffer zone of the Cotacachi-Cayapas reserve [9], characterized by lush vegetation, of which, a part is destined for conservation.

The area where this community is located is very humid and its climate is tropical rainy, with an average annual temperature of 25 °C, [9]. The tourists who visit it, both national and foreign, show interest in making sporadic visits to observe how the indigenous people cook panda fish while speaking in their native language, chapalá [18].

For its part, Zapallo Grande is located at a height of 449 m above sea level. This community is located in a very humid zone and its climate is tropical rainy, its annual average temperature is 25 °C. Its flora is in the humid forest type. Ranconchal is an area also characteristic of this ecosystem. They are extensions periodically flooded by high tides or by heavy rains, which are covered by a species of bush fern that can exceed 2 m in height. Regarding its characteristic fauna, the artisanal exploitation of many of its species by adjacent communities has sustained their economies for decades [8]. About hydrographic characteristics, the rivers that cross it are: El Santiago, Cayapas, which are the largest and its representative tributaries are: Zapallo Grande, Chimbagal, Barbudo, Agua Clara, Bravo Grande, and Hoja, Blanca.

The tourist activity in Zapallo Grande is characterized by religious celebrations in tribute to San Martín de Porres, held every year on November 3. The same impact on tourism has the typical gastronomy of the community which has a diversity of dishes, whose basis for the preparation are seafood [19].

Once the field research was carried out, the following generalities of the Loma Linda and Zapallo Grande communities were defined about the data of interest for the work:

Both communities are self-identifying Chachi indigenous ethnic groups, their houses are generally simple the roofs are of zinc and the material that predominates in the walls of their houses is wood. Inside they have a space to cook and the main source of light is the public electric company, cooking their food is done through gas, it was also identified that they do not have an exclusive shower space and their type of service Hygienic is commonly a latrine [19].

The main access route to the house is through the river in canoes since the communities are located on the banks of the Cayapas River.

As they do not have potable water, the communities do not have a water meter. Commonly the source of drinking water is in the yard or lot of the house, they do not indicate that there are working children, diseases due to lack of access and water quality have increased, all consider that lack of access and water quality affects their family, within the communities do not participate in political activities, neighborhood league committee, and others.

2.2 Results and Discussion

The results of the survey applied in the communities studied are presented below in Table 2.

Table 2. A person who answers the survey – absolute frequencies

Answers	Loma Linda	Zapallo Grande	Total
Head of household and/or family	29%	60%	54%
Spouse	38%	31%	33%
Otros	33%	9%	13%

Source: Research finding

87% of the total respondents were the heads of the household or their spouses, with the heads of the household having the highest percentage in the survey (54%).

In 73% of the surveyed houses, there is only one family (52% in Loma Linda and 77% in Zapallo Grande. It is mostly made up of houses with two families, as shown in Table 3 below.

Table 3. Number of families living in the home – absolute frequencies

Number of families living in the home	Loma Linda	Zapallo Grande	Total
1	52%	77%	73%
2	38%	19%	22%
3	10%	3%	4%
6	0%	1%	1%

Source: Research finding

Families of Zapallo Grande and Loma Linda are made up of more than 4 members, most of them, as well as numerous families, lies reach up to 20 people and homes that are only inhabited by one person, extremes that obtain a lower percentage as shown in Table 4.

94% of the surveyed homes are owned by their residents. The state of these from the situation of ceilings and floors reflects that between 65 and 75% of these are between fair and good, the rest are declared with a state that goes from bad to lousy, being the community Zapallo Grande the one with the highest incidence of houses in poor condition. 63% of the surveyed homes have rooms destined for dormitories. In the rest of the houses (37% of the total), in the same room, several functions are combined such as kitchen-dining room-bedroom, reflecting a notorious level of overcrowding in them.

The 67% of the homes evaluated have bathrooms, highlighting the community of Loma Linda where 84% of them have it. Within 78% of these homes, there is no productive activity. 62% of these homes have 4 or more lights for lighting, highlighting

Table 4. Number of family members - absolute frequencies

Family members	Loma Linda	Zapallo Grande	Total
Between 1 and 3	16%	14%	15%
Between 4 and 6	42%	50%	49%
More than 6	42%	36%	37%

Source: Research finding

Loma Linda where 43% of their homes have 5 or more lights. In the rest of the surveyed homes, lighting conditions can be evaluated from fair to poor.

Table 5 shows the ways of eliminating household waste generated in both communities:

Table 5. The main way to remove garbage – absolute frequencies

The main way to remove garbage	Loma Linda	Zapallo Grande	Total
Municipal service	0%	0%	0%
Bounce to the street/stream/river	5%	17%	15%
Burning/burying	42%	66%	63%
Community Agreement	53%	16%	22%

Source: Research finding

The main way to eliminate garbage (63%) is by burning or burying it, followed by agreements between the community, where Loma Linda stands out with 53%. It cannot be ignored that 15% of the respondents dispose of the waste they generate to the street, streams, or surface water sources located in their environment, constituting a direct source of contamination.

Regarding the dimension of water supply and sanitation, the results of the survey are presented below in Table 6:

Table 6. Shower service – absolute frequencies

Shower service	Loma Linda	Zapallo Grande	Total
Exclusive	42%	5%	11%
Shared with other Homes	58%	95%	89%

Source: Research finding

In 89% of the surveyed homes, the shower service is shared with other homes, reaching 95% in the Zapallo Grande community. The situation in the community of Loma Linda is a little more favorable since 42% of the houses have exclusive shower service, which generates better hygiene conditions and greater comfort for the inhabitants of this community.

The hygienic service conditions are shown in Table 7.

Table 7. Hygienic service of the house - absolute frequencies

Hygienic service of the house	Loma Linda	Zapallo Grande	Total
Toilet and sewer	0%	0%	0%
Toilet and septic tank	0%	0%	0%
Toilet and blind well	32%	37%	36%
Latrina	68%	63%	64%

Source: Research finding

The hygienic service of the dwellings is basically through latrines (64%), the percentage being higher in Loma Linda (68%). Hence, the rest of the houses (36%) have a toilet and a blind well; without the septic tank or sewer service being declared as existing in the sample.

The most frequent type of latrine is a pit without a slab/open pit through a rudimentary hole in the ground (43% of the total sample), the value in Loma Linda being higher with 57%. In 68% of cases, the latrine/hole has never been emptied, the value in Loma Linda is higher with 81% of cases.

In 58% of the houses surveyed for the Loma Linda community and 52% in the case of Zapallo Grande, the inhabitants of these go to the mountains, the countryside or throw the garbage in a package, and 47% of the total surveyed use facilities nearby as a loan.

Table 8 shows the analysis of the waste disposal sites.

Table 8. Where the waste ends – absolute frequencies

Where the waste ends	Loma Linda	Zapallo Grande	Total
Doesn't respond	43%	25%	28%
Some open places (river, ravine, ditch, street, patio, open field)	14%	13%	10%
Remain in the septic tank/blind pit and then are buried	38%	55%	52%
Another part if it is not an open site	10%	3%	4%
Don't know	0%	3%	2%

Source: Research finding

The 28% of respondents did not answer the question shown in Table 8, indicating a refusal to acknowledge the problem. The 52% declared that the waste remains in the blind well to be buried later, with the prevalence of this situation in the Zapallo

Grande community (55%). 85% of the respondents declare their willingness to contribute capital, labor, and/or construction materials to health development through the construction or improvement of latrines since in this case, they recognize the discomfort and unhealthiness that these practices generate for your everyday life.

As the main source for supplying water to their homes, the respondents stated what is shown in Table 9:

Table 9. The main source of household water supply – absolute frequencies

Main source	Loma Linda	Zapallo Grande	Total
Public network	0%	1%	1%
Pile or faucet	0%	2%	2%
Water well	0%	4%	3%
Rain	14%	13%	13%
River/spring/ditch	86%	80%	81%

Source: Research finding

The main source of water supply for the surveyed homes is the Cayapas River (86% in Loma Linda and 80% in the Zapallo community. 13% of the respondents state that they satisfy their domestic needs from rainwater. If we take into account the significant percentage of homes for both communities that dispose of their domestic waste and their sewage in the environment, we will have a clear idea of the low quality of the supply water, as well as the danger to gastrointestinal diseases to which they are exposed. Exposed the inhabitants of these. The results of Table 10 reinforce these comments considering the sources used in both sites to obtain the water they use for drinking.

94% of those surveyed did not respond when asked about the routes used to get water to their homes. Only 6% of them declare the use of external or internal pipes. These results lead us to believe that the means of transporting water to homes is another of the causes of its low quality and the hygienic-sanitary problems present in both communities, this is reinforced by the criteria of 79% of those surveyed, which recognize that the water they consume can cause illness. The 56% of these homes have reservoirs for water storage, the rest carry it at the time of using it, which is extremely cumbersome in the normal operation of these homes, although 89% of those surveyed stated that they only take between 1 to 10 min to reach the source of the water they use.

The results shown in Table 11, reflect that 41% of the total respondents are exposed to diseases because they directly consume the water without prior treatment, those who chlorinate state that they use sodium hypochlorite without a certain dosage, which does not certify the effectiveness of this method of disinfection of drinking water, and in the case of those that boil the water later they do not filter it, which is effective for organic contamination, but not for the presence of salts in the water to consume.

80% of the respondents expressed their willingness to contribute to the financing for the implementation of safe water supply sources, as well as the installation of efficient drainage systems for the liquid waste generated in their homes.

Table 10. The main source for drinking water - absolute frequencies

The main source for drinking water	Loma Linda	Zapallo Grande	Total
Public network	0%	0%	0%
Pile or public key	0%	0%	0%
Cased Well/Protected Well	0%	0%	0%
Unprotected well	0%	0%	0%
Non-protected spring/spring	17%	23%	22%
River or ditch	50%	46%	46%
Delivery car	0%	0%	0%
They collect rainwater	22%	13%	15%
Bottled or bottled water	0%	0%	0%
Water in a nylon sheath	11%	18%	17%

Source: Research finding

Table 11. How they drink water - absolute frequencies

How they drink water	Loma Linda	Zapallo Grande	Total
They drink it as it arrives at home	43%	40%	41%
Boil	43%	32%	34%
Add chlorine	14%	24%	22%
Other (Filtration)	0%	4%	3%

Source: Research finding

From the socio-economic point of view, the economy of the studied communities is based especially on agriculture (74% of the heads of families); followed by the commercial activity to which 9% of them are dedicated. 66% of the remaining family members are also engaged in agricultural activities, and 13% of the total respondents do not respond, which may mean that they are unemployed or engaged in some type of illegal activity.

The 12% of residents have some type of disability, and only 21% of all respondents are affiliated with social security. The main items to which family money is dedicated are the following: food (76%), clothing (8%), education (6%), and transportation 5%. Items such as electric energy, water, telephone, and health stand out with very low values. The main diseases that affect residents of both communities according to the survey results are diarrheal (45%), parasitosis (22%), respiratory (14%), and skin infections with 7%. 83% of the sick go to medical services and 15% of them are treated by healers or by home remedies.

81% of the surveyed homes have access to radio and TV channels, 60% of the inhabitants have cell phones as a means of communication and in 7% of the homes they have computers and Internet access. 31% of the total surveyed do not have any electronic device. For 64% of the respondents, their level of participation in social and political spaces varies from regular to almost nil, the rest have adequate participation in this type of activity.

The 64% of those surveyed have never participated in training programs for the management of drinking water, hygiene, health, or environmental education, which is reflected in the type of attitude they present towards the problems of unhealthiness and present contamination in both communities. Those who have received some type of training in this regard have been through the municipality, the councils, and specific education centers.

Table 12 shows the variables with a dependency relationship, based on the Pearson's Chi-square test calculation; after having analyzed the relationships between the variables: community; who answers the survey; the number of families in the dwelling and number of family members, versus the rest of the questions in the questionnaire. As can be seen in it, the way garbage is disposed of in the home and the type of latrine available are dependent on the community; the type of shower service in the study community, who answers the question, and the number of families in the home. The fate of the family's money depends on who answers the question and the number of families in the home, the latter also shows influence with the state of the roof of the home. Finally, it was determined that the means of communication used by the family and the type of housing depending on the number of family members.

Table 12. Pearson's Chi-square test

Variables		Level of significance
Community	The main way to remove garbage	0.0020
	Type of shower service	0.0000
	Type of latrine that the home has	0.0380
Who answers the question?	Type of shower service	0.0190
	Family money destination	0.0040
Number of families in the dwelling	Type of shower service	0.0190
	Destination of money in the family	0.0040
Number of family members	State of the roof of the house	0.0050
	Media used by the family	0.0330
	Housing type	0.0320

Source: Research finding

With the calculation of Spearman's Rho correlation coefficient, a considerable (direct) positive relationship was found between the variables: level of participation of families in the community and how family members drink water; the result of interest for future actions from the social and political point of view in the communities under study.

Additionally, positive (direct) medium-type relationships were found between the following variables:

- Number of people living in the home and the type of toilet service.
- Main source where you get water and where waste from the septic tank/well ends up.
- Distance from the house to the water source and type of toilet service.
- Economic activities of the rest of the family members and where the waste from the septic tank/well ends up.
- Where wastewater from the septic tank/well ends up and diseases that most frequently affect family members.
- How family members drink water and diseases that affect family members most often.
- Level of the participation of families in the community and diseases that most frequently affect family members.
- Place where training programs are carried out in institutions and how family members drink water.

Negative (inverse) relationships of medium type were determined between the following variables:

- Time to arrive and return to the water source and type of shower service.
- Time to arrive and return to the water source and how family members drink the water.

3   Conclusions

The communities studied are self-identifying Chachi and are located on the banks of the Cayapas River. The investigation showed effects related to access to water and sanitation, about the fact that they do not have access to drinking water, they drink water from the river without treatment, and latrines are the predominant type of hygienic service, among other factors. The effect of the poor quality of drinking water on the number of diseases was recognized, which increase over time, and which are mainly digestive and respiratory.

Agricultural activities are the main source of economic income for both communities, where the level of affiliation to social security is very low. Family income is mainly dedicated to the acquisition of food, with low items for health, education, clothing, water, etc.; which, together with the poor housing conditions, overcrowding, and other aspects evaluated, made it possible to reveal the complex socioeconomic conditions of the families studied. Added to this is low participation in social and political spaces, as well as in training programs on the management of drinking water, hygiene, health, or environmental education.

The influence of socioeconomic variables such as the number of families in the home, the number of family members, level of participation in social and political spaces, economic activities, and the destination of income was determined in aspects that denote serious problems in terms of access to water and sanitation, such as the way to dispose of solid waste, the type of toilet and shower, the way they drink water and diseases that affect them. The foregoing should be taken into consideration for the definition of public policies aimed at achieving better levels of access and water quality in the Loma Linda and Zapallo Grande communities.

References

1. Universidad Andina Simón Bolívar. Revealing disenchantment. Editions Abya-Yala, Quito (2010)
2. PAHO. WHO regional office. Water and sanitation. Evidence for public policies with a focus on human rights and public health results (2011). https://www.paho.org/tierra/images/pdf/agua_y_saneamiento_web.pdf
3. ECLAC. Diagnosis of water statistics in Ecuador. Water secretary, Quito (2012)
4. ESPOL. Preparation of the Hydrogeological Map at a scale of 1:250,000. Guayaquil (2014). http://qa-ide.ambiente.gob.ec:8080/geonetwork/srv/api/records/1535d6a9-57ec-49af-94d3-f2e8e2dc2a43
5. WHO. Water. WHO Press Center. (2019). www.who.int/es/news-room/fact-sheets/detail/drinking-water
6. GAD Eloy Alfaro. Plan for the Development and Territorial Ordering of the Eloy Alfaro Canton 2014–2022 (2015)
7. INEC. Results of the 2010 Population and Housing Census in Ecuador. https://www.ecuadorencifras.gob.ec/wp-content/descargas/Manu-lateral/Resultados-pr
8. GAD La Tola. Flora and Fauna (2014). http://latola.gob.ec/index.php/ct-menu-item-16/ct-menu-item-38
9. Go Raymi. Telembí (2019). https://www.goraymi.com/es-ec/telembi/telembi-a3dbc421b
10. INEC. Form on Water of the National Survey of Employment, Unemployment, and Underemployment - ENEMDU 2010 - 2018. (2018). https://www.ecuadorencifras.gob.ec/documentos/web-inec/EMPLEO/2018/Septiembre-2018/ENEMDU_Metodologia%20Encuesta%20Nacional%20de%20Empleo%20Desempleo%20y%20Subempleo.pdf
11. ESPE. Report on the Linkage with Society Project: Promotion of the generation of sectoral policies through technical advice for updating and monitoring the baseline of priority attention groups in the Rumiñahui cantón (2020)
12. Peru. Test No. 1 With home connection. Socio-economic survey. Lima: Ministry of Economy and Finance. (2016). https://www.mef.gob.pe/contenidos/inv_publica/docs/instrumentos_metod/saneamiento/_1_Formato_encuesta_socioeconomicas_CC.doc
13. Calero, A.: Statistics III. La Habana: Editions Félix Valera (2003)
14. Kendall, M., Babington, B.: Randomness and random Sampling numbers. J. Royal Stat. Soc. 101(1), 147–166 (1939)
15. Cronbach, L.: Coefficient alpha and internal structure of tests. Psychometrika 16(3), 297–334 (1951)
16. Oviedo, C., Campo, A.: Approach to the use of Cronbach's alpha coefficient. Colombian J. Psychiatry 34(4), 572–580 (2005)
17. Sampieri, R., Fernández, C., Baptista, P.: Investigation methodology. Bogotá. McGraw-Hillinternamericana de México (1991)
18. WordPress. Afro-Ecuadorians. Afro Esmeraldeñas Festive Customs (2008). https://afros.wordpress.com/cultura/costumbres-festivas-afroesmeraldenas/
19. Ecu Red. Eloy Alfaro Canton (2016). https://www.ecured.cu/Cant%C3%B3n_Eloy_Alfaro_(Ecuador)

Application of Ecuadorian Ferrotitaniferous Sands in Reinforcing Epoxy Composites

Katherine Aguinzaca[1] ⓘ, Alex Tamayo-Aguilar[1] ⓘ, Marco V. Guamán[2] ⓘ,
Víctor H. Guerrero[1] ⓘ, and Patricia I. Pontón[1](✉) ⓘ

[1] Department of Materials, Escuela Politécnica Nacional, 170517 Quito, Ecuador
patricia.ponton@epn.edu.ec
[2] Department of Mechanical Engineering, Escuela Politécnica Nacional, Quito, Ecuador

Abstract. Ecuadorian ferrotitaniferous sands (FS), an abundant natural resource, can be considered as promising fillers for polymer matrixes due to their inherent mechanical properties and magnetic nature. Until now, this raw and underrated resource has only been used as a cement clinker additive and agro-industrial fertilizer, but not as a polymer reinforcement. Thus, epoxy composites were prepared by incorporating 2, 4 and 6 wt.% of chemically untreated and ball-milled FS, with the purpose of assessing the effects of the reinforcing particles on the mechanical and thermal properties of the as-prepared composites. Through microindentation, the optimum FS content was defined as being 6 wt.%, which increased both the elastic modulus and hardness in ~6% when compared to the neat matrix. Micromechanical models viz., the modified rule of mixtures and Halpin-Tsai predicted the Young's modulus of the composites and supported the experimental results. The epoxy composite reinforced with the optimum FS content also presented the highest increase in storage modulus (E'), as evaluated by dynamic mechanical analysis (DMA). Additionally, the damping parameter (tanδ) for all composites was maintained, indicating that impact absorption and the glass transition temperature of the matrix was unaffected by the FS filler.

Keywords: Black mineral sands · Low cost fillers · Mechanical properties

1 Introduction

Low-cost ceramics are deemed as promising fillers in the field of polymer composites. Submicronic iron oxide-based minerals have attracted the attention of the scientific and industrial sectors due to their intrinsic magnetic properties and characteristic gamma and x-ray attenuation [1]. Among them, naturally occurring black beach sands, also known as ferrotitaniferous sands (FS), composed primarily of ilmenite raise special interest [2, 3]. In South America, FS are prevalent along the coastlines of various countries, and traditionally, FS deposits have been mostly exploited with the purpose of obtaining TiO_2 [4–6]. However, the low TiO_2 recovery rate is still insufficient to justify the FS mining process. In Ecuador, FS can be localized primarily along its Pacific coast with an estimated commercial value of \$24 per ton [2] and have been conventionally used only as a cement clinker additive and agro-industrial fertilizer [2]. Recently, FS have been employed as a low-cost precursor for the synthesis of iron-titanium oxide-based nanostructures [3] and ferrous oxalate [6] via soft chemistry approaches. However, applications of Ecuadorian FS without chemical treatments have still not been reported in the literature as far as the authors are aware.

A previous study determined that Ecuadorian FS are an ilmenite-hematite solid solution (0.6 $FeTiO_3 \cdot 0.4$ Fe_2O_3) [2]. As a matter of fact, solid solutions between ilmenite ($FeTiO_3$) and hematite (Fe_2O_3) display both semiconducting and ferromagnetic behavior, resulting in a non-traditional magnetic semiconductor with conceivable spintronic and ionizing radiation-barrier applications [7, 8].

In the field of polymer composites, epoxy resin is an extensively used thermoset that exhibits engineering properties thanks to its densely crosslinked chains and chemical structure. Besides, epoxy resin presents low density, lack of volatile curing byproducts, easy processing and a hydrophilic nature [9, 10]. This resin is mainly used as an insulator, coating, adhesive, and for advanced composites. When reinforced with ceramic oxide fillers, such as TiO_2 [11] and Fe_2O_3 [12], several mechanical properties of epoxy have proven to be enhanced at the optimum filler content, becoming suitable fillers for reinforcing this thermoset matrix. Nevertheless, these fillers are generally obtained through environmentally harmful mineral extraction or complex synthesis routes [6].

Since it has been proven that metal oxide-based ceramics are viable reinforcements for epoxy matrices some studies have focused on finding their natural substitutes [13]. As a matter of fact, the actual trend in preparing polymer composites is to employ ceramic-based fillers derived from natural resources without the need for further complex refinement processes. For instance, $CaCO_3$, found in eggshells [14] and seashells [15], has been incorporated in a polymer matrix, such as epoxy to improve its mechanical, thermal, and physical properties. In light of this concept, other fillers such as volcanic ash, mainly composed of SiO_2 and Al_2O_3, have also been used for this purpose [16]. Thus, a variety of popular ceramic reinforcements can be found constituting natural resources as is the case of FS. Therefore, FS, a raw, abundant, cheap, and naturally occurring iron-titanium oxide, can be considered as a potential substitute for traditional inorganic fillers. However, up until now, the feasibility of reinforcing epoxy resin with FS has not yet been considered, even though the filler's mechanical and magnetic properties can be imparted to the composite. Apart from that, both $FeTiO_3$ and Fe_2O_3, have proven to successfully attenuate gamma ray and neutron radiation on polymer matrixes [17, 18], showing potential as a non-toxic lead substitute. Moreover, the surface hydroxyl groups on the FS, a common functional group on metal oxides, produce a hydrophilic affinity that could benefit its compatibility with other hydrophilic matrixes, such as epoxy resin [10]. Their mutual hydrophilic nature would enhance the composite dispersion state and interfacial interactions, favoring the filler-matrix load transfer [19–21]. Hence, this work is intended to evaluate the effect of FS in reinforcing an epoxy resin through microindentation and dynamic mechanical analysis (DMA). These characterizations are important to define the optimum FS content based on the mechanical performance. Micromechanical models were used to predict the Young's modulus of the as-prepared composites to elucidate the FS reinforcement effect. The storage and loss modulus of the composites were also determined, together with the damping parameter to gain an insight into their viscoelastic behavior.

This study is a framework for the exploration of the mechanical and thermal response of the as-prepared composites as a valuable step towards expanding the applications of FS in this research area.

2 Materials and Methods

2.1 Materials

Diglycidyl ether of bisphenol A prepolymer (EPON 828, Hexion), and diethylenetri-amine hardener (EPIKURE 3223, Hexion) were used as the matrix and curing agent in a 100:12 mass ratio.

Ecuadorian FS, the selected fillers, were collected from El Ostional beach (Mompiche-Esmeraldas) [2], and ground under the conditions described by Lagos et al. [3]. Briefly, 5.5 g of FS were placed in a stainless-steel jar and ball milled employing a RETSCH PM 400 equipment, with 20:1 mass ratio of ball-to-FS at 300 rpm speed for 9 min, at 3 min intervals. Finally, the submicronic size of the milled FS was confirmed by dynamic light scattering (DLS) with a Brookhaven 90 Plus equipment (see Fig. 1).

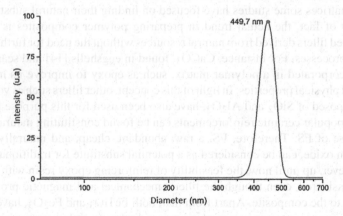

Fig. 1. DLS curve of milled FS sample.

2.2 Preparation Procedure of FS/Epoxy Composites

The composites were obtained following the procedure described by Tamayo-Aguilar et al. [10]. In a determined amount of epoxy resin, FS were added. The FS contents used were 2, 4 and 6 wt.%. Then, FS were dispersed by sonication in an ice bath. Afterwards, the curing agent was added to the as-prepared dispersion and manually stirred during 5 min. The composites were shaped by casting in acrylic molds. Finally, the upper spec-imen surface was polished to improve the surface quality. The as-prepared composites were denoted as EP-FS-2%, EP-FS-4% and EP-FS-6%. Considering both the filler and matrix densities as 4.69 [5] and 1.16 g cm^{-3} [10], respectively, the corresponding volume loadings were computed as being 0.5, 1.0 and 1.6 vol. %. The scheme of the composite preparation is presented in Fig. 2.

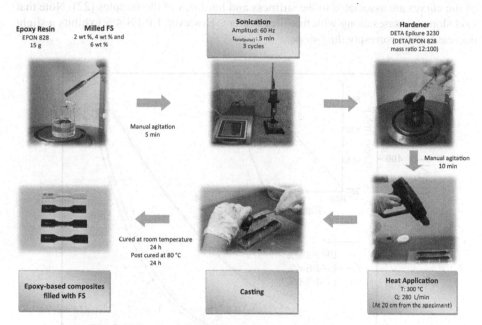

Fig. 2. Scheme of the procedure for the composite preparation.

2.3 Characterization Techniques

The control sample (neat epoxy) and composites specimens were tested through microindentation (MHT:S/N:01-02802 CSM Instrument). The Poisson ratio and elastic modulus of the Berkovich indenter were 0.07 and 1140 GPa, respectively. The test conditions were the following: i) the contact load: 10 mN, ii) lineal maximum load: 500 mN and iii) loading and unloading rates: 1200 mN min^{-1} with 70 s pauses. The indentations were recorded by tracing the load as a function of the displacement curve. Both the elastic modulus and hardness were computed employing the Oliver-Pharr method [22], using a Poisson ratio equal to 0.35 for the matrix [23].

Dynamic mechanical analyses (DMA) were carried out to quantify the storage modulus (E'), loss modulus (E"), damping factor (tanδ = E"/E') and glass transition temperature (T$_g$). The analyses were performed in a TA DMA 850 equipment using a single cantilever configuration, in the interval from 20 to 180 °C, 3 °C min^{-1} heating rate, 30 μm amplitude and 1 Hz frequency. The specimen dimensions were 30x13x1.5 mm.

3 Results and Discussion

The load vs. displacement curves of the polymer matrix and the as-prepared composites are exhibited in Fig. 3. It is important to point out that the slopes of the unloading section of the curves are associated to the stiffness and hardness of the samples [22]. Note that said slope increases along with the filler content. However, EP-FS-4% exhibits a slight decrease on its corresponding slope.

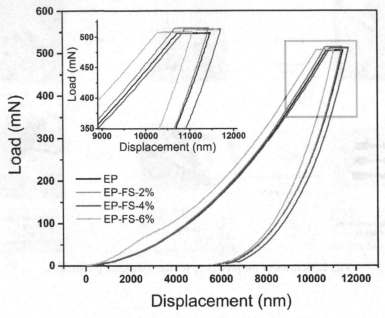

Fig. 3. Load as a function of displacement for the epoxy matrix and composites filled with FS.

The values of the elastic modulus and hardness of the bare matrix and composites reinforced with FS were quantified applying the Oliver-Pharr methodology [22] and are presented in Fig. 4 and Fig. 5, respectively.

The reinforcement effect was evident for 6 wt. % FS, since the Young's modulus of this composite (3.51 GPa) increased 6% in comparison to the neat epoxy (3.30 GPa), as seen in Fig. 4. On the other hand, the effect of FS appeared to be less pronounced at 2 and 4 wt. % FS, loadings that led to a slightly increase of 3% and a decrease of 2% of the Young's modulus, respectively. Previous studies have reported similar results for low contents of related iron oxide fillers ($\leq$ 4 wt. %), demonstrating the difficulty of enhancing the matrix stiffness even at nanometric dimensions. For instance, epoxy composites filled with 4 wt. % Fe_2O_3 practically did not increase the Young's modulus when compared with the control sample [24]. In the case of core-shell nanoparticles (Fe@FeO) the Young's modulus decreased 4.2% after the incorporation of this filler at 1 wt. % into an epoxy matrix. Although, at a 5 wt. % of Fe@FeO the Young's modulus raised 9.8% [25]. This suggests that a filler content boundary must be overcome for this type of particles to produce a reinforcement effect.

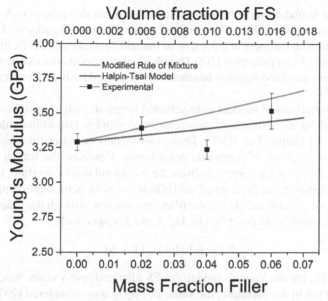

Fig. 4. Elastic moduli of the epoxy matrix and composites filled with FS.

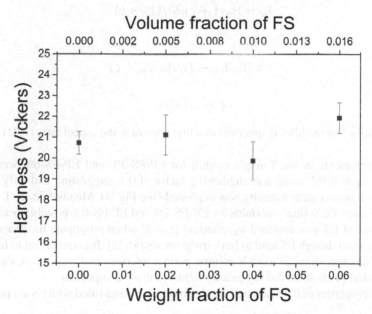

Fig. 5. Hardness of the epoxy matrix and composites filled with FS.

Regarding hardness of the as-prepared composites, a trend similar to that displayed by the Young's modulus was observed in Fig. 5. Merely the composite filled with 6 wt. % FS increased in hardness (~ 6% in comparison with the neat matrix), implying that a filler content boundary must be surpassed to also boost this property. A comparable decrease in hardness for EP-FS-4% was presented by Tamayo-Aguilar et al. who found a slight reduction on hardness at 0.5 wt. % of titanate nanotubes (TTNT), fillers derived from an anatase (TiO_2) precursor [10]. That work also supports the existence of a filler content frontier since the composite hardness was improved for higher contents of TTNT (up to 3 wt. %).

Two micromechanical models were selected to get an insight into the effect of FS on the elastic modulus of the composites reinforced with FS: i) modified rule of mixture (MROM) and ii) Halpin-Tsai (H-T). These two models consider the elastic modulus and the volume fractions of composite constituents. However, the former considers a strengthening factor (β_f), a correction from the traditional rule of mixture, that contemplates filler orientation and finite length and is best suited for particulate composites [26]. The later takes the shape and size of the filler into account through the shape parameter (ς) [27]. These models are described by Eq. 1 and 2, respectively:

$$E_c = \beta_f E_f \phi + E_m (1 - \phi) \tag{1}$$

where E_f and E_m are the Young's moduli for FS filler and epoxy resin. Since E_f has not been reported yet in the literature, the value of Fe_2O_3 was considered (237 GPa) [28]. The value of 3.29 GPa was used as E_m [10]. Also, ϕ is the FS volume fraction.

$$E_c = E_m (1 + \varsigma \eta \phi)/(1 - \eta \phi) \tag{2}$$

where,

$$\eta = (E_f/E_m - 1)/(E_f/E_m + \varsigma) \tag{3}$$

$$\varsigma = 2(L/D) \tag{4}$$

Assuming that the filler is spherical as a first approach, the aspect ratio (L/D) is equal to 1.

The increments in the Young's moduli for EP-FS-2% and EP-FS-6% were aptly predicted by MROM, using a strengthening factor of 0.1, suggesting that only 10% of the filler's reinforcement capacity was exploited (see Fig. 4). Meanwhile, H-T slightly underestimates the Young's modulus for EP-FS-2% and EP-FS-6% possibly because the morphology of FS was assumed as spherical ($\varsigma = 2$) when proposing the shape fitting parameter, even though FS tend to have irregular shapes [2]. It is important to highlight that both micromechanical models assume perfect interface and dispersion, the reason why theorical predictions did not exactly adjust to these composites.

DMA properties of the neat matrix and epoxy composites filled with FS are presented in Fig. 6.

The storage modulus (E') quantify the elastic response of the composite, that is, its capacity to store energy and then liberate it when the load is removed. As seen in Fig. 6a, at low FS loadings, the E' of epoxy was slightly improved for 2 wt. % and practically unaltered for 4 wt. %. A FS content of 6 wt. % was defined as the optimum value since it increased the E' in 5.3% at room temperature in comparison with the neat matrix, while the rise in this property was 7.3% at T_g (~145 °C). The E' increment for EP-FS-6% is

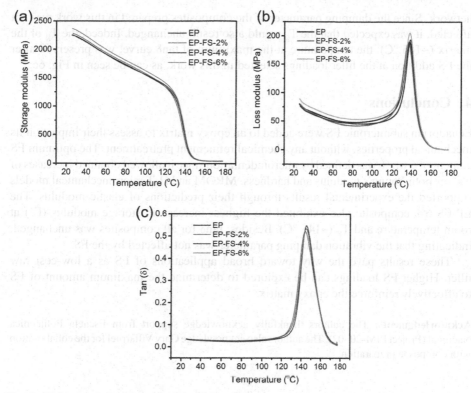

Fig. 6. DMA properties: (a) storage modulus, (b) loss modulus and (c) vibration damping of the neat matrix and the composites reinforced with FS.

constant within the glassy plateau. In the case of similar iron-oxide based fillers, such as core-shell nanoparticles (Fe@FeO), for a filler loading of 20 wt. % an increase of 4% in E' was observed at 60 °C in the glassy region [25]. Thus, the outcome presented in this work highlights the potential of FS to enhance the elastic properties of an epoxy matrix.

The loss modulus (E''), which measures the viscous response of the composite, represents the material's capacity to dissipate energy. The E'' increased in 13% at room temperature and 7.3% at T_g (~145 °C) for an FS content of 6 wt. %, as presented in Fig. 6b. Therefore, since both E'' and E' experience similar increases at T_g, the tanδ value was the same as the matrix indicating that the vibration damping parameter (impact absorption) of the matrix was not affected (see Fig. 6c). Generally, the incorporation of a stiffer phase results in a disproportional increase of the elastic response in comparison with the viscous response, consequently resulting in a decrease in tanδ. Such disproportional change between E' and E'' was evident for core-shell nanoparticles (Fe@FeO) that caused a decrease in tanδ peak size regarding that of the epoxy matrix [25]. Similar results were observed with composites reinforced with Fe_3O_4 with filler loadings of 2, 5, 10 and 15 wt. % [29], as well as for 3 and 4 wt. % of Fe_2O_3 functionalized with amino phenol formaldehyde resin [24]. In these cases, a shift in the T_g accompanies the tanδ peak change, as both properties are related to the chain movement inside the polymer network. Since the damping parameter of the composites prepared in this work was not affected, it was expected that the T_g would also result unchanged. Indeed, the T_g of the matrix ($\sim$145 °C), the temperature at the maximum of tanδ curve, was preserved after the FS addition at the filler loadings selected in this work, as can be seen in Fig. 6c.

4   Conclusions

Ecuadorian submicronic FS were added to an epoxy matrix to assess their impact on its mechanical properties, without any chemical refinement pretreatment. The optimum FS content of 6 wt. % was defined by microindentation since it allowed obtained increases of 6% for both Young's modulus and hardness. MROM and H-T micromechanical models supported the experimental results through their predictions of elastic modulus. The EP-FS-6% composite also exhibited the highest increase in storage modulus (E') at room temperature and T_g ($\sim$145 °C). Besides, tanδ for all composites was unchanged, indicating that the vibration damping parameter was not affected by the FS.

These results pave the way toward broad applications of FS as a low-cost raw filler. Higher FS loadings can be explored to determine the maximum amount of FS to effectively reinforce the epoxy matrix.

Acknowledgments. The authors thankfully acknowledge support from Escuela Politécnica Nacional (Project PIM-20–02). The authors also acknowledge Gary Villarruel for the collaboration with composite preparation.

References

1. Srinivasan, K., Samuel, E.: Evaluation of radiation shielding properties of the polyvinyl alcohol/iron oxide polymer composite. J. Med. Phys. **42**, 273–278 (2017). https://doi.org/10.4103/jmp.JMP_54_17
2. Lagos, K.J., et al.: Data on phase and chemical compositions of black sands from "El Ostional" beach situated in Mompiche. Ecuador. Data Br. (2020). https://doi.org/10.1016/j.dib.2020.106214
3. Lagos, K.J., et al.: Towards iron-titanium oxide nanostructures from ecuadorian black mineral sands. Minerals. **11**, 1–17 (2021). https://doi.org/10.3390/min11020122
4. Perez, S.M., Sharadqah, S.: Successive methods for the separation of titanium oxide from the black sands of Ecuador. J. Ecol. Eng. **19**, 186–190 (2018). https://doi.org/10.12911/22998993/79417
5. Trujillo, D., Manangon, L.: Titanium Dioxide Recovery from Ilmenite Contained in Ferroti-taniferous Sands from Mompiche-Ecuador. J. Geol. Resour. Eng. **4**, 175–183 (2016). https://doi.org/10.17265/2328-2193/2016.04.003
6. Valdivieso-Ramírez, C.S., Pontón, P.I., Dosen, A., Marinkovic, B.A., Guerrero, V.H.: One-step synthesis of iron and titanium-based compounds using black mineral sands and oxalic acid under subcritical water conditions. Minerals **12**, 306 (2022)
7. Pandey, R.K., Droopad, R., Stern, H.P.: Magnetic field sensor based on varistor response. IEEE Sens. J. **19**, 8635–8641 (2019). https://doi.org/10.1109/JSEN.2019.2918270
8. Naresh, N., Bhowmik, R.N.: Structural, magnetic and electrical study of nano-structured α-Fe1.4Ti0.6O3. J. Phys. Chem. Solids. **73**, 330–337 (2012). https://doi.org/10.1016/j.jpcs.2011.10.014

9. Kocijan, A., Conradi, M., Hočevar, M.: The influence of surface wettability and topography on the bioactivity of TiO2/epoxy coatings on AISI 316L stainless steel. Materials (Basel) 12, (2019). https://doi.org/10.3390/ma12111877

10. Tamayo-Aguilar, A., et al.: Mechanical properties of amine-cured epoxy composites reinforced with pristine protonated titanate nanotubes. J. Mater. Res. Technol. 9, 15771–15778 (2020). https://doi.org/10.1016/j.jmrt.2020.11.019

11. Goyat, M.S., Rana, S., Halder, S., Ghosh, P.K.: Facile fabrication of epoxy-TiO2 nanocomposites: A critical analysis of TiO2 impact on mechanical properties and toughening mechanisms. Ultrason. Sonochem. 40, 861–873 (2018). https://doi.org/10.1016/j.ultsonch.2017.07.040

12. Kausar, A.: Polymeric materials filled with hematite nanoparticle: current state and prospective application. Polym. Technol. Mater. 59, 323–338 (2020). https://doi.org/10.1080/257 40881.2019.1647238

13. Sienkiewicz, N., Dominic, M., Parameswaranpillai, J.: Natural Fillers as Potential Modifying Agents for Epoxy Composition : A Review. 1–17 (2022)

14. Mohan, T.P., Kanny, K.: Thermal, mechanical and physical properties of nanoegg shell particle-filled epoxy nanocomposites. J. Compos. Mater. 52, 3989–4000 (2018). https://doi. org/10.1177/0021998318773445

15. Owuamanam, S., Cree, D.: Progress of bio-calcium carbonate waste eggshell and seashell fillers in polymer composites: A review. J. Compos. Sci. 4 (2020). https://doi.org/10.3390/jcs 4020070

16. Pratiwi, H.: The effects of Mt. Kelud volcanic ash on morphological and mechanical properties of hemp fabric reinforced polyester and epoxy composites. In: AIP Conference Proceedings of 2014 (2018). https://doi.org/10.1063/1.5054498

17. Turhan, M.F., Akman, F., Polat, H., Kaçal, M.R., Demirkol, İ.: Gamma-ray attenuation behaviors of hematite doped polymer composites. Prog. Nucl. Energy. 129 (2020). https://doi.org/ 10.1016/j.pnucene.2020.103504

18. Haque, M.M., Shamsuzzaman, M., Uddin, M.B., Salahuddin, A.Z.M., Khan, R.A.: Fabrication and Characterization of Shielding Properties of Heavy Mineral Reinforced Polymer Composite Materials for Radiation Protection. 4, 15–20 (2019)

19. Matsuura, K., Umahara, Y., Gotoh, K., Hoshijima, Y., Ishida, H.: Surface modification effects on the tensile properties of functionalised graphene oxide epoxy films. RSC Adv. 8, 9677–9684 (2018). https://doi.org/10.1039/c8ra00252e

20. Wu, Q., Zhao, R., Xi, T., Yang, X., Zhu, J.: Comparative study on effects of epoxy sizing involving ZrO2 and GO on interfacial shear strength of carbon fiber/epoxy composites through one and two steps dipping routes. Compos. Part A Appl. Sci. Manuf. 134, 105909 (2020). https://doi.org/10.1016/j.compositesa.2020.105909

21. Chhetri, S., et al.: Investigation of the mechanical and thermal properties of L-glutathione modified graphene/epoxy composites. Compos. Part B Eng. 143, 105–112 (2018). https://doi. org/10.1016/j.compositesb.2018.02.004

22. Oliver, W.C., Pharr, G.M.: An improved technique for determining hardness and elastic modulus using load and displacement sensing indentation experiments. J. Mater. Res. 7, 1564–1583 (1992). https://doi.org/10.1557/JMR.1992.1564

23. Ahangari, M.G., Fereidoon, A.: Micromechanical properties and morphologies of self-healing epoxy nanocomposites with microencapsulated healing agent. Mater. Chem. Phys. 151, 112–118 (2015). https://doi.org/10.1016/j.matchemphys.2014.11.044

24. Sun, T., Wang, Y., Yang, Y., Fan, H., Liu, M., Wu, Z.: A novel Fe2O3@APFS/epoxy composite with enhanced mechanical and thermal properties. Compos. Sci. Technol. 193, 108146 (2020). https://doi.org/10.1016/j.compscitech.2020.108146

25. Zhu, J., Wei, S., Ryu, J., Sun, L., Luo, Z., Guo, Z.: Magnetic epoxy resin nanocomposites reinforced with core - Shell structured Fe@FeO nanoparticles: Fabrication and property analysis. ACS Appl. Mater. Interfaces. 2, 2100–2107 (2010). https://doi.org/10.1021/am100361h

26. Papageorgiou, D.G., Kinloch, I.A., Young, R.J.: Hybrid multifunctional graphene/glass-fibre polypropylene composites. Compos. Sci. Technol. **137**, 44–51 (2016). https://doi.org/10.1016/j.compscitech.2016.10.018

27. Halpin, J.C., Kardos, J.L.: The Halpin-Tsai equations: A review. Polym. Eng. Sci. **16**, 344–352 (1976). https://doi.org/10.1002/pen.760160512

28. Chicot, D., et al.: Mechanical properties of magnetite (Fe3O4), hematite (α-Fe2O3) and goethite (α-FeO·OH) by instrumented indentation and molecular dynamics analysis. Mater. Chem. Phys. **129**, 862–870 (2011). https://doi.org/10.1016/j.matchemphys.2011.05.056

29. Gu, H., et al.: Polyaniline stabilized magnetite nanoparticle reinforced epoxy nanocomposites. ACS Appl. Mater. Interfaces. **4**, 5613–5624 (2012). https://doi.org/10.1021/am301529t

Behavior of Influencing Parameters of the Fused Deposition Modeling Process in Dissimilar Combinations: Polymer-3D Printer

Marcelo Tulio Piovan[1] (iD) and Patricio G. Riofrío[2](✉) (iD)

[1] UTN-FRBB, 11 de Abril 461, Bahía Blanca, Argentina
mpiovan@frbb.utn.edu.ar

[2] DCEM-Universidad de las Fuerzas Armadas-ESPE, Av. Rumiñahui s/n, Sangolqui, Ecuador
pgriofrio@espe.edu.ec

Abstract. The proliferation of 3D printers and the availability of low-cost polymeric materials has allowed the Fused Deposition Modeling (FDM) process to expand its participation in the Additive Manufacturing (AM) market. In this work, the mechanical properties of typical polymers are characterized using two dissimilar material and FDM printer combinations, contrasting a low cost combination with a higher cost one. The modulus of elasticity and the tensile strength of acrylonitrile butadiene styrene (ABS) and polylactic acid (PLA) polymers are determined with standardized ASTM and ISO tests considering the effect of the infill density, layer thickness and filament color. It was mainly found that the increase in layer thickness generates appreciable reductions in the modulus of elasticity and tensile strength in the range of 12–17% considering the two polymers and that the influence of the filament color produces the widest range of variation, between 3% and 19% in the mechanical properties. In the previous ranges, the highest values correspond to PLA polymer and the lowest to ABS polymer, this may be due to the difference in quality of the polymers.

Keywords: FDM · ABS and PLA polymers · Mechanical properties · Low-cost 3D printing

1   Introduction

Nowadays, Fused Deposition Modeling (FDM) is considered a mature technology of Additive Manufacturing (AM) due to its versatility and variety of applications both with industrial printers and with low-cost printers called three-dimensional printers [1]. After the development between the years 1980–1990 under the concept of rapid prototyping, the FDM grew due to the incorporation of cheap control platforms and due to the commercial opening thanks to the cessation of patents. There are currently several 3D printing technologies available, each with advantages and limitations [2], however; FDM, due to the proliferation of very low-cost 3D printers (which can be less than USD 1000.00 and even below USD 400.00), covers a wide market, from the industrial segment to the one dedicated to hobby [3].

© The Author(s), under exclusive license to Springer Nature Switzerland AG 2023
M. Botto-Tobar et al. (Eds.): ICAT 2022, CCIS 1756, pp. 159–171, 2023.
https://doi.org/10.1007/978-3-031-24971-6_12

The FDM process consists in dropping a thermoplastic semi-liquid filament on a platform through an extrusion nozzle, following a layer-by-layer construction according to the slicing of a computer aided design (CAD) three-dimensional model. The filament deposition process in each layer follows a predefined path by default or according to the user's decision.

A crucial aspect of FDM-3D printing is the time spent printing complex or bulky parts. To reduce the time it is possible to increase the layer thickness, build the piece with different density in its parts and increase the head speed. A solid infill on the surface and a low infill density on the inside are generally used. The sketches in Fig. 1 show the cross-section of a FDM printed specimen, its regions (left) and typical infills or internal supports (right). In region (1) there is a type of deposition with longitudinal filament that forms the perimeter or contour of the piece, region (2) and region (3) are internal parts of the contour which are arranged at a given angle, generally at 45°, but it can be at 0° or 90° with respect to the filaments of region (1). Finally, region (4) can have different patterns and infill densities that depend on the technology of the printer and the control program. Thus, in details (a), (b) and (c) of Fig. 1 are represented a solid fill (or 100% infill density), a low-density hollow (LDH) (which can be equivalent to 25% infill density), and a high-density hollow (HDH) (which can be equivalent to 75% infill density), respectively.

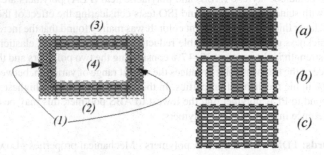

Fig. 1. Cross-sectional cut of a generic specimen showing regions (left) and infills (right).

The mechanical properties of parts printed by FDM today are of vital importance considering that the additive manufacturing process has evolved from rapid prototyping for visual evaluation (in the eighties) to a manufacturing process that imparts the final properties of the product (nowadays). Several authors have carried out characterization studies of mechanical properties in specimens built with various 3D printing techniques and have also proposed simple mathematical models that represent the mechanical strength and stiffness of materials and printed parts [4–9]. Specimens that meet ISO 527-2, ASTM D638 or other standards have been used in these studies, although each study followed the experimental criteria of only one standard. Unlike the works mentioned, Tymrak et al. [10] carried out characterization studies of parts built with various types of machines and experimental methodologies and with different construction features such as: filament color, layer thickness and raster angle. In addition to the above parameters, the printing speed, nozzle temperature, infill density and infill pattern stand out as influential parameters in the mechanical properties of printed pieces by FDM [11–13].

Acrylonitrile Butadiene Styrene (ABS) polymer due to its reasonable cost, high mechanical strength and resistance to temperature [14] and Polylactic Acid (PLA) polymer due to its low cost and easy printing [15] are two polymers widely used in FDM-3D printing. In the already cited work, Tymrak et al. [10] found that the raster angle parameter, in solid infill specimens, has an important influence on the modulus of elasticity since the dispersion amplitude was 8.5% for ABS and 2.9% for PLA. Similar observations emerge from the articles of Rodríguez et al. [4], Oksmana et al. [7] and Lee and Huang [9].

Although in the literature there are various works related to the mechanical characterization of polymers printed by FDM, a large majority are dedicated to test pieces or specimens with solid infill and, on the other hand, there are few works aimed at comparing the mechanical properties of pieces printed with machines and polymers used in the industrial field with those resulting from low-cost machines and polymers. Thus, in this work the mechanical properties of two commonly used polymers are characterized: ABS and PLA, using two types of printers: on one hand, an industrial-grade-professional printer and, on the other hand, a low-cost-semiprofessional printer. Tensile strength and modulus of elasticity are determined by standard tensile experimental tests, considering the effect of the infill density, the layer thickness and the filament color.

2   Materials and Procedure

Since FDM printed parts can have different mechanical behavior due to the features of printing machines (i.e. the technology to control the deposition process) and the associated software to perform the slicing procedure of the 3D computational model; two dissimilar material and 3D printing machine combinations are used in this work to print specimens by FDM. The first combination comprises low-cost generic PLA material from the provider High QS 3D-printing and a Replikat® open-source printer which employs the Kisslicer© program, meanwhile; in the second combination, a certified ABS polymer and a professional Stratasys® printer were used, both from the same manufacturer. The Stratasys machine employs the Catalist© software.

The determination of the mechanical properties: modulus of elasticity and tensile strength, were carried out under the guidance of the standards for tensile tests on plastics: ASTM D638 [16] and ISO 527-2 [17]. Figure 2 shows the geometry and essential dimensions of the specimens used in this work. Figure 2 also shows the specimen in accordance with ISO 178 standard [18], which, although it corresponds to the bending behavior of plastics, since it proved to be very useful for tensile tests in the case of non-solid sections. Figure 2 includes the three types of specimens printed according to ABS-Stratasys® printer combination. Similar specimens were printed under the PLA-Replikat® combination except that in this case the ASTM D638 specimens were not used.

The tensile tests of the specimens were carried out in two different testing machines: the PLA specimens, in a computerized test equipment (designated as ME1) developed at the Universidad Tecnológica Nacional of Argentina, while the ABS specimens were

ASTM D638

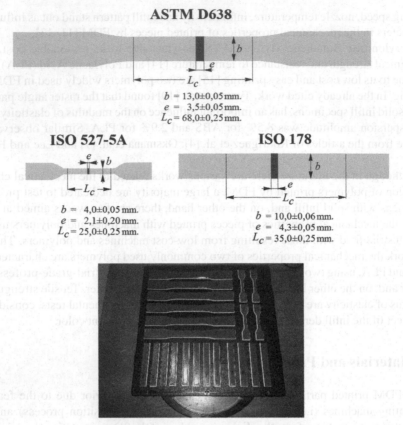

$b = 13,0\pm0,05$ mm.
$e = 3,5\pm0,05$ mm.
$L_c = 68,0\pm0,25$ mm.

ISO 527-5A

$b = 4,0\pm0,05$ mm.
$e = 2,1\pm0,20$ mm.
$L_c = 25,0\pm0,25$ mm.

ISO 178

$b = 10,0\pm0,06$ mm.
$e = 4,3\pm0,05$ mm.
$L_c = 35,0\pm0,25$ mm.

Fig. 2. Geometry and essential dimensions of the specimens used in the tests (top) and specimens printed in ABS-Stratasys® printer combination (bottom).

tested in an AMSLER plastic testing machine (identified as ME2) of the Universidad de las Fuerzas Armadas-ESPE of Ecuador. Furthermore, in order to observe the replicability of the experimental results, PLA specimens were tested in the ME1 machine and ABS specimens were tested in the ME2 machine. Specimens used for the latter purpose are designated as witness specimens.

For each factor examined (filament color, layer thickness and infill density) 4 to 6 specimens were tested. A minimum speed of 5 mm/min was used in the heads of the test machines according to works of other authors [10, 19].

Table 1 presents for each polymer tested, types of specimens, printers, testing machines and printing attributes employed. The infill density is identified in two ways (related to the nomenclature of Kisslicer© or Catalist© programs): by percentage, for PLA specimens, and by name (solid, LDH, HDH), for ABS specimens.

To determine the longitudinal elasticity modulus (E) and the tensile strength (σ_{max}) from the experimental results, expressions (1) and (2) are used, which are based on the standards already mentioned.

Table 1. Relevant aspects and attributes of PLA and ABS polymers tests

Aspect or attribute	PLA	ABS
Specimen type	ISO 527-5A, ISO 178	ISO 527-5A, ISO 178, ASTM D638
Testing machine	ME1	ME2
Printing machine	Replikat®	Stratasys®
Filament diameter (mm)	0.4	0.254
Layer thickness (mm)	0.2, 0.3	0.254, 0.332
Filament color	Black, orange	Grey, white
Infill density	25%, 100%	Solid, LDH, HDH

$$E = \left(\frac{F}{\delta}\right)\frac{L_c}{be} \qquad (1)$$

$$\sigma_{max} = \frac{(F)}{be\kappa} \qquad (2)$$

In the above expressions, the measurable values are discriminated between parentheses, being F the force and δ the strain in the elastic range or the maximum values depending on the case of determining E or σ_{max}; b, e, and L_c are the width, thickness, and gage length of the specimen, respectively. The κ factor introduced in expression (2) is useful in the analysis of infill density as a factor correlated to the effective loaded section, taking a unit value when correspond to solid condition.

3 Results and Discussion

In the following sections, the results corresponding to the modulus of elasticity and tensile strength for PLA and ABS under different test conditions are presented in order to determine the effect of the infill density, filament color and layer thickness as highlighted in Table 1.

3.1 Solid Fill. Overall Results

Figure 3 shows the results of the tensile strength (σ_{max}) corresponding to the ABS specimens in its solid filling condition and tested on the ME2 machine (yellow bar). The results correspond to the entire set of specimens according to Table 1, but only for the layer thickness of 0.254 mm. For comparison purposes, Fig. 3 also includes the results of the ABS witness (control) specimens executed on the ME1 testing machine and the results of previous studies by other authors (blue bars). Figure 3 stands out, for all cases, the mean values (red squares) as well as the maximum and minimum values (black diamonds).

Figure 4 shows the results of the tensile strength reached by the specimens of the PLA material in its solid configuration. The results corresponding to the present work appear in green bars (ME1 and ME2 machines).

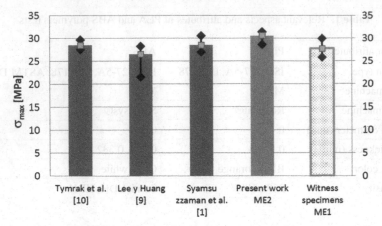

Fig. 3. Tensile strength of the ABS material in the two test machines and according to other authors (Color figure online)

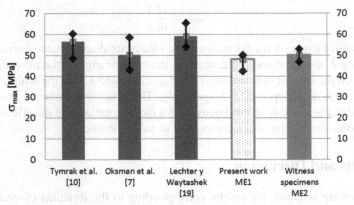

Fig. 4. Tensile strength of the PLA material in the two test machines and according to other authors (Color figure online)

In Figs. 3 and 4, it is observed that the results of the tensile tests according to the two machines (ME1 and ME2) are comparable. It was found that the averages differ in order of 9% for ABS and 4% for PLA. Therefore, the replicability between machines is acceptable. On the other hand, the comparison between the results of this study with the data of other authors shows a low dispersion in the case of the ABS material and a higher dispersion in the case of the PLA material, this can be explained because the ABS polymer is a certified material by the manufacturer Stratasys®, while the PLA material is generic without certification of its properties and constituents.

Quantitatively, the differences of the mean values of other references, which are depicted in Figs. 3 and 4, with the results of this present study, show absolute differences between 6% and 13% for the ABS (measured in ME2) and the 2% to 5% (measured in ME1) while, from 4% to 23% for PLA (measured in ME1) and from 0% to 18% (measured in ME2). In addition, in Fig. 4, it is noted an important dispersion among the values of the reference works (within 43.0 to 65.0 MPa) and the experimental results obtained in the present investigation. The reason of this dispersion is connected with the variability in the manufacturing process of filament makers and consistent with what was reported in two studies [2, 20].

Table 2 presents the values of the modulus of elasticity for ABS and PLA polymers found in the present study considering the entire space of experimental samples. Table 2 includes the results corresponding to other studies for comparison. The mean, maximum and minimum values are displayed for all cases except for the research of Li et al. [5] where only the mean value was reported.

Table 2. Modulus of elasticity obtained in this study and reported by other authors. Units in GPa

Works	Polymer	Mean	Maximum	Minimum
Tymrak et al. [10]	ABS	1.81	1.88	1.74
Li et al. [5]	ABS	1.78	–	–
Rodriguez et al. [4]	ABS	1.76	1.87	1.59
Present work ME2	ABS	1.71	1.76	1.65
Witness specimens ME1	ABS	1.81	1.98	1.64
Tymrak et al. [10]	PLA	3.37	3.48	3.28
Oksman et al. [7]	PLA	3.40	3.70	3.20
Lechter and Waytashek [19]	PLA	3.71	3.82	3.00
Present work ME1	PLA	3.36	3.51	3.15
Witness specimens ME2	PLA	3.60	3.70	3.50

Table 2 shows that the values obtained in the present study are close to the reference studies, thus, in terms of the mean values, the maximum percentage differences in relation to those of other authors are 5% and 10% for ABS and PLA polymers, respectively. The greater level of dispersion of PLA can be associated, as already highlighted in Figs. 3 and 4, to the fact that this material is of a generic type, unlike the ABS material.

3.2   Solid Infill. Effect of the Type of Specimen and the Filament Color

Table 3 shows the results for modulus of elasticity and tensile strength of all types of specimens highlighting the filament color. These results correspond to solid section and the smallest layer thickness of those indicated in Table 1. It can be seen that for each color and material, the percentage differences of the mean values for both properties between different types of specimens are less than 11%. For example, the absolute percentage difference in the mean values of the modulus of elasticity of white ABS between the ASTM D638 and ISO178 and with ISO 527A specimens is of the order of 3.2% and 1.3%, respectively. Meanwhile, the maximum percentage difference in the use of various test pieces is given in the comparison of the average values of the tensile strength between ISO 527A and ISO 178 specimens for orange PLA with a value of 11.4%.

Table 3. Modulus of elasticity [MPa] and tensile strength [MPa] of PLA and ABS according to the filament color

Polymer	Standard	Property (color)	Mean	Maximum	Minimum
ABS	ASTM D638	E (white)	1 720	1 732	1 710
		E (grey)	1 765	1 856	1 684
		σ_{max} (white)	31.90	33.40	30.60
		σ_{max} (grey)	33.00	35.40	32.60
	ISO 178	E (white)	1 775	1 795	1 732
		E (grey)	1 845	1 883	1 763
		σ_{max} (white)	30.50	34.20	27.90
		σ_{max} (grey)	31.20	31.40	30.70
	ISO 527A	E (white)	1 698	1 705	1 677
		E (grey)	1 820	1 845	1 756
		σ_{max} (white)	28.80	30.20	26.80
		σ_{max} (grey)	30.10	30.30	29.70
PLA	ISO178	E (orange)	3 205	3 450	2 725
		E (black)	3 880	3 950	3 750
		σ_{max} (orange)	44.30	46.40	41.80
		σ_{max} (black)	48.20	50.90	45.50
	ISO 527A	E (orange)	3 170	3 365	2 955
		E (black)	3 700	3 831	3 250
		σ_{max} (orange)	43.80	45.50	42.30
		σ_{max} (black)	47.80	49.50	46.20

In relation to the influence of the filament color, for the same polymer, according to Table 3, for grey ABS, the averages of the modulus of elasticity and the tensile strength are 1810 MPa and 31.4 MPa, respectively, and for white ABS, the values are 1731 y 30.4 MPa. Consequently, for ABS material, the influence of the filament color between white and grey is between 3.4% and 4.6% in relation to the average values of the tensile strength and the modulus of elasticity.

For the orange PLA, an average of 3188 MPa was obtained for the modulus of elasticity and an average of 44.1 MPa for tensile strength, while in the case of black PLA, the corresponding values were 3790 MPa and 48.0 MPa, respectively. Consequently, for the PLA polymer analyzed, it can be mentioned that there is a percentage difference between 9.0% and 19% for the black and orange pigments evaluated. This shows, in the first instance, the existence of an influence of the pigments that give color to the raw polymers, in relation to the mechanical properties of the prints, especially in the case of generic PLA polymer.

3.3 Solid Infill. Effect of the Layer Thickness

To examine the influence of the layer thickness on the modulus of elasticity and the tensile strength the layer thicknesses indicated in Table 1 were used, the increase from thin to thick layer corresponds to 31% and 50% for ABS and PLA polymers, respectively. For both materials, the ISO 527-2 type 5A specimen with solid section, in grey color for ABS and in black color for PLA, were used.

Figure 5 shows the comparison of the modulus of elasticity and the tensile strength according to the layer thickness. In the case of the results for the thick layer, in addition to the average value, the variation with the maximum and minimum values is also shown. The values for the thin layer correspond to the means shown in Table 3.

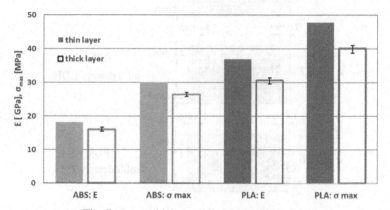

Fig. 5. Layer thickness effect on solid sections

As can be seen in Fig. 5, the increase in layer thickness leads to a decrease in both values (modulus of elasticity and tensile strength) in both polymers. In particular, the mean values of E and σ_{max} for the ABS decreased by 12% for both values, in relation to the mean values reported in Table 3; while for PLA, the mean values of E and σ_{max} decrease by 17% and 16%, respectively, in relation to the homonymous mean values in Table 3. This important decrease in the mechanical properties has also been observed in the investigation of Syamsuzzaman et al. [1], though these authors compared only high and low cost polymers.

3.4 Effect of Infill Density

For specimens in a non-solid fill condition, the main aspect to take into account is how to determine the effective resistant area and the κ factor that is used in Eq. (2) to calculate the tensile strength (maximum stress). Determining κ a priori involves the geometric evaluation of the specimen section using the impression model dissection program and a geometric analysis program. In effect, with an image of a resistant cross-section of the specimen (taken from the printer's own 3D model dissection program) and knowing the thickness of the sectional contour, layer thickness and type of internal infill, the effective area is determined by means of operations booleans between images (that of the nominal solid area and that of the hollow one) with the use of the Mathematica® program, see Chap. 1 from Trott [21].

Figure 6 shows the characteristics and dimensions of the sections of hollow ISO 178 test pieces for ABS (grey color) and PLA (black color) that have been used in this study. There is also indicated the type of infill that is used for each case and the value of κ corresponding to each case.

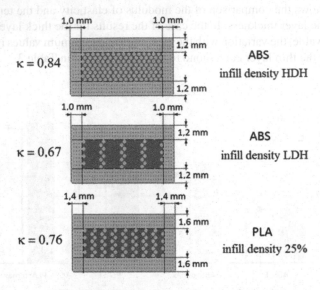

Fig. 6. Hollow sections: sizes and κ factors

Table 4 shows the values of the modulus of elasticity E and the tensile strength σ_{max} obtained for the ISO 178 type specimens with hollow sections, consigning the average, maximum and minimum values of each set of samples. In relation to the tensile strength, Table 4 shows both the value that resulted without including the κ factor and when the κ factor was included.

As it can be seen in Table 4, the values of the modulus of elasticity and the tensile strength of ABS and PLA polymers are quite similar to those of Table 3. Note that, the sample set for ABS or PLA polymers are more dispersed than their counterparts of solid sections in Table 3. This greater dispersion, even in the cases of the professional printer with high quality certified material, can be attributed to the possible irregularity of the internal pattern and its effect on the lack of cohesion between the infill and the outer shell perimeter.

The use of ISO 178 specimens to perform tensile test has proved to be a good choice in the case of hollow infills in comparison to the conventional dog-bone shapes of ASTM 638 and ISO 527-5A specimens. The reason of this lies in the experimental observation that dog-bone specimens with non-solid infill have frequent drawbacks; breaking outside the calibrated length L_c, which invalidates the test. On the contrary ISO 178 specimens under tensile test always broke inside the calibrated length. This particular is an important finding with respect to other previous reports.

Table 4. Modulus of elasticity [MPa] and tensile strength [MPa] of PLA and ABS according to the infill density

Material	Infill density	Property	Mean	Maximum	Minimum
ABS	HDH	E	1 680	1 707	1 639
		σ_{max}	29.60	30.00	28.80
		σ_{max} (without κ)	24.86	25.20	24.19
	LDH	E	1 802	1 882	1 749
		σ_{max}	31.80	31.90	31.60
		σ_{max} (without κ)	21.32	21.37	21.17
PLA	25%	E	3 719	3 820	3 652
		σ_{max}	47.40	48.40	46.20
		σ_{max} (without κ)	36.02	36.78	35.11

4   Conclusions

In this work, the tensile mechanical behavior of ABS and PLA polymers printed by FDM in dissimilar printing equipment was characterized, considering different types of specimens, infill density, layer thickness and using different filament colors. From the set of tests carried out, it is possible to draw the following conclusions:

- Although the materials are polymers that can present a significant dispersion in their properties because they come from different manufacturers, they have been contrasted with the experimental results of other authors, both for ABS and PLA. Such a contrast reflects percentage differences in a band from 0% to 23% for elastic properties. The biggest differences occurred in the use of generic type PLA. However, it is emphasized that there is not enough information regarding the specific chemical composition of the PLA used in the comparison references.
- The testing machines and their inherent methods have not shown (the interested reader can see References [20, 22]) -beyond their load capacity- a difference that can be considered substantial in the tests carried out, since the control specimens reflected percentage differences of the order of 4% to 9% for the evaluated properties; which can be considered experimentally and statistically acceptable within the context of prevailing uncertainty in the use of polymers for 3D printing.
- The use of test pieces of different shapes, once the data has been normalized has shown not to be very sensitive to dispersions with a percentage differences of the mean values for both properties less than 11% and showing the PLA polymer higher values in relation to the ABS polymer.
- The color effect in PLA (generic type) has shown to have an important variability calculated between 9% and 19% between the evaluated colors: black and orange. On the other hand, in the case of ABS (from the manufacturer Stratasys®) this variability is much lower, reaching a maximum of 4.6%, clearly associated with product quality control. Although in this study comparisons were made between a few filament colors, it can be noted that there is an important influence in the case that filaments with adequate quality control cannot be counted on.

- The effect of the layer thickness is notorious, both the modulus of elasticity and the tensile strength decrease with increasing layer thickness, however it has a greater effect on the tensile strength.
- The fact of using a generic polymer (in this case PLA), leads to a wider range of variability of the mechanical properties which is evident in the results of most of the factors considered.
- The use of ISO 178 shape specimens proved to be useful to characterize the material properties under tensile test in the case of non-solid infill.

Acknowledgements. The authors wish to acknowledge the sponsorship of the Universidad de las Fuerzas Armadas-ESPE and SENESCYT of Ecuador and the Universidad Nacional Tecnológica and CONICET of Argentina. In turn, we wish to thank the Ings. David Loza and Francisco Navas from the DCEM of the Universidad de las Fuerzas Armadas- ESPE for their assistance in the construction of specimens and execution of tests.

References

1. Syamsuzzaman, M., Mardi, N.A., Fadzil, Y.: Investigation of layer thickness effect on the performance of low-cost and commercial fused deposition modelling printers. Mater. Res. Innov. **18**(6), 485–489 (2014). https://doi.org/10.1179/1432891714Z.0000000001030
2. Dizon, J.R., Espera, A.H., Chen, Q., Advíncula, R.C.: Mechanical characterization of 3D printed polymers. Addit. Manuf. **20**, 44–67 (2018). https://doi.org/10.1016/j.addma.2017.12.002
3. Savolainen, J., Collan, M.: Additive manufacturing technology and business model change-a review of literature. Addit. Manuf. **32**, 1–13 (2020). https://doi.org/10.1016/j.addma.2020.101070
4. Rodriguez, J.F., Thomas, J.P., Renaud, J.E.: Mechanical behavior of acrylonitrile butadiene styrene (ABS) fused deposition materials. Rapid Prototyping J. **7**(3), 148–158 (2001). https://doi.org/10.1108/13552540110395547
5. Li, L., Sun, Q., Bellehumeur, C., Gu, P.: Composite modelling and analysis for fabrication of FDM prototypes with locally controlled properties. J. Manuf. Process. **4**(2), 129–141 (2002). https://doi.org/10.1016/S1526-6125(02)70139-4
6. Ahn, S.H., Montero, M., Odell, D., Roundy, S., Wright, P.K.: Anisotropic material properties of fused deposition modeling ABS. Rapid Prototyping J. **8**(4), 248–257 (2002). https://doi.org/10.1108/13552540210441166
7. Oksmana, K., Skrifvars, M., Selin, J.F.: Natural fibers as reinforcement in polylactic acid (PLA) composites. Compos. Sci. Technol. **63**, 1317–1324 (2003). https://doi.org/10.1016/S0266-3538(03)00103-9
8. Bijarimi, M., Ahmad, S., Rasid, R.: Mechanical, thermal and morphological properties of PLA/PP melt blends. In: International Conference on Agriculture, Chemical and Environmental Sciences (ICACES 2012), pp. 115–117. Dubai, Emiratos Arabes Unidos (2012). https://doi.org/10.1177/0095244310362403
9. Lee, J., Huang, A.: Fatigue analysis of FDM materials. Rapid Prototyping J. **19**(4), 291–299 (2013). https://doi.org/10.1108/13552541311323290
10. Tymrak, B.M., Kreiger, M., Pearce, J.: Mechanical properties of components fabricated with open-source 3-D printers under realistic environmental conditions. Mater. Des. **58**, 242–246 (2014). https://doi.org/10.1016/j.matdes.2014.02.038

11. Kumar, R.K., Mohanavel, V., Kiran, K.: Mechanical properties and characterization of poly-lactic acid/carbon fiber composite fabricated by fused deposition modeling. J. Mater. Perform., 1–10 (2020).https://doi.org/10.1007/s11665-021-06566-7

12. Palanisami, C., Raman, R., Dhanraj, P.: Adittive manufacturing: a review on mechanical properties of polyjet and FDM printed parts. Polymer Bull., 1–52 (2021).https://doi.org/10.1007/s00289-021-03899-0

13. Samykano, M.: Mechanical property and prediction model for FDM-3D Printed Polylactic Acid (PLA). Arab. J. Sci. Eng. 46(8), 7875–7892 (2021). https://doi.org/10.1007/s13369-021-05617-4

14. He, F., Khan, M.: Effects of printer parameters on the fatigue behavior of 3D-printed ABS under dynamic thermos-mechanical loads. Polymers 13(2362), 1–25 (2021). https://doi.org/10.3390/polym13142362

15. Amendola, C., et al.: Optical characterization of 3D printed PLA and ABS filaments for diffuse optical applications. PLoS ONE 16(6), 1–14 (2021). https://doi.org/10.1371/journal.pone.0253181

16. ASTM D638-14: Standard test method for tensile properties of plastics. American Society for Testing and Materials. 2014. doi:https://doi.org/10.1520/D0638-10

17. ISO 527-2.: Plastics – Determination of tensile properties – Part 2: Test conditions for molding and extrusion plastics. International Standard Organization (2012)

18. ISO 178.: Plastics-Determination of flexural properties. International Standard Organization (2010)

19. Lechter, T., Waytashek, M.: Material property testing of 3D-printed specimen of PLA on an entry-level 3D printer. In: Proceedings of the ASME International Mechanical Engineering Congress and Exposition IMECE. Montreal, Canada. IMECE2014-39379 (2014). https://doi.org/10.1115/IMECE2014-39379

20. Romero, A., et al.: Tensile properties of 3D printed polymeric pieces: comparison of several testing setups. Ingeniería e Investigación 41(1) (2021). https://doi.org/10.15446/ing.investig.v41n1.84467

21. Trott, M.: The Mathematica GuideBook for Numerics, 1st. edn. Springer, New York (2006). https://doi.org/10.1007/0-387-28814-7

22. Mainetti, C., Romero, A., Piovan, M.: Development of automated testing machine for poly-mers used in 3D printing. Revista Tecnología y Ciencia 38, 50–66 (2020). https://doi.org/10.33414/rtyc.38.50-66.2020

Bamboo Cellulose Textile Filament "Angustifolia" Floating Root Resin

Willam Ricardo Esparza Encalada[✉] ⓘ, Wilson Adrián Herrera Villarreal ⓘ,
and Luis Adalberto Chamorro Ortega ⓘ

Universidad Técnica del Norte, Ibarra Imbabura, Ecuador
{wresparza,waherrera,lachamorro}@utn.edu.ec

Abstract. The purpose of the research was to manufacture bamboo cellulose textile filament "Angustifolia" (BCTF) incorporating anionic resin (IR), and to determine its performance in its properties of recovery to doubling (RTD), elongation (E), resistance (R), to be applied in hydroponic floating root crops. The applied process was developed by extruding and forming textile filament with bamboo cellulose (BC) and resin (AR). The BC was placed in a glass container and combined with AR in a 1:10 ratio respectively by stirring with a rod until a homogeneous solution was obtained. Then, the solution of BC and AR is placed at the end of a manual extruder (EM) polyester syringe (PET) of 1 cm in diameter, 12 cm in length and capacity for 10mL, it is manually compressed while at the other end there is an orifice of 1mm in diameter through which the solution is extruded producing BCTF, then it is dried in the environment for 30 min at a temperature of 29.2 °C and relative humidity (RH) 42%. The data provided has a reliability of 95% ($p > 0.05$) using past 4 statistical software. Concluding that it has a great RTD capacity with a statistical average (139.28°) (CV = 3.22), while the E has a statistical average of stretching (18. 38 mm), (25.15%) in relation to its length (CV = 50.97), opposite case occurs with resistance (N) (1.58 N) (CV = 29.02) decreases N in relation to its titer (T) (g/m) where BCTF samples acquire good flexibility and stretching capacities when mixed with AR.

Keywords: Textile filament · Cellulose · Bamboo · Floating root · Extruder

1 Introduction

The study deals with a process of elaboration of continuous filament regenerated by extrusion from bamboo cellulose (Angustifolia), resin and determine the behavior to the resistance and elongation of its structure with applications in floating root crops. The process starts from pulverized bamboo culms with particle size of 1mm from which the cellulose base can be extracted in different concentrations. For this process of manufacturing biodegradable regenerated fibers, cellulose is obtained as raw material, which is, a natural organic polymer most abundant on Earth and exists widely in the cell wall of green plants and algae. In addition, some species of bacteria secrete it to form biofilms [23].

M. Botto-Tobar et al. (Eds.): ICAT 2022, CCIS 1756, pp. 172–182, 2023.
https://doi.org/10.1007/978-3-031-24971-6_13

One of the promising materials is polymer cellulose which has been widely studied for chemical and mechanical modification to obtain cellulose based nanomaterials due to its diverse properties, availability in nature, biodegradability and non-toxicity [17]. Bamboo cellulose has long been widely used as a reinforcement for polymers or template material for composite manufacturing due to its high strength-to-weight ratio and biodegradability that performs better in mechanical properties and thermal stability [12]. Bamboo is now widely used in construction, paper making, textiles, furniture and other fields due to its renewable process, fast growth, high strength, high yield and easy processing [7]. And because of the demand for cellulose fibers in the near future and its main source is wood pulp, cellulose was isolated from six agro-industrial wastes: corn cob, corn husk, grape stalk, pomegranate peel, arbutus pomace and bean pods the corn cob cellulose showed the highest extraction yield (26%) [21]. To extract the cellulose find procedures from the bamboo fiber (50 g) was immersed in a 17.5% sodium hydroxide solution (300 ml) and heated for 3 h with constant stirring to dissolve the pectin and hemicellulose. The mixture was filtered and rinsed separately with deionized water [5]. While using a similar mechanical extrusion process to improve the mechanical and thermal properties of polypropylene (PP) matrix composites, ultrafine bamboo carbon (UFBC) was introduced into PP by twin-screw extrusion and injection molding [25]. Also, the antibacterial activity with blended bamboo and cotton fibers was qualitatively evaluated. It was found that the incorporation of regenerated bamboo fiber did not drastically increase the antibacterial property of the resulting fabric. In fact, a limited bacteriostatic property was observed in the case of the sample containing up to 75% bamboo fiber [2]. Also bamboo fiber was treated with alkali and bleached to produce cellulose, which was then modified with ethylene and propylene oxides and CuO nanoparticles, the cellulosic material impregnated with CuO nanoparticles exhibited the highest stability, The raw bamboo fiber appeared as stacked porous nanotubes [5]. In addition, it can be mixed in the dispersion state of polystyrene/CF composites produced by two different processing methods, a well-dispersed CF cellulose filament network was obtained, while from 5 to 15% by weight. CF% were agglomerated, leading to a network of agglomerated fibers for concentrations higher than 15 wt.% [6]. Meanwhile keratin filaments have been regenerated from white duck feathers by effectively restoring disulfide crosslinks using a dithiol reducing agent and the tenacity and elongation at break were 160.7 MPa and 14%, respectively [13]. The use of renewable biomass cellulose in the treatment of heavy metal ion (HMI) pollution is one of the most important and attractive strategies, as it simultaneously satisfies sustainable development and solves increasing environmental problems [27]. Regenerated cellulose aerogels (RCA), the typical eco-friendly sustainable 3D cellulose products, have numerous merits including high surface area, high porosity, low density, high mechanical strength, 3D network structure and abundant oxygen-containing groups, which make them ideal candidates as eco-friendly. Matrices to support various active nanomaterials for the development of novel functional nanocomposites [23]. The cellulose nanofibrils (CNF) obtained in the combined process of enzymatic hydrolysis and grinding (EG-CNF), the strength of the CNF network and pulp properties were critical factors affecting the mechanical strength of CNF-enhanced paper [26]. In this study, a new type of regenerated cellulose fiber composite reinforced with cellulose nano fibrils (CNFs) and nano silica (nano-SiO2).

Adding 1% CNFs and 1% nano-SiO2 to pulp/AMIMCl improved the tensile strength of the cellulose composite by 47.46% [24]. New raw materials such as cellulose algae exist as a novel, biocompatible and environmentally friendly biomaterial, with structural variations that hold great potential for various biomedical applications, while promoting aquaculture and the green agenda [3]. When continuous yarns and viscose (rayon) filaments were treated with polymeric diphenylmethane diisocyanate (pMDI) or a pMDI-based hardener for polyurethane resins, the treatment resulted in a reduced molecular weight of cellulose, presumably due to hydrolytic cleavage caused by the hydrochloric acid produced as an impurity in pMDI [20]. By bamboo/resin bonding significantly influences the preparation and final properties of bamboo scrimber composites (BSC), with different molecular weights of brominated phenol-formaldehyde resin [15]. Also paper mill sludge (PMS) is a cellulosic by-product dissolved in an ionic liquid, 1-ethyl-3-methylimidazolium diethylphosphate, with the aid of a co-solvent dimethyl sulfoxide (DMSO), centrifuged into continuous filaments for textile production and the mechanical properties of paper sludge are competitive with commercial viscose [1]. For the spinning of cellulosic fibers, 1-ethyl-3-methylimidazolium octanoate ([C2C1im] [Oc]) was dissolved in ionic liquid (IL) using a thin film evaporator in a continuous process, the fibers were spun by dry jet wet spinning and an extruder instead of a spinning pump [22]. In addition, hexamethylolmelamine was used as a crosslinking agent to graft 3-(dimethylphosphono)-N-methylolpropionamide (MDPA) ontoLyocellfibers in a post-treatment process to reduce flammability. The processing conditions on the mechanical properties and P content of the fibers were examined [14]. In addition, these continuous yarns and viscose (rayon) filaments were treated with polymeric diphenyl methane di isocyanate (pMDI) or a pMDI-based hardener for polyurethane resins [17]. With these methods of obtaining regenerated filaments, the objective of the research is to obtain extruded filament based on bamboo cellulose and resin for possible application in hydroponic crops as a biodegradable floating medium, being, soilless crops an agricultural alternative to marginal soils with low water availability, Hydroponics has worldwide high productivity per unit area, water saving and crop cycles throughout the year [9]. As an example, lettuce (Lactuca sativa L.) is a leafy vegetable grown in nutrient solution in two growing seasons and lettuces are grown in a hydroponic floating root system [8]. This procedure is applied because of a shortage of O2 which can be detrimental to plants. As when rice is flooded and grown in deep water with dysfunctional roots in the soil, the root tip has no diffusion barriers and receives O2 from the stem and flood water, which improves root aeration [11].

1.1 Methodology

The methods used are based on methodologies according to bamboo cellulose (BC) continuous filament (CF) analysis standards to determine the tensile strength (N) and elongation (E) parameters of bamboo cellulose textile filament (BCTF) and anionic resin (AR) by applying the standards:

– ISO 13934–2 (2014): Tensile strength and elongation.
– ISO 2313 Standard: Double recovery

1.2 Materials and Equipment

The materials and equipment were used to achieve the formation and obtainment of BCTF:

– Bamboo cellulose base particle size 1 mm
– Anionic patching resin
– Glass container
– Wooden stirring rod
– Extruder (10 mL syringe)
– Laser thermometer
– Dynamometer (Titan 5)
– Double recovery equipment (SN 150/2106)

1.3 Process

For the selection of the samples to characterize the BCTF with AR and determine its acquired properties, it was from the raw material of bamboo culm "Angustifolia" obtained from the tropical zone with a temperature of 15 to 22 °C at an altitude of 1639 m above sea level, using the process flow chart shown (see Fig. 1).

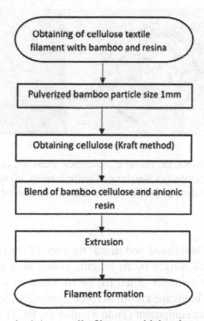

Fig. 1. Process for obtaining textile filament with bamboo cellulose and resin.

Bamboo stalk was pulverized into 1 mm by means of a circular disc adhered sand-paper and its subsequent obtaining of bamboo cellulose base by the alkaline method by means of sodium hydroxide flakes. 2 g of BC obtained by hand are placed in a glass container and mixed with 20 g of anionic resin AR resin in a 1:10 ratio of BC and AR respectively, stirring with a wooden rod until a homogeneous solution was obtained. Then, the solution of BC and AR is placed at the end of a manual extruder EM PET polyester syringe of 1 cm in diameter, 12 cm in length and capacity for 10 mL, immediately compressed manually at room temperature 29.2 °C and relative humidity (RH) 42% while at the other end there is an orifice of 1mm in diameter through which the solution is extruded producing BCTF textile filament, then it is dried at room temperature for 30 min at 29.2 °C as the 30 min' elapse, the filament acquires a dark brown color due to the drying and oxidation process of the resin until reaching its stability (see Fig. 2).

Fig. 2. Materials and equipment. (a) Balance, container, glass jar, resin and bamboo cellulose. (b) Weighing of bamboo cellulose. (c) Weighing of anionic resin. (d) Bamboo resin and cellulose. (e) Agitation of bamboo cellulose and resin. (f) Formation of extruded filament (g) Measurement of filament temperature.

After the BCTF was stabilized and dried, its titer (T) was determined in number (ktex), that is, dividing its weight by its length, giving as a result its T in g/m. This titration was used for the diameter of the BCTF of 1 mm to which it was extruded, in addition, the resistance to breakage known as force applied before breaking was found by means of the dynamometer equipment (Titan 5), also the BCTF samples were submitted to the double recovery equipment (SN 150/2106) to check its recovery to double (see Fig. 3).

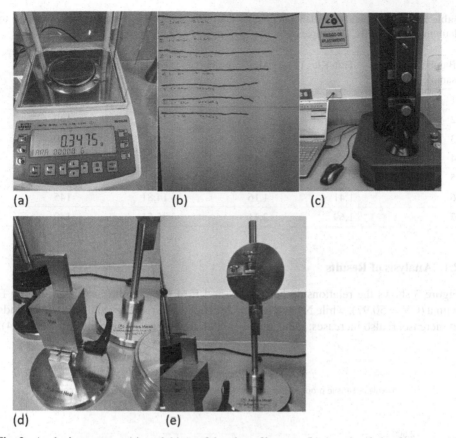

Fig. 3. Analysis process. (a) weighing of bamboo filament. (b) length of the filament. (c) Dynamometer equipment (Titan 5). (d) Recovery equipment at double compression (SN 150/2106). (e) Recovery angle measuring equipment.

2   Results and Discussion

With the seven samples obtained in the laboratory tests, the behavior of the BCTF was established by means of the titer (T), force (N), elongation (E) and recovery to doubling (RTD) tests indicated in Table 1.

The data found from the BCTF were entered and analyzed in the statistical software Past 4 with the purpose of validating the data of the seven samples analyzed in the parameters T, N, E and RTD, through the variance and normality test of the data that influenced the decision making, finding that the distributions of the data obtained are within a normality and reliability of 95% (P > 0.05), with no significant differences between their data.

Table 1. Data obtained from laboratory tests: titer (T), force (N), elongation (E), recovery to doubling (RTD) of BCTF samples.

Bamboo filament sample	Title Ktex (T)	Maximum Force (N)	Elongation at Max. Force (%)	Recovery to doubles (°)
1	1,44	1,99	33,87	130
2	1,46	1,13	16,32	140
3	1,49	1,17	12,02	140
4	1,54	1,44	18,38	140
5	1,37	2,07	45,14	140
6	1,41	1,16	14,81	145
7	1,69	2,11	35,51	140

2.1 Analysis of Results

Figure 3 shows the relationship between N and E of the samples analyzed, finding E with a (CV = 50.97), while N has a (CV = 28.92), it is also observed that while N tends to increase, E also increases, indicating that N is directly proportional to E (see Fig. 4).

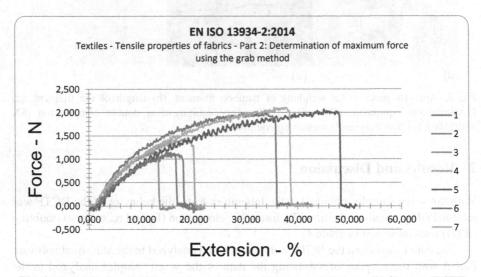

Fig. 4. Ratio of strength (N) and elongation (E) of bamboo cellulose textile filament (BCTF)

In the figure matrix plot it can be observed the similarities of the BCTF samples and in the findings it is found that T (CV = 7.08), and N (CV = 28.92) are very similar and are very related to each other respectively, while the elongation has variations between its samples (CV = 50.97), opposite case happens with RTD are very similar (CV = 3.22), there is a significant difference with the rest of parameters, while in E decreases, but increases its (CV = 50.97), surely this variation happened by its manual way of extruding where it is not possible to control its pressure in a uniform way to obtain its title in relation to the weight and its mass, Therefore, increasing the resin content to bamboo is important to improve the extrusion capacity of the bamboo mass. Furthermore, it was revealed that the pre-compression treatment effectively improves the resin permeability and formability of the resin impregnated bamboo volume PF [18]. Likewise, the title is found with minimum variation (CV = 7.08) showing that there is not much variation in relation to its N (CV = 28.92) (see Fig. 5).

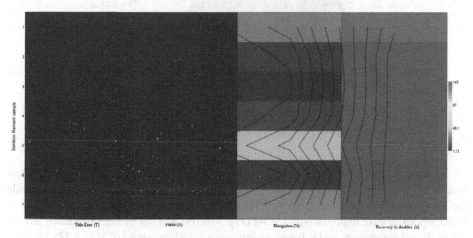

Fig. 5. Similarity of samples in relation to titer (T), force (N), elongation (E) and recovery to doubles (RTD)

In the ternary plot and scatter plot we find the relationship of the analyzed parameters of N, E and RTD, finding that the RTD (CV = 3.22) of the samples are similar, but is significantly different (p < 0.05) and has greater influence compared to the rest of the parameters N and E, in addition the RTD also has good relationship with the E (p > 0.05) are significantly similar despite having a (CV = 50.97) this elongation variation originates the resin used and at the same time helps RTD in its flexibility, phthalonitrile (PN) oligomeric resins are desirable materials for many high temperature applications because they show good structural performance over a wide temperature range, have low thermal conductivity and water absorption [4], while N (CV = 28.92) is inversely proportional to RTD and E, indicating the main component that most influences BCTF the RTD and consecutively E, as the molecular weight of resin increased, the water resistance of BSC gradually increased, flexural performance and compressive strength gradually decreased, shear strength [15], Furthermore it coincides with the shape memory property by calculating the shape recovery ratio for 60 min at 37 °C. Indicating that TC-85 photo-curable resin can constantly apply light force, due to its flexibility and visco-elastic properties [10], and with reactive resins, it was found that the parameters for the optimized processes at maximum tear strength were with, bath ratio 12.22:1, resin concentration 183 g/L, cure temperature as 140 °C and cure time as 12 min 20 s. [16] (see Fig. 6).

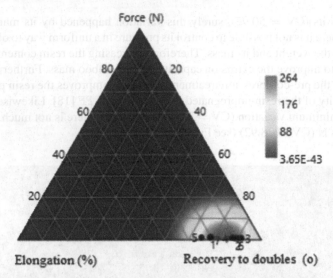

Fig. 6. Incidence of N, E, RTD principal component on CBTF formation.

In the trend and bar graph it is observed that the N found in the samples is very low with a slight tendency to increase (CV = 28.92) being very similar (p > 0.05), while the T of the extruded filaments (p > 0.05) remain stable with a slight variation (CV = 7.08), opposite case happens with the RTD (p < 0.05) and has greater influence among the analyzed parameters and is found maintaining a uniform trend (CV = 3.22), keeping a slight correlation with E (p > 0.05) and slight variations between them (CV = 50.97) with a tendency to remain stable, coincide with the fiber cross section shapes on the bending behavior of the continuous yarns compared with the bending behavior of the

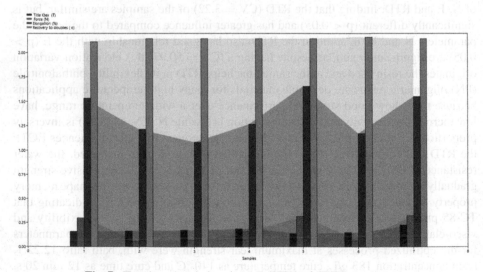

Fig. 7. Trends and variations in N, E, RTD and CBTF parameters.

fabric to study the effect of the cross section shapes and remained constant [19] (see Fig. 7).

3 Conclusions

In the formation of bamboo cellulose textile filament (BCTF) with anionic resin (AR) for possible applications in hydroponic crops, it was found that it has a great capacity of recovery to doubles (RTD) with a statistical average of (139.28°) in a range from 0 to 180° means very high with (CV = 3. 22), while the elongation has a statistical average of stretching (18.38 mm), (25.15%) in relation to its length and (CV = 50.97), opposite case occurs with the breaking strength (1.58 N) and (CV = 29.02) low resistance in relation to its titer (T) (g/m). It was concluded that the (BCTF) samples acquire good flexibility and stretching capacities when mixed with anionic AR resin.

Thanks

A cordial thanks to the North Technical University, textile career for financing and providing the laboratory equipment to conclude the research.

References

1. Adu, C., et al.: Continuous and sustainable cellulose filaments from ionic liquid dissolved paper sludge nanofibres. J. Clean. Prod. 280 (2021). https://doi.org/10.1016/j.jclepro.2020. 124503
2. Ali, M., et al.: An investigation into the antibacterial properties of bamboo/cotton blended fabric and potential limitations of the test method AATCC 147. J. Nat. Fibers. 18(1), 51–58 (2021). https://doi.org/10.1080/15440478.2019.1612305
3. Bar-Shai, N., et al.: Seaweed cellulose scaffolds derived from green macroalgae for tissue engineering. Sci. Rep. 11, 1 (2021). https://doi.org/10.1038/s41598-021-90903-2
4. Butler, T., et al.: Molecular weight effects on the processing, thermal, and mechanical properties of oligomeric bisphenol a phthalonitrile resins. In: Anderson, A.K., et al. (eds.) International SAMPE Technical Conference. Soc. for the Advancement of Material and Process Engineering (2019). https://doi.org/10.33599/nasampe/s.19.1471
5. Elemike, E.E., Onwudiwe, D., Ivwurie, W.: Structural and thermal characterization of cellulose and copper oxide modified cellulose obtained from bamboo plant fibre. SN Applied Sciences 2(10), 1–8 (2020). https://doi.org/10.1007/s42452-020-03503-6
6. Genoyer, J., et al.: Effect of the addition of cellulose filaments on the relaxation behavior of thermoplastics. J. Rheol. (N. Y. N. Y). 65(5), 779–789 (2021). https://doi.org/10.1122/8.000 0228
7. Hao, X., et al.: The effect of oil heat treatment on biological, mechanical and physical properties of bamboo. J. Wood Sci. 67(1), 1–14 (2021). https://doi.org/10.1186/s10086-021-019 59-7
8. Lara-Izaguirre, A.Y., et al.: Growth and NO3- accumulation in hydroponic lettuce with nitrate/ammonium ratios in two cultivation seasons. Rev. Fitotec. Mex. 42(1), 21–30 (2019). https://doi.org/10.35196/RFM.2019.1.21-29
9. Lazo, R.P., Gonzabay, J.Q.: Economic analysis of hydroponic lettuce under floating root system in semi-arid climate. Granja. 31(1), 121–133 (2020). https://doi.org/10.17163/LGR. N31.2020.09

10. Lee, S.Y., et al.: Thermo-mechanical properties of 3D printed photocurable shape memory resin for clear aligners. Sci. Rep. **12**, 1 (2022). https://doi.org/10.1038/s41598-022-09831-4

11. Lin, C., et al.: Oxygen in the air and oxygen dissolved in the floodwater both sustain growth of aquatic adventitious roots in rice. J. Exp. Bot. **72**(5), 1879–1890 (2021). https://doi.org/10.1093/jxb/eraa542

12. Lin, Q., et al.: Effects of extraction methods on morphology, structure and properties of bamboo cellulose. Ind. Crops Prod. **169** (2021). https://doi.org/10.1016/j.indcrop.2021.113640

13. Mi, X., et al.: Transferring feather wastes to ductile keratin filaments towards a sustainable poultry industry. Waste Manag. **115**, 65–73 (2020). https://doi.org/10.1016/j.wasman.2020.07.022

14. Peng, K., et al.: Flame-retardant treatment of Lyocell fibers and effects on various fiber properties. Fire Mater. **46**(2), 487–495 (2022). https://doi.org/10.1002/fam.2993

15. Rao, F., et al.: Influence of resin molecular weight on bonding interface, water resistance, and mechanical properties of bamboo scrimber composite. Constr. Build. Mater. **292** (2021). https://doi.org/10.1016/j.conbuildmat.2021.123458

16. Rim, C., et al.: Optimization of the pre-application process of a reactive resin before direct dyeing for imparting reserve effects on Elastane/cotton pant garments. Alexandria Eng. J. **61**(12), 9365–9376 (2022). https://doi.org/10.1016/j.aej.2022.02.048

17. Sayyed, A.J., et al.: Cellulose-based nanomaterials for water and wastewater treatments: a review. J. Environ. Chem. Eng. **9**, 6 (2021). https://doi.org/10.1016/j.jece.2021.106626

18. Seki, M., Yashima, Y., Miki, T., Kiryu, T., Tanaka, S., Kanayama, K.: Effects of resin content and precompression treatment on bulk bamboo extrusion. Int.J. Mater. Form. **13**(3), 331–339 (2019). https://doi.org/10.1007/s12289-019-01497-0

19. Singh, M.K., Behera, B.K.: Effect of fibre cross-sectional shape on bending behaviour of yarns and fabrics; part I. J. Text. Inst. **113**(5), 810–823 (2025). https://doi.org/10.1080/00405000.2021.1906488

20. Ungerer, B., et al.: Chemical and physical interactions of regenerated cellulose yarns and isocyanate-based matrix systems. Sci. Rep. **11**, 1 (2021). https://doi.org/10.1038/s41598-021-91115-4

21. Vallejo, M., et al.: Recovery and evaluation of cellulose from agroindustrial residues of corn, grape, pomegranate, strawberry-tree fruit and fava. Bioresour. Bioprocess. **8**(1), 1–12 (2021). https://doi.org/10.1186/s40643-021-00377-3

22. Vocht, M.P., et al.: High-performance cellulosic filament fibers prepared via dry-jet wet spinning from ionic liquids. Cellulose **28**(5), 3055–3067 (2021). https://doi.org/10.1007/s10570-021-03697-x

23. Wan, C., et al.: Functional nanocomposites from sustainable regenerated cellulose aerogels: a review. Chem. Eng. J. **359**, 459–475 (2019). https://doi.org/10.1016/j.cej.2018.11.115

24. Xue, Y., et al.: High-strength regenerated cellulose fiber reinforced with cellulose nanofibril and nanosilica. Nanomaterials **11**, 10 (2021). https://doi.org/10.3390/nano11102664

25. Yao, W., et al.: Fabrication and properties of polypylene matrix composites reinforced by ultrafine bamboo-char. Fuhe Cailiao Xuebao/Acta Mater. Compos. Sin. **34**(12), 2661–2667 (2017). https://doi.org/10.13801/j.cnki.fhclxb.20170314.004

26. Zeng, J., et al.: Cellulose nanofibrils manufactured by various methods with application as paper strength additives. Sci. Rep. **11**, 1 (2021). https://doi.org/10.1038/s41598-021-91420-y

27. Zhao, N.-D., et al.: Fabrication of cellulose@Mg(OH)2 composite filter via interfacial bonding and its trapping effect for heavy metal ions. Chem. Eng. J. **426** (2021). https://doi.org/10.1016/j.cej.2021.130812

Development of a Settlementmeter for the Control and Monitoring of Embankments Through the Use of Artificial Intelligence

Tania Gissela Casa-Toctaguano, Byron Omar Morales-Muñoz, and Theofilos Toulkeridis[✉] [iD]

Universidad de las Fuerzas Armadas ESPE, Sangolquí, Ecuador
ttoulkeridis@espe.edu.ec

Abstract. The current study presents a methodology to monitor the behavior of embankments in addition to the development and implementation of an on-site settlementmeter in a given study area. This equipment is a portable system of easy installation, connection and operation that fulfills the specific function of monitor the vertical movement (settlement) of the soil in embankments. The electronic system includes two sensors, the operating equipment and an anchor spider. The sensor captures the orthogonal distance in millimeters or centimeters, from the reference point where it is placed to the bottom of the ground and is coupled to the anchor spider, the same ones that are inserted into a hole with a diameter of 4 in. that a once the spider plates are anchored to the ground. Through an LCD screen that is part of the operating equipment, the respective value of the length can be manually observed and recorded, thus initiating the control and monitoring of possible progressive settlements in a previously established time interval. Each of the elements of this geotechnical instrumentation is secured in a protective casing made of PLA material to prevent any damage from climate change.

Palabras clave: Settlementmeter · Sensors · Operation equipment · Anchor spider · LCD screen · Control · Monitoring

1 Introduction

Knowing the risks and reliability of highway embankments has led man to develop different techniques, methods and procedures that allows a greater certainty about the causes, consequences and possible effects of failures in earth structures in the face of some variations within the conditions that they can occur in their environment either due to the construction of works or due to natural phenomena [1–13]. In order to ensure the good condition and behavior of the embankments, it is essential to comply with a set of activities within the stages of the project, both in planning and execution and throughout its useful life [14–17]. Thus starting with the geotechnical study, selection of materials, geometric design, construction techniques, execution and evolutionary supervision of its performance [18–20].

M. Botto-Tobar et al. (Eds.): ICAT 2022, CCIS 1756, pp. 183–195, 2023.
https://doi.org/10.1007/978-3-031-24971-6_14

During this pre and post construction process the action of the soil triggers an important role of stability so that the embankment is kept in optimal conditions of use but the lack of control and monitoring of settlements in its infrastructure after its construction has caused mistakes to keep them in good condition that, when controlled at a tolerable level, can improve their performance, reduce repair costs and avoid catastrophic scenes that present economic, material or human losses [21–23].

Therefore, the implementation of such equipment performs an efficient and timely method for the evaluation of significant variables by quantitatively recording in millimeters or centimeters the vertical settlements in real time due to different actions on the ground, thus allowing to know the deformation-time relationship of the embankment, which through graphical statistical analysis methods for their pertinent interpretation.

2   Materials, Methods and Installation Procedure

2.1   Materials

The devices that compose all the geotechnical instrumentation are measurement sensors, operating equipment and anchor spider as illustrated in Figs. 1 and 2. The corresponding operation equipment records the orthogonal measurements from the point where the sensor is placed with the anchor spider in the embankment drilling, thus initiating the control and monitoring of vertical settlements, see (see Fig. 3 and 4). Hereby, the devices that compose it are a 16×2 LCD screen. It is a small device with a liquid crystal display that has two rows of sixteen characters each, which is used to display alphanumeric information visually [24] (see Fig. 3). The specifications are a JANSANE of 16×2, a Blue LCD screen, a IIC I2C module interface adapter for Raspberry pi 2 Pack equipment and a display area size of 6.5×1.5 cm.

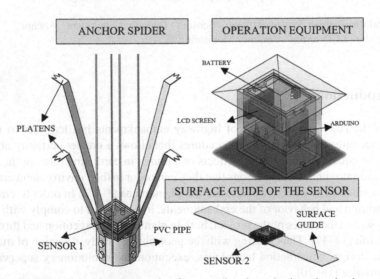

Fig. 1. Geotechnical instrumentation for control and monitoring of embankments.

Fig. 2. Implementation and supply of a settlementmeter on site.

Fig. 3. 16x2 LCD Screen (upper left; Arduino (upper right); Lithium battery (lower left); Jumpers (lower center); Wire AWG 18 (lower right) [25]

Furthermore, there is included an Arduino (Arduino R3 CON ATMEGA328 DIP with USB cable), which is a board with 13 digital signals that is able function as both input and output of a microcontroller that are programmed by an open platform algorithm [26]. There is also a lithium battery, which supplies power. This battery has a minimum capacity of 1000 mAh, a weight of 97 g, a size of 74 × 34 × 21 mm and a XT60

Connector. The Jumpers create its own circuit on a board, therefore no soldering is required [27]. It ranges of approximate 5.8 in./5.8 cm. Finally, there is also an AWG 18 cable. It is a cable (18 gauge wires) that connects the different electronic devices, see (see Fig. 3 and 4).

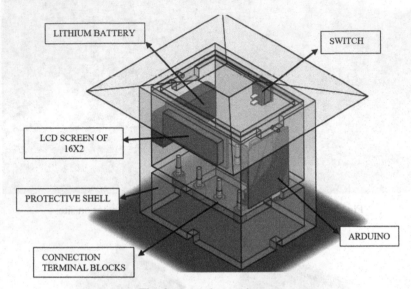

Fig. 4. Operation equipment

Additionally, there are the settlementmeter measurement sensors that capture the orthogonal measurement in cm or mm from the reference point where it is placed (see Fig. 5). It contains a Sensor HC-SR04. This electronic instrument that uses ultrasound measures distance up to 450 cm [28]. The dimension of the sensor are of about 45 * 20 * 15 mm, with a Sensor precision of ± 3 mm and a Minimum waiting time for the calculation between one measurement and the start of another 20 ms (recommended 50 ms).

Fig. 5. HC-SR04 sensor (left); Seat meter measurement sensors (right).

Finally there is the anchor spider with plates for the floor walls. This instrument is used to guide the sensor inside the drill (see Fig. 6 and 7). It is composed of 2-in. PVC pipe, which allows fixing the steel plates to build the anchoring spider (see Fig. 8). It has the size of 2 in. and a height of 5 cm, made of PVC. The screws and nuts are elements to secure the position of the steel plates, with sizes of 7/8 in. There is also the Steel Plate is a component that will serve as an anchor in the soil walls at a certain depth of excavation. It has a height of 33 cm, with blades at the upper end and a thickness of 2 mm (see Fig. 8).

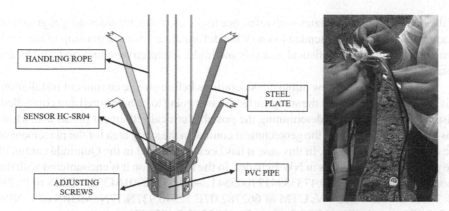

Fig. 6. Spider with anchoring plates for the walls of the floor, in situ.

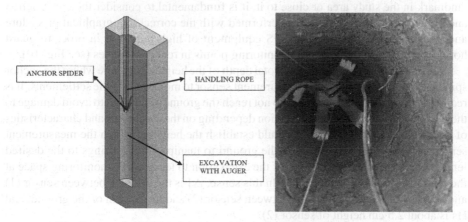

Fig. 7. Installation of the anchor spider in the depth of the ground, in situ.

2.2 Methods

The equipment conducts a progressive evaluation of the behavior of the embankment in terms of its vertical movement in the previously established time interval to record its possible settlements and its horizontal monitoring will be guarded based on the control

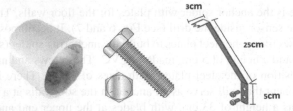

Fig. 8. 2-inch PVC pipe (left); Bolts and nuts (center); Steel platen (right)

of the real location coordinates with reference to the cairn that includes the geographical plaque. In this way, it is intended to know the deformation-time relationship of the earth structure, that through statistical analysis methods, interpretive values and graphs are obtained.

However, there are a few initial considerations before on-site equipment installation. It is fundamental to delimit the study surface that is going to be monitored and controlled. Visually and strategically determining the possible critical settlement points and where it is convenient to perform the geotechnical control in the study area for the placement of the equipment (see Fig. 9), In this case it has been considered in the Quinindé canton of the province of Esmeraldas in NW Ecuador. In the road section it is encountered with the coordinates: Lat Long of 0.4733894177005541, −79.53722901642323; DMS of 0° 28' 24.2" N | 79° 32' 14.02" W; UTM of 662782.07E 52340.937N 17N; MGRS of 17NPA 62782 52341 and CRS of EPSG:4326 -79.5372283 0.4733853.

In case of not having the materialization of a geographical point with a plaque and landmark in the study area or close to it, it is fundamental to consider the construction and obtaining a geospatial control performed with the correct topographical procedure and with the implementation of GPS equipment of high precision in order to guard horizontal displacements and the monitoring points in real coordinates (see Fig. 10).

There is also the definition of the total depth of the height of the hole where the anchor spider is going to enter with the measurement sensor to monitor possible settlements. It is recommended that the excavations do not reach the groundwater level to avoid damage to the devices. However it is a free decision depending on the conditions and characteristics of the ground (see Fig. 11). One should establish the height at which the measurement sensor is going to be submerged in the ground to manipulate the strings to the desired length, considering the total depth of the excavation to leave a free monitoring space at the bottom of the hole (see Fig. 11). In this sense, $\Delta 1$ is the distance between sensor (1) and sensor (2); $\Delta 2$ is the distance between sensor (2) and the bottom of the ground, and Hs is about 2.5 cm height of sensor (2).

There are some additional parameters to be measured and controlled with the Sttlementmeter. Although it is true that a single piece of equipment has two measurement sensors, it is possible to place them in different styles depending on the professional's decision, however these two options are recommended. The first is the measurement of vertical displacements (settlements) in the ground at various points in the same horizontal direction (see Fig. 12). The second is the measurement of vertical displacements (settlements) in the ground at various points on the same vertical level (see Fig. 13).

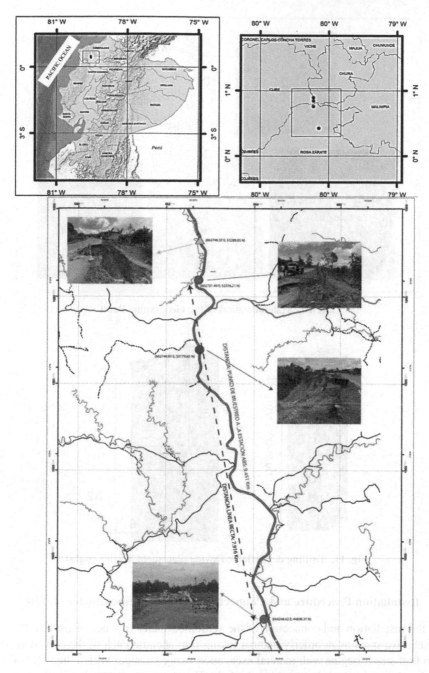

Fig. 9. Study area and installation point location

Fig. 10. Materialization of the Geographic Point

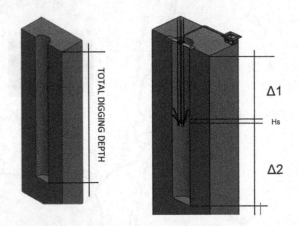

Fig. 11. Drilling depth (left); Device placement heights (right)

2.3 Installation Procedure and Connection of the Settlementmeter on Site

For the installation and connection of the settlementmeter it is necessary to follow six consecutive steps in an orderly manner taking into account each of the considerations. As a first step it begins with manual excavation using an auger with a diameter of 4 in. previously established the depth of the hole. For the second step, before entering the anchoring spider with the sensor, it is recommended to identify the connection cables of the sensors to the operating equipment where the measurement values will be reflected through the LCD screen. Both positive and negative devices and in turn receivers and transmitters. In the third step, once the connection cables have been identified, the ends

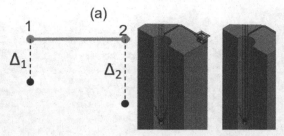

Fig. 12. Measurement of vertical displacements (settlements) of the soil in the horizontal direction.

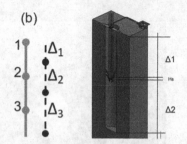

Fig. 13. Measurement of vertical displacements (settlements) of the soil in the vertical direction.

of the plates are joined with the rope, making a shoelace-type knot with only one end so that when the sensor is inserted with the spider at the required depth, pull said rope and thus the action of the plates will be released under pressure against the walls of the floor and will remain anchored to them. It needs to be noted, as it is recommended not to over-tighten the cord knot to make it easier to instantly untie.

For the fourth step, considering the strings found at the ends of the PVC pipe, the entrance of the sensor is directed and manipulated with the anchoring spider up to the established depth, taking care that the connection cables are not disconnected, which is important that they dive at the same time. In the fifth and sixth steps, once the sensor is immersed in the hole, we pull the rope from the ends of the plates where the blades are located to obtain the desired anchorage in the walls and consequently, once the monitoring system is installed inside the hole, the operating equipment is turned on to display the LCD screen and record the first orthogonal reference measurements that will serve as a starting point for the next taking of values in the interval of set time, being either daily, weekly, monthly or as the custodian professional considers it to control the behavior of the embankment. This is freely chosen in order to obtain progressive records and depending on the conditions in which the earth structure is found.

3 Results and Discussion

After the understanding about the operation, the supply and installation of the settlement-meter, the development of the methodology for evaluating the behavior of the embankment over time is ensured, which will allow, at a technical level, to identify unstable

Fig. 14. Field site (upper part). Entry of the sensor with the spider with the manipulation of the strings at the ends (central left). Spider anchored to soil walls for embankment monitoring (central central part); Connection of the sensors to the operating equipment (central right); Screen display for data logging (lower part)

embankments or those close to being unstable according to the risk they present and thus be able to implement corrective or maintenance actions in road sections of the first order and between other earth structures or civil works. The measurement results according to the time interval that are recorded are part of a database system that will work efficiently and in a timely manner according to the number of cumulative values that are obtained by future actions on the embankment where the analysis and interpretation of the numerical information is made based on a growth trend that indicates a clear interpretation of deformations in the event of a progressive failure in the soil and that under this processing of data collected through statistical methods, the relationship between deformation-time will hereby be clearly identified (see Fig. 14).

4 Conclusions

The management of the equipment and measurement system is easy to handle. This instrumentation will allow making correct decisions on pavement structures under construction, maintenance or repair. In addition, being controlled at a tolerable level will avoid possible reversible consequences in the event that an embankment fails.

The implementation of the settlementmetric structure control and monitoring equipment for an instability level classification evaluation is designed to reflect the potential risk created by the various factors based on the severity that they present in an embankment of a highway section. However it should not be used as a mathematical model to predict the probability of a very severe failure in a study area, rather than to manage and, with the information obtained, give solution plans.

The database and monitoring follow-up is part of a system that will perform efficiently and optimally, according to the number of settlement values that are collected according to the future behavior of the embankment that will be evaluated with interpretive graphic and statistical analysis methods.

The installation costs of the embankment settlement measurement equipment with destructive drilling with an auger is $525.06, which includes the materialization of the landmark with the geographic plate. The supply and preparation of the equipment has a price of $118.86 and the monitoring by a professional for each data collection is estimated at a value of $15, thus giving a total of $643.93 in early 2022.

References

1. Christian, J.T.: Geotechnical engineering reliability: How well do we know what we are doing? J. Geotech. Geoenviron. Eng. 130(10), 985–1003 (2004)
2. De Mello, V.F.: Reflections on design decisions of practical significance to embankment dams. Géotechnique 27(3), 281–355 (1977)
3. Galvão, N., Matos, J.C., Oliveira, D.V.: Human Error-Induced Risk in Reinforced Concrete Bridge Engineering. J. Perform. Constr. Facil. 35(4), 04021026 (2021)
4. Rodriguez, F., Toulkeridis, T., Sandoval, W., Padilla, O., Mato, F.: Economic risk assessment of Cotopaxi volcano, Ecuador, in case of a future lahar emplacement. Natural Hazards 85(1), 605–618 (2017)

5. Sandoval-Erazo, W., Toulkeridis, T., Rodríguez-Espinosa, F., Mora, M.M.: Velocity and time of concentration of a basin–a renewed approach applied in the Rio Grande Basin, Ecuador. In: IOP Conference Series: Earth and Environmental Science, vol. 191, no. 1, p. 012117. IOP Publishing (October 2018)
6. Poma, P., Usca, M., FdzPolanco, M., GarciaVillacres, A., Toulkeridis, T.: Landslide and environmental risk from oil spill due to the rupture of SOTE and OCP pipelines, San Rafael Falls, Amazon Basin, Ecuador. Int. J. Adv. Sci. Eng. Inf. Technol. 11(4), 1558–1566 (2021)
7. Segura-Alcívar, M., Rodriguez-Espinoza, F., Toulkeridis, T.: Potential risk analysis of fuel storages in central Quito, Ecuador. In: Proceedings of the International Conference on Natural Hazards and Infrastructure 2019, 2nd International Conference on Natural Hazards and Infrastructure, ICONHIC 2019; Chania; Greece; 23 June 2019 through 26 June 2019; Code 257429 (2019)
8. Matheus-Medina, A.S., Toulkeridis, T., Padilla-Almeida, O., Cruz-D´Howitt, M., Chunga, K.: Evaluation of the tsunami vulnerability in the coastal Ecuadorian tourist centers of the peninsulas of Bahia de Caráquez and Salinas. Science of Tsunami Hazards 38(3), 175–209 (2018)
9. Matheus Medina, A.S., Cruz D´Howitt, M., Padilla Almeida, O., Toulkeridis, T., Haro, A.G.: Enhanced vertical evacuation applications with geomatic tools for tsunamis in Salinas, Ecuador. Sci. Tsunami Hazards 35(3), 189–213 (2016)
10. Navas, L., Caiza, P., Toulkeridis, T.: An evaluated comparison between the molecule and steel framing construction systems – Implications for the seismic vulnerable Ecuador. Malaysian Construct. Res. J. 26(3), 87–109 (2018)
11. Toulkeridis, T.: The Evaluation of unexpected results of a seismic hazard applied to a modern hydroelectric center in central Ecuador. J. Struct. Eng. 43(4), 373–380 (2016)
12. Zafrir Vallejo, R., et al.: Numerical probability modeling of past, present and future landslide occurrences in northern Quito, Ecuador – Economic implications and risk assessments. In: 2018 5th International Conference on eDemocracy and eGovernment, ICEDEG 2018 8372318, pp. 117–125 (2018)
13. Jaramillo Castelo, C.A., Padilla Almeida, O., D´Howitt, C., Toulkeridis, M.T.: Comparative determination of the probability of landslide occurrences and susceptibility in central Quito, Ecuador. In: 2018 5th International Conference on eDemocracy and eGovernment, ICEDEG 2018 8372318, pp. 136–143 (2018)
14. Correia, A.G., Winter, M.G., Puppala, A.J.: A review of sustainable approaches in transport infrastructure geotechnics. Transportation Geotechnics 7, 21–28 (2016)
15. Momtaz, S.: Environmental impact assessment in Bangladesh: a critical review. Environ. Impact Assess. Rev. 22(2), 163–179 (2002)
16. Pagano, A., Pluchinotta, I., Pengal, P., Cokan, B., Giordano, R.: Engaging stakeholders in the assessment of NBS effectiveness in flood risk reduction: a participatory System Dynamics Model for benefits and co-benefits evaluation. Sci. Total Environ. 690, 543–555 (2019)
17. Malano, H.M., Chien, N.V., Turral, H.N.: Asset management for irrigation and drainage infrastructure–principles and case study. Irrig. Drain. Syst. 13(2), 109–129 (1999)
18. Gomes Correia, A., Cortez, P., Tinoco, J., Marques, R.: Artificial intelligence applications in transportation geotechnics. Geotech. Geol. Eng. 31(3), 861–879 (2013)
19. Katzenbach, R., Leppla, S., Vogler, M., Seip, M., Kurze, S.: Soil-structure-interaction of tunnels and superstructures during construction and service time. Procedia Eng. 57, 35–44 (2013)
20. Shi, Z., Huang, M., Hambleton, J.P.: Possibilities and limitations of the sequential kinematic method for simulating evolutionary plasticity problems. Comput. Geotech. 140, 104449 (2021)
21. Ladd, C.C.: Stability evaluation during staged construction. J. Geotechn. Eng. 117(4), 540–615 (1991)

22. Johnson, S.J.: Precompression for improving foundation soils. J. Soil Mech. Found. Div. **96**(1), 111–144 (1970)
23. Zhang, F., et al.: A rapid loess mudflow triggered by the check dam failure in a bulldoze mountain area, Lanzhou China. Landslides **16**(10), 1981–1992 (2019)
24. Hetpro-store. https://hetpro-store.com/lcd-16x2-blog/. Accessed 15 Nov 2021
25. AMAZON.   https://www.amazon.com/-/es/americano-cremallera-amplificador-cableado-conexión/dp/B07428NBCW?th=1. Accessed 21 Feb 2022
26. Fernández.   https://www.xataka.com/basics/que-arduino-como-funciona-que-puedes-hacer-uno. 03 Jan 2021
27. AVElectronics, https://avelectronics.cc/producto/65-cables-jumper/.Accessed 12 Dec 2021
28. Naylammechatronics. https://naylampmechatronics.com/sensores-proximidad/10-sensor-ultrasonido-hc-sr04.html. Accessed 17 Nov 2021

Removal of Arsenic and Heavy Metals from Contaminated Water with Emerging Sorbents

Erika Murgueitio⬛, Luis H. Cumbal Flores⬛, and Theofilos Toulkeridis(✉)⬛

Universidad de las Fuerzas Armadas ESPE, Sangolquí, Ecuador
ttoulkeridis@espe.edu.ec

Abstract. The current research arose due to an oil spill in the Papallacta Sub-basin, in the Amazonian area of Ecuador. Hereby, we were based to implement a baseline of the corresponding waters and sediments by searching an effective and low-cost treatment for the removal of arsenic and heavy metals from the lagoon water matrix. First steps included the synthesis of the hybrid sorbent (double lamellar hydroxides-metal oxides) for the selective removal of arsenical species, removal tests of As and heavy metals from the water matrix using the synthesized hybrid sorbent. Subsequently, the material was calcined and resulted in a material with metal oxides, then these were conditioned with ferric chloride to bind the hydrated iron oxides. In the synthesis of the hybrid sorbent, technical grade and reactive grade reagents were used to reduce the manufacturing costs of hybrid sorbents and four types of sorbents were obtained. The results indicated that the removal of arsenic and heavy metals can be attributed to inner sphere complexes by coulombic reactions and Lewis acid base. Balance tests were conducted applying the Langmuir and Freundlich models, being the Freundlich model the one that presented the best results. The data from the kinetic tests are adjusted to first-order kinetics and a half-life of 60 min. The intraparticle diffusion gives a value of 1.0×10^{-9} cm^2/s, which indicates that it is a fast kinetics. Both reactive and technical grade sorbents performed well in reducing arsenic and heavy metals in synthetic water.

Keywords: Papallacta Sub-basin · Heavy metal removal · Arsenic · Emerging sorbents · Langmuir model

1 Introduction

Arsenic is distributed in the environment with various oxidation states, where it appears in natural waters in the inorganic form predominantly as oxyanions of trivalent arsenite [As(III)] or pentavalent arsenate [As(V)] [1]. It is one of the most dangerous metalloids, whose origin is due to anthropogenic activities such as metal smelting, coal burning, mining activity (between 100–500 mg/L), and the use of pesticides that contain arsenic in their composition [2], or natural sources with high thermal and volcanic activity [3]. Chronic ingestion of arsenic causes gastrointestinal damage, disturbance to the

M. Botto-Tobar et al. (Eds.): ICAT 2022, CCIS 1756, pp. 196–211, 2023.
https://doi.org/10.1007/978-3-031-24971-6_15

functions of the cardiovascular and nervous systems, or death [4]. These evidences confirm the need to maintain the concentration of arsenic in drinking water at levels that meet the requirements established by official standards. The maximum permissible arsenic concentration in the world ranges between values of 10 $\mu g/L$ and 50 $\mu g/L$. Various populations are exposed to higher than allowed levels, of which a great amount of some six millions reside in India [5]. In the United States, more than 350,000 people drink water whose content is greater than 0.5 mg/L of arsenic and more than 2.5 million people receive water with arsenic content greater than 0.025 mg/L [6]. In Argentina, Chile, Mexico, El Salvador, Nicaragua, Peru and Bolivia, at least four million people permanently drink water with levels of arsenic that put their health at risk [6]. Arsenic concentrations in lake water are typically close to or less than those found in river water, with baseline concentrations being less than 1 mg/L in Mexico [7].

Water has been contaminated with arsenic in Ecuador, when the spill of 12,000 barrels of oil occurred in the area of Papallacta, a water catchment of the Tuminguina River, on April 8, 2003. This source of natural water, was considered as one of the best quality in the area. An average of one thousand liters per second were captured, which were used in Quito, Ecuador´s capital city [8]. Subsequently, analyzes were conducted on the drinking water of the Tumbaco parish where a concentration of 126 mg/L of As was found [8]. Considering this issue, the current research evaluated technological options that allow efficient removal of arsenic from natural waters, beginning with existing ones, such as precipitation with alum or with iron(III) salts, that have operational limitations due to their physical characteristics of the precipitates formed. Therefore, we introduced an innovative approach with the use of lamellar double hydroxide with metal oxides, which appears to offer an interesting alternative to traditional techniques.

2 Methodology

2.1 Reagents

The reagents used in the investigation were of reagent and technical grade, including magnesium sulfate trihydrate ($MgSO_4.3H_2O$), aluminum sulfate octadecahydrate ($Al_2(SO_4)3.18H_2O$), potassium carbonate solution (K_2CO_3) and potassium hydroxide. potassium (KOH).

2.2 Preparation and Characterization of the Hybrid Sorbent: Lamellar Double Hydroxides-Mixed Oxides

The synthesis was based on the technique developed by [9], coprecipitation at pH between 7.0–9.5 using two solutions, being aqueous solution of $MgSO_4.3H_2O$ and $Al_2(SO_4)_3.18H_2O$ and carbonate solution potassium and potassium hydroxide. The prepared solutions maintained a molar Mg/Al ratio of 1:4 under the following stoichiometry: $[MgaAlb(OH)_2(a+b)](CO_3)b/2.mH_2O$ [9].

The physical characterization of the sorbent included humidity using the gravimetry method, gravity by the pycnometer method and by calculating the total and effective porosity. Additionally, scanning electron microscopy was used to determine the surface morphology of the hybrid sorbent and the approximate size of the pores and their distribution. In the preparation of the sample, the "freeze-drying" technique was used for 16 h and giving it a subsequent coating with gold to increase the secondary emission of electrons. In the process, gold was used as cathode for 20 s of discharge and then microphotographs were taken.

2.3 Arsenic Removal from Synthetic Water

The tests were performed under the following conditions: i) different sorbents to compare their arsenic removal efficiency, ii) two times of agitation (2 h and 2 d) and iii) use of synthetic water with different concentrations of arsenic and competing ions. Four types of lamellar double hydroxides with metal oxides (HOM) were used, being i) HOM technical grade (HOM-T), ii) HOM reactive grade (HOM-R), iii) HOM with iron oxides technical grade (HOM-T-OFH) and iv) HOM with reactive grade iron oxides (HOM-R-OFH). With the HMO coated with iron oxides, the tests were conducted in batches, for which 1 g of each support material was placed in a polyethylene bottle with 1 L of synthetic water. The pH was set at 7.0 ± 0.5 and stirred for 2 h. Samples of the supernatant were filtered and analyzed in the Perkin Elmer Model AA 100 Atomic Absorption equipment.

The on line tests were performed in an Eldex PN 1243 universal fraction collector, with a glass column with an internal diameter of 11 mm and a length of 30 cm, and a constant flow stainless steel peristaltic pump. In the column, a bed of 4.5 cm^3 of sorbent coated with iron oxides was placed on a layer of natural cotton for uniform flow distribution. The size of the packed hybrid sorbent was 14 mesh (1.40 mm) to avoid wall effects in the flow through the bed. The synthetic arsenic solution was prepared in a 25 L tank and fed to the column with a peristaltic pump at a constant flow rate of 1 mL/min. A hydraulic retention time of 20 min in the bed was chosen and the superficial liquid velocity (VSL) and the empty bed contact time (TCLV) were recorded. The effluent was collected in test tubes placed in the collector and the volume control for each sample was set at 20 mL. The samples for analysis were taken every 10 or 20 tubes. Samples were taken at different hours of column operation, to observe the evolution of the arsenic concentration in the treated water with respect to time. The operation of the system was stopped when the concentration of arsenic in the effluent reached the saturation of the medium (inlet concentration equal to outlet concentration). The collected samples were analyzed for pH determination and quantification of total Fe and As.

2.4 Adsorption Isotherms

In order to estimate the maximum adsorption capacity of As in the hybrid sorbent, several solutions of known concentration of As(V) (100 to 400 µg/L), pH ≈ 7 and competing anions were prepared. In each of these solutions (200 mL), a fixed and known amount of adsorbent (500 mg of HOM) was added. The solutions were left stirring (40 rpm) at constant temperature for 48 h. The concentrations of As(V) remaining in the liquid phase were then determined. From these data, the amount of As(V) adsorbed per gram of the hybrid sorbent was estimated, through Eq. 1:

$$q_{eq} = \frac{V}{m}(C_i - C_{eq}) \tag{1}$$

where: q_{eq} is the equilibrium arsenic adsorption (mg/g) or (μg/g), V volume of the solution (L), C_i the initial concentration of arsenic in solution (mg/L) or (μg/L), C_{eq} equilibrium concentration of the metalloid in the liquid phase (mg/L) or (μg/L) and m mass of the sorbent (g).

The experimental data of the variation of the adsorbed solute concentration in the adsorbent solid phase as a function of the equilibrium concentration in the liquid phase were adjusted by the Langmuir and Freundlich models [10]. The Langmuir equation applied to adsorption data in solution is as follows:

$$\frac{C_{eq}}{q_{eq}} = \frac{1}{b.Q_{max}} + \frac{1}{Q_{max}}C_{eq} \tag{2}$$

where: q_{eq} is the amount of metal captured by the hybrid sorbent (mg/g) or (μg/g), C_{eq} is the concentration of arsenic in the liquid phase (mg/L) or (μg/L), b is the constant of Langmuir, Q_{max} the maximum adsorption capacity (mg/g) or (μg/g), On the other hand, the Freundlich isotherm is expressed by the following equation:

$$q_e = K_F.C_e^n \tag{3}$$

where: C_e is the equilibrium concentration of the solute in the liquid phase (mg/L) or (μg/L), q_e is the amount of solute adsorbed in the solid phase, (mg/g) or (μg/g), K_F and n = constants related to adsorption capacity and adsorption intensity, respectively.

The parameters of the Langmuir isotherm, b and Q_{max} were found from the linearization of the equation of the graph C_e/q_e vs. C_e, their values were estimated from the intersection with the C_e/q_e axis and from the slope of the line, respectively. The parameters of the Freundlich isotherm, K_F and n were obtained from the graph ln q_e vs. ln C_e. The selection of the model that best fit the experiment was based on the best value of the correlation coefficient.

2.5 Regeneration of the Absorbent Medium

For regeneration, 500 mL of 3% NaOH and 2% NaCl solution were used in proportion. The test was conducted in two cycles. In the first cycle, 15 bed volumes were allowed to pass, collecting in test tubes with 2.5 mL of aliquot, from volume 16 to 60 volumes, 10 mL of aliquot were collected and from volume 61 to bed volume 100, 20 mL aliquots were collected. In the second cycle, the procedure was modified in order to extract a greater amount of arsenic, so that up to 35 bed volumes, 5 mL of aliquot was collected and from there, up to 130 volumes, 10 mL of aliquot was collected. The regenerating solution was fed to the fixed bed column at a flow rate of 0.5 mL/min and the effluent was collected every five minutes in the fraction collector. Subsequently, the collected aliquots were used to analyze the concentration of As. The regenerated granules were washed with 8 bed volumes of a 10% HCl solution to be reused.

2.6 Kinetic Tests

These tests were conducted by weighing 1.0 g of the hybrid sorbent loaded with hydrated iron oxides (OFH) and contacted with 1 L of synthetic water at pH $\approx$ 7.0. The content was mechanically shaken at 1000 rpm to remove the effects of diffusion resistance imposed by the liquid film surrounding HMO granules. Aliquots of 5 mL were taken every 15 min and analyzed in the AA100 to determine the concentration of arsenic. With the data of As concentration versus time, the reaction order of As (V) decrease in the liquid phase was determined. The modeling of the sorption kinetics of trace solutes in the HOM-OHF sorbent assumes the following simplifications: i) intra-particle diffusion of As(V) through the HOM-OHF sorbent ii) affinity and intra-particle diffusivity in the arsenate sorption. The composition of the liquid phase for the kinetic tests was 100 µg/L As(V) together with 90 mg/L of chloride and 120 mg/L of sulfate at pH equal to 7.0. The kinetic tests were performed using the hybrid sorbent particles with an average diameter of 1.4 mm. The capture rate of As(V) in the kinetic assays, where intra-particle diffusion is the limiting phase, is denoted as:

$$\frac{\partial q_{As(V)}}{\partial t} = \overline{D}_{eff}(\frac{\partial^2 q_{As(V)}}{\partial r^2} + \frac{2}{r}\frac{\partial q_{As(V)}}{\partial r}) \tag{4}$$

For a variable surface concentration model, the following initial and boundary conditions apply:

$$\frac{a}{K}\frac{\partial q_{As(V)}}{\partial t} = \rho_P \overline{D}_{eff}\frac{\partial q_{As(V)}}{\partial r} \tag{5}$$

$$\frac{\partial q_{As(V),t}}{\partial r}\bigg|_{r=0} = 0 \tag{6}$$

$$0 < r < r_o;\, t = 0\, q_{As(V)} = 0 \tag{7}$$

where, a is the ratio of the volume and surface area of the particle and K is the partition coefficient of As(V) between the solid and liquid phases (linear equilibrium coefficient). Then the fractional capture rate of As(V), F, under the experimental conditions can be approximated by the following equation [11].

$$F = \frac{\partial q_{As(V),t}}{\partial q_{As(V),\infty}} = 1 - \sum_{n=1}^{\infty}\frac{6\omega(\omega+1)\exp(-\overline{D}_{eff}\beta_n^2 t/r_0)}{9+9\omega+\beta_n^2\omega^2} \tag{8}$$

$Q_{As(V)}$, is the capture of As(V) by the HOM under equilibrium conditions, the values of β_n, are the positive roots of the transcendental equation:

$$Tan\beta_n = \frac{3\beta_n}{3+\omega\beta_n^2} \tag{9}$$

the values of β can be estimated with the relation of the final capture fraction:

$$\frac{q_{As(V),\infty}}{VC_{As(V),0}} = \frac{1}{1+\omega} \tag{10}$$

2.7   Determination of Arsenical and Metal Species

In the determination of metals, the considerations given by [12, 13] were followed. To quantify arsenic, the hydride generation method was used, coupled to atomic absorption equipment equipped with an electron discharge lamp and associated equipment. For the determination of Fe, Ni and Cu metals, the air-acetylene flame method was used, direct method of nitrous oxide acetylene flame for Ba. The instruments used were the Perkin Elmer Atomic Absorption equipment, AA100, for iron and heavy metals (Cu, Ni, Ba), hollow cathode lamps at different wavelengths were used and the reagents are of analytical grade FLUKA brand. Calibration curves were made for each element and data were accepted when the correlation coefficient was greater than 0.999. Data quality control was performed by blank analysis between sample readings and a standard every ten samples for calibration verification.

3   Results and Discussion

Compounds HOM-R and HOM-T-OFH were characterized using scanning microscopy and chemical analysis. Microphotographs were taken for this purpose, with a magnification of 1 μm. The size of the granules is between 1.5 to 2.5 mm and the range of the pore is between 1 μm to 2 μm. The surface of the HOM-T is less pore compared to that of the HOM-R. This can be attributed to impurities in technical grade sorbent synthesis materials, and HOM-R has a larger surface area than HOMR OHF. The surface area could be better observed if the resolution was at least 0.1 μm.

The results of the chemical analysis of the HOM-T and HOM-T-OFH samples are detailed in Table 1. Note that the concentration of aluminum and magnesium are found in greater proportion in the two samples. However, traces of iron (0.17%) are also observed in the HOM-T samples. The presence of this metal may derived from impurities contained in technical grade chemicals.

Table 1. Chemical analysis

Sample HOM-T-OHF		Sample HOM-T	
Determination	Results	Determination	Results
Calcium	0,08%	Calcium	0,12%
Magnesium	5,17%	Magnesium	9,97%
Aluminum	10,38%	Aluminum	7,57%
Sodium	5,09%	Sodium	9,17%
Iron	1,33%	Iron	0,17%

In the removal of heavy metals, the percentage ranges between 71.9 and greater than 99.0% with the four types of HOM using synthetic water contaminated with barium, nickel, copper and barium in known concentrations (Table 2). No significant difference is observed in the percentage of removal with HMOs loaded with iron oxides, this may be associated with the positive charge that iron oxides have at pH less than 8 and that, when in contact with heavy metals, these are repelled.

The removal of heavy metals with the HOM is produced by the action of the mixed oxides existing in the Lamellar Double Hydroxides (HDL). These oxides have basic sites of the type: OH^-, pairs $Mg^{2+}-O^{2-}$, $Al^{3+}-O^{2-}$ that bind with heavy metals through electrostatic attractions. Apparently, the FeOH functional group of hydrated iron oxides does not favor removal because at pH $= 7.0$ this functional group has no charge and does not affect electrostatic attraction or repulsion with heavy metal ions (Ba^{2+}, Cd^{2+}, Ni^{2+}, Cu^{2+}), consequently, there is no significant difference in the removal with the hybrid materials containing hydrated iron oxides Eq. 11.

$$2 \equiv [OH]^- + [Ba]^{2+} \rightarrow \equiv 2[OH]^- Ba^{2+} \tag{11}$$

Through batch tests, the removal percentage of As(V) applying the four types of hybrid sorbents, being HOM-T, HOM-R, HOM-T-OFH AND HOM-R-OFH, ranging from 43% to 88%. of As(V). The HOM (technical and reactive grade) reach equilibrium at 48 h, unlike those conditioned with iron oxides that need two h and have a higher percentage of As removal (Tables 3 and 4). Thus, of the four types of hybrid sorbents, those that remove the greatest amount of As (V) are those loaded with iron oxides (Table 3).

Table 2. Table captions should be placed above the tables. *MPL: Maximum permitted limit, *ND: not detectable. All results correspond to arithmetic means

Metals	C_i	*MPL	HOM-T	Removal	HOM-T-OFH	Removal
	mg/L	Mg/L	Cf, mg/L	%	Cf, mg/L	%
Ba^{2+}	2	1	°ND	>99	°ND	>99
Ni^{2+}	1	0,025	0,211	78,9	0,02	98
Cu^{2+}	1	1	<0,05	>95	<0,05	95
Cd^{2+}	1	0,01	<0,012	>95	<0,012	98,8
			HOM-R	M	**HOM-R-OFH**	
			Cf, mg/L		**Cf, mg/L**	
Ba^{2+}	2	1	*ND	>99	*ND	>99
Ni^{2+}	1	0,025	0,281	71,9	0,188	71,9
Cu^{2+}	1	1	0,093	90,7	0,18	82
Cd^{2+}	1	0,01	<0,012	>98,8	<0,012	>98,8

The removal of As(V) by applying the hybrid sorbents is performed through two types of intersections, being ion exchange and Lewis acid-base reaction. Using the hybrid sorbent (technical and reagent grade) without hydrated iron oxides, two $H_2AsO_4^-$ ions are exchanged for a CO_3^{2-} ion and one $HAsO_4^{2-}$ ion for a carbonate ion to compensate

Table 3. As removal using HOMS with stirring time of two H

C_i	HOM-R Cf	HOM-R-OFH Cf	HOM-T Cf	HOM-T-OFH Cf
µg/L	µg/L	µg/L	µg/L	µg/L
25	14,0	3,3	14	5,1
50	23,2	6,3	23.2	8,7
100	50,7	16,3	50.7	17,0
200	105,6	23,5	106	57,7

for the positive charge of the inner sphere. Equations 12 and 13 theoretically represent this removal mechanism. The metal oxides found in the HOM have acidic and basic active centers on their surface that facilitate the removal of cations and anions (arsenates and arsenites) through electrostatic attraction reactions.

$$[Mg_{(1-x)}Al_x(OH)_2](CO_3^{2-})_{\frac{x}{n}}.mH_2O + 2H_2AsO_4^- \\ \rightarrow [Mg_{(1-x)}Al_x(OH)_2](H_2AsO_4^-)_{\frac{x}{n}}(H_2AsO_4^-)_{\frac{x}{n}}.mH_2O + CO_3^{2-} \quad (12)$$

$$[Mg_{(1-x)}Al_x(OH)_2](CO_3^{2-})_{\frac{x}{n}}.mH_2O + 2H_2AsO_4^{2-} \\ \rightarrow [Mg_{(1-x)}Al_x(OH)_2](H_2AsO_4^{2-})_{\frac{x}{n}}.mH_2O + CO_3^{2-} \quad (13)$$

Table 4. As removal using HOMS with stirring time of two days

Ci	HOM-R		HOM-R-OFH		HOM-T		HOM-T-OFH	
	Cf	Removal	Cf	Removal	Cf	Removal	Cf	Removal
µg/L	µg/L	%	µg/L	%	µg/L	%	µg/L	%
25	5.2	79.2	5.1	79.6	5,2	79,4	3.3	86.8
50	13.1	73.8	8.7	82.6	13,1	73,8	6.3	87.4
100	26.8	73.2	17	83	26,8	73,2	16.3	83.7
200	52.2	73.9	58	71	52,1	74	23.5	88.25

Reagent and technical grade hybrid sorbents remove arsenic by combining Lewis acid-base and coulombic interactions with the ligands arsenate diacid $H_2AsO_4^-$ and arsenate acid $HAsO_4^{2-}$, in the first coordination sphere. The competing ions Cl^-, SO_4^{2-}, HCO_3^- in both cases are located in the second coordination sphere and do not join in the first sphere, as they are not reactive. Equations 14 and 15 describe the capture of As using the hybrid sorbent:

$$\equiv FeOH + H_2AsO_4^- + H_2O \xrightarrow{L.A.B} \equiv FeOH_2^+(H_2AsO_4^-) + OH^- \quad (14)$$

$$2(\equiv FeOH) + H_2AsO_4^- + 2H_2O \overset{L.A.B}{\rightarrow} \equiv FeOH_2^+ (H_2AsO_4^-) + 2OH^- \qquad (15)$$

Fixed bed column tests were performed for both technical and reagent grade sorbents. It is observed that the HOM-R-OFH sorbent is saturated approximately at 16,000 bed volumes equivalent to 76 L of synthetic water. And the maximum adsorption capacity is 1431 ug/g, obtained by evaluating the area on the curve (Fig. 2). After the end of the first cycle, the column packed with HOM-R-OHF was regenerated and a second sorption cycle was conducted under the same experimental conditions as above. In this cycle it was possible to pass 10714 volumes of contaminated water equivalent to 50.9 L and the maximum adsorption capacity is 876.68 ug/g. Comparing the first cycle with the second, it is observed that the removal capacity decreases by approximately 40% (Fig. 3). The drop in removal capacity can be attributed to the presence of hydroxyls (OH^-) in the matrix of the hybrid sorbent after balancing the pH and to the loss of iron oxides [12].

The column loaded with HOM-T-OFH was saturated at 9683 volumes of equivalent to 46 L of synthetic water. Note that in the first 6000 volumes of fixed bed, the concentration reaches 15 $\mu g/L$ of arsenic and then increases rapidly to 80 $\mu g/L$, the maximum adsorption capacity of this type of hybrid sorbent is 1099.2 $\mu g/L.g$ (Fig. 4). As(V) removal using HOM-T-OFH is 23% lower than HOM-R-OFH (Fig. 5). This difference may be associated with the technical grade hybrid sorbent preparation method, since the hybrid sorbent granules did not have the same reactive surfaces and consequently less Fe oxides were deposited in the HOM. This assumption was confirmed by calculating the amount of total iron stored in the technical grade hybrid sorbent (20 mg/g) and in the reagent grade hybrid sorbent (30 mg/g). Note that the amount of iron oxides deposited in the HOM plays a very important role in the As removal capacity, since in the first removal cycle with HOM-R-OFH it is possible to accumulate 1431 ug As(V)/g sorbent compared with the 1099 ug As(V)/g of HOM-T-OFH (Fig. 1).

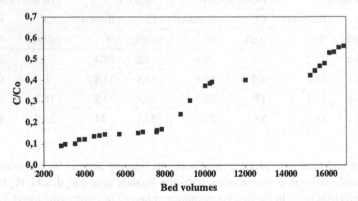

Fig. 1. First As(V) sorption cycle in a fixed bed column using H.O.M.R.OHF

In order to demonstrate the feasibility of recovering the capacity of the sorbent material to remove arsenic, the H.O.M.R.OHF granules were reused, previously conditioning them at pH7 using four to six volumes of 10% hydrochloric acid, where the functional groups of the Fe (III) oxides that cover the HMO granules are protonated again, regenerating the column packed with H.O.M.R.OHF, obtaining a 97.58% release of As. A second regeneration of the H.O.M.R.OHF was performed, obtaining 98.40% release of As. Note that the regeneration in the second cycle has the same efficiency. (Fig. 6). The use of 0.2 N NaOH as a regenerant increases the pH of the system and consequently the net charge of the iron oxides becomes negative. The arsenical species at basic pH are also anions so that they are repelled from the hybrid sorbent phase. Note that the peak As concentration in the first regeneration is remarkably high compared to that in the second regeneration. Certainly, a good amount of OH- groups were not removed in the conditioning of the sorbent after the first regeneration and this situation causes a decrease in the sorption capacity in the second cycle and also hinders its subsequent regeneration.

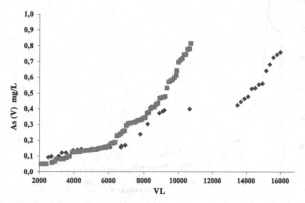

Fig. 2. Comparison between As(V) sorption cycles in a fixed bed column using HOM-R-OFH. In blue: Max.Cap.Ad. 1431 ug/g of first cycle; In red: Max.Cap.Ad. 876.68 ug/g of second cycle (Color figure online).

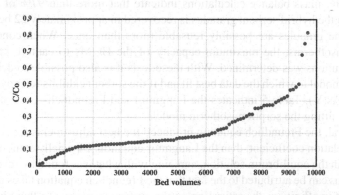

Fig. 3. First As(V) sorption cycle in a fixed bed column using HOM-T-OHF

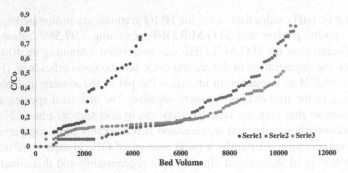

Fig. 4. Comparison of As(V) removal in fixed bed column using HOM-R-OFH and HOM-T-OFH

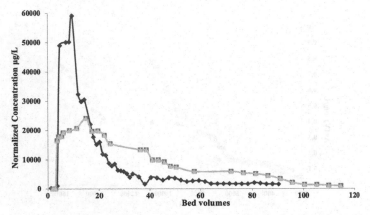

Fig. 5. Comparison of As(V) desorption with the two fixed-bed column cycles using HOM-R-OFH. Blue is first cycle, while green is the second cycle (Color figure online)

Therefore, mass balance calculations indicate that more than 97% of the arsenic adsorbed on the hybrid sorbent granules is recovered in approximately 22 bed volumes, therefore, the granules are possibly reusable more than once. When conducting the adsorption isotherms, the maximum capacity of the HOMs to capture arsenic from aqueous solutions was determined. With these tests it is also possible to determine the adsorption model to which the data best fit and if the sorbent exhibits selectivity to retain the solute, As(V). Table 5 indicates the Langmuir and Freundlich constants that were obtained by fitting the sorption isotherm models.

In general, the Freundlich equation produced the best adjustments for adsorbed As, higher correlation coefficient, than the Langmuir equation, especially at high concentrations of As in the equilibrium solution, agreeing with what was found by several authors [14–19]. This can be attributed to the fact that the Freundlich equation takes into account the decrease in affinity as the saturation on the surface increases, so there is a better fit at high concentrations. At low concentrations, it was observed that the Langmuir model presented a better behavior, because this model includes a series of assumptions that are mostly difficult to verify (uniform solid surfaces, adsorbed molecules move along the surface, etc.) while the Freundlich equation was obtained from empirical data.

Table 5. Constants of Langmuir and Freundlich

Hybrid sorbent	Langmuir		
	Qmax	K_L	R^2
	µg/g	L/mg	
HOM-R	454,54	$2,384 \times 10^{-3}$	0,999
HOM-R-OHF	370,37	$1,460 \times 10^{-2}$	0,860
HOM-T	322,58	$1,107 \times 10^{-2}$	0,690
HOM-T-OHF	505,05	$1,026 \times 10^{-2}$	0,836
Hybrid sorbent	Freundlich		
	N	K_F	R^2
HOM-R	1,1792	1,8750	0,999
HOM-R-OHF	1,1223	7,5509	0,989
HOM-T	1,1507	4,4259	0,991
HOM-T-OHF	1,2626	7,4302	0,938

To model the capture of As by H.O.M in the sorbent, the intra-particle diffusion mechanism of a multi-component system was used. The disappearance of As from the liquid phase is linear, since the fit of the experimental results is $R^2 = 0.9628$. So the model that best describes the results is a first order kinetics ($k = 0.7868 \text{ min}^{-1}$) (Fig. 7). Furthermore, it follows that the half-life time, $t_{1/2}$, in the disappearance of As(V) is 60.205 min. In the modeling of the intra-particle diffusivity during the selective sorption of As(V) with the HOM-T-OFH, the experimental results were obtained and applying Eq. 8 (Table 6) it was determined that the best fit of the effective intra-particle diffusivity corresponds to $1.0 \times 10^{-9} \text{ cm}^2/\text{s}$ for the HOM-T-OFH (Fig. 7).

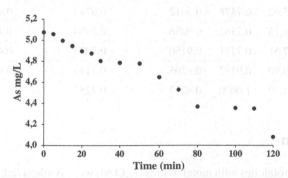

Fig. 6. Removal of As(V) in the liquid phase as a function of time during kinetic tests using HO.M.R.OHF

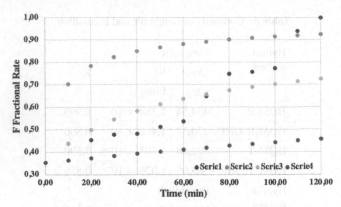

Fig. 7. Kinetic Data and Estimated Intra-particle Diffusivity of Best-Fit Curves: As(V) Fractional Sorption Versus Time Using HOM-R-OFH

Table 6. Experimental data of intraparticle diffusion

t	C	q	F exp	F adjust		
min	ug/L	ug/g		$D = 1.0 \times 10^{-8}$	$D = 1.0 \times 10^{-9}$	$D = 1.0 \times 10^{-10}$
0	80.06	0.00	0.0000	0.3526	0.3526	0.3526
10	47.37	32.59	0.4381	0.7027	0.4363	0.3631
20	46.19	33.77	0.4540	0.7829	0.4982	0.3734
30	44.41	35.54	0.4778	0.8234	0.5453	0.3832
40	44.17	35.78	0.4810	0.8492	0.5822	0.3927
50	41.92	38.03	0.5112	0.8675	0.6119	0.4019
60	40.03	39.91	0.5365	0.8813	0.6363	0.4107
70	31.74	48.18	0.6476	0.8922	0.6568	0.4193
80	24.27	55.62	0.7478	0.9012	0.6743	0.4276
90	23.64	56.25	0.7562	0.9086	0.6894	0.4356
100	22.38	57.51	0.7731	0.9150	0.7027	0.4433
110	9.95	69.90	0.9397	0.9205	0.7146	0.4508
120	5.45	74.39	1.0000	0.9253	0.7251	0.4581

4   Conclusions

Four types of hydrotalcites with metal oxides (H.O.M) were synthesized, being H.O.M.T technical grade, H.O.M.R reactive grade, H.O.M.T.OHF with iron oxides technical grade and H.O.M.R.OHF with iron oxides reactive grade. The size of the H.M.O is between 1.5 to 2.5 mm and the pore range between 1 to 2 μm. The H.O.M.T has less porous surface than the H.O.M.R and can be attributed to the impurities that the synthesis materials of the sorbent prepared with technical grade materials have. X-ray diffraction concluded that the synthesized sorbents are amorphous.

Batch tests synthesized materials removed As (V) from initial concentrations of 25 to 200 g/L in a period of 2 h, in a range of 43% to 88%, being H.O.M.R.OHF and H.O.M.T.OHF. those that remove more arsenic.

In the tests on fixed bed columns, HOMROHF was tested in two cycles, in the first it was saturated with approximately 16000 bed volumes with a maximum adsorption capacity of 1431 μg/g., after regeneration it was subjected to to a second sorption cycle the HOMROHF, in which it was possible to pass 11000, determining a maximum adsorption capacity of 870.68 μg/g, decreasing the sorption capacity with respect to the first cycle by 40%, this can be attributed to the decrease in surface area due to the presence of hydroxyls (OH-) in the hydrotalcite matrix after balancing the pH and to the loss of iron oxides.

In order to demonstrate the feasibility of recovering the capacity of the sorbent material to remove arsenic, the HOMROHF granules were reused, previously conditioning them at pH7 using four to six volumes of 10% hydrochloric acid, where the functional groups of the Fe (III) oxides that cover the HMO granules are protonated again, regenerating the column packed with HOMROHF, obtaining a 97.58% release of As.

A second regeneration of the H.O.M.R.OHF was performed, obtaining 98.40% release of As. Note that the regeneration in the second cycle has the same efficiency.

The H.O.M.T.OHF was tested with a single cycle. It was saturated at 9683 volumes, and the maximum adsorption capacity of this type of hydrotalcite is 1099.2 μg/g.

Compared to the reagent grade material, the removal of As (V) is lower by 23%, such a difference may be associated with the quality of the technical grade reagents, since on the H.O.M. Fewer Fe oxides were deposited on its surface. To confirm this assumption, it was determined that the amount of iron was lower in the technical grade (20 mg/g) than in the reagent grade (30 mg/g).

To determine adsorption isotherms. This test was carried out for the following reasons: i) to determine the maximum capacity of the H.O.M. to capture arsenic from aqueous solutions at different concentrations ii) to estimate the type of adsorption and iii) to determine if the adsorbent exhibits selectivity to retain the solute (As (V)). Two Langmuir and Freundlich models were used, the Freundlich equation being the one that produced the best fits and the highest correlation coefficient. This can be attributed to the fact that the Freundlich equation takes into account the decrease in affinity as the saturation on the surface increases, so there is a better fit at high concentrations.

In the modeling of the adsorption kinetics of As (V) with H.O.M.R.OHF in the liquid phase, the disappearance of As (V), from the water matrix, the model that best described the results was the pseudo first order equation. The pseudo model is applied because in synthetic water, the concentrations of the competing ions undergo very slight changes.

To model the capture of As by H.O.M in the sorbent, the intra-particle diffusion mechanism of a multi-component system was used. From the experimental data it was determined that the best fit of the effective intra-particle diffusivity is equal to 1×10^{-9} cm^2/s for the H.O.M.T.OHF and indicates that it has a fast kinetics at the beginning and then it becomes slow.

Heavy metal removal percentages range from 71.9 to >99% with the four types of HMO using synthetic water contaminated with barium, nickel, copper and barium in known concentrations, the removal occurs through electrostatic attractions of the existing mixed oxides in HDL they present basic sites of type: OH^-, pairs $Mg^{2+}-O^{2-}$, $Al^{3+}-O^{2-}$ with heavy metals.

No significant difference in removal percentage is observed with HMOs charged with iron oxides. This can be attributed to the fact that the FeOH functional group, which is dominant at pH 7, has no charge and therefore does not carry out electrostatic attraction or repulsion with the ions of heavy metals (Ba^{2+}, Cd^{2+}, Ni^{3+}, Cu^{2+}) therefore there is no significant difference in removal with white hybrid materials.

References

1. Goyer, R.A., Clarkson, T.W.: Toxic effects of metals. Casarett Doull's Toxicol Basic Sci. Poisons **5**, 691–736 (1996)
2. O'Day, P.A.: Chemistry and mineralogy of arsenic. Elements **2**(2), 77–83 (2006)
3. Tapia, J., et al.: Naturally elevated arsenic in the Altiplano-Puna, Chile and the link to recent (Mio-Pliocene to Quaternary) volcanic activity, high crustal thicknesses, and geological structures. J. S. Am. Earth Sci. **105**, 102905 (2021)
4. Abernathy, C.O., Thomas, D.J., Calderon, R.L.: Health effects and risk assessment of arsenic. J. Nutr. **133**(5), 1536S-1538S (2003)
5. Massey, M.S.: Investigating the quantity and form of heavy metal contaminants for improved risk analysis and mitigation. In: Siegel, M., Selinus, O., Finkelman, R. (eds.) Practical Applications of Medical Geology, pp. 169–191. Springer, Cham (2021). https://doi.org/10.1007/978-3-030-53893-4_5
6. de Esparza, M.C.: The presence of arsenic in drinking water in Latin America and its effect on public health. Nat. Arsenic Groundwater Lat. Am. **1**, 17–29 (2009)
7. Razo, I., Carrizales, L., Castro, J., Díaz-Barriga, F., Monroy, M.: Arsenic and heavy metal pollution of soil, water and sediments in a semi-arid climate mining area in Mexico. Water Air Soil Pollut. **152**(1), 129–152 (2004)
8. El Comercio. (20 de septiembre de 2014). El agua se somete a pruebas de arsénico. Obtenido de https://www.elcomercio.com/tag/agua
9. Reichle, W.T.: Synthesis of anionic clay minerals (mixed metal hydroxides, hydrotalcite). Solid State Ionics **22**(1), 135–141 (1986)
10. Reed, B.E., Matsumoto, M.R.: Modeling cadmium adsorption by activated carbon using the Langmuir and Freundlich isotherm expressions. Sep. Sci. Technol. **28**(13–14), 2179–2195 (1993)
11. Esteban, L.S., Archila, F.P.: Estrucplan (2004). Obtenido de https://estrucplan.com.ar/hidrot alcitas-precursores-de-materiales-adsorbentes-de-sox/
12. American Society for testing and Materials. Annual book of Standards: Determinacion de Alcalinidad del agua metodo ASTM D 1067-92. APHA, New York (1994)
13. Crank, J.: The mathematics of diffusion. Oxford University Press (1979)
14. Cumbal, L., et al.: Desarrollo de una Técnologia para la recuperación de las aguas de la laguna de Papallacta contaminadas con arsénicoy metales pesados usando sorbentes emergentes. CENCI, Reporte técnico, Quito (2008)
15. Cumbal, L., Murgueitio, E., Aguirre, Chávez, C., Tipán, I.: The origin of arsenic in waters and sediments from Papallacta Lagoon. In: Taller de distribución de As en Iberoamérica, pp. 85–86. Libro de Resumenes (2006)

16. Poma, P., Usca, M., Fdz-Polanco, M., Garcia-Villacres, A., Toulkeridis, T.: Landslide and environmental risk from oil spill due to the rupture of SOTE and OCP pipelines, San Rafael Falls, Amazon Basin, Ecuador. Int. J. Adv. Sci. Eng. Inf. Technol. 11(4), 1558–1566 (2021)
17. Heredia-R, M., et al.: Multitemporal analysis as a non-invasive technology indicates a rapid change in land use in the Amazon: the case of the ITT Oil block. Environments 8(12), 139 (2021)
18. Lozano, P., Cabrera, O., Peyre, G., Cleef, A., Toulkeridis, T.: Plant diversity and composition changes along an altitudinal gradient in the isolated volcano Sumaco in the Ecuadorian amazon. Diversity 12(6) (2020). Article number 229
19. Toulkeridis, T., et al.: Climate change according to Ecuadorian academics–perceptions versus facts. La Granja 31(1), 21–49 (2020)

Implementation of the CAESAR-Lisflood Cellular Automated Landscape Evolution Model to Determine Possible Flood Areas in the Portoviejo River Sub-basin, Coastal Ecuador

Diego Sebastián Moncayo-Galárraga ⓘ, Alexander Alfredo Robayo-Nieto ⓘ,
Oswaldo Padilla ⓘ, and Theofilos Toulkeridis[✉] ⓘ

Universidad de las Fuerzas Armadas ESPE, Sangolquí, Ecuador
ttoulkeridis@espe.edu.ec

Abstract. In the Portoviejo canton of the province of Manabí of coastal Ecuador, floods have historically occurred as a result of extreme rainfall events and the overflow of the Portoviejo River. Nowadays, hydrodynamic models constitute a tool that allows simulating the flow of water in hydrographic basins. The zones with the possibility of flooding at different return periods were determined in the Colón parish of the Portoviejo canton using the CAESAR-Lisflood two-dimensional model in its two modes, being the Catchment and Reach Mode. The inputs used for the simulation were rainfall and flow data at different return periods (historical and probable maximum) as well as the size of the sediments that were obtained from granulometric analysis by sieving and a Digital Elevation Model of ALOS PALSAR with a resolution of 24.5 m and were later compared to HEC-RAS. With the one-factor ANOVA statistical technique, it was determined that there are no significant differences between the means of the affected areas and flow depths. The flood hazard analysis was performed on the buildings of Colón, considering two main factors. The first has been the probability of occurrence depending on the return period (10, 25, 50, 100 and 500 years), where the greater the return period, the less probability of occurrence, while the second has been the intensity that is classified as low, medium and high depending on the depth of the water flow, when educational institutions, health centers and homes were the buildings of interest to analyze the medium and high hazard.

Keywords: Flood hazard · Hydrodynamic models · CAESAR-Lisflood · HEC-RAS · Return period · Ecuador

1 Introduction

Massive flooding belongs between the natural disasters with the greatest death toll and a potentially massive destruction of assets, infrastructure and socio-economic activities [1, 2]. The causes and origins of floods such as river overflows can be multiple, however the catastrophic result is the same [3, 4]. In certain regions such as the western part of South America in general and of Ecuador in particular, floods occur temporarily and in phases of extraordinary phenomena such as "El Niño" [5–9]. The success in managing and preventing these hydrometeorological processes by the corresponding authorities and the affected population is always a challenge with an unknown outcome [10–15].

For some decades, hydrodynamic models have been used as a tool for the analysis and prevention of floods in the lower areas of hydrographic basins [16–20]. In Ecuador around 35% of the population lives in areas threatened by floods, besides other potential disasters which affect an even higher percentage of the public [21–37]. In the lower basins of the Coast and the Amazon basin, floods have been more frequent than in the Andean region [38–40]. In the coastal region of Ecuador, at the beginning of February 2017, occurred high volumes of precipitation, as a consequence of a variety of factors associated with the El Niño phenomenon, such as thermal anomalies in the equatorial Pacific, in which the temperature reached close to 2 °C above usual values, the formation of cloudy systems due to the displacement of the intertropical convergence zone towards the equator and the atmospheric instability of the Amazon [41]. In the province of Manabí, 2,500 families were affected by the floods as a result of the heavy rains. The cantons that suffered the most damage were Santa Ana, Portoviejo, Rocafuerte, Chone [42].

Portoviejo, capital of Manabí, had rainfall records that exceeded historical averages. This caused the overflow of the Portoviejo River and streams, in addition to landslides and interruptions of drinking water, collapse of the sewage and irrigation system [41]. In the months of extreme rains, the flow and draft of the Portoviejo River increased, and consequently the river overflowed its limits [43], which became a major problem as the populations settle in the plains of flooding, which are easily accessible, fertile, with a flat topography, belonging to the characteristics that usually allow urban development [44]. The flow of water that overflowed from the Portoviejo River moved at high speeds and at different heights through the floodplains, affecting buildings such as homes, health centers, schools, colleges, agricultural land, and human lives [45–48].

From 1990 to 2014, the Portoviejo river basin has had a loss of its forest in approximately 35,624 Ha [49, 50]. Consequently, without vegetation there was no water retention, and the rain began to erode the soil, reducing its infiltration rate. Therefore, surface runoff increases, which carries with it mud, large volumes of material and debris, filling quickly the riverbeds, followed by their overflowing, causing floods. The problem of floods is aggravated because the population does not have adequate knowledge about risk management and prevention. Thus, there is no adequate final disposal of the solid waste they generate, which obstructs storm sewers and riverbeds. In addition, the lack of urban planning policies causes buildings to be built in flat areas or with low slopes and that they are susceptible to flooding [51]. The construction of the Poza Honda dam was done in order to store water for agricultural irrigation and drinking water, and prevent flooding. However, in times of heavy rains it has not helped to minimize the impact of floods, quite the contrary. The Poza Honda dam has suffered up to 30% of silt deposition and therefore its storage capacity has been reduced, which caused large volumes of water to be evacuated, causing floods [52].

Based on the aforementioned, a rural parish of Portoviejo named Colón has been chosen, as it suffers by a great vulnerability to floods. In this study area has been an urgent need to model the possible flood zones, where we decided to apply the Automated Cellular Model of Evolution of the CAESAR-Lisflood landscape, as a prospective tool. This, since, without the exact delimitation of the flood areas, the population of the Colón parish is exposed to further damage to its infrastructure, economic losses and even loss of lives. The results of the modeling may be used to propose a plan of activities for the relevant decentralized autonomous governments to establish adequate urban planning, territorial reorganization and improved and more efficient land use.

2 Study Area

The Portoviejo canton extends to an area of 967 km^2, comprising 16 parishes, of which nine are urban and seven are rural (see Fig. 1). The present study was performed in the Colón parish, one of the rural parishes of Portoviejo. Colón, composed of 12 districts, has a large production of crops of corn, peanuts, tomatoes, wood production, which is why it is considered an area with great fertility and influence for the industrial development of the canton.

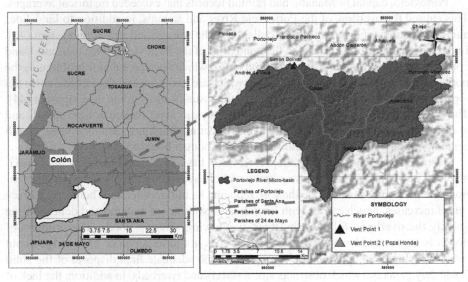

Fig. 1. Location of the Portoviejo canton and Colón parish within in central-western Ecuador (left) and the Portoviejo river micro-basin (right)

The Portoviejo river basin is located in the province of Manabí and includes the cantons of Portoviejo, Santa Ana, Rocafuerte, 24 de Mayo and Jipijapa. It contains three sub-basins, being the upper sub-basin of the Portoviejo River which has 13 micro-basins, as well as the lower sub-basin of the Portoviejo River and of the Chico River which are made up of three micro-basins each. The Colón parish is part of the Portoviejo river micro-basin (see Fig. 1), which extends to an area of 430.97 km^2, to which the morphometric, hydrological and hydrometric characterization was realized.

3   Methodology

The upper sub-basin of the Portoviejo River was divided into several micro-basins, using a 12.5 m Digital Terrain Model ALOS PALSAR from the Japan Aerospace Exploration Agency (JAXA) [53, 54]. In other words, each of the micro-basins of the upper sub-basin of the Portoviejo River was delimited. The existing depressions were eliminated with the "Fill" tool. The flow direction and accumulation files of the digital terrain model were generated from them, with the "Watershed" tool, using the flow direction and each flow direction as input data. One of the outlet points was obtained for each of the micro-basins that compose the area of the upper sub-basin of the Portoviejo River, of which the most fundamental are the micro-basins of the Portoviejo River and the micro-basin of the Poza Honda Dam. Once the Portoviejo river micro-basin was delimited, its morphometric parameters were calculated, such as shape, relief and drainage.

Two methods were used to determine the average rainfall of the Portoviejo river micro-basin, being Thiessen and Isohyetal polygons [55, 56]. For this, it was necessary to use the information of monthly rainfall provided by the National Institute of Meteorology and Hydrology (INAMHI) of nine meteorological stations that are close to the study micro-basin, until the year 2013 [57]. In addition, the free Climate Engine web application was used to obtain average precipitation data from 2014 to 2020 [58].

Probable maximum daily rainfall was calculated using the Gumbel distribution function, which allowed for the Intensity-Duration and Frequency Curves and from them the hyetograms were made at return periods (10, 25, 50, 100, 500 years) of the meteorological stations of Portoviejo UTM (M005), SANCAN (M449), 24 de Mayo (M447) and La Teodomira (M1208) [59–61]. To determine the probable maximum flows at different return periods, we entered in the HEC-HMS software the values of the calculated hyetograms, the approximate concentration time of three hours, based on the equations of Témez, Kirpich and delay and the number curve value of 77.28 [62, 63].

In order to realize the flood modeling with CAESAR-Lisflood, a resample Digital Elevation Model (DEM) of 24.5 m was used (64–66). ALOS PALSAR in ASCII format and a bedrock DEM in the same format, delimited in the Colón parish. In the catchment mode five files were used in.txt format of precipitation values (historical and probable maximums at different return periods) and the sizes of the sediments of point 5 (adjacent to the Colón parish zone of flood modeling) that were obtained from a granulometric analysis by sieving. While in the Reach Mode, five files in.txt format of flow values (historical and probable maximum at different return periods) were used, as well as the size of the sediments from point 5. In addition, we configured vegetation parameters, such as vegetation resistance to being washed away, growth rate and erosion rate; slope parameters: creep rate, slope above which landslides can occur. This followed the flow parameters, being minimum flow to calculate depth, maximum flow to calculate a depth limit, depth at which erosion starts to occur, cell slope, evaporation rate, Froude number, and Manning's n value [67, 68]. Finally the model was run.

After several attempts to run the CAESAR-Lisflood model, the corresponding corrections were realized when the flooding areas and water heights that could affect the Colón parish of the Portoviejo canton in the event of maximum rainfall or maximum flows were obtained at different return periods. In addition, we performed an analysis of the areas of affectation of buildings by the flow of water. These results were compared with those obtained previously by [69] in which the one-dimensional HEC-RAS model was used [70, 71]. In order to generate the comparison, an analysis of variance (ANOVA) was used, which is a statistical technique with which the mean values of a dependent variable can be compared, according to the variation of independent variables, also called factors [72, 73]. In order to evaluate the hazard of flooding in the Colón parish of the Portoviejo canton, the criteria for determining the level or degree of hazard were considered, which are found in the River Flood Risk Estimation Manual [74, 75], in which it is referred that the hazard of flooding is based on the probability of occurrence and intensity of the same. Three types of intensity were considered according to the height or depth of the water, being high intensity, with depths greater than 1.2 m, medium intensity with depths between 0.6 to 1.2 m and low intensity, with depths less than 0.6 m. The probability of occurrence is given by the return period or frequency, the greater the return period, the less probability of occurrence (Table 1).

Table 1. Flood hazard as a function of intensity level and probability of occurrence or frequency

	Frequency		
	High 5 < Pr < 15	Medium 15 < Pr < 50	Low 50 < Pr < 200 or more
High (H > 1.2)	High	High	High
Medium (0.6 < H < 1.2)	High	Medium	Low
Low (H < 0.6)	Medium	Low	Low

4   Results and Discussion

4.1   Analysis of Significant Differences Between the Affected Areas and Differences Between Flood Heights

When comparing the affected areas that were determined with the Reach Mode of the CAESAR-Lisflood two-dimensional model, with those obtained with the HEC-RAS one-dimensional model, it can be observed that from the Reach Mode of cellular automaton CAESAR-Lisflood slightly smaller affected areas were determined. The areas obtained using the CAESAR-Lisflood Catchment Mode are slightly larger than those obtained with HEC-RAS, however, the differences are shortened compared to the Reach Mode (see Fig. 2).

In order to determine if there are significant differences between the affected areas that were obtained with the CAESAR-Lisflood Model in its two mentioned modes and those obtained by [69] with HEC-RAS, a test was performed. The ANOVA, of one factor with a significance level of 95%. The sum of the squares, degrees of freedom and average of the squares were calculated for each of the factors or independent variables. Finally, Fc (calculated F) and critical F (table F) were calculated. According to Table 2, the critical F is greater than Fc, therefore, H_0 is accepted, that is, there is no significant difference between the affected areas if the CAESAR-Lisflood model is used in its two modes, being Catchment Mode, Reach Mode or HEC-RAS [76].

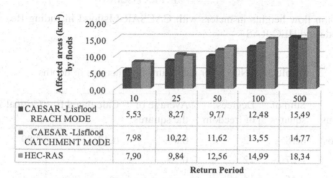

	10	25	50	100	500
■ CAESAR -Lisflood REACH MODE	5,53	8,27	9,77	12,48	15,49
■ CAESAR -Lisflood CATCHMENT MODE	7,98	10,22	11,62	13,55	14,77
■ HEC-RAS	7,90	9,84	12,56	14,99	18,34

Return Period

Fig. 2. Affected areas (km^2) in the Colón-Portoviejo parish Reach, Catchment Mode and HEC-RAS

Table 2. Analysis of variance (ANOVA) for affected areas

Origin of the variations	Sum of squares	Degrees of freedom	Average of the squares	Calculated F	Critical value for F
between groups	14.66	2	7.33	0.56	3.89
within groups	156.01	12	13.00		
Total	170.67	14			

An analysis of ANOVA was performed with a significance level of 95%, in order to determine whether or not there are significant differences in flow heights or depths when using the two CAESAR-Lisflood modes and the one-dimensional HEC-RAS model. As listed in Table 3, the Critical F is 3.89 and is greater than the Fc, therefore, the null hypothesis (H_0) is accepted. All the mean maximum heights are equal in each of the groups or models and there are no significant differences (see Fig. 3).

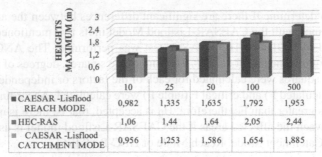

	10	25	50	100	500
CAESAR -Lisflood REACH MODE	0,982	1,335	1,635	1,792	1,953
HEC-RAS	1,06	1,44	1,64	2,05	2,44
CAESAR -Lisflood CATCHMENT MODE	0,956	1,253	1,586	1,654	1,885

RETURN PERIOD

Fig. 3. Maximum flow heights in meters with CAESAR-Lisflood including Reach as well as Catchment Mode and HEC-RAS

Table 3. ANOVA for maximum flow heights or depths

Origin of the variations	Sum of squares	Degrees of freedom	Average of the squares	Calculated F	Critical value for F
between groups	0.18	2	0.09	0.47	3.89
within groups	2.27	12	0.19		
Total	2.45	14			

4.2 Percentage of Affected Areas by Districts of Colón Parish with CAESAR-Lisflood, Reach Mode and Catchment Mode

It was determined what percentage of the total flood area would affect the twelve neighborhoods of the Colón parish using the Reach Mode (see Fig. 4), and with the Catchment Mode (see Fig. 5). The districts most affected by a possible flood are Los Ángeles de Colón, La Mocora, El Cadi, San Ignacio, El Naranjo and Centro de Colón. While the least affected neighborhoods are Mapasingue, Pachinche and El Pollo.

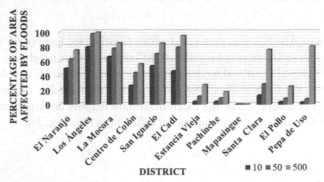

Fig. 4. Percentage of affected areas in the neighborhoods of the Colón parish with the CAESAR-Lisflood-Reach Mode

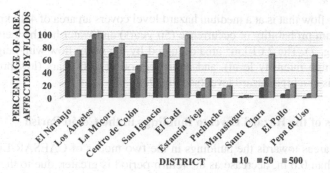

Fig. 5. Percentage of affected areas in the neighborhoods of the Colón parish with the CAESAR-Lisflood-Catchment Mode

Areas with depths or heights of water less than 0.6 m decrease from the return period of 50 years to the return period of 500 years, this is because the area that decreases, moves and occupies another place at a depth larger when the return period is larger (see Fig. 6). The areas that contain water heights between 0.6 to 1.2 m or greater than 1.2 m, increase as the return period increases, due to the increase in maximum flow. For a return period of 100 years, the probability of occurrence is low for the water to occupy an area of 3.06 km^2 and with water flow heights greater than 1.2 m (high intensity level). Therefore, it is in a high hazard level (see Fig. 6).

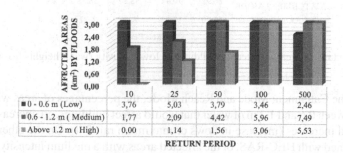

	10	25	50	100	500
■ 0 - 0.6 m (Low)	3,76	5,03	3,79	3,46	2,46
■ 0.6 - 1.2 m (Medium)	1,77	2,09	4,42	5,96	7,49
■ Above 1.2 m (High)	0,00		1,14	1,56	3,06	5,53

RETURN PERIOD

Fig. 6. Flood hazard according to water height (m), CAESAR -Lisflood-Reach Mode

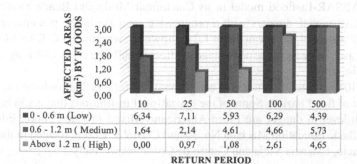

	10	25	50	100	500
■ 0 - 0.6 m (Low)	6,34	7,11	5,93	6,29	4,39
■ 0.6 - 1.2 m (Medium)	1,64	2,14	4,61	4,66	5,73
■ Above 1.2 m (High)	0,00	0,97	1,08	2,61	4,65

RETURN PERIOD

Fig. 7. Flood hazard according to water height (m) -CAESAR-Lisflood-Cathment Mode

The water flow that is at a medium hazard level covers an area of 4.42 km^2, because it has a medium probability of occurrence (50 years) and water heights between 0.6 to 1.2 m (see Fig. 7). The 2.61 km^2 area occupied by the water flow with heights greater than 1.2 m (high intensity level), and return period of 100 years (low probability of occurrence), is at a high hazard level (see Fig. 7).

4.3 Analysis of the Hazard Level to Buildings in the Colón Parish

The affected areas towards the buildings in the two modes of CAESAR-Lisflood with heights less than 0.6 m, decrease as the return period is greater, due to the increase in maximum flows or maximum rainfall. With the HEC-RAS model, however, the percentages of areas that would be affected by water heights of less than 0.6 m also decrease (see Fig. 8).

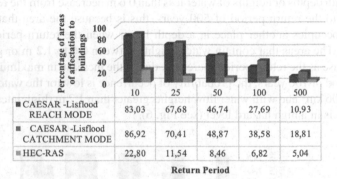

	10	25	50	100	500
■ CAESAR -Lisflood REACH MODE	83,03	67,68	46,74	27,69	10,93
■ CAESAR -Lisflood CATCHMENT MODE	86,92	70,41	48,87	38,58	18,81
■ HEC-RAS	22,80	11,54	8,46	6,82	5,04

Return Period

Fig. 8. Percentage of areas affected by buildings at low intensity (water heights less than 0.6 m)

Within the Catchment Mode and Reach Mode, the percentages of areas with heights of water between 0.6 and 1.2 m of water that would affect buildings, are increasing, as the return period increases (increase in flows or maximum rainfall). On the other hand, the results obtained with HEC-RAS, of the affected areas with a medium intensity, increases from 77.20% to 84.16% at return periods of 10 and 25 years respectively, however, from the return period of 50 years, the percentage of involvement decreases.

The CAESAR-Lisflood model in its Catchment Mode and Reach Mode, as with the HEC-RAS model, appears with a progressive increase in the percentage of areas occupied by water heights greater than 1.2 m, however, with the HEC-RAS Model there is a more drastic increase in the percentage of affected building areas with a high intensity type (see Fig. 9).

Figure 10 illustrates the amount of educational institutions that could be affected with a high level of flood hazard. Some of the educational institutions that could be affected with a high level of danger are Liceo Americano Mixed Private School, Educational Center for Basic Education Machala No. 30 and Cristóbal Colón, located in the districts of San Ignacio, Estancia Vieja and Centro de Colón respectively.

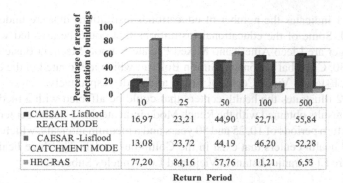

Fig. 9. Percentage of affected areas at a high intensity (water heights greater than 1.2 m)

	10	25	50	100	500
■ CAESAR -Lisflood REACH MODE	16,97	23,21	44,90	52,71	55,84
■ CAESAR -Lisflood CATCHMENT MODE	13,08	23,72	44,19	46,20	52,28
■ HEC-RAS	77,20	84,16	57,76	11,21	6,53

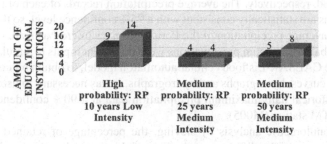

Fig. 10. Educational Institutions with high flood hazard. Reach mode (blue), Catchment (blue) (Color figure online).

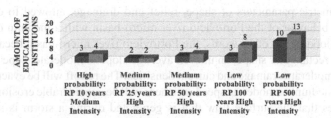

Fig. 11. Educational institutions with medium flood hazard

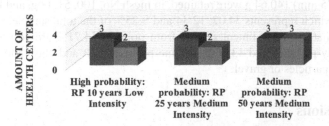

Fig. 12. Health centers with medium flood hazard

Figure 11 indicates the number of educational institutions that are under medium flood hazard. Some of the educational institutions that could be affected with a high level of danger are Liceo Americano Mixed Private School, Machala Basic Education Center No. 30, Cristóbal Colón and Simón Bolívar, which are located in the districts of San Ignacio, Estancia Vieja, Center of Colón and Cadi, respectively.

Figure 12 illustrates the health centers that could be affected with a medium flood hazard. The results obtained with the Reach Mode indicate that 3 health centers could be affected at return periods of 10, 25 and 50 years and a medium intensity, which represents 42.85% of 7 health centers that exist in the Columbus parish. The three health centers mentioned are El Naranjo, Estancia Vieja and Los Angeles Subcenter.

4.4 General Evaluation

The morphometric parameters of shape, relief and drainage, allowed to evaluate the hydrological behavior of the Portoviejo river micro-basin with a medium or moderate tendency to flooding. In other words, the Portoviejo river micro-basin because it has a widened and rectangular shape, an uneven average slope, a moderate slope of the main channel and moderate drainage and current densities. The runoff will be evacuated by the currents at a medium or moderate speed and there will be considerable erosion processes, which implies that the surface flow that is generated during a storm is significantly influenced by the morphometric parameters, mainly by the relief parameters.

Furthermore, the average rainfall of the Portoviejo river micro-basin is 913.84 and 911.48 mm according to the results obtained by the Thiessen Polygon method and the Isohyet method, respectively. The average precipitation records of each of the meteorological stations are statistically consistent with a 95% confidence level, so the calculated values of the average precipitation of the Portoviejo river micro-basin are reliable. The flows and probable maximum precipitations were important inputs to simulate the flood flows with the CAESAR-Lisflood cellular automaton model, to obtain precise precipitation intensity curves, hyetographs and hydrographs, it was necessary to use statistically consistent historical daily maximum precipitation data at a 90% confidence, from the Portoviejo UTM station (M005).

In the granulometric analysis by sieving, the percentage of retained weight and passing percentage in the different mesh sizes of the five sediment samples from the main channel of the Portoviejo River were determined. In the sample of point 5, in mesh No. 200 (0.075 mm) 140.64 g were retained, in mesh No. 100, 51.43 g, and in mesh No. 60, 34.11 g, which represents 34.02, 12.44 and 8.25% of the total sample, respectively. This means that, in the sediment sample from point 5, 54.71% are very fine, fine or medium sandy particles and 43.45% are fine particles (silt and clay) and the rest are coarse sandy particles or gravel.

5 Conclusions

From the areas of the flood zones at different return periods, which were obtained with the CAESAR-Lisflood two-dimensional model in its two Catchment and Reach Modes, the districts that would be most affected in a possible flood were determined. Most of the buildings are located within them, so the authorities should take corrective actions to prevent damage in these districts, which are more vulnerable.

From ANOVA, it was determined that there are no significant differences between the affected areas, heights or depths of flow and the percentage of affected building areas (dependent variables), using three types of methods CAESAR Lisflood in its Catchment and Reach Mode and HEC-RAS (independent variables).

Despite the absence of significant differences between the areas and heights of flooding, the CAESAR-Lisflood two-dimensional model considers erosion and sediment deposition according to the amount of water in each of the cells, as it models the landscape in a way that is close to reality, while one-dimensional HEC-RAS lacks to consider these processes and discretizes the river as a line that is divided into cross sections.

High or medium flood hazard areas are the highest priority to take preventive actions to avoid their infrastructures such as educational institutions, health centers, homes, from having structural damage due to the speed and height of the water and compromise the well-being of the inhabitants of the Colón parish of the Portoviejo canton.

References

1. Hamidifar, H., Nones, M.: Global to regional overview of floods fatality: the 1951–2020 period. In: Natural Hazards and Earth System Sciences Discussions, pp, 1–22 (2021)
2. Kundzewicz, Z.W., Takeuchi, K.: Flood protection and management: quo vadimus? Hydrol. Sci. J. 44(3), 417–432 (1999)
3. Kron, W., et al.: How to deal properly with a natural catastrophe database–analysis of flood losses. Nat. Hazard Earth Syst. Sci. 12(3), 535–550 (2012)
4. Jonkman, S.N., et al.: Integrated hydrodynamic and economic modelling of flood damage in the Netherlands. Ecol. Econ. 66(1), 77–90 (2008)
5. Mato, F., Toulkeridis, T.: The missing Link in El Niño's phenomenon generation. Sci. Tsunami Haz. 36, 128–144 (2017)
6. Toulkeridis, T., et al.: Climate change according to Ecuadorian academics–perceptions versus facts. La Granja 31(1), 21–49 (2020)
7. Trenberth, K.E.: The definition of el nino. Bull. Am. Meteor. Soc. 78(12), 2771–2778 (1997)
8. Covey, D.L., Hastenrath, S.: The pacific el nino phenomenon and the Atlantic circulation. Mon. Weather Rev. 106(9), 1280–1287 (1978)
9. Philander, S.G.H.: El Nino southern oscillation phenomena. Nature 302(5906), 295–301 (1983)
10. Poku-Boansi, M., et al.: What the state does but fails: Exploring smart options for urban flood risk management in informal Accra, Ghana. City Environ. Interact. 5, 100038 (2020)
11. Zia, A., Wagner, C.H.: Mainstreaming early warning systems in development and planning processes: multilevel implementation of Sendai framework in Indus and Sahel. Int. J. Disaster Risk Sci. 6(2), 189–199 (2015)
12. Morss, R.E., et al.: Flash flood risks and warning decisions: a mental models study of forecasters, public officials, and media broadcasters in Boulder, Colorado. Risk Anal. 35(11), 2009–2028 (2015)
13. Li, W., et al.: Risk assessment and sensitivity analysis of flash floods in ungauged basins using coupled hydrologic and hydrodynamic models. J. Hydrol. 572, 108–120 (2019)
14. Pathan, A.I., et al.: Application of new HEC-RAS version 5 for 1D hydrodynamic flood modeling with special reference through geospatial techniques: a case of River Purna at Navsari, Gujarat, India. Model. Earth Syst. Environ. 7(2), 1133–1144 (2021)

15. Scionti, F., et al.: Integrated methodology for urban flood risk mitigation in Cittanova, Italy. J. Water Resour. Plan. Manag. **144**(10), 05018013 (2018)

16. Fang, H., Han, D., He, G., Chen, M.: Flood management selections for the Yangtze River midstream after the Three Gorges Project operation. J. Hydrol. **432**, 1–11 (2012)

17. Fleischmann, A., Collischonn, W., Paiva, R., Tucci, C.E.: Modeling the role of reservoirs versus floodplains on large-scale river hydrodynamics. Nat. Hazards **99**(2), 1075–1104 (2019)

18. Reguero, B.G., et al.: Effects of climate change on exposure to coastal flooding in Latin America and the Caribbean. PLoS ONE **10**(7), e0133409 (2015)

19. Hidalgo-Bastidas, J.P., Boelens, R.: The political construction and fixing of water over-abundance: rural–urban flood-risk politics in coastal Ecuador. Water Int. **44**(2), 169–187 (2019)

20. Calil, J., et al.: Comparative coastal risk index (CCRI): a multidisciplinary risk index for Latin America and the Caribbean. PLoS ONE **12**(11), e0187011 (2017)

21. Echegaray-Aveiga, R.C., et al.: Effects of potential lahars of the Cotopaxi volcano on housing market prices. J. Appl. Volcanol. **9**, 1–11 (2019)

22. Yépez, V., Toledo, J., Toulkeridis, T.: The armed forces as a state institution in immediate response and its participation as an articulator in the risk management in Ecuador. Smart Innov. Syst. Technol. **181**, 545–554 (2020)

23. Toulkeridis, T., Buchwaldt, R., Addison, A.: When volcanoes threaten, scientists warn. Geotimes **52**, 36–39 (2007)

24. Toulkeridis, T., et al.: Evaluation of the initial stage of the reactivated Cotopaxi volcano - analysis of the first ejected fine-grained material. Nat. Hazards Earth Syst. Sci. **3**(11), 6947–6976 (2015)

25. Rodriguez, F., et al.: The economic evaluation and significance of an early relocation versus complete destruction by a potential tsunami of a coastal city in Ecuador. Sci. Tsunami Haz. **35**(1), 18–35 (2016)

26. Toulkeridis, T., et al.: Causes and consequences of the sinkhole at El Trébol of Quito, Ecuador - implications for economic damage and risk assessment. Nat. Hazards Earth Sci. Syst. **16**, 2031–2041 (2016)

27. Toulkeridis, T.: The evaluation of unexpected results of a seismic hazard applied to a modern hydroelectric center in central Ecuador. J. Struct. Eng. **43**(4), 373–380 (2016)

28. Rodriguez, F., et al.: Economic risk assessment of Cotopaxi volcano Ecuador in case of a future lahar emplacement. Nat. Hazards **85**(1), 605–618 (2017)

29. Toulkeridis, T., et al.: The 7.8 M_W Earthquake and Tsunami of the 16th April 2016 in Ecuador - seismic evaluation, geological field survey and economic implications. Sci. Tsunami Haz. **36**, 197–242 (2017)

30. Jaramillo Castelo, C.A., et al.: Comparative determination of the probability of landslide occurrences and susceptibility in central Quito, Ecuador. In: 2018 5th International Conference on eDemocracy and eGovernment, ICEDEG 2018, vol. 8372318, pp. 136–143 (2018)

31. Zafrir Vallejo, R., et al.: Numerical probability modeling of past, present and future landslide occurrences in northern Quito, Ecuador – economic implications and risk assessments. In: 2018 5th International Conference on eDemocracy and eGovernment, ICEDEG 2018, vol. 8372318, pp. 117–125 (2018)

32. Sandoval-Erazo, W., et al.: Velocity and time of concentration of a basin – a renewed approach applied in the Rio Grande Basin, Ecuador. IOP Conf. Ser. Earth Environ. Sci. **191**(1), 012117 (2018)

33. Sandoval-Erazo, W., et al.: Sedimentological study of the reservoir of the Manduriacu hydroelectric project, northern Ecuador. IOP Conf. Ser. Earth Environ. Sci. **191**(1), 012119 (2018)

34. Chunga, K., et al.: Characterization of seismogenetic crustal faults in the Gulf of Guayaquil, Ecuador. Andean Geol. **46**(1), 66–81 (2019)

35. Toulkeridis, T., et al.: Two independent real-time precursors of the 7.8 Mw earthquake in Ecuador based on radioactive and geodetic processes—powerful tools for an early warning system. J. Geodyn. **126**, 12–22 (2019)
36. Suango Sánchez, V., et al.: Use of geotechnologies and multicriteria evaluation in land use policy – the case of the urban area expansion of the city of Babahoyo, Ecuador. In: 2019 6th International Conference on eDemocracy and eGovernment, ICEDEG 2019, pp. 194–202 (2019)
37. Toulkeridis, T., Echegaray-Aveiga, R.C., Martinez-Maldonado, K.P.: Shock metamorphism in volcanic rock due to the impact of the Miguir-Cajas meteorite in 1995 and its importance for Ecuador. Geoj. Tourism Geosites **35**(2), 315–321 (2021)
38. Espinoza Villar, J.C., et al.: Spatio-temporal rainfall variability in the Amazon basin countries (Brazil, Peru, Bolivia, Colombia, and Ecuador). Int. J. Climatol. J. R. Meteorol. Soc. **29**(11), 1574–1594 (2009)
39. Latrubesse, E.M., et al.: Damming the rivers of the Amazon basin. Nature **546**(7658), 363–369 (2017)
40. Laraque, A., et al.: Heterogeneous distribution of rainfall and discharge regimes in the Ecuadorian Amazon basin. J. Hydrometeorol. **8**(6), 1364–1381 (2007)
41. Pacheco, H., et al.: Causes and consequences of the extraordinary rainfall of 2017 on the Ecuadorian coast: the case of the province of Manabí. Boletín de Investigaciones Marinas y Costeras-INVEMAR **48**(2), 45–70 (2019)
42. El Comercio: Unas 2 500 familias afectadas por inundaciones por lluvia en Manabí (2017). https://www.elcomercio.com/actualidad/ecuador/familias-afectados-inundaciones-lluvia-manabi.html
43. Medina Espinoza, E.G., Panduro Sisniegas, S.C.: Estimación de la vulnerabilidad por inundaciones en la quebrada El León y propuesta de mejora con fines de protección en el centro poblado El Milagro-La Libertad, 2020. Puce unpublished thesis, 141 p. (2021)
44. García, C.L.G., Loor, A.M.A.: Evaluación de zona urbana educativa ante amenazas de riesgo de inundación. Río Portoviejo. Revista de Investigaciones en Energía, Medio Ambiente y Tecnología: RIEMAT **6**(2), 51–66 (2021). ISSN 2588-0721
45. Romano, J., Coral, B.V.: Public management, private management and collective action in the Portoviejo river basin: visions and conflicts. Sustainability **12**(13), 5467 (2020)
46. Giler, B.I.C., et al.: Water quality of the Poza Honda Dam and other water points down. J. Coll Univ. **2454**, 2261 (2017)
47. Cedeno, A.C., et al.: Estimation of the runoff of the hills of the city of Portoviejo-Ecuador to assess the degree of flooding in the region. IOP Conf. Ser. Mater. Sci. Eng. **675**(1), 012020 (2019)
48. Pacheco, H.A., et al.: Soil erosion risk zoning in the Ecuadorian coastal region using geotechnological tools. Earth Sci. Res. J. **23**(4), 293–302 (2019)
49. Ortiz-Hernández, E., Chunga, K., Pastor, J.L., Toulkeridis, T.: Assessing susceptibility to soil liquefaction using the standard penetration test (SPT)—a case study from the city of Portoviejo, Coastal Ecuador. Land **11**(4), 463 (2022)
50. Delgado, D., Sadaoui, M., Pacheco, H., Méndez, W., Ludwig, W.: Interrelations between soil erosion conditioning factors in basins of Ecuador: contributions to the spatial model construction. In: da Costa Sanches Galvão, J.R., et al. (eds.) ICoWEFS 2021, pp. 892–903. Springer, Cham (2021). https://doi.org/10.1007/978-3-030-75315-3_94
51. Burgos, B., et al.: Análisis de la vulnerabilidad a inundaciones de la parroquia Santa Ana de Vuelta Larga, Ecuador. Investigaciones Geográficas **98**, 3–11 (2019)
52. Caballero, G.B., et al.: Water quality of the Poza Honda Dam and other water points down. Int. Res. J. Eng. IT Sci. Res. (IRJEIS) **3**(3), 2454–2261 (2017). http://ijcu.us/online/journal/index.php/irjeis

53. Bakiev, M., Khasanov, K.: Comparison of digital elevation models for determining the area and volume of the water reservoir. Int. J. Geoinf. **17**(1), 37–45 (2021)
54. Rosenqvist, A., et al.: Operational performance of the ALOS global systematic acquisition strategy and observation plans for ALOS-2 PALSAR-2. Remote Sens. Environ. **155**, 3–12 (2014)
55. Fiedler, F.R.: Simple, practical method for determining station weights using Thiessen polygons and isohyetal maps. J. Hydrol. Eng. **8**(4), 219–221 (2003)
56. Şen, Z.: Average areal precipitation by percentage weighted polygon method. J. Hydrol. Eng. **3**(1), 69–72 (1998)
57. INAMHI: Anuario Meteorológico 2013. № 53-2013 Quito, Ecuador. 165 p. (2017)
58. Hegewisch, K., et al.: Climate engine-monitoring drought with Google Earth Engine. In: AGU Fall Meeting Abstracts, vol. 2016, p. IN51B-1841 (2016)
59. Leese, M.N.: Use of censored data in the estimation of Gumbel distribution parameters for annual maximum flood series. Water Resour. Res. **9**(6), 1534–1542 (1973)
60. Fadhel, S., et al.: Uncertainty of intensity–duration–frequency (IDF) curves due to varied climate baseline periods. J. Hydrol. **547**, 600–612 (2017)
61. Témez, J.R.: Control de la erosión fluvial en puentes. Ministerio de Obras Públicas y Urbanismo (MOPU), Madrid, Espana (1988)
62. Cuevas, J.G., Arumí, J.L., Dörner, J.: Assessing methods for the estimation of response times of stream discharge: the role of rainfall duration. J. Hydrol. Hydromech. **67**(2), 143–153 (2019)
63. Kirpich, Z.P.: Time of concentration of small agricultural watersheds. Civil Eng. **10**(6), 362–368 (1940)
64. Coulthard, T.J., et al.: Integrating the LISFLOOD-FP 2D hydrodynamic model with the CAESAR model: implications for modelling landscape evolution. Earth Surf. Proc. Land. **38**(15), 1897–1906 (2013)
65. Feeney, C.J., Chiverrell, R.C., Smith, H.G., Hooke, J.M., Cooper, J.R.: Modelling the decadal dynamics of reach-scale river channel evolution and floodplain turnover in CAESAR-Lisflood. Earth Surf. Proc. Land. **45**(5), 1273–1291 (2020)
66. Wilson, M.D., Coulthard, T.J.: Tracing and visualisation of contributing water sources in the LISFLOOD-FP model of flood inundation. In: Geoscientific Model Development Discussions, pp. 1–28 (2021)
67. Jia, Y.: Minimum Froude number and the equilibrium of alluvial sand rivers. Earth Surf. Proc. Land. **15**(3), 199–209 (1990)
68. García Díaz, R.: Analysis of manning coefficient for small-depth flows on vegetated beds. Hydrol. Process Int. J. **19**(16), 3221–3233 (2005)
69. Sandoval, W., et al.: Risk and vulnerability analysis of flood hazards in the Colón Parrish, western Ecuador based on HEC-RAS numerical simulation. In: Proceedings of CIT 2021, Smart Innovation, Systems and Technologies (SIST) (2022, accepted, in press)
70. Ghimire, E., Sharma, S., Lamichhane, N.: Evaluation of one-dimensional and two-dimensional HEC-RAS models to predict flood travel time and inundation area for flood warning system. ISH J. Hydraul. Eng. **28**(1), 110–126 (2022)
71. Gibson, S., et al.: New one-dimensional sediment features in HEC-RAS 5.0 and 5.1. In: World Environmental and Water Resources Congress 2017, pp. 192–206 (2017)
72. St, L., Wold, S.: Analysis of variance (ANOVA). Chemom. Intell. Lab. Syst. **6**(4), 259–272 (1989)
73. Alvan Romero, N., Cigna, F., Tapete, D.: ERS-1/2 and Sentinel-1 SAR data mining for flood hazard and risk assessment in Lima. Peru. Appl. Sci. **10**(18), 6598 (2020)
74. Greiving, S., et al.: Participatory assessment of multi risks in urban regions—the case of critical infrastructures in Metropolitan Lima. Sustainability **13**(5), 2813 (2021)

75. Mallma, S.F.T.: Mainstreaming land use planning into disaster risk management: trends in Lima, Peru. Int. J. Disaster Risk Reduct. **62**, 102404 (2021)
76. Van De Wiel, M.J., et al.: Embedding reach-scale fluvial dynamics within the CAESAR cellular automaton landscape evolution. Geomorphology **90**(3–4), 283–301 (2007)

Exergetic Analysis of Reheating and Regeneration Alternatives in Steam Cycles for the Generation of Electricity from Municipal Solid Waste

N. Y. Castillo-Leon[1]([⊠]) (iD), B. E. Tarazona-Romero[1,2] (iD),
C. L. Sandoval-Rodriguez[1] (iD), A. D. Rincon-Quintero[1] (iD),
and J. G. Ascanio-Villabona[1,2] (iD)

[1] College of Natural Sciences and Engineering, Unidades Tecnológicas de Santander,
Bucaramanga, Colombia
nycastillo@correo.uts.edu.co
[2] Energy Engineering Department, University of the Basque Country, Bizkaia, Spain

Abstract. The present study aims to apply a conventional exergy analysis to different configurations of the Rankine cycle incorporating regeneration and reheating processes through an analytical approach, together with mathematical models governed by the second law of thermodynamics and CoolProp™ software, three scenarios were evaluated, quantifying the irreversibilities of the system with higher exergy destruction and the processes that generate them. The steam parameters of the Rankine cycles were estimated at 40 bar and 380 °C, with a Low Heating Value (LHV) of Municipal Solid Waste (MSW) of 8,786 kJ/kg. The energy analysis identified the plant's energy destruction of about 55.6 MW, of which 90% is produced in the waste boiler. The incorporation of a reheating stage increases the energy efficiency by 0.73%, and the configuration with three regenerators increases the energy efficiency by 0.63%, delivering 88.5 GWh of electricity per year to the grid.

Keywords: Exergetic analysis · Rankine cycle · Incineration · Electricity generation · Municipal solid waste

1 Introduction

The economic and demographic growth of countries and cities brings with it the challenges of energy security and proper waste management. Globally in 2016 around 2,010 million tons of MSW were generated and it is expected that in 2030 and 2050 the world will generate 2,590 and 3,400 million tons of MSW respectively, currently this waste is disposed of 40% in controlled landfills and 30% in open dumps [1], This disposal method is the last option in the hierarchy for sustainable waste treatment [2] and is considered a source of greenhouse gases 20 times more potent than carbon dioxide (CO_2) due to the methane (CH_4) contained in the biogas, a product of the biological decomposition

© The Author(s), under exclusive license to Springer Nature Switzerland AG 2023
M. Botto-Tobar et al. (Eds.): ICAT 2022, CCIS 1756, pp. 228–242, 2023.
https://doi.org/10.1007/978-3-031-24971-6_17

of organic matter and contains volatile organic compounds that are harmful to human health [3–5]. Colombia is no stranger to this trend; around 12 million tons of MSW are produced annually, with a per capita generation of 0.85 kg/day per inhabitant [6]. The predominant final disposal model is the disposal of waste through open landfills, where 7.5% of these have already finished their useful life and 15% end their useful cycle in less than a decade [6], reasons why this situation invites the scientific community, along with legislators to develop sustainable alternatives, this study proposes to evaluate at an Exergetic level the WtE technology that uses part of the problem, such as MSW in the solution fuel, in what is called waste to energy (WtE).

Biomass-to-energy conversion has grown rapidly in recent years, including energy valorization of MSW through thermal treatments (incineration, pyrolysis and gasification) and biochemical conversions (anaerobic digestion and fermentation), mainly motivated by hygienic waste disposal, renewable energy production and reductions of environmental impacts [7, 8]. Combustion processes with energy production (electricity, district heating and in some cases, district cooling) represent the most mature technology, tested in more than 2000 WTE plants worldwide, treating about 250 million tons annually and is expected according to estimate of the International Solid Waste Association (ISWA) and the United Nations Environment Programme (UNEP) an increase of 500% in installed capacity for the next decade [9]. Among the above technologies, direct MSW incineration (MSWI) stands out as the most dominant in the WtE industry, with a capacity to process a total of more than 700,000 metric tons per day and 1179 plants installed worldwide [10]. As an added value the MSWI incineration plants have a double objective: reduce the amount of waste sent to landfills and simultaneously recover energy from the waste by means of an energy cycle (steam Rankine cycle) producing electricity or steam as required, However, this technology has technical limitations, perhaps the most relevant, goes through the heterogeneity of MSW that influences the low energy content (LHV) and high humidity, which, Another technical reason that prevents higher percentages of efficiency in WtE plants is observed in the simplicity of configurations used in the steam generation cycles [11, 12].

In the bibliographic review carried out, a field of study to be explored is revealed, a space that this research intends to take, having the possibility of identifying and quantifying thermodynamic performances from an exergetic approach in MSWI WtE plants, incorporating combined regeneration and reheating systems. As an added value, this study did not use specialized commercial software, which are usually expensive and inaccessible for students or researchers from less privileged educational institutions, on the contrary, the results of this study were achieved with an analytical approach, allowing observing the methodologies, assumptions and equations involved in a second law thermodynamic evaluation.

2 Methodology

2.1 Characterization of the Simulated Systems

In order to evaluate the thermal performance and perform the Exergetic analysis on the implementation of the reheating and regeneration alternatives in the steam cycle, four scenarios were defined, simulating 3 plants with different Rankine cycle schemes and configurations, named:

1. Scenario (C0), base case
2. Scenario (C1), Reheating
3. Scenario (C2), Regeneration lution.

Description and Cycle Configuration Used as Base Case (C0)

The plant layout considered for the base or conventional scenario is shown in Fig. 1. Steam cycle schemes for MSW incineration are usually simple, due to the low steam parameters penalized by corrosive agents in the convective heat transfer zone of the boiler. The plant operates as follows. The working fluid leaves pump 2 (compressed liquid) passing through the economizer (saturated steam) and superheater (superheated steam) of the boiler, the superheated steam enters the turbine (stream 5), where it expands to condensing pressure (stream 7). An extraction in the turbine is performed providing the steam necessary for deaerator operation (stream 6). The condensed steam enters pump 1 (stream 1) which increases the water pressure to the deaerator operating pressure (stream 2). Finally, the water enters pump 2, through stream 3, closing the cycle.

In the boiler, the exhaust gases circulate as follows (green dotted line): the exhaust gases exhage energy with the steam generator and enter the superhearter to exchange heat with the steam coming from the bolier. After passing through the superheater, the gases enter the economizer to exchange heat with the water from pump. The exhaust gases exit the economizer and enter the air prehearter, where the combustion air is heated.

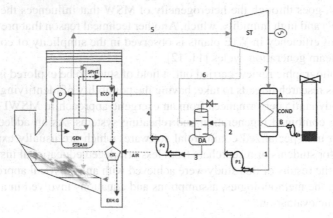

Fig. 1. Base case configuration (C0)

Description and Configuration of Cycle with Superheat (C1)

Figure 2 shows a steam cycle considering a reheat stage. The purpose of introducing a reheat stage in this scenario is to reduce the moisture content of the steam in the final stage of expansion in the turbine and thus increase the cycle efficiency, an optimum reheat pressure is determined by means of a sensitivity calculation, iterating pressure values in the turbine extraction as a function of the maximum thermal efficiency of the cycle as considered by [13]. The plant operates as follows. The working fluid leaves pump 2 with stream 4, (compressed liquid) passing through the economizer (saturated steam) and superheater (superheated steam) of the boiler, the superheated steam enters the high pressure turbine (stream 5), where it expands to reheat pressure and returns to the boiler (stream 5″) where it is reheated to constant pressure reaching the same inlet temperature of the high pressure turbine. Stream 5″ enters the low turbine, expanding to condensing pressure (stream 7). An extraction in the turbine is performed providing the steam necessary for deaerator operation (stream 6). The condensed steam enters pump 1 (stream 1) which increases the water pressure to the deaerator operating pressure (stream 2). Finally, the water enters pump 2, through stream 3, closing the cycle.

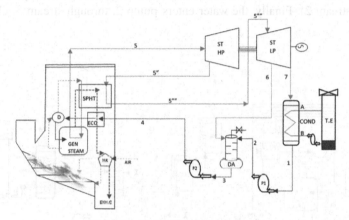

Fig. 2. Reheating configuration (C1)

Description and Configuration of Cycle with Regeneration (C2)

The proposed steam cycle with regeneration (Fig. 3), is characterized by including the two types of regeneration most used in thermoelectric plants (open feed water and backward cascade drainage). Closed heaters with backward cascade drainage can be of two types, saturated or slightly undercooled; the feedwater temperature at the outlet of a closed type regenerator cannot reach the inlet temperature of steam extracted from the turbine. Therefore, there is a terminal temperature differential (TTD) between 4 and 6 °C which depends on the design properties of the regenerator [14]. The TTD can be defined as the difference between the steam extraction inlet temperature for saturation conditions and the feed or drain water outlet temperature [15], the TTD adopted in this work was 5 °C, according to recommendations proposed by Ref. [14, 16]. The maximum efficiency is reached when the feedwater heaters reach the optimal temperature difference Δt opt, which can be calculated with Eq. 1.

$$\Delta \text{topt} = \frac{(\text{TSat})_{\text{BOIL}} - (\text{TSat})_{\text{COND}}}{n + 1} \tag{1}$$

The plant operates as follows. The working fluid leaves pump 2 (stream 4) at boiler pressure, passing through the regenerators R1, R2 and R3 of closed characteristics, leaving the regenerator R3 (stream 7) enters the economizer (saturated steam) and superheater (superheated steam) of the boiler, the superheated steam enters the turbine (stream 8), where it expands to condensing pressure (stream 19). Four extractions in the turbine are performed providing the steam necessary for the operation of the deaerator (stream 18), regenerator R1 (stream 15), regenerator R2 (stream 12) and regenerator R3 (stream 9). The extraction pressure of the regenerators was calculated using the method [14], after leaving regenerator R3, stream 10 undergoes an isoenthalpic process in valve 3 (V3) reaching the pressure of R2 (stream 11). Stream 13 enters valve 2 (V2), which by means of an isentropic process reaches the pressure of R1. (stream 14). Stream 16 enters valve 1 (V1), which reaches the deaerator pressure (stream 17). The condensed steam enters pump 1 (stream 1) which increases the water pressure to the operating pressure of the deaerator (stream 2). Finally, the water enters pump 2, through stream 3, closing the cycle.

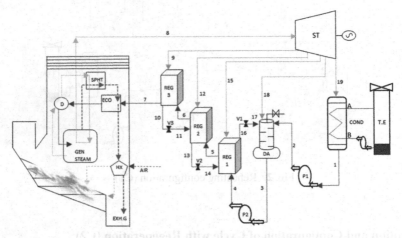

Fig. 3. Regeneration configuration (C2)

2.2 Exergy Analysis

For this study, a conventional exergy analysis was performed, allowing the quantification of system irreversibilities that can be (i) internal, such as friction and heat transfer within the system; or (ii) external, such as heat transfer from the system to its surroundings (e.g., cooling water leaving the condenser, flue gas emissions), which makes it necessary to identify the devices in the system with the highest exergy destruction and the processes that cause it, the efficiency of the devices can be improved by reducing their exergy destruction due to technological constraints. The methodology used in the exergy analysis of the proposed scenarios is shown in Fig. 6, using second law thermodynamic concepts it is possible to calculate the chemical exergy of the MSW, the exergy flows, and the exergy destroyed per device. Once the initial parameters of the plant have been defined (see Table 1), an energy analysis allows to calculate the main thermody-namic properties in each state of the cycle, Pressure (P), Temperature (T), Enthalpy (h), Entropy (s). For this purpose, the software CoolProp [17] was used. The assumptions of the calculations are: (I) The system operates in steady state; (II) Each component of the system is analyzed as a control volume; (III) Kinetic and potential energy variations are negligible; (IV) The higher internal electricity consumption is taken into account; (V) Mechanical and electrical losses in the turbine and electric generator, boiler blowdown, incomplete combustion and steam losses through joints are not considered; (VI) Pressure drops in the boilers and piping are not considered (Fig. 4).

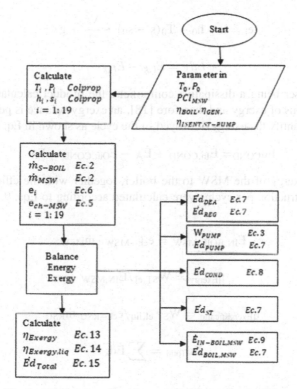

Fig. 4. Methodology used in analysis Exergetic calculations.

Considering thermodynamic concepts and principles of mass and energy conserva-tion, the steam production of the boiler and waste flows entering the furnace can be calculated by means of Eq. 2.

$$\dot{m}_{S,OUT,BOIL} = \frac{\dot{m}_{RSU} \cdot \eta_{BOIL} \cdot PCI_{RSU}}{(h_{OUT,BOIL} - h_{IN,BOIL})} \tag{2}$$

The calculation of the pump works is described in Eq. 3.

$$w_{PUMP} = v_{IN} \cdot (P_{OUT} - P_{IN})/\eta_{Isent-PUMP} \tag{3}$$

The exergy of each stream was calculated as the sum of the physical and chemical exergies, according to Eq. 4.

$$e = e_{ch} + e_{ph} \tag{4}$$

The calculation of the chemical exergy of MSW is determined by means of Eq. 5.

$$e_{ch-MSW} = (LHV_{MSW} \cdot \beta) + (bchs - Cs) \cdot zs + bcha \cdot za + bchw \cdot zw \tag{5}$$

The exergy fluxes in the different process streams and the exergy destruction for each component are calculated with Eqs. 6 and 7 respectively.

$$e_i = h - h_0 - T_0(s - s_0) + \frac{V^2}{2} + gz \tag{6}$$

$$\dot{E}d_k = \dot{E}_{I,k} - \dot{E}_{P,k} \tag{7}$$

The condenser being a dissipative component, the product calculation cannot be expressed in terms of exergy and therefore [18], an exergy balance is performed in the condenser to quantify the exergy destroyed in the cycle as shown in Eq. 8.

$$\dot{E}d_{COND} = \dot{E}_{In,COND} + \dot{E}_A - \dot{E}_{Out,COND} - \dot{E}_B \tag{8}$$

The input exergy of the MSW to the boiler, together with the efficiency and the total exergy destruction per cycle, were calculated according to Eqs. 9, 10, 11 and 12 respectively.

$$\dot{E}_{IN,BOIL,MSW} = e_{ch-MSW} \cdot \dot{m}_{MSW} \tag{9}$$

$$\eta_{Exergy} = \dot{W}_{ST,el}/\dot{E}_{IN,MSW} \tag{10}$$

$$\eta_{Exergéticaliq} = \dot{W}_{ST,el,liq}/e_{ch-RSU} \cdot \dot{m}_{RSU} \tag{11}$$

$$\dot{E}d_{Total} = \sum \dot{E}d_k \tag{12}$$

3   Theory/Calculation

3.1   Plant Operation Parameters

In the present study, the energetic and physical conditions of the solid urban waste flows that enter the El Carrasco landfill, located in the city of Bucaramanga (Colombia), which manages the final disposal of waste from the metropolitan area of Bucaramanga (Girón, Piedecuesta, Floridablanca), were taken as a reference case. The plant electrical power ($\dot{W}_{ST,el}$) was set for all scenarios at 15 MW, with which we can represent the efficiency of the plant in terms of using less fuel (MSW) and maintaining the electrical power, the landfill receives an average of 1000 t of MSW per day. The plant parameters considered are shown in Table 1.

Table 1. Parameters considered in simulation of steam plant.

Parameter		Value	Ref
Ambient temperature	$(T_0)°C$	25	[19]
Ambient pressure	$(P_0)kPa$	101.325	[19]
Furnace temperature	$(T_{Furnace})$ °C	1,150	[20]
MSW fuel LHV	$(LHV_{MSW})kJ/kg$	8,786	[21]
Steam temperature	$(T_{ST}).°C$	380	[22]
Boiler pressure	$(P_{ST})kPa$	4,000	[22]
Boiler Efficiency	$(\eta_{BOIL})\%$	75	[9]
Generator Efficiency	$(\eta_{Gen})\%$	96	[23]
Pump isentropic Efficiency	$(\eta_{Isent-PUMP})\%$	85	[24]
Steam turbine isentropic Efficiency	$(\eta_{Isent-ST})\%$	85	[25]
Condensing pressure	(P_{COND}) kPa	15	[26]
Deareador pressure	(P_{DEA}) kPa	350	[14]
Installed power	$(\dot{W}_{ST,el})MW$	15	[27]
Hours of operation	(Hrs/year)	8,000	[28]
Electric energy consumed plant	$(EECP)kWh/t_{RSU}$	150	[27]

3.2 Mass and Energy Balances

Based on the concepts in the first law of thermodynamics, the properties of the main flows of the proposed plants were calculated, the results are shown in reference [29]. By means of a mass and energy balance for each component of the system, the energy yields described in Table 2 were calculated.

3.3 Exergetic Analysis

In order to calculate the exergy efficiency and identify which equipment and devices contribute most to the exergy destruction of the different scenarios, an analysis was carried out on each of the plant components, initially calculating the exergies of the fuels. In this work, the reference pressure (P_0) is one atmosphere (101,325 kPa) and the reference temperature is (T_0) is 25 °C. It is considered that the intensive properties of the environment do not change significantly with the interaction of any process in question, thus remaining a reference environment without irreversibilities. The exergy of each stream was calculated as the sum of the physical and chemical exergies, according to Eq. 4. If the kinetic and potential components of the exergy are ignored, the physical flow exergy can be calculated according to Eq. 13.

$$e_{Ph} = h - h_0 - T_0(s - s_0) \qquad (13)$$

MSW Fuel Chemical Exergy

For all evaluated scenarios the input exergy of MSW was considered. The MSW chemical exergy was calculated for the solid components C, H, O, N, using Eqs. 5 and 14 [27]. Where, *bcha* is the chemical exergy of ash which is generally discriminated, *bchw.zw* is the standard chemical exergy of water; zs, za and zw are the mass fraction of sulphur, ash and water respectively. Finally, the expression (*bchs* − *Cs*) from standard values found in the [30], where *bchs* is the standard chemical exergy of sulfur [27]. The physical composition of MSW in this study was determined by averaging three studies conducted at the el carrasco landfill, [21, 31]. Lacking a study on the chemical composition of MSW entering the carrasco, the chemical composition of MSW from Santo André was taken as a reference with previous evaluation, taking into account their socioeconomic similarities [32].

$$\beta = \frac{1.044 + 0.016\left(\frac{H}{C}\right) - 0.3493\left(\frac{O}{C}\right)\left[1 + 0.0531\left(\frac{H}{C}\right)\right] + 0.0493\left(\frac{N}{C}\right)}{1 - 0.4124\left(\frac{O}{C}\right)} \tag{14}$$

Calculation of Exergy Destroyed by Each Component and Cycle Exergy Efficiency

With the calculated exergy flows followed by mass and exergy balances, it was possible to determine the exergy destructions per device, the total exergy destroyed and the exergy efficiency per scenario. The exergy entering a component is equal to the exergy of products, plus Exergy destroyed, plus Exergy losses, as shown in Eq. 15.

$$\dot{E}_{F,tot} = \dot{E}_{P,tot} + \dot{E}_{d,tot} + \dot{E}_{l,tot} \tag{15}$$

Exergy losses, $\dot{E}_{l,tot}$ should not be confused with exergy destruction, exergy losses consist of exergy flowing into the surroundings, while exergy destruction indicates exergy loss within the process boundaries due to irreversibilities. For each device there is an input (fuel) and an output, the exergy destruction is determined by the difference input minus output in each device [29].

4   Results and Discussion

In this study, alternatives have been implemented in the plant design, such as regeneration devices and reheating techniques of recirculated steam in the MSW boiler, three scenarios were established in which there is a base or conventional scenario, against which the results found will be contrasted. In order to quantify the efficiency gains in each scenario, an energy analysis was carried out, from which the first law thermal efficiency was obtained together with other useful parameters of the evaluated systems. For the scenarios studied, the best thermal performance is achieved in C1, obtaining a thermal efficiency of 23.41%, generating approximately 418 kWh for each ton of waste entering the furnace and delivering 88.5 GW per year to the grid. The other parameters of the energy analysis are presented in Table 2.

Table 2. Main results of mass and energy balances.

Parámeter		C0	C1	C2
Steam production	TON$_{Steam}$/hr	5.352	4.607	6.075
Plant Capacity	TON$_{MSW}$/day	651.346	629.99	633.4
Thermal efficiency	%	22.6	23.41	23.3
Electricity to grid	GWh/year	87.433	88.500	88.32
Specific MSW consumtion	kg/kWh	1.810	1.749	1.759
Net electricity generation	kWh/t$_{MSW}$	402.701	421.43	418.3

The calculation of exergy yields shows a higher exergy efficiency and lower exergy destruction in C1, about 1% and 2.4 MW respectively, compared to the base case C0, presenting the best performance in terms of exergy lost. The other results are presented in Table 3.

Table 3. Exergy performance per scenario

Parámeter		C0	C1	C2
Exergetic Efficiency	%	20.37	21.1	21
MSW to Exergy	MW	73.6	71.2	71.6
Destroyed exergy	MW	57.9	55.5	55.7
Exergy losses	MW	0.7	0.69	0.92

In the methodology of the exergy analysis applied in this study, it was proposed to determine the exergy destruction of each device in the different scenarios, the results show that the greatest exergy destruction occurs in the boiler, about 90% of the total exergy destruction. The problem with this device lies in the steam parameters (4. 0 MPa/380 °C), which are penalized by corrosion problems [33], there is little that can be done to reduce the irreversibilities that occur in this device; however, technological advances regarding materials with higher corrosion resistance (Inconel) among others [34], would allow reducing the exergy destroyed in the boiler, which would be reflected in the exergy yield of the cycle. Table 4, together, with Figs. 7, 8 and 9, show the percentages of exergy destroyed by each component (Fig. 5).

In this study, the option of modifying the plant configurations was addressed, thus, regeneration, reheat and the simultaneous incorporation of reheat and C3 regeneration in the steam cycle were implemented. In scenario C1, the incorporation of a reheat stage that recirculates steam in the boiler and expands in the steam turbine with higher quality, allows reducing the exergy destruction in the boiler and steam turbine by 2,020 kW and 200 kW, respectively, compared to the base scenario C0.

Table 4. Value and percentage of exergy destroyed by component

Devices	C0		C1		C2	
	Ed (kW)	% Ed	Ed (kW)	% Ed	Ed (kW)	% Ed
P1	1.71	0.003	1.50	0.003	0.897	0.002
DEA	508.78	0.878	444.61	0.801	221.228	0.397
P2	31.38	0.054	27.01	0.049	11.039	0.020
R1					15.089	0.027
R2					22.174	0.040
R3					82.971	0.149
BOIL	52,481.4	90.60	50,460.83	90.88	50,393.08	90.51
ST-HP	2,407.66	4.157	467.71	0.842	2,422.580	4.351
ST-LP			1,747.74	3.148		
COND	2,492.55	4.303	2,374.07	4.276	2,480.978	4.456
V1					15.042	0.027
V2					7.402	0.013
V3					4.116	0.007

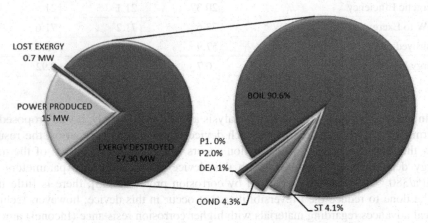

Fig. 5. Percentage of exergy destroyed per components (C0)

With the modification made in scenario C2, which integrated three regenerators and allows the preheating of the boiler feed water by means of steam extractions in the turbine, the exergy destruction in the boiler is reduced by 2,088 kW and 287.5 kW in the deaerator with respect to the base case; however, new devices such as regenerators and throttling valves appear, which add up to exergy destruction in the system and a lost exergy of 200 kW.

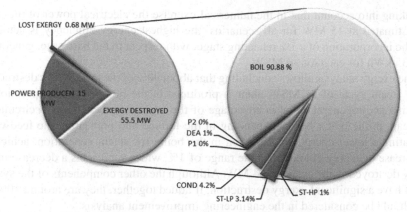

Fig. 6. Percentage of exergy destroyed per components (C1)

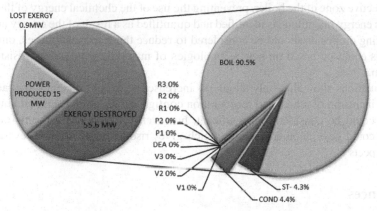

Fig. 7. Percentage of exergy destroyed per components (C2)

Although other components do not have significant exergy destruction, they should be analyzed to quantify an exogenous exergy destruction value associated with them, which can contribute to improved plant performance, but this can only be achieved through advanced exergy analysis [27].

5   Conclusions

The methodology used in the exergetic analysis of the three simulated scenarios, where steam cycle configurations such as regeneration and reheating were implemented, allowed determining favorable thermodynamic performances individually and comparatively and identifying the devices of the generation cycle where the highest irreversibilities are presented.

Taking into account that in the numerical exercise the electrical power of the plant was estimated at 15 MW for all scenarios, the highest energy efficiency is achieved with the incorporation of a 1% reheating stage, with respect to the base case, generating 421,435 kWh for each ton of MSW.

The exergy analysis allows concluding that about 90% of the total exergy destruction in the steam cycle of an MSW plant is produced in the boiler, the incorporation of reheating and regeneration takes advantage of the synergistic benefits of recirculating the steam in the boiler before expanding in the turbine and preheating the feedwater, generating a lower energy consumption in the boiler for steam generation, achieving an increase in exergy efficiency in the range of 1%, which represents a decrease in the exergy destroyed in the cycle of 3.4 MW. Although the other components of the system do not have a significant exergy destruction, if added together, they are around 10%, so they should be considered in the engineering improvement analysis.

A limitation in the thermodynamic performance of direct waste incineration plants is determined by the steam parameters, these parameters are penalized by corrosion in the convective zone of the boiler, preventing the use of the chemical energy of the waste, once this energy magnitude is identified and quantified as a result of the exergy analysis, engineering proposals should be considered to reduce these irreversibilities, one of the proposals could be based on new technologies of materials with greater resistance to corrosion.

Calculations show that only about 1% increase in energy efficiency was achieved with the inclusion of reheat and regeneration configurations, at first sight and in energy terms it could be considered insignificant, however, in economic and environmental terms it could have another reading, which gives rise to future work to evaluate the above aspects.

References

1. Kaza, S., Yao, L., Bhada-Tata, P., Van Woerden, F.: What a waste 2.0. A Global Snapshot of Solid Waste Management to 2050. Washington, DC: World Bank (2018)
2. Wang, D., Tang, Y., Long, G., Higgitt, D., He, J., Robinson, D.: Future improvements on performance of an EU landfill directive driven municipal solid waste management for a city in England. Waste Manag. 102, 452–463 (2020)
3. Glikson, A.: The methane time bomb. Energy Procedia 146, 23–29 (2018). International Carbon Conference 2018, ICC 2018, 10–14 September 2018, Reykjavik, Iceland
4. Nair, A.T., Senthilnathan, J., Nagendra, S.M.S.: Emerging perspectives on VOC emission from landfill sites: impact on tropospheric chemistry and local air quality. Process Saf. Environ. Prot. 121, 143–154 (2018)
5. Wu, C., Liu, J., Liu, S., Li, W., Yan, L., Shu, M.: Chemosphere assessment of the health risks and odor concentration of volatile compounds from a municipal solid waste land fill in China. Chemosphere 202, 1–8 (2018)
6. Universidad Nacional de Colombia: Colombia debe superar etapa de rellenos sanitarios (2017)
7. Cutz, L., Haro, P., Santana, D., Johnsson, F.: Assessment of biomass energy sources and technologies: the case of Central America. Renew. Sustain. Energy Rev. 58, 1411–1431 (2016)
8. Beyene, H.D., Werkneh, A.A., Ambaye, T.G.: Current updates on waste to energy (WtE) technologies: a review. Reinf. Plast. 24(00), 1–11 (2018)

9. Kalogirou, E.N.: Waste-to-Energy Technologies and Global Applications, 1ª Edición. Taylor & Francis Group, Boca Ratón (2017)
10. Makarichi, L., Jutidamrongphan, W., Techato, K.: The evolution of waste-to-energy incineration: a review. Renew. Sustain. Energy Rev. **91**, 812–821 (2018)
11. Lausselet, C., Cherubini, F., del Alamo, G., Serrano, M.B., Strømman, A.H.: Life-cycle assessment of a Waste-to-Energy plant in central Norway: current situation and effects of changes in waste fraction composition. Waste Manage. **58**, 191–201 (2016)
12. Coelho, S.T., Diaz-chavez, R.: Best Available Technologies (BAT) for WtE in Developing Countries. Elsevier Inc. (2020)
13. Dincer, I., Al-Muslim, H.: Thermodynamic analysis of reheat cycle steam power plants. Int. J. Energy Res. **25**(8), 727–739 (2001)
14. Badr, O., Probert, S.D., O'Callaghan, P.: Rankine cycles for steam power-plants. Appl. Energy **36**(3), 191–231 (1990)
15. Suresh, M.V.J.J., Reddy, K.S., Kolar, A.K.: Energy for sustainable development 4-E (energy, exergy, environment, and economic) analysis of solar thermal aided coal- fi red power plants. Energy Sustain. Dev. **14**(4), 267–279 (2010)
16. Palacio, C.E., Venturini, O.J., Martínez, A.M., Rúa, D.J., Silva, E.E.: Thermodynamic and economic evaluation of reheat and regeneration alternatives in cogeneration systems of the Brazilian sugarcane and alcohol sector. Energy **152**, 247–262 (2018)
17. Bell, I.H., Wronski, J., Quoilin, S., Lemort, V.: Pure and pseudo-pure fluid thermophysical property evaluation and the open-source thermophysical property library CoolProp. Ind. Eng. Chem. Res. **53**(6), 2498–2508 (2014)
18. Santos, J., Nascimento, M., Lora, E., Reyes, A.M.: On the Negentropy application in thermoeconomics: a fictitious or an exergy component flow? Int. J. Thermodyn. **12**(4), 163–176 (2009)
19. Lazar, R., Eder, J.: Estudio sobre el clima urbano en Bucaramanga. Universidad Industrial de Santander, UIS (2001)
20. Comisión Europea·Mejores Técnicas Disponibles de Referencia Europea Para Incineración de Residuos (2011)
21. EMAB, E.D.A.D.B.S.A.-E.: "INVITACIÓN PÚBLICA PARA LA SELECCIÓN DE LA NUEVA TECNOLOGÍA, SU IMPLEMENTACIÓN Y OPERACIÓN, PARA EL TRATAMIENTO ALTERNATIVO DE LA DISPOSICIÓN FINAL Y EL APROVECHAMIENTO DE LOS RESIDUOS SÓLIDOS URBANOS (RSU) EN LA CIUDAD DE BUCARAMANGA, DEPARTAMENTO DE SAN," p. 202 (2017)
22. Branchini, L.: Advanced waste-to-energy cycles. Alma Mater Studiorum – Università di Bologna Research (2012)
23. Gohlke, O., Martin, J.: Drivers for innovation in waste-to-energy technology. Waste Manag. Res. **25**(3), 214–219 (2007)
24. Moran, M., Shapiro, H.: Fundamentals of Engineering Thermodynamics, 7th edn. New Jersey (2011)
25. Nag, P.K., Deshmukh, R.: Scilab Textbook Companion for Engineering Thermodynamics. Tata McGraw - Hill Education Pvt. Ltd., New Delhi (2008)
26. Barigozzi, G., Perdichizzi, A., Ravelli, S.: Wet and dry cooling systems optimization applied to a modern waste-to-energy cogeneration heat and power plant. Appl. Energy **88**(4), 1366–1376 (2011)
27. Trindade, A.B., et al.: Advanced exergy analysis and environmental assesment of the steam cycle of an incineration system of municipal solid waste with energy recovery. Energy Convers. Manage. **157**, 195–214 (2018)
28. Lombardi, L., Carnevale, E., Corti, A.: A review of technologies and performances of thermal treatment systems for energy recovery from waste. Waste Manag. **37**, 26–44 (2015)

29. Castillo, N.: Evaluación termodinámica y económica para la generación eléctrica por medio de la incineración de residuos sólidos urbanos. UDES (2019)
30. Szargut, J., Morris, D.R., Steward, F.R.: Exergy Analysis of Thermal, Chemical, and Metallurgical Processes. Hemisphere (1988)
31. Szanto, M., Rodriguez, J.: CONSORCIO BIO-INGE 2015 CONTRATO DE CONSULTORÍA ESPECIALIZADA No 193 DE 2015 FORMULACION DE LA REGION-ALIZACIÓN DE LA PRESTACIÓN DE SERVCIO PÚBLICO DE ASEO EN RECOLEC-CIÓN , TRANSPORTE , TRANSFERENCIA, APROVECHAMIENTO Y DISPOSICION FINAL EN EL MARCO DE LA, Bucaramanga (2015)
32. Nordi, G.H., Palacios-bereche, R., Gallego, A.G., Nebra, S.A.: Electricity production from municipal solid waste in Brazil (2017)
33. Viklund, P., Hjörnhede, A., Henderson, P., Stålenheim, A., Pettersson, R.: Corrosion of superheater materials in a waste-to-energy plant. Fuel Process. Technol. **105**, 106–112 (2013)
34. Dal Magro, F., Xu, H., Nardin, G., Romagnoli, A.: Application of high temperature phase change materials for improved efficiency in waste-to-energy plants. Waste Manag. **73**, 322–331 (2018)

Water Quality and Dynamic Time Series Based on Meteorological Variables at the Muisne Station Located in the Bunche Enclosure, Esmeraldas, Ecuador

David Carrera-Villacrés[1]([✉]), Mayra Mercedes Chicaiza[2],
Carlos Anibal Choloquinga[2], Sisa Maribel Ramos[2], Leandro Jair Unda[2],
and Felipe Carrera-Villacrés[3]

[1] Departamento de Ciencias de la Tierra y la Construcción y Departamento de Ciencias Exactas, Universidad de Las Fuerzas Armadas ESPE, Av. General Rumiñahui s/n, Sangolquí, Ecuador
dvcarrera@espe.edu.ec
[2] Facultad de Ingeniería en Geología Minas Petróleos y Ambiental FIGEMPA, Carrera de Ambiental, Universidad Central del Ecuador, Av. Universitaria, Quito, Ecuador
[3] Facultad de Ciencias de la Vida, Carrera Ingeniería en Ecosistemas, Universidad Regional Amazónica IKIAM, Av. Km 7 Vía Alto Tena, Tena, Ecuador

Abstract. The study of climate is important over time since it allows to forecast the behavior of climatic variables, being necessary to have climatological records of at least 30 years. The community of Bunche has faced deficiencies in drinking water in their homes, taking into account that water is an increasingly scarce resource in the world, it was necessary to build a fog collector system to be able to capture water and meet the different needs in the population, thus, the exploratory analysis of data (EAD) was carried out to understand the behavior of meteorological variables: precipitation, temperature, relative humidity and wind speed of Muisne station (M153). The information was collected from the National Institute of Meteorology and Hydrology and the remote sensor TERRACLIMATE from the period 1990 to 2020, after that, recurrence maps were generated, and the ACP multivariate analysis was developed to filter the variables with the greatest correlation. Consequently, climate forecasts were made by applying the ARIMA model by coding in the R-Studio software. The results allowed predicting accumulated monthly rainfall ranging between 100–200 mm and average monthly temperatures between 25–26 °C by 2022, ensuring a high amount of water collected, which was suitable for human consumption and agricultural use according to the water quality analyses carried out and which were evaluated about the standards established in Ministerial Agreement 097-A from Ecuador.

Keywords: Recurring maps · ARIMA · Meteorological variables · Fog collector systems

© The Author(s), under exclusive license to Springer Nature Switzerland AG 2023
M. Botto-Tobar et al. (Eds.): ICAT 2022, CCIS 1756, pp. 243–257, 2023.
https://doi.org/10.1007/978-3-031-24971-6_18

1 Introduction

Over time, it is important to study the meteorological variables to make accurate weather forecasts. In climatology, the meteorological data that determine the behavior of the climate are obtained by comparing the annual averages with the average value of 30 years. During this period, the seasonal, annual, and multiannual variations associated with climatic oscillations are averaged, for example, phenomena named Niño that cause increased rainfall, mass movement, floods, droughts among others, causing damage to the population, infrastructures, affectation to the supply and demand of drinking water and irrigation due to the decrease in the quality of the water resource [1].

The community of Bunche is located in the tropical zone of Ecuador being more prone to natural phenomena. The enclosure has a culture dedicated to the extraction of marine and mangrove resources, agriculture and agroforestry systems. At the same time, it goes through different socio-environmental problems such as the lack of access to basic services and their quality, which generates health problems in the population due to lack of water resources [2].

The knowledge obtained in the present research allowed us to have a better idea of the behavior of the most influential meteorological variables in the climate of Muisne, in this way to know and disseminate widely the detailed climatology of the meteorological phenomena that influence the quality and quantity of the water resource whose Qualitative information is fundamental, not only for the evaluation of the behavior of the variables but also for real-time decision-making through the analysis of the data where a series of statistical processes and methods intervene [3].

1.1 Measurement Techniques of the Chaos

Chaos theory is a theoretical model that attempts to explain the behavior of dynamical systems that initially seem to develop randomly, proposing a new way of studying and understanding reality, it is defined as "the study of aperiodic behavior in nonlinear dynamical systems". One of the benefits of studying chaos is that it can make more accurate short-term predictions and show the feasibility of making long-term predictions. Chaos research can help improve systems modeling [4].

1.2 Phase Space

Reconstructing the phase space in a system from measured data is a standard procedure in the analysis of nonlinear time series. Each point in phase space belongs to a unique state and the evolution in time of the system creates a path or orbit [3]. For the reconstruction of the trajectory of the phase space, the time delay method is used, which consists of embedding the observed scalar time series $\{X_t\}_{t \in I}$ in an n-dimensional space:

$$X_n^\tau(t) = \left(X_t, X_{t+\tau}, \ldots X_{t+(p-1)\tau} \right) \tag{1}$$

For $t \in I$, where τ is the time delay for reconstruction, n is the embedding dimension, and I is a set of time indices of cardinality T. Note that the number of points embedded in the n-dimensional space is $N = T - (n - 1)\tau$ and all the dynamic properties such as dependencies, periodicity and complexity changes can be extracted from it.

To determine the delay time (τ) it was based on the autocorrelation function or ACF method described below [3]:

$$AC(\tau) = \frac{\sum_{i=1}^{L}\left(X_{i+\tau} - \tilde{X}\right)\left(X_i - \tilde{X}\right)}{\sum_{i=1}^{L}\left(X_{i+\tau} - \tilde{X}\right)^2} \qquad (2)$$

This function makes it possible to measure the degree to which past values are similar to subsequent values, within a delayed time series [3].

1.3 Recurring Maps

In 1987, Eckmann, Oliffson-Kamphorst, and Ruelle first included recurrence maps as a simple graphical tool to represent the basic dynamical characteristics of time series, it is defined as a matrix of points (i, j) where each point is recursive and flagged if the distance between the lag vectors $\overrightarrow{x_i}$ and $\overrightarrow{x_j}$ is less than a given threshold ($\in$), the distance is calculated by the norm between all combinations of lag vectors [3]. It is represented by the Eq. (3) of García, Uddin, and Torresen [5]:

$$R_{i,j}(x) = \begin{cases} 1 \text{ if } \left\| \overrightarrow{x_i} - \overrightarrow{x_j} \right\| \le \in \\ 0 \qquad \text{otherwise} \end{cases} \qquad (3)$$

where x are the states, . is a norm, and $\in$ is a threshold. $R_{i,j}(x)$ will be one if $\overrightarrow{x_i} \approx \overrightarrow{x_j}$ except for an error of $\in$, which forms a diagonal line called the identity line. The $\in$ is important as systems often don't exactly fall back to a previously visited state so the threshold is selected as the value so that 20% of locations will have points plotted if they are not mentioned. This value is known as the recurrence rate [6].

1.4 Normality Test

The Kolmogorov-Smirnov test was used to test the normality of the sample data, which is useful mainly in non-linear and interactive physical processes since these lead to non-Gaussian distributions. The Kolmogorov-Smirnov test is applied to test the hypothesis of population normality and is represented by Eq. (4) [7].

$$d = Max|f_\infty - E_\infty| \qquad (4)$$

where, f_∞ is the normal cumulative distribution function (cdf) and E_∞ is the empirical cfd. If the maximum observed d is greater than a critical value (CV), it is proved that E_∞ differs from the theoretical distribution f_∞ with a level of significance (α). A null hypothesis is established H_0: The data have a normal distribution ($d < CV_{(\infty,L)}$), and H_A: The data do not have a normal distribution $\left(d \ge CV_{(\infty,L)}\right)$ [3].

1.5 Multivariate Principal Component Analysis (PCA)

The technique of Principal Component Analysis (PCA), has been used in several meteorological and climatological studies, the main objective is the reduction of the number of variables, that is, the dimensions of the data set. These main components are determined through the linear combination of the original variables, which have to be linearly independent [8]. The graph used for the analysis of the ACP is the circle of correlations, which indicates the relationship between the variables, that is, of each of the meteorological parameters, the angle formed between the arrows of the variables is taken into account, if they are close to each other, this indicates a strong and positive correlation, if the angle is close to $90°$ it means that there is no correlation, and if the arrows are opposite to the origin they have a strong and negative correlation [9].

1.6 Integrated Autoregressive Moving Average Model (ARIMA)

The reason for the introduction of ARIMA models arises because you cannot work with a non-stationary time series. It is said that a series is stationary when its mean, variance, and self-covariance are time-invariant, this being optimal to apply the methodology of the ARIMA models [10]. In general, a time series Yt is said to support an integrated autoregressive and moving average representation of orders p, d, q respectively, and is denoted by ARIMA (p, d, q) [10]. It is represented by the following equation:

$$Y_1 = c + \emptyset_1 y_{dt-1} + \emptyset_p y_{dtp} + ... + \emptyset_1 e_{t-1} + \emptyset_q e_{tq} + e_t \tag{5}$$

where $\emptyset$ corresponds to the autoregressive coefficient to be determined, θ is the moving average coefficient to be determined, the error term, and $Ydtp$ is the normalized log of the series to be modeled. For the spread term, an evaluation of the order must be considered, "p" denotes the number of autoregressive terms, "d" is the number of times the series must be differentiated to make it stationary, and q is the number of terms of the invertible moving average [11]. The construction of the models is carried out iteratively through a process in which four stages can be distinguished: identification, differentiation analysis of the time series, adjustment of an Arima model, and, finally, prediction.

1.7 Water Quality

It is important to check that the water is free of polluting elements and that it is not a means for the transmission of diseases; In addition, its definition depends on the final use that will be given, that is, that water for human consumption or as a habitat for aquatic fauna demand higher levels of purity while for irrigation the quality standards are less strict [12]. To determine water quality, physical, chemical, and microbiological parameters must be analyzed to compare their results with current environmental regulations.

The objectives of this work were to analyze the behavior of the meteorological variables: precipitation, temperature, relative humidity, and wind speed of the M0135 station located in the Bunche enclosure, province of Esmeraldas, to establish the dynamics of time series through the development of recurrence maps and normality tests, perform the multivariate analysis (PCA) that allows the identification of the variables most correlated, apply Arima models to obtain short-term weather forecasts and estimate the amount of monthly precipitation accumulated in the following year using coding in the R-Studio software. In addition to this, determine if the quality of water collected by the fog catcher system is suitable for human consumption and agricultural use.

This work is ordered as follows: First, the necessary meteorological data was collected from the M135 station in Bunche. Second, data analysis was performed to observe their behavior through recurrence maps and the normality test. Third, the Principal Component Analysis was applied to obtain the best correlation between the meteorological variables, the result of which served to make forecasts with the ARIMA model. This research's importance consists of identifying the climatic variables that influence the quality and quantity of the water collected by a fog catcher system.

2 Methodology

2.1 Study Area

In the canton Muisne, the province of Esmeraldas is the community of Bunche of the parish of San Francisco. In this area, there are trade winds from the west. The relative humidity is approximately 85.6%, in the sector, there are average annual temperatures of 24.7 °C, but they can vary between 17 °C to 27 °C [2]. Figure 1 shows the map of the study area where the main climatological station of Muisne is observed, hydrological information whose geoinformation metadata was obtained from: http://www.geoportal igm.gob.ec/portal/ [13].

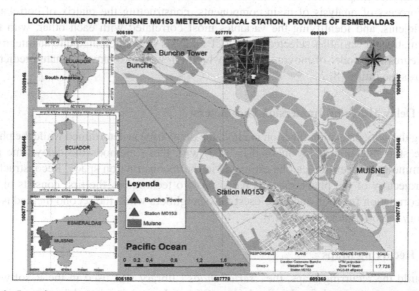

Fig. 1. Location map of the place of study, commune Bunche parish San Francisco Canton Muisne, Province of Esmeraldas, Ecuador, Southamerica.

2.2 Data Collected

For the study, local and satellite information was collected, obtaining 372 monthly data corresponding to precipitation (mm), temperature (°C), relative humidity (%), and wind speed (m/s) from 1990 to 2020, which were obtained from the meteorological yearbooks provided by the National Institute of Meteorology and Hydrology (INAMHI) specifically from the M153 Muisne station, and the Terraclimate satellites with a spatial resolution of 4638.3 m [14].

However, missing data were identified that were essential when working with continuous series, so the simple linear regression methodology and R-Climatol were used, methods proposed by the World Meteorological Organization in the WMO Climatological Practice Guide No. 100 for the filling and homogenization of missing data. It is recommended to estimate monthly and annual data [15] and be the best methodology for filling data in time series for the Andean and coastal regions of Ecuador. The data filling was validated using the Pearson correlation coefficient that allows measuring the linear dependence between local and satellite data.

2.3 Data Analysis

A descriptive and exploratory analysis of the data was carried out by coding in R-Studio and the different statistical parameters were determined, mainly the covariance since this allowed us to accept or reject the KS test normality test to establish whether or not the data set is governed by Gaussian distributions being represented graphically in recurrence maps. Once the behavior of the data set was identified, it was subjected to a process of analysis of main components, constructing the matrix of correlation coefficients, and identifying the variables most correlated with each other, with this information the variables selected in the ACP analysis were integrated into an integrated autoregressive model of moving average which allowed to make a climate prediction towards the future [8].

2.4 Delay Time and Immersion Parameters

Using the autocorrelation function method, the delay time is determined while the phase space stops the time delay method is used, with these methods the delay time and the immersed dimension can be estimated in the reconstruction space. Reconstructing the trajectory of the phase space is based on two techniques, the first consists of the autocorrelation function and the closest false neighbors while the second method is the sensory region of determinism [3].

2.5 Recurring Maps

To build the recurring maps, the *"series chaos"* library was used in the R software. The parameters were defined as the dataset (Climatological dataset), delay time, and the immersed dimension of Table 1. In addition, the same threshold of 0.1 was set for all variables, thus obtaining the maps of recurrence of precipitation, temperature, relative humidity, and wind speed. The threshold allows to better find the transitions of the regime in non-stationary systems or to conclude the adjustment between dynamical systems.

Table 1. Delay time and immersed dimension

Variable	Delay time (t)	Immersed dimension (n)
Precipitation	4	5
Temperature	2	3
Relative humidity	2	3
Wind speed	4	7

Source: (Ayala et al., 2018)

2.6 Multivariate Principal Component Analysis (PCA)

To identify the best correlation between the four variables analyzed, the analysis of Principal Components was performed, for which the Studio software was used, using the *"prcomp"* parameter, and the multivariate analysis was performed. In addition, the library *"factoextra"* and *"factoMineR"* are used for the realization of the correlation circle graph.

2.7 Integrated Autoregressive Moving Average Model (ARIMA)

The modeling in ARIMA was carried out through five stages. The first stage consists of data processing, after this, the code *"Rstudio tsclean"* is used to reduce atypical data and move averages for better smoothing of monthly data. In the second stage, seasonality is sought using the Dickey-Fuller test (ADF). This test handles hypothesis contrast where H0 means non-stationary and H1 stationary. Next, autocorrelations of the data are applied using the ACF and PACF [16].

In series with low seasonality, differentiation is performed, then the Dickey-Fuller test is performed for verification. The p-value obtained must be $0.01 < 0.05$ so H0 is rejected and the H1 hypothesis is adopted where the time series is stationary. The model is adjusted using the *"auto. Arima"* function and residual elements are removed with the *"tsdisplay"* function. Finally, the forecast for the model is obtained [10].

2.8 Water Quality

For the analysis of water quality, 7 main parameters were studied, each with the methods observed in Table 2.

Table 2. Determination of water quality parameters

Parameter	Method
Temperature, pH	HANNA HI 2210
Conductivity	ORION STAR A212
Evaporated dry residue (CSR) and calcined (CSR)	Gravimetric
Hardness	EDTA Titrimetric
Nitrate and sulfates	HACH DR Spectrophotometer
Fecal and total coliforms	Most Likely Number or NMP

Source: Khanh, Mäkelä, Schreithofer & Dahl [17]

3   Discussion and Results

3.1   Normality Test

The shape of the dataset was identified to compare them according to the classification given in Fig. 2 and it was determined that the variables relative humidity, wind speed, and temperature have a symmetrical shape with random dynamics and periosteal precipitation.

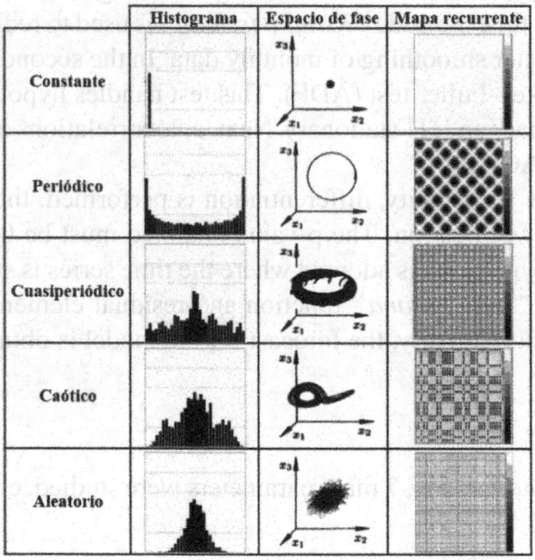

Fig. 2. Classification of histograms, phase spaces, and recurrent maps according to their dynamics.

As shown in Table 3, the K-S normality test was performed, where it was demonstrated whether or not the data are from a Gaussian distribution for each of the climatological variables studied.

Table 3. Results of the normality test of each of the climatological variables

Variable	Form	K-s test	Ho	Distribution
Precipitation	Positive asymmetric	d = 0.18 hp = 0.04	d < CV α = 5% rejected	Non-Gaussian
Temperature	Symmetrical	d = 0.076 hp = 0.038	d > CVSe rejected	Non-Gaussian
Relative humidity	Positive symmetrical	d = 0.11 hp = 0.35	d < CV α = 5% not rejected	Gaussian
Wind speed	Negative symmetric	d = 0.078 hp = 0.0435	d < CV α = 5% rejected	Non-Gaussian

3.2 Recurrence Maps

Based on the normality test performed, the behavior of the recurrence maps presented in Fig. 3 was corroborated, for the temperature variable (a), interruptions or white stripes can be visualized, which means the existence of extreme events in the time series. These white dots correspond to the years 1997, 1998, and 2000 which coincides with the period where the presence of the "El Niño" phenomenon was had [3] On the other hand, it is observed that the variable temperature is quasiperiodic. The variable precipitation (b), shows equal repetitive structures so it is classified as a periodic series. In this map, the

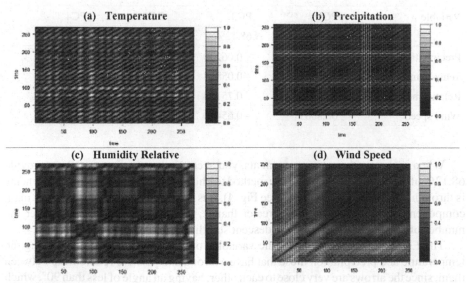

Fig. 3. Recurrence maps of the variables: (a) Temperature, (b) Precipitation, (c) Relative Humidity, and (d) Wind Speed.

white stripes stand out in the years 2010 and 2012 when the phenomenon of "La Niña" occurred.

In the map of recurrence of relative humidity (c), it is observed that the white stripes correspond to the years from 1997 to 2001, groupings of vertical and horizontal lines with identifiable patterns are also distinguished in the case of a chaotic series. Finally, there is the variable wind speed (d) the white stripes stand out from 1990 to approximately 1999 where diagonal lines and interrupted lines were identified causing isolated points. In general, the years where extreme events are identified correspond to ENSO phenomena [18].

3.3 Multivariate Principal Component Analysis (PCA)

Once the classification of the data according to its dynamics has been identified through the recurrence and normality test maps, the order of magnitude of each of the variables concerning the main components is shown in Table 4, the first component provides a similar weighting and gives greater weight to the variables temperature and precipitation reaching an index very close to 0.7 indicating that they are highly correlated with each other, in the same way, the second main component gives greater weight to the relative humidity and wind speed, but in the same way provides a magnitude similar to precipitation and temperature, indicating a relationship between them [19]. Hiruta [1] mentions that the increase in temperatures produces an increase in evapotranspiration, which means that there is more water available to precipitate, therefore there is talk of a directly proportional relationship.

Table 4. Principal component analysis

Variable	PC1 41.7%	PC2 68.12%	PC3 89.44%	PC4 100%
Precipitation	−0.63617	0.06230	0.40597	0.65313
Temperature	−0.67617	−0.05843	0.11606	−0.72518
Relative humidity	0.24425	0.75104	0.58152	−0.19519
Wind speed	0.28001	−0.65470	0.69536	−0.09703

When analyzing the main components, you access to use the first two, these provide 68.12% of the initial information. The method to choose the number of main components is through the sedimentation graph (see Fig. 4), it is observed that only the first two main components have variance values greater than 1, it is also advisable to consider the number of components in which the descent stabilizes.

The Fig. 5 indicates how much the variables of the study are correlated, being the temperature and precipitation those that have a strong and positive relationship between them, since the arrows are very close to each other, having an angle of less than 90°, which means that they are the ones that best represent the dataset. The exponential regression achieves a coefficient of determination of 0.49 indicating that there is dependence on the

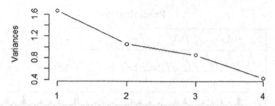

Fig. 4. Sedimentation graph to obtain main components

variables, Explains water harvesting because if there are days where high temperatures are reached, that is, very hot days, rainfall is more likely to increase due to which water vapor is produced [20].

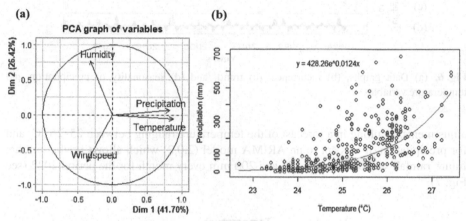

Fig. 5. (a) Graph of principal components between individuals and variables (correlation circle) (b) Exponential scatter plot between the variable precipitation and temperature.

3.4 ARIMA Model

Based on the results obtained from the ACP se evaluated the historical records of the variables temperature and precipitation taken from the Muisne station from 1990 to 2020 since a good exponent correlation between them was observed. With this information, the ARIMA statistical model was used to properly represent the time series, starting with a preliminary analysis of the behavior of the data (see Fig. 6).

The variables precipitation and temperature present seasonality, but not a clear trend since the values grow and decrease continuously.

After observing the behavior of the series, analyses are performed to check seasonality with the Dickey-Fuller test. The next step is to determine the appropriate values (p, d, q) that form the ARIMA model con which performed the prognosis [10]. The results obtained for the temperature data were governed by a model (5,1,2) with the relevant

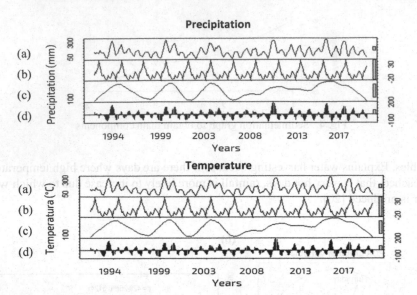

Fig. 6. (a) Data graphs, (b) recurrence, (c) trend, and (d) seasonality of precipitation and temperature variables

adjustments, resulting in a forecast of the temperature ranging between 25–26 °C, and for precipitation, it was apt to an ARIMA model (2,0,2) which allows predicting that future rainfall will be between 100 and 200 mm every month for the period 2022 (see Fig. 7).

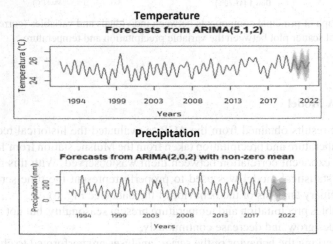

Fig. 7. ARIMA model predictions for temperature and precipitation.

3.5   Water Quality

The analysis carried out on the water from the prototype quadratic tower of Pichincha complies with the normative for the use of [21] 1 [21] as observed in Table 5, therefore, all water quality parameters are within the maximum permissible limits. According to Gómez-Gutierrez [22], they mention that the low concentration of hardness and fecal coliforms present is because it is free of wastewater and acid rain because the collection of water comes from the haze goes directly to a collection tank.

Table 5. Water quality parameters for human consumption in the quadratic tower of the City of Quito.

Parameter	Units	Quadratic	Max limits Permissible
Temperature	°C	13,7	Absence
pH	Absence	6,98	6,5–9,5
Electrical conductivity	µS/cm	93,215	540
Evaporated dry residue	mg/L	100	Absence
Calcined dry residue	mg/L	34	Absence
Hardness	mg/L	8	200
Nitrates	mg/L	1,35	50
Phosphates	mg/L	0,281	Absence
Fecal coliforms	UFC	0	1000
Total coliforms	UFC	240	2000

4   Conclusion

Through the development of the different statistical methods, it was possible to determine a good exponential correlation between the meteorological variable's temperature and precipitation, whose behaviors were quasi-periodic and periodic respectively, being the main components to explain their influence on the Bunche climate. In addition, accumulated monthly rainfall ranging between 100–200 mm and monthly average temperatures between 25–26 °C were forecast for the year 2022, with these values high and medium rainfall is predicted during the year. Therefore, the supply of the liquid will be high and according to the analysis of water quality, it was suitable for human consumption and agricultural use according to the standards established in Ministerial Agreement 097.

Acknowledgements. The construction of the fog collector systems has been carried out with financing from Switzerland with the program: Leading House for the Latin American Region, from Germany with the GIZ: 4th Call for the Innovation Fund and PUCESE, Catholique University, Esmeraldas.

References

1. Hiruta, Y., Ishizaki, N.N., Ashina, S., Takahashi, K.: Hourly future climate scenario datasets for impact assessment of climate change considering simultaneous interactions among multiple meteorological factors. Data Br. **42**, 108047 (2022). https://doi.org/10.1016/j.dib.2022.108047
2. Carrera Villacrés, F., Vernaza Quiñónez, L., Vicente da Silva, E.: Fortalecimiento del turismo comunitario a través del diagnóstico paisajístico en Bunche – Muisne. Fipcaec **6**(3), 367–392 (2021)
3. Ayala, M.F., Tierra, A.R., Carrera-Villacrés, D.: Análisis de la Dinámica de Series Temporales de Variables Meteorológicas en la Estación Climatológica Chone, Ecuador, December 2021 (2018)
4. Liang, Y., Gao, N., Liu, T.: Suppression method of inter-symbol interference in communication system based on mathematical chaos theory. J. King Saud Univ. Sci. **32**(2), 1749–1756 (2020). https://doi.org/10.1016/j.jksus.2020.01.012
5. Garcia-Ceja, E., Uddin, Z., Torresen, J.: ScienceDirect classification of recurrence plots' distance matrices with a convolutional neural network for activity recognition. Procedia Comput. Sci. **130**, 157–163 (2018)
6. Hirata, Y.: Recurrence plots for characterizing random dynamical systems. Commun. Nonlinear Sci. Numer. Simul. **94**, 105552 (2021). https://doi.org/10.1016/j.cnsns.2020.105552
7. Tapia-Flores, C.E., Cevallos-Flores, K.L.: Pruebas Para Comprobar La Normalidad De Datos En Procesos Productivos : Anderson-Darling, Ryan-Joiner, Shapiro-Wilk Y Kolmogórov-Smirnov, Tests to verify the normality of data in production processes : Anderson-Darling, Ryan-Joiner, Shapiro-Wilk. Societas **23**(2), 83–97 (2021)
8. Zhong, R., Liu, S., Li, H., Zhang, J.: Robust functional principal component analysis for non-Gaussian longitudinal data. J. Multivar. Anal. **189**, 104864 (2022). https://doi.org/10.1016/j.jmva.2021.104864
9. Boudou, A., Viguier-Pla, S.: Principal components analysis and cyclostationarity. J. Multivar. Anal. **189**, 104875 (2022). https://doi.org/10.1016/j.jmva.2021.104875
10. Ahmar, A.S., et al.: Implementation of the ARIMA(p,d,q) method to forecasting CPI data using forecast package in R software. J. Phys. Conf. Ser. **1028**(1), 012189 (2018). https://doi.org/10.1088/1742-6596/1028/1/012189
11. Salman, A.G., Kanigoro, B.: Visibility forecasting using autoregressive integrated moving average (ARIMA) models. Procedia Comput. Sci. **179**(2019), 252–259 (2021). https://doi.org/10.1016/j.procs.2021.01.004
12. Carrera-Villacrés, D.V., Robalino, I.C., Rodríguez, F.F., Sandoval, W.R., Hidalgo, D.L., Toulkeridis, T.: An innovative fog catcher system applied in the Andean communities of Ecuador. Trans. ASABE **60**(6), 1917–1923 (2017). https://doi.org/10.13031/trans.12368
13. IGM, GeoportalIGM
14. INAMHI, Instituto Nacional de Meteorología e Hidrología
15. Campo-Portacio, D.M., Guerrero-Velásquez, L.F., Castillo-García, A.P., Orozco-Méndez, K., Blanco-Tuirán, P.J.: Detección de Toxoplasma gondii en agua para el consumo humano proveniente de jagüeyes del área rural del municipio de Sincelejo. Biomédica **41**(Suppl. 1), 82–99 (2021). https://doi.org/10.7705/biomedica.5858
16. Yonggang, D., Huan, W., Mingqiang, W., Linjiang, T., Tao, Y.: Application of ARIMA-RTS optimal smoothing algorithm in gas well production prediction. Petroleum (2022). https://doi.org/10.1016/j.petlm.2021.09.001
17. Le, T.M.K., Mäkelä, M., Schreithofer, N., Dahl, O.: A multivariate approach for evaluation and monitoring of water quality in mining and minerals processing industry. Miner. Eng. **157**, 106582 (2020). https://doi.org/10.1016/j.mineng.2020.106582

18. Singh, S., Abebe, A., Srivastava, P., Chaubey, I.: Effect of ENSO modulation by decadal and multi-decadal climatic oscillations on contiguous United States streamflows. J. Hydrol. Reg. Stud. **36**, 100876 (2021). https://doi.org/10.1016/j.ejrh.2021.100876
19. Carrera-Villacrés, D., Pazmiño, M.: Determinación de la calidad agrícola de los suelos en la zona del proyecto propósito múltiple Chone fase II (2018)
20. Chakravarty, T., Gupta, S.: Assessment of water quality of a hilly river of south Assam, north east India using water quality index and multivariate statistical analysis. Environ. Challenges **5**, 100392 (2021). https://doi.org/10.1016/j.envc.2021.100392
21. Mae, M.D.A.: Acuerdo_Ministerial_97a.Pdf (2017)
22. Gómez-Gutiérrez, A., Miralles, M.J., Corbella, I., García, S., Navarro, S., Llebaria, X.: La calidad sanitaria del agua de consumo. Gac. Sanit. **30**, 63–68 (2017). https://doi.org/10.1016/j.gaceta.2016.04.012

Electronics

An Electronic Equipment for Monitoring, Detection and Warning of Pitch Motion of Vehicle Drivers

Luis Alzamora⬛, Josue Espino⬛, Rubén Acosta⬛, Manuel Márquez⬛,
and Guillermo Kemper⁽⊠⁾⬛

Universidad Peruana de Ciencias Aplicadas, Av. Prolongación Primavera, 2390 Santiago
de Surco, Lima, Peru
{u201313692,u201315421,pcelraco,pcelmmar}@upc.edu.pe,
guillermo.kemper@upc.pe

Abstract. Long and monotonous journeys during the transport of goods can generate tiredness and/or fatigue in the driver, generating a potential vehicle accident where the driver can enter a state of micro-sleep, losing control of the vehicle for a period of time. Within the state of the art, it is observed that most of the solutions have as their fundamental axis the analysis of the ocular muscle, being these vulnerable to the variation of light intensity and facial accessories that the driver can use. On the other hand, other studies analyze EEG signals being intrusive and disturbing the driving skills of the driver. This work presents a driver fatigue monitoring system based on the angular movement of the head, the main characteristic prior to the state of micro-sleep, located in a safety helmet. To do this, an analysis of the angular movement of the driver's head is carried out, thus avoiding the use of cameras, potential lighting problems and intrusive driving disturbances. The device will detect the nodding symptom and will issue an auditory alert with a message via Telegram to a third party to alert the presence of driver fatigue with an error rate of less than 22%, having as auditory alert response time a period of 500 ms equivalent to the distance of 8 m if the vehicle moves at 60 km/h. The validation was carried out by comparing the angles between the device located in the helmet and a reference accelerometer.

Keywords: Driver · Fatigue · Helmet · Movement · Pitch · Trajectory · Vehicle

1 Introduction

Sleep deprivation is the inadequate amount of sleep that negatively affects the brain and its cognitive functions, causing memory loss, confusion, malaise, irritability, headache, hand tremors and yawning. This causes, in people, attention deficit and increases the reaction response time, therefore, the National Sleep Foundation recommends sleeping an average of 7 to 9 h a day [1]. In Peru alone, the SUTRAN specifies that, between 2018 and 2019, there were approximately between 90,000 and 96,000 traffic accidents in Peruvian territory, where 74% of them were caused by human factors [2]. In addition,

M. Botto-Tobar et al. (Eds.): ICAT 2022, CCIS 1756, pp. 261–273, 2023.
https://doi.org/10.1007/978-3-031-24971-6_19

according to a study carried out by the MTC on 238 interprovincial drivers, it was revealed that approximately a little more than half sleep less than 6 h a day and that 80% of them confess to having had an accident or almost had an accident; in the case of bus and taxi drivers in Lima, the percentage drops to 32.7% [3]. Faced with this problem, the Ministry of Transport and Communications (MTC) regulated the driving hours of heavy-duty vehicle drivers in Peruvian territory, where they are currently allowed to perform this service for a maximum of 12 h per day [3]. However, despite the fact that they can take a break every 6 h, the long journeys and monotonous roads during the transport of goods cause vehicle accidents. Currently there are commercial devices, such as the Resqme, this device is placed on the driver's ear and detects the angular movements of the head, considering possible fatigue when detecting an angular movement of 20° [4]. However, this device is only limited to detecting frontal movements of the head, which is insufficient because during fatigue the person's head is not limited to moving to one side. In addition, it is a very sensitive device causing possible false alarms. In other proposed solutions, the use of processing and images is also found, for example, in the proposal by Li et al. In [5], a fatigue detection system based on the driver's facial characteristics is presented using a YOLOv3-tiny convolutional neural network to capture facial regions. Detection by can give optimal results. However, in order to reach an optimal result, it requires various processes for the proper taking of the face, generating a greater computational load, increasing the cost of this system.

Chao Zhang et al. in [6] propose a fatigue detection system by detecting blinking, yawning and blood volume pulse (BVP). For the acquisition of facial characteristics and BVP signals, image processing is used, adhering to a known photoplethysmography method. For the identification of fatigue, Zhang proposes the method of second-order blind separation (SOBI) for detection, which allows the matrices to be analyzed separately, allowing a more accurate detection. However, as in the case of Li, this proposal depends on several factors that must be processed for a correct detection. Also, results may vary depending on the driver's facial features or whether the driver wears glasses. It is necessary to explore and develop other alternatives for fatigue monitoring in order to provide the driver and third parties with a system that safeguards their physical integrity. Therefore, a device that does not depend on several factors for a correct detection is necessary, and it must not alter the cabin of the vehicle or be invasive for the driver. In this sense, the present work proposes a driver fatigue monitoring system based on the driver's pitch movement, where it has been found that state-of-the-art proposals present weaknesses and limitations both in the variation of light intensity, intrusiveness in the driver as well as being solutions that do not alert third parties but only personally.

The proposed method is based on the analysis of head tilt angles, which will be measured by a gyroscope located in a helmet that does not exceed the allowed weight. These data will be sent to a small board computer for analysis and detection, which will be indicated by an audible alarm. The parts that make up the proposed equipment will be described in the following sections.

2   Description of the Proposed Equipment

Figure 1 shows the block diagram of the proposed device for the proposed equipment. The process begins as soon as it is turned on and the correct remote connection is made between the system for pitch detection and the local vehicle registration station. Figure 2 shows a view of the driver using the device.

The driver's head tilt angle sensing begins by preprocessing the information to be sent to the local station (see Fig. 2). Once the information is collected through the shortwave signal, the local station performs the main processing to determine if there is pitching to issue an audible alert and send an alert through a Bot chat on Telegram. The details of each stage are described in the following sections.

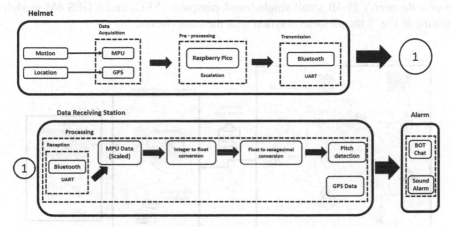

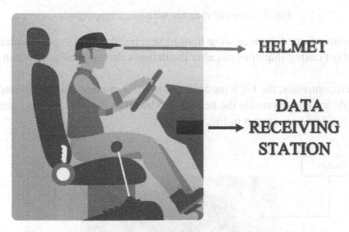

Fig. 1. Block diagram of the proposed equipment.

Fig. 2. Final view of the conductor using the proposed system.

2.1 Materials

The device measures the inertial movement of a driver's head in real time while driving a vehicle, therefore, it is taken into account that the device should not alter driving skills, thus avoiding the driver having to retire the proposed device. A Raspberry Pi Pico, a microcontroller with Python language of small dimensions (21 mm × 51.3 mm and 3gr) was used for collecting the inclination angles of the MPU6050 inertial module (wide support through widely distributed libraries for immediate use, including the measurement of 6 degrees of freedom, incorporating a voltage regulator at 3.3 V and pull-up resistors for direct use by I2C) and then transmit it via Bluetooth, using the HC-05 module (based on the IEEE 802.15 1 standard, endorsed by the American Cancer Society as not being a health hazard) to the local vehicle registration station that is made up of a Raspberry Pi 4B small single-board computer (SBC) and a GPS 6M module, showing in Fig. 3 the pictorial diagram with the components.

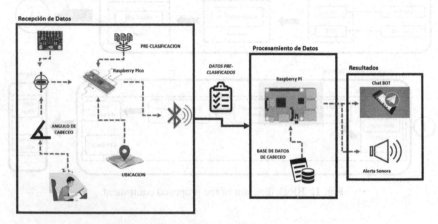

Fig. 3. Pictorial diagram with the components.

The aforementioned devices were housed in a helmet prototype in order to have a solid and robust casing that does not alter the driver's driving skills. This can be seen in Fig. 3.

The microcontroller, the GPS module, the inertial module and the Bluetooth transmitter module are housed inside the helmet, as shown in Fig. 4. Likewise, the electrical diagram of the device is shown in Fig. 5.

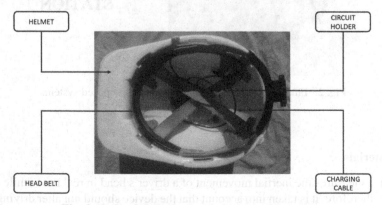

Fig. 4. Safety helmet for the pitch monitoring system.

2.2 Data Acquisition

For the acquisition of angular movement data of the head, an MPU6050 inertial module was used, which has a gyroscope, which is located in a helmet prototype shown in Fig. 3. The helmet prototype is based on a safety helmet for mine workers based on the NTP228 standard [5].

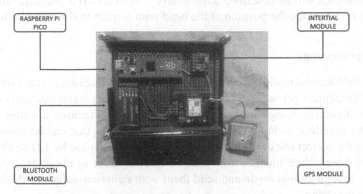

Fig. 5. Electronic circuit for monitoring the pitch of the driver in a safety helmet.

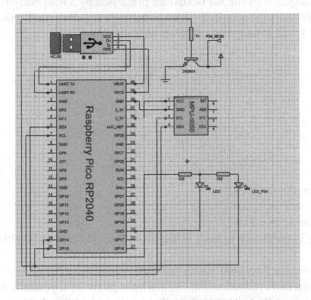

Fig. 6. Circuit diagram of the device located in the helmet.

The user must place the helmet on his head when driving a vehicle, in this way, the movement that the driver makes while driving is collected by the MPU6050 inertial module. The information is collected every 10 ms because it is required to have a fast response for pitch detection as it triggers a micro-sleep that can last in a range of milliseconds to seconds where control of the pitch can be lost vehicle, being established by the participants as not having a significant difference if the frequency of monitoring lean angles is increased. In addition, in order to simplify the analysis of information, it was established that the best option is the use of sexagesimal degrees, taking the axis of gravity as the main axis. The Raspberry Pi Pico microcontroller must have input and output in 12 bits while the MPU6050 works with 16 bits, therefore, to standardize the information and its correct communication, the use of 8 bits was established.

In the following sections, the processing stages to which the obtained inclination data are subjected will be described sequentially. The first step is the acquisition of tilt angle data to determine the position of the head with respect to the axis of gravity.

2.3 Pre-processing

The MPU6050 inertial module has various information reading ranges that vary between 250 and 2000 degrees per second. Therefore, in order to have greater ease and not have to work with values that change due to the high sensitivity of this sensor, a scaling is carried out in order to reduce and/or have practical working ranges that can be transmitted in 8-bit string for correct use of information that is why it is divided by 127 to obtain 8-bit data. Then these values must be converted to float in order to obtain their respective equivalent in sexagesimal angle and send them with delimiter values of the beginning and end of the string.

The values acquired by the MPU6050 are processed by a Raspberry Pico microcontroller. Where, initially the acquired values go through a scaling stage which can be seen in (1), (2) and (3) since the gyroscope gives us values both in x, y y z.

$$a_x = \frac{a_x}{127} \tag{1}$$

$$a_y = \frac{a_y}{127} \tag{2}$$

$$a_z = \frac{a_z}{127} \tag{3}$$

where:

a_x = Magnitude on x axis

a_y = Magnitude on y axis

a_z = Magnitude on z axis

The scaling is necessary to have values from 0 to 255 and to be able to work at 8 bits.

The measurement threshold and/or maximum limit established between 0 and 90 sexagesimal degrees is related to the circular movement of a person's head, which is divided into 6 types: Flexion (43°–73°), Extension (33°–77°), Right Lateral Flexion (FLD) (43°–73°), Left Lateral Flexion (FLI) (43°–73°), Right Rotation (RD) (60°–86°), Left Rotation (RI) (60°–86°).

The main function of pre-processing is to reduce computational load as well as the elimination of redundant information to avoid sending it constantly over a period of time, in other words, the pre-processing stage is an information filtering stage that follows the following sequence:

Step 1: The head position value is located with respect to the gravity axis.

Step 2: Redundant data or similar information is eliminated. This process is carried out by comparing a chain of 10 samples that are equivalent to 1 s of information.

Step 3: Finally, all the data where a significant variation occurs is stored in the chain.

2.4 Transmission

The transmission is developed using the Bluetooth protocol, sending the data obtained by the Raspberry Pi Pico to the Raspberry Pi 4B where it receives the values of lateral, longitudinal and vertical movement of the inertial module, receiving the angles formed between the driver's head and the axis of gravity.

2.5 Processing

In this stage, the data sent goes through a processing stage that follows the following steps:

Step 1: Integer to float conversion.

Data sent via Bluetooth and previously scaled requires an integer to float conversion using Eqs. (1), (2), and (3) for the x, y and z axes, respectively, it must be multiplied by 1.0 because the values are previously as integers and by multiplying them by 1.0 we ensure that they will be in float format. In this way the data can be divisible and can later be transformed into sexagesimal values.

$$a_x = (accel_x - 127) \times 1.0 \tag{4}$$

$$a_y = (accel_y - 127) \times 1.0 \tag{5}$$

$$a_z = (accel_z - 127) \times 1.0 \tag{6}$$

where:

$accel_x$: Acceleration on x axis
$accel_y$: Acceleration on y axis
$accel_z$: Acceleration on z axis

Step 2: Conversion to sexagesimal values.

Once the data has been converted to floats, they must go through a sexagesimal conversion, in this way they can be classified and detected. For this, Eqs. (7), (8) and (9) were used.

For a correct mapping and analysis of the movement of the head, the axes of the plane will be taken as a reference, where any aircraft is capable of rotating on 3 axes perpendicular to each other, having its center of gravity as its midpoint, these are known as Pitch (rotation on lateral x axis), Yaw (Rotation on longitudinal y axis) and Roll (rotation on vertical z axis).

$$pitch = 180 \times \frac{\tan^{-1}\left(\frac{a_x}{\sqrt{a_y^2 + a_z^2}}\right)}{\pi} \tag{7}$$

$$roll = 180 \times \frac{\tan^{-1}\left(\frac{a_y}{\sqrt{a_x^2 + a_z^2}}\right)}{\pi} \tag{8}$$

$$yaw = 180 \times \frac{\tan^{-1}\left(\frac{a_z}{\sqrt{a_x^2 + a_y^2}}\right)}{\pi} \tag{9}$$

Regarding the GPS data, these do not require any processing and only collect information depending on whether the pitch has been detected.

2.6 Detection

The threshold to determine the pitching symptom in a driver was established at 40° in a spherical manner, that is, in the axis of rotation of a person's head, taking into account the various road conditions that may be encountered on the journey, steep slope, poor road conditions and the correct body movement of a driver behind the wheel was also considered. After obtaining the angle of inclination of the driver and determining that he has a pitching symptom, a continuous auditory alert is emitted until the driver has an adequate posture behind the wheel, in addition to sending a notification through a Telegram Bot chat indicating the location, time and the presence of driver fatigue. Figure 6 shows the message that is sent through a Bot chat via Telegram indicating the presence of driver fatigue, its location and the registration time.

Finally, although the collection of information is every 10 ms, the maximum response time of the system, after completing the pre-processing, processing and alert stages, has a maximum period of 500 ms, taking into account the time from that the MPU6050 inertial module begins to detect the magnitude of interest until the audible alert is issued. Likewise, once the pitch alert is activated, the audible alarm is activated for a period of 3 s and the pitch detection is turned off for the same period, giving enough time, time established by the participants, for the driver to return to a correct position behind the wheel.

3 Results

The driver fatigue detection performance test was conducted through a graphical interface that displayed the location and tilt of the driver's head in real time. The interface indicated the presence of the driver's pitching symptom and subsequently issued an audible alert and a message to a mobile application. The interface is shown in Fig. 8. To verify the correct operation of the proposed method, the participating driver was required to travel with the vehicle through a controlled road at a speed not exceeding 60 km/h. The data for this test was collected by the local vehicle registration station, a laptop and a mobile phone with the Telegram application. The graphic interface showed through the laptop the inclination of the driver's head, his location in real time and if he had symptoms of fatigue. Finally, the pitching simulations were carried out where,

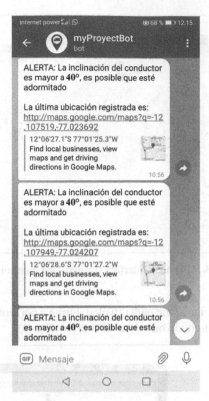

Fig. 7. Alert vía chat Bot Telegram

when this symptom was detected, the driver was alerted through an auditory alert and a message through Telegram.

All the criteria for pitch detection are based on a good detection of the angle of inclination, with which the percentage of error in the detection of the inclination angle has been validated. The error rate exceeded 22% for a total of 60 randomly selected samples. Also, the maximum error distance was 21 m, due to the accuracy of the sensor. Finally, the accuracy of the test exceeded 96.15% when the driver's pitch simulations were performed. For this, Eq. (10) was used.

$$\%Error = \frac{|V_e - V_i|}{V_i} \times 100\% \tag{10}$$

V_e = Experimental value of head tilt by the system.
V_i = Reference value of head tilt by Bosch sensor.

Figure 7 shows the graphical interface that was used to monitor the lean angle and driver location in real time. In order to verify the state of rest and the calibration of the sensor, a participant was positioned in the state of rest behind the wheel as shown in Fig. 8.

Figure 10 shows the angles obtained by the inertial module of the proposed device and the Bosch referential inertial module, in Fig. 11 the percentage of error obtained

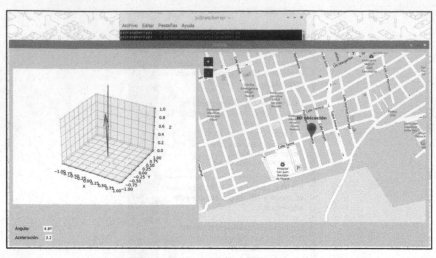

Fig. 8. Graphical interface for real-time monitoring.

between samples and in Fig. 12 the path traveled during a performance test of the system recording latitude and longitude based on GPS error (Fig. 9).

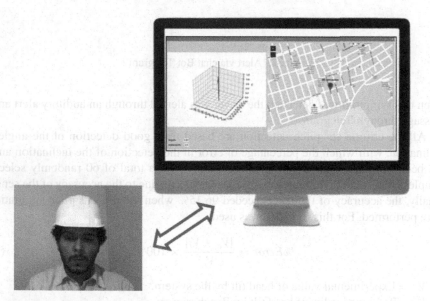

Fig. 9. Participant in resting state for calibration. Image authorized by the participant.

Figure 10 shows the results of the performance test in angles for both the inertial module of the helmet and the reference Bosch sensor, where it can be seen that there are small variations in magnitude between the two. Likewise, Fig. 11 shows the error

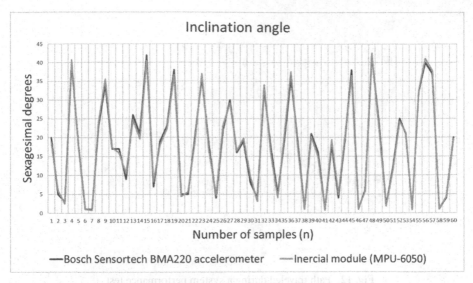

Fig. 10. Angle of inclination obtained by inertial modules of the system and referential

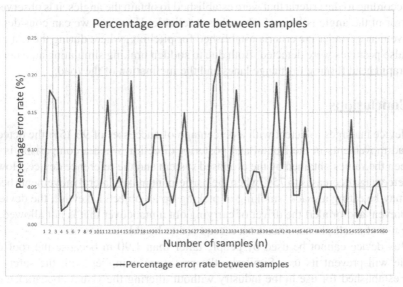

Fig. 11. Percentage of error between samples.

percentage between samples where the maximum error does not exceed 22% during this test, carried out with speed variations between 0 and 60 km/h.

Although the initial tests were carried out with ideal cervical movements, these must be varied in order to obtain a greater amount of data for later analysis, helping to obtain a better notion regarding the cervical movement of people and thus be able to see their physical limitations of according to the body dimensions of each participant.

Fig. 12. Path traveled during a system performance test.

According to the criteria that were established to obtain the angles, it is observed that the error of the angle is low, which makes it reliable. However, we can consider some inconveniences under the criteria established for pitching, where during the test carried out, false positives were detected. Both due to sudden braking simulating an emergency stop, rapid head turning to change lanes and the inclination of the road.

4 Conclusions

The device manages to detect with a percentage of successes of 96.15% the detections of head movements in the frontal and posterior direction when a comparison is made between the values obtained by the proposed system and the reference device. However, this percentage decreases to 75% when the participant makes lateral movements because they may be eating a snack, smoking or picking up an object. Likewise, the device can also prevent and/or alert the driver of carrying out a maneuver that is not allowed, such as the use of a cell phone, since a tilt is required to be able to view it.

This device cannot be used by people taller than 1.90 m because the roof of the vehicle will prevent its use. Similarly, the prototype complies with the safety standards established for use in the industry without altering the visual appearance of the collaborator.

The use of the Bluetooth protocol allows a successful transmission between devices because they are at a short distance, less than 5 m. However, it must be taken into account that if the driver leaves and enters the vehicle, there will be a reconnection delay of no more than 10 s. Likewise, the time it takes to send an alert to a third party depends on the connectivity capacity in the area, being affected by tunnels, places without a mobile network connection.

In the future, the aim is to improve the results by using artificial intelligence algorithms to detect pitching states more accurately.

Acknowledgements. The authors would like to thank the Dirección de Investigación of Universidad Peruana de Ciencias Aplicadas for funding and logistical support with Code UPC-D-2022.

References

1. How to build a better bedtime routine for adults. Sleep Foundation, 8 January 2021. https://www.sleepfoundation.org/sleep-hygiene/bedtime-routine-foradults
2. (n.d.) YouTube. Accessed 10 May 2022. https://www.youtube.com/results?search_query=sut ran+como+prevenir+accidentes
3. (N.d) Gob.pe. Accessed 10 May 2022. https://portal.concytec.gob.pe/images/stories/portal/are asinstitucion/pyp/plan_nac_ctei/plan_nac_ctei_2006_2021.pdf
4. Alertme Drowsy Driver Device. Resqme Inc., 26 March 2016. https://resqme.com/product/ale rtme/
5. Li, K., Gong, Y., Ren, Z.: A fatigue driving detection algorithm based on facial multi-feature fusion. IEEE Access Pract. Innov. Open Solutions **8**, 101244–101259 (2020). https://doi.org/10.1109/access.2020.2998363
6. Zhang, C., Wu, X., Zheng, X., Yu, S.: Driver drowsiness detection using multi-channel second order blind identifications. IEEE Access Pract. Innov. Open Solutions **7**, 11829–11843 (2019). https://doi.org/10.1109/access.2019.289197

Pose Estimation for Nonlinear Visual Servo Control of an Omnidirectional Platform

Rodriguez Jhon[✉], Pilatasig Marco[✉], and Mendoza Dario[✉]

Universidad de las Fuerzas Armadas ESPE, Sangolqui, Ecuador
{jcrodriguezh,mapilatagsig,djmendoza}@espe.edu.ec

Abstract. This paper developed a nonlinear visual servo control using the reverse kinematic model of the omnidirectional platform with mecanum wheels for trajectory tracking using visual feedback for pose estimation based on binary markers. Control actions are sent from the computer to the platform using a wireless communication channel (Zigbee Protocol). The experimental results obtained show that the errors converge asymptotically to values close to zero, demonstrating that the proposed controller works correctly and responds adequately to external disturbances.

Keywords: Control servo visual · Pose estimation · Omnidirectional platform

1 Introduction

Mobile robots are used in education, research, industry, and defense because they can move in a specific space and perform activities such as exploration and navigation due to their excellent performance in speed, maneuverability, and balance [1, 2]; mobile robots are classified into terrestrial, aquatic, and aerial. In terrestrial robots, there are omnidirectional robots that are characterized by their excellent maneuverability and mobility in complex scenarios that make them suitable for different fields [3, 4], for example, in the military field, they are used in dangerous environments and are difficult to access for people [5].

Pose estimation (position and orientation) in omnidirectional robots is important for trajectory tracking in structured and unstructured environments [6], one of the techniques used for this purpose is odometry, which involves using information about the rotation of the wheels to estimate changes in position over time [7]. Odometry is based on simple equations that can be easily implemented and that use data from encoders located on the robot's wheels; it is also based on the assumption that the revolutions of the wheels can be translated into a linear displacement relative to the ground [8]. Another technique for pose estimation is visual servo control, which uses visual information to control the movement of a robot. This information can be pixels in an image, lines, or an area of an image; the camera can provide visual information [9, 10]. The camera can be mounted on the mobile robot or fixed in its working environment [11].

M. Botto-Tobar et al. (Eds.): ICAT 2022, CCIS 1756, pp. 274–285, 2023.
https://doi.org/10.1007/978-3-031-24971-6_20

In mobile robots, different control algorithms can be implemented to fulfill specific tasks and act efficiently in the presence of disturbances [12], he non-linear controllers are implemented depending on the kinematic and dynamic model of the mobile robot; how can they be a sliding mode, neural, diffuse, etc. [13–16].

In this context, there are several works related to pose estimation as in [17], the proposed algorithm effectively improves the accuracy of position estimation based on triangulation and reduces position uncertainty. In [18], the position of a mobile robot is estimated recursively based on the optimal Kalman filter. In [19], an adaptive algorithm is presented to estimate the position of a mobile robot with high precision in an unknown and unstructured environment by merging images from an omnidirectional vision system with odometry measurements and inertial sensors. In [20], a simple and effective method based on an adaptive estimator is proposed to estimate the position and linear speed of a mobile robot in an unknown and unstructured environment, using inertial sensors and visual feedback. In [21], it is demonstrated by simulations that the simultaneous position estimates of two mobile robots using an Extended Kalman Filter, with the relative distance information presents an improvement compared to the independent estimates. In [22], taking into account the estimation of the position of the vehicle, the conventional method is Dead-Reckoning, whose estimation accuracy is almost good. But once the vehicle slip occurs, this method loses accuracy due to wheel slippage.

The present research work proposes a visual servo system using a pose estimation method based on binary markers to solve the problem of trajectory tracking, using a nonlinear controller based on the inverse kinematic model of an omnidirectional platform.

The article is organized into 4 Sections, including the Introduction: Sect. 2 material and method; Sect. 3 presents results and discussions; Finally, the conclusions are presented in Sect. 4.

2   Material and Method

2.1   Kinematic Modeling

To obtain the kinematic model, the schematic representation of Fig. 1. Where you can see an omnidirectional platform that moves to the frame of reference using two linear velocities referring to the front and side axis, respectively $<O> \mu_l, \mu_f$; in addition, there is an angular velocity ω_ψ which allows the rotation of the system around the axis z'. These speeds are applied at the reference point $< \mathcal{R}_a >$, which is displaced one distance a from the inertial center $<\mathcal{R}>$ of the omnidirectional platform.

The kinematic model of the omnidirectional platform considering the displacement of the operating point is defined as:

$$
\begin{bmatrix} \dot{x}_a \\ \dot{y}_a \\ \dot{\psi} \end{bmatrix} = \begin{bmatrix} \cos(\psi) & -\sin(\psi) & -a\sin(\psi) \\ \sin(\psi) & \cos(\psi) & a\cos(\psi) \\ 0 & 0 & 1 \end{bmatrix} \begin{bmatrix} \mu_f \\ \mu_l \\ \omega_\psi \end{bmatrix} \tag{1}
$$

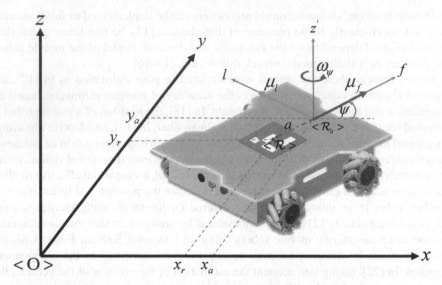

Fig. 1. Schematic representation of the omnidirectional platform.

The abbreviated representation of the kinematic model can be written as:

$$\dot{\boldsymbol{\eta}}_{\mathbf{a}}(t) = \mathbf{J}(\psi)\boldsymbol{\mu}(t) \qquad (2)$$

where, $\dot{\boldsymbol{\eta}}_{\mathbf{a}} \in \Re^m$ con $\dot{\boldsymbol{\eta}}_{\mathbf{a}}(t) = [\dot{x}_a \ \dot{y}_a \ \dot{\psi}]^T$ is the vector that contains the speeds of the omnidirectional platform from the frame of reference $<O>$, $\boldsymbol{\mu} \in \Re^n$ with $\boldsymbol{\mu}(t) = \left[\mu_f \ \mu_l \ \omega_\psi\right]^T$ is the velocity vector applied at the shifted operating point $<\mathcal{R}_a>$ and finally $\mathbf{J}(\psi) \in \Re^{m \times n}$ is the Jacobian matrix that establishes the relationship between both velocity vectors.

2.2 Servo Visual Environment

This section discusses the stage corresponding to visual feedback, for example, the omnidirectional platform's pose estimation. Implementing a camera as a feedback system to close the control loop of the visual servo system has multiple advantages because, unlike the system based on odometry, it does not physically dependent on the surface (inclination, roughness, imperfections, etc.) through which the mobile robot moves. However, working with this type of system where the camera is used as a measuring instrument requires a previous calibration stage that identifies an accurate model that describes the projection of a three-dimensional point on the image plane.

2.3 Camera Calibration

The calibration of the camera is an indispensable task that aims to extract the intrinsic parameters of the chamber necessary to perform the projection of a point $\mathbf{p}_w \in \Re^3$ with $\mathbf{p}_w = \left[x_w \ y_w \ z_w\right]^T$ of the world corresponding to a point $\mathbf{p}_i \in \Re^2$ con $\mathbf{p}_i = \left[u_i \ v_i\right]^T$ at the image plane, the transformation in question is known as the full perspective model and is defined as:

$$
\begin{bmatrix} u_i \\ v_i \\ 1 \end{bmatrix} = \begin{bmatrix} f_x & 0 & c_x \\ 0 & f_y & c_y \\ 0 & 0 & 1 \end{bmatrix} \begin{bmatrix} r_{11} & r_{12} & r_{13} & t_1 \\ r_{21} & r_{22} & r_{23} & t_2 \\ r_{31} & r_{32} & r_{33} & t_3 \end{bmatrix} \begin{bmatrix} x_w \\ y_w \\ z_w \\ 1 \end{bmatrix}
\tag{3}
$$

$$
\mathbf{p}_i = \mathbf{K}_c \big[\mathbf{R}_c | \mathbf{t}_c \big] \mathbf{p}_w
\tag{4}
$$

where, $\mathbf{K}_c \in \Re^{3\times3}$ represents the matrix of intrinsic parameters that it contains: f_x, f_y y c_x, c_y that define the focal lengths and coordinates of the center of the camera in pixels, respectively; $\mathbf{R}_c \in \Re^{3\times3}$ is the generalized rotation matrix and $\mathbf{t}_c \in \Re^3$ the translation vector, both responsible for defining the position and orientation of the camera.

For this work, the calibration process was carried out using an identification algorithm that receives as input a set of images of a chessboard in different positions. As a result of the calibration process is obtained: 1) The intrinsic parameters of the chamber necessary to complete the model that allows the linear transformation described in Eq. (3). 2) The distortion coefficients responsible for correcting the re-projection error due to the radial distortion presented by the camera lens due to its construction.

2.4 Pose Estimation

Pose estimation is made from the identification of an object in the environment from which the characteristics of interest are to be extracted and analyzed. For this work, the task in question has been carried out through binary markers due to how easy it is to estimate the rotation vectors $\mathbf{r}_{vec} \in \Re^3$ and translation $\mathbf{t}_{vec} \in \Re^3$ of such markers. However, to obtain the angle of rotation concerning the axis z of the marker, it is necessary to convert the received rotation vector into a generalized rotation matrix. To perform this operation, the matrix expression known as Rodrigues' formula is used:

$$
\mathbf{R}_i = \cos(\theta)\mathbf{I} + (1 - \cos(\theta))\mathbf{r}_i\mathbf{r}_i^T + \sin(\theta) \begin{bmatrix} 0 & -r_z & r_y \\ r_z & 0 & -r_x \\ -r_y & r_x & 0 \end{bmatrix}
\tag{5}
$$

where, $\mathbf{R}_i \in \Re^{3\times3}$ represents the rotation matrix; $\mathbf{r}_i \in \Re^3$ is the unit vector of the rotation vector and is the norm of the rotation vector θ. So, the orientation angle (yaw) is obtained by means of $\psi = \tan^{-1}(r_{21}/r_{11})$, where r_{11}, r_{21} are elements of the rotation matrix $\mathbf{R}_i$.

The proposed visual servo environment consists mainly of two binary markers, as shown in Fig. 2: the first allows estimating the position and orientation of the inertial center of the omnidirectional platform $<\mathcal{R}>$ concerning the camera coordinate system $<C>$; the second marker is fixed and allows a referential system to be anchored to the surface on which the mobile robot moves, with the aim that the omnidirectional platform performs the task of tracking trajectories concerning the reference frame $<O>$ fixed by the marker.

From the position and estimated orientation of the markers located in $<O>$ y $<\mathcal{R}>$ concerning the camera reference system $<C>$ (see Fig. 2), the matrix expression that

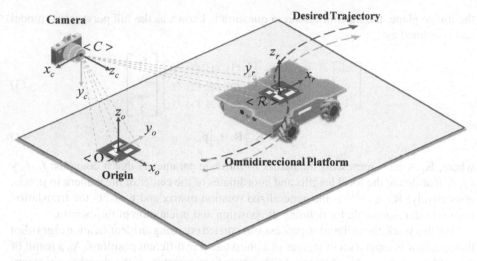

Fig. 2. Visual servo environment

describes the transformation of homogeneous coordinates that allows obtaining the translation vector of the omnidirectional platform is obtained $<\mathcal{R}>$ concerning the origin fixed in $<O>$, Like this:

$$^O\eta_R = {}^C\mathbf{R}_O^T\left({}^C\mathbf{t}_R - {}^C\mathbf{t}_O\right) \tag{6}$$

where, ${}^C\mathbf{t}_R \in \mathfrak{R}^{3\times1}$ is the translation vector of the inertial center of the omnidirectional platform; ${}^C\mathbf{t}_O \in \mathfrak{R}^{3\times1}$ the estimated translation vector of the reference frame of origin and ${}^C\mathbf{R}_O^T \in \mathfrak{R}^{3\times3}$ its estimated transposed rotation matrix, all concerning the frame of reference of the chamber; and ${}^O\eta_R \in \mathfrak{R}^{3\times1}$ is the translation vector of the platform expressed in the referential system of the origin.

From Eq. (6) the displacement of the operating point along the axis of the x coordinate system is made $<\mathcal{R}>$ (see Fig. 1), Like this:

$$^O\eta_{aR} = \begin{bmatrix} a\cos(\psi) & 0 & 0 \\ 0 & a\sin(\psi) & 0 \\ 0 & 0 & 1 \end{bmatrix} {}^C\mathbf{R}_O^T\left({}^C\mathbf{t}_R - {}^C\mathbf{t}_O\right) \tag{7}$$

$$^O\eta_{aR} = \mathbf{M_a} {}^C\mathbf{R}_O^T\left({}^C\mathbf{t}_R - {}^C\mathbf{t}_O\right) \tag{8}$$

where, $\mathbf{M_a} \in \mathfrak{R}^{3\times3}$ is the matrix that makes the displacement of the operating point concerning the axes x, y of the referential frame $<O>$.

The orientation of the omnidirectional platform is determined based on the matrices obtained from the estimated rotation vectors for each of the markers, as well as:

$$^O\mathbf{R}_R = {}^C\mathbf{R}_O^T{}^C\mathbf{R}_R \tag{9}$$

where, ${}^C\mathbf{R}_R \in \mathfrak{R}^{3\times3}$ the rotation matrix of the referential $<\mathcal{R}>$ respect to the camera and ${}^O\mathbf{R}_R \in \mathfrak{R}^{3\times3}$ is the rotation matrix of the reference frame $<\mathcal{R}>$ concerning the reference of the origin $<O>$.

2.5 Kinematic Controller

The proposed control scheme shown in Fig. 3 consists mainly of a non-linear controller which is based on the reverse kinematic model described above; this controller allows solving the trajectory tracking problem of the omnidirectional platform through the control actions that are generated based on the error present between the desired references and the estimated position and orientation data within the stage of the visual servo environment.

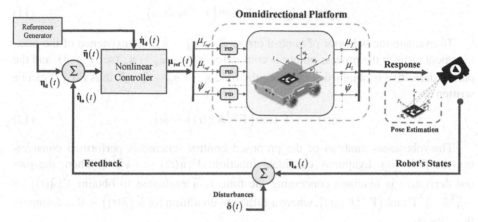

Fig. 3. Visual servo control schematic

2.6 Design Controller

The design of the nonlinear controller is developed from the reverse kinematic model of the omnidirectional platform; the controller has the following inputs: 1) The error defined as $\tilde{\boldsymbol{\eta}}(t) = \boldsymbol{\eta_d}(t) - \hat{\boldsymbol{\eta}}(t)$ where, $\boldsymbol{\eta_d} \in \Re^3$ with $\boldsymbol{\eta_d}(t) = \begin{bmatrix} \eta_{x_d} & \eta_{y_d} & \eta_{\psi_d} \end{bmatrix}^T$ represents the desired states of position and orientation generated from time-parameterized curves and, $\hat{\boldsymbol{\eta}}_\mathbf{a} \in \Re^3$ with $\hat{\boldsymbol{\eta}}_\mathbf{a}(t) = \begin{bmatrix} \hat{\eta}_{x_a} & \hat{\eta}_{y_a} & \hat{\eta}_{\psi_a} \end{bmatrix}^T$ represents the estimated states of the frame of reference $<\mathcal{R}_a>$ concerning the origin located in $<O>$. 2) The change ratio of the desired reference, i.e., the vector of desired velocities of the point of interest defined as $\dot{\boldsymbol{\eta}}_\mathbf{d} \in \Re^3$ with $\dot{\boldsymbol{\eta}}_\mathbf{d}(t) = \begin{bmatrix} \dot{\eta}_{x_d} & \dot{\eta}_{y_d} & \dot{\eta}_{\psi_d} \end{bmatrix}^T$. Consequently, the goal of the proposed nonlinear controller focuses on generating a vector of control velocities described as $\boldsymbol{\mu}_\mathbf{ref} \in \Re^3$, that allows the error to converge asymptotically to zero, that is, $\lim\limits_{t \to \infty} \tilde{\boldsymbol{\eta}}(t) = 0$.

Therefore, the proposed control law for omnidirectional platform trajectory tracking is defined as:

$$\boldsymbol{\mu}_\mathbf{ref}(t) = \mathbf{J}^{-1}\left(\dot{\boldsymbol{\eta}}_\mathbf{d}(t) + \boldsymbol{\Gamma} \tanh\left(\boldsymbol{\Gamma}^{-1}\mathbf{K}\,\tilde{\boldsymbol{\eta}}(t)\right)\right) \tag{10}$$

where, $\mathbf{J}^{-1}(\psi)$ is the inverse Jacobian matrix; $\boldsymbol{\Gamma} \in \Re^{3x3}$ y $\mathbf{K} \in \Re^{3x3}$ are constant diagonal matrices defined positive. In addition, the function $\tanh(.)$ performs the task of saturation of control errors, which directly influences the smooth behavior of the signals applied to the actuators.

2.7 Robustness Analysis

The analysis of the robustness of the visual servo control is an essential part of this work because, through this study, it is possible to determine the validity and consistency of the proposed control scheme in the face of errors produced in the pose estimation stage. This is based on the consideration that the mobile robot moves at the same maneuverability speed generated by the controller. $\mu = \mu_{ref}$, replacing (10) in (2) the equation is obtained in closed loop:

$$\dot{\eta}_a(t) = \dot{\eta}_d(t) + \Gamma \tanh\left(\Gamma^{-1} K \tilde{\eta}(t)\right) \tag{11}$$

To evaluate the behavior of control errors $\tilde{\eta} = \eta_d - \hat{\eta}_a$, the existence of the measurement error in the process output is considered as $\delta = \hat{\eta}_a - \eta_a$ (see Fig. 3), and the partial derivative is obtained concerning the time $\dot{\eta}_a = \dot{\eta}_d - \dot{\tilde{\eta}} - \dot{\delta}$, thus Eq. (7) can be written as:

$$\dot{\tilde{\eta}}(t) = -\Gamma \tanh\left(\Gamma^{-1} K \tilde{\eta}(t)\right) - \dot{\delta}(t) \tag{12}$$

The robustness analysis of the proposed control scheme is performed considering the following Lyapunov candidate function: $V\left(\tilde{\eta}(t)\right) = \frac{1}{2}\tilde{\eta}^T \tilde{\eta}$. Then, the partial derivative is obtained concerning the time is $\dot{\tilde{\eta}}$ evaluated to obtain: $\dot{V}\left(\tilde{\eta}(t)\right) = -\tilde{\eta}^T\dot{\delta} - \tilde{\eta}^T\Gamma \tanh\left(\Gamma^{-1} K \tilde{\eta}(t)\right)$, where a sufficient condition for $\dot{V}\left(\tilde{\eta}(t)\right) < 0$ is definitely negative is,

$$\left|\tilde{\eta}^T\Gamma \tanh\left(\Gamma^{-1} K \tilde{\eta}(t)\right)\right| > \left|\tilde{\eta}^T\dot{\delta}\right| \tag{13}$$

Analyzing for large values of $\tilde{\eta}(t)$, the above expression can be reduced by considering that $\Gamma \tanh\left(\Gamma^{-1} K \tilde{\eta}(t)\right) \approx \Gamma$, then $\dot{V}\left(\tilde{\eta}(t)\right)$ is a negative defined function if, $\|\Gamma\| > \left\|\dot{\delta}\right\|$. Ensuring that the error decreases, while for reduced values of $\tilde{\eta}(t)$, can be approximated $\tanh\left(\Gamma^{-1} K \tilde{\eta}(t)\right) \approx \tanh(\kappa_{aux})\tilde{\eta}(t)/\kappa_{aux}$, therefore, Eq. (13) is represented as:

$$\|\tilde{\eta}\| < \frac{\kappa_{aux}\left\|\dot{\delta}\right\|}{\tau \lambda_{\min}(K)\tanh(\kappa_{aux})}; \text{ with } 0 < \tau < 1 \tag{14}$$

The behavior of control errors $\tilde{\eta}(t)$ (Eq. (14)), depends directly on the change rate of the measurement error $\dot{\delta}$ considered in the pose estimation stage, this error will depend on the quality of the work done in the calibration phase and parameter estimation of the camera. However, it is connected to $\left\|\dot{\delta}\right\| < \kappa_\delta$, where κ_δ So it can be concluded that the controller will absorb the error produced by the estimate, ensuring an asymptotically stable behavior. For example, $\lim_{t \to \infty} \tilde{\eta}(t) = 0$.

3 Results and Discussions

This section presents the evaluation and validation of the proposed control scheme (see Fig. 3). To this end, a prototype of an omnidirectional platform with Mecanum wheels has been developed for experimental tests (see Fig. 4), To this end, a prototype of an omnidirectional platform with Mecanum wheels has been developed for experimental tests (Zigbee Protocol). On the other hand, a PC is used in charge of image processing (OpenCV C++), pose estimation and the generation of control actions that are subsequently sent wirelessly to the platform each $t_s = 0.1$ s.

Fig. 4. Omnidirectional Platform.

To evaluate the stability and performance of the proposed controller, whose parameters have been defined as: $\mathbf{\Gamma} = diag\left[\,0.7\ 0.7\ 0.7\,\right]$ and $\mathbf{K} = diag\left[\,0.9\ 0.9\ 0.9\,\right]$, the resolution of the trajectory tracking problem was raised, where the omnidirectional platform starts from an initial condition $\mathbf{\eta_0}(t)$ to make your position estimated $\mathbf{\eta_a}(t)$ converge to the time-parameterized curve that represents the desired references $\mathbf{\eta_d}(t)$. The above parameters are summarized in Table 1.

Table 1. Desired task and initial parameters.

Initial conditions		Desired task	
η_{0x_a}	0.83 [m]	η_{x_d}	$0.7\sin(0.16t) + 1.2\,[m]$
η_{0y_a}	1.02 [m]	η_{y_d}	$0.49\sin(0.16t)\cos(0.16t) + 0.45\,[m]$
$\eta_{0\psi_a}$	$\pi\,/\,2\,[rad]$	η_{ψ_d}	$0\,[rad]$
a	0.15 [m]	$\upsilon_{\max}$	$0.5\,[m/s]$

Figure 5 shows the image resulting from the projection of three-dimensional points $\Re^3$ that make up the actual trajectory $\mathbf{\eta_a}(t)$ and the desired trajectory $\mathbf{\eta_d}(t)$, onto the plane of the image $\Re^2$. Such a transformation is described in Eq. (3).

The experimental results obtained are shown in Fig. 6, where it can be observed that the trajectory described by the omnidirectional platform converges to the desired trajectory demonstrating that the proposed controller works optimally.

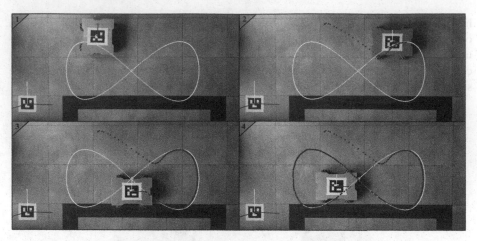

Fig. 5. Projection of trajectory tracking points on the image.

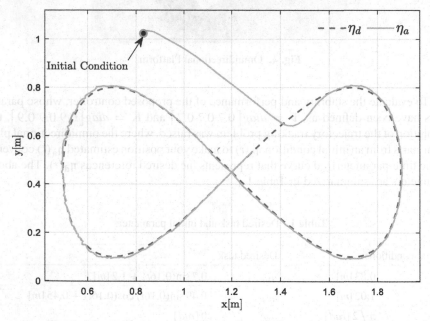

Fig. 6. Movement executed by the platform during trajectory tracking.

Figure 7 shows how the trajectory traveled by the offset operating point of the omnidirectional platform $\eta_a(t)$ resembles the desired trajectory $\eta_d(t)$ with respect to the x and y axes individually, thus fulfilling the controller's objective for the selected gains.

Figure 8 shows the evolution of control errors $\tilde{\eta}(\tilde{\eta}_x, \tilde{\eta}_y, \tilde{\eta}_\psi) \in \Re^3$, where it is observed that these errors occur asymptotically at values close to zero.

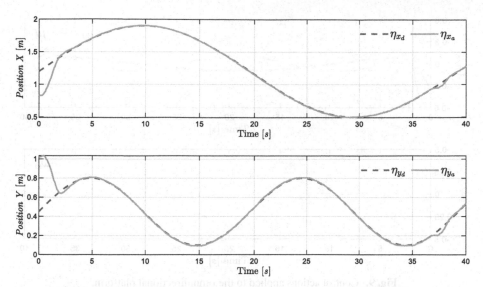

Fig. 7. Evolution of the trajectory described by the omnidirectional platform.

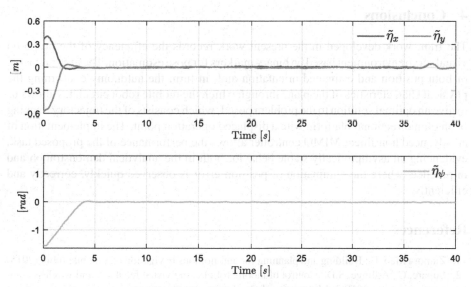

Fig. 8. Evolution of control errors.

Figure 9 shows the maneuverability velocities generated by the controller for the execution of the desired task, where it is observed that the speeds sent to the omnidirectional platform do not exceed the previously defined maximum values (see Table 1).

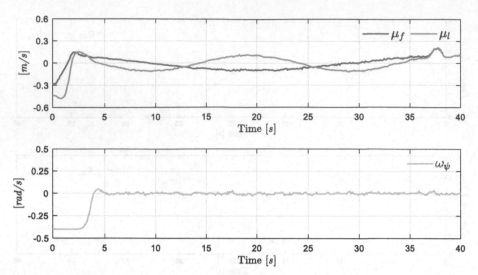

Fig. 9. Control actions applied to the omnidirectional platform.

4   Conclusions

The framework developed in the present work records the efficiency of the proposed visual servo environment based on binary markers for pose estimation. The high precision of both position and estimated orientation and, in turn, the autonomy concerning the physical characteristics of the plane through which the mobile robot circulates allows us to give an optimal solution to the problem posed, which consists of the trajectory tracking of an omnidirectional platform with a displaced operation point. The implementation of an advanced non-linear MIMO controller allows the performance of the proposed task, evidencing an asymptotically stable behavior both in the analytical demonstration and in practice, where the elimination of position error is observed quickly, correctly and efficiently.

References

1. Zamora Mao, E.: Building and planning for autonomous navigation of a mobile robot (2015)
2. Supare, C., Adlinge, S.D.: Control of mobile robot using visual feedback and wireless communication. In: 2018 3rd International Conference for Convergence in Technology (I2CT), pp. 1–5 (2018)
3. Chen, W., Yang, C., Feng, Y.: Shared control for omnidirectional mobile robots. In: 2019 Chinese Control and Decision Conference (CCDC), pp. 6185–6190 (2019)
4. Comasolivas, R., Quevedo, J., Escobet, T., Escobet, A., Romera, J.: Low level control of an omnidirectional mobile robot. In: 2015 23rd Mediterranean Conference on Control and Automation (MED), pp. 1160–1166 (2015)
5. Morales, S., Magallanes, J., Delgado, C., Canahuire, R.: LQR trajectory tracking control of an omnidirectional wheeled mobile robot. In: 2018 IEEE 2nd Colombian Conference on Robotics and Automation (CCRA), pp. 1–5 (2018). https://doi.org/10.1109/CCRA.2018.858 8146

6. Zhang, M., Chen, Y., Li, M.: SDF-Loc: signed distance field based 2D relocalization and map update in dynamic environments. In: Proceedings of American Control Conference, pp. 1997–2004 (2019)
7. Censi, A., Franchi, A., Marchionni, L., Oriolo, G.: Simultaneous calibration of odometry and sensor parameters for mobile robots. IEEE Trans. Robot. **29**(2), 475–492 (2013)
8. Huai, Z., Huang, G.: Robocentric visual-inertial odometry. In: Proceedings of IEEE/RSJ International Conference on Intelligent Robots and Systems, pp. 6319–6326 (2018)
9. Abadianzadeh, F., Derhami, V., Rezaeian, M.: Visual servoing control of robot manipulator in 3D space using fuzzy hybrid controller. In: 2016 4th International Conference on Robotics and Mechatronics (ICROM), pp. 61–65 (2016)
10. Rodrigues, R.T., Miraldo, P., Dimarogonas, D.V., Aguiar, A.P.: A framework for depth estimation and relative localization of ground robots using computer vision. In: 2019 IEEE/RSJ International Conference on Intelligent Robots and Systems (IROS), pp. 3719–3724 (2019)
11. Park, K., Ha, H., Rameau, F., Kweon, I.S.: Fused robot pose estimation using embedded and external cameras. In: 2015 12th International Conference on Ubiquitous Robots and Ambient Intelligence (URAI), pp. 375–376 (2015)
12. Pawitan, G.A.H., Mutijarsa, K., Adiprawita, W.: Three-wheeled omnidirectional robot controller implementation. In: 2016 International Conference on Information Technology Systems and Innovation (ICITSI), pp. 1–4 (2016)
13. Alakshendra, V., Chiddarwar, S.S.: Design of robust adaptive controller for a four wheel omnidirectional mobile robot. In: 2015 International Conference on Advances in Computing, Communications and Informatics (ICACCI), pp. 63–68 (2015)
14. Andreev, A., Peregudova, O.: On the trajectory tracking control of a wheeled mobile robot based on a dynamic model with slip. In: 2020 15th International Conference on Stability and Oscillations of Nonlinear Control Systems (Pyatnitskiy's Conference) (STAB), pp. 1–4 (2020)
15. Manel, M., Faouzi, B.: Predictive control based on dynamic modeling of omnidirectional mobile robot. In: 2017 International Conference on Engineering & MIS (ICEMIS), pp. 1–6 (2017)
16. Al Mamun, M.A., Nasir, M.T., Khayyat, A.: Embedded system for motion control of an omnidirectional mobile robot. IEEE Access **6**, 6722–6739 (2018). https://doi.org/10.1109/ACCESS.2018.2794441
17. Yan, W., Wang, K., Li, R.: A method for position estimation of mobile robot based on data fusion. In: 2019 Chinese Control and Decision Conference (CCDC), pp. 5568–5572 (2019)
18. Xu, Z., Chen, H., Xiang, Z., Liu, J.: Position estimation for a mobile robot with augmented system state. In: 2005 International Conference on Neural Networks and Brain, pp. 366–370 (2005)
19. Li, L., Liu, Y., Wang, K., Fang, M.: Estimating position of mobile robots from omnidirectional vision using an adaptive algorithm. IEEE Trans. Cybern. **45**(8), 1633–1646 (2015)
20. Li, L., Liu, Y., Wang, K., Fang, M.: A simple algorithm for position and velocity estimation of mobile robots using omnidirectional vision and inertial sensors. In: 2014 IEEE International Conference on Robotics and Biomimetics (ROBIO 2014), pp. 1235–1240 (2014)
21. Gualda, D., Ureña, J., García, J.C., Pérez, M.C., Díaz, E.: Study of cooperative position estimations of mobile robots. In: 2017 International Conference on Indoor Positioning and Indoor Navigation (IPIN), pp. 1–7 (2017)
22. Kondo, M., Ohnishi, K.: Constructing a platform of robust position estimation for mobile robot by ODR. In: The 8th IEEE International Workshop on Advanced Motion Control, AMC 2004, pp. 263–268 (2004)

Design of a Model Based Predictive Control (MPC) Strategy for a Desalination Plant in a Hardware in the Loop (HIL) Environment

E. Panchi-Chanatasig, W. Tumbaco-Quinatoa(✉), J. Llanos-Proaño, and D. Ortiz-Villalba

Universidad de las Fuerzas Armadas ESPE, Sangolquí, Ecuador
{eipanchi,wwtumbaco,jdllanos1,ddortiz5}@espe.edu.ec

Abstract. The desalination process using the reverse osmosis technique is important for the production of drinking water, but its control is a great challenge due to its nonlinear and multivariable nature. In academia, the implementation of physical industrial processes represents a considerable cost, taking this into account, in recent years the technology has evolved and boomed called the "metaverse", where it is proposed to create a virtual representation of reality. This research work proposes a hardware-in-the-loop (HIL) environment which consists of a virtual reverse osmosis industrial process and designs and implements the control algorithm in a programmable logic controller (PLC), which is common in the industry. The system is versatile to implement different control algorithms and opens the door to the use of different control devices for its implementation. The design methodology to be used consists of three sections. The first section is the mathematical model of the industrial process. The second section is the implementation of the virtual process in Unity3D software. The third section is the implementation of two control strategies: Proportional Integral Derivative Control (PID) and Model-Based Predictive Control (MPC). Finally, a comparison of the performance of the implemented controllers for both the permeate flow variable (F) and conductivity (C), in transient and steady state, is performed.

Keywords: Hardware in the loop · Advanced control · PID · Virtual laboratory · Reverse osmosis

1 Introduction

At present, almost 700 million people in 43 different countries suffer from a lack of water, and the problem is even worse in the future since it is estimated that by 2025, 1.8 billion people will have absolute water shortages and two-thirds of the world's population will be living under water stress [1]. What is worrying is that, after decades of efforts to address the situation, these figures are still very high [2, 3]. Seawater desalination appears as a viable solution for the population, which consists of extracting clean, pure, and ready-to-drink water.

© The Author(s), under exclusive license to Springer Nature Switzerland AG 2023
M. Botto-Tobar et al. (Eds.): ICAT 2022, CCIS 1756, pp. 286–299, 2023.
https://doi.org/10.1007/978-3-031-24971-6_21

Desalination is declared as the separation of salt from a substance, economically it favors the drinking water companies of each country, being for some countries their only source of obtaining this liquid, for this, several techniques help to separate the water from the salt which is: distillation, freezing, flash evaporation, electrodialysis, thermal de-application and reverse osmosis, the latter being the most widely used in desalination processes, due to its benefits such as high water purity and use of ocean water [4, 5].

Reverse osmosis desalinization plants generally use traditional controllers, which do not ensure efficient performance in the transient state of the variables to be controlled in the process, causing clogging in the membranes and thus higher energy consumption, lowering permeate production and reducing its quality. There are several traditional controllers used for the reverse osmosis process, for example, the PI and PID controller using the Ziegler-Nichols tuning method which shows that the flow output has overshoot [6, 7], this could be improved with the use of more sophisticated controllers, such as model-based predictive control (MPC), such as model-based predictive control (MPC), used for example in a horizontal three-phase separator [8], a horizontal two-phase separator [9]. Another controller implemented is the fuzzy controller using a pilot plant in the R&D laboratories, concluding that fuzzy controllers prove to be more efficient than traditional PI and PID controllers in steady-state error and the more damped response of the manipulated variables [10], also used for a combined cycle thermal power plant [11] and flow processes [12].

Therefore, the design of control strategies to optimize the reverse osmosis process and operate efficiently in the face of changes in influent water quality and changes in the plant's operating environmental conditions is important. In addition, the aim is to achieve plant profitability and compliance with product quality standards while being environmentally responsible and seeking to maximize profits by optimizing existing processes. This can be achieved with the design of advanced control algorithms, which in this work is designed (MPC). These controls have the following advantages: increased product profitability, reduced energy consumption, increased information flow in the system, improved product quality and consistency, reduced waste, increased system response speed, improved process safety, and reduced environmental emissions [13].

Over time it has been concluded that the so-called advanced controllers have better performance than PI or PID controllers, especially for MIMO processes, from control in oil refineries [14], to water treatment, since the controllers are becoming more sophisticated according to the needs of the industry. Normally, advanced controllers are not implemented in these devices (PLC), since the manufacturer's software does not allow it or does not have simple tools for its implementation. In addition, for the design of advanced control is necessary, knowledge in this area and therefore learning time for development. Therefore, among the new technological tools, which have a strong impact on today's society, is virtual reality, such as the virtual workstation for level and temperature process control [15], which stimulates students in the learning process and encourages interest in exploring things more attractively compared to the typical teaching concept of the last decades, that is why 3D virtual environments are evolving exponentially, due to their great usefulness in the work field as well as in the academic field [16], allowing the development of a plant similar to reality. However, these industrial processes being virtual will have an ideal environment which does not happen in practice, considering this, the controllers are implemented in a physical industrial control device within the simulation loop [17].

In this research project, a HIL environment is designed for an industrial reverse osmosis desalination process, controlled by a programmable logic controller (PLC). There is the ability to connect to other devices by coupling the communication between the virtualized plant and the control device. A comparison is made between advanced and traditional control versus multivariable industrial processes. It provides the following contributions: i) A realistic linear MIMO model of an industrial desalination process, ii) The design of an MPC control for a MIMO desalination process, iii) A methodology to implement the MPC control in a physical industrial control device.

2   Reverse Osmosis Process

This section describes the operation and analysis of the industrial reverse osmosis process.

2.1   Description of Reverse Osmosis Process Operation

The operation of the industrial reverse osmosis process is explained with the piping and instrumentation diagram (P&ID), which details the instrumentation and equipment (see Fig. 1).

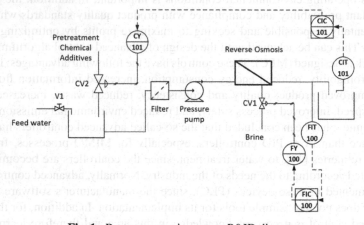

Fig. 1. Reverse osmosis process P&ID diagram.

The reverse osmosis process (See Fig. 1), includes a constant water input, and the desalination process includes two control loops: 100 and 101. The control loop 100 is to control the permeate flow which starts by taking the permeate flow reading through a flow indicator transmitter (FIT-100), whose signal enters the flow indicator controller (CIF-100), the output of the flow controller passes through an electric to the pneumatic signal converter (FY-100) and reaches the actuator which is a control valve (CV1). Loop 101 is responsible for controlling the conductivity of the permeate flow and requires a conductivity indicator transmitter (CIT-101), whose signal enters the conductivity indicator controller (CIC-101), the output goes through an electrical to a pneumatic signal converter (CY-101) which is connected to the actuator which is a control valve (CV2).

Osmosis is a natural process that occurs in plant and animal tissues. It can be said that when two solutions of different concentrations (composed of a solvent and a solute dissolved in a solvent), are joined by a membrane that allows the passage of the solvent, but not a solute, there is a natural circulation of solvent through the membrane, minus the solution. The height difference obtained is converted into a pressure difference, called osmotic pressure. However, concerning the solution, an external pressure greater than the osmotic pressure of the solution is applied. On the other hand, the process can be reversed, recycling the solvent from a more concentrated solution to a solution with a lower concentration will eventually yield water of acceptable purity [18]. In membrane separation processes, the solute to be separated accumulates on the membrane surface due to concentration polarization (solute retained in the membrane) or fouling phenomena (such as pore clogging, adsorption, etc.) [19]. For this reason, both the pressure and the pH supplied to the membrane must be controlled, thus extending its useful life. For this, at the beginning of the process, the pH is regulated by adding sulfuric acid or hydrochloric acid, and the pressure by throttling the valve (CV1) that controls the pressure exerted on the membrane.

2.2 Mathematical Model

Several theoretical models of reverse osmosis membranes have been developed over the past decades. When developing a theoretical model to predict the performance of a reverse osmosis membrane, one of the first aspects to consider is the selection of a transport model that describes the flow of water and salt through the membrane [20]. Although most reverse osmosis models use process identification and obtain plant dynamics, this only corresponds to a SISO model. Others take into account the mass balance and the concentrations of the inflow and outflow, there are some models that due to the computational time are not able to simulate the process in real-time [21], based on the above and the comparative study carried out in [22]. In this research work, we use the model described in [23] (see Fig. 2), because it represents a real plant with relation to the influence of pH on the quality of permeate obtained from the reverse osmosis process, using real data from a laboratory plant. The model [23] is multivariable and uses feed water pressure and pH as manipulated variables, and the variables to be controlled are permeated flow and conductivity.

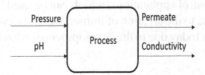

Fig. 2. Reverse osmosis process input and output diagram

The dynamic model of the plant obtained is described by Eqs. (1) and (2), where the inputs of the reverse osmosis process (U) are pressure and pH. The outputs (Y) are permeated flux and conductivity, where G_p are the gains: (3) shows the transfer function relating permeate flux (F) to pressure (P). Equation (4) is zero since the relationship that exists between the pH input does not affect the permeate flux, (5) similarly relates the conductivity (C) to the pressure exerted on the membrane, and (6) the transfer function of conductivity (C) to pH. The model described above serves for the implementation of the HIL, since it has the dynamics of the real process variables. It should be noted that to implement this model in the virtual environment it must be in the time domain, so the inverse Laplace transform is applied [24].

$$Y = G_p U \tag{1}$$

$$\begin{bmatrix} F \\ C \end{bmatrix} = \begin{bmatrix} G_{p11} & G_{p12} \\ G_{p21} & G_{p22} \end{bmatrix} \begin{bmatrix} P \\ pH \end{bmatrix} \tag{2}$$

$$\frac{F}{P} = G_{p11} = \frac{0.002(0.56s + 1)}{0.003s^2 + 0.1s + 1} \tag{3}$$

$$\frac{F}{pH} = G_{p12} = 0 \tag{4}$$

$$\frac{C}{P} = G_{p21} = \frac{-0.51(0.35s + 1)}{0.213s^2 + 0.7s + 1} \tag{5}$$

$$\frac{C}{pH} = G_{p22} = \frac{-57(0.32s + 1)}{0.6s^2 + 1.8s + 1} \tag{6}$$

3 HIL Environment Design for the Industrial Reverse Osmosis Process

La Hardware in the Loop simulation is a well-established technique used in the design and evaluation of control systems. The idea of HIL simulation is to add a part of the real hardware into the simulation loop. Instead of testing the control algorithm on a purely mathematical model of the system, the real hardware (if available) can be used in the simulation loop [17]. Using such a technique connects the actual signals from the controller to a test system to a computer, which has a virtual representation of the plant developed in Unity 3D software. Such software allows the creation of realistic 2D and 3D environments, and control applications, which can be used for educational purposes of industrial processes due to the creation of immersive experiences in environments that are heard more frequently today due to the development of what is known as 'metaverse'.

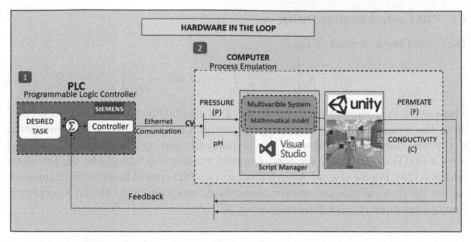

Fig. 3. Hardware in the Loop reverse osmosis process system.

HIL (see Fig. 3) consists of two stages, stage 1 corresponds to a Programmable Logic Controller (PLC), where the control algorithms are programmed, which can be PID, MPC, and others, using the TIA Portal programming software for the PLC S7-1200 AC/DC/RLY and uploading the program to the device. There is also the possibility of using any control device by coupling the communication with the virtualized environment. On the other hand, stage 2 is the virtualized industrial process; communication is via Ethernet. In the first stage, the desired values (SP) and the values of the flow and conductivity variables at that instant are taken, these enter the PLC, then provides the control values (CV) that are sent by Ethernet communication to the second stage, in which is the mathematical model of Sect. 2.2 implemented through lines of Visual Studio 2019 code in Unity 3D, the control values excite the plant making it evolve by modifying the process variables (PV) and these are sent back to the first stage to close the control loop.

The virtualized reverse osmosis process is based on a piping and instrumentation diagram (P&ID) of a real plant (see Fig. 1). For the modeling of the instruments in a virtual way (CAD), it is implemented with the help of software such as Autocad Plant 3D, SketchUp, Blender where the instrumentation involved in the reverse osmosis process is designed. The files are converted into.fbx format to later import them into the Unity 3D software, placing each one in its respective place as close to reality as possible. The mathematical model implemented in Visual Studio 2019 interacts with the environment developed in Unity 3D and this process works together with the physical control device (PLC).

4   Reverse Osmosis Process Control Algorithms Design

After having designed and validated the virtual plant, we proceed to incorporate the controllers.

4.1   PID Control Strategy Design

The control law is defined by Eq. 7

$$u(t) = K_p\left[e(t) + \frac{1}{T_i}\int_0^t e(t)dt + T_d\frac{de(t)}{dt}\right] \tag{7}$$

where $u(t)$ is the control value, K_p is the gain, T_i is integral time, and T_d is the differential time. The tuning method to be used is Aggressive Lambda tuning. Where this tuning is a special case of pole assignment that is frequently used in the process industry, this is for a FOTD model, where the controller performance is influenced by the parameter selection [24]. For the reverse osmosis process, two PID control loops are implemented, one for the flow variable and one for conductivity, as shown in the closed-loop reverse osmosis industrial process diagram (see Fig. 4).

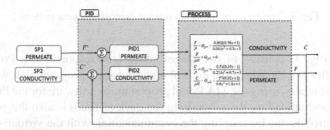

Fig. 4. PID control loop for industrial reverse osmosis process.

4.2   Control Design Based on the MPC Model

For the design of the MPC control it is needed: a prediction horizon, a control horizon, an objective function, restrictions, error weights and control actions [25, 26]. This in turn relies on the plant model to predict the future values of the variables to be controlled as in this case are the permeate flow and conductivity minimizing their errors $(F * -F(t))y(C * -C(t))$. . Depending on the weights, the control actions are more aggressive or soft (see Fig. 5).

An objective function $J(k)$ defined in Eq. (8) is responsible for minimizing the errors, where the first term $\left[\hat{F}(k + i|k) - F * (k + i|k)\right]^2$ is the squared error between the desired value and the predicted value of the permeate to minimize permeate flow errors, $\delta_1(k)$ which is the weight for the first control target. The second control objective is to minimize the conductivity error $\left[\hat{C}(k + i|k) - C * (k + i|k)\right]^2$ with the corresponding weight $\delta_2(k)$. Subsequently, control objectives are included that minimize the changes in control actions to protect the actuator, therefore, the objective function includes $[\Delta u_1(k + i - 1)]^2$, which is the variance of the quadratic control value for the permeate control variables, is the weight for the control targets, likewise for $[\Delta u_2(k + i - 1)]^2$, with its respective weight $\lambda_2(k)$. Where k represents a sample, N_p is the prediction horizon, and N_c is the control horizon.

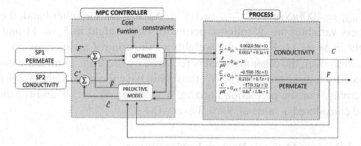

Fig. 5. MPC control loop for industrial reverse osmosis process

$$J(k) = \sum_{i=N_f}^{N_p} \delta_1(k) \Big[\hat{F}(k+i|k) - F*(k+i|k)\Big]^2 + \delta_2(k) \Big[\hat{C}(k+i|k) - C*(k+i|k)\Big]^2$$

$$+ \sum_{i=0}^{N_c-1} \lambda_1(k)[\Delta u_1(k+i-1)]^2 + \lambda_2(k)[\Delta u_2(k+i-1)]^2 \tag{8}$$

Also, $\hat{F}(k+i|k)$ is the predicted permeate output, $\hat{C}(k+i|k)$ is the predicted output of conductivity, $F*(k+i|k)$ is the desired permeate value, $C*(k+i|k)$ is the desired conductivity value, and finally we have the variations of the control actions $\Delta u_n(k+i-1)$ corresponding to the pressure and pH [8].

The optimization problem is subject corresponding to pressure and pH inequality constraints through an upper bound and a lower bound for the permeate: $F_{min} \leq F(t) \leq F_{max}$, F_{min} for the minimum value of the permeate flow rate like F_{max} for maximum permeate flow rate and for conductivity: $C_{min} \leq C(t) \leq C_{max}$, C_{min} for the minimum conductivity value like C_{max} for maximum conductivity. In addition, the restrictions of the control value variables are included by establishing maximum and minimum limits. The restriction of the maximum limits (Δu_{max}) and minimal (Δu_{min}) of the control value for the permeate control variables are shown as follows: $\Delta u_{min} \leq \Delta u_1 \leq \Delta u_{max}$ and likewise Δu_2 for the second departure.

The implementation of this type of advanced control (MPC) in the PLC S7 1200 is not possible only with the manufacturer's software must resort to the help of Matlab Simulink for the design and exploitation of the code in.scl file, using the PLC coder tool and then import the TIA Portal software, with this programming blocks are generated to finally load the physical control device.

5   Reverse Osmosis Process Operating Results

This section describes the results of the control strategies applied to the desalination process in a Hardware in the Loop simulation environment. Considering the following parameters for the MPC control: The values of the constraints are: $\Delta u_{1\,min} = 0$, $\Delta u_{1\,max} = 1\,000$ for pressure and $\Delta u_{2\,min} = 0$, $\Delta u_{2\,max} = 14$ for pH; limits of the permeate are: $F_{min} = 0.85[gpm]$ y $F_{max} = 2[gpm]$, the conductivity restrictions are given by $C_{min} = 400[uS/cm]$ y $C_{max} = 1000[uS/cm]$. On the other hand, the weights of the process variables are as follows: permeate flow weight in $\delta_1 = 11$ and conductivity weight in $\delta_2 = 11$. Finally, the weights of the control actions are: $\lambda_1 = 0.07$ y $\lambda_2 = 0.07$. Moreover, the other parameters required by the MPC control are control and horizon prediction, these are given by N_p, those that have the same samples for permeate and conductivity. For the prediction horizon, a value of $N_f = 10$, and for the control horizon, we considered a value of $N_c = 3$ every 0.1 s.

5.1 Virtual Reverse Osmosis Process Environment

After implementing the HIL, through the interaction of the programmable logic controller (PLC) and the virtual plant of the reverse osmosis desalination process, the following results were obtained.

Figure 6 shows the virtual environment of the reverse osmosis process, which contains its instruments and monitoring area similar to a real process.

Fig. 6. Virtual environment of the reverse osmosis process.   **Fig. 7.** Monitoring and control area

Figure 7, corresponds to the monitoring area which consists of three screens in which you can see the trends of control variables permeate flow, conductivity, as well as the parameters of the designed controllers, desired values (SP), which are part of the PID or MPC control.

Figure 8 shows the HIL implementation, which is composed of the physical programmable logic controller (PLC) and connected by Ethernet communication to the virtualized process for controller validation.

Fig. 8. Connection between the S7-1200 PLC and the virtualized process

The PLC and the computer communicate via an Ethernet connection so the two devices must be within the same network, considering this it is necessary to check the

IP address, otherwise the virtual environment will not run and will launch a message informing the connection error.

5.2 Performance of the Proposed Control Strategies for the Reverse Osmosis Process

Figure 9a, shows the performance of the permeate flow variable against different control strategies, a PID control (green) and an MPC controller (blue). A constant set point of 1.40 gpm is used to evaluate the permeate control in the reverse osmosis process. The PID controller presents an overshoot of 3.57%, and a settling time of 62 s, from this point on there is a steady state control error of gpm. While the MPC controller presents no overshoot, and settles at 60 s, from that instant, there is a steady state error of gpm. As for the control actions, Fig. 9b shows the manipulated variable pressure. In the PID controller, it acts from time 0 s to reach a steady state with a pressure of 277 psi. While the MPC control does not act quickly, this is because, in the formulation of the controller model, the effect of the conductivity process is considered.

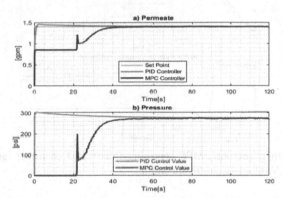

Fig. 9. a) Permeate flow response, Set Point (red), PID controller (green), MPC controller (blue), b) Manipulated variable with PID control action (green) and MPC control value (blue). (Color figure online)

Table 1 compares the results of control parameters such as overshoot, settling time, and steady-state error of the PID and MPC controllers implemented in the reverse osmosis process corresponding to permeate.

Figure 10 shows the analysis of the conductivity variable of the reverse osmosis process, where: the Set Point (red), the application of a PID controller and its respective control value (green), and finally the evolution of the MPC controller and its respective control value (blue). For conductivity control, a constant set point value of 450 uS/cm was taken (see Fig. 10a). The PID controller has an overshoot of 4.23% and stabilizes at 60 s. When the controller reaches its adjustment time, the control error in the stable state is uS/cm. On the other hand, the MPC controller presents an overshoot of 6% and stabilizes at 46 s. Regarding the control action (see Fig. 10b). The MPC is faster allowing it to stabilize the system in a shorter time. As can be seen during the conductivity transient

Table 1. Performance of control algorithms to the permeate flow variable.

Parameters	PID controller	MPC controller
	Permeate	Permeate
Overshoot [%]	3.57	0
Settling time [s]	62	60
Steady-state error [gpm]	1×10^{-3}	6.4×10^{-5}

in the permeate variable there is no change, because the pressure affects the conductivity, stabilizing first the conductivity loop and then the permeate flow loop.

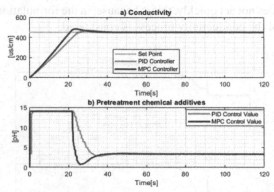

Fig. 10. a) Conductivity response, MPC controller (blue), PID controller (green), b) PID CV (green), and MPC CV (blue). (Color figure online)

Table 2 compares the results of the control parameters such as overshoot, time adjustment, and steady-state error of the PID and MPC controllers of the conductivity variable. With this comparison it can be seen that the MPC control has better performance as it controls both control variables (pressure and pH) to control the conductivity, prioritizing this as the conductivity determines the quality of the liquid obtained at the process output. In addition, if the pressure is too high, the membrane lifetime is affected by polarization causing plugging of the membrane, which MPC has a favorable performance in controlling the pressure.

For robustness analysis of controllers against disturbances, a disturbance is added by reducing the pressure to the membrane at the inlet. Figure 12 shows the performance of the controllers against this disturbance that affects the entire system because the pressure decrease is related to the conductivity affecting the two control loops.

It has been subjected to a perturbation representing a pressure leakage to the membrane at a value of 50 psi in the second 150 in (see Fig. 11) where the performance of the PID and MPC controllers can be observed. With the MPC controller, permeate and conductivity are not affected to a great extent, while the PID controller shows larger

Table 2. Performance of the control algorithms to the conductivity variable.

Parameters	PID controller	MPC controller
	Conductivity	Conductivity
Overshoot [%]	4.23	6
Settling time [s]	60	46
Steady-state error [uS/cm]	8×10^{-3}	7×10^{-3}

variations when the perturbation occurs in the permeate loop. Since the MPC controller infers that the pressure control action will affect the second control loop of conductivity, it increases the pressure, making the control in this case of conductivity that determines the quality of water better, unlike the PID controller that by performing a faster action in the pressure control loop produces oscillations to the conductivity loop, in this way, it is verified that in MIMO systems the control actions affect the rest of the system, thus verifying the multivariable characteristic of the designed controller.

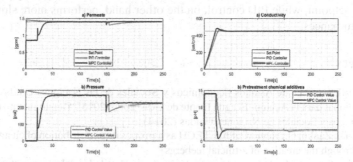

Fig. 11. Process with disturbance (pressure leakage).

6 Conclusions

The HIL technique allows the integration of PLC-programmed control algorithms operating in real-time with virtual environments of industrial processes in this case of reverse osmosis, which works in conjunction with the implemented control algorithms, reducing the cost to real processes in laboratory environments.

Input-output models based on real industrial plant measurements allow the implementation of a virtual environment similar to the industrial process with equal dynamics of the variables to be controlled within an immersive environment. This allows the application of different control algorithms, such as linear and nonlinear controllers and multivariable or more complex ones. Allowing it to be a very useful and accessible tool for learning and professional training.

The MPC controller shows a better performance in the operation of the controlled variables permeate flow and conductivity for the PID control strategy, for parameters such as overshoot, settling time, and steady-state error. Regarding the permeate flow, the PID controller presents a higher overshoot of 3.57%, while with the MPC it is 0%. The settling time of the MPC controller is 60 s, which is less in comparison to the PID which is 62 s. In both cases, the steady-state error is small and very close to zero. Regarding the conductivity, the MPC control presents an overshoot of 6% higher than the PID of 4.23%, likewise, the settling time is lower with a value of 46 s compared to the PID which is 60 s.

The MPC controller presents a better response in the control action being smoother than that produced by the PID controller, which is reflected in a better operation of the actuators as seen in the permeate loop. In addition, since the MPC controller includes the prediction model of the plant, it can be noted that in terms of the value of the controlled variables it takes into consideration the effect of pressure on conductivity. Therefore, it stabilizes the conductivity variable first and then the permeate flow, it is important to note that the conductivity determines the quality of the output liquid and the MPC controller prioritizes this variable unlike the PID, which considers each loop as an independent process.

MPC control is robust to disturbances since it corrects the error quickly while maintaining the setpoint, while PID control, on the other hand, performs more slowly in the face of disturbances.

References

1. ONU-DAES and D. de Asuntos Económicos y Sociales de las Naciones Unidas, "Decenio Internacional para la Acción 'El agua fuente de vida' 2005–2015." Departamento de Asuntos Económicos y Sociales de Naciones Unidas (2014)
2. Ramos, D., Zanko, G.: Review of ICETECH as a proposal for distribution of clean, drinkable water through the creation of artificial icebergs
3. Benavides Ortiz, C.A.: Diseño y construcción de un destilador solar con sistema de lente Fresnel destinado a la desalinización de agua de mar. Universidad de Guayaquil. Facultad de Ingeniería Química (2020)
4. Dévora-Isiordia, G.E., González-Enríquez, R., Ruiz-Cruz, S.: Evaluación de procesos de desalinización y su desarrollo en México. Tecnol. y Ciencias del Agua 4(3), 27–46 (2013)
5. Latina, A.: Publicado en el 2010 por el Programa Hidrológico Internacional (PHI) de la Oficina Regional de Ciencia para Instrucciones a los autores (2010). http://www.unesco.org.uy/phi/aqualac
6. Asuntha, Jana, I., Selvam, K., Srinivasan, A., Arc, J.O.X.: Reverse osmosis (RO) desalination systems using PID tuning. Res. J. Pharm. Biol. Chem. Sci. 8(2), 2548–2556 (2017)
7. Guna, G., Prabhakaran, D., Thirumarimurugan, M.: Design, implementation, control and optimization of single stage pilot scale reverse osmosis process. Water Sci. Technol. 84, 2923 (2021). https://doi.org/10.2166/wst.2021.302
8. Aimacaña Cueva, L.E., Auqui, G., Jonathan, O.: CIT 2022-International Congress on Science and Technology Advanced Control Algorithms for a Horizontal Three-Phase Separator in a Hardware in the Loop Simulation Environment
9. Flores-Bungacho, F., Guerrero, J., Llanos, J., Ortiz-Villalba, D., Navas, A., Velasco, P.: Development and application of a virtual reality biphasic separator as a learning system for industrial process control. Electronics 11(4), 636 (2022)

10. Ampuero Atamari, E.A.: Diseño de un controlador difuso sintonizado con computación evolutiva para una planta de desalinización de agua de mar por Osmosis Inversa. Univ. Nac. San Agustion Arequipa **8**(5), 55 (2019). http://repositorio.unsa.edu.pe/handle/UNSA/9326. Accessed 2 Dec 2021
11. Dennis, B., Orrala, T., Llanos, J., Ortiz-Villalba, D., Diego, A.A., Ponce, C.: Fuzzy and PID controllers performance analysis for a combinedcycle thermal power plant. CIT (2020)
12. Pruna, E., Escobar, I., Llanos, J., Navas, A., Zambrano, J.: Evaluación del desempeño de los controladores lógico y difuso y proporcional integral derivativo en una estación de caudal. Rev. Científica INFOCIENCIA. ESPE extensión Latacunga, vol. 8, pp. 72–77 (2014)
13. Rivas Mendoza, R.E., et al.: ¿Qué es el control avanzado? Rev. tecnológica. **3**(3), 31–33 (2010)
14. Ramos Azpilcueta, G.G.: Aplicación de un control predictivo tipo matriz dinámica en una refinería de petróleo (2004)
15. Feijoo, J.D., Chanchay, D.J., Llanos, J., Ortiz-Villalba, D.: Advanced controllers for level and temperature process applied to virtual Festo MPS®PA workstation. In: 2021 IEEE International Conference on Automation/XXIV Congress of the Chilean Association of Automatic Control (ICA-ACCA), pp. 1–6 (2021)
16. Campos Soto, M.N., Navas-Parejo, M.R., Moreno Guerrero, A.J., Campos Soto, M.N., Navas-Parejo, M.R., Moreno Guerrero, A.J.: Realidad virtual y motivación en el contexto educativo: Estudio bibliométrico de los últimos veinte años de Scopus. ALTERIDAD. Rev. Educ. **15**(1), 47–60 (2020). https://doi.org/10.17163/ALT.V15N1.2020.04
17. Bacic, M.: On hardware-in-the-loop simulation. In: Proceedings 44th IEEE Conference on Decision and Control European Control Conference CDC-ECC 2005, vol. 2005, pp. 3194–3198 (2005). https://doi.org/10.1109/CDC.2005.1582653
18. Álvarez, G.S., Benavides, M.S.: Desalación de agua de mar mediante sistema Osmosis Inversa y Energía Fotovoltaica para provisión de agua potable en Isla Damas, Región de Coquimbo. Unesco **1**, 71 (2013). http://www.unesco.org.uy/phi/biblioteca/archive/files/e733e28fc539e3c010d06c64bf298dcc.pdf
19. Algado, P.G.: Estudio de la capa de polarización formada en diferentes procesos: Osmosis inversa en flujo cruzado y ultrafiltración por cargas. Aplicación de la interferometría holográfica clásica y digital. Universitat d'Alacant-Universidad de Alicante (2010)
20. Moreno, J.: Diseño de planta de tratamiento de agua de osmosis inversa para la empresa Dober Osmotech de Colombia Ltda. Univ. Autónoma Occident. **1**, 136 (2011)
21. Armijo, J., Condorhuamán, C.: Simulación Dinámica De Sistemas De Osmosis Inversa. Rev. Peru. Química e Ing. Química **15**(1), 21–37 (2012). http://revistasinvestigacion.unmsm.edu.pe/index.php/quim/article/view/4758
22. Gambier, A., Krasnik, A., Badreddin, E.: Dynamic modeling of a simple reverse osmosis desalination plant for advanced control purposes. In: Proceedings of American Control Conference, pp. 4854–4859 (2007). https://doi.org/10.1109/ACC.2007.4283019
23. Alatiqi, I.M., Ghabris, A.H., Ebrahim, S.: System identification and control of reverse osmosis desalination. Desalination **75**(C), 119–140 (1989). https://doi.org/10.1016/0011-9164(89)85009-X
24. Guano Bermeo, A.R.: Diseño de un Sistema Virtual 3D de una estación de control de presión enfocado a la sintonía de controladores PI-PID (2021)
25. Camacho, E.F., Bordons, C.: Generalized predictive control. Advanced Textbooks in Control and Signal Processing, no. 9781852336943, pp. 47–79 (2007). https://doi.org/10.1007/978-0-85729-398-5_4
26. Model Predictive Control System Design and Implementation Using MATLAB® (2009). https://doi.org/10.1007/978-1-84882-331-0

Modeling of a Robotic Arm for the Application of Welding Processes

César A. Olovache[1], Jorge S. Sánchez[1]([⊠]), Carlos R. Sánchez[1],
and María S. Mendoza[2]

[1] Universidad de Las Fuerzas Armadas ESPE, Sangolquí 171103, Ecuador
{caolovache,jssanchez,crsanchez9}@espe.edu.ec
[2] Escuela Superior Politécnica del Chimborazo, Riobamba 060155, Ecuador
mmendoza@espoch.edu.ec

Abstract. Through this work, it is expected to contribute to the development and research of industrial robots with different welding processes used in the productive industry in our country, in order to shorten the gap between global technological innovation and knowledge, thus improving the level of same. In the welding process, with the development of the control algorithm based on the kinematic model of the manipulator, it is also expected to provide information simple enough for people interested in further studying these topics. The algorithm is a method developed using numerical knowledge and linear algebra. The results obtained by running the algorithm are tested in simulations, graphs and determination of zero convergence errors in different tasks assigned to the robot (robotic arm).

Keywords: Mathematical model · Robotic arm · Welding process

1 Introduction

Increasing the productivity rates, having high quality products and decreasing labor costs gradually have been the principal reasons why the big industries have been technifying their production processes with the implementation of industrial robots. A classic example is the controlled industrial robot which is manipulated by a controller. This robot is formed by different rigid elements (links) which are connected in a serie through prismatic or rotative joints [1–4]. The robotic arms or industrial robots (got this name since they were used massively in the industry) which introduced the era of Robots in the 60s [5].

In the last years people have tried to make robots work collaboratively since various robots working together on different tasks in a coordinated way makes the process more efficient than working only with one specialized robot. The cooperative robotics is defined as the set of theoretical and practical knowledge which forms, carries out and automates the systems based on intelligent polyarticulated mechanical structures which will be part of the industrial production or men substitution in several tasks [6–10].

© The Author(s), under exclusive license to Springer Nature Switzerland AG 2023
M. Botto-Tobar et al. (Eds.): ICAT 2022, CCIS 1756, pp. 300–313, 2023.
https://doi.org/10.1007/978-3-031-24971-6_22

Humans have always tried to control everything. So they have been investigating and experimenting in order to know more and be able to establish ways to control processes of different matters. Besides, with the increase of the use of robots in the different fields of the industry; it has been necessary to implement an automatic control system which is an interconnection of elements called system. Through this control theory humans are looking for a system which follows a predetermined behavior. This means following the specific conditions of its design correctly [11–15].

A robotic arm of 4 DOF was designed with a cinematic model with algorithm control which can perform different processes like welding (one of the most relevants). In Sect. 2 we check the analyzed problem of the investigation, in Sect. 3 and 4 the mathematic model is presented and also the algorithm and control of the robotic arm mentioned before. Finally, in Sect. 5 we can see the results of the arm robot performance on three specific tasks; also the results from the verification of the mathematic model, algorithm and control proposed in this document.

2 Structure of the Problem

The formation of MIG competent and efficient welders for the different processes of welding needs a lot of time. There are basic concepts we know but it is always important to study more through books and seminars. To become efficient in this welding art people need to create habits, become accustomed to it, manual dexterity, hand-eye synchronization and the essential control motor skills to weld correctly and systematically.

Robotic welding is considered as a development system of technology and competitive market which is adapted to a growing number of processes in the industries that require appropriate welding processes in their productive system.

The results obtained from this investigation will definitely ease the unstoppable insertion of the new robotized processes in the welding industry. This will lead to a faster and optimal series of procedures for these new processes designed specifically for he robotized welding and with a solid metallurgical basis which guarantees quality.

In this document there is a proposal to establish an analysis of the process GMAW (Gas, Metal, Arc Welding) through the use of a robotic arm optimizing its translation and rotation movements using a mathematical model and the simulation of virtual scenarios where conditions will be established according to the most possible reality.

Therefore, this investigation will be focused on analyzing the cinematic of the robot considering the fundamental parts of the direct kinematics and reverse kinematics.

After that, a control algorithm based on the Dynamic models of the controller will be proposed. As a result, different laws that control the desired robot functioning will be created.

3 Mathematical Model and Algorithm

The development of the control algorithm is based on the cinematic modeling of the selected robotic arm. This has four independent free movements and one gripper.

3.1 Mathematical Modeling and Control Algorithm

Considering the necessities of each procedure involved in the welding process tasks we have one robotic arm (Fig. 1).

Fig. 1. Proposed Robotic Arm of 4 DOF

The cinematic model is established according to Denavit – Hartemberg theory. The parameters to obtain the model are specified in the Table 1. These parameters will be useful to determine the transformation matrix presented in Eq. (1).

Table 1. Parameters of Denavit – Hartemberg for the Robot of 4DOF

Joints	θ_i	d_i	a_i	α_i
1	q_1	l_1	0	0°
2	q_2	l_2	0	90°
3	q_3	0	l_3	0°
4	q_4	0	l_4	0°

$$\mathbf{h}(t) = \begin{cases} h_1 = [0\,0\,0] \\ h_2 = [0\,0\,l_1] \\ h_3 = [l_2C_1 + l_2C_2; \, l_2S_1C_2; \, l_1 + l_2S_2] \\ h_4 = [l_2C_1C_2 + l_3C_1C_{23}; \, l_2S_1C_2 + l_3S_1C_{23}; \, l_1 + l_2S_2 + l_3S_{23}] \\ h_5 = [l_2C_1C_2 + l_3C_1C_{23} + l_4C_1C_{234}; \, l_2S_1C_2 + l_3S_1C_{23} + l_4S_1C_{234}; \, l_1 + l_2S_2 + l_3S_{23} + l_4S_{234}] \end{cases}$$

$$(1)$$

where,

$$C_\alpha = \cos(\alpha); \; C_{\alpha\beta} = \cos(\alpha + \beta); \; C_{\alpha\beta\gamma} = \cos(\alpha + \beta + \gamma);$$

$$S_\alpha = \sin(\alpha); \; S_{\alpha\beta} = \sin(\alpha + \beta); \; S_{\alpha\beta\gamma} = \sin(\alpha + \beta + \gamma);$$

l_1; l_2; l_3; yl_4, which represent the length of each link.

Equation (1) permits to determine the position of the final effector $\mathbf{h}(t) \in R^m$ with $m_a = 3$.

The initial position $\mathbf{h}(t)$ from the operating end of the controller robot with respect to R_0 will be represented by its coordinates in the Eq. (2).

$$\mathbf{h}(t) = \begin{cases} h_x(1) = l_2 C_1 C_2 + l_3 C_1 C_{23} + l_4 C_1 C_{234} \\ h_y(1) = l_2 S_1 C_2 + l_3 S_1 C_{23} + l_4 S_1 C_{234} \\ h_z(t) = l_1 + l_2 S_2 + l_3 S_{23} + l_4 S_{234} \end{cases} \tag{2}$$

That is to say if we consider that $\mathbf{h}(t) = f(q)$, then its temporal derived Eq. (3), will be expressed by the derivative $h(t)$ with respect to the time t.

$$\frac{d}{dt}\mathbf{h}(t) = \frac{d}{dt}f(t) \tag{3}$$

The linear speed of the final actuator in function of the angular speed each link will have been represented in the following expression (4).

$$\dot{\mathbf{h}}(t) = \frac{d}{dt}\mathbf{h}(t), \tag{4}$$

$$\dot{h}(t) = \begin{cases} \dot{h}_x(t) = -(l_2 S_1 C_2 + l_3 S_1 C_{23} + l_4 S_1 C_{234})\dot{q}_1 + (l_2 C_1 C_2 + l_3 C_1 C_{23} + l_4 C_1 C_{234})\dot{q}_2 \\ \qquad +...(l_3 C_1 C_{23} + l_4 C_1 C_{234})\dot{q}_3 + (l_4 C_1 C_{234})\dot{q}_4 \\ \dot{h}_y(t) = (l_2 C_1 C_2 + l_3 C_1 C_{23} + l_4 C_1 C_{234})\dot{q}_1 + (l_2 S_1 C_2 + l_3 S_1 C_{23} + l_4 S_1 C_{234})\dot{q}_2 \\ \qquad +...(l_3 S_1 C_{23} + l_4 S_1 C_{234})\dot{q}_3 + (l_4 S_1 C_{234})\dot{q}_4 \\ \dot{h}_z(t) = -(l_2 S_2 + l_3 S_{23} + l_4 S_{234})\dot{q}_2 - (l_3 S_{23} + l_4 S_{234})\dot{q}_3 - l_4 S_{234}\dot{q}_4 \end{cases} \tag{5}$$

Lasly, the cinematic model is represented in its matrix form through the Eq. (6),

$$\dot{\mathbf{h}}(t) = \mathbf{J}(q)\dot{\mathbf{q}}(t) \tag{6}$$

Here $\dot{\mathbf{h}}(t)$ representing the linear speed of the operating end linear speed (m/s) y $\mathbf{J}(q) \in R^{mxn}$, con $m = 3$ y $n = 4$.

For obtaining $\dot{\mathbf{q}}(t)$, the reverse pseudo of $\mathbf{J}(q)$ is used, represented by $\mathbf{J}^\#(q)$, since the Jacobian matrix is not a square matrix, so the angular speed is represented by the expression (7).

$$\dot{\mathbf{q}}(t) = \mathbf{J}^\#(q)\dot{\mathbf{h}}(t) \tag{7}$$

Expression in which $\dot{\mathbf{q}}(t)$ is the angular speed of each link (rad/s); $\mathbf{J}^\#(q)$ is the reverse pseudo of the Jacobian matrix.

3.2 Control Algorithm

For the development of the control algorithm we take into account a control algorithm which is considered as a minimum norm controller that is determined with the use of the following expression (8).

$$\dot{\mathbf{q}}_{ref}(t) - \mathbf{J}^\#\left(\dot{\mathbf{h}}_d + k\tilde{\mathbf{h}}\right) \tag{8}$$

Expression where $\dot{q}_{ref}(t)$; represents the angular speed of the links; $J^{\#}$ is the reverse pseudo matrix; $\dot{h}_d$ the movement linear speed of the operating end; k is a matrix $\in R^{mxm}$, defined as positive $k > 0$; y $\tilde{h}$ is the control error.

After developing this equation, we can determine the formulation of the control law which is expressed through the expression (9).

$$\dot{q}_{ref}(t) = J^{\#}\left(\dot{h}_d + k\tilde{h}\right) + \left(I - J^{\#}{*}J\right) * \eta \qquad (9)$$

where, J the Jacobian matrix; y η is the null vector.

The expression (9) represents the control law which through its implementation ensures the correct functioning of the robotic arm in a specific task assigned along the term calculation $J^{\#}\left(\dot{h}_d + k\tilde{h}\right)$ of the expression and additionally to this process we can determine the achievement of secondary with the calculation of the second terms of the expression; this term is $\left(I - J^{\#}{*}J\right) * \eta$, For example the optimization of energy through the achievement of the task in the least possible movements done by the operating end of the robot, it will avoid the robot to be marked as a normal singular robot as well.

4   Results

In order to verify the effiency of the control algorithm; tasks where the final effector follows given trajectorieswere implemented. A simulation in Matlab has been also implemented to observe its functioning. Following these parameters:

Simulation Conditions:

- Type of simulation in (seg.): tfin = 60
- Period of sampling in (seg.): To = 0.1
- The evolution in each To (seg.): t = [0:To:tfin]

Initial conditions of the Controller Robot.

- q1 = 0; Joint position of link 1 in [rad]
- q2 = −pi/6; Joint position in link 2 in [rad]
- q3 = pi/4; Joint position in link 3 in [rad]
- q4 = −pi/5; Joint position in link 4 in [rad]

Physical parameters of the Controller Robot.

- l1 = 0.125; Distance of link 1 in [m]
- l2 = 0.275; Distance of link 2 in [m]
- l3 = 0.275; Distance of link 3 in [m]
- l4 = 0.15; Distance of link 4 in [m]

These are some of the assigned tasks:

- Welding of a trajectory "line in space"
- Welding of a trajectory "circular in space"
- Welding of a trajectory "saddle"

4.1 Welding Simulation of a Trajectory "Straight Line in Space"

Figure 2 shows the movement control of the controller robot. The evidence reveals that the robot performs the task correctly.

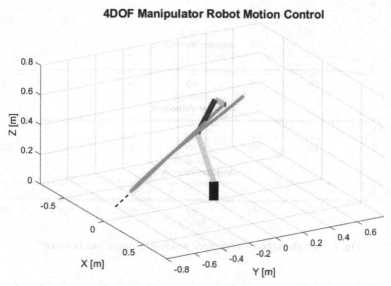

Fig. 2. Movement Control - Welding simulation of a trajectory "straight line in space"

Figure 3 shows the trajectory made by the operating end of this robot when finishing the complete trajectory.

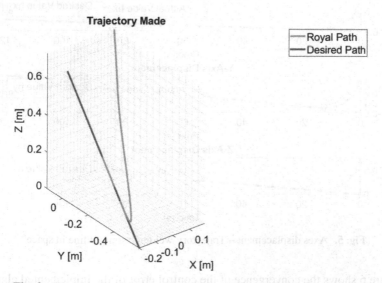

Fig. 3. Completed trajectory – Trajectory welding "straight line in space"

Figure 4 shows the angular speed of each link of the robot in the performance of the task.

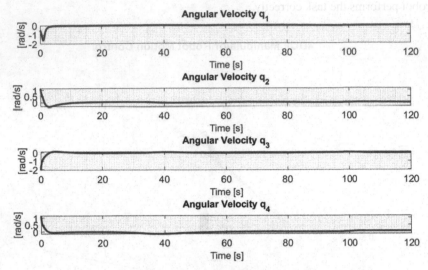

Fig. 4. Angular speed – Trajectory welding "straight line in space"

Figure 5 shows the displacement the axes have in the operating end of the robot when achieving the desired trajectory.

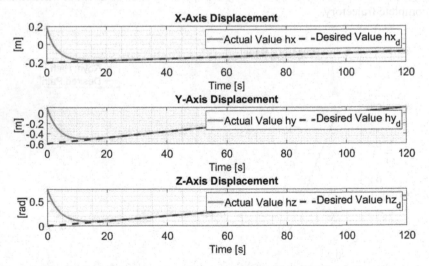

Fig. 5. Axes displacement – Trajectory welding "straight line in space"

Figure 6 shows the convergence of the control error of the implemented algorithm. The evidence reveals that with the application of the algorithm this tends to be zero.

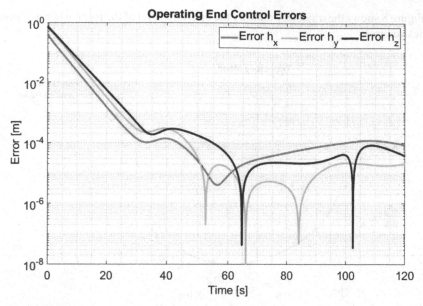

Fig. 6. Control error – Trajectory welding "straight line in space" – logarithmic scale

4.2   Simulation of the Welding Task of a Trajectory "CIRCular in Space"

Figure 7 shows the movement control of the controller robot. This evidence shows the robot achieves the desired task.

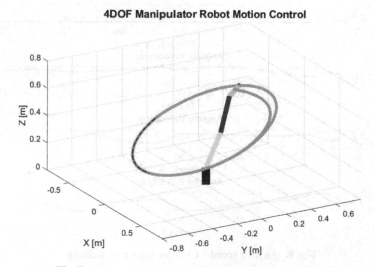

Fig. 7. Movement control – Circular trajectory welding

Figure 8 shows the trajectory done by the operating end of the robot when achieveing the desired task.

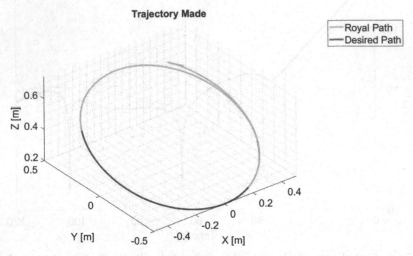

Fig. 8. Completed trajectory – Circular in space welding

Figure 9 shows the angular speed of each link of the robot when achieving the desired task.

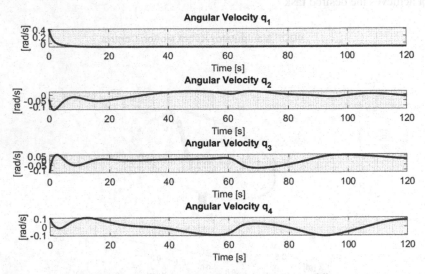

Fig. 9. Angular speed – Circular trajectory welding

Figure 10 shows the displacement the axes have in the operating end of the robot when achieving the desired task.

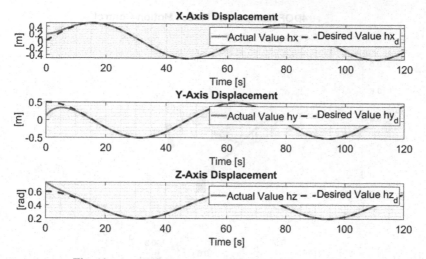

Fig. 10. Axes Displacement – Circular trajectory welding

Figure 11 shows the convergence of the control error of the control algorithm implemented. The evidence shows that with the application of this algorithm; it tends to be zero.

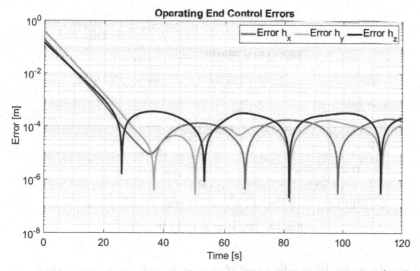

Fig. 11. Control error – Circular trajectory welding – logarithmic scale

4.3   Simulation of the Welding Task of a Trajectory "SADDle"

Figure 12 shows the movement control of the controller robot. This evidence shows the robot achieves the desired task.

4DOF Manipulator Robot Motion Control

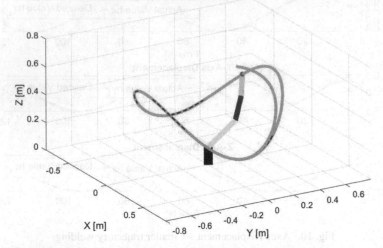

Fig. 12. Movement control of the controller robot 4DOF

Figure 13 shows the trajectory done by the operating end of the robot when achieving the desired task.

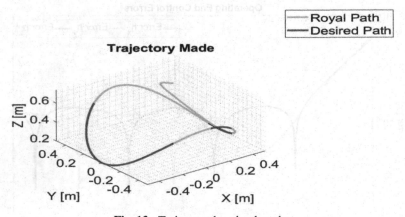

Fig. 13. Trajectory done by the robot

Figure 14 shows the angular speed of each of the links of the robot when achieving the desired task.

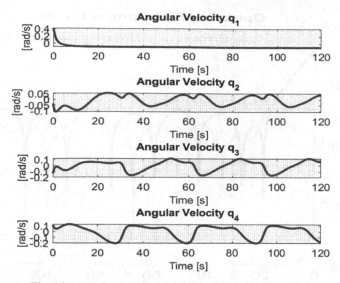

Fig. 14. Angular speed of the links of the controller robot

Figure 15 shows the displacement the axes have in the operating end of the robot when achieving the desired trajectory.

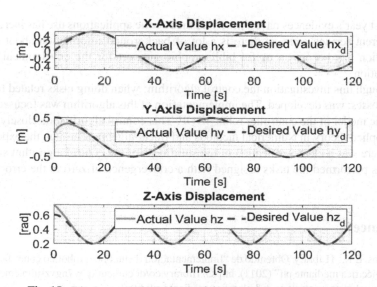

Fig. 15. Displacement in the axes of the operating end of the robot

Figure 16 shows the convergence of the control error of the implemented algorithm. This evidence shows that with the application of the algorithm; this tends to be zero.

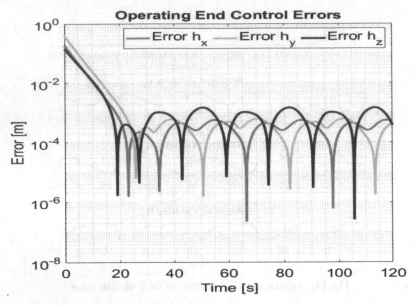

Fig. 16. Errors of the control of the operating end of the robot – Logarithmic scale

5 Conclusion

In the last year's evidences have shown that the robotic applications use has increased in the different service areas so there is a lot of background information about it. This information has become a useful bibliographic support for the development of this investigation.

Through this investigation the control algorithm; when doing tasks related to welding processes; was developed. The implementation of this algorithm was focused on the cinematic model of the controller robot 4DOF. This control algorithm is closely related to the applied theory in Numerical methods and linear algebra. Through the experimentation there was a clear verification of the sturdiness of the control algorithm since the robot has performed the tasks assigned with a convergence of zero in the errors of the control.

References

1. Vimos, E.R.: 1Library. Obtenido de "Implementación de un brazo robótico controlado por la red eléctrica mediante plt" (2011). https://1library.co/document/q7w7ngvz-implementacion-brazo-robotico-controlado-red-electrica-mediante-plt.html
2. López, L.F.: Modelación y Simulación dinámica de un brazo robótico de 4 grados de libertad para tareas en un plano horizontal (2009). https://www.slideshare.net/EliasBacilio/lopez-luis-modelacionbrazorobotico
3. Cruz, H.: Robot de tracción diferencial con navegación mediante seguidor de línea y posicionamiento GPS. Robot de tracción diferencial con navegación mediante seguidor de línea y posicionamiento GPS. Instituto Politécnico Nacional (Tesis), México (2013)

4. Andaluz, G., Andaluz, V., Rosales, A.: Modelación, Identificación y Control de robots móviles. Escuela Politécnica Nacional, Quito, Tesis de Ingeniería en Electrónica y Control (2011)
5. Pascual, J.R.G.: Robótica: Estado del arte. Universidad de Deusto (2010)
6. Bekey, G.A., et al.: Robotics: state of the art and future challenges (2008)
7. Andaluz, V., Rampinelli, V.T.L., Roberti, F., Carelli, R.: Coordinated cooperative control of mobile manipulators. In: 2011 IEEE International Conference on Industrial Technology, pp. 300–305. IEEE (2011)
8. Caballero, J.P.: Una visión del campo de la robótica. Una visión del campo de la robótica. Mongra
9. Sanderson, A.C.: A distributed algorithm for cooperative navigation among multiple mobile robots. Adv. Robot. **12**(4), 335–349 (1997)
10. Cao, Y.U., Fukunaga, A.S., Kahng, A.B.: Cooperative mobile robotics: antecedents and directions. Auton. Robot. **4**, 1–23 (1997)
11. Polania, L.A.: Teoría de Control (2000). file:///C:/Users/PC/Downloads/Dialnet-TeoriaDelControl-7835981.pdf
12. Gaviño, R.H.: Introducción a los sistemas de control (2010). http://lcr.uns.edu.ar/fcr/images/Introduccion%20a%20Los%20Sistemas%20de%20Control.pdf
13. Moreno, R.P.: Evolución Histórica de la Ingeniería de Control (1999). http://automata.cps.unizar.es/regulacionautomatica/historia.PDF
14. Pérez, M., Pérez, A., Pérez, E.: Introducción a los sistemas de control y Modelo Matemático para Sistemas Lineales Invariantes en el tiempo (2008). http://dea.unsj.edu.ar/control1b/teoria/unidad1y2.pdf
15. Martin del Campo, L.: Manual de Laboratorio de Teoría de Control y Robótica (2021). http://olimpia.cuautitlan2.unam.mx/pagina_ingenieria/electronica/prac/practicas/2/M_Teoria_Control_Robotica_2021-1.pdf

Passive Positioning of Autonomous Underwater Vehicles

Enrique V. Carrera[⊠]🆔 and Diego Guevara

Departamento de Eléctrica, Electrónica y Telecomunicaciones,
Universidad de las Fuerzas Armadas – ESPE, Sangolquí 171103, Ecuador
{evcarrera,deguevara1}@espe.edu.ec

Abstract. Currently, autonomous underwater vehicles (AUVs) show a high potential to work in surveillance tasks, as well as in payload delivery through rivers, lakes or seas. However, AUVs have some limitations that prevent them from fully relying on their autonomous functions. In particular, unlike unmanned aerial vehicles, AUVs do not have precise positioning mechanisms like GPS to work underwater. Although inertial navigation systems have been developed for the positioning of these vehicles, smaller and cheaper alternatives for modern micro-AUVs are still required. Furthermore, the possibility of passively detecting the location of an AUV (*i.e.*, detecting it without emitting any additional signal) opens up new alternatives for military and defense-oriented applications with these vehicles. Thus, this work proposes a passive positioning system for underwater vehicles using the acoustic signals already emitted by the AUVs themselves. To do this, the initial challenges associated to the positioning of AUVs through trilateration techniques are analyzed, and the final proposals are evaluated in a real scenario. The results show that the method known as TDoA is easier to implement and presents a more precise positioning.

Keywords: Passive positioning · Underwater positioning · Autonomous underwater vehicles · TDoA

1 Introduction

In the same way as unmanned aerial vehicles or drones have rapidly grown in popularity over the past few years [3], unmanned underwater vehicles are breaking barriers in traditional industries dedicated to surveillance tasks, search and rescue operations, payload delivery, etc. Even in security and defense-oriented applications, these unmanned vehicles have important contributions in the fight against organized crime, or any other threat that could alter personal or citizen safety [5, 7].

Unmanned underwater vehicles are commonly divided into *remotely operated vehicles* (ROVs) and *autonomous underwater vehicles* (AUVs) [2]. The ROVs are controlled by a remote human operator, while the AUVs do no include direct human intervention. Thanks to the technological innovations in recent years,

© The Author(s), under exclusive license to Springer Nature Switzerland AG 2023
M. Botto-Tobar et al. (Eds.): ICAT 2022, CCIS 1756, pp. 314–325, 2023.
https://doi.org/10.1007/978-3-031-24971-6_23

small and inexpensive underwater vehicles, called micro-AUVs, are now becoming a reality [17]. These AUVs must be based entirely on autonomous functions, offering capabilities and applications that no other platform can offer [1].

However, existing AUVs face several challenges such as position uncertainty, limited and noisy communication, and bounded time autonomy [12]. In particular, this work is aimed at proposing an alternative for the underwater positioning of AUVs. This is a challenging task as GPS positioning is not available on submersed devices [14]. Current AUVs use inertial navigation systems, which require regular updates using some form of GPS positioning. AUV positioning without GPS access using bottom-terrain maps or using a set of acoustic beacons in an LBL network has also been proposed [11].

Despite of all this, smaller and cheaper positioning alternatives are still required for modern and compact micro-AUVs. Moreover, the possibility of passively detecting the location of the underwater vehicles (*i.e.*, the detection of AUVs without emitting any additional signal) opens up new alternatives for military and defense-oriented applications with these submersed vehicles.

Based on the above, this paper analyzes and evaluates the implementation of common trilateration techniques for AUV positioning through acoustic signals, but in a passive configuration. More specifically, the positioning of the underwater vehicles does not use any additional sound source other than the AUV itself. To do this, we describe the challenges involved in implementing the RSSI (Received Signal Strength Indication) and TDoA (Time Difference of Arrival) techniques [4,6], and then our final proposals of passive positioning are evaluated in a real scenario. The results show that TDoA is easier to implement and has the best accuracy when four hydrophones are employed.

The rest of this paper is organized as follows. Section 2 introduces the positioning of underwater vehicles through trilateration techniques. Section 3 analyzes the challenges and alternatives for passive AUV positioning. The main results and their implications are discussed in Sect. 4. Finally, Sect. 5 concludes the paper and proposes some future works.

2   AUV Positioning

Many AUVs have been developed in the last decades, varying in size, autonomy range, navigation technology and built-in sensors [2]. As it was already mentioned, there are still many technological problems to be solved, specially if these devices are going to be utilized in military missions.

A particular problem to be discussed here is the positioning of AUVs, which in the simplest case can be done using acoustic signals [5]. In fact, acoustic signals propagate faster in the water than in the air (the speed of sound in the water is approximately 1480 m/s at 20 °C), and the absorption of the acoustic power at low frequencies is small, making water a good conductor for acoustic waves [9]. Obviously, the propagation of sound in the water depends on various parameters such as salinity, acidity, depth, temperature, frequency, and so on [8], but several already established relationships determine the influence of all these parameters on the propagation of sound in water [19]. For instance, it is well known that the sound spreads around in such a way that its intensity decreases exponentially with the distance.

Based on this, it is possible to apply trilateration techniques to determine the position of a given underwater audio source [18]. When it is feasible to establish the intensity (*i.e.*, the instantaneous power) of the emitted sound, the most common trilateration techniques are RSSI, ToA (Time of Arrival) and TDoA. However, when it is possible to establish the angle of arrival of the emitted sound, the trilateration technique knows as AoA (Angle of Arrival) can be employed [15]. Furthermore, an interesting way of positioning an AUV in a passive way is by using the sound emitted by the vehicle itself. This type of positioning is interesting since it does not require to radiate any additional signal in the environment.

Thus, in our proposal, an infrastructure-based positioning is considered, where the underwater vehicle normally emits a specific sound and N hydrophones in the surrounding area are listening to that emission. In the case of passive positioning, the AUV does not need to emit any extra sound, which simplifies the overall consumption of energy in the AUV, but also complicates the implementation of the trilateration techniques that require time information. Therefore, ToA is not going to be considered in this work, since it requires strict time synchronization between the sound transmitter and receivers [5]. Similarly, AoA is not considered here because our hydrophones have an omni-directional reception pattern and cannot determine the angle of arrival.

2.1 RSSI

This technique measures the strength of the signals received by the hydrophones located at known positions. Since the intensity of a signal is attenuated by the traveled distance, the distance of each source can be modeled as a function of the received intensity [16]. However, this modeling is hard to achieve accurately due to multi-path interference, path loss, Doppler distortion, and other fading effects. In the case of passive positioning, an additional problem is the fact that the sound emitted by the AUV is not constant, which requires additional hydrophones to solve the resulting system of linear equations. However, an important advantage of this technique is that no time synchronization is required between the AUV and the audio receivers.

2.2 TDoA

This trilateration technique determines the position of the underwater vehicle by measuring the time differences between each pair of received signals. Knowing the actual position of the hydrophones, the difference in time between each pair of sound receivers generates a hyperbola of possible positions where the AUV could be, but using three or more receivers, the intersection of these hyperbolas determine a single estimated position for the underwater vehicle [13]. This technique requires that only the acoustic receivers are synchronized with each other,

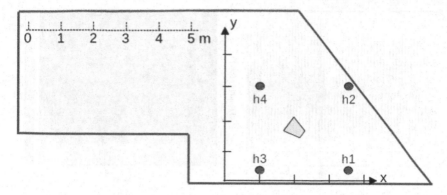

Fig. 1. Diagram of the geometry used for the AUV positioning inside a pool, including the used reference axes.

being clearly advantageous the initially proposed infrastructure-based positioning, since there is only one acoustic source to track. In the case of passive positioning, an additional problem is the fact that there is no single beginning and end of the sound emitted by the AUV, as we will see in the following sections.

3   Passive Underwater Positioning

3.1   Positioning Infrastructure

The scenario implemented to analyze and evaluate the passive positioning of AUVs consists of a pool of irregular dimensions containing approximately $65\,m^3$ of water, as shown in Fig. 1. Inside the pool, there is a PowerVision Power-Ray underwater drone navigating in a remotely controlled way. The scenario also includes four DolphinEar DE200 hydrophones connected to a Behringer U-phoria UMC404HD audio interface with a cumulative sampling rate of 192 kHz and 24-bit samples. All the hydrophones include an analog amplifier that feeds the 4-input audio interface. Using the Reaper v6 software, the four audio signals coming from the hydrophones are captured in a synchronized way at an individual sampling rate of 48 kHz on each channel. All the *a posteriori* processing of the captured audios is implemented in Matlab®.

The diagram showing the position of the hydrophones relative to the marked reference axes and the pool is shown in Fig. 1. The hydrophones are located at the bottom of the pool at the coordinates $(3.5, 0.5)$, $(3.5, 3.0)$, $(1.0, 0.5)$, and $(1.0, 3.0)$, respectively. In most of the audio recordings, the underwater drone hovers 0.5 m above the bottom of the pool.

3.2   Initial Audio Processing

Considering as the default configuration, the case where the 4 hydrophones are located as indicated in Fig. 1, and the underwater drone is located at position

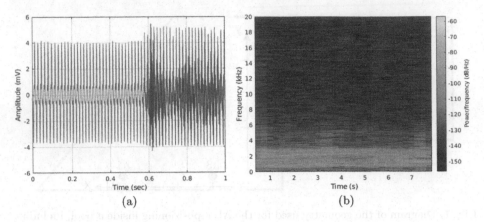

(a)   (b)

Fig. 2. Audio received at the hydrophone No. 3: (a) original signal, and (b) spectrogram of the original signal.

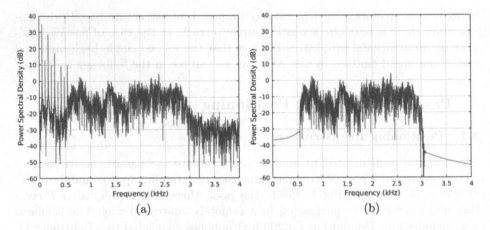

(a)   (b)

Fig. 3. Power spectral density of the (a) original audio, and (b) filterer audio.

(2.0, 1.5)-m, according to the reference axes also shown in Fig. 1, we proceeded to record the 4-channel audio signals. Thus, Fig. 2 shows the signal received at the hydrophone No. 3 and its corresponding spectrogram. As we can see in Fig. 2(a), a frequency 60 Hz, which corresponds to the electrical power that feeds the electronic devices, produces various harmonics. Note also in Fig. 2(b) that most of the energy is concentrated approximately 500 Hz and below 3 kHz. In order to better visualize this behavior, Fig. 3(a) shows the power spectral density of the original audio signal, showing that the highest energy of the audio produced by the underwater drone (*i.e.*, values above −10 dB) is 570 Hz and 2.9 kHz, approximately.

Based on the above, we have implemented a band-pass filter with cutoff frequencies of 560 and 3000 Hz. Figure 3(b) shows the power spectral density of the filtered audio, showing that after this process, the audio signal contains

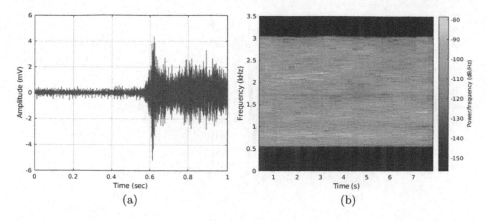

Fig. 4. Audio signal after using a band-pass filter: (a) filtered signal, and (b) spectrogram of the filtered signal.

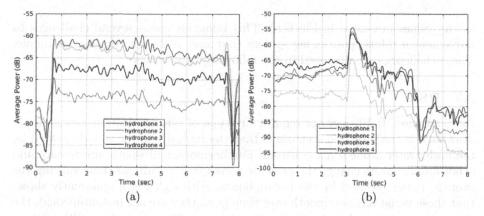

Fig. 5. Average power of the audio signals captured by the 4 hydrophones using 100-ms windows: (a) a controlled scenario, and (b) a more general case.

exclusively the sound emitted by the underwater drone. This assertion was audibly verified by listening to the resulting audios after filtering the original signals. Figure 4 shows the filtered signal and the corresponding spectrogram of the audio previously presented in Fig. 2. Note that the harmonics 60 Hz have disappeared and only the frequencies 560 Hz and 3 kHz remain.

In order to apply any positioning technique based on trilateration, the system basically needs to computed the average power of the sound received at each hydrophone. In this case, the average power is computed used a temporal sliding window whose size is initially set to 100 ms and with a window overlap of 50 ms. In a very controlled environment, like the one analyzed so far, we obtain measurements like those presented in Fig. 5(a), but due to the variation of propulsion power in the motors of the underwater drone, in order to keep it still or sometimes move it around, the power measurements can change as much

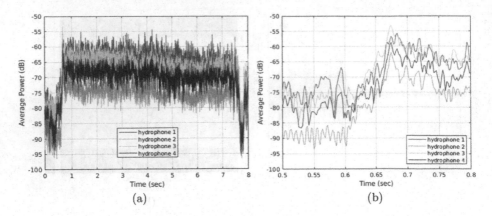

Fig. 6. Average power of the audio signals captured by the 4 hydrophones using 4-ms windows: (a) the entire signal, and (b) zoom around 0.65 s.

as the values presented in Fig. 6(b). This behavior opens several challenges to implement a robust positioning system that uses some trilateration technique. These challenges are discussed in the following subsections.

3.3   RSSI

As mentioned, RSSI does not require any type of synchronization, but its main drawback in the proposed scenario is that the intensity of the sound emitted by the underwater drone is not constant. Furthermore, multi-path interference and other fading effects change the acoustic waves very rapidly in time, varying the average power received by the hydrophones. Although Fig. 5 apparently shows that these variations are smooth over time (*i.e.*, they are not instantaneous), the average power plotted in that figure correspond to 100-ms windows with a 50-ms overlap. However, Fig. 6 shows what happens to the average power when using 4-ms windows with only 2-ms overlap. In this case, the average power fluctuations are much more abrupt, making it difficult to have a stable positioning of the underwater drone.

Since RSSI does not require an exact time reference for the positioning of the drone, and we need to keep the sound intensity received by the hydrophones almost constant, we decided to use a window large enough to compute the average intensity of the audio source, 100 ms in this case. Moreover, since the actual intensity of the audio source P_0 is unknown, because it varies continuously as the propulsion power of the drone changes, that value becomes one more variable to determine in the system of equations described by:

$$P_0/d_i^2 = I_i \quad \text{with} \quad d_i < 3.5 \quad \text{for} \quad i = 1, \dots, 4$$

where d_i is the Euclidean distance from the drone to the hydrophone i, and I_i is the relative intensity perceived at hydrophone i. To reduce the number of required hydrophones (and equations), we need to restrict the navigation area of the vehicle in order to find an approximated location.

3.4   TDoA

This trilateration technique has the drawback that we need to know when the underwater drone generates a specific sound in order to compute the time difference between the hydrophones in receiving that particular sound. Although the sounds received by the hydrophones are synchronized, we need to distinguish some specific event throughout all the signals. Therefore, if we pay attention to Fig. 6(b), we see that some peaks and valleys in the signals are identifiable, for instance the peak at 0.674 s. In this way, we can use the time at which those peaks and valleys occur to calculate the perceived time difference between each pair of hydrophones.

However, although the abrupt changes in power can be used as events to compute time differences, the values presented in Fig. 6 are not useful at all due to the small time gap between consecutive measurements. In the case of Fig. 6, the power samples are spaced just 2 ms. In fact, the four peaks in Fig. 6(b) appear at exactly 0.674 s in all four signals. Given that the maximum separation between hydrophones is 3.5 m in our scenario, and considering the speed of sound in water of 1480 m/s, the maximum time difference between hydrophones will be 2.4 ms. Therefore, we need to compute the average power using shorter windows with higher overlap to increase the temporal resolution of the computed differences.

We have tested windows as short as $200\,\mu s$ (*i.e.*, around 10 audio samples) with almost complete overlap to produce a power value at each new sample (*i.e.*, a 20-μs time resolution). In other words, we can discriminate distances as short as 30 cm. Moreover, besides the system of linear equations needed to determine the position of the underwater drone, we have evaluated a method based on Taylor series that requires an initial clue of where the vehicle might be [10].

4   Main Results

In order to determine the accuracy of each algorithm, we have captured audio signals from the underwater drone at several established positions and used RSSI and TDoA to compute the estimated final positions for the drone in each case. At the end, the distance between the current position and the estimated position is calculated as our error metric. The following subsections summarize the obtained results for the two trilateration techniques.

4.1   RSSI

For this positioning technique, we compute the average power in synchronized windows of 100 ms. The four values corresponding to the average power perceived at each hydrophone are used to find the most likely position of the underwater drone. The perceived sound intensities are identified by I_1, I_2, I_3 and I_4, and despite the sudden changes in acoustic power and the fact that the acoustic power emitted by the drone is not constant, the RSSI algorithm is quite useful because we are using four hydrophones to achieve a 2-D positioning. While three

Table 1. Estimated position and error (in meters) for several established locations of the underwater drone using RSSI

Actual position (meters)		Perceived intensity ($\times 10^{-6}$)				Estimated position (meters)		Error in
x	y	I_1	I_2	I_3	I_4	$\hat{x}$	$\hat{y}$	meters
1.0	1.0	0.14	0.11	2.80	0.27	1.16	1.66	0.68
1.0	2.0	0.15	0.16	0.36	1.08	1.64	2.13	0.65
1.5	0.5	0.28	0.10	3.15	0.11	1.56	1.18	0.68
1.5	2.5	0.10	0.28	0.24	1.65	1.85	2.77	0.44
2.0	0.5	0.35	1.10	0.99	0.10	2.63	1.87	1.51
2.0	1.5	0.35	0.46	0.39	0.24	2.36	1.77	0.45
2.5	1.0	1.04	0.20	0.46	0.20	2.09	1.77	0.87
2.5	2.0	0.42	0.86	0.26	0.54	2.84	1.77	0.41
3.0	2.0	0.32	1.31	0.75	0.16	2.52	1.93	0.49
3.0	3.0	0.13	3.86	0.10	0.23	3.12	2.60	0.41
						Average error		0.66

hydrophones are enough to find a 2-D fixed position, the fourth hydrophone provides some redundancy that improves the precision of this proposal considering that the underwater drone is inside the region defined by the hydrophones.

Therefore, Table 1 summarizes the results for the 10 configurations tested in the real environment described in Sect. 3. Note that the constraints mentioned above make this positioning technique noisy and unstable, reaching errors of up to 1.5 m in the presented examples. Since multi-path interference and other fading effects change very rapidly over time, it is necessary to smooth *a posteriori* the reported positions to decrease the average error, which in our evaluation is approximately 66 cm.

4.2   TDoA

In the case of TDoA, we identify the most relevant peaks of acoustic power in the four synchronized signals obtained from the hydrophones. The window used to calculate the average power is very short, approximately $200\,\mu s$. Thus, each window only has 10 audio samples and the overlap between windows is 8 samples. In this way, we have an average power measurement every $42\,\mu s$. Since the timing of each peak is relative in TDoA, we assign the time $0.00\,s$ to the appearance of the first peak in the 4-signal sequence, and the time of the other three peaks is computed relative to that first peak. Moreover, in order to use TDoA we apply two different methods: the first one uses the traditional system of linear equations, while the second method employs the Taylor series [10] considering that the probable position is constrained to be inside the region defined by the hydrophones (*i.e.*, the initial guess corresponds to the centroid of the area covered by the hydrophones).

Table 2. Estimated position and error (in meters) for several established locations of the underwater drone using TDoA

Actual position (meters)		Registered time (msec)				Estimated position with Taylor (meters)		Error (meters)	
x	y	t_1	t_2	t_3	t_4	$\hat{x}$	$\hat{y}$	Lineal	Taylor
1.0	1.0	1.47	2.14	0.00	1.39	0.96	0.80	0.52	0.21
1.0	2.0	1.18	0.84	0.04	0.00	1.16	2.00	1.80	0.16
1.5	0.5	0.88	1.81	0.00	1.18	1.42	0.69	2.10	0.21
1.5	2.5	1.34	0.84	0.80	0.00	1.64	2.32	0.32	0.22
2.0	0.5	0.17	1.22	0.00	1.09	2.09	0.64	2.52	0.16
2.0	1.5	0.29	0.63	0.00	0.55	2.02	1.32	0.23	0.18
2.5	1.0	0.00	0.71	0.34	0.84	2.53	1.08	0.43	0.09
2.5	2.0	0.21	0.00	0.55	0.34	2.61	1.97	0.48	0.11
3.0	2.0	0.55	0.00	1.13	0.76	2.92	2.26	0.48	0.27
3.0	3.0	1.39	0.00	1.93	1.13	3.02	3.00	0.27	0.02
						Average error		0.92	0.16

Table 2 summarizes the results of the TDoA technique when the relative times of the peaks are observed at t_1, t_2, t_3 and t_4, using the system of linear equations and the Taylor series. We can see that because the time resolution is a little bit coarse (*i.e.*, 42 µs) the precision of the system of linear equations is worse than that achieved by the RSSI technique. The fact that the system of linear equations does not incorporate any heuristic for the positioning of the drone limits the accuracy of this method. However, as the Taylor series initially guesses that the drone is likely to be in the center of the region defined by the hydrophones, this technique achieves better precision with an average error of 16 cm. This last result place to TDoA based on Taylor series as the best trilateration technique in this study, obtaining a maximum error of 27 cm. We could also reduce the error presented here, using a higher number of hydrophones o using a higher sampling frequency of the acoustic signals, but we are convinced that an error below 20 cm is quite good for the considered scenario.

5   Conclusions

The positioning of underwater vehicles using acoustic signals and simple trilateration techniques is very accurate, especially if TDoA is used. This work goes a step further by attempting a passive positioning without requiring any other acoustic source than the AUV itself. This technology is primarily useful for military and defense-oriented applications after solving the challenges initially outlined in this paper with a couple of proposed alternatives.

In fact, this work is a proof of concept that the issues existing in passive positioning are controllable, achieving average errors as small as 16 cm when the

TDoA mechanism with Taylor series is used. However, there are many extensions to this work that need to be studied in the near future. Basically, we would like to evaluate the AoA technique employing hydrophone arrays and combining AoA and TDoA to reduce the degree of uncertainty in the positioning of the AUVs. In addition, we require a deeper statistical analysis to explain the possible causes of the large errors reached when using automatic detection of the sudden power changes in each acoustic signal. Finally, we must assess the capacity of passive positioning when two or more AUVs navigate in the same area.

Acknowledgments. This work was partially supported by the Universidad de las Fuerzas Armadas – ESPE under Research Grant 2019-PIC-007-INV.

References

1. Allard, Y., Shahbazian, E.: Unmanned underwater vehicle (UUV) information study. Technical report, DRDC-RDDC-2014-C290, OODA Technologies Inc., Montreal, Canada (2014)
2. Antonelli, G.: Underwater Robots, 4 edn. Springer, Cham (2018). https://doi.org/10.1007/978-3-319-02877-4
3. Baek, H., Lim, J.: Design of future UAV-relay tactical data link for reliable UAV control and situational awareness. IEEE Commun. Mag. **56**(10), 144–150 (2018)
4. Carrera, E.V., Mena, E., Arciniega, P., Padilla, A., Paredes, M.: Analysis and evaluation of sound-based positioning techniques for short distances. In: 2020 IEEE ANDESCON, pp. 1–6. IEEE (2020)
5. Carrera, E.V., Paredes, M.: Analysis and evaluation of the positioning of autonomous underwater vehicles using acoustic signals. In: Rocha, Á., Pereira, R.P. (eds.) Developments and Advances in Defense and Security. SIST, vol. 152, pp. 411–421. Springer, Singapore (2020). https://doi.org/10.1007/978-981-13-9155-2_33
6. Carrera, E.V., Perez, M.S.: Event localization in wireless sensor networks. In: Central America and Panama Convention (Concapan 2014), IEEE, pp. 1–6. IEEE, Panama (2014)
7. Damian, R.G., Jula, N., Paturca, S.V.: Autonomous underwater vehicles - achievements and current trends. Sci. Bull. Naval Acad. **21**(1), 85–89 (2018)
8. Doonan, I.J., Coombs, R.F., McClatchie, S.: The absorption of sound in seawater in relation to the estimation of deep-water fish biomass. ICES J. Mar. Sci. **60**(5), 1047–1055 (2003)
9. Etter, P.C.: Underwater Acoustic Modeling and Simulation. CRC Press (2018)
10. Jose, D., Sebastian, S.: Taylor series method in TDOA approach for indoor positioning system. Int. J. Electric. Comput. Eng. **9**(5), 3927 (2019)
11. Khan, R., et al.: Underwater navigation using maneuverable beacons for localization. In: OCEANS 2016 MTS/IEEE, pp. 1–5. IEEE, Monterey (2016)
12. Li, D., Du, L.: AUV trajectory tracking models and control strategies: a review. J. Mar. Sci. Eng. **9**(9), 1020 (2021)
13. Li, S., Sun, H., Esmaiel, H.: Underwater TDoA acoustical location based on majorization-minimization optimization. Sensors **20**(16), 4457 (2020)
14. Paull, L., Saeedi, S., Seto, M., Li, H.: AUV navigation and localization: a review. IEEE J. Oceanic Eng. **39**(1), 131–149 (2014)

15. Perez, M.S., Carrera, E.V.: Acoustic event localization on an arduino-based wireless sensor network. In: IEEE Latin-America Conference on Communications (Latincom 2014), IEEE, pp. 1–6. IEEE, Cartagena (2014)
16. Qin, Q., Tian, Y., Wang, X.: Three-dimensional UWSN positioning algorithm based on modified RSSI values. Mob. Inf. Syst. **2021** (2021)
17. Rodriguez, J., Castañeda, H., Gordillo, J.: Design of an adaptive sliding mode control for a micro-AUV subject to water currents and parametric uncertainties. J. Mar. Sci. Eng. **7**(12), 445 (2019)
18. Stojanović, D., Stojanović, N.: Indoor localization and tracking: Methods, technologies and research challenges. Facta Universitatis Ser. Autom. Control Rob. **13**(1), 57–72 (2014)
19. Wong, G.S., Zhu, S.M.: Speed of sound in seawater as a function of salinity, temperature, and pressure. J. Acoust. Soc. Am. **97**(3), 1732–1736 (1995)

Hybrid Storage System Based on Rectenna and Photovoltaic Cells for Low Power IoT Wireless Devices

Myriam Cumbajín[1] ⓘ, Milton Valle[2] ⓘ, Carlos Gordón[2(✉)] ⓘ, and Carlos Peñafiel[3] ⓘ

[1] SISAu Research Group, Facultad de Ingeniería, Industria y Producción, Universidad Indoamérica, 180103 Ambato, Ecuador
myriamcumbajin@uti.edu.ec
[2] GITED Research Group, Facultad de Ingeniería en Sistemas, Electrónica e Industrial, Universidad Técnica de Ambato, UTA, 180207 Ambato, Ecuador
{mvalle7921,cd.gordon}@uta.edu.ec
[3] Facultad de Ingeniería, Universidad Nacional de Chimborazo, UNACH, 060108 Riobamba, Ecuador
carlospenafiel@unach.edu.ec

Abstract. This article presents the results of a research project, in which a system for harvesting Radio Frequency energy in the Wi-Fi frequency and a system for harvesting solar energy were developed, later they were connected. The two voltage sources collected in series to add them and an MT3608 circuit was added to its output, to have a regulated voltage between 5 to 27 V at the system output and charge a 3.7 V lithium battery at 300 mA, and a 9 V battery. The antenna that was designed was a patch-type Sierpinski carpet until the second interaction, which together with a two-stage Cockcroft Walton multiplier is improved to acquire up to 254 mV, the solar panel on the other hand was a 6 V at 150 mA, when implementing the entire system, 27 V were acquired at the output, a voltage that, thanks to the MT3608 regulator, can be regulated to obtain a sufficiently voltage at the output of the system. To carry out several systems loads tests in different day conditions such as: cloudy, sunny and at night, managing to charge 90% 3.7 V and 9 V batteries in 4 h.

Keywords: Fractal antenna · Photovoltaic cells · IoT · Wireless

1 Introduction

There are different sources of renewable energy, among which are wind, sunlight, vibrations, electromagnetic wave sources, among others. To summarize, the amount of energy that some of these sources can provide, the following previous works are analized. Alex Moupai, Nadir Hakem and Gilles Delisle, in their article "A new approach to design of RF energy harvesting system to enslave wireless sensor networks" [1] indicate that it can get from 0.4 to 1 mW/cm^3 of the air flow and from 0.2 to 1 mW/cm^2 in electromagnetic waves.

© The Author(s), under exclusive license to Springer Nature Switzerland AG 2023
M. Botto-Tobar et al. (Eds.): ICAT 2022, CCIS 1756, pp. 326–339, 2023.
https://doi.org/10.1007/978-3-031-24971-6_24

An RF energy harvesting system is mainly composed of 4 stages. First there is the antenna, the one in charge of receiving the RF signals, then comes the impedance matching stage, this is the one in charge of adapting the impedance of the antenna to the subsequent circuits to avoid loss of energy, followed by this stage comes the voltage rectifier circuit which oversees converting the alternating current voltage received by the antenna into direct current and finally there is the amplification stage.

In this project, an RF energy harvesting system was implemented using an antenna with a fractal design that works at a frequency of 2.4 to 2.5 GHz, a 5-stage wave rectifier multiplier, followed by a solar energy harvesting system, with a monocrystalline solar panel of 6 V at 150 mA to finally go through a dc-dc converter MT3608 and thus be able to have a controlled voltage of between 5 to 27 V at the output.

The aim of the present work is the development of the Hybrid Storage System based on Rectenna and Photovoltaic Cells for Low Power IoT (Internet of Things) Wireless Devices. In which, the RF energy harvesting is carried out at the 2.4 GHz frequency. Considering the implemented system, various load tests were carried out on a capacitor, with 3.7 and 9 V batteries, the measurements were taken every 30 min for an hour and a half, with which it was determined that only the antenna carried out a load in 90 min. of 140 mV in a 9 V battery and 40 mV in a 3.7 V battery, the solar panel was able to charge 710 mV in a 9 V battery and 131 mV in a 3.7 V battery, while with the implemented system it was possible to charge 840 mV in a 9 V battery and 208 mV in a 3.7 V battery, it should also be added that in a capacitor the antenna was able to harvest 261.4 mV and the complete system can provide up to 27 V at its output.

2 Methodology

2.1 Bibliographic Review

Analyzing some previous articles in which energy harvesting projects were developed, some results were found, for example, in a study in which they applied a rectangular patch type antenna that operated in GSM (Global System for Mobile), UMTS (Universal Mobile Telecommunications System), LTE (Long-Term Evolution) and Wi-Fi (Wireless Fidelity) frequencies, managed to obtain up to 600 mV [2], similarly, in an article published in IEEE in 2017 in which a 18 rectenna array system was developed, they managed to acquire up to 41 mW/m^2 [3]. In the same way, with a circular antenna operating from 135 MHz to 2.45 GHz and the application of step-up converters in the article RF Energy Harvesting for Ubiquitous, Zero Power Wireless Sensors, they managed to get up to 12 V [4].

2.2 Design and Calculation

Design of the System to be Implemented. For the development of this project, the following components are used: a solar panel of 6 V at 150 mA, a patch type antenna with fractal design that operates in the frequency of 2.4 GHz, a 5 stage Cockcroft Walton multiplier that uses HSMS 286C schottky diodes, a step-up dc - dc converter MT3608, a 3.7 V and a 9 V battery; the project diagram can be seen in Fig. 1.

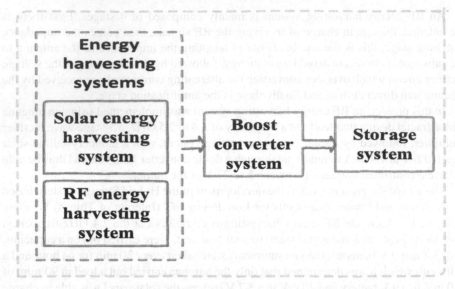

Fig. 1. Logic diagram of the system to be implemented.

Solar Energy Harvesting System. There are mainly three types of solar panels. First, the polycrystalline ones that are made of small particles of silicon which provide an efficiency of 16% in good light conditions, which is increased when the light does not directly affect them. Second, the monocrystalline solar panels are composed of a purer silicon crystal, which gives it an efficiency of up to 20% in conditions in which the light strikes them directly, which also allows small-sized solar panels to achieve large amounts of energy. Third, there are also thin-film solar panels, which, unlike the two previously mentioned, are made up of by very thin layers of sackcloth next to a substrate that can be plastic, metal or glass, which makes them optimal for application in projects where little space is available, its efficiency is approximately 10%. For this project, a monocrystalline solar panel has been chosen since it has the highest efficiency of the 3 mentioned above in conditions in which the light strikes it directly [5].

RF Energy Harvesting System. The RF energy harvesting is carried out in the 2.4 GHz frequency, this is because with the increase in technology and wearable devices, the Wi-Fi and Bluetooth bands are increasingly used, which provides a greater amount of energy to be harvested. There are different types of patch-type antennas, each one with its different advantages and disadvantages. In this article, an antenna with a fractal design, specifically the Sierpinski carpet is used, this is because the fractal design offers some advantages such as: the great bandwidth and the significant reduction in size that is achieved with this design. In order to verify the performance, the calculations of the dimensions are made to design a patch-type rectangular antenna which serves as the basis for the design of the Sierpinski carpet. Later, when designing the antenna, It is necessary reduction of the size of the Sierpinski carpet until it works at 2.4 GHz, which also serve to see how much you can reduce the size of an antenna when applying the fractal design. Next, a Cockcroft Walton multiplier circuit made up of 5 stages is connected to the antenna output with the purpose of implementing the rectenna and increasing the voltage harvested by the antenna [6–11].

Boost Converter System. The MT3608 step-up dc - dc converter can provide a regulated output voltage higher than the input voltage. As features, it can withstand a current of up to 2 Amps and with an input of 2 to 24 V you can have at your disposal output a voltage between 2 to 27 V which is regulated to keep it fixed against input voltage variations with a linear potentiometer found in the same device, which allows the prototype to charge 3.7 and 9 V batteries as long as between the solar panel and the antenna harvest at least 2 V.

Storage System. Currently, the most used batteries are 3.7 V, since this is present in cell phones, portable speakers, smart home devices such as: equipment compatible with the Google assistant, equipment for Alexa, etc. Tests are also carried out on a 9 V battery to determine its charging time and finally storage measurements are taken in a capacitor as a sample of the amount of voltage that each energy harvesting system implemented in this study can provide. The physical diagram of the system to be implemented can be seen in the following figure (Fig. 2).

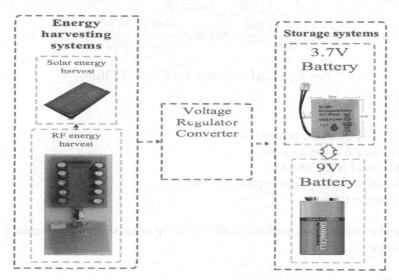

Fig. 2. Physical diagram of the system.

Design Equations of a Sierpinski Carpet Fractal Antenna. The formulas for the development of a Sierpinski carpet fractal antenna are detailed below.

K: Interaction number.

8^k: indicates the number of squares remaining after each interaction.

$\frac{1}{3^k}$: Give the length of each square for each interaction.

$\left(\frac{8}{9}\right)^k$: Give the area of each resulting Sierpinski rug.

Calculations of a Rectangular Microstrip Antenna for 2.4 GHz. With the help of the book Microstrip Patch Antennas second edition by Kai Fong Lee, the equations that allow obtaining the dimensions of the antenna for its design are obtained, since the substrate is FR4 $\varepsilon_r = 4.3$, the lengths of the sides are in centimeters (cm), the frequency in GHz and the speed of light as 30 [12, 13].

$$w = \frac{\lambda}{2}\sqrt{\frac{2}{\varepsilon_r + 1}} = \frac{12.5}{2}\sqrt{\frac{2}{4.3 + 1}} = 3.8[cm]$$

$$\varepsilon_{ef} = \frac{\varepsilon_r + 1}{2} + \frac{\varepsilon_r - 1}{2}\frac{1}{\sqrt{1 + 12\frac{h}{w}}} = \frac{4.3 + 1}{2} + \frac{4.3 - 1}{2\sqrt{1 + 12\frac{0.16}{3.8}}} = 4.08$$

$$\lambda_g = \frac{\lambda}{\varepsilon_{ef}} = \frac{12.5}{3.39} = 3.06\,cm$$

$$L = L_{ef} - 2\Delta L[cm]$$

$$L_{ef} = \frac{15}{f\sqrt{\varepsilon_{ef}}} = \frac{15}{2.4\sqrt{4.08}} = 3.09\,cm$$

$$\Delta L = 0.412h\frac{(\varepsilon_{ef} + 0.3)(\frac{w}{h} + 0.264)}{(\varepsilon_{ef} - 0.258)(\frac{w}{h} + 0.8)} = 0.412(0.16)\frac{(4.08 + 0.3)\left(\frac{4.08}{0.16} + 0.264\right)}{(4.08 - 0.258)\left(\frac{4.08}{0.16} + 0.8\right)} = 0.13\,cm$$

$$L = L_{ef} - 2\Delta L = 3.09 - 2 * 0.13 = 2.83[cm]$$

where:

ε_{ef} = Effective dielectric permittivity
λ_s = Wavelength in the substrate
L_{ef} = Electrical patch length
ΔL = Length differential due to patch current
f_r = Resonance frequency

With the formulas indicated above, the following dimensions were obtained for the design of the antenna.

W: 3.8 cm
L: 2.83 cm

The calculated values of W and L are for the design of a patch-type rectangular antenna that operates at a frequency of 2.4 GHz, in this project, we start from these measurements to design the fractal Sierpinski carpet antenna, from which with the help of the optimometrics offered by the software, the measurements of W and L are be reduced until the Sierpinski carpet works at the frequency of 2.4 GHz, also verifying that applying a fractal design to an antenna reduces its size. Once the design was done, it was possible to get the antenna to work at the Wi-Fi frequency with the following dimensions. All the dimensions are summarized in Table 1.

Table 1. Antenna dimensions.

Variable	Dimension [mm]
SW	40
SL	40
W	10
L	9
WLTX	2
LLTX	18
LGND	7
WGND	11
WLTG	1

Transmission Line Calculations. To obtain the values of width and length of the transmission line, the TX Line Calculator software was used, which allows us to calculate the dimensions of the transmission line, entering the parameters of the substrate such as: dielectric constant, type of material, frequency and tangent of substrate loss. In this project FR4 is used with a dielectric constant of 4.3, loss tangent of 0.02, the conductive material is copper, and the working frequency is 2.4 GHz, applying these values in the software, the length of the transmission line must be 18 mm and the width 2 mm.

Multiplier Circuit Calculations. In the system to be implemented, a Cockcroft Walton multiplier circuit is designed using HSMS 286C diodes that are low in consumption and can work at high frequencies. The calculation was also carried out to determine the minimum width that the tracks must have to transmit.

The tracks are required to be designed for a current of 200 mA and Printed Circuit Board (PCB) type FR4 has a copper thickness of 35 um, so the calculation of the width of the tracks was based on the ANSI-IPC 2221 standard, whose formulas and constants are detailed below.

$$\text{Área} = \frac{I_{máx}}{k3 * (k1 * \Delta Tk2)} = \frac{0.200}{0.6732 * (0.0647 * 10 * 0.4281)} = 1.0725\,\text{mm}^2$$

$$Ancho = \frac{área}{L * 1.378} = \frac{1.0725}{35 * 1.3787} = 0.22\,\text{mm}$$

As indicated in the calculations, the minimum width of the tracks must be 0.2 mm, which is within the range indicated by the ANSI-IPC 2221 standard to transmit voltages less than 15 V, but since the tracks are designed by a CNC, the multiplier circuit with a width of tracks that is 1.3 mm, this so that the CNC can design the tracks without problems.

2.3 Simulation

Antenna Simulation. The antenna was simulated in the CST studio software, starting with the previously calculated dimensions and then, with the help of the optimetrics offered by the CST studio software, it was possible to modify their values until a good bandwidth was achieved with a central frequency of 2.4 GHz. Once finished with the simulation of the antenna in the software depicted in Fig. 3, a bandwidth ranging from 2.34 to 2.437 GHz and a central working frequency of 2.403 GHz were achieved, as can be seen in Fig. 4.

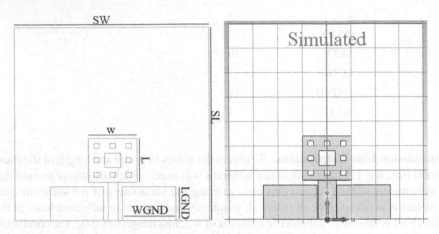

Fig. 3. Antenna design in CST studio.

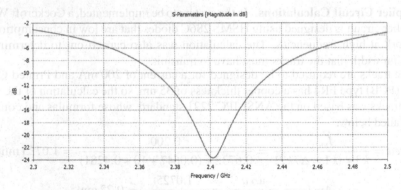

Fig. 4. Reflection coefficient of the antenna designed in CST study.

Simulation of the Multiplier Circuit. The multiplier circuit was simulated using Proteus software and its schematic diagram can be seen in Fig. 5.

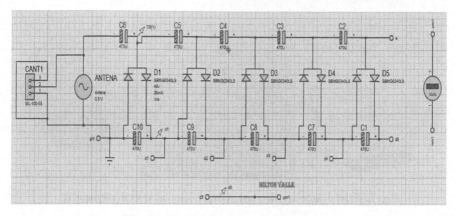

Fig. 5. Simulation of the multiplier circuit.

The tracks in the PCB layout were also designed to be able to have a 3D view of the finished product, which is made up of 5 HSMS 286C diodes and 10 capacitors of 470 uF at 10 V as can be seen in Fig. 6.

Fig. 6. Multiplier circuit design.

2.4 System Implementation

Implementation of the Antenna. Once the antenna was implemented, the Nano VNA V2.2 vector network analyzer was used to be able to see the reflection coefficient of the antenna and the central working frequency. With which it was observed that the antenna has a central frequency of 2.4 GHz (see Fig. 7) with a bandwidth that goes from 2.37 GHz to 2.5 GHz. The simulated vs. implemented reflection coefficient of the antenna is you can see in Fig. 8.

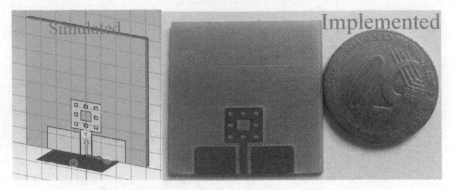

Fig. 7. Fractal Antenna Sierpinski Carpet, simulated vs implemented.

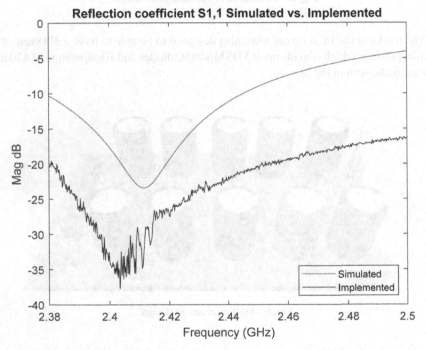

Fig. 8. Reflection coefficient of the implemented antenna vs simulated antenna.

The simulated central frequency is 2.412 GHz and the central frequency that was obtained when implemented is 2.403 GHz, which provides a deviation error percentage of the central frequency between the simulated and the implemented equal to 0.34%.

Implementation of the Multiplier Circuit. The multiplier circuit was implemented with the help of a CNC to then weld the respective components. In Fig. 9, you can see the simulated multiplier circuit and the implemented one.

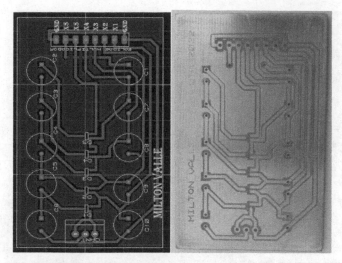

Fig. 9. Simulated vs implemented multiplier circuit.

Implementation of the Solar Panel. A monocrystalline solar panel of 6 V at 150 mA was implemented, later measurements of the voltage that it can deliver in different conditions of the day were carried out. Which can be seen in the Table 2.

Table 2. Voltages provided by the solar panel.

#	Sunny	Foggy	Time Hrs: Min	Place	Measured voltaje [v]
1		X	10:19	Inside	4.37
2		X	10:27	Outside	7.00
3	X		12:00	Inside	3.84
4	X		12:07	Outside	7.12
5	X		14:00	Inside	2.47
6		X	18:30	Outside	1.90

System Implementation. After completing the stages of the Cockcroft Walton multiplier circuit, the solar panel and the Fractal Antenna, the system was implemented in an acrylic box since it allows light to enter the solar panel, see Fig. 10.

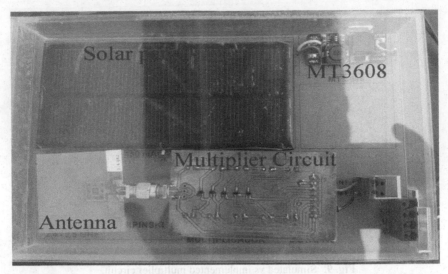

Fig. 10. RF energy harvesting system.

3 Results

When the system was implemented, a measurement was made of the voltage that it can deliver to its output in its maximum operating condition, that is, when there is enough light, with which it was possible to obtain up to 27 V at the output of the MT3608 converter. It was also determined that this voltage can only be acquired when the solar panel manages to harvest at least 2 V of solar energy. At night the system only manages to provide the voltage harvested by the antenna, making the solar panel like a load, since when giving 0 V and being connected in series with the antenna, it becomes more of a resistance, so it is possible to measure a lower voltage than the one delivered by the antenna at its output.

The voltages that were collected in the 3.7 V and 9 V batteries are indicated in Table 3. The voltages that can be obtained directly in a capacitor are also indicated.

Subsequently, tests were carried out with the system on a cloudy, sunny day and at night, the results of which are indicated in Tables 4, 5 and 6, respectively.

As an observation, in the charge of the 3.7 V battery, it was possible to notice that from the start time, after 90 min it was already charged at 4.03 V and after 2 h it reached 4.12 V from hence the charging speed decreases due to the current needed by the source and the amount of light that exists outside.

In the tests carried out at night, it can be seen that the energy stored in the batteries is only that provided by the antenna, in addition to having the panel connected in series, this becomes one more load for the battery, reducing the amount of energy supplied to storage devices.

Table 3. Voltages stored with the system.

Metered system		Voltage initial [V]	Voltage [mV]			Voltage harvested [mV]
			30 min	60 min	90 min	
Battery 9 V	Antenna	8.5	8.59	8.62	8.64	140
	Solar panel	8.44	8.86	9.12	9.15	710
	Implemented system	8.4	9.02	9.16	9.28	840
Capacitor	Antenna	0	254	258	26.4	261.4
	Implemented system	27	x	x	x	27 000
Battery 3.7 V	Antenna	3.71	3.72	3.74	3.75	40
	Solar panel	3.73	3.77	3.84	3.861	131
	Implemented system	3.66	3.748	3.802	3.868	208

Table 4. Stored voltages on a cloudy day.

	Voltage Initial [v]	Voltage Harvested 90 min [v]	End voltage [v]	Time [hours]
Battery 9 V	8.64	9.28	9.44	4
Battery 3.7 V	3.74	3.97	4.01	4

Table 5. Stored voltages on a sunny day.

	Voltage Initial [v]	Voltage Harvested in 90 min [v]	End voltage [v]	Time [hours]
Battery 9 V	8.52	9.31	9.45	4
Battery 3.7 V	3.75	4.03	4.12	4

Table 6. Voltages stored at night.

	Voltage Initial [v]	Voltage in 90 min [v]
Battery 9 V	8.13	8.23
Battery 3.7 V	3.69	3.72

4 Conclusions

In the present work, 261 mV was obtained from the antenna designed to harvest from 2.4 GHz frequency energy. With the help of the solar panel, it was possible to increase the output voltage of the system. Later, thanks to the dc-dc converter, can have a controlled voltage between 5–27 V at the output, which allows regulating the voltage that you want to apply to any battery whose charge limit is less than 27 V. During the tests of the system, it was possible to appreciate that by adding a solar panel the amount of energy harvested can be exponentially increased, achieving a 90% charge of a 3.7 V battery in 4 h. It was also observed that the solar panel provides 3.84 V indoors while outdoors it can provide 7 V so faster charging times were achieved outdoors on sunny days between 10 AM to 4 PM. The main advantages that could be found when adding a solar panel to the RF energy harvesting system are: First, obtaining sufficient voltage to be able to charge any battery used in IoT devices whose charge threshold is less than 27 V. Second, reduction of charging times to charge on sunny days. And third, more optimal charging processes for the batteries, ensuring that the charging cycles of the batteries are not affected.

Acknowledgments. The authors thank the Technical University of Ambato and the "Dirección de Investigación y Desarrollo" (DIDE) for their support in carrying out this research, in the execution of the project "Captación de Energía Limpia de Baja Potencia para Alimentación de Dispositivos de Quinta Generación (5G)", approved by resolution "Nro. UTA-CONIN-2022-0015-R". Project code: SFFISEI 07.

References

1. Mouapi, A., Hakem, N., Delisle, G.Y.: A new approach to design of RF energy harvesting system to enslave wireless sensor networks. ICT Exp. **4**(4), 228–233 (2018)
2. Shen, S., Chiu, C.Y., Murch, R.D.: A dual-port triple-band L-probe microstrip patch rectenna for ambient RF energy harvesting. IEEE Antennas Wirel. Propag. Lett. **16**, 3071–3074 (2017)
3. Erkmen, F., Almoneef, T.S., Ramahi, O.M.: Electromagnetic energy harvesting using full-wave rectification. IEEE Trans. Microw. Theory Techn. **65**(5), 1843–1851 (2017)
4. Saeed, W.: RF energy harvesting for ubiquitous, zero power wireless sensors. Int. J. Antennas Propag. 11–14 (2018)
5. Mellit, A., Benghamen, M.: A Practical Guide for Advanced Methods in Solar Photovoltaic Systems, pp. 139–163. Springer, Cham (2020)
6. Wagih, M., Hillier, N., Yong, S., Weddell, A.S., Beeby, S.: RF-powered wearable energy harvesting and storage module based on E-textile coplanar waveguide rectenna and supercapacitor. IEEE Open J. Antennas Propag. **2**, 302–314 (2021)
7. Sharma, H., Ahteshamul, H., Zainul, A.: An efficient solar energy harvesting system for wireless sensor nodes. In: IEEE International Conference on Power Electronics, Intelligent Control and Energy Systems (ICPEICES), pp. 1–4 (2018)
8. Aznar, A.C., et al.: Antenas. Univ. Politéc. De Cataluya, pp. 391–416 (2004)
9. Fang, D.G.: Antenna Theory and Microstrip Antennas, pp. 783–867. CRC Press (2017)
10. Domínguez, A., Armando, G.: Cálculo de Antenas: Antenas de última generación para tecnología digital y métodos de medición, 4th edn. Marcombo, Barcelona (2010)
11. Trikolikar, A., Lahudkar, A.: A review on design of compact rectenna for RF energy harvesting. In: 2020 International Conference on Electronics and Sustainable Communication Systems (ICESC), pp. 651–264 (2020)

12. Balanis, C.A.: Antenna Theory Analysis and Design, 4th edn, pp. 783–867. Wiley (2016)
13. Filiz, S., Yunus, U.: A comparative study: voltage multipliers for RF energy harvesting system. Reserchgate 1–11 (2019)

Design and Construction
of an Anthropomorphic Robotic Head
with Gestural Projection

Cristhian Masabanda, Ana Oña, David Loza, Byron Cortez[(✉)],
and Alejandra Alban

Universidad de las Fuerzas Armadas "ESPE", Quito, Ecuador
bhcortez@espe.edu.ec

Abstract. The following document presents the design and construction of an anthropomorphic robotic head with gestural projection named Kyle. Kyle's main elements are structure, human-machine interaction systems, and gestural projection. The structure is composed of the carcass and the neck mechanism. Reverse kinematics is presented through the neck mechanism as it is responsible for head mobility to achieve better control. It is fully programmed in Python language and making use of the Robotic Operative System, the nodes and topics generated and implemented in the robot can be observed in order to allow different interactions with the user such as natural language, and tracking through artificial vision. The most important part is the use of projection technology in order to present of gestures and feelings. Kyle was tested in various aspects such as mechanical, through movement tests and usability. It was assessed using a survey carried out on users that allowed to verify that it is a robot of acceptable anthropomorphism and has an adequate level of interaction towards different users.

Keywords: Robotic head · Anthropomorphism · Actions units

1 Introduction

To define the concept of a robotic head is necessary to start from the definition of a social robot. A social robot [5], is one that achieves communication with the human being, understands and even relates to people in a personal way. It also has the ability to understand humans and in turn, make themselves understood by them. The definition of a robotic head is a social robot [6], whose objective is to simulate or pretend expressions of the human face, to facilitate human-robot interaction, through the use of different technologies such as mechanical actuators, avatars on screens or projections of light. To generate a better predisposition of users towards the robot, allowing it to perform better in the task to which it has been assigned. Currently, social robots have had a constant evolution in the study of human-robot interaction in various areas such as education [9], care, entertainment [4,7], health [11] among others. However, there are still some problems to be solved, such as the cost of construction and maintenance, current robots still do not have the emotional and social capacities necessary for interaction with human beings, and the appropriate degree of anthropomorphism [1]. Due to the aforementioned problems, it was decided to design and build a flexible anthropomorphic robotic head, moderate cost and acceptable anthropomorphism implemented to the head the senses and gestures through gestural projection.

Regarding previous researches, the head has certain advantages. It is well known that the development of new prototypes represents a significant expense due to the consumption of resources such as time and money, the head has a low cost, reducing this mainly with the use of rapid prototyping (3D printing) in this way also saves time since changes can be made in an agile way. The use of free software is an important contribution to reducing money, mainly to the use of Blender software, which has a very high design capacity that offers flexibility when making animations and that presents additional advantages. The main advantage is that it has a programming block that is compatible with the Python language.

A very important aspect is the anthropomorphism of the head, this has been achieved with the size, at present, electrical devices (projector, motors, cameras) have chosen to reduce their size to the point of achieving greater portability but without leaving Performance aside. This has allowed the head to have a size very similar to that of a middle-aged human, thus avoiding the use of large projectors that greatly impaired the aesthetics and anthropomorphy of previous developments. The paper is organized as follows. Section 2 describes the design and construction of the robotic head, taking as the most important points the neck mechanism, the inverse kinematics, the gestural projection system and ending with the animations. Section 3 presents the tests of mechanism, usability and the confusion matrix. Finally, Sect. 4 presents the conclusions and future work on the project.

2   Evolution of Robotic Heads

The study of robotic heads in the last 20 years has allowed the birth of several prototypes, which seek to cover the main function of emulating the traits and emotions of people, analyzing and predicting behaviors, that is a considerable interaction between human-machine. Then, a timeline is observed in which all the robots are presented, starting with heads of rear projection technology, going through mechatronic heads and androids and ending with Furhat System: Tengai [15]. The advances in technology in the different prototypes of both mechatronic and projected heads are presented. The beginning of the rear projection is born in the projected image in the haunted house of Walt Disney where the moving image of a woman was projected on a face shaped screen, resulting in a 3D projection. However, the projected material was only based on a film, it was not yet implemented in robotic applications. Kismet [3], a robotic head that appeared in 2002, built at MIT by Dr. Cynthia Breazeal, the robot can imitate certain human gestures and also move the eyes, eyebrows and mouth, later the robot named Grace [21] built by RWI, has an expressive face on a panoramic platform. Grace can speak with a high quality speech synthesizer and understand the responses with her microphone and speech recognition software. During 2005 there are some prototypes such as iCat [4], it was developed by Philips Company, an emotionally intelligent user interface robot. Another type of construction is androids, a first approach, is the Albert Hubo robot [19], it was a robot-humanoid created by Kaist, its main characteristic is to use synthetic skin, in order to obtain a more real resemblance. Other academics create Chit Chat Club [13] a projected retro robot that combines a physical and virtual environment.

In the latest research on rear projection, Socibot [18] implemented in 2014 is found to be a compact and sociable robot designed to interact between humans and robots with the ability to detect faces, features, emotions, speech and gestures. In 2018, the Furhat System was developed: Tangai [15] that uses projection technology to transfer a face to a mobile base with the shape of a head, has visual tracking in real time. A camera tracks whoever is communicating with Furhat, allowing the head, with three degrees of freedom, to move naturally (similar to a person) in order to maintain eye contact.

After reviewing the different heads, it can be concluded that each type of head has advantages and disadvantages. Avatars are low-cost developments, which are easy to present emotions, but their lack of naturalness due to being a flat face greatly limits the interaction with people. On the other hand, mechatronic heads present a greater naturalness but the production costs are too high due to the large number of mechanical and electronic elements needed. The mixed models known as back-projected robots allow the ease of elaboration and presentation of different gestures of the avatar's face, as well as the natural movement that mechatronic heads present when simulating the human neck.

Kyle is an anthropomorphic head with gestural projection consisting of 3 main parts which are the mobility mechanism, the projection system and the robot housing. It is similar to Furhat: Tangai, but the big difference is cost reduction.

3   Desing and Construction

To the design and construction, several interesting aspects were taken into account, among which we can find the following:

- **Low Costs**: mechatronic and android systems use a large amount of resources from the large number of actuators for the simulation of the movements of the eyes, sight and face, the control cards and the complexity of the mechanisms for their movement.
- **Gestural Projection**: the technology of gestural projection has a great number of advantages with respect to the movement mechanisms that use androids or mechatronic heads. First, it presents a great flexibility at the time of the design and presentation of the human face, allowing a better acceptance with the people generating a greater anthropomorphism.
- **Open Source Software**: open source allows a cost reduction and has powerful programs such as Blender, ROS an operating system for robotics and Python a programming language.

3.1   Mobility Mechanism

The mobility mechanism is designed in order to simulate the movement of the neck that a person has, that is to allow flexion, extension and rotation movements and to support the rear projection system and carcass. Taking these considerations into account, a parallel RSSR configuration mechanism was designed as shown in Fig. 1. It has 5 main parts which are: 1) The upper platform which allows the attachment of the outer part of the head and serves as a support for the projector and fisheye lens (They are lenses with a wide angle of vision that produce a large visual distortion in order to generate a panoramic image). 2) The lower platform serves as the base for the motors. 3) The universal joint that allows the upper platform to rotate in two degrees of freedom. 4) The connecting rods are two parallel axes that are attached to the upper and lower platform by means of a swivel system and allow the pitch and roll movement. Finally 5) the lower base which is the support of the robot and contains the motor that allows the rotational movement in the missing axis of the 3 which is yaw.

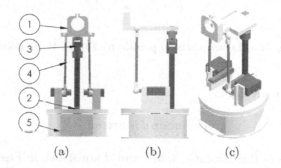

(a)   (b)   (c)

Fig. 1. Three-degree-of-freedom RSSR parallel mechanism a) Side View b) Front View c) Isometric View 1) Upper Platform, 2) Lower Platform, 3) Universal Joint, 4) Tie Bars, 5) Lower Base

3.2   Inverse Kinematics of the Mechanism

The inverse kinematics of the robot was carried out by means of the graphic method, using rotation matrices and vectors as shown in Fig. 2. The method allows generating a polygon of vectors, which once solved, showed the following results for the first two degrees of rotation: that is to say θ_1 and θ_2. In the Fig. 3, you can see the points that were taken into account for the generation of vectors, in ref fig: points a, the lower platform is observed taking as point 0,0 start of the base in the center of the bar, in ref fig: points b, the upper platform is observed and the values of the points can be observed. Each distance will contribute to the values obtained in the equations representing a, b, c, d.

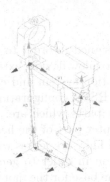

Fig. 2. Three-degree-of-freedom RSSR parallel mechanism

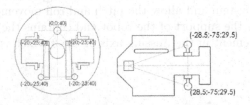

Fig. 3. a) Lower platform points. b) Top platform points

Giving as a result Eq. 1:

$$\theta_1 = \arcsin d - \arctan \frac{a}{b} \tag{1}$$

where the values of the constants a, b, c and d are shown in Eqs. 2, 3, 4 y 5:

$$a = 28.5 S\theta_3 S\theta_4 - 78.0 C\theta_3 - 33.0 C\theta_4 S\theta_3 + 25.0 \tag{2}$$

$$b = 33.0 C\theta_3 C\theta_4 - 78.0 S\theta_3 - 28.5 C\theta_3 S\theta_4 + 120.4 \tag{3}$$

$$c = 28.5 C\theta_4 + 33.0 S\theta_4 - 33.75 \tag{4}$$

$$d = \frac{153.59^2 - 54.7^2 - c - a^2 - b^2}{109.4\sqrt{a^2 + b^2}} \tag{5}$$

For the case of θ_2, the result is shown in Eq. 6:

$$\theta_2 = \arcsin d_1 - \arctan \frac{a_1}{b_1} \tag{6}$$

where the values of the constants $a1$, $b1$, $c2$, $d2$ and are shown in Eqs. 7, 8, 9 y 10:

$$a_1 = -28.5 S\theta_3 S\theta_4 - 78.0 C\theta_3 - 33.0 C\theta_4 S\theta_3 + 25.0 \tag{7}$$

$$b_1 = 33.0 C\theta_3 C\theta_4 - 78.0 S\theta_3 + 28.5 C\theta_3 S\theta_4 + 120.4 \tag{8}$$

$$c = -28.5 C\theta_4 + 33.0 S\theta_4 + 35.75 \tag{9}$$

$$d = \frac{153.59^2 - 54.7^2 - c_1 - a_1{}^2 - b_1{}^2}{109.4\sqrt{a_1{}^2 + b_1{}^2}} \tag{10}$$

It can be seen that the results are a combination of sines and cosines, due to the rotation matrices used. It also depends on the angles of inclination of the universal joint as well as the ends of the connecting bars. For the angle θ_3, the design of the system allows the calculation to be suppressed, since it takes the value directly from the servo motor that controls it.

The inverse kinematics allows obtaining the equations of movement, in order to achieve the best control of the mechanism, avoiding sudden or jerky movements that could cause a negative reaction from the users. On the contrary, more harmonic and continuously movements raise the level of acceptance and allow to meet the objective of anthropomorphism.

3.3   Gestural Projection System

One of the most important systems of the robot, is the gestural projection shown in Fig. 4, the system consists of 4 parts each one with a specific task that are described below:

1. The carcass is the external part, its main task is to contain and to protect the internal parts from external actions that may damage them in any way.
2. The projector is in charge of generating the image to be presented. It receives the designed image in the software that is sent by an HDMI connection from a computer
3. The main task of the fisheye lens is to generate concavity to the image, allowing it to fit to the projection mask and to generate a higher level of acceptance to people.
4. The projection mask allows the image to be shown to people, generated by a thermoforming process in opal acrylic material.

3.4   Animations

The animations were created in Software Blender [10], a program for modeling, rendering, animation and creation of three-dimensional graphics. It also allows the handling of animations through programming codes in Python language. First, it is necessary to talk about certain Blender concepts such as:

- **Shape Keys:** The Shape Keys are tools used for the deformation of objects such as meshes, curves and surfaces. They are commonly used in facial animations. In Fig. 5 you can see the creation process, on the left the original version, in the center the selection of surfaces, and on the right the final position.
- **Frame:** It is a basic element for animation of elements in blender, it can be analogously considered as a real skeleton and it has several bones. In Fig. 6 you can see the frame for the generation of gestures.

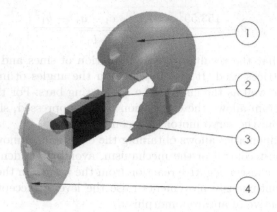

Fig. 4. Projection system composed of: 1) Carcass 2) Projector 3) Fish-eye lens 4) Projection Mask

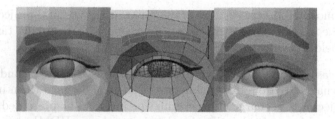

Fig. 5. Creation process of a shape key

- **Bones:** These are basic elements that are linked to the frames and allow to control the movement depending on the shape key to which they are associated with. In Fig. 6 a) you can see the bones used for the movement of gestures.

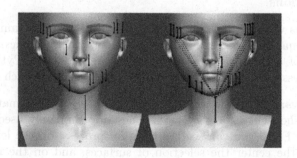

Fig. 6. Bones attached to the base of the face and attached to the frame

Keeping the mentioned concepts clear, a total of 13 Shape Key were defined, each with its respective bone and connected to a general frame for movement. After defining the Shape Keys, we proceeded to define 13 units of action, which are defined as actions performed by the face in order to transfer information through facial expressions. In Table 1 is shown a description of the action units, shape key and movements.

Table 1. Actions units implemented to the robot

Action units	Shape key	Movements
AU1	1	To open mouth
AU2	2	Lips up
AU3	3	Lips down
AU4	4	To close eyes
AU5	5	To open eyes
AU6	6	To open right eye
AU7	7	To raise eyebrow
AU8	8	To low eyebrow
AU9	9	Eye movement 1
AU10	10	Eye movement 2
AU11	11	To move cheekbone
AU12	12	To raise eyebrow
AU13	13	Nose movements

The anthropomorphic head has several gestures that are born from the combination of different action units among the most important we can find happiness, anger, sadness and surprise and are shown in the Table 2 below.

Table 2. Combination of action units to the generation of expressions

Expression	Action units
Happiness	AU2, AU11, AU11, AU13
Anger	AU4
Surprise	AU1, AU9, AU7
Sadness	AU3, AU4
Wink	AU6
Blink	AU5

3.5 Programming Architecture

The robot was fully programmed in the ROS environment, it has a total of 18 nodes which are separated in order to fulfill specific functions. The most important nodes are that allow the entry of data from the world that are located in the left part enclosed in blue. The nodes in the center located in the red part are the nodes that process the information and transform it into information to be sent abroad Fig. 7. Among the most important nodes can find artificial vision, rosserial. On the right side, there are the connection bridges of the ROS system to the outside world, considering the most important nodes such as the bridge with blender and the Arduino micro controller for controlling the servomotors and allowing kyle's mobility as can be seen in Fig. 7.

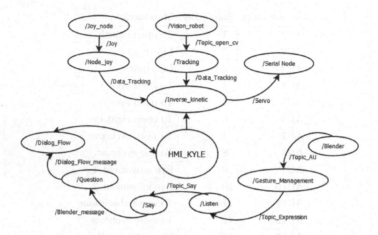

Fig. 7. Kyle's node architecture

The nodes are structured in such a way that they fulfill the specific tasks below. Each node is described with its respective task that it fulfills, and the function that their combination generates.

Natural Language. The nodes described below are used for the person-Kyle dialogue:

- Listening: It is the node that allows Kyle to interpret what a person says and translates it into text. It is done using the Google Speech to Text packages.
- Dialog Flow: It is a natural language platform used to implement conversational interfaces, through the question-answer system, which allows Kyle to create his answers to everyday questions and to add more questions and answers quickly and easily.
- Gestures is a combination of action units, which allows to show eye and mouth movements for presentation on the face.

Gestures. The generation of gestures is carried out through the following nodes:

- Gestures: Interprets series of data that are sent by the bridge between ros and blender, and later to process and to transform them into movements that will be presented on Kyle's face.

- ROS Bridge: It is a bridge between ros and blender that is generated through the client-server configuration and python libraries in order to allow communication for sending data between blender and ros.
- Visemes: For the transformation of text in movements for its later sending through the node.
- Blender: In charge of generating movement on the face, it uses the program's own functions that will be explained clearly later.

Movement. The set of nodes below generates the kyle movement depending on the mode chosen and the function it is fulfilling.

- Ros Joy: It is a node that allows the interpretation of the actions carried out by the user in the command control ("Joystick"), to transform them later, into movements that are sent to the inverse kinematics in the form of an arrangement of 3 angles for each of the robot freedom degrees.
- Artificial Vision: It is a node that allows the detection of people's faces, and takes the nose of a person as a reference to send coordinates to the tracking node.
- Tracking: Allows the transformation of the coordinates to angles that can be interpreted by the inverse kinematics of the robot.
- Inverse Kinematics: calculates from the angles sent by the tracking node, the value that each of the actuators should turn, using Eqs. 1 and 6, and send it to the node found on the Arduino control board.
- Ros Serial: it is ROS's own node that allows communication with Arduino cards through the serial port, and by sending an array of 3 data that are the values to be rotated by each of the motors.
- Arduino: it is in charge of moving the 3 motors, each one at the indicated angle by the inverse kinematics node.

4   Test and Results

Figure 8 shows the integration of the system, in which all the aforementioned systems have been implemented, such as mobility with the mechanism, the projection system and the different gestures. For this, the system uses two sensors: microphone and camera, for the simulation of the senses of sight and hearing, in addition to a computer and an Arduino control board for the management of the motors.

4.1   Animation Tests

The animation tests were done in order to calibrate projector and lens positions, and at the same time to find the ideal values for the filters of the blender software in order to achieve the best presentation. In Fig. 9, the gestures can be seen on the right: happiness, anger, sadness, surprise.

As can be seen in the faces on the left. These are already implemented in the robot, the lens and fisheye set give the image a certain concavity and the way in which the projection mask was created allows a complete passage of light, allowing the face to be shown in a natural way and the emotions to be easily recognized.

Fig. 8. Complete integration of the robot

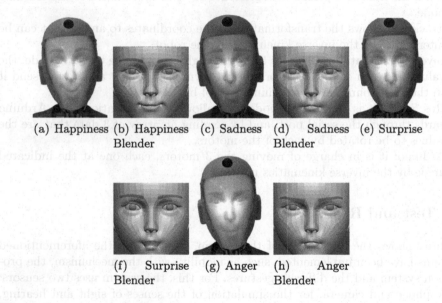

(a) Happiness (b) Happiness (c) Sadness (d) Sadness (e) Surprise
                    Blender   Blender

(f) Surprise (g) Anger (h) Anger
    Blender   Blender

Fig. 9. Comparison between software gestures and implementation of animations: a), c), e) and g) Animations implemented on the robot, b), d), f) and h) Animations designed in Blender

4.2 Mechanism Test

The 3 degrees of freedom mechanism, in order to check the validity of its inverse kinematics, a system was designed that consisted of a gyroscope that was coupled to the upper platform and entered rotation values in roll, pitch and yaw that were processed by inverse kinematics and sent to the rotation of the motors and at the end check if the motors reached the same value that was assigned in the test. The results obtained are shown in Table 3 below.

As can be seen in the angle column, obtained by the gyroscopic sensor, the error presented by the mechanism is a low error and is mainly due to the range of the servo motors and the precision of the signal sent by the Arduino microcontroller.

Table 3. Results of mechanism tests

Results of mechanism tests			
Test 1			
	Initial position	Angle required	Angle obtained
Yaw	0	15	15.2
Pitch	0	0	0
Roll	90	90	90
Test 2			
	Initial position	Angle required	Angle obtained
Yaw	0	0	0.2
Pitch	0	−15	−14.8
Roll	90	90	90.2
Test 3			
	Initial position	Angle required	Angle obtained
Yaw	0	0	0
Pitch	0	0	0
Roll	90	120	120.2
Test 4			
	Initial position	Angle required	Angle obtained
Yaw	0	−10	−10.2
Pitch	0	10	9.8
Roll	90	75	90.2

4.3 Usability

The usability of the robot was evaluated by the SUS (System Usability Scale) method [14], which is a tool that allows to measure the usability of an object, device or application. The results obtained are reliable. The SUS survey was conducted on 22 people who ranged in age from 22 to 26 years. All the people chosen had experience in handling technology, as well as some approach to social robots, but it was the first time they had an interaction with the robotic head Kyle. Before starting the test everyone received an explanation of the basic functioning of Kyle. Once the introduction was finished, each participant obtained a questionnaire containing the aforementioned questions and to which they could answer on a SUS scale: 1) Effectiveness System, 2) Efficiency and 3) Easy to use. The questions were taken from the original test of the Usability.gov page [2] and attached to the place that was chosen, the mechatronics laboratory of the University of the Armed Forces "ESPE".

- I would use the lab assistant frequently.
- I find the lab assistant unnecessarily complex.
- I find the lab assistant easy to use.
- The assistance of a technical support person is required when using the laboratory assistant.
- The assistance of a technical support person is required when using the laboratory assistant.
- I find the lab assistant to be very inconsistent.
- I think that people would learn to use the lab assistant quickly.
- I felt uncomfortable using the lab assistant.
- I am confident using the lab assistant.
- You need a previous knowledge of the laboratory assistant to be able to use it.

After the 22 surveys that were answered anonymously, the interpretation was carried out using the aforementioned scale, giving the results of the surveys of 82.5 out of 100 that indicates that its acceptability is excellent. Although, it is necessary to clarify that since it is a prototype, it still has several aspects in which it can be improved, placing emphasis especially on aspects such as user friendliness that are not related or knowledge about technology, as well as expanding the range of people selected from children to older adults.

5   Results

According to the results, the main objective of the project was achieved. Kyle is a low-cost anthropomorphic head with gestural projection that has an acceptable level of usability, a good level of interaction, as well as an acceptable level of anthropomorphism due to the animations of the face and the controlled movement of its neck mobility mechanism.

As can be seen in the Figs. 8 and 4, Kyle is a compact robot, similar in appearance and size to a human and also has an emotion simulation system, which It was carried out using the action units system through the Blender software, resulting in a total of 13 action units, which, when combined allow the robot to present emotions such as: joy, sadness, surprise and anger. In addition to emotions, the robot has the ability to simulate and hold a conversation. The conversation system is based on Dialog Flow, a Google application that allows generating questions and answers. The same in combination with the emotion simulation system, allows you the ability to start a conversation.

According to the results of the usability tests shown in Sect. 4, the questions where Kyle has the most difficulty are referring to assistance and previous knowledge for the use of the robot. Something very valid as it is a prototype that may have several improvements or future work. Similarly, it has great advantages especially in questions 1, 3, 7, 9, in which it obtains a perfect score in aspects more related to constant use of the robot, comfort of use and acceptance of part of it. Resulting in an average of 82.5 out of 100 points that indicates an excellent level of acceptance.

6   Conclusions

The main theme of the document is the design and construction of Kyle, an anthropomorphic head with gestural projection has a parallel mechanism of 3 degrees of freedom that allows it to simulate the movement of a human neck, a gestural projection system and sensors for emulation of the sense of sight and hearing. One of the most important systems is the gesture projection system, which was developed in blender and allows the robot a more fluid interaction with people, as well as a question and answer system that was implemented through Dialog Flow through the use of libraries from Google Assistant.

Kyle has two main advantages over commercial robots that have similar functions. The first: flexibility, present in the generation of gestures, allowing the number of gestures to be increased and decreased. Another aspect where kyle's flexibility comes into play is the application for which it is intended, being a prototype robot. It was designed in such a way that it can be used for various purposes; this is thanks to the use of Dialog Flow, which allows generating questions and answers for any topic and of great complexity. The second advantage is its low cost. It is a system under development but compared to current systems on the market the cost is extremely low. Largely, thanks to the large amount of free software that was used.

Kyle's usability as a whole was tested by 22 people, who rated the robot through the SUS scale, obtaining a result of 82.5. This allows us to conclude that the robot has acceptable usability, that is, it complies with the parameters of effectiveness, efficiency and ease of use.

References

1. Abdollahi, H., et al.: A pilot study on using an intelligent life-like robot as a companion for elderly individuals with dementia and depression, pp. 541–546 (2017). https://doi.org/10.1109/HUMANOIDS.2017.8246925
2. Assistant Secretary for Public Affairs, July 2013. https://www.usability.gov/
3. Breazeal, C.: Toward sociable robots. Rob. Auton. Syst. **42**(3–4), 167–175 (2003)
4. van Breemen, A., Yan, X., Meerbeek, B.: iCat: an animated user-interface robot with personality, pp. 143–144, January 2005. https://doi.org/10.1145/1082473.1082823
5. Chaminade, T., et al.: Motor interference between humans and humanoid robots: effect of biological and artificial motion, pp. 96–101, August 2005. ISBN: 0-7803-9226-4. https://doi.org/10.1109/DEVLRN.2005.1490951
6. Delaunay, F.: A retro-projected robotic head for social human-robot interaction. Ph.D. thesis, October 2015

7. Delaunay, F., Belpaeme, T.: Refined human-robot interaction through retro-projected robotic heads, pp. 106–107, May 2012. https://doi.org/10.1109/ARSO.2012.6213409

8. Duffy, B., et al.: Social robot architecture: a framework for explicit social interaction, January 2005

9. Espinoza E., N.A., Almeida G, R.P., Escobar, L., Loza, D.: Development of a social robot NAR for children's education. In: Botto-Tobar, M., León-Acurio, J., Díaz Cadena, A., Montiel Díaz, P. (eds.) ICAETT 2019. AISC, vol. 1067, pp. 357–368. Springer, Cham (2020). https://doi.org/10.1007/978-3-030-32033-1_33

10. Blender Foundation: Home of the Blender project - Free and Open 3D Creation Software. https://www.blender.org/

11. Alonso, S.G., et al.: Social robots for people with aging and dementia: a systematic review of literature. Telemedicine e-Health **25**(7), 533–540 (2019). PMID: 30136901. https://doi.org/10.1089/tmj.2018.0051

12. Hashimoto, M., Kondo, H., Tamatsu, Y.: Gaze guidance using a facial expression robot. Adv. Rob. **23** (2009). https://doi.org/10.1163/016918609X12518783330162

13. Karahalios, K., Dobson, K.: Chit chat club: bridging virtual and physical space for social interaction, pp. 1957–1960 (2005). https://doi.org/10.1145/1056808.1057066

14. Kaya, A., Ozturk, R., Altin Gumussoy, C.: Usability measurement of mobile applications with system usability scale (SUS). In: Calisir, F., Cevikcan, E., Camgoz Akdag, H. (eds.) Industrial Engineering in the Big Data Era. LNMIE, pp. 389–400. Springer, Cham (2019). https://doi.org/10.1007/978-3-030-03317-0_32

15. Kukulska-Hulme, A.: Intelligent assistants in language learning: friends or foes? In: Proceedings of World Conference on Mobile and Contextual Learning 2019, p. 20, July 2019

16. Kuratate, T., et al.: "Mask-bot": a life-size robot head using talking head animation for human-robot communication, pp. 99–104, October 2011. https://doi.org/10.1109/Humanoids.2011.6100842

17. Nishio, S., Ishiguro, H., Hagita, N.: Geminoid: teleoperated android of an existing per- son, June 2007. ISBN: 978-3-902613-00-4.10.5772/4876

18. Marks, P.: Robot head disguises itself as your friends. In: New Scientist 221, p. 20, March 2014

19. Oh, J., et al.: Design of android type humanoid robot albert HUBO. In: 2006 IEEE/RSJ International Conference on Intelligent Robots and Systems, pp. 1428–1433 (2006)

20. Salvador, M., Silver, S., Mahoor, M.: An emotion recognition comparative study of autistic and typically-developing children using the Zeno robot. In: Proceedings - IEEE International Conference on Robotics and Automation 2015, pp. 6128–6133, June 2015. https://doi.org/10.1109/ICRA.2015.7140059

21. Simmons, R., et al.: Grace: an autonomous robot for the AAAI robot challenge. AI Mag. **24**, 51–72 (2003)

Energy Harvesting: Energy Sources, Excitation Type and Conversion Mechanisms

M. A. Duran-Sarmiento[1,3]($\boxtimes$) , C. Borras-Pinilla[2] ,
and L. A. Del Portillo-Valdes[2]

[1] Unidades Tecnológicas de Santander, Bucaramanga 680005, Colombia
aduran@correo.uts.edu.co
[2] Industrial University of Santander, Bucaramanga 680002, Colombia
[3] University of the Basque Country, 20018 Vizcaya, Spain

Abstract. The growing demand for energy has led to technological developments focused on the transformation of energy from renewable sources, where strategies capable of converting energy efficiently according to the nature of the energy have emerged. This paper presents a classification of energy sources, excitation types and energy conversion mechanisms used in energy harvesting.

Keywords: Energy · Harvesting · Conversion

1 Introduction

Currently, the growing world population puts pressure on land use due to the increasing demand for food in world markets and energy production to satisfy the human consumption of more than 8600 million people estimated for the year 2030, expecting by 2050 a 60% growth for the inhabitants of megacities[1] [1].

These pressures lead to economic impacts and increased environmental risks due to the impact on the climate change category, considering that by 2016 the CO_2 content in the atmosphere reached its highest level in recent history [2]. New models of renewable energy and food production are needed to simultaneously decrease greenhouse gas (GHG) emissions, use land more efficiently and replace large amounts of fossil fuels.

The strategies for harvesting energy vary depending on the type of excitation and conversion mechanisms, these strategies can be implemented in various applications, from the environmental scale such as ocean and wind energy, structures, machines and the movement of the human body [3].

This paper presents an overview of the strategies currently used for energy harvesting, classifying them according to their energy source, their type of excitation and the mechanisms used in energy transformation.

---

[1] With more tan 10 million population.

2 Energy Harvesting

The use of energy from various sources must be sustainable, environmentally friendly and has become one of the great challenges in the world, taking into consideration that some traditional sources of energy such as oil, coal and gas, are agents that contribute to the production of greenhouse gases, climate change and pollution [4].

Energy harvesting promises to be a viable solution to current and future problems related to the responsible use of energy and its impact on the environment. The following is a classification of energy harvesting strategies according to energy sources, type of excitation and energy conversion mechanisms (Fig. 1).

Energy Harvesting
Energy Sources
Excitation Type
Energy Conversion Mechanisms

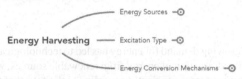

Fig. 1. Energy harvesting classification.

2.1 Energy Sources

Energy sources can be classified if they come from a natural phenomenon and have not been transformed like primary energy. (Sun energy [4], biomass [5], wave energy [6], wind energy [7] and others) or if they are the result of some intentional transformation of the primary ones, called secondary ones. The following are some types of energy (primary and secondary) where strategies and devices capable of collecting energy have been implemented and where they are classified according to their nature (Fig. 2).

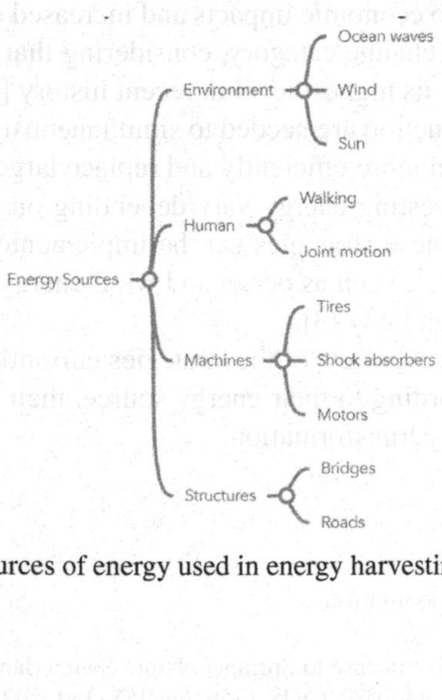

Energy Sources
Environment
Ocean waves
Wind
Sun
Human
Walking
Joint motion
Machines
Tires
Shock absorbers
Motors
Structures
Bridges
Roads

Fig. 2. Sources of energy used in energy harvesting systems.

2.1.1 Environment

Wave Energy

Ping Cheng et al. [8] uses a soft-contact spherical triboelectric nano-generator made with a spherical acrylic shell, two copper foil electrodes and a silicon sphere with water inside, in order to provide a larger contac-to surface. The simulations yielded higher charge and voltage for an excitation frequency of 2 Hz (110 nC and 280 V) with a displacement of 50 mm. The diameters of the acrylic and silicon spheres are 7 and 5 cm respectively.

Steven L Zhang et al. [9] develops a triboelectric nano-generator based on rolling electrification and uses the Pelamis energy harvesting mechanism, the maximum power density achieved was 3 W/m^3, Li Min Zhang et al. [10] presents a dodecahedron structure with twelve layers (wave-shaped copper-kapton-copper) of triboelectric nano-generators. The output characteristics at different wave radii and kapton layer thickness were compared for a 0.64 MW average on a surface of 1 km^2 at a depth of 5 m. The 2 mm wave radius configuration and 25 μm thickness has the best results.

Solar Energy

Yusuf Shi et al. [4]The photothermal three-dimensional cylindrical structure is implemented to recover the diffuse reflection and thermal radiation lost by a two-dimensional structure. This two-dimensional structure uses a material with high sunlight absorption. Twenty mixtures of metal oxide (MMO) were tested. This material (MMO) has high stability under strong sunlight. The test results showed that the cylindrical system recovered diffuse reflection and thermal radiation. George Ni et al. [11] implemented a receiver with a variety of available low cost materials that can generate saturated steam at 100 °C. The model used generates steam more economically than with solar concentrators at a cost of approximately US $6/m^2, which can be reduced in the future to about US $2/m^2, compared to the cost of solar concentrators that can reach up to US $200/m^2.

Wind Energy

Muhammad Iqbal, Farid Ullah Khan [11] proposes a hybrid model capable of converting the low vibration frequencies of bridges and ambient air currents into energy using piezoelectric and electromagnetic mechanisms. The device has three resonance frequencies at 12.5, 34 and 45 Hz. The 12.5 Hz frequency corresponds to the upper beam, the 34 Hz frequency corresponds to the magnet and airfoil assembly, and the 45 Hz frequency corresponds to the lower beam. The maximum voltage obtained was 401 mV and a power of 2214.32 μW for the electromagnetic part, the maximum voltage and maximum power for the piezoelectric part were 6279 mV and 155.7 μW. It is suggested to implement a rectifier circuit and fatigue analysis on the beams in the prototype.

2.1.2 Human

From the natural movement and heat given off by human beings, such as walking, daily activities, and even facial expressions, part of this energy can be transformed into useful energy [12].

Xiong Pu et al. [13] presents the development of a textile composed of two units, a generator (triboelectric nano generator) and a storage unit (super capacitor). The composition of the textile has a nickel layer and a graphene oxide reduction film, covered with wool that acts as a super capacitor (13.0 mF/cm, 72.1 mF/cm^2), presenting 96% stability for 10000 cycles. The polyester (wool) has a diameter of 500 μm and a resistance of 1.48 Ω/cm. The surface power density achieved was 2.42 mW/cm^2.

2.1.3 Machines

Machines in general involve a considerable consumption of energy, in some cases the energy is used in unnecessary displacements or in which it is not possible to take advantage of the work done by these forces in those displacements, some methods have been developed to transform part of this energy into usable energy. [14].

Jaeyun Lee and Bumkyoo Choi developed a piezoelectric nano generator inside the vehicle's tires. The tire used is a conventional one (komho Co., 235/60 R18) and the piezoelectric has a surface area of 10 mm * 60 mm. The actual tests characterized the loads on each wheel with the vehicle in motion (456 kgf, 484 kgf, 606 kgf and 597 kgf). The piezoelectric generated 380.2 μJ per revolution under a load of 500 kgf. The power density in this mechanism was 1.37 μW/mm^3, which makes it feasible for application in wireless sensors.

2.1.4 Structures

Structures generally remain immobile, at rest or in equilibrium. In some cases, small deformations occur that can be translated into usable energy by means of various mechanisms that will be explained below [15].

Paul Cahill et al. [16] implements a piezoelectric device driven by forced dynamic excitations in a bridge. The piezoelectrics have cantilever beam arrangement and have been calibrated with sine loads in the laboratory. The acceleration response for the tests yielded peak accelerations of 0.34 m/s^2 and 0.63 m/s^2, as well as occasional peaks due to the passage of trains at the time of the test, with a maximum peak of 1.81 m/s^2.

Other work related to energy harvesting, depending on its sources (Table 1):

Table 1. Energy sources articles

Energy source	Title
Environment	Largely enhanced triboelectric nanogenerator for efficient harvesting of water wave energy by soft contacted structure [8]
	Self-powered intelligent buoy system by water wave energy for sustainable and autonomous wireless sensing and data transmission [17]
	Spring-Assisted Triboelectric Nanogenerator for Efficiently Harvesting Water Wave Energy [18]
	Wave energy device and breakwater integration: A review[19]
	Rationally designed sea snake structure based triboelectric nanogenerators for effectively and efficiently harvesting ocean wave energy with minimized water screening effect [9]
	Ocean wave energy harvesting with a piezoelectric coupled buoy structure [20]

(*continued*)

Table 1. (*continued*)

Energy source	Title
	Self-cleaning hybrid energy harvester to generate power from raindrop and sunlight [21]
Human	Piezoelectric energy harvesters for biomedical applications [22]
	Fiber-Based Energy Conversion Devices for Human-Body Energy Harvesting [12]
	Optimizing orientation of piezoelectric cantilever beam for harvesting energy from human walking [23]
	Shape Memory Polymers for Body Motion Energy Harvesting and Self-Powered Mechanosensing [24]
	Impact of contact pressure on output voltage of triboelectric nanogenerator based on deformation of interfacial structures [25]
Machines	Energy-harvesting potential of automobile suspension [26]
	Development of a piezoelectric energy harvesting system for implementing wireless sensors on the tires [27]
	A novel approach to energy harvesting from vehicle suspension system: Half-vehicle model [28]
	Energy harvesting sensitivity analysis and assessment of the potential power and full car dynamics for different road modes [29]
Structures	Vibration energy harvesting based monitoring of an operational bridge undergoing forced vibration and train passage [16]
	Energy harvesting technologies in roadway and bridge for different applications – A comprehensive review [15]
	Harvesting kinetic energy from roadway pavement through an electromagnetic speed bump [30]

2.2 Excitation Type

The type of excitation of a device is what conditions the mechanism of energy transformation, it is the final effect of the energy source that can be translated into a fluid current [31, 32], an oscillation [33], an impact or a movement [34] which may be of different nature (Fig. 3).

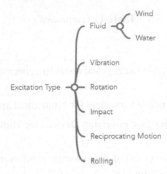

Fig. 3. Excitation type classification

2.2.1 Fluid

Dongwhi Choi et al. [35] implements a triboelectric device that uses the contact between a liquid (water) and a solid (aluminum tube with hydrophobic characteristics). The aluminum used in the device was subjected to cleaning with ethanol and deionized water, then underwent an anodization process for 6 h with oxalic acid at 70 V.

The triboelectric generation process is carried out in a manner similar to that of a syringe (initially) so that the water inside the tube can rise and fall, since when contact is made between water and a triboelectric material with negative polarity, negative charges are induced at the interface of the material and positive charges at the interface of the water.

The same mechanism was also implemented, consisting of two aluminum tubes, one of which is "bare" aluminum and the other Teflon-coated, separated by an insulator (the tubes are concentrically aligned and can store water inside, which can move freely between the two aluminum tubes, this device does not use the vacuum principle like syringes for its operation, but manual agitation), under a frequency of 13 Hz a peak current of 1.3 μA and a peak voltage of 18 V can be produced.

2.2.2 Vibration

Junlei Wang et al. [36] uses air-induced vibration on a body at the end of a piezoelectric cantilever beam. The vibration-inducing air stream is generated in a wind tunnel and the beam is subjected to vortex-induced vibration and galloping phenomena. Three different prototypes were tested on the body located at the free end of the piezoelectric cantilever beam and four angles of attack for the wind to determine their influence. The geometry of the body consists of cuboid and cylinder segments (the cuboid is used to generate galloping and the cylinder is used to generate vorticity induced vibration). The mathematical model was successfully validated with an experimental test.

2.2.3 Rotation

Kangqi Fan et al. [37] uses linear reciprocating displacement to generate rotational motion by means of a rotor driven by two ropes.

The rotor is 15 mm in diameter and 6 mm thick and is contained within a tube with an internal diameter of 18 mm and a length of 51 mm. The ropes are made of polyester and are 0.2 mm in diameter. The experimental tests were developed taking into account the movement of the arms and legs in a person, as a source of energy, with direct actuation from the hands (i.e. pulling the device) and also with the vibrations produced on a ca-mining belt. The results obtained yielded 3.4 mW for arm movement (natural movement), 4.9 mW for leg movement, 15.9 mW for direct actuation with the hands, and 5.4 mW with treadmill vibration.

2.2.4 Rolling

Yanchao Mao et al. [38] presents the design of a single-electrode triboelectric nano generator with the purpose of harnessing the energy of vehicle tires. It is shown that the output power depends on the speed and the load on the wheel. The maximum instantaneous power obtained was 179 mW with a resistance of 10 MΩ, obtaining a conversion efficiency of 10.4%. The 1 cm $\times$ 1 cm $\times$ 120 μm flexible triboelectric nano-generator was attached to the surface of a 7 cm diameter rubber wheel. The voltage increased from 0.3 V up to 4.2 V as the velocity increased from 0.1 m/s up to 0.5 m/s. Increasing the load also produced an increase in voltage from 2.3 V to 3.7 V with the load variation up to 2.2 kg. Under the curve fit obtained, it can be estimated that, for a 1 kg increase in load, the peak voltage increases by 0.7 V.

Other work related to energy harvesting as a function of excitation types include (Table 2).

Table 2. Excitation type articles

Excitation type	Title
Fluid	Energy harvesting model of moving water inside a tubular system and its application of a stick-type compact triboelectric nanogenerator [35]
	Effect of mass-ratio, damping, and stiffness on optimal hydrokinetic energy conversion of a single, rough cylinder in flow induced motions [39]
	Energy harvesting by means of flow-induced vibrations on aerospace vehicles [32]
Rolling	Single-electrode triboelectric nanogenerator for scavenging friction energy from rolling tires [38]
Rotation	A string-suspended and driven rotor for efficient ultra-low frequency mechanical energy harvesting [37]
	A methodology for low-speed broadband rotational energy harvesting using piezoelectric transduction and frequency up-conversion [40]

(continued)

Table 2. (*continued*)

Excitation type	Title
	Two-dimensional rotary triboelectric nanogenerator as a portable and wearable power source for electronics [41]
	Design and experimental investigation of a magnetically coupled vibration energy harvester using two inverted piezoelectric cantilever beams for rotational motion [42]
	A rotational pendulum based electromagnetic/triboelectric hybrid- generator for ultra-low-frequency vibrations aiming at human motion and blue energy applications [43]
Vibration	Hybrid wind energy scavenging by coupling vortex-induced vibrations and galloping [36]
	A comprehensive review on vibration energy harvesting: Modelling and realization [28]

2.3 Energy Conversión Mechanisms

These are the physical phenomena through which the transformation of energy takes place, in this case only those phenomena in which the final result is electrical energy are being considered (Fig. 4).

- Piezoelectricity: A physical phenomenon by which mechanically stressed crystals generate potential differences [33].
- Electromagnetism: Describes the interaction of charged particles with electric and magnetic fields [44].
- Triboelectricity: It is called triboelectricity (from the Greek tribein, "to rub" and ἤλεκτρον, electron, "amber") to the phenomenon of electrifi-cation by rubbing. Electrostatics can be produced by rubbing or by electrostatic induction (not to be confused with electromagnetic induction) [45].
- Thermoelectricity: Thermoelectricity is any form of electricity generation through the use of heat, which is used to generate steam, the pressure of which feeds the movement of a turbine that, connected to a generator, transforms this mechanical energy into electricity [46–48].
- Pyroelectricity: Electrical charge on the surface of certain crystals, such as tourmaline, topaz, tartaric acid, etc., when subjected to temperature variation [49, 50].
- Photovoltaic: Photovoltaic energy is the direct transformation of solar radiation into electricity. This transformation takes place in devices called photovoltaic panels [51,52]

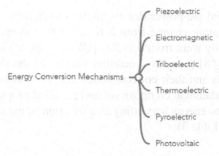

Fig. 4. Energy conversion mechanisms classification.

2.3.1 Piezoelectric

Junlei Wang et al. [53] analytically and experimentally compares the effect of a "Y" shaped attachment to the body (cylinder) subjected to aerodynamic load, the use of the attachment causes the aerodynamic face to produce the "galloping" phenomenon and without the attachment there is vibration induced by vorticity. For the vorticity-induced vibration it has an optimum operating speed range between 1 m/s and 1.42 m/s, while for the "galloping" phenomenon it is for speeds higher than 1.28 m/s.

2.3.2 Electromagnetic

Wei Wang et al. [54] used an adjustable magnetic spring to harvest energy through an electromagnetic device. The device consists of a tube with two fixed magnets at its ends and a set of moving magnets inside. By adjusting the mass of the moving magnet assembly and the effective length of movement, the resonant frequency can be adjusted to the movement of the human body. The maximum voltage at a harmonic excitation of 9.155 Hz was 0.86 V.

Yiming Cao et al. [55] models photovoltaic cells with titanium oxide (TiO2) films achieving an efficiency of 13.21% under solar radiation of 100 mW/cm^2 (sunlight) and 32% for ambient light (1000 lux).

2.3.3 Triboelectric

Kai Dong et al. [56] develops a stretchable and washable triboelectric nano-generator for use in energy harvesting and as a pressure sensor. It is fabricated as a network of silver-coated nylon conductive wires and a silicon membrane.

The maximum power density obtained was 230 mW/m^2. The device has the ability to monitor pressure as well as pulsations in real time. It highlights the ability to recognize vocalization signals according to the monitoring of the muscles used when speaking.

2.3.4 Thermoeléctric

Jing Liu et al. [57] obtained hydrogel fibers under the process of gelation and subsequent treatment with organic solvents, such material has the ability to convert heat into electricity when there is a temperature difference. The results of the experimental tests show that both the voltage and the power density increase when the temperature difference increases, for a temperature change from 5 K to 60 K, voltage went from 2.4 mV to 21 mV and power density went from 0 to 500 μW/cm^2 approximately.

Yuan Wang et al. [58] presents a detailed review of the development of flexible thermoelectric materials and their collection devices, also relating the performance of such materials to their chemical composition and physical properties.

Other work related to energy harvesting as a function of the conversion mechanisms include the following (Table 3):

Table 3. Energy conversion mechanisms

Conversion mechanism	Title
Electromagnetic	Thermally Driven Transport and Relaxation Switching Self-Powered Electromagnetic Energy Conversion [59]
	Magnetic-spring based energy harvesting from human motions: Design, modeling and experiments [54]
	Scaling and power density metrics of electromagnetic vibration energy harvesting devices [60]
Photovoltaic	Transparent Polymer Photovoltaics for Solar Energy Harvesting and Beyond [52]
	Direct Contact of Selective Charge Extraction Layers Enables High-Efficiency Molecular Photovoltaics [55]
	Enhanced photovoltaic energy conversion using thermally based spectral shaping [51]
Piezoelec	High-Performance Piezoelectric Energy Harvesters and Their Applications [61]
	Flexible Nanogenerators for Energy Harvesting and Self-Powered Electronics [62]
	High-performance piezoelectric wind energy harvester with Y-shaped attachments [53]
Thermoele	Flexible Thermoelectric Materials and Generators: Challenges and Innovations. [58]
	Highly Conductive Hydrogel Polymer Fibers toward Promising Wearable Thermoelectric Energy Harvesting [57]
	Flexible thermoelectric materials and devices [47]
Triboelectric	Fiber/Fabric-Based Piezoelectric and Triboelectric Nanogenerators for Flexible/Stretchable and Wearable Electronics and Artificial Intelligence [63]
	A Stretchable Yarn Embedded Triboelectric Nanogenerator as Electronic Skin for Biomechanical Energy Harvesting and Multifunctional Pressure Sensing [56]

3   Conclusions

Energy harnessing can be achieved by correctly choosing the energy transformation mechanism according to the energy source. The energy potential to be transformed involves an assiduous process of identifying the relationship between the type of excitation and the transformation mechanism, e.g., rotation-electromagnetism.

The energy sources are of diverse nature, some of them depend on the operation of machinery, the use of structures or even daily activities, others do not even depend on the seasons as in the case of the energy coming from the waves of the sea.

Excitation methods go hand in hand with transformation mechanisms, where devices capable of using such excitation in energy transformation were found.

The document presented grouped various energy transformation strategies and classified them according to the nature, characteristics, type of excitation and conversion mechanism, providing an overview of the technologies used in energy harvesting.

References

1. Facchini, A., Kennedy, C., Stewart, I., Mele, R.: The energy metabolism of megacities. Appl. Energy **186**(2017), 86–95 (2017). https://doi.org/10.1016/j.apenergy.2016.09.025
2. Magazzino, C., Mele, M., Schneider, N.: A machine learning approach on the relationship among solar and wind energy production, coal consumption, GDP, and CO2 emissions. Renew. Energy **167**, 99–115 (2021). https://doi.org/10.1016/j.renene.2020.11.050
3. Zou, H.X., et al.: Mechanical modulations for enhancing energy harvesting: principles, methods and applications. Appl. Energy **255**, 113871 (2019). https://doi.org/10.1016/j.apenergy.2019.113871
4. Shi, Y., et al.: A 3D photothermal structure toward improved energy efficiency in solar steam generation. Joule **2**(6), 1171–1186 (2018). https://doi.org/10.1016/j.joule.2018.03.013
5. Moharamian, A., Soltani, S., Rosen, M.A., Mahmoudi, S.M.S., Morosuk, T.: A comparative thermoeconomic evaluation of three biomass and biomass-natural gas fired combined cycles using organic Rankine cycles. J. Clean. Prod. **161**, 524–544 (2017). https://doi.org/10.1016/j.jclepro.2017.05.174
6. Pang, Y., Chen, S., Chu, Y., Wang, Z.L., Cao, C.: Matryoshka-inspired hierarchically structured triboelectric nanogenerators for wave energy harvesting. Nano Energy **66**, 104131 (2019). https://doi.org/10.1016/j.nanoen.2019.104131
7. Chen, B., Yang, Y., Wang, Z.L.: Scavenging wind energy by triboelectric nanogenerators. Adv. Energy Mater **8**(10), 1–13 (2018). https://doi.org/10.1002/aenm.201702649
8. Cheng, P., et al.: Largely enhanced triboelectric nanogenerator for efficient harvesting of water wave energy by soft contacted structure. Nano Energy **57**, 432–439 (2019). https://doi.org/10.1016/j.nanoen.2018.12.054
9. Zhang, S.L., et al.: Rationally designed sea snake structure based triboelectric nanogenerators for effectively and efficiently harvesting ocean wave energy with minimized water screening effect. Nano Energy **48**, 421–429 (2018). https://doi.org/10.1016/j.nanoen.2018.03.062
10. Zhang, L.M., et al.: Multilayer wavy-structured robust triboelectric nanogenerator for harvesting water wave energy. Nano Energy **22**, 87–94 (2016). https://doi.org/10.1016/j.nanoen.2016.01.009

11. Iqbal, M., Khan, F.U.: Hybrid vibration and wind energy harvesting using combined piezo-electric and electromagnetic conversion for bridge health monitoring applications. Energy Conv. Manag. **172**, 611–618 (2018). https://doi.org/10.1016/j.enconman.2018.07.044

12. Huang, L., et al.: Fiber-based energy conversion devices for human-body energy harvesting. Adv. Mater. **32**(5), 1–20 (2020). https://doi.org/10.1002/adma.201902034

13. Pu, X., et al.: Wearable self-charging power textile based on flexible yarn supercapacitors and fabric nanogenerators. Adv. Mater. **28**(1), 98–105 (2016). https://doi.org/10.1002/adma.201504403

14. Zou, J., Guo, X., Abdelkareem, M.A.A., Xu, L., Zhang, J.: Modelling and ride analysis of a hydraulic interconnected suspension based on the hydraulic energy regenerative shock absorbers. Mech. Syst. Signal Process. **127**, 345–369 (2019). https://doi.org/10.1016/j.ymssp.2019.02.047

15. Wang, H., Jasim, A., Chen, X.: Energy harvesting technologies in roadway and bridge for different applications – a comprehensive review. Appl. Energy **212**, 1083–1094 (2018). https://doi.org/10.1016/j.apenergy.2017.12.125

16. Cahill, P., Hazra, B., Karoumi, R., Mathewson, A., Pakrashi, V.: Vibration energy harvesting based monitoring of an operational bridge undergoing forced vibration and train passage. Mech. Syst. Signal Process. **106**, 265–283 (2018). https://doi.org/10.1016/j.ymssp.2018.01.007

17. Xi, F., et al.: Self-powered intelligent buoy system by water wave energy for sustainable and autonomous wireless sensing and data transmission. Nano Energy **61**, 1–9 (2019). https://doi.org/10.1016/j.nanoen.2019.04.026

18. Jiang, T., Yao, Y., Xu, L., Zhang, L., Xiao, T., Wang, Z.L.: Spring-assisted triboelectric nanogenerator for efficiently harvesting water wave energy. Nano Energy **31**, 560–567 (2017). https://doi.org/10.1016/j.nanoen.2016.12.004

19. Mustapa, M.A., Yaakob, O.B., Ahmed, Y.M., Rheem, C.K., Koh, K.K., Adnan, F.A.: Wave energy device and breakwater integration: a review. Renew. Sustain. Energy Rev. **77**, 43–58 (2017). https://doi.org/10.1016/j.rser.2017.03.110

20. Wu, N., Wang, Q., Xie, X.D.: Ocean wave energy harvesting with a piezoelectric coupled buoy structure. Appl. Ocean Res. **50**, 110–118 (2015). https://doi.org/10.1016/j.apor.2015.01.004

21. Jeon, S.B., Kim, D., Yoon, G.W., Yoon, J.B., Choi, Y.K.: Self-cleaning hybrid energy harvester to generate power from raindrop and sunlight. Nano Energy **12**, 636–645 (2015). https://doi.org/10.1016/j.nanoen.2015.01.039

22. Ali, F., Raza, W., Li, X., Gul, H., Kim, K.H.: Piezoelectric energy harvesters for biomedical applications. Nano Energy **57**, 879–902 (2019). https://doi.org/10.1016/j.nanoen.2019.01.012

23. Izadgoshasb, I., Lim, Y.Y., Lake, N., Tang, L., Padilla, R.V., Kashiwao, T.: Optimizing orientation of piezoelectric cantilever beam for harvesting energy from human walking. Energy Conv. Manag. **161**, 66–73 (2018). https://doi.org/10.1016/j.enconman.2018.01.076

24. Liu, R., et al.: Shape memory polymers for body motion energy harvesting and self-powered mechanosensing. Adv. Mater. **30**(8), 1–8 (2018). https://doi.org/10.1002/adma.201705195

25. Seol, M.L., Lee, S.H., Han, J.W., Kim, D., Cho, G.H., Choi, Y.K.: Impact of contact pressure on output voltage of triboelectric nanogenerator based on deformation of interfacial structures. Nano Energy **17**, 63–71 (2015). https://doi.org/10.1016/j.nanoen.2015.08.005

26. Múčka, P.: Energy-harvesting potential of automobile suspension. Veh. Syst. Dyn. **54**(12), 1651–1670 (2016). https://doi.org/10.1080/00423114.2016.1227077

27. Lee, J., Choi, B.: Development of a piezoelectric energy harvesting system for implementing wireless sensors on the tires. Energy Conv. Manag. **78**, 32–38 (2014). https://doi.org/10.1016/j.enconman.2013.09.054

28. Wei, C., Jing, X.: A comprehensive review on vibration energy harvesting: modelling and realization. Renew. Sustain. Energy Rev. **74**, 1–18 (2017). https://doi.org/10.1016/j.rser.2017. 01.073

29. Abdelkareem, M.A.A., et al.: Energy harvesting sensitivity analysis and assessment of the potential power and full car dynamics for different road modes. Mech Syst Signal Process **110**, 307–332 (2018). https://doi.org/10.1016/j.ymssp.2018.03.009

30. Gholikhani, M., Nasouri, R., Tahami, S.A., Legette, S., Dessouky, S., Montoya, A.: Harvesting kinetic energy from roadway pavement through an electromagnetic speed bump. Appl. Energy **250**, 503–511 (2019). https://doi.org/10.1016/j.apenergy.2019.05.060

31. Seol, M.L., et al.: Vertically stacked thin triboelectric nanogenerator for wind energy harvesting. Nano Energy **14**, 201–208 (2015). https://doi.org/10.1016/j.nanoen.2014.11.016

32. Li, D., Wu, Y., da Ronch, A., Xiang, J.: Energy harvesting by means of flow-induced vibrations on aerospace vehicles. Prog. Aerosp. Sci. **86**, 28–62 (2016). https://doi.org/10.1016/j.paerosci. 2016.08.001

33. Toyabur, R.M., Salauddin, M., Cho, H., Park, J.Y.: A multimodal hybrid energy harvester based on piezoelectric-electromagnetic mechanisms for low-frequency ambient vibrations. Energy Conv. Manag. **168**, 454–466 (2018). https://doi.org/10.1016/j.enconman.2018.05.018

34. Azam, A., et al.: Design, fabrication, modelling and analyses of a movable speed bump-based mechanical energy harvester (MEH) for application on road. Energy **214**, 118894 (2021). https://doi.org/10.1016/j.energy.2020.118894

35. Choi, D., Lee, S., Park, S.M., Cho, H., Hwang, W., Kim, D.S.: Energy harvesting model of moving water inside a tubular system and its application of a stick-type compact triboelectric nanogenerator. Nano Res. **8**(8), 2481–2491 (2015). https://doi.org/10.1007/s12274-015-0756-4

36. Wang, J., et al.: Hybrid wind energy scavenging by coupling vortex-induced vibrations and galloping. Energy Conv. Manag. **213**, 112835 (2020). https://doi.org/10.1016/j.enconman. 2020.112835

37. Fan, K., et al.: A string-suspended and driven rotor for efficient ultra-low frequency mechanical energy harvesting. Energy Conv. Manag. **198**, 111820 (2019). https://doi.org/10.1016/j.enc onman.2019.111820

38. Mao, Y., Geng, D., Liang, E., Wang, X.: Single-electrode triboelectric nanogenerator for scavenging friction energy from rolling tires. Nano Energy **15**, 227–234 (2015). https://doi. org/10.1016/j.nanoen.2015.04.026

39. Sun, H., Kim, E.S., Nowakowski, G., Mauer, E., Bernitsas, M.M.: Effect of mass-ratio, damping, and stiffness on optimal hydrokinetic energy conversion of a single, rough cylinder in flow induced motions. Renew. Energy **99**, 936–959 (2016). https://doi.org/10.1016/j.renene. 2016.07.024

40. Fu, H., Yeatman, E.M.: A methodology for low-speed broadband rotational energy harvesting using piezoelectric transduction and frequency up-conversion. Energy **125**, 152–161 (2017). https://doi.org/10.1016/j.energy.2017.02.115

41. Kuang, S.Y., Chen, J., Cheng, X.B., Zhu, G., Wang, Z.L.: Two-dimensional rotary triboelectric nanogenerator as a portable and wearable power source for electronics. Nano Energy **17**, 10–16 (2015). https://doi.org/10.1016/j.nanoen.2015.07.011

42. Zou, H.X., et al.: Design and experimental investigation of a magnetically coupled vibration energy harvester using two inverted piezoelectric cantilever beams for rotational motion. Energy Conv. Manag. **148**, 1391–1398 (2017). https://doi.org/10.1016/j.enconman.2017. 07.005

43. Hou, C., et al.: A rotational pendulum based electromagnetic/triboelectric hybrid-generator for ultra-low-frequency vibrations aiming at human motion and blue energy applications. Nano Energy **63**, 103871 (2019). https://doi.org/10.1016/j.nanoen.2019.103871

44. Gholikhani, M., Shirazi, S.Y.B., Mabrouk, G.M., Dessouky, S.: Dual electromagnetic energy harvesting technology for sustainable transportation systems. Energy Conv. Manag. **230**, 11380 (2021). https://doi.org/10.1016/j.enconman.2020.113804
45. He, J., et al.: Triboelectric-piezoelectric-electromagnetic hybrid nanogenerator for high-efficient vibration energy harvesting and self-powered wireless monitoring system. Nano Energy **43**, 326–339 (2018). https://doi.org/10.1016/j.nanoen.2017.11.039
46. Dehkordi, A.M., Zebarjadi, M., He, J., Tritt, T.M.: Thermoelectric power factor: enhancement mechanisms and strategies for higher performance thermoelectric materials. Mater. Sci. Eng. R Rep. **97**, 1–22 (2015). https://doi.org/10.1016/j.mser.2015.08.001
47. Du, Y., Xu, J., Paul, B., Eklund, P.: Flexible thermoelectric materials and devices. Appl. Mater. Today **12**, 366–388 (2018). https://doi.org/10.1016/j.apmt.2018.07.004
48. Kim, T.Y., Negash, A.A., Cho, G.: Waste heat recovery of a diesel engine using a thermo-electric generator equipped with customized thermoelectric modules. Energy Conv. Manag. **124**, 280–286 (2016). https://doi.org/10.1016/j.enconman.2016.07.013
49. Zi, Y., et al.: Triboelectric-pyroelectric-piezoelectric hybrid cell for high-efficiency energy-harvesting and self-powered sensing. Adv. Mater. **27**(14), 2340–2347 (2015). https://doi.org/10.1002/adma.201500121
50. Wang, S., Wang, Z.L., Yang, Y.: A one-structure-based hybridized nanogenerator for scavenging mechanical and thermal energies by triboelectric-piezoelectric-pyroelectric effects. Adv. Mater. **28**(15), 2881–2887 (2016). https://doi.org/10.1002/adma.201505684
51. Bierman, D.M., et al.: Enhanced photovoltaic energy conversion using thermally based spectral shaping. Nat. Energy **1**(6) (2016). https://doi.org/10.1038/nenergy.2016.68
52. Chang, S.Y., Cheng, P., Li, G., Yang, Y.: Transparent polymer photovoltaics for solar energy harvesting and beyond. Joule **2**(6), 1039–1054 (2018). https://doi.org/10.1016/j.joule.2018.04.005
53. Wang, J., Zhou, S., Zhang, Z., Yurchenko, D.: High-performance piezoelectric wind energy harvester with Y-shaped attachments. Energy Convers Manag **181**, 645–652 (2019). https://doi.org/10.1016/j.enconman.2018.12.034
54. Wang, W., Cao, J., Zhang, N., Lin, J., Liao, W.H.: Magnetic-spring based energy harvesting from human motions: design, modeling and experiments. Energy Conv. Manag. **132**, 189–197 (2017). https://doi.org/10.1016/j.enconman.2016.11.026
55. Cao, Y., Liu, Y., Zakeeruddin, S.M., Hagfeldt, A., Grätzel, M.: Direct contact of selective charge extraction layers enables high-efficiency molecular photovoltaics. Joule **2**(6), 1108–1117 (2018). https://doi.org/10.1016/j.joule.2018.03.017
56. Dong, K., et al.: A stretchable yarn embedded triboelectric nanogenerator as electronic skin for biomechanical energy harvesting and multifunctional pressure sensing. Adv. Mater. **30**(43), 1–12 (2018). https://doi.org/10.1002/adma.201804944
57. Liu, J., et al.: Highly conductive hydrogel polymer fibers toward promising wearable thermo-electric energy harvesting. ACS Appl. Mater. Interfaces **10**(50), 44033–44040 (2018). https://doi.org/10.1021/acsami.8b15332
58. Wang, Y., et al.: Flexible thermoelectric materials and generators: challenges and innovations. Adv. Mater. **31**(29), 1–47 (2019). https://doi.org/10.1002/adma.201807916
59. Cao, M., Wang, X., Cao, W., Fang, X., Wen, B., Yuan, J.: Thermally driven transport and relaxation switching self-powered electromagnetic energy conversion. Small **14**(29), 1–8 (2018). https://doi.org/10.1002/smll.201800987
60. Moss, S.D., Payne, O.R., Hart, G.A., Ung, C.: Scaling and power density metrics of electromagnetic vibration energy harvesting devices. Smart Mater. Struct. **24**(2), 23001 (2015). https://doi.org/10.1088/0964-1726/24/2/023001
61. Yang, Z., Zhou, S., Zu, J., Inman, D.: High-performance piezoelectric energy harvesters and their applications. Joule **2**(4), 642–697 (2018). https://doi.org/10.1016/j.joule.2018.03.011

62. Fan, F.R., Tang, W., Wang, Z.L.: Flexible nanogenerators for energy harvesting and self-powered electronics. Adv. Mater. **28**(22), 4283–4305 (2016). https://doi.org/10.1002/adma.201504299
63. Dong, K., Peng, X., Wang, Z.L.: Fiber/fabric-based piezoelectric and triboelectric nanogenerators for flexible/stretchable and wearable electronics and artificial intelligence. Adv. Mater. **32**(5), 1–43 (2020). https://doi.org/10.1002/adma.201902549

Experimental Study of a Flat Solar Collector with Thermal Energy Storage, Applying Improvements Based on Bibliometric Review and CAD Simulation

A. D. Rincon-Quintero[1,2](✉) ⓘ, W. L. Rondon-Romero[1] ⓘ, J. G. Maradey-Lazaro[3] ⓘ,
O. Lengerke[1] ⓘ, C. L. Sandoval-Rodriguez[1] ⓘ, and O. A. Acosta-Cardenas[1] ⓘ

[1] Faculty of Natural Sciences and Engineering, Unidades Tecnológicas de Santander, Student Street 9-82, Bucaramanga 680005, Colombia
{arincon,wrondon,olengerke,oacosta}@correo.uts.edu.co

[2] Department of Energy Engineering, University of the Basque Country, Plaza Ingeniero Torres Quevedo n°1, 48013 Bilbao, Spain

[3] Mechatronic Engineering Program, Universidad Autónoma de Bucaramanga, Avenida 42#48-11 Cabecera del Llano, Bucaramanga 680003, Colombia
jmaradey@unab.edu.co

Abstract. The research shows the development process of a 3 m^2 flat solar collector, composed of three modules of 1 m^2 each, with labyrinth trap geometry, turbulence ridges and thermal energy storage tanks, the latter using different types of phase change materials (PCM), specifically two types of paraffins with melting points in the range of 48 to 58 °C. Additionally, one of its modules filled with motor oil.

During the first phase, a bibliometric exploration methodology is carried out with VOSviewer Software, identifying prominent technologies in the subject, which allows the design and simulation of a prototype using CAD Software. Subsequently, when implementing it, an analysis of the behavior of the vacuum collector with respect to the use of thermal energy storage is carried out, identifying the advantages in the use of PCM. Among the results, a working power close to 450 W and an approximate efficiency of 25% stand out, contrasting with the simulation, the importance of PCMs in increasing the efficiency of these devices used in different applications is concluded.

Keywords: Flat solar collector · PCM - Phase Change Materials · Thermal energy storage VOSviewer

1 Introduction

Flat solar collectors for drying food have been studied over the years [1–3] due to the simplicity to take advantage of the fundamental concepts of heat transfer, such as conduction, convection and radiation of thermal energy [4–7]. On the other hand, due to its implementation advantages, the scientific community has opportunely highlighted its usefulness, using these devices for heating the air as a moisture extracting fluid and the efficiency that contributes to the reduction of drying times and the conservation of food products [8].

With the recent social challenges that have been framed in the replacement of fossil energies, solar energy and its capture through flat solar collectors, have become a remarkable technology to be developed in an important industry such as the production of food. Despite the frequent research and academic achievements found in the specialized literature in the last decade, these advances are not evident in the productive use of small and medium-scale farmers [6, 7].

In this technological development work, a methodology for accelerated bibliographic exploration and implementation of concepts that contribute to improving the efficiency of food drying, using flat collectors, is established. In this sense, two fundamental principles are established:

First, the design of the collector layout and configuration, which refers to the mechanisms used to improve heat convection between the absorber plate and the surrounding air inside the collector [11–13]. Designs that have favored this thermal behavior have shown progress in improving device efficiency [14–16].

Second, the use of the phase change material (PCM), whose contribution is oriented as a thermal energy store, additionally contributes to the stabilization of the temperature, maintaining the specific ranges of the process. In the exploration of the bibliography, different proposed materials are found that cover both sensible and latent heat and some alternatives of how they should be coupled to the solar collector or within the drying system [17–21].

On the other hand, to apply these principles, the use of a computational simulation that shows the behavior of the fluids used in the development of the collector is required, which requires an establishment of the operating conditions and the thermal properties of the participating elements. In addition, with the construction and operation of the air heating system with energy storage, it was possible to extract a series of data, including thermodynamic properties, to later be processed and graphed in the results section.

2   Materials and Methods

2.1   Bibliometrics Applied to Solar Collectors with Thermal Storage Used in Food Drying

In the bibliographic exploration, a work methodology is implemented using specialized software in bibliometric networks called VOSviewer. The topic of interest is the sustainable drying of food in rural areas and in preliminary reviews, the flat solar collector was established as a sustainable equipment that increases drying efficiency due to the use of heat transfer concepts. Additionally, as an improvement to the process, the storage of thermal energy has been proposed to extend the drying times, seeking to continue the process during night hours or cloudy hours. The search words implemented were "dry* AND thermal storage AND collector". With this fence of information, data analysis is carried out through software, elaborating the corresponding bibliographic networks that allow having a clearer image of the progress of this technology, for this document the following networks are exposed [22].

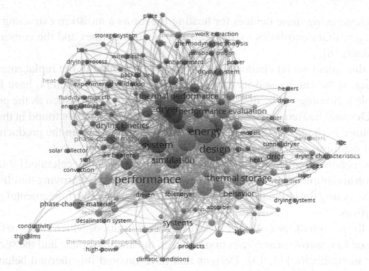

Fig. 1. Keyword co-occurrence map (155 nodes, 3 groups, 1704 links)

With this network (see Fig. 1) of 155 keywords that have at least 2 matches within the articles, it is possible to show the content of the studies of the documents. Three general lines of research are established in the network, the first and broadest focuses on drying, linked to issues such as systems, simulations, thermal efficiency and the analysis of the drying process, which is mainly divided into two stages: surface drying that is the most accelerated and internal drying, which requires more elaborate processes such as movement, or prolonged times at constant temperatures that encourage the movement of water particles outside the product to be extracted by the surrounding air.

The second line of research focuses on design, energy and storage. In this an approach is made to the study of the dryers taking into account the energy consumed, the constant improvement of the systems, analyzing the behavior of the air that is the main fluid used in the drying of food, the construction methods, materials among others aspects to consider when designing a drying cycle using the sun with collectors.

The third line of research focuses on solar thermal collectors, efficiency and energy storage. Being this last line the one of greater interest for the project, for having the most important topics for the design of the collector. It highlights key words such as changes in phase of state, conductivity, technologies, climatic conditions and other important characteristics for the construction of a solar collector used in food drying.

2.2 Solar Collector Characteristics

One of the first and most outstanding documents of interest for this research is the one carried out by [23] where it is established how there are different types of solar collectors used for the absorption of solar radiation, going from collectors not concentrators such as the flat solar collector, which takes advantage of the sun's direct radiation to heat fluids using metals or other materials analyzed in the academy; to concentrators that use mirrors to direct the radiation and concentrate it in a point or area, achieving higher temperatures and improvements in the efficiency of the system. On the other hand, advances in the design of solar systems for food drying have as their main value that this activity consumes about 25% of the energy needed in food production at an industrial level [24]. For this reason, they emphasize that the implementation of these becomes a necessary contribution to the future of humanity in terms of climate change. Regarding systems with energy storage [23] and [25], recommend the application of Phase Change Materials (PCM), because with this, the heat transfer times to the working fluid are increased, specifically in hybrid dryers., where a thermal source complements a continuous process. In addition, they highlight the importance in the selection of construction materials for the collector.

2.2.1 Improvements for Flat Collectors

Regarding the design of solar collectors for air heating, it can be stated that there are models or designs that significantly improve drying times, an example of this is reflected in different works [26], in which the great importance in the design of the absorber plate as it is the source of heat transmission. This review shows evidence of multiple investigations that use the concepts of thermal conductivity to improve the efficiency of the collector, highlighting two fundamental aspects in the improvements for a solar collector. First, the recirculation of the air, what is sought is to increase the time or length of air flow inside the solar collector to achieve the desired temperatures or the required work margins. Second is the increase in the heat transfer area, in the context of the absorber plate, even if a recirculation configuration is used, the heat transfer area remains the same, but if conductive fins are added to the absorber plate, the heat transmission it will be more efficient when it comes to heating the air internally. The designs explored by [26], led them to conclude different ideas or concepts. The variation of the air flow is directly proportional to its efficiency; the corrugated V-shaped collector is the most efficient and the flat plate collector (without any alterations in its design) is the least efficient; Thermal energy storage by Phase Change Materials (PCM) is beneficial for increasing drying times in hours without sunlight [27].

2.2.2 Collector Sizing

With the information found in the databases, different research projects are identified that are oriented towards the implementation of solar collectors for drying food, among these, those published by [28–35], the collectors used, the materials and working methods expose together with the results obtained.

The solar collector is made up of three main components: the metal plate, the wooden box or thermal insulation and the glass cover, the first of which is the metal plate, which for the purposes of this project has two essential functions, the first is absorption of solar radiation to transfer heat to thermal fluids, which in the case of food drying would be the materials for energy storage and air; the second function is to contain the fluids used to store thermal energy. For this reason, what goes from being an absorption plate to being an absorption tank is designed [36].

To define the dimensions of the absorption tank, two aspects must be taken into account: the first is the absorption area, which is the area over which the irradiation falls on the solar collector, and the second factor is the volume of the material used for the absorption. Energy storage.

When talking about PCM it is necessary to reach melting temperatures, as is the case of paraffin, the main material for this research normally requires temperatures above 40 °C, as established by the literature [37]. Using as a basis the difference between the temperature levels and the size of commercial metal sheets, it is decided to design a 1 m² tank that allows assembly with other containers and thus be able to use different types of materials for storage, in each one of them.

2.3 Computational Fluid Simulation

Additionally, the issue of numerical simulations of fluids is addressed by reading some articles that apply specialized software for the design of solar collectors. Among these works, those published by [38–41] can be highlighted, they identify the different conditions of borders necessary for the correct simulation of a solar collector, such as irradiation, materials, flow, fluids, among other variables necessary for the software.

Within the literature, it is highlighted that phase change materials have a greater capacity to store energy because it absorbs heat in large quantities during the phase change stage and releases it efficiently when it returns to its original state.

In the databases there are different types of materials used for energy storage, but each of these must be used based on the specific requirements of the application, such as the operating temperature, the construction materials due to possible oxidations or chemical reactions, toxicity, costs, among others. Under these criteria, different authors [37, 42, 43] and [39] point out the advantage that paraffin has for drying applications due to its low cost, long useful life, its melting temperature below 60 °C and low toxicity. Due to its properties, it can have thousands of energy charge and discharge cycles without undergoing changes in its composition.

Additionally, the boundary conditions for the simulation are listed below (Fig. 2):

- Ambient Temperature T_{amb} 20.5 °C.
- Inicial fluid temperature (Air and paraffin) 20.5 °C.
- Solar Irradiation of 500–800 W/m², angle of incidence (θ) at 0° to emphasize the thermal study of the collector.
- The air velocity inside the collector is varied for analysis.

As can be seen in the simulation under a constant air flow at 0.014 m³/s, the collector manages to maintain outlets close to 60 °C, which is an ideal temperature for drying food. Air heating is progressive inside the collector and is a reflection of the temperatures reached by the thermal energy storage material. Taking into account the different temperatures in each of the absorption modules or tanks, the decision is made to implement three different types of thermal storage materials that are distributed based on the melting temperatures, materials that are described later.

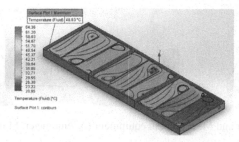

Fig. 2. Simulation of fluids in the collector 0.014 m^3/s a 500 W/m^2

2.4 Collector Implementation

The construction process of the collector involves the recreation of the profile of the corrugated plate in "V" that encourages the dynamics of heat transfer, increasing the area and generating turbulence, as can be seen (see Fig. 3). In this process it is important to highlight the materials used: iron sheet, wood, glass, PVC pipe (2″ in diameter, for air inlet and outlet) and black liquid silicone. Once assembled, a black anticorrosive paint coating is applied, which withstands temperature to give the following result.

2.4.1 Energy Storage Material

For the storage of thermal energy, three materials were selected, which are located respectively in each of the quadrants of the collector. In the first, at the air inlet, a used thermal motor oil is stored. In the second quadrant, a paraffin whose melting temperature is 48 °C is located, and in the last quadrant, at the air outlet, a paraffin whose melting temperature is 58 °C is stored. This based on the temperature variation along the collector. The simulations show that in the first quadrant temperatures that allow the melting of the paraffin are not reached and for this reason its properties are not used for the required purpose. Thermal oil has superior conductivity and allows accelerated heat transfer in the first quadrant of the solar collector.

2.4.2 Implemented Test Methodology

In this equipment development project for food drying, two tests are applied: one for the analysis of the behavior of the collector without energy storage and another that involves a data acquisition and visualization system with an Arduino card and LabVIEW software, the which are described below.

2.4.3 Collector Tests Without Thermal Energy Storage

The data collection process in this stage is applied by measuring equipment for thermodynamic variables such as a thermometer, anemometer and pyranometer.

The process consists of taking data from the different variables of interest every 15 min to monitor the behavior of the system, tabulating the information to be processed.

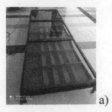

a)   b)

Fig. 3. Solar collector and Measurement equipment (Anemometer, Multimeter, Pyranometer)

2.4.4 Collector Tests with Energy Storage

With the implementation of the Arduino card and a PC with LAbVIEW software, the data is stored, to be processed and analyzed later. The following table shows the census variables (Table 1).

Table 1. Equivalence of variables

Irradiation	Solar energy incident on the collector
T_{inD}	Temperature at dryer inlet
H_{inD}	Humidity at dryer inlet
T_{amb}	Ambient air temperature
H_{amb}	Ambient air humidity
T_{out}	Air temperature at manifold outlet
H_{out}	Humidity of the air at the collector outlet
T_{oil}	Temperature of stored oil
T_{t1}	Tank 1 surface temperature
T_{k48}	Stored 48 °C kerosene temperature
T_{t2}	Tank 2 surface temperature
T_{k58}	Stored 58 °C kerosene temperature
T_{t3}	Tank 3 surface temperature
T_{air3-2}	Air temperature between bin 3 and 2
T_{air2-1}	Air temperature between drawer 2 and 1
T_{g1}	Glass surface temperature 1
T_{g2}	Glass surface temperature 2
T_{g3}	Glass surface temperature 3

With this information it is possible to have a more detailed understanding of the phenomena that occur within the solar collector for the development of technology.

2.4.5 Efficiency Calculation

For collector efficiency calculation purposes, the equations used in [38], are applied, which correspond to:

$$Q = \dot{m} * C_p(\Delta T) \tag{1}$$

where Q is the heat generated or absorbed, $\dot{m}$ is the air mass flow that can be calculated with the product between the air speed and the inlet area. C_p is the specific heat at constant pressure that is tabulated in the literature and ΔT is the difference between the outlet and inlet temperatures. Once the heat generated by the collector has been calculated, the efficiency is found using the following equation:

$$\eta = Q_a/Q_T \tag{2}$$

where η is the efficiency, Q_a is the heat absorbed by the air and Q_T is the solar power on the collector obtained by multiplying the total area by the irradiation, neglecting the losses due to reflection and transmittance.

3 Results and Discussion

3.1 Results Without Thermal Storage

To begin with, an analysis of the behavior of the collector without energy storage is made, seeking to give a general idea of its functionality with an absorber plate and air recirculation (see Fig. 3).

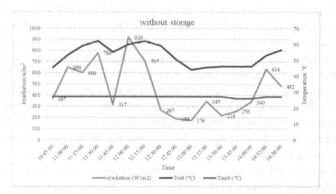

Fig. 4. Air behavior in the solar collector without storage

In Fig. 4, it is possible to analyze the changes generated by the variability of solar radiation, due to climatic factors. Among the most notable data are the values of the air temperature, which manages to reach 62 °C at the collector outlet around 12:15 p.m., when there is an irradiation of approximately 850 W/m², from At this point a drastic decrease in solar radiation is established, going from 920 W/m² at 12:00 p.m. up to

176 W/m2 at 12:45 p.m. which is reflected in the air that lowers its temperature from 62 °C to 44 °C in approximately 45 min, having a drop of 18 °C. Under these working conditions, the collector maintains an average efficiency of 26.77%. The air velocity in these tests was 6.2 m/s.

3.2 Results with Thermal Storage

With the storage of thermal energy, the behavior of the collector changes significantly, this can be evidenced by observing the graphs generated with the test data (see Fig. 5).

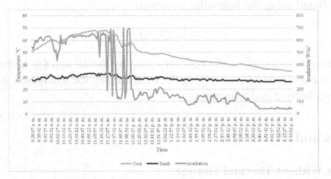

Fig. 5. Air behavior in the solar collector with energy storage

In the Fig. 5 shows the behavior of the studied thermodynamic variables. Among these, those with the highest priority are observed, which is the instantaneous irradiation, the ambient temperature and the temperature at the collector outlet. As can be seen, the ambient temperature has a small variation over time, it rises and falls along with the radiation present, going from 26 °C to 31 °C. The irradiation has a high variability, in the morning hours it has the highest intensity passing from 550 W/m^2 to 700 W/m^2, in the hours after noon the intensity drops, varying between 200 W/m^2 to 50 W/m^2. The variable of greatest interest for the investigation is the temperature at the outlet of the solar collector. In the morning hours when the intensity of the irradiation is greater, it has a temperature that varies between 50 and 68 °C, at a constant flow of 6.5 m/s. In the afternoon hours, due to the decrease in irradiation, the air begins a progressive drop in temperature, going from 58 to 35 °C over 4 h.

Figure 6 shows two moments of accelerated changes in the air temperature at the collector outlet, one between 11:35 and 11:55, in this space of time the irradiation decreases from 700 to 120 W/m^2 and the other from 12:00 in which it goes from an irradiation of 700 to 100 W/m^2. In these spaces, the air temperature changes in a not so abrupt way due to the storage of energy in the fluids (oil and paraffin).

The power of this collector is calculated at 450 W, with an approximate efficiency of 25%.

3.3 Fluid Behavior Analysis

The purpose of this research is to analyze the behavior of the fluids used for the storage of thermal energy, with the installation of thermocouples inside the tanks it is possible to monitor their changes, variations that can be seen in the following figures:

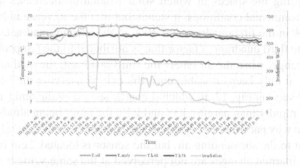

Fig. 6. Temperature variation in storage fluids

In Fig. 7 it is possible to analyze the changes in the temperature of the thermal storage fluids over 3 and a half hours. In the first hour and 15 min the irradiation reaches a maximum of 640 W/m², with this energy the collector begins to heat the fluids, a fact that is manifested in the rising values, reaching approximate ranges of 45 °C for the oil located in the first quadrant at the air inlet, 41 °C for the k48 paraffin located in the central quadrant and 40 °C for the k58 paraffin located in the final quadrant at the air outlet. The fluid with the highest thermal conductivity and that is used for this property in engine cooling is oil, this characteristic stands out when observing the loss of heat when the irradiation decreases, for which it is established that this fluid delivers a greater amount of energy. Into the air in the energy discharge period.

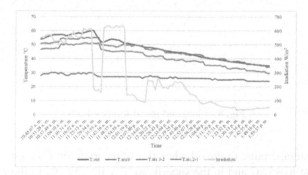

Fig. 7. Behavior of the air inside the collector

In Fig. 8 allows a precise analysis of the heat gain by the air when entering the solar collector. The first notable characteristic is established in the temperature increase of the first quadrant, over time it is shown that the air heats up mostly in the first quadrant where the oil is stored. When there is high intensity irradiation with values above 500 W/m², the thermal gain in quadrants 2 and 3 is approximately 5 °C, and in the first quadrant it is 17 °C. This heat transfer phenomenon can be attributed to the charge represented in the paraffin, being in a solid state and constantly absorbing thermal energy, the heat delivered to the air is less than in the first quadrant.

When analyzing the spaces in which solar irradiation decreases abruptly due to changes in environmental conditions, it stands out that the increase in heat in the air is reflected in 70% in the first quadrant and 30% in the second quadrant, being approximately 0% in the third quadrant, a factor that is attributed to the temperature difference in the heat exchange, when the air enters the third quadrant, the medium paraffin does not give it heat, it only keeps it stable until the exit, conserving the heat. This can be evidenced by observing Fig. 12, in which it can be seen how the temperature of the oil decreases more rapidly than paraffin k58 and k48, the latter being almost constant over time. The reason why paraffins do not have such a notable variation as oil is because they also deliver heat to the surrounding air, but the sensor is located 2 cm from the surface metal plate and thermal changes are not perceived at the same velocity than that of the oil.

Oil, thanks to its heat transfer qualities, allows thermal changes to be observed more precisely over time. But the paraffins present different temperatures depending on the height between the surface plate and the bottom of the tank, for this reason it is necessary to state that in the upper part when the sun delivers a high irradiation intensity (700 W/m²), the paraffin in contact with the metal it absorbs heat and changes state, but the paraffin furthest from the metal plate is still in a solid state. This phenomenon can be seen in the following graph.

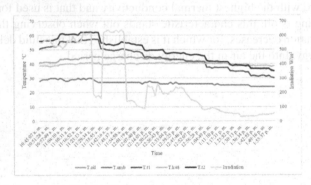

Fig. 8. Fluid and metal temperatures

Finally, the temperature of the oil when the solar irradiation is high with 600 W/m2 has values close to 45 °C and in the superficial T.t1 it is 57 °C, in the case of paraffin (K48) it has a approximate temperature of 40 °C that remains almost constant over time and the surface temperature of the T.t2 reaches 63 °C. With the passage of time, as solar irradiation decreases, the temperature differences begin to reverse their positions, the stored fluid having a greater amount of heat than the surface plate of each of the quadrants.

4 Conclusions

With the performance of functionality tests it was possible to compare the behavior of a corrugated solar collector in V, with and without thermal energy storage using phase change materials (PCM), the paraffin used shows two important improvements in the generation of hot air. The first focuses on temperature stability, for those moments when solar irradiation drops by 80%, the acceleration of change in air temperature with storage is logarithmic and for the case in which this is not available, it is linear. The second is the storage of energy, it has a very important value for the functionality of the dryer, with this it is possible to continue drying up to 4 h when there has been an irradiation of magnitudes greater than 500 W/m^2 for more than 5 h in the course of the day. The delivery of heat during times with low irradiation, by the storage fluids, allows for hot air at the outlet of the collector that is 10 °C higher than the ambient air. This capacity allows to extend the drying times and take care of the quality of food products.

Due to the heat transfer characteristics of paraffin and oil, a higher energy exchange is identified in the first quadrant. With the variability of solar irradiation, the collector remains in a transitory state for both energy charging and discharging. In the tests carried out, it is not observed that all the stored paraffin changes state and if it behaves as a thermal load for the system.

By identifying that thermal fluids do not manage to change state (solid-liquid), it is recommended for energy storage to use mainly k48 paraffin and thermal engine oil. In the case of k58 paraffin, its melting point and heat transfer properties do not favor energy exchange. In case you want to incorporate k58 paraffin, it is recommended to use a metallic sponge filling in the tank, by increasing the thermal conductivity inside the storage tank, the disadvantages with respect to oil are overcome.

References

1. Fudholi, A., Sopian, K., Ruslan, M.H., Alghoul, M.A., Sulaiman, M.Y.: Review of solar dryers for agricultural and marine products. Renew. Sustain. Energy Rev. **14**(1), 1–30 (2010). https://doi.org/10.1016/j.rser.2009.07.032
2. El-Sebaii, A.A., Shalaby, S.M.: Solar drying of agricultural products: a review. Renew. Sustain. Energy Rev. **16**(1), 37–43 (2012). https://doi.org/10.1016/j.rser.2011.07.134
3. Saxena, A.V., El-Sebaii, A.A.: A thermodynamic review of solar air heaters. Renew. Sustain. Energy Rev. **43**, 863–890 (2015). https://doi.org/10.1016/j.rser.2014.11.059
4. Tomar, V., Tiwari, G.N., Norton, B.: Solar dryers for tropical food preservation: thermophysics of crops, systems and components. Sol. Energy **154**, 2–13 (2017). https://doi.org/10.1016/j.solener.2017.05.066
5. Rodriguez, C.L.S., Correa-Quintana, E.A., Tarazona-Romero, B.E., Rincón-Quintero, A.D., Maradey-Lazaro, J.G.: Characterization of mechanical vibrations in a metal structure using the transform Cepstrum. Period. Eng. Nat. Sci. (PEN) **9**(4), 767 (2021). https://doi.org/10.21533/pen.v9i4.1994
6. Cárdenas, C., Sandoval, C., Rincón, A., Galván, D., Téllez, H.: Data collector design for vibration analysis by raspberry pi 3B embedded system means for industrial applications. J. Phys.: Conf. Ser. **2224**(1), 012032 (2022). https://doi.org/10.1088/1742-6596/2224/1/012032
7. Mendoza-Calderón, K.D., Jaimes, J.A.M., Maradey-Lazaro, J.G., Rincón-Quintero, A.D., Cardenas-Arias, C.G.: Design of an automatic palletizer. J. Phys.: Conf. Ser. **2224**(1), 012095 (2022). https://doi.org/10.1088/1742-6596/2224/1/012095

8. Kalogirou, S.A., Karellas, S., Braimakis, K., Stanciu, C., Badescu, V.: Exergy analysis of solar thermal collectors and processes. Prog. Energy Combust. Sci. **56**, 106–137 (2016). https://doi.org/10.1016/j.pecs.2016.05.002
9. Garrido-Silva, G., Maradey-Lazaro, J.G., Rincón-Quintero, A.D., Lengerke-Pérez, O., Sandoval-Rodriguez, C.L., Cardenas-Arias, C.G.: Estimation of the energy consumption of an electric utility vehicle: a case study. In: Botto Tobar, M., Cruz, H., Díaz Cadena, A. (eds.) CIT 2020. LNEE, vol. 763, pp. 257–272. Springer, Cham (2021). https://doi.org/10.1007/978-3-030-72212-8_19
10. Rincón-Quintero, A.D., Meneses-Jacomé, A., Del Portillo-Valdés, L. A.: Obtención de un modelo termoplástico, aprovechando la ceniza de la biomasa proveniente del despulpado del cacao y el reciclaje de PET, mediante un horno compresor automatizado con Software LabView y Hardware Arduino. In: Tecnologías Útiles para la Sustentabilidad Energética para Beneficio de la Sociedad, pp. 229–234 (2019)
11. Sansaniwal, S.K., Sharma, V., Mathur, J.: Energy and exergy analyses of various typical solar energy applications: a comprehensive review. Renew. Sustain. Energy Rev. **82**, 1576–1601 (2018). https://doi.org/10.1016/j.rser.2017.07.003
12. Fudholi, A., Sopian, K.: A review of solar air flat plate collector for drying application. Renew. Sustain. Energy Rev. **102**, 333–345 (2019). https://doi.org/10.1016/j.rser.2018.12.032
13. Lingayat, A., Balijepalli, R., Chandramohan, V.P.: Applications of solar energy based drying technologies in various industries – a review. Sol. Energy **229**, 52–68 (2021). https://doi.org/10.1016/j.solener.2021.05.058
14. Kamarulzaman, A., Hasanuzzaman, M., Rahim, N.A.: Global advancement of solar drying technologies and its future prospects: a review. Sol. Energy **221**, 559–582 (2021). https://doi.org/10.1016/j.solener.2021.04.056
15. Gorjian, S., et al.: Recent advancements in technical design and thermal performance enhancement of solar greenhouse dryers. Sustain. **13**(13), 1–32 (2021). https://doi.org/10.3390/su13137025
16. Rincón-Quintero, A.D., Lengerke-Pérez, O., Maradey-Lazaro, J.G., Garrido-Silva, G., Sandoval-Rodriguez, C.L., Osorio-Lizarazo, J.A.: Determination of heat transfer coefficients in natural and forced convection for different geometric configurations, using a prototype controlled by labview software and arduino hardware. In: Botto Tobar, M., Cruz, H., Díaz Cadena, A. (eds.) CIT 2020. LNEE, vol. 762, pp. 223–237. Springer, Cham (2021). https://doi.org/10.1007/978-3-030-72208-1_17
17. Ahmadi, A., et al.: Energy, exergy, and techno-economic performance analyses of solar dryers for agro products: a comprehensive review. Sol. Energy **228**, 349–373 (2021). https://doi.org/10.1016/j.solener.2021.09.060
18. Bhardwaj, A.K., Kumar, R., Kumar, S., Goel, B., Chauhan, R.: Energy and exergy analyses of drying medicinal herb in a novel forced convection solar dryer integrated with SHSM and PCM. Sustain. Energy Technol. Assess. **45**, 101119 (2021). https://doi.org/10.1016/j.seta.2021.101119
19. Cetina-Quiñones, A.J., López López, J., Ricalde-Cab, L., Amina El Mekaoui, L., San-Pedro, A. Bassam.: Experimental evaluation of an indirect type solar dryer for agricultural use in rural communities: relative humidity comparative study under winter season in tropical climate with sensible heat storage material. Solar Energy **224**, 58–75 (2021). https://doi.org/10.1016/j.solener.2021.05.040
20. Srinivasan, G., Rabha, D.K., Muthukumar, P.: A review on solar dryers integrated with thermal energy storage units for drying agricultural and food products. Sol. Energy **229**, 22–38 (2021). https://doi.org/10.1016/j.solener.2021.07.075
21. Madhankumar, S., Viswanathan, K., Wu, W.: Energy, exergy and environmental impact analysis on the novel indirect solar dryer with fins inserted phase change material. Renew. Energy **176**, 280–294 (2021). https://doi.org/10.1016/j.renene.2021.05.085

22. Rincón-Quintero, A.D., Portillo-Valdés, L.A., Meneses-Jácome, A., Sandoval-Rodríguez, C.L., Rondón-Romero, W.L., Ascanio-Villabona, J.G.: Trends in technological advances in food dehydration, identifying the potential extrapolated to cocoa drying: a bibliometric study. In: Tobar, Miguel Botto, Cruz, Henry, Cadena, Angela Díaz. (eds.) CIT 2020. LNEE, vol. 763, pp. 167–180. Springer, Cham (2020). https://doi.org/10.1007/978-3-030-72212-8_13

23. Mohana, Y., Mohanapriya, R., Anukiruthika, T., Yoha, K.S., Moses, J.A., Anandharamakrishnan, C.: Solar dryers for food applications: concepts, designs, and recent advances. Sol. Energy 208, 321–344 (2020). https://doi.org/10.1016/j.solener.2020.07.098

24. Romero, B.E.T., Celador, A.C., Rodriguez, C.L.S., Villabona, J.G.A., Quintero, A.D.R.: Design and construction of a solar tracking system for linear fresnel concentrator. Period. Eng. Nat. Sci. 9(4), 778–794 (2021). https://doi.org/10.21533/pen.v9i4.1988

25. Sandali, M., Boubekri, A., Mennouche, D.: Improvement of the thermal performance of solar drying systems using different techniques: a review. J. Solar Energy Eng. 141(5), 050802 (2019). https://doi.org/10.1115/1.4043613

26. Kabeel, A.E., Hamed, M.H., Omara, Z.M., Kandeal, A.W.: Solar air heaters: design configurations, improvement methods and applications – a detailed review. Renew. Sustain. Energy Rev. 70, 1189–1206 (2017). https://doi.org/10.1016/j.rser.2016.12.021

27. Lázaro, J.G.M., Rincón-Quintero, A.D., Sandoval-Rodriguez, C.L., Lengerke-Perez, O., Castellanos-Hernández, J.F.: Design and set up of a pulverized panela machine. Period. Eng. Nat. Sci. (PEN) 9(4), 812 (2021). https://doi.org/10.21533/pen.v9i4.1989

28. Baniasadi, E., Ranjbar, S., Boostanipour, O.: Experimental investigation of the performance of a mixed-mode solar dryer with thermal energy storage. Renew. Energy 112, 143–150 (2017). https://doi.org/10.1016/j.renene.2017.05.043

29. Kareem, M.W., Gilani, S.I., Habib, K., Irshad, K., Saha, B.B.: Performance analysis of a multi-pass solar thermal collector system under transient state assisted by porous media. Sol. Energy 158, 782–791 (2017). https://doi.org/10.1016/j.solener.2017.10.016

30. Tiwari, Sumit, Sanjay Agrawal, G.N., Agrawal, S.: PVT air collector integrated greenhouse dryers. Renew. Sustain. Energy Reviews 90, 142–159 (2018). https://doi.org/10.1016/j.rser.2018.03.043

31. Chaouch, W.B., Khellaf, A., Mediani, A., Slimani, M.E.A., Loumani, A., Hamid, A.: Experimental investigation of an active direct and indirect solar dryer with sensible heat storage for camel meat drying in Saharan environment. Sol. Energy 174, 328–341 (2018). https://doi.org/10.1016/j.solener.2018.09.037

32. Bhardwaj, A.K., Kumar, R., Chauhan, R.: Experimental investigation of the performance of a novel solar dryer for drying medicinal plants in Western Himalayan region. Sol. Energy 177, 395–407 (2019). https://doi.org/10.1016/j.solener.2018.11.007

33. Ortiz-Rodríguez, N.M., García-Valladares, O., Pilatowsky-Figueroa, I., Menchaca-Valdez, A.C.: Solar-LP gas hybrid plant for dehydration of food. Appl. Therm. Eng. 177, 115496 (2020). https://doi.org/10.1016/j.applthermaleng.2020.115496

34. Pankaew, P., Aumporn, O., Janjai, S., Pattarapanitchai, S., Sangsan, M., Bala, B.K.: Performance of a large-scale greenhouse solar dryer integrated with phase change material thermal storage system for drying of chili. Int. J. Green Energy 17(11), 632–643 (2020). https://doi.org/10.1080/15435075.2020.1779074

35. Kamfa, I., Fluch, J., Bartali, R., Baker, D.: Solar-thermal driven drying technologies for large-scale industrial applications: state of the art, gaps, and opportunities. Int. J. Energy Res. 44(13), 9864–9888 (2020). https://doi.org/10.1002/er.5622

36. Rincón-Quintero, A.D., et al.: Manufacture of hybrid pieces using recycled R-PET, polypropylene PP and cocoa pod husks ash CPHA, by pneumatic injection controlled with LabVIEW software and arduino hardware. IOP Conf. Ser. Mater. Sci. Eng. 844(1), 1–12 (2020). https://doi.org/10.1088/1757-899X/844/1/012054

37. Kahwaji, S., Johnson, M.B., Kheirabadi, A.C., Groulx, D., White, M.A.: A comprehensive study of properties of paraffin phase change materials for solar thermal energy storage and thermal management applications. Energy **162**, 1169–1182 (2018). https://doi.org/10.1016/j.energy.2018.08.068

38. Bellos, E., Korres, D., Tzivanidis, C., Antonopoulos, K.A.: Design, simulation and optimization of a compound parabolic collector. Sustain. Energy Technol. Assess. **16**, 53–63 (2016). https://doi.org/10.1016/j.seta.2016.04.005

39. Iranmanesh, M., Akhijahani, H.S., Jahromi, M.S.B.: CFD modeling and evaluation the performance of a solar cabinet dryer equipped with evacuated tube solar collector and thermal storage system. Renew. Energy **145**, 1192–1213 (2020). https://doi.org/10.1016/j.renene.2019.06.038

40. Korres, D.N., Tzivanidis, C.: Investigation of a novel small-sized bifacial cavity PTC and comparison with conventional configurations. Therm. Sci. Eng. Prog. **17**, 100355 (2020). https://doi.org/10.1016/j.tsep.2019.100355

41. Rincón-Quintero, A.D., Del Portillo-Valdés, L.A., Meneses-Jácome, A., Ascanio-Villabona, J.G., Tarazona-Romero, B.E., Durán-Sarmiento, M.A.: Performance evaluation and effectiveness of a solar-biomass hybrid dryer for drying homogeneous of cocoa beans using labview software and arduino hardware. In: Botto Tobar, M., Cruz, H., Díaz Cadena, A. (eds.) CIT 2020. LNEE, vol. 762, pp. 238–252. Springer, Cham (2021). https://doi.org/10.1007/978-3-030-72208-1_18

42. Devahastin, S., Pitaksuriyarat, S.: Use of latent heat storage to conserve energy during drying and its effect on drying kinetics of a food product. Appl. Therm. Eng. **26**(14), 1705–1713 (2006). https://doi.org/10.1016/j.applthermaleng.2005.11.007

43. Parsazadeh, M., Duan, X.: Numerical study on the effects of fins and nanoparticles in a shell and tube phase change thermal energy storage unit. Appl. Energy **216**, 142–156 (2018). https://doi.org/10.1016/j.apenergy.2018.02.052

Implementation of PID and MPC Controllers for a Quadruple Tank Process in a 3D Virtual System, Using the Hardware in the Loop Technique

Jonathan F. Amaguaña⬭, Milton J. Sánchez$^{(\boxtimes)}$ ⬭, Edwin P. Pruna⬭, and Ivón P. Escobar⬭

Universidad de las Fuerzas Armadas ESPE, Sangolquí, Ecuador
{jfamaguana,mjsanchez10,eppruna,ipescobar}@espe.edu.ec

Abstract. In this article, the design of an advanced MPC controller and a PID control have been proposed and implemented in a programmable logic controller (PLC) for a quadruple process of tanks, developing a comparison between the 2 controllers. The design of the controllers is carried out from the initial conditions of the process, the same conditions that must have an opening value of the valves between 60%–80% to have interaction between the 4 interconnected tanks, the PID controllers were developed in Tia Portal V16 by means of programming in Ladder language using PID blocks for process control, while the MPC controller was designed using structured language SCL exported from Matlab-Simulink to Tia portal V16. The industrial process was virtualized in a unity 3D graphic engine, using the hardware in the loop technique and the Profinet protocol as well, it was possible to establish communication between the virtualized plant and the PLC. Finally, different tests were developed between the controllers, allowing to show that the MPC controller presents an optimal settling time and better compensation before disturbances.

Keywords: Quadruple tank process · MPC · PID · HIL · PLC · Matlab · Unity 3D · SCL

1 Introduction

Nowadays, Industry 4.0 is related to the fourth Industrial Revolution because of the appearance and introduction of new technologies and work methods enabling machines, people and devices to be digitized and connected to each other. Nevertheless, technological advances and developments require new control algorithms for the automation of nonlinear systems using PLCs [1]. Virtualization is a technology that lets us to save hardware, electricity and maintenance [2].

In [3] the use of the Hardware in the loop (HIL) technique allows the development and testing of controlled systems to manage complex machines and processes, likewise this technique enables replacing a physical part with software.

© The Author(s), under exclusive license to Springer Nature Switzerland AG 2023
M. Botto-Tobar et al. (Eds.): ICAT 2022, CCIS 1756, pp. 385–398, 2023.
https://doi.org/10.1007/978-3-031-24971-6_28

Ever since level systems are the most useful processes in the industry, as well as in the field of control and automation teaching, the implementation of level controllers for SISO and MIMO processes is essential. Hence, being very frequent in the industry, an analysis is required to increase the efficiency of the controllers [4]. In [5] the development of the mathematical model of a quadruple process of interconnected tanks is presented, from which a non-linear model was disposed and an analysis was carried out to adjust its parameters, to minimize the differences between the measurements. Experimental data and the predictions obtained by the model. Likewise, in [6] it is mentioned that the use of the mathematical model for the quadruple tank process, which was used to implement a controller in linear algebra. These models have been used frequently for the control of power plants, hydrographic processes, chemical processes and biotechnological industries.

To work out the control of a quadruple process of tanks, the use of classic controllers has been studied, one of the strategies was that [7] where a decentralized multivariable control with two PI controllers was designed, giving as a result a response that conforms the right specifications. There are investigations that make use of advanced controllers as presented in [8], where the study and design of a model-based predictive controller (MPC) was made to check and control the speed of a motor using the tool Matlab/Simulink concluding from the experimentation that the controller had better results than a self-adjusted PID controller, as well.

In [9] it is noted how the PLC is essential in industrial automation since they are very robust, but they have the limitation in view of computing performance, memory and deficiency when programming, which forces it currently searching new methods to implement more efficient and tunable control algorithms. Hence, in [10] the usage of the Structured Control Language (SCL) is explained, which has few studies given its complexity and low popularity in small and medium-sized industries, however, they are suitable for programs that require calculations of mathematical equations. Evenly, the research shows a clear guide for the use of the Matlab/Simulink PLC-Coder tool to export a mathematical function block to a programming language with the international standard IEC 61131 understandable by PLCs [11]. For industrial communication between hardware (PLC) and software (virtualized plant) the Industrial protocol Profinet is used.

This work provides a methodology for the design of the advanced MPC controller and implementation in a PLC S7-1200 programmable logic controller, providing a low-cost solution in automatic process control; considers the educational approach, it will help to fight the problem of training automation and control from students for using the process, control and techniques with simulated plants.

This article is organized as follows: Sect. 2 presents the virtual environment; Sect. 3 presents the mathematical model; Sect. 4 presents the design of the controllers; then, Sect. 5 contains the experimental results. Finally, the conclusions are set in Sect. 6.

2 Virtual Environment

This section illustrates the methodology used for the virtualization quadruple tank process, which is divided into four main stages: reference models; 3D modeling; programming and visualization; and Profinet communication with the PLC as shown in Fig. 1.

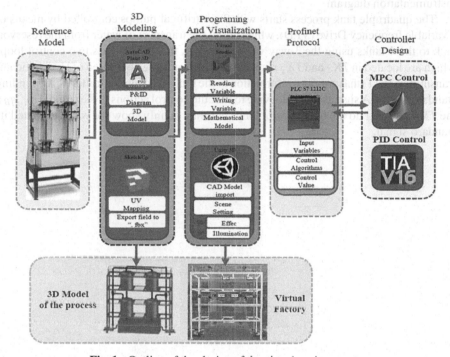

Fig. 1. Outline of the design of the virtual environment.

In the first stage, a reference model was looked for which considers features and aspects of a real industrial factory. In the second stage, called 3D modeling, the design of the quadruple tank process is worked out with AutoCAD Plant 3D software, where layers are defined to distribute the equipment and devices (tanks, flanges, pipes, structure, meshes) as well as the dimensions of the design, structures containing the tanks are created, valves and pumps are placed, the file created has the extension.dwg. To change the format, the native AutoCAD Plant 3D file must be opened in SketchUp software, which helps to get the file in extension fbx which is recognized by Unity 3D software.

In the Programming and virtualization of the 3D industrial environment, the different features of the process are incorporated, such as transmitters, frequency variators, control room, liquid filling, sounds and visual effects using the Unity 3D graphic engine and object-oriented programming in Visual Studio, enabling the virtualized plant having a greater resemblance to the real plant.

The last stage, Industrial communication with the PLC uses the Profinet protocol where the virtualized plant reads an IP address generated by the PLC to be able to write and read the data from the MPC and PID controller implemented in the PLC, this is how the system by means of the hardware in the loop (HIL) technique.

2.1 P&ID Diagram

The structure of the quadruple tank process is shown in Fig. 2, with a piping and instrumentation diagram.

The quadruple tank process starts with 2 centrifugal pumps controlled by means of a variable frequency Drive (VFD), which allow the transport of water from the reservoir tank to the 4 tanks using the 3-way valves (y_A, y_B), this process has two control loops which are located in TK_1 and TK_2 respectively, the same are composed of level indicator transmitters (LIT) that provides information to the multivariable controller (UIC) sending standard 4–20 mA signals thus achieving to execute control actions to the pumps (q_A, q_B), the TK_3 and TK_4 do not have control loops but they mainly show the water level and its standard signal.

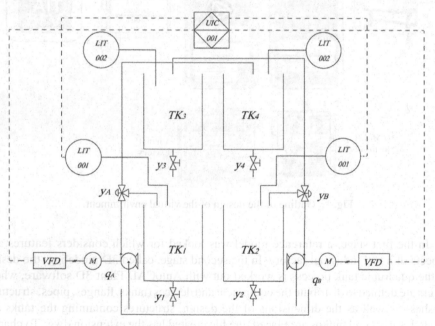

Fig. 2. P&ID diagram of the quadruple tank process

3 Mathematical Modelling

The mathematical model is based on some physical principles such as volumetric flow, mass balance equation, Torricelli's theorem and Bernoulli's principle [12]. The quadruple level tank process is shown in Fig. 2, consisting of four tanks (TK_1, TK_2, TK_3, TK_4)

two centrifugal pumps (q_A, q_B) to control the flow of water between tanks, six manual valves ($y \in R[0\ 1]$), which are distributed in two three-way valves and four liquid release valves.

A continuous and constant inlet flow is assumed, while Torricelli's theorem is used for the outlet of the tanks, which relates the fluid speed to the cross-sectional area and its flow rate is limited by the centrifugal pumps.

The amount of flow through any section of pipe 1 or 2 is constant, so it follows that

$$Q_o = A_i v_i$$
$$Q_{oi} = A_i \sqrt{2gh_i} \quad \text{where} \quad i = 1, 2, 3, 4 \tag{1}$$

Once the operating principles have been analyzed, a mathematical expression of 4 non-linear equations is arrived at, which represent the mathematical model of the quadruple tank process.

$$A_1 \frac{dh_1}{dt} = y_A k_A q_A + y_3 k_3 \sqrt{2gh_3} - y_1 k_1 \sqrt{2gh_1}$$

$$A_2 \frac{dh_2}{dt} = y_B k_B q_B + y_4 k_4 \sqrt{2gh_4} - y_2 k_2 \sqrt{2gh_2}$$

$$A_3 \frac{dh_3}{dt} = (1 - y_B) k_B q_B - y_3 k_3 \sqrt{2gh_3}$$

$$A_4 \frac{dh_4}{dt} = (1 - y_A) k_A q_A - y_4 k_4 \sqrt{2gh_4} \tag{2}$$

where:

A_1, A_2, A_3, A_4: Area of thanks
$k_A, k_B, k_1, k_2, k_3, k_4$: Valve constants
$y_A, y_B, y_1, y_2, y_3, y_4$: Valve opening
h_1, h_2, h_3, h_4: Tanks height.

The mathematical model in Fig. 2 is expressed in the form of a matrix, with the corresponding values of the control valve openings as well as the load valve:

$$
\begin{bmatrix} \dot{h}_1 \\ \dot{h}_2 \\ \dot{h}_3 \\ \dot{h}_4 \end{bmatrix}
=
\begin{bmatrix}
-\frac{y_1 k_1 \sqrt{2gh_1}}{A_1} & 0 & \frac{y_3 k_3 \sqrt{2gh_3}}{A_1} & 0 \\
0 & \frac{-y_2 k_2 \sqrt{2gh_2}}{A_2} & 0 & \frac{y_4 k_4 \sqrt{2gh_4}}{A_2} \\
0 & 0 & -\frac{y_3 k_3 \sqrt{2gh_3}}{A_3} & 0 \\
0 & 0 & 0 & -\frac{y_4 k_4 \sqrt{2gh_4}}{A_4}
\end{bmatrix}
+
\begin{bmatrix}
\frac{y_A k_A}{A_1} & 0 \\
0 & \frac{y_B k_B}{A_2} \\
0 & \frac{(1-y_B) k_B}{A_3} \\
\frac{(1-y_A) k_A}{A_4} & 0
\end{bmatrix}
\begin{bmatrix} q_A \\ q_B \end{bmatrix}
\tag{3}
$$

Figure 3 shows the validation of the performance of the mathematical model for the quadruple tank process.

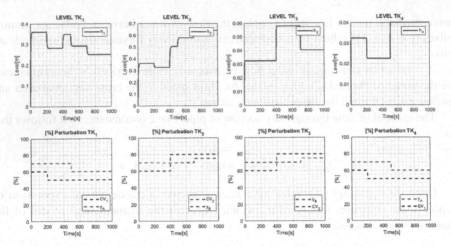

Fig. 3. Validation of the mathematical model.

For the validation of the mathematical model of the quadruple tank process, we start with initial conditions of level $0[m]$ for each tank, then:

At time $0[s]$ 3-way valves start with an initial value of $y_A = y_B = 70\%$ and control actions $CV_1 = CV_2 = 60\%$, which generates the tanks to increase their water level. Then at time $200[s]$ a decrease of CV_1 by 10% is generated, decreasing the level of TK_1, TK_2 and TK_4.

For the time $400[s]$ the value of CV_2 is increased by 20% so it is observed that the level of TK_1, TK_2 and TK_3 increases.

At $500[s]$ a perturbation of y_A with minus 10% is generated and it is observed that the level of TK_1 decreases and TK_4, TK_2 increases. Finally, at the time $700[s]$ a perturbation of y_B with plus 10% is generated and it is visualized that TK_2 increases and TK_1, TK_3 decreases.

4 Controller Design

This section presents the design of an advanced MPC controller and a classical PID controller for quadruple tank process control. Moreover, the performance of the control algorithms in the quadruple tank process is analyzed as well.

4.1 MPC Controller

Model-based predictive control (MPC) is an optimization strategy that uses a model of a process to foretell the effect of the control action on the quadruple tank process.

For the design of the MPC controller, the nonlinear model of the plant is included, creating a subsystem in Matlab/Simulink, where the inputs and outputs of the subsystem enter the MPC block of the controller. In this way, trial and error tests can be developed to find the right constants of the controller and it can be exported through the PLC encoder with the international standard IEC 61131 understandable by PLCs.

The target function applicable to MIMO systems explained in (4), searches to minimize the level error in tank 1 and tank 2, in addition to optimizing the abrupt control actions of the actuators (centrifugal pumps), this Eq. (4) serves for the simultaneous control of two process variables to determine the control actions.

$$
J(k) = \sum_{\substack{i=N_w}}^{N_p} \delta_1(k)[h_1(k+i|k) - hd_1(k+i|k)]^2 + \delta_2(k)[h_2(k+i|k) - hd_2(k+i|k)]^2
$$

$$
+ \sum_{j=1}^{N_c-1} \lambda_1(k)\big[\Delta q_A(k+i-1)\big]^2 + \lambda_2(k)\big[\Delta q_B(k+i-1)\big] \tag{4}
$$

where:

$$
\Delta q_{min} \leq \Delta q_A \leq \Delta q_{max}
$$
$$
\Delta q_{min} \leq \Delta q_B \leq \Delta q_{max} \tag{5}
$$

$$
h_{min} \leq h_1 \leq h_{max}
$$
$$
h_{min} \leq h_2 \leq h_{max} \tag{6}
$$

where N_w y N_p are the starting of the prediction horizon and the number of samples of the prediction horizon, N_c is the control horizon which should be less than the prediction horizon., $h_1(k+i|k)$ is the predicted level output of tank level 1, $h_2(k+i|k)$ is the predicted level output of tank level 2, $hd_1(k+i|k)$ is the desired value of tank level 1 and $hd_2(k+i|k)$ is the desired value of tank level 2.

To stand the inequality constraints in the optimization function they were entered as the constraints of the quadruple tank process, Eq. 5 represents the percentage of the control variable that is input to the final control elements in charge of manipulating the level of both TK_1 and TK_2, the two have the maximum value is $\Delta q_{max} = 100\%$ and the minimum value is $\Delta q_{min} = 0\%$. Equation 6 is the inequality constraint for the tank level limits, in this case they are $h_{min} = 0[m]$ y $h_{max} = 1[m]$.

The values of δ_1, δ_2 (error weight) and the values of the constants λ (weight of the control actions variations) were determined by the trial-and-error method, which are presented in Table 1.

Table 1. MPC controller design parameters.

Parameters	Tank 1	Tank 2
Prediction horizon (N_w)	12	12
Horizon control (N_c)	3	3
Rate weight – input (δ_1, δ_2)	6.5	6.5
Weight – input (λ)	0.001	0.001
Weight –output (λ)	0.9	0.85

The diagram in Fig. 4 represents the implementation of the MPC control loop for the level of TK_1 and TK_2.

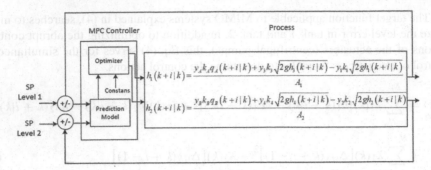

Fig. 4. Diagram of the implementation of the MPC control loops.

4.2 PID Controller

The Lambda tuning method was used to design the PID controller since it is robust and does not generate overshoot. Therefore, the dynamic model of the quadruple tank process must be determined. For de system, a first-order transfer function will be used, as shown in Eq. 7.

$$G(s) = \frac{k_p}{1 + sT} e^{-sL} \tag{7}$$

where k_p represents the static gain of the process, L is the dead time and T is the time constant. These parameters were calculated by obtaining a transfer function using the mathematical model of the quadruple tank process with the help of the linmode function of Matlab, it possible to linearize the nonlinear model of the process and thus obtain the transfer function that represents the behavior of the quadruple tank process.

The transfer function representing the behavior of tank 1 and tank 2 are represented by Eq. 8.

$$G(s) = \frac{0.06015}{1 + 0.821s} e^{-0.01s} \tag{8}$$

PID Controller Tuning

For the tuning of PID controllers, the aggressive lambda tuning method is used because of its high performance in the process industry. The closed-loop response time Tc1 is the design parameter, which will be set Tc1 = T as denoted in [13].

The parameters describing the Lambda tuning constants are listed in Table 2. For this purpose, the constants K_p, T_i, T_d are calculated.

The diagram in Fig. 5 shows the implementation of the PID level control loops for TK_1 and TK_2.

Table 2. Values of the constants for the PID controller with Lambda tuning.

Constants	Tank 1	Tank 2
k_p	16.62	16.62
T_i	0.78 seg	0.78 seg
T_d	0 seg	0 seg

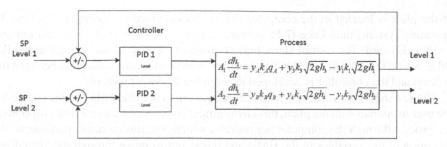

Fig. 5. Diagram of the implementation of the control loops.

5   Experimental Results

This section presents the implementation of the HIL technique for the virtualization and control of the quadruple process of tank in Fig. 2, the virtual environment consists of industrial equipment and instruments as shown in Table 3. The mathematical model

Table 3. Industrial equipment and instruments

Centrifugal pump	Manual valve	Factory
Level transmitters (LIT)	Variable Frequency Drive	Tank (*TK*)
Hardware In the loop (HIL)		
Quadruple tank process ——— [image] ——— PLC S7-1200 ——— Profinet Protocol		

of the plant is located in the computer that is characterized by having a Windows 10 operating system, Intel Core i7 Processor, 12 GB Ram memory, fifth generation and 2 GB video card. The control algorithms are found in a programmable logic controller (PLC S7-1200 CPU 1212 AC/DC/RL), while the industrial communication between the process and the controller is developed through the Profinet protocol.

Table 4 shows the virtual environment carried out in the Unity 3D graphic engine for the user to interact with the plant, this environment consists of a control room (to control the process through the computer peripherals) which contains monitors (to observe the evolution of the variables in the HMI) and the avatar to move through the virtualized process. The development of the virtual environment contains effects to give more realism to the quadruple tank process, such as: visual effects, surround sounds and the filling in the tanks.

Table 4. Control Room quadruple tanks

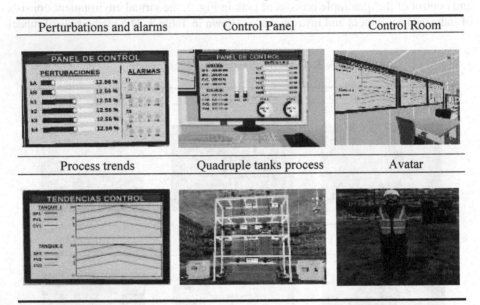

Perturbations and alarms	Control Panel	Control Room
Process trends	Quadruple tanks process	Avatar

5.1 PID and MPC Controller Performance

Figure 6 illustrates the performance of the advanced control algorithm MPC and classical PID for different setpoint values, and in Table 5 you can see the values of the simulation parameters placed in the Unity 3D graphics engine.

Table 5. Parameters of the quadruple-tank.

Parameters	Value	Unit	Description
h_{max}	1	m	Maximum level in all tanks
h_{min}	0.01	m	Minimum level in all tanks
q_{max}	3.1	V	Maximum voltage in q_A and q_B
q_{min}	0	V	Minimum voltage in q_A and q_B
K_1, K_2, K_3, K_4	0.033	m^2/Vs	Discharge constant in all valves
K_A, K_B	0.0314	m^2/Vs	Discharge constant in 3-way valve
y_1, y_2, y_3, y_4	0.5	–	Parameter in all valves
y_A, y_B	0.7	–	Parameter of the 3-way valve

The process starts with $SP1 = SP2 = 0.5[m]$, the evolution of the level with the MPC controller is fast and does not present overshoot. From 220 [s] a set point change of $SP1 = 0.4[m]$ and $SP2 = 1[m]$ is observed, the difference between the controllers is noticeable as the PID controller reaches its set point slower compared to the MPC controller. Finally, at time 450 [s] another set point change occurs, from $SP1 = 1[m]$ and $SP2 = 0.2[m]$ in which the controllers have very similar PV responses, although the MPC controller reaches the desired value earlier, in Table 6 and Table 7 the settling time and the overshoot of the tanks level are shown.

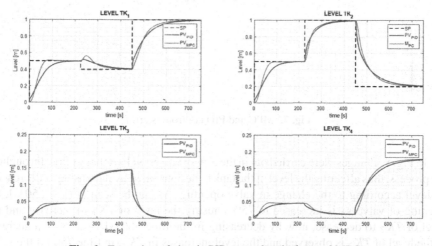

Fig. 6. Execution of classic PID control and advanced MPC.

Figure 7 shows the plant response to changes in the set point "SP". The simulation of the virtualized process indicates that the error tends to reduce to zero asymptotically, with the advanced MPC control being faster than the classical PID control.

Table 6. Controller Response Analysis in Tank 1

	Controllers	Set point 0.5 m		Set point 0.4 m		Set point 1.0 m	
		OS (%)	T_S (s)	OS (%)	T_S (s)	OS (%)	T_S (s)
TK_1	MPC	0.9	120	0	140	0	210
	PID	0	200	0	195	0	250

Table 7. Controller Response Analysis in Tank 2

	Controllers	Set point 0.5 m		Set point 1 m		Set point 0.2 m	
		OS (%)	T_S (s)	OS (%)	T_S (s)	OS (%)	T_S (s)
$TK2$	MPC	0	100	0	145	0	230
	PID	0	255	0	175	0	285

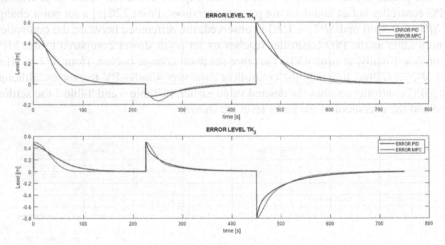

Fig. 7. MPC and PID controllers error.

In Fig. 8, changes were carried out in the 3-way valves, valves that in-flow throughout the process, thus affecting the level of the tank to be controlled by increasing or decreasing its level according to the change in valve opening. As can be seen at time 250 [s], the opening of valve y_A is increased to 75% causing the level of TK_1 to increase and the level of TK_2 to decrease, now by decreasing in the time 500 [s] y_B to 65% a decrease in the level of TK_2 is observed and the level increases in TK_1, in time 750 [s] the value of y_A decreases to 70% causing the level in TK_1 to decrease and the level in TK_2 to increase, Finally increasing the valve y_B to 70% in time 1000 [s] causes a level increase in TK_2 and level in TK_1 to decrease.

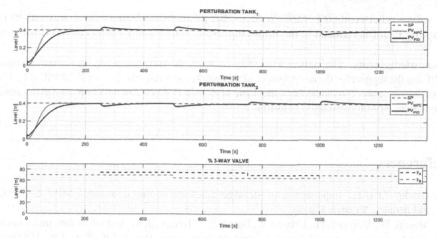

Fig. 8. Perturbation in the quadruple tank process.

6 Conclusions

In this work, the achievement of the mathematical model of the quadruple process of tanks has been shown, which has allowed the implementation of the MPC and PID controller, in addition to obtaining the transfer function, a correct tuning for the PID controller was carried out.

For the design of the MPC controller, the use of mathematical software (Matlab/Simulink) was necessary, since it allowed exporting and loading the function block (SCL language) to a programming language understandable by PLCs, while for the design of the controller PID, the Tia Portal V16 software was needed to place the tuning constants in the PID block.

The design and connection of the industrial devices and equipment in Unity 3D were worked out with the use of standard instrumentation, to give users a real environment of the quadruple process of tank and managing to control the variables through a panel located in a control room. The Profinet protocol of the PLC S7-1200 CPU 1212 AC/DC/RL allowed the communication between the PLC and the virtualized plant, achieving the sending and receiving of data for the correct operation of the control algorithms that act in the process.

To demonstrate the efficiency of the proposed algorithms, 2 tests were developed, the first one where no perturbations were considered and only the response of the controllers to set point changes was analyzed, and the second where there is a constant set point and perturbation are performed in the (y_A, y_B) valves. The design parameters that were chosen for the MPC control algorithm in tank 1 and tank 2 presented faster settling times, better reaction to perturbations and set point changes compared to the PID controller. Nevertheless, both controllers were adjusted to the user's requirements.

Finally, it was observed that the quadruple tank process being an interacting process has several restrictions at the time of the design of the controllers, one of them and the most important are the initial conditions (y_A, y_B) after many tests it was determined that: the value of the valves (y_A, y_B) cannot be less than 50%, the range of variation between the valves is between 60%–80%. With a value greater than 80% of the 3-way valves the coupling factor is reduced in the liquid ingress in tanks 3 and 4 tends to be eliminated.

Acknowledgements. The authors would like to thank the Universidad de las Fuerzas Armadas ESPE for the support for the development of this work, especially the project 2020-PIC-017-CTE "Simulación de proceso industriales, mediante la técnica Hardware in the Loop, para el desarrollo de prácticas en Automatización Industrial".

References

1. Grado, T.F.D.E.: Implementación de algoritmos de control avanzados MPC EN PLC's industriales. Valencia (2019)
2. Martín, D., Marrero, M., Urbano, J., Barra, E., Moreiro, J.A.: Virtualización, una solución para la eficiencia, seguridad y administración de intranets. Prof. la Inf. **20**(3), 348–355 (2011)
3. Tebani, K., Mehdi, G.: Hardware-In-the-Loop Simulation for Validating PLC Programs Hardware-In-the-Loop Simulation for Validating PLC Programs, Algeria, pp. 1–5 (2015)
4. Morilla García, F., Isabel, A., Sánchez Moreno, J.: Entorno de experimentación sobre control de nivel y control de caudal. Madrid (2002)
5. Loyarte, A.S., Clementi, L.A.: Sistema de Control de Niveles con Cuatro Tanques Interconectados: Modelado Matemático y Estimación de Parámetros. XIV Reunión de Trabajo en Procesamiento de la Información y Control. Argentina (2014)
6. Sásig, E.R., et al.: An implementation on matlab software for non-linear controller design based on linear algebra for quadruple tank process. In: Rocha, Á., Adeli, H., Reis, L.P., Costanzo, S. (eds.) WorldCIST'18 2018. AISC, vol. 746, pp. 333–340. Springer, Cham (2018). https://doi.org/10.1007/978-3-319-77712-2_32
7. Castelo, G., Garrido, J., Vazquez, F.: Ajuste, Configuración y control de cuatro tanques acoplados. Univ. Córdoba (2011)
8. Verdés Kairuz, R., González Santos, A.: Controladores MPC y PID con autoajuste para un proceso de dinámica rápida a través de MATLAB®/Simulink® y OPC. Rev. Científica Ing. Electrónica, Automática y Comun. **36**(3), 80–93 (2015)
9. Käpernick, B., Graichen, K.: PLC implementation of a nonlinear model predictive controller. IFAC Proc. **19**, 1892–1897 (2014)
10. Páez-Logreira, H.D., Zamora-Musa, R., Bohórquez-Pérez, J.: Programación de Controladores Lógicos (PLC) mediante Ladder y Lenguaje de Control Estructurado (SCL) en MATLAB. Rev. Fac. Ing. **24**(39), 109 (2015)
11. Delgado Sobrino, D.R., Ružarovský, R., Holubek, R., Velíšek, K.: Into the early steps of Virtual Commissioning in Tecnomatix Plant Simulation using S7-PLCSIM Advanced and STEP 7 TIA Portal. In: MATEC Web Conference, vol. 299, p. 02005 (2019)
12. Johansson, K.: The quadruple-tank process: a multivariable laboratory process with an adjustable zero. IEEE Trans. Control Syst. Technol. **8**, 456–465 (2000)
13. Cayo, L., Pilicita, A.: Desarrollo de Algoritmos de control avanzado, y creación de un entorno virtual 3D, para el control de procesos de flujo y presión. Universidad de las Fuerzas Armadas, Thesis (2021)

Advanced Control Algorithms for a Horizontal Three-Phase Separator in a Hardware in the Loop Simulation Environment

L. Aimacaña-Cueva⊕, O. Gahui-Auqui(✉)⊕, J. Llanos-Proaño⊕,
and D. Ortiz-Villalba⊕

Universidad de las Fuerzas Armadas ESPE, Sangolqui, Ecuador
{leaimacana1,ojgahui,jdllanos1,ddortiz5}@espe.edu.ec

Abstract. The three-phase separator has a fundamental role in oil production, due to its multivariable and nonlinear characteristics, controlling it represents a major challenge. In the engineering training academy, having a real industrial process represents a significant cost, however, thanks to technological advances, providing a virtual industrial process is possible. In this research work, a hardware in the loop simulation (HIL) environment is proposed, which includes a three-phase horizontal separator, and its controllers implemented in a physical control device. The proposed system is flexible enough to perform different control algorithms and implement them in any control device. The design methodology of the proposed system includes three sections. In the first section, the nonlinear multivariable mathematical models of the industrial process are obtained. The second section corresponds to the development of the virtual environment, in which the 3D modeling of the industrial process is performed. In the third section, the control strategies are proposed, designed and implemented in a physical control device. To validate the applicability and performance of the variables to be controlled, two control strategies are implemented: a traditional proportional integral derivative (PID) control, and a multivariable model predictive control (MPC). Finally, a comparison of the implemented controllers performance is made for the controlled variables: water level $h(t)_w$, oil level $h(t)_l$ and separator pressure $P(t)$.

Keywords: Advanced control · Hardware in the loop · Multivariable dynamics · Three-phase separator · PID · Virtual laboratory

1 Introduction

In an oil production industrial process, the separator has the function of separating in phases (water, oil, and gas), liquids from gas, and free water from oil [1]. There are different types of separators, vertical, horizontal, and spherical [1,2], which can be two-phase or three-phase. The two-phase separators have the disadvantage that extra processes are needed to obtain oil, generating problems in the oil separation, which does not happen with the three-phase separators since they optimize the division process and improve the quality of the final product. Within the study of three-phase separators, concepts from hydrodynamics to thermodynamics and the law of energy conservation are involved [3]. From a point of view of process control, three-phase separators are much more efficient than two-phase. However, since it is a multivariable nonlinear system, the variables to be controlled are correlated with each other, this is a control challenge. Usually the control strategies for three-phase separators have been designed considering them as SISO systems when in fact their dynamics is multivariable, and also traditional linear controllers are used, so the performance of the industrial process is not as efficient in the transient state as expected, therefore it is proposed the development of multivariable and advanced control algorithms, in order to optimize the operation and performance of the separator.

There are several traditional controllers used for the three-phase separator, for example, the PID controller, whose purpose is to maintain a stable pressure inside the separator [4,5]. As is the case of the research work in which a PID controller with Particle Swarm Optimization (PSO) tuning is chosen to improve the system response of the three-phase separator [4], however, the system is still considered as linear and single-variable when in fact the real dynamics of the industrial process is multivariable, which means that its variables are correlated.

Another of the controllers used is the PI controller in order to maintain the required water level, since this type of control works appropriately for first-order processes, as is the case of the water level and SISO systems [6]. Although the proposal shows a minimum error, in the transient state, an overshot is produced, this could be improved with the use of advanced controllers, such as model predictive control (MPC) with feedforward action that is applied to a three-phase separator [7], which is efficient, however, it does not consider the real dynamics of the system because it is modeling based on transfer functions; when in fact the system is highly nonlinear. On the other hand, advanced control techniques such as fuzzy control are used in the regulation of variables in the separator, the results show a higher efficiency and lower sensitivity to the effect of gases [8].

It has been shown that advanced controllers have a better performance than traditional PI or PID controllers in industrial processes with nonlineal and multivariable dynamics, for instance, the control of cycle-combined process [9,10] or reactor multivariable with control of temperature and level [11]. However, in the industry, these controllers are unusually implemented, this is mainly because the control devices are mostly programmable logic controllers (PLC) that do not have simple tools to implement these strategies. On the other hand, the design of advanced control strategies requires knowledge and experience. Therefore, during the engineering learning in the area of process control, design and experimentation are required, considering real industrial processes, which are very expensive. For this reason, it has been useful and appropriate the fact of creating industrial processes or virtual laboratories, as they allow to have environments similar to real processes such as a two-phase separator [9], a virtual laboratory multivariable for temperature and level control [12], or a pressure process in order to implement advanced controllers [13]. However, these virtual industrial processes do not allow interaction with physical controllers, therefore, the hardware technique has been implemented, so the user can experiment with the virtualized process and with the physical control device.

In this research project, a hardware in the loop environment is designed for a horizontal three-phase separator which can be controlled from any physical control device, for instance, a programmable logic controller (PLC). In addition, traditional and advanced controllers are compared to validate the impact of advanced controllers in nonlinear multivariable industrial processes. The main contributions of this research work are: i) A hardware in the loop design methodology that can be replicated in other industrial processes. ii) A realistic nonlinear multivariable modelling of a three-phase separator. iii) The design of an advanced control strategy for the efficient operation of the three-phase separator. iv) A methodology to implement an advanced MPC control in a programmable logic controller (PLC) for industrial use.

2   Description and Mathematical Modeling of the Three-Phase Separator

In this section, the operation of the three-phase separator is described and analyzed. In addition, the description of the mathematical models is shown.

2.1   Description of the Three-Phase Separator Operation

To understand the behavior of the three-phase separator, the piping and instrumentation diagram (P&ID) for the horizontal three-phase separator is used (Fig. 1), where the instrumentation and process equipment are shown.

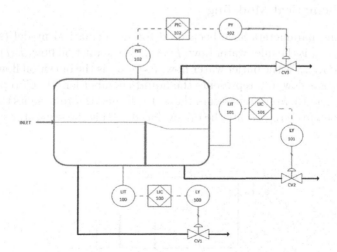

Fig. 1. Three-phase separator P&ID diagram.

In Fig. 1 there is a constant oil inlet (INLET), the separation process includes three control loops: 100, 101 and 102. The control loop 100 is responsible for controlling the water level and also requires a level indicator transmitter (LIT-100), whose signal enters to the level indicator controller (LIC-100), the output is connected to the actuator which is a control valve (CV1), and passes through an electric to a pneumatic signal converter, which in this case is a level relay (LY-100). The control loop 101 is responsible for controlling the oil level and requires a level indicator transmitter (LIT-101), whose signal enters to the level indicator controller (LIC-101), the output is connected to the actuator which is a control valve (CV2), and passes through an electrical to pneumatic signal converter, which in this case is a level relay (LY-101). The control loop 102 is responsible for controlling the pressure inside the separator and requires a pressure transmitter (PT-102), whose signal enters the pressure indicating controller (PIC-102), the output is connected to the actuator which is a control valve (CV3), and passes through an electrical to pneumatic signal converter, which in this case is a pressure relay (PY-102).

The operating principle of the three-phase separator is based on the separation by gravity action, this process starts when the inlet fluid stream, coming directly from the oil producing wells, then, this fluid enters to the separator, where the first stage occurs when the oil flow hits the flow diverter, where the separation of gas and liquids occurs due to the change of momentum and the difference of their densities [1]. It is important that the liquid collection section has the volume and time necessary to separate the oil and emulsion from the water. The layer of oil and emulsion that forms on top of the water is called the oil pad. The weir controls the level of the oil pad, and the interface controller controls the water level through the water outlet valve. Oil and emulsion flow over the weir and into the oil accumulation section, where their level is controlled by a level controller through the oil outlet valve [1,3].

2.2   Mathematical Modeling

The following parameters have been used for mathematical model (see Fig. 2), where: $F(t)_{w\_in}$ is the inlet water flow, $F(t)_{l\_in}$ is the inlet oil flow, $F(t)_{g\_in}$ is inlet gas flow, $F(t)_{w\_out}$ is the outlet water flow, $F(t)_{l\_out}$ is the outlet oil flow, $F(t)_{g\_out}$ is the outlet gas flow, C_w represents the liquid chamber length, C_l represents the oil chamber length, $h(t)_w$ represents the water level, $h(t)_t$ represents the water-oil interface level, $h(t)_l$ represents the oil level and $P(t)$ is the separator pressure.

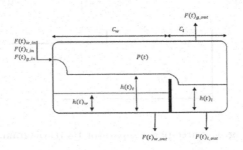

Fig. 2. Three-phase separator schematic diagram.

On the other hand, the differential equations that represent the dynamic model of a three-phase separator are given in terms such as $h(t)_w$, $h(t)_l$, $h(t)_t$ and $P(t)$. The differential equation to determine the water level inside the separator is given by Eq. 1

$$\frac{dh(t)_w}{dt} = \frac{F(t)_{w\_in} - F(t)_{w\_out}}{2C_w\sqrt{(D - h(t)_w)h(t)_w}} \tag{1}$$

where D is the separator diameter. For the oil-water interface level model, the dynamics of $h(t)_t$ is defined and described by the differential Eq. 2:

$$\frac{dh(t)_t}{dt} = \frac{F(t)_{w\_in} + F(t)_{l\_in} - F(t)_{vert} - F(t)_{w\_out}}{2C_w\sqrt{(D - h(t)_t)h(t)_t}} \tag{2}$$

where $F(t)_{vert}$, is the weir flow. For the oil level model, the dynamics of $h(t)_l$ is defined as shown in the following differential Eq. 3

$$\frac{dh(t)_l}{dt} = \frac{F(t)_{vert} - F(t)_{l\_out}}{2C_l\sqrt{(D - h(t)_l)h(t)_l}} \tag{3}$$

For pressure mathematical model, it is defined the dynamics of $P(t)$, described by the Eq. 4:

$$\frac{dP(t)}{dt} = \frac{P(t)[F(t)_{g\_in} + F(t)_{w\_in} + F(t)_{l\_in} - F(t)_{g\_out} - F(t)_{w\_out} - F(t)_{l\_out}]}{V_{3\phi} - V(t)_w - V(t)_l} \tag{4}$$

where $V_{3\phi}$, is the total volume of the separator, $V(t)_w$, is the volume of the water chamber and $V(t)_l$ is the volume of the oil chamber. The total volume of the three-phase separator is defined by Eq. 5.

$$V_{3\phi} = \pi \left(\frac{D}{2}\right)^2 C \tag{5}$$

where C is the total length of the three-phase separator.

For modeling the control of water, oil and gas outlet valves, an unidirectional flow is considered [14,15]. The water flow outlet F_{w_out} is given by Eq. 6, which represents the valve that allows water level control.

$$F(t)_{w\_out} = 2.4 \times 10^{-4}k_w a(t)_w \sqrt{P(t) - P_a} \tag{6}$$

where: k_w is the constant of the water level control valve, $a(t)_w$ is the water level control valve opening, $P(t)$ is the separator pressure and P_a is the pressure upstream of the valve.

Similarly, the oil outflow $F(t_{l\_out})$ is represented by Eq. 7 which represents the valve that allows oil level control.

$$F(t)_{l\_out} = 2.4 \times 10^{-4}k_l a(t)_l \sqrt{\frac{P(t) - P_a}{\frac{\rho_l}{\rho_{H2O\_15°C}}}} \tag{7}$$

where: k_l is the oil level control valve constant, $a(t)_l$ is the oil level control valve opening, ρ_l is the oil density and ρ_{H20} is the specific density of water at a temperature of $15,5\,°C$. Finally the gas flow is represented by Eq. 8.

$$F(t)_{g\_out} = 2.88 \times 10^{-4} k_g a(t)_g \sqrt{\frac{(P(t) - P_a)(P(t) + P_b)}{\dfrac{\rho(t)_g}{\rho_{H2O\_15°C}}}} \tag{8}$$

where: k_g is the gas control valve constant, $a(t)_g$ is the gas flow control valve opening, P_b is the upstream pressure and $\rho(t)_g$ is the gas density, which is given by Eq. 9, where M_g is the molecular weight of the gas, T is the temperature inside the separator and R is the gas constant.

$$\rho(t)_g = \frac{P(t) M_g}{RT} \tag{9}$$

The mathematical model represents the real dynamics of the process and it is necessary for the virtual process as it is part of the hardware in the loop environment.

3 Hardware in the Loop System Design for Three-Phase Horizontal Separator

The HIL technique is a simulation of the required system or process in real time. The real signals of the controller are connected to a test system using a computer in which there is a virtual representation of the process designed in Unity 3D software, which is used to develop 2D and 3D projects, as well as control applications, allowing the creation of solutions in industrial areas, such as training, simulation and immersive experiences in these environments. In this section, the scheme of the HIL environment and the methodology for the implementation of controllers of a three-phase separator are described. (see Fig. 3).

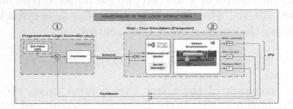

Fig. 3. Hardware in the Loop system for a three-phase separator.

The HIL system shown in Fig. 3 consists of two sections, Sect. 1 corresponds to the Programmable Logic Controller block, where the control algorithm is implemented, it could be PID, MPC and others, using the most appropriate software depending on the type of control device to be used, for instance the TIA portal software for Siemens S7 family, and then load it into the control device, in this case, the PLC S7-1500. It is also important to emphasize that you can use any control device. On the other hand, Sect. 2 refers to the virtualized industrial process; the connection between Sect. 1 and Sect. 2 is via Ethernet communication. From Sect. 1, the control values (CV) are sent to the three-phase separator control valves. The mathematical models obtained in Sect. 2.2 are incorporated into the virtual process by means of Visual Studio scripts in order to interact with the virtual environment developed in the Unity 3D software. The three-phase separator sends the process variables (PV), which are feedbacked to the control device, thus closing the control loop.

On the other hand, the methodology used for the virtualization of the three-phase separator starts from a piping and instrumentation diagram (P&ID) of an industrial process, in this case, the three-phase separator (see Fig. 1), the next step is the computer aided modeling (CAD) using Autocad Plant 3D software, where the measuring instruments involved in the three-phase separator are designed. Then, the previously created .fbx files are imported to the Unity 3D software, placing all necessary elements to make the virtual environment as realistic as possible. The models implemented in Visual Studio work jointly with the process designed in Unity 3D, at the same time this process works with the physical control device, thus, the Hardware in the Loop environment is conformed.

4   Three-Phase Separator Control Algorithms Design

After the virtual process is designed and validated, it is linked to the controllers, so this section describes the development of the control algorithms.

4.1   Traditional PID Control Strategy Design

The control law is given by the following Eq. 10

$$u(t) = K \left[e(t) + \frac{1}{T_i} \int_0^t e(t)\mathrm{d}t + T\frac{de(t)}{dt} \right] \qquad (10)$$

where $u(t)$ is the control value, K is the gain, T_i is the integral time and T_d is the differential time. To design this control, the Lambda tuning method was used, which uses Pole-zero cancellation to achieve the response in a closed-loop control system [16]. Three PID control loops are implemented in the three-phase separator, one for each variable, as shown in the closed loop diagram (Fig. 4).

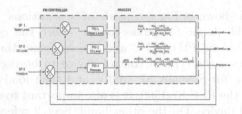

Fig. 4. PID control loop for the horizontal three-phase separator.

4.2   Model Predictive Control MPC Design

The advanced control law includes an objective function, constraints, a prediction horizon and a control horizon. The MPC control law includes predictive models that are responsible for predicting the behavior of a future controlled variable over a prediction horizon when applying control actions [17,18]. The predictive control based on MPC models includes an objective function that minimizes the errors of water level $h(t)_w$, oil level $h(t)_l$ and pressure $P(t)$ in the separator. Also, it minimizes the abrupt control actions to increase the life of the actuators as shown in Fig. 5.

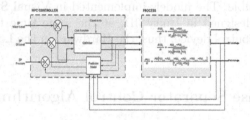

Fig. 5. MPC control loop for the horizontal three-phase separator.

The objective function $J(k)$ defined in Eq. 11 is responsible for minimizing the errors, where the first term $[\hat{h}_w(k+i \mid k) - h_{wd}(k+i \mid k)]^2$ is the squared error between the desired value and predicted value of level for minimizing water level errors, $\delta_1(k)$ is the weight for the first control objective, The second and third control objectives are similar to the first term for the oil level and pressure, followed by the variations of the control values, which must be minimal to protect the actuator, therefore the objective function includes $[\Delta u_1(k+i-1)]^2$, which is the variation of the quadratic control value for the water level control valve, $\lambda_1(k)$ is the weight for the control objectives, in the same way for $[\Delta u_2(k+i-1)]^2$, $[\Delta u_3(k+i-1)]^2$, and their respective weights $\lambda_2(k)$, $\lambda_3(k)$.

$$J(k) = \sum_{i=N_w}^{N_p} \delta_1(k) \left[\hat{h}_w(k+i \mid k) - h_{wd}(k+i \mid k)\right]^2 + ..$$

$$\delta_2(k) \left[\hat{h}_l(k+i \mid k) - h_{ld}(k+i \mid k)\right]^2 + \delta_2(k) \left[\hat{P}(k+i \mid k) - P_d(k+i \mid k)\right]^2 +$$

$$\sum_{i=0}^{N_c-1} \lambda_1(k) \left[\Delta u_1(k+i-1)\right]^2 + \lambda_2(k) \left[\Delta u_2(k+i-1)\right]^2 + ..$$

$$\lambda_3(k) \left[\Delta u_3(k+i-1)\right]^2$$

$$(11)$$

Furthermore, $\hat{h}_w(k+i \mid k)$ is the water level predicted output, $\hat{h}_l(k+i \mid k)$ is the oil level predicted output, $\hat{P}(k+i \mid k)$ is the pressure predicted output, $h_{wd}(k+i \mid k)$ is the desired value of water level, $h_{ld}(k+i \mid k)$ is the desired value of oil level, $Pd(k+i \mid k)$ is the desired value of pressure, and finally we have the variations of the control actions $\Delta u_n(k+i-1)$ corresponding to the three control valves.

The optimization problem is subject to inequality constraints, through an upper limit and a lower limit, for water level: $h_{wmin} \le h(t)_w \le h_{wmax}$, for oil level: $h_{lmin} \le h(t)_l \le h_{lmax}$ and finally for pressure: $P_{min} \le P \le P_{max}$. In addition, the constraints of the control value variations are included by setting maximum limits and minimum limits. The restriction of maximum (Δu_{max}) and minimum (Δu_{min}) limits of control value for water level control valve are shown in this way: $\Delta u_{min} \le \Delta u_1 \le \Delta u_{max}$, and in the same way for Δu_2, and Δu_3 for the other variables.

The constraints values are: $\Delta u_{min} = 0$, and $\Delta u_{max} = 1$; the water level limits are: $h_{w\_min} = 0[m]$ and $h_{w\_max} = 1.2[m]$, the oil level constraints are given by $h_{l\_min} = 0[m]$ and $h_{l\_max} = 1.2[m]$, and the pressure constraints are given by $P_{min} = 7[bar]$ and $P_{max} = 20[bar]$. On the other hand, the values corresponding to the weights of the process variables are the following: water level weight at $\delta_1 = 1$, oil level weight at $\delta_2 = 1.8$ and pressure weight at $\delta_3 = 0.4$. Finally, control actions weights are: $\lambda_1 = 0.005$, $\lambda_2 = 0.1$ and $\lambda_3 = 0.1$. In addition the other parameters required by the MPC control are control and prediction horizon, these are given by N_p, which have the same samples for water level, oil level and pressure. For prediction horizon a value of $N_w = 15$ was considered and for control horizon a value of $N_c = 3$ every 0.1 seconds was considered.

On the other hand, if it is required to implement this controller (MPC) in a PLC device, this does not have a toolbox or tools that allow us to implement directly. However, in this work, the following methodology used in order to advanced controllers can be implemented in PLC devices that are widely used in the industry: i) Implement the nonlinear process model by using Simulink toolbox ii) Design the MPC controller using the Matlab Simulink toolbox iii) Transform the MPC controller designed in Simulink to a structured code by using the PLC Coder tool in order to generate the control block, which is compatible with TIA portal software.

5   Analysis Results

This section analyzes the control strategies applied to the three-phase separator in a Hardware in the Loop simulation environment.

5.1   Virtual Environment of the Hardware in the Loop System

After implementing the HIL strategy, the following results were obtained regarding the virtual environment of three-phase separator and the interaction with the programmable logic controller (PLC).

Figure 6 shows the three-phase separator virtual environment that is similar to a real process, it has the respective instrumentation components, monitoring and control area and the multivariable nonlinear process dynamics animation.

Fig. 6. Three-phase separator virtual environment.

Regarding the monitoring and control area (Fig. 7), there are six screens distributed for the three control variables, which are: water level, oil level and pressure, in which the different parameters of the designed controllers can be observed, such as: set point, process variable, control value, disturbances and trends where the evolution of the PID and MPC controller is shown.

Fig. 7. Monitoring and control area.

Figure 8 shows the implementation of the hardware in the loop strategy, thus, the connection of the physical controller (PLC) where the designed controllers are implemented, with the virtualized process through Ethernet communication to validate the control algorithms is presented.

Fig. 8. Connection between the physical controller and the virtualized process.

In order to be able to communicate between the devices, it is necessary to know the Internet Protocol (IP) address of the programmable logic controller (PLC SIEMENS S7-1500) in order to create a link port between the virtualized process and the controller, which allows sending and receiving data to observe the nonlinear and multivariable dynamics of the process when a control action is applied.

5.2 Performance and Comparative Analysis Between the Strategies Control Proposed for the Three-Phase Horizontal Separator

The parameters used in the virtualized three-phase separator are: (see Sect. 2.2): $C = 8$ m, $D = 3$ m, $k_w = 410$, $k_l = 1024$, $k_g = 120$, $P_a = 6bar$, $P_b = 6bar$, $\rho_l = 850$ kg/L, $\rho_{H2O} = 999,19$ kg/L, $Mg = 0.029$ kg/mol, $C_l = 3$ m, $C_w - 5$ m, $g = 9.81$ m/s^2, $R = (0.08314474barL)/(mol°K)$, $T = 303.15°K$, $V = 56,6$ m^3. In addition, the initial conditions for the three variables to be controlled are: water level $h(t)_w = 0.1m$, oil level $h(t)_l = 0.1$ m, oil-water interface level $h(t)t = 1.5$ m, initial condition of pressure $P = 8bares$ and the inlet flows, water flow $F(t)_w = 0.1$ m^3/s, oil flow $F(t)_l = 0.1$ m^3/s and finally the gas flow $F(t)_g = 8$ m^3/s.

Figure 9a, shows the analysis of the water level variable, where the water level control in relation to a set point (red), the evolution of PID controller and its respective control value (green) and finally, the evolution of MPC controller and its respective control value (blue) are presented.

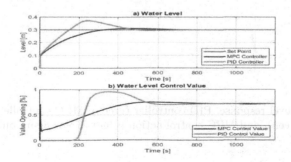

Fig. 9. a) Water level response, PID controller (green), MPC controller (blue). b) PID control value (green), and MPC control value (blue). (Color figure online)

For the water level control, there is a constant set point value at 0.3 m (Fig. 9.a), where the response for PID controller shows a overshoot at 233 s and it presents a slight oscillation until 750 s, where the controller reaches its settling time and remains constant from that time, the control error at steady state is within the tolerable range of 1%. On the other hand, the MPC controller does not present an overshoot, and has a settling time of 626 s, from this time the errors in the steady state are within the tolerable range of 1%.

Regarding the control values (Fig. 9b), it can be observed that with PID controller, the water control valve starts to act from 200 s and tends to open at 90% of its total value and at 800 s it maintains a constant opening of 75%. In contrast, with MPC controller, the control valve starts to act from 0 s, and tends to open at 75% of its total value and from 800 s it maintains a constant opening of 75%, showing a smoother response for the actuators.

Table 1 compares the results of the control parameters such as overshoot, settling time and steady-state error of PID and MPC controllers implemented in the three-phase separator.

Figure 10a, shows the analysis of three-phase separator oil level variable, where the oil level control in relation to a set point (red), the evolution of the PID controller and its respective control value (green) and finally, the evolution of the MPC controller and its respective control value (blue) are presented.

Table 1. Performance of the control algorithms in relation to the water level variable.

Parameters	PID controller	MPC controlle
	Water level	Water level
Overshoot [%]	20	0
Settling time [s]	750	625
Steady-state error [m]	2.9×10^{-4}	1.17×10^{-5}

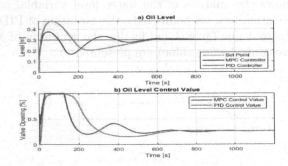

Fig. 10. a) Oil level response, PID controller (green), MPC controller (blue). b) PID control value (green), and MPC control action (blue) (Color figure online)

For the oil level control, a constant set point value of 0.3 m was taken (Fig. 10a). The PID controller has a overshoot at 66 s and it presents an oscillation until 890 s, when the controller reaches its settling time, the control error in steady state is within the tolerable range of 1%. On the other hand, the MPC controller presents a overshoot at 47 s, oscillating up to 675 s. The time where the controller reaches its settling time and from that its steady-state control error is within the range is a tolerable value of 1%.

Regarding the control values (Fig. 10b), it can be observed that with the PID controller, the oil level control valve starts to act from 0 s. It tends to open to 98% of its total value and at 900 s maintains a constant opening of 25%. In contrast, with the MPC controller, the control valve starts to act from 0 s, and tends to open completely and from 800 s maintains a constant opening of 25%, presenting a smoother response for the actuators.

Table 2 compares the results of the control parameters such as overshoot, settling time and steady-state error of PID and MPC controllers.

Figure 11a, shows the analysis of Variable Pressure of the three-phase separator, where the pressure control in relation to a set point (red), the evolution of the PID controller and its respective control value (green) and finally, the evolution of the MPC controller and its respective control avalue (blue) are presented.

Table 2. Performance of control algorithms in relation to the oil level variable

Parameters	PID controller	MPC controlle
	Water level	Water level
Overshoot [%]	56.6	16.6
Settling time [s]	890	675
Steady-state error [m]	26.6×10^{-4}	6.7×10^{-4}

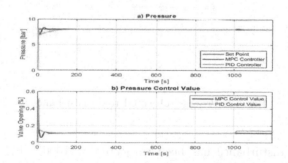

Fig. 11. a) Pressure response, PID controller (green), MPC controller (blue). b) PID control value (green), and MPC control action (blue). (Color figure online)

For the separator pressure control, a constant set point value of 8 bar is used (Fig. 11a). Where the PID controller presents a overshoot at 25 s, and a settling time of 188 s, from this time there is an steady-state control error within the tolerable range of 1%. While the MPC controller presents a maximum overshoot

at 30 s, and stabilizes at 55 s, from that instant, there is a steady state control
error within the tolerable range of 1%.

Regarding the control values (Fig. 11b), it can be observed that with the PID
controller, the pressure control valve starts to act from 0 s and tends to open
at 55% of its total value and at 900 s maintains a constant opening of 17%. In
contrast, with the MPC controller, the control valve starts to act from 0 s and
tends to open 19% and from 800 s maintains a constant opening of 12%, showing
a smoother response for the actuators.

Table 3 compares the results of the control parameters such as overshoot,
settling time and steady state error of PID and MPC controllers. Regarding
the controllers robustness analysis against to disturbances, a disturbance by
means of a gas flow (Fg(t)) at the inlet has been subjected. Figure 12 shows an
enlargement in the graph of disturbance and what it causes to the controlled
variables.

Table 3. Performance of the control algorithms in relation to the pressure variable.

Parameters	PID controller	MPC controlle
	Water level	Water level
Overshoot [%]	1.25	3.75
Settling time [s]	188	55
Steady-state error [m]	3.1×10^{-3}	5.91×10^{-4}

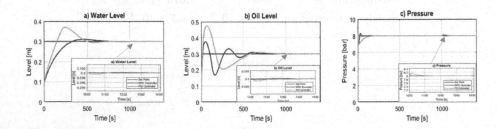

Fig. 12. Process subjected to a disturbance.

A gas flow disturbance has been subjected at 1000 s (Fig. 12) where the
behavior of PID and MPC controllers can be observed. The MPC controller
is not affected and remains at the set point, while the PID controller does show
variations when the disturbance occurs. Since the implemented process has multivariable nonlinear models, when a disturbance is made in one of the controlled
variables, this disturbance affects the other variables, thus validating the multivariable characteristic of the designed controller.

6 Conclusions

The HIL strategy design methodology allows obtaining an immersive virtual environment of the three-phase separator process, which worked together with the control algorithms designed and implemented in a physical control device, significantly reducing the cost of working with real processes from the academic point of view.

From the nonlinear multivariable mathematical models of the three-phase separator, it was possible to obtain a virtual environment similar to the real industrial process with similar dynamics in the virtualized system. In addition, different controls algorithms can be applied, for instance, lineal controllers or more complex multivariable and nonlinear controllers.

The MPC controller has a better performance as it has an average overshoot of 6.78% among the three variables compared to the PID controller whose average overshoot is 25.95%. It also has a lower settling time than the traditional controller and a minimum steady-state error. Therefore the MPC controller has a better response in nonlinear and multivariable processes.

Regarding the control value, it is observed that with the MPC controller, the control valves have a better response because their control value is smoother compared to the control values of the PID controller, which are a little more abrupt. Thus, by implementing the MPC controller, longer life of the actuators can be achieved.

Regarding the disturbance analysis, it is determined that the MPC controller does not show variations and remains at the set point, which is not the case with the PID controller when the disturbance occurs.

The proposed HIL system is flexible enough and allows not only to connect the PLC control device but any other device as it would only change the programming of the control algorithms depending on the language that handles the controller device. Moreover, it is flexible to implement any control algorithm, including advanced controllers.

References

1. Abdel-Aal, H.K., Aggour, M.A., Fahim, M.A.: Petroleum and Gas Field Processing. CRC Press (2003)
2. Mendoza Barahona, M.E., Rueda Villón, J.C., et al.: Simulación del control de un separador de producción trifásico de petróleo, B.S. thesis, Espol (2018)
3. Sayda, A.F., Taylor, J.H.: Modeling and control of three-phase gravity separators in oil production facilities. In: 2007 American Control Conference, pp. 4847–4853. IEEE (2007)
4. Mendes, P., Normey-Rico, J.E., Plucenio, A., Carvalho, R.: Disturbance estimator based nonlinear MPC of a three phase separator. IFAC Proc. Vol. 45(15), 101–106 (2012)
5. Backi, C.J., Skogestad, S.: Virtual inflow monitoring for a three phase gravity separator. In: 2017 IEEE Conference on Control Technology and Applications (CCTA), pp. 1499–1504. IEEE (2017)

6. Ajuste de un controlador de nivel de separador trifásico mediante algoritmo de optimización de enjambre de partículas. In: 2018 International Conference on Recent Trends in Electrical, Control and Communication (RTECC) (2018)
7. Viñan Andino, M.F.: Diseño e implementación de un sistema de control para operación automática de separadores de petróleo trifásicos. B.S. thesis, QUITO/EPN/2013 (2013)
8. Júnior, J.I.S.S., da Silva Linhares, L.L., da Silva, P.K.F., de Araújo, F.M.U.: Logica fuzzy para controle de vaso separador trifasico em plantas de processamento primario de petroleo, UFRN. Natal (2011)
9. Ortiz-Villalba, D., Arcos-Aviles, D., Poncc, C.: Fuzzy and PID controllers performance analysis for a combined-cycle thermal power plant. In: Recent Advances in Electrical Engineering, Electronics and Energy: Proceedings of the CIT 2020 Volume 1, vol. 762, p. 78 (2021)
10. Orrala, T., Burgasi, D., Llanos, J., Ortiz-Villalba, D.: Model predictive control strategy for a combined-cycle power-plant boiler. In: 2021 IEEE International Conference on Automation/XXIV Congress of the Chilean Association of Automatic Control (ICA-ACCA), pp. 1–6. IEEE (2021)
11. Feijoo, J.D., Chanchay, D.J., Llanos, J., Ortiz-Villalba, D.: Advanced controllers for level and temperature process applied to virtual Festo MPS® pa workstation. In: 2021 IEEE International Conference on Automation/XXIV Congress of the Chilean Association of Automatic Control (ICA-ACCA), pp. 1–6. IEEE (2021)
12. Chanchay, D.J., Feijoo, J.D., Llanos, J., Ortiz-Villalba, D.: Virtual Festo MPS® PA workstation for level and temperature process control. In: Botto Tobar, M., Cruz, H., Díaz Cadena, A. (eds.) CIT 2020. LNEE, vol. 762, pp. 164–180. Springer, Cham (2021). https://doi.org/10.1007/978-3-030-72208-1_13
13. Llanos-Proaño, J., Pilatasig, M., Curay, D., Vaca, A.: Design and implementation of a model predictive control for a pressure control plant. In: 2016 IEEE International Conference on Automatica (ICA-ACCA), pp. 1–7. IEEE (2016)
14. Pinto, D.: Estratégias de controle contra intermitência severa na alimentaçao de separadores offshore. Federal University of Rio de Janeiro, Rio de Janeiro (2009)
15. Proaño Cardenas, J.C.: Simulación numérica de un proceso de separación trifásico para una corriente de hidrocarburos, Master's thesis, UCE, Quito (2015)
16. Pruna, E., Andaluz, V.H., Proaño, L.E., Carvajal, C.P., Escobar, I., Pilatásig, M.: Construction and analysis of PID, fuzzy and predictive controllers in flow system. In: 2016 IEEE International Conference on Automatica (ICA-ACCA), pp. 1–7. IEEE (2016)
17. Camacho, E.F., Alba, C.B.: Model Predictive Control. Springer, London (2013). https://doi.org/10.1007/978-0-85729-398-5
18. Gómez Ortega, M.A., Correa Cely, C.R.: Implementacion de un sistema de control predictivo multivariable en un horno, Dyna (2009)

Appropriate Technology for Solar Thermal Desalination by Concentration Applied the Humidification-Dehumidification Method

B. E. Tarazona-Romero[1]([envelope]) [iD], A. Campos-Celador[2] [iD], O. Lengerke-Perez[1] [iD],
N. Y. Castillo-Leon[1] [iD], and A. D. Rincon-Quintero[1] [iD]

[1] College of Natural Sciences and Engineering, Unidades Tecnológicas de Santander,
Bucaramanga, Colombia
{btarazona,olengerke,arincon}@correo.uts.edu.co
[2] Energy Engineering Department, University of the Basque Country, Bizkaia, Spain
alvaro.compos@ehu.eus

Abstract. There is an urgent need to develop technologies that purify available water resources in territories that have limited access to fresh water. As a result, it was possible to analyze the suitability of desalination technology by the humidification-dehumidification method (HDH) for a given context, based on the appropriate technology paradigm, defined as technologically decentralized, labor-intensive, environmentally sustainable solutions. And economically, autonomous and energetically efficient This article evaluates the configurations of the desalination method by HDH energetically fed by solar concentration systems under the paradigm of appropriate technology. To do this, it defines the system in two parts: HDH desalination subsystem and solar concentration subsystem. Each subsystem will be evaluated based on compliance with 7 attributes. A specific literature review has been developed to analyze each subsystem as appropriate technology by means of a matrix. The information analysis method was based on the formal concept analysis methodology using the Concep Explorer tool. The analysis shows that the combination of closed water cycle HDH desalination systems in water, open in air and water cycle, open in water and air, integrated with Linear Fresnel systems are considered the best option to meet the requirements of appropriate technology as a single freshwater production system. Finally, it is important to highlight that the developed methodology has proven to be an adequate tool for the evaluation of technologies as a first step to identify advantages and disadvantages in each one of them, through a deterministic set of attributes.

Keywords: Formal analysis of concepts · Linear fresnel reflector · Solar desalination · Solar concentrators

1 Introduction

The desalination process is perceived as one of the most viable and oldest to face the problem posed by the United Nations Organization (ONU), which projects a water shortage for the year 2050, in which around 7 million people in 60 countries will be affected [1]. Desalination consists of removing salts or other minerals and contaminants from seawater and brackish water, to obtain fresh water for human consumption [2]. Sea water differs from brackish water by the levels of saline concentration that vary in ranges of 35 a 50 g/l and 0,5 a 35 g/l respectively [3].

For its part, the solar thermal desalination process consists of the integration of desalination techniques and renewable energy technologies that includes: photovoltaic and thermal systems [4]. The uses of photovoltaic and thermal systems are necessary to operate desalination units, due to the consumption of electrical energy by the control and monitoring systems of centralized or large-scale systems, as well as thermal systems, which directly feed the desalination processes [5].

Additionally, the solar thermal desalination process has two methods: direct or indirect. On the one hand, the direct thermal solar desalination technique captures normal solar radiation (DNI), generating heat that makes a phase change from liquid to gas of the saline water contained in the system in a single stage.

In turn, solar collection systems take advantage of the DNI and are divided into technologies: 1D that reach temperatures of up to 100 °C, 2D concentration technologies that reach temperatures up to 500 °C and 3D that reach temperatures of up to 1000 °C, for centralized systems [6]. These technologies, in decentralized or small-scale applications, have different characteristics: 1D technology has performance problems and the ability to supply sufficient flows to feed small or scalable desalination units [7]. 2D technology operates with efficiencies less than 50% of centralized equipment, but offers appropriate temperatures and flows to feed small-scale solar desalination units [8].

As a result of the need for the development of decentralized technologies, capable of carrying out the desalination process, emerging technological alternatives arise, including techniques such as [9]; Humidification-dehumidification (HDH) [10] and solar stills [11]. The HDH solar thermal desalination technique does not present the restrictions of centralized technologies [12] and has advantages over solar stills such as: simple structure, work at low temperatures and pressures, without fuel consumption and with energy recovery capacity [10]. Therefore, the HDH solar thermal desalination system is a promising technique applicable for freshwater production in small remote areas with favorable solar normal radiation (DNI) conditions [13].

Considering the socio-economic situation present in isolated regions with problems of fresh water shortage, the concept of Appropriate Technology (AT) arises, which promotes the adaptation of technologies on a large scale, based on social, economic, environmental and cultural aspects of the specific regions targeted [14]. Eade and Williams describe appropriate technologies with general characteristics that include: low investment of money, prioritization of locally available materials, labor intensive, applied on a small scale, controlled and maintained by personnel without a high level of specific qualification, manufactured locally, flexible and with adaptation to socio-cultural contexts and friendly to the environment [15]. For example, if we compare centralized desalination technologies with HDH desalination technology, we see that, given its technological and material simplicity, the latter is better suited to the development of local solutions, reducing dependency on specialized industry. In the same way, the investment cost is lower and its integration with 2D solar radiation concentration systems for its operation, allows the generation of a sustainable system, with greater energy flows and, therefore, lower material needs per production unit.

Given the context, there is a need to link AT characteristics in the design of integrated HDH desalination techniques to 2D indirect concentrating solar systems (ICST). This work aims to contribute to it by providing a review of the types of HDH technologies, their integration with ICST 2D and, subsequently, analyzing their applicability as TA in isolated regions. It is important to mention that currently, there is no systematic method in the literature that allows the selection of the appropriate technology (AT). Additionally, both ICST 2D and HDH desalination systems each have variations in terms of complexity, environmental impact, energy and material needs, etc., so they will be analyzed in detail.

2   Methodology

AT is presented as a viable option over time for decentralized technological developments, taking advantage of local resources for component manufacturing, operation and maintenance, reducing investment costs. Currently there is no general definition for AT, but this work takes into consideration a series of specific characteristics: i) use of local skills for manufacturing, operation and maintenance; ii) benefits for the community, with minimal negative effects; iii) sustainable to operate in the long term; iv) low impact of environmental resources; v) application of simple and flexible systems, with small-scale capabilities and the possibility of scalability over time.

It is important to mention that AT is not a closed set of very clear specific characteristics, but rather a paradigm that is fulfilled to a greater or lesser extent. To be classified as AT, the subsystems are evaluated according to the following attributes:

A1. The system presents application in small units efficiently scalable in the future
A2. The system has low energy requirements (energy sustainable system)
A3. The system presents flexibility in construction and use of resources at the local level
A4. The system presents operability and maintenance of easy development, including local work with low previous technical requirements
TO 5. The system has low cost of initial implementation and long-term maintenance
A6 The system generates a low environmental impact
A7. The system is efficient in small-scale units

Considering the two subsystems that make up the HDH desalination technology by 2D solar concentration, a search for literary information is carried out, identifying the characteristics that satisfy the attributes stated above, to be within the AT category. The set of attributes described above will allow the development of a selection matrix and the identification of technological solutions that meet the AT requirements, generating a qualitative analysis of the subsystems.

In this document, FCA analyzes the subsystems and their integration, establishing through a separate matrix the variables that satisfy the AT levels. The analysis is carried out by applying the open access software "Concept Explorer" [16], which allows evaluating the existing relationships between objects and attributes, previously defined within the formal concept analysis (FCA).

3   2D Indirect Solar Desalination Technologies HDH by 2D Concentration

The set of systems that make up the HDH desalination technology by 2D solar concentration, are described through two subsystems: HDH desalination and 2D solar concentration. Additionally, the projects are analyzed at the level of experimentation with prototypes that integrate the two subsystems at a centralized and decentralized level.

3.1   HDH Desalination Subsystem

Humidification-dehumidification (HDH) is an emerging process favorably used in small-scale desalination plants. The main advantage of HDH configurations is that they operate efficiently under low temperature and low pressure conditions [17, 18], as well as the possibility of integrating with renewable and sustainable energy sources, applying low-level technologies [19]. Additionally, HDH cycles use separate components for each thermal process, generating flexibility when designing each element of the system [17]. Added to this, the manufacturing and operation prices are reasonable, and they can operate in a wide range of water quality, without complex maintenance needs [20], considered as appropriate technologies, for processes with low capital investment and limited technical support [19].

The conventional HDH process has three main components (See Fig. 1): humidifier, dehumidifier and heat supply system [19]. The humidifier consists of three components: spray nozzle, packed and Brine drainage container.

The dehumidifier on the other hand, is used for the condensation of the water vapor present in the humid air. It can contain copper coils with fins or without fins[21], through which the saline water is transferred at low temperature to condense the water vapor of the humid air coming from the humidifier. The most widely used dehumidifiers are flat plate and finned tube [22]. Additionally, pumps and fans are used to pump water and air, respectively.

In a simple water-heated configuration (See Fig. 1), the operation of the HDH system is as follows: the air flows in a closed circuit while the water flows in an open circuit. The salt water is pumped through the heat exchanger into the dehumidifier to recover energy from the moist condensing air. Coming out of the dehumidifier, the preheated water is further heated in a water heater. Hot water in the humidifier is sprayed onto a packing material in order to increase the heat and mass transfer area. Air flows through the humidifier in counter current through the packing material. The air is heated and humidified through its direct contact with the sprayed water [23]. Coming out of the humidifier, it almost approaches the saturation condition. The warm, moist air flows into the dehumidifier where the water vapor condenses to produce fresh water and the cool air is drawn back to the humidifier by a fan to repeat the cycle [24].

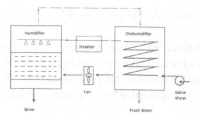

Fig. 1. HDH system [9]

In the literature there are investigations that present design configurations of HDH systems. These configurations are made up of different components and cycles. Thus, HDH systems are classified depending on the heating fluid (water/air), as well as the type of circuit through which the fluid is transferred (Open or closed). The classification can also be according to the energy source used, such as wind, geothermal, solar, electric or hybrid systems and the nature of the flow [25]; natural or forced, the latter being the preferred method to produce reasonable levels of water [26]shows the classification of Basic HDH desalination systems (Fig. 2).

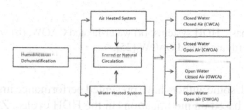

Fig. 2. Basic HDH desalination systems

Additionally, Fig. 3 shows the basic schemes of HDH systems by means of line diagrams. Figure 3(a) presents an open water, water heated closed air (OWCA) HDH system described above and presented in more detail in Fig. 3. For its part, Fig. 3(b) resents a system Closed Outdoor Heated Water (CWOA) Water HDHs; Its principle of operation is similar to CAOW, except that the water recirculates and the air leaves the system after condensing the steam. On the other hand, Fig. 3(c) shows the schematic of an open water, closed air and air heated (OWCA) HDH system, where the air heater is located between the humidifier and dehumidifier, to heat the air that enter the humidifier. Finally, Fig. 3(d) shows an open-air, heated-by-air (OWOA) closed-air HDH system, where the heater is only connected to the bottom of the humidifier [25].

Lawal and Qasem, in 2020, highlight that the "OWCA and CWOA" water-heated systems circulate the heating water through a pumping system and have excellent water production, low water cost related to production and optimum operating performance; differing, in that the OWCA system additionally requires a fan or compressor to circulate the air inside the cycle, while CWOA requires a pump to circulate the water inside the cycle [25]. On the other hand, the energy required by the pumping systems can easily be replaced by a thermosyphon to cover the flow demand. In turn, the water-heated OAOW cycle always outperforms the water-heated CAOW cycle regardless of ambient relative Humidity [23].

Additionally, "OWCA and CWOA" air-heated systems circulate heating air through a forced draft system fed by a fan or compressor and have lower water production, cost, and performance than air-heated systems water [27]. Generally, the air-heated CAOW cycle outperforms the OAOW cycle except when the ambient relative humidity approaches 100% [25].

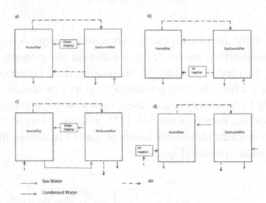

Fig 3. Schematics of basic HDH systems: (a) water-heated CAOW, (b) water-heated OACW, (c) air-heated CAOW, and (d) air-heated OAOW [25].

On the other hand, some authors have presented performance improvement studies of basic HDH systems, based on modifications in the HDH cycles. Zubair et al., modified a CWOA HDH system with hot water, where a large amount of seawater circulates through the dehumidifier to improve the condensation of water vapor, from moist air, in turn, a small amount of seawater It serves as a replenishment to compensate for the amount of seawater that evaporates and dilute the high levels of salt concentration in the brine [19].

Finally, it is important to note that Lawal and Qasem in 2020 compiled the main packing materials used in HDH configurations, highlighting that their application can be carried out in any configuration and improves device performance. The materials with the greatest application are [25]: Cellulose paper, Canvas, Wood surface, Plastic packaging, Ceramic corrugated packaging [28], Plastic screens, "aluminum foil" zigzag packaging, jute and sawdust sack, jute cloth, cross-ribbed film padding, Wood, PVC, fabric jute, HD Q-PAC, wooden slate packaging and wood cellulose.

When evaluating the attributes applying the methodology presented in Sect. 2, the matrix of Table 1 is built. The HDH configurations fed by air appear with the abbreviation "Air" and those fed by water with the abbreviation "Water". The attributes that are fulfilled are identified within the matrix with an X.

Table 1. Attribute matrix for the HDH desalination subsystem.

Technology	A1	A2	A3	A4	A5	A6	A7
Air_CWCA	X		X		X	X	
Air_CWOA	X		X		X	X	
Air_OWCA	X		X		X	X	
Air_OWOA	X		X		X	X	
Water_CWCA	X		X		X	X	X
Water_CWOA	X	X	X	X	X	X	X
Water_OWCA	X		X		X	X	X
Water_OWOA	X	X	X	X	X	X	X

3.2 2D Solar Concentration Subsystem

2D solar concentration systems take advantage of normal solar radiation (DNI) and reflect the solar rays in a linear focal point [29]. They are made up of two specific technologies: parabolic trough collectors (PTC) and linear Fresnel reflectors (LFC) [30]. The two technologies handle high operating temperatures and large flows in centralized systems, difficult to maintain on a small scale [31]. On the other hand, small-scale or decentralized systems compensate for the decrease in temperature with large flows, which makes them attractive for integration with small desalination units [32].

Linear Fresnel reflectors (LFC) and parabolic trough collectors (PTC) differ mainly in terms of construction: PTCs are made of parabolic-cylindrical mirrors that concentrate the sun's rays at the focal point (See Fig. 4b) [33] and the LFC are formed by strips of flat or slightly curved mirrors, which reflect and concentrate the solar rays in the focal point (See Fig. 4a) [34].

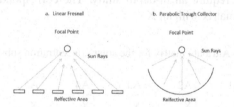

Fig. 4. 2D Concentration systems [26]

Regarding the characteristics in common regarding their integration with HDH desalination units, the two technologies share the flexibility to scale to different sizes, without incurring a significant increase in cost and manufacturing materials [35]. he scalability of these systems is generally given by varying the opening area of the reflecting mirrors. Both systems require energy to autonomously carry out solar tracking and heat transfer fluid pumping, but this can be supplied without generating functionality problems through manual tracking of the reflection area with respect to the solar path and applying a thermosiphon to ensure the flow of water during the commissioning of the device [36].

The two technologies basically use the same components, which are [32]: support structure of the reflection area, reflection surface "mirrors" and linear concentration receiver. The materials of each component may vary depending on the local scope, reducing the difficulty in maintenance, at the expense of a decrease in system performance. Generally, performance is higher in parabolic trough (PTC) technology [37, 38], implying that the investment cost is lower compared to LFC technology, but both technologies are commercially available and in great demand at a centralized level.. In the case of decentralized systems, the opposite happens, LFC technology has advantages of simplicity and flexibility when built locally; since, in this case, its manufacture does not depend on commercial maturity, but on the complexity of the system [39].

Additionally, the nature of solar collection between both options does not present a great difference, they only differ in the modularity of the collection area, where LFC has an advantage over PTC [40]. On the other hand, the maintenance of both devices refers to the superficial cleaning of the reflectors and the direct repair of components when they break down; less complex tasks in the LFC technology mirrors, which can be carried out by local personnel, without major requirements for specialized technical training [41].

Finally, the construction flexibility of the LFC systems has a positive effect against the transport of the device, allowing it to be disassembled into smaller and easier to mobilize components, compared to the reflection area of a PTC system [42]. Additionally, LFC technology allows adaptability in terms of the simplest reflection field, varying the number of mirrors, allowing it to be adapted to specific applications determined according to the needs of the region. On the other hand, in the case of PTC technology, the variation of the reflection area is not so simple and a new design is required to modify the devices [43].

Table 2 presents the attribute matrix for the two 2D concentrating solar technologies. Attribute 6 is not evaluated, because the two technologies generate an environmental impact that does not require an in-depth study. The corresponding attributes will be identified within the matrix with an X.

Table 2. Attribute matrix for the solar concentration subsystem 2d.

Technologies	A1	A2	A3	A4	A5	A6	A7
LFC	X	X	X	X	X	N/A	X
PTC		X		X	X	N/A	X

3.3   2D Technological Advances in HDH Desalination Systems by 2D Solar Concentration

Zubair et al., in 2018 presents the comparison of several basic systems and HDH modifications powered by solar concentrators in terms of performance (See Table 3), concluding that the air-heated and modified CAOW and CWOA system present a higher GOR index [19].

Table 3. Comparison of basic HDH systems [13].

Basic Systems	GOR
CAOW – Air Heated Cycle	0,78
CAOW – Multi-Stage Air Heated Cycle	0,85
CAOW – Modified Air Heated Cycle	3,5
CAOW – Water Heated Cycle	2,5
CWOA – Water Heated Cycle	2,6
CWOA – Modified Heated Cycle Air	3,5

Additionally, in 2020, Lawal and Qasem presents an analysis of the basic HDH systems (CWCA, CWOA, OWCA and OWOA) powered by thermal and concentrating solar systems with FPC, ETC, FLC and PTC technologies, concluding [25]: solar water heaters have better water production conditions than air systems, as well as higher performance and systems with air heaters are not very applicable due to problems of low air density and little tightness.

Finally, Alnaimat et al., in 2021 presents a review of recent advances in HDH technologies using solar energy, highlighting that solar-powered HDH systems are the future of small-scale freshwater production, presenting improvements in production costs. Investment and reduction of environmental impact. Highlighting that the PTC technology presents greater technological and experimental development integrated to HDH systems, than the LFC concentration technology [27].

4 Discussion

This section develops the critical evaluation of the review carried out in Sect. 3 applying the Formal Concept Analysis (FCA) method. Figure 5 presents the graphic diagram of the FCA output corresponding to the classification of the desalination subsystem by the Humidification-Dehumidification (HDH) method, based on the attribute matrix in Table 1. This diagram relates 8 HDH configurations with those 7 attributes that characterize a technology as appropriate. The nodes that appear in the diagram are identified as follows: white-blue are attribute-only containers, white-black are technology-only containers, and blue-black are attribute-related technology containers.

Given the above, understanding the diagram is simple. Each type of HDD configuration relates to all the attributes that connect up to the source node. Thus, the Water_OWCA and Water_OWOA configurations represent the option that connects with the greatest number of attributes, since it is related to the 7 attributes. Specifically, Water_OWCA and Water_OWOA are the only options with low energy requirements (A2) and easy maintenance and operation, including labor intensive (A4). Additionally, it shares an attribute with Water_OWCA and Water_CWCA, showing that HDH cycles by water are efficient in small-scale units (A7). The remaining 4 attributes are shared by all water HDH cycles with all air HDH cycles. Finally, all the HDH air cycle technologies have applications in small units with scalability (A1), have flexibility in construction and use of local resources (A3), their construction implies low capital investment (A5) and the system generates low environmental impacts (A6).

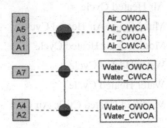

Fig. 5. FCA diagram for HDH desalination unit cycles

From this analysis, it can be seen that HDH technologies operated by air cycles have sought to provide solutions in a more centralized way, with intensive use of energy resources and levels of automation when operating and maintaining the unit, limiting their use to developing regions. As an alternative to this approach, we can state that the HDH cycles Water_OWOA and Water_CWOA are more suitable, followed by Water_OWCA and Water_CWCA. Among these, the advantage lies in the flexibility when operating the units and in the minimum energy requirements.

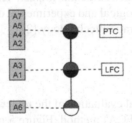

Fig. 6. FCA diagram for solar concentration subsystems

Analogously, Fig. 6 represents the graphic diagram of the formal analysis of concepts corresponding to the solar collection subsystem. In this case, the analysis is very simple because the objects are the PTC and LFC concentrating solar technologies. Linear Fresnel Reflectors (LFC) are the most suitable option for the current case study, connected to 6 attributes, of which it is individually connected to two attributes, standing out for its applicability in small units with future scalability (A1) and flexibility. in construction and use of local resources (A3). Additionally, LFC shares attributes with parabolic trough collectors (PTC), which means that LFC is currently the most attractive option to integrate with desalination systems using the Humidification and Dehumidification

(HDH) method. It is important to highlight that this type of system does not produce direct environmental impacts, therefore attribute A6 was not a direct part of the analysis.

In general, PTC is currently the option with the greatest application at a centralized level, specifically in solar thermal plants for the production of electrical energy. In these applications, the requirements are opposite to the systems developed under the paradigm of appropriate technology, since they are developed in developed regions with considerable capital investments. Consequently, PTC is presented within linear concentrating solar technologies as the most mature. However, LFC is also found in some large-scale systems as a renewable option for generation plants, however, it has favorable characteristics to adapt to the needs of isolated regions under the paradigm of appropriate technology, opening a window to increase its application. And reach technological maturity in the medium term.

5 Conclusions

The integration of desalination systems and renewable technologies take advantage of the large amounts of solar radiation that commonly exist in those territories that lack water. For this reason, the different cycles of desalination systems have been evaluated by the Humidification and Dehumidification (HDH) method, integrated with linear solar concentration technologies, using the formal concept analysis (FCA) methodology directed especially for this purpose. The HDH systems were divided into 8 operation cycles and the linear concentration systems were divided into two technologies. From the analysis of the information, the following conclusions were obtained:

HDH air cycles are targeted solutions for medium scale units, so when it comes to appropriate technology applications, HDH water cycles are more suitable solutions as they are highly efficient at small scale. Currently, the HDH Water_OWOA and Water_CWOA cycles lack maturity, however, external energy requirements are minimal and their operation is simple, easily supplied with local human resources. There is still a need to expand technology development with the different configurations of HDH cycles to achieve technological consolidation, with commercially viable alternatives.

In the analysis presented in this document, only the linear concentration options for the energy supply were considered, because it is simple to adapt them to the energy demands of the HDH units. Of the two technologies analyzed under the appropriate technology approach, although LFC has neither the maturity nor the efficiency of PTC technology, it has characteristics such as modularity, application in small units with acceptable efficiencies, flexibility in construction and operability with local human resource. However, despite these favorable factors, technological developments are still required to improve the efficiency of the system using materials that are easily available in isolated areas.

On the other hand, the results show that there are post-improvement characteristics in the development of technologies under the paradigm of appropriate technology, that is, there is a social and economic need to develop alternative systems according to the context of impoverished regions. Finally, the FCA methodology applied for the analysis of the information has proven to be a useful tool to evaluate the integration of dispersed technologies, serving as an initial phase to relate common characteristics of various alternatives through attributes or deterministic characteristics.

References

1. Ihsanullah, T.L., et al.: Novel anti-microbial membrane for desalination pretreatment: a silver nanoparticle-doped carbon nanotube membrane. Desalination **376**, 82–93 (2015). https://doi.org/10.1016/j.desal.2015.08.017
2. Jalihal, P., Venkatesan, R.: Chapter 4 - Advanced desalination technologies. In: Galanakis, C.M., Agrafioti, E. (eds.) Sustainable Water and Wastewater Processing, pp. 93–131. Elsevier (2019). https://doi.org/10.1016/B978-0-12-816170-8.00004-1
3. Kress, N.: Chapter 2 - Desalination technologies. In: Kress, N. (ed.) Marine Impacts of Seawater Desalination, pp. 11–34. Elsevier (2019). https://doi.org/10.1016/B978-0-12-811953-2.00002-5
4. Abu El-Maaty, A.E., Awad, M.M., Sultan, G.I., Hamed, A.M.: Solar powered fog desalination system. Desalination **472**, 114130 (2019). https://doi.org/10.1016/j.desal.2019.114130
5. Anand, B., Shankar, R., Murugavelh, S., Rivera, W., Midhun Prasad, K., Nagarajan, R.: A review on solar photovoltaic thermal integrated desalination technologies. Renew. Sustain. Energy Rev. **141**, 110787 (2021). https://doi.org/10.1016/j.rser.2021.110787
6. Sakthivadivel, D., Balaji, K., Dsilva, D., Rufuss, W., Iniyan, S., Suganthi, L.: Chapter 1 - solar energy technologies: principles and applications. In: Ren, J. (ed.) Renewable-Energy-Driven Future, pp. 3–42. Academic Press (2021). https://doi.org/10.1016/B978-0-12-820539-6.00001-7
7. Aktaş, A., Kirçiçek, Y.: Chapter 1 - solar system characteristics, advantages, and disadvantages. In: Aktaş, A., Kirçiçek, Y. (eds) Solar Hybrid Systems, pp. 1–24. Academic Press (2021). https://doi.org/10.1016/B978-0-323-88499-0.00001-X
8. Lovegrove, K., Stein, W.: Chapter 1 - Introduction to concentrating solar power technology. In: Lovegrove, K., Stein, W. (eds.) Concentrating Solar Power Technology, 2nd edn, pp. 3–17. Woodhead Publishing (2021). https://doi.org/10.1016/B978-0-12-819970-1.00012-8
9. Hernandez, R.D.T.: Identificación De Las Tecnologías Alternativas De Desalinización De Agua De Mar Que Involucren Sistemas Termo Solares Y De Destilación (2020). Accedido: 3 de mayo de 2021. http://repositorio.uts.edu.co:8080/xmlui/handle/123456789/4860
10. Essa, F.A., Abdullah, A.S., Omara, Z.M., Kabeel, A.E., El-Maghlany, W.M.: On the different packing materials of humidification–dehumidification thermal desalination techniques – a review. J. Clean. Prod. **277**, 123468 (2020). https://doi.org/10.1016/j.jclepro.2020.123468
11. Srithar, K., Rajaseenivasan, T., Karthik, N., Periyannan, M., Gowtham, M.: Stand alone triple basin solar desalination system with cover cooling and parabolic dish concentrator. Renew. Energy **90**, 157–165 (2016). https://doi.org/10.1016/j.renene.2015.12.063
12. Anand, B., Murugavelh, S.: Performance analysis of a novel augmented desalination and cooling system using modified vapor compression refrigeration integrated with humidification-dehumidification desalination. J. Clean. Prod. **255**, 120224 (2020). https://doi.org/10.1016/j.jclepro.2020.120224
13. Narayan, G.P., Sharqawy, M.H., Lienhard, John H., Zubair, S.M.: Thermodynamic analysis of humidification dehumidification desalination cycles. Desalination Water Treat. **16**(1–3), 339–353 (2012). https://doi.org/10.5004/dwt.2010.1078
14. Parnwel, M.: Intermediate technology, pp. 523–528 (2009). https://doi.org/10.1016/B978-008044910-4.00103-6
15. Eade, D., Williams, S.: The Oxfam Handbook of Development and Relief, vol. 1. Oxfam, Londres (1995)
16. Source Forge. The Concept Explorer (2021). http://conexp.sourceforge.net/. Accedido 18 de mayo de 2021

17. Prakash Narayan, G., Sharqawy, M.H., Summers, E.K., Lienhard, J.H., Zubair, S.M., Antar, M.A.: The potential of solar-driven humidification–dehumidification desalination for small-scale decentralized water production. Renew. Sustain. Energy Rev. **14**(4), 1187–1201 (2010). https://doi.org/10.1016/j.rser.2009.11.014

18. Klausner, J.F., Li, Y., Darwish, M., Mei, R.: Innovative diffusion driven desalination process. J. Energy Res. Technol. **126**(3), 219–225 (2004). https://doi.org/10.1115/1.1786927

19. Ifras Zubair, M., Al-Sulaiman, F.A., Antar, M.A., Al-Dini, S.A., Ibrahim, N.I.: Performance and cost assessment of solar driven humidification dehumidification desalination system. Energy Conv. Manag. **132**, 28–39 (2017). https://doi.org/10.1016/j.enconman.2016.10.005

20. Al-Sulaiman, F.A., Ifras Zubair, M., Atif, M., Gandhidasan, P., Al-Dini, S.A., Antar, M.A.: Humidification dehumidification desalination system using parabolic trough solar air collector. Appl. Thermal Eng. **75**, 809–816 (2015). https://doi.org/10.1016/j.applthermaleng.2014.10.072

21. Chafik, E.: Design of plants for solar desalination using the multi-stag heating/humidifying technique. Desalination **168**, 55–71 (2004). https://doi.org/10.1016/j.desal.2004.06.169

22. El-Agouz, S.A., Abugderah, M.: Experimental analysis of humidification process by air passing through seawater. Energy Conv. Manag. **49**(12), 3698–3703 (2008). https://doi.org/10.1016/j.enconman.2008.06.033

23. Sharqawy, M.H., Antar, M.A., Zubair, S.M., Elbashir, A.M.: Optimum thermal design of humidification dehumidification desalination systems. Desalination **349**, 10–21 (2014). https://doi.org/10.1016/j.desal.2014.06.016

24. Ettouney, H.: Design and analysis of humidification dehumidification desalination process. Desalination **183**(1–3), 341–352 (2005). https://doi.org/10.1016/j.desal.2005.03.039

25. Lawal, D.U., Qasem, N.A..A..: Humidification-dehumidification desalination systems driven by thermal-based renewable and low-grade energy sources: a critical review. Renew. Sustain. Energy Rev. **125**, 109817 (2020). https://doi.org/10.1016/j.rser.2020.109817

26. Tarazona-Romero, B.E., Campos-Celador, A., Maldonado-Muñoz, Y.A.: Can solar desalination be small and beautiful? a critical review of existing technology under the appropriate technology paradigm. Energy Res. Social Sci. **88**, 102510 (2022). https://doi.org/10.1016/j.erss.2022.102510

27. Alnaimat, F., Ziauddin, M., Mathew, B.: A review of recent advances in humidification and dehumidification desalination technologies using solar energy. Desalination **499**, 114860 (2021). https://doi.org/10.1016/j.desal.2020.114860

28. Gang, W., Zheng, H., Ma, X., Kutlu, C., Yuehong, S.: Experimental investigation of a multistage humidification-dehumidification desalination system heated directly by a cylindrical Fresnel lens solar concentrator. Energy Conv. Manag. **143**, 241–251 (2017). https://doi.org/10.1016/j.enconman.2017.04.011

29. Meyer, R., Schlecht, M., Chhatbar, K., Weber, S.: Chapter 3 - Solar resources for concentrating solar power systems. In: Lovegrove, K., Stein, W. (eds.) Concentrating Solar Power Technology, 2nd edn., pp. 73–98. Woodhead Publishing (2021). https://doi.org/10.1016/B978-0-12-819970-1.00014-1

30. Santos, J.J.C.S., Palacio, J.C.E., Reyes, A.M.M., Carvalho, M., Freire, A.J.R., Barone, M.A.: Chapter 12 - concentrating solar power. In: Yahyaoui, I. (ed.) Advances in Renewable Energies and Power Technologies, pp. 373–402. Elsevier (2018). https://doi.org/10.1016/B978-0-12-812959-3.00012-5

31. Häberle, A., Krüger, D.: Chapter 18 - Concentrating solar technologies for industrial process heat», In: Lovegrove, K., Stein, W. (eds.) Concentrating Solar Power Technology, 2nd edn., pp. 659–675. Woodhead Publishing (2021). https://doi.org/10.1016/B978-0-12-819970-1.00011-6

32. El Bassam, N.: Chapter Seven - solar energy: technologies and options. In: El Bassam, N. (ed.) Distributed Renewable Energies for Off-Grid Communities, 2nd edn., pp. 123–147. Elsevier, Boston (2021). https://doi.org/10.1016/B978-0-12-821605-7.00015-5

33. Malekan, M., Khosravi, A., El Haj Assad, M.: Chapter 6 - parabolic trough solar collectors. In: Assad, M.E.H., Rosen, M.A. (eds.) Design and Performance Optimization of Renewable Energy Systems, pp. 82–100. Academic Press (2021). https://doi.org/10.1016/B978-0-12-821602-6.00007-9

34. Abbas, R., Martínez-Val, J.M.: A comprehensive optical characterization of linear Fresnel collectors by means of an analytic study. Appl. Energy 185, 1136–1151 (2017). https://doi.org/10.1016/j.apenergy.2016.01.065

35. El Gharbi, N., Derbal, H., Bouaichaoui, S., Said, N.: A comparative study between parabolic trough collector and linear Fresnel reflector technologies. Energy Procedia 6, 565–572 (2011). https://doi.org/10.1016/j.egypro.2011.05.065

36. López, J.C., Escobar, A., Cárdenas, D.A., Restrepo, Á.: Parabolic trough or linear fresnel solar collectors? an exergy comparison of a solar-assisted sugarcane cogeneration power plant. Renew. Energy 165, 139–150 (2021). https://doi.org/10.1016/j.renene.2020.10.138

37. Anish Malan, K., Kumar, R.: A comprehensive review on optical analysis of parabolic trough solar collector. Sustain. Energy Technol. Assess. 46, 101305 (2021). https://doi.org/10.1016/j.seta.2021.101305

38. Famiglietti, A., Lecuona, A.: Small-scale linear Fresnel collector using air as heat transfer fluid: experimental characterization. Renew. Energy 176, 459–474 (2021). https://doi.org/10.1016/j.renene.2021.05.048

39. Abbas, R., Valdés, M., Montes, M.J., Martínez-Val, J.M.: Design of an innovative linear Fresnel collector by means of optical performance optimization: a comparison with parabolic trough collectors for different latitudes. Solar Energy 153, 459–470 (2017). https://doi.org/10.1016/j.solener.2017.05.047

40. Montes, M.J., Rubbia, C., Abbas, R., Martínez-Val, J.M.: A comparative analysis of configurations of linear Fresnel collectors for concentrating solar power. Energy 73, 192–203 (2014). https://doi.org/10.1016/j.energy.2014.06.010

41. Vouros, A., Mathioulakis, E., Papanicolaou, E., Belessiotis, V.: On the optimal shape of secondary reflectors for linear Fresnel collectors. Renew. Energy 143, 1454–1464 (2019). https://doi.org/10.1016/j.renene.2019.05.044

42. Fuqiang, W., Ziming, C., Jianyu, T., Yuan, Y., Yong, S., Linhua, L.: Progress in concentrated solar power technology with parabolic trough collector system: a comprehensive review. Renew. Sustain. Energy Reviews 79, 1314–1328 (2017). https://doi.org/10.1016/j.rser.2017.05.174

43. Abdulhamed, A.J., Adam, N.M., Ab-Kadir, M.Z.A., Hairuddin, A.A.: Review of solar parabolic-trough collector geometrical and thermal analyses, performance, and applications. Renew. Sustain. Energy Rev. 91, 822–831 (2018). https://doi.org/10.1016/j.rser.2018.04.085

Practical Framework for Optimal Planning of Microgrids for Production Processes

J. Llanos, D. Ortiz-Villalba$^{(\boxtimes)}$, M. Saltos-Rodríguez, C. Chipantiza-Punguil, and R. Guaita-Rojano

Universidad de las Fuerzas Armadas ESPE, Sangolqui, Ecuador
{jdllanos1,ddortiz5}@espe.edu.ec

Abstract. The communities face some energy problems, but the reliability and power quality are still challenging. In addition, hundreds of communities lack access to energy entirely, affecting production activities and community development. This paper proposes a methodology for the optimal planning microgrids considering distributed energy resources (DERs) such as photovoltaic systems (PV), wind turbine (WT), micro-hydro (MH) systems, battery energy storage systems (BESS), gas generator sets (GGS) and Diesel generators sets (DGS). In addition, we consider the flexible loads of production processes and non-controllable demands of production processes. The proposed methodology was validated in the rural area "Los Laureles" in the province of Sucumbios in Ecuador, considering the Pitajaya production process. The results show that our methodology can obtain a microgrid planned with an optimal mix of DERs and reduce the powering-up time of the water pumps (flexible loads) associated with the washing of Pitajaya due to maximizes the use of renewable energy resources available. Our methodological framework might be used in any communities to maximize the technical-economic benefits and minimize operating and investment costs.

Keywords: Distributed energy resources · Microgrids · Optimal planning · Production processes

1 Introduction

Universal access to electricity is deemed critical for improving living standards, allowing eradication of poverty, ensuring access to health and education through growth sustainable in the production processes and achieving society's development[1]. However, it is estimated that approximately 10.47% of people do not have continuous access to electric power in the world [2]. According to the International Energy Agency, the electrification rate has reached 92.3% in Latin America, leaving 33.8 million people without access to this service [3]. In Ecuador, 2.67% of its population does not have electric power access [4]. This part of the population lives in rural and isolated areas that are not considered

M. Botto-Tobar et al. (Eds.): ICAT 2022, CCIS 1756, pp. 429–444, 2023.
https://doi.org/10.1007/978-3-031-24971-6_31

for electrification projects due to the high investment costs and social-technical challenges. Microgrids emerge as an alternative that can significantly contribute to achieving the electrification goals. Microgrids can provide reliable electricity to rural areas at a lower cost than traditional electrification solutions [5]. In particular, a microgrid integrates and coordinates energy sources with proper voltage and frequency control strategies, including the active participation of the local community [6].

Microgrids can help ensure that rural, off-grid communities have increased access to electricity and the opportunity to grow their communities' economies through the agriculture industry. For instance, the authors in [7] show how the microgrid of the Huatacondo community located in the Atacama desert in northern Chile impacts production activities. Most community people said it was possible to undertake new economic activities or enhance existing ones with the microgrid implementation. In particular, 27% reported that the project benefited tourism development and associated services. 23% said it benefited agriculture through irrigation technology; 18% suggested that it benefited construction activities due to the extended period in which electrical tools could be used. Likewise, there are researches and projects on distributed energy sources (DERs), and microgrids focused on the improvement and sustainability of productive processes in rural areas [8,9]. They demonstrate that microgrids focused on productive processes are a feasible proposal for the development of rural communities. However, only a few studies have addressed the microgrids planning focused on productive processes.

This paper proposes a practical framework for planning microgrids considering productive processes solving a mixed-integer linear programming (MILP) optimization problem. Candidate DERs consider within the optimization problem includes photovoltaic power plant (PV), wind turbine (WT), micro-hydro (MH), battery energy storage systems (BESS), gas and diesel generator set (GGS and DGS, respectively). In addition, we consider the management of flexible loads of productive processes, residential electricity demand, and non-controllable loads of productive processes.

The remainder of this paper is organized as follows: Sect. 2 presents the proposed methodological framework for planning microgrids considering productive processes. The case study is presented in Sect. 3. Section 4 presents the results, and the main conclusions and contributions are summarized in Sect. 5.

2   Methodology

The proposed methodological framework for optimal planning of microgrids for production processes is illustrated in Fig. 1 and contains three main stages that are explained in detail below.

2.1   Input Data

In this stage, the renewable energy sources availability is analyzed in the area under study. Moreover, the regulation policies, economics and productive aspects are analyzed together with local producers and the community leaders to identify the productive processes of the community. Thus an energy problems assessment is carried out to obtain requirements and characterize the demand profile.

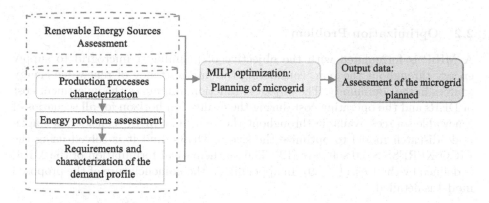

Fig. 1. The proposed methodological framework for optimal planning of microgrids for production processes.

Renewable Energy Sources Assessment. To assess the availability of renewable sources in the planning of the microgrid, we considered a typical meteorological year (hourly data samples) of each renewable energy source, such as solar irradiation, wind speed, and hydrologies, among others. They are obtained from historical data or from software and websites that provide georeferenced information, such as the photovoltaic geographical information system (PVGIS) [10].

Production Processes Characterization. The socioeconomic aspects analysis is carried out with the producers and community leaders to identify potential production processes that might contribute to the development of the community [11]. Surveys and/or interviews and meetings with the producers and the community population are applied to identify problems and necessities of the production processes. The characterization of the production processes includes the seasonal farm products, identification of critical tasks in the production chain, and critical production times, among others.

Energy Problems Assessment. The communities face some energy problems, such as the lack of access to energy entirely in off-grid communities, in which the energy production is carried out through fossil fuel power generators, which leads to producing greenhouse gas emissions. On the other hand, reliability and power quality are still a challenge for power distribution companies in on-grid communities. Due to these situations, it is critical to recognize the energy problems in the communities to obtain a microgrid that assists ensure that rural communities have increased access to electricity. In this methodological sub-stage, the primary energy problems are identified.

Requirements and Characterization of the Demand Profile. Based on the production processes and energy problems assessment, the demand profile is characterized by an estimate of the total demand of the community and an extrapolation of the electricity demand focused on productive processes.

2.2 Optimization Problem

A MILP is formulated with the objective of planning a microgrid to supply energy throughout the year, considering the intermittency of renewable energy sources in the community. The objective function minimizes the investment cost of DERs and the operating cost during the evaluation horizon for all scenarios of renewable sources available throughout the year. The MILP considers a single-node dispatch model to optimize the size of DERs, and it is solved using the FICO XPRESS 8.8.0 software [12]. The mathematical formulation of the MILP is defined by the Eqs. (1)–(29). In appendix A, the nomenclature of the proposed model is detailed.

Objective Function. The objective function is presented in Eq. (1), where investment costs (IC) and operating costs (OC) are minimized. Equation (2) shows the investment costs for the total capacity power of DERs to be installed. Equation (3) shows the OC of each DERs considered in the planning problem. It is worth mentioning that PV, WT, are not considered, because they are negligible. In addition, the cost of the energy not supplied (ENS) and the curtailment cost of PV, WT, and MH are also included to avoid an oversizing of these technologies. Finally, the costs for CO_2 emissions from the fossil fuel consumption are modelled. Thus, the fossil fuel power generation is dispatched when the availability of renewable sources is low and for supply the peak demand, therefore the environmental impact is reduced.

$$Min\{IC + OC\} \tag{1}$$

$$IC = \frac{CRF}{8760}T[c^{PV}P^{PV,inst} + c^{WT}P^{WT,inst} + c^{MH}P^{MH,inst}$$
$$+ c^{BESS}P^{BESS,inst} + c^{fuel,inst}P^{fuel,inst}] \tag{2}$$

$$OC = \sum_{t=1}^{T}[c^{ENS}ENS_t + c^{curt}(P_t^{PV,curt} + P_t^{WT,curt} + P_t^{MH,curt})$$
$$+ c^{MH,op}P_t^{MH} + c^{fuel}P_t^{fuel} + c^{CO_2}E_t^{CO_2}] \tag{3}$$

PV Model. The active power injection from a PV system (P_t^{PV}) is defined by Eq. (4) and depends on the solar irradiance (I_t), the area ($Area_{panel}$) and efficiency (η_{panel}) of PV panel. Equation (5) determines the $Area_{panel}$ through the panels number to be installed (N_{panels}) and dimensions of the PV panel.

Equation (6) calculates the PV power installed capacity considering N_{panels} and the PV panel rated power ($P^{panel,rated}$). (7) is a constraint related to PV power curtailment. Finally, PV active power limits are defined by constraint (8).

$$P_t^{PV} = I_t[kW/m^2] \cdot A_{panel}[m^2] \cdot \eta_{panel} \tag{4}$$

$$A_{panel}[m^2] = N_{panels} \cdot Width_{panel}[m] \cdot Length_{panel}[m] \tag{5}$$

$$P^{PV,inst} = N_{panels} \cdot P^{panel,rated} \tag{6}$$

$$P_t^{PV,curt} \leq P_t^{PV} \tag{7}$$

$$P_t^{PV} \leq P^{PV,inst} \tag{8}$$

Wind Turbine Model. The power output of a WT system (P_t^{WT}) is given by the Eqs. (9)–(11). In which $P^{WT,rated}$ represents the WT rated power, and v_{CI}, v_R, and v_{CO} are cut-in, rated and cut out speeds, respectively. v_t^{wind} is the wind speed at hour t. (12) is a constraint related to WT power curtailment and WT active power limits are defined by constraint (13). This model is used in [13].

$$P_t^{WT} = 0 \qquad\qquad \forall v_t^{wind} \leq v_{CI} \ or \ v_t^{wind} \geq v_{CO} \tag{9}$$

$$P_t^{WT} = N^{WT} P^{WT,rated} \frac{v_t^{wind} - v_{CI}}{v_R - v_{CI}} \qquad \forall v_{CI} \leq v_t^{wind} \leq v_R \tag{10}$$

$$P_t^{WT} = N^{WT} P^{WT,rated} \qquad\qquad \forall v_R \leq v_t^{wind} \leq v_{CO} \tag{11}$$

$$P_t^{WT,curt} \leq P_t^{WT} \tag{12}$$

$$P_t^{WT} \leq P^{WT,inst} \tag{13}$$

BESS Model. The proposed model in [14–16] can be implemented to determine optimal sizing of BESS. The amount of energy available in the BESS is defined by Eqs. (14) and (15). Constraints (16)–(17) represent the BESS charging and discharging limits, and in (18), it is established that the SOC of the batteries will be 20% , thus ensuring that the lifespan of the BESS is extended.

$$E_{s,t} = E_0 + \eta^{inv,BESS} P_t^{BESS,cha} - \frac{P_t^{BESS,dis}}{\eta^{inv,BESS}} \tag{14}$$

$$E_t = E_{t-1} + \eta^{inv,BESS} P_t^{BESS,cha} - \frac{P_t^{BESS,dis}}{\eta^{inv,BESS}} \qquad t \geq 1 \tag{15}$$

$$0 \geq -P_t^{BESS,cha} \geq -\frac{P^{BESS,inst}}{\eta^{inv,BESS}} \tag{16}$$

$$0 \leq P_t^{BESS,dis} \leq \eta^{inv,BESS} P^{BESS,inst} \tag{17}$$

$$0.2 P^{BESS,inst} \leq E_t \leq P^{BESS,inst} \tag{18}$$

Micro-Hydro Model. The estimation of power output of the MH system is given by Eq. (19) used in [17]. Equation (19) represents the power supply by MH that depends on gravity (g), water density (ρ), height (h), flow (Q_t) and MH efficiency (η^{MH}). Constraint (20) denotes the active power output limits of MH system. Finally, constraint (21) represents the power curtailment by MH.

$$P_t^{MH} = g\rho h Q_t \eta^{MH} \tag{19}$$

$$0 \leq P_t^{MH} \leq P^{MH,inst} \tag{20}$$

$$0 \leq P_t^{MH,curt} \leq P_t^{MH} \tag{21}$$

Fossil Fuel Power Generation Model. The fossil fuel power generation model proposed in [18,19] is considered, it is modeled by the Eqs. (22)–(24). The Eq. (22) corresponds the fossil fuel consumption (f_t^{fuel}), where P_t^{fuel} is the output power from power generation, u^{fuel} is the energy density of the fossil fuel consumed by power generation in kWh/kg, and η^{fuel} is the power efficiency of power generation. The Eq. (23) represents the CO_2 emissions. ($E_t^{CO_2}$) and depends of the carbon footprint for the energy produced (K^{CO_2}). Finally, the constraint (24) represents the power supply limits by power generation.

$$f_t^{fuel} = \frac{P_t^{fuel}}{u^{fuel}\eta^{fuel}} \tag{22}$$

$$E_t^{CO_2} = K^{CO_2} u^{fuel} f_t^{fuel} \tag{23}$$

$$0 \leq P_t^{fuel} \leq P^{fuel,inst} \tag{24}$$

Productive Processes Model. This work considers a productive agricultural process consisting of farm products washing systems with water storage tanks and water pumps. The optimization problem formulation aims to minimize the powering up time of the water pumps considering the available renewable resources and the water demand for a farm product. The amount of water available in the storage tank is defined by Eqs. (25) and (26), where the constraint (25) represents the initial state of water level ($Level_t^{water}$), in which is considered that the initial water level is the maximum capacity storage tank ($Level^{max}$). (26) defines the amount of water available considering the water demand ($Demand_t^{water}$) for the agricultural process and water charging of storage tank through capacity water pumping ($Pumping^{water}$), which depends on the binary decision variable T_t^{on} that represents the powering up ($T_t^{on} = 1$) and down ($T_t^{on} = 0$) of the water pumps at the time t. The constraint (27) denotes the storage limits of the water storage tank.

$$Level_t^{water} = Level^{max} - Demand_t^{water} + Pumping^{water} T_t^{on} \qquad t = 0 \tag{25}$$

$$Level_t^{water} = Level_{t-1}^{water} - Demand_t^{water} + Pumping^{water} T_t^{on} \qquad t \geq 1 \tag{26}$$

$$Level^{min} \leq Level_t^{water} \leq Level^{max} \tag{27}$$

Balance Equation. Equation (28) represents the balance equation of the system where the power supplied by the PV, WT, MH, BESS and fossil fuel power generation are considered, denoted by P_t^{PV}, P_t^{WT}, P_t^{MH}, $P_t^{BESS,dis}$, P_t^{fuel} respectively, the power charge of the BESS ($P_{s,t}^{BESS,char}$), the ENS, the system demand ($Demand_t$), and the production process demand, in this case in particular the water pumps demand ($Demand_{pumps}$) that depends on T_t^{on}. Finally, constraint (29) denotes that the ENS should be a positive value lower than the total demand of the community considering production process demand.

$$P_t^{PV} + P_t^{WT} + P_t^{MH} + P_t^{BESS,dis} + P_t^{fuel} = P_t^{BESS,char} - ENS_t$$
$$+ Demand_t + Demand_{Pumps}T_t^{on} \tag{28}$$

$$ENS_t \leq Demand_t + Demand_{Pumps}T_t^{on} \tag{29}$$

2.3 Assessment of the Microgrid Planned

Finally, a techno-economic analysis is carried out to assess the planned microgrid, evaluating the IC and OC expected considering renewable sources throughout the year.

3 Case Study

To validate the proposed methodology, it is implemented in "Los Laureles" a rural community located in the province of Sucumbios (Ecuador) (latitude: −1.7672, longitude: −77.9764). There are located 20 houses and 7 Pitajaya production centres to export, in which there is low reliability of energy supply.

The production centres focus on the washing of the Pitajaya. To this end, each centre has water storage tanks with a total capacity of 5000 [l], which obtain their water supply from the Palora River through a water pump of 3 hp (2,238 kW) with a flow rate of 135 [l/min]. The water stored in the tanks is used for washing the Pitajaya. The planning horizon considered was one year where the months of high production (from December to April), medium production (from June to August) and low production (from September to November) were identified to determine the water demand profile for washing the Pitajaya. Figure 2 shows the water demand profile of the production centers in a month of high production of pitahaya (January).

To the aim of characterizing the electric power demand profile of the community, it considers the residential, the public services and the production processes demand in the months in which there is high, medium and low production of the Pitajaya. Note that we considered a representative daily power demand profile of one weekday and one weekend day because residential demand varies significantly. Figure 3 shows the electric power demand profile projected for 20 years of the community in a month of high production of Pitahaya (January) for one weekday Fig. 3(a) and one weekend day Fig. 3(b).

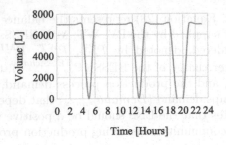

Fig. 2. Water demand profile to the Pitajaya washed process in a month of high production (January).

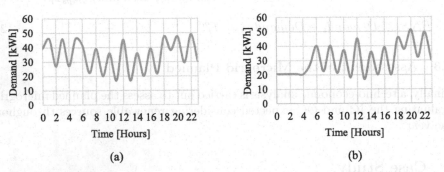

Fig. 3. Electric power demand profile of the community in a month of high production of Pitahaya (January) for (a) one weekday, and (b) one weekend day in a month of high production (January).

In order to cover the variability of the solar, wind and water sources throughout the year, representative hourly solar irradiation and wind speed curves for each month of the community were used obtained from PVGIS available in [10]. And the hourly flow curve of the Palora River was obtained in [20]. Finally, the costs per installed kW [USD/kW] are: $C^{PV} = 871$ [21], $C^{BESS} = 1800$ [22], $C^{MH} = 3263$ [23] , $C^{GGS} = 894$ [24], $C^{DGS} = 448$ and $C^{WT} = 1266$ in addition, the CRF is calculated with a payment term of 10 years at an interest rate of 10%.

4   Analysis Results

Four scenarios were considered to evaluate the investment portfolios (see Table 1). The flexible load powering up of the productive process (water pump) is assumed as a decision variable within the MILP for scenarios S-II and S-IV. In contrast, for scenarios S-I and S-III, powering up is considered a parameter within the MILP.

The results obtained for the sizing of DERs, IC and annuity for each scenario are shown in Table 2. As can be seen, the IC in the scenarios in which the powering up and down of the water pump is considered as a variable decision (S-II and S-IV) is lower than the IC of the scenarios where it was regarded as a parameter (S-I and S-III). Therefore, these IC results show that considering the flexible loads of the productive process as a decision variable in the optimization problem leads to a better investment solution.

Table 1. Scenarios considered in the microgrid planning

Scenario	DERs	Flexible load (water pump)
S-I	PV, WT, MH, BESS, GGS, DGS	Parameter
S-II	PV, WT, MH, BESS, GGS, DGS	Variable
S-III	PV, MH, BESS, DGS	Parameter
S-IV	PV, MH, BESS, DGS	Variable

Table 2. Results of DER Installed Capacity and IC

Scenario	PV [kW]	WT [kW]	BESS [kW]	MH [kW]	GGS [kW]	DGS [kW]	Annuity [USD]	IC [USD]
S-I	51,26	1,75	12,73	16,26	36,13	9,96	33.824	159.603
S-II	51,26	1,09	0,00	16,26	33,39	0,02	29.077	128.940
S-III	51,26	–	31,30	16,26	–	35,43	40.411	169.932
S-IV	51,26	–	0,00	16,26	–	33,41	26.876	112.668

Table 3 shows the water demand values in litres per day estimated that the production process requires in the months of high, medium and low production of Pitajaya. The powering-up of water pumps for S-I and S-III is determined according to the surveys carried out. In the month of the Pitajaya high output, the water pump powering-up approximately 3 hours per day. In the month of medium production, the water pump is only powered up three times a day (45 minutes per period). Finally, the water pump is not powered-up during the low production season. On the other hand, in scenarios S-II and S-IV, the powering-up of water pumps are recognised as a decision variable within MILP. The results show that the powering-up time of the water pumps is reduced when our methodology is applied to maximising the use of renewable energy resources available.

Figure 4(a) and 4(b) show the energy supply of the DERs on a representative day in January for scenarios S-I and S-II, respectively. As can be seen, in both cases, the energy supply to the demand is carried out through MH and GGS when there is no solar resource availability. However, when there is solar resource availability from 6:00 A.M. to 6:00 P.M., electricity demand is supplied through PV, BESS and MH, which allows displacing the GGS and thus reduce the OC. Note that the WT energy supply to the microgrid is deficient, while MH remains constant throughout the day due to the flow characteristics of the Palora River. On the other hand, in S-II, it is observed that the community demand (dotted line) does not vary when considering the flexible electricity demand of the productive process (continuous line) in the planning of the microgrid, which leads to a reduction of peaks demand compared to S-I. Therefore, BESS is not installed, and thus S-II has a lower investment cost (see Table 2).

Table 3. Results of water pump powering up time

Month	Production	Water demand [l/day]	Water pump powering up Scenario S-I, S-III [Hours/day]	Scenario S-II, S-IV [Hours/day]
January	High	140000	3	2,22
April	Medium	63000	2,25	1,11
July	Medium	63000	2,25	1,11
October	Low	–	–	–

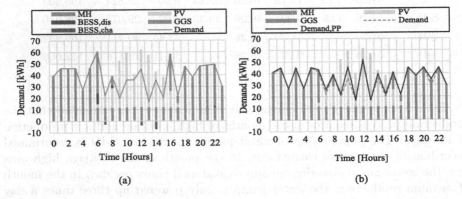

(a)   (b)

Fig. 4. DERs energy supply in a month of high production of Pitahaya (January) for one weekday for (a) S-I and (b) S-II

Figure 5 shows the DERs energy supply of a day in the months of high (January), medium (April-July) and low (October) production of Pitajaya for S-I (see Fig. 5(a)) and S-II (see Fig. 5(b)). As can be seen in both scenarios in January, there is low renewable resources availability leading to 48% of the energy supply by GGS while the supply of PV, MH and BESS is 19% 30%, 3% respectively. In April, the availability of renewable resources growth, thus allowing to displace GGS to 18% and increase the energy supply of PV, MH and BESS to 23%, 54% and 5%, respectively. On the other hand, in July the solar resource in the community decreases, thereby the supply of GGS increases to 30%. Finally, in October, the energy supply is carried out mainly by MH with 75% due to a high water resource availability. Note that the BESS energy supply is low for S-I; however BESS is essential to cover the power supply peak demand, as can be seen in the Fig. 4(a).

The energy supply of DERs in a month of high production for S-III and S-IV are shown in Fig. 6(a) and Fig. 6(b), respectively. As can be seen, the energy supply is similar to the results obtained for S-I and S-II. However, the energy supply is carried out through DGS when renewable resources are unavailable in these scenarios. Noticed, for the case S-II and S-IV, the water pumps are powering on during the hours when there is an excedent of solar renewable resources. Therefore, the energy supply for the flexible loads of the productive process is carried out through PV, unlike S-I and S-III, where flexible loads are supplied by GGS and DGS.

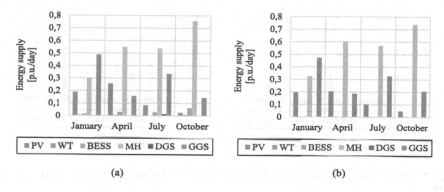

Fig. 5. DERs energy supply in a day representative by month for (a) S-I and (b) S-II

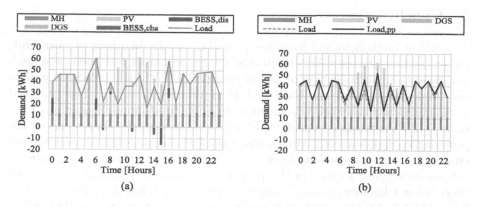

Fig. 6. DERs energy supply in a month of high production of Pitahaya (January) for one weekday for (a) S-III and (b) S-IV

In S-III and S IV, it is observed that in the months where there is no hydro and solar sources (January), the energy supply is carried out by DGS (See

Fig. 7(a) and Fig. 7(b)). However, during the months April to October where the highest hydro sources are available, the electricity demand is mainly supplied by MH and PV.

These results show that our methodology can be used according to the community requirements to obtain an optimal sizing of DERs and thus supply the community's energy throughout the year. It also shows that when considering the flexible loads of the production process in the optimization problem, lower investment solutions are reached, where the flexible loads are powering on when there is a surplus of renewable energy. Thus, it allows for a reduction of peak demand and, therefore, OC due to not using fossil fuel generation to cover the peak demand.

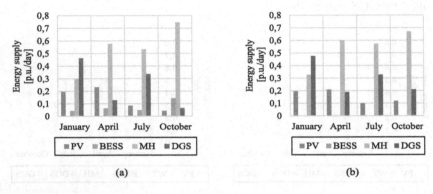

(a)   (b)

Fig. 7. DERs energy supply in a day representative by month for (a) S-III and (b) S-IV

5 Conclusions

A practical methodological framework for the optimal planning of microgrids for production process using distributed energy resources has been presented. An investment portfolio was proposed considering PV, MH, BESS, as well as the implementation of gas GGS and DGS to energy supply. The proposed methodological framework was formulated as a mixed-integer linear programming (MILP) in which it considered binary decision variables that represent the powering up and down of flexible loads of production processes. To evaluate the efficiency of the proposed methodology, it was implemented in "Los Laureles" a rural community located in the province of Sucumbios (Ecuador), in which there is low reliability of energy supply. In this community, there are located 20 houses and 7 Pitajaya production centers focused on washing the Pitajaya to export. To this end, each center has water storage tanks that obtain their water supply from the Palora River through a water pump. Four investment scenarios were evaluated, where S-I and S-III considered the powering up of water pump as a parameter in the optimization problem and S-II and S-IV considered the flexible load as a binary decision variable. S-I and S-II consider PV, WT, MH,

BESS, GGS and DGS; while S-III and S-IV consider only PV, MH, BESS and DGS. The results showed that the investment solution in the scenarios where the powering up of flexible load is a decision variable is lower than in the scenarios where the flexible load is assumed as a parameter within the optimization problem. This practical framework might be used by system planners for microgrids planning that can help ensure that rural, off-grid communities have increased access to electricity and the opportunity to grow their communities' economies through the agriculture industry.

Acknowledgment. This work is supported by the project Control and Optimal Management of Isolated Microgrids 2020-PIC-014-CTE, and 2020-EXT-007 from the Research Group of Propagation, Electronic Control, and Networking (PROCONET) of Universidad de las Fuerzas Armadas ESPE. This work has been partially supported by VLIR-UOS project number EC2020SIN322A101. In addition, the authors would like to thank to "Academic Partner Program" (APP) of FICO Xpress Optimization Suite.

Appendix A

Nomenclature

A. Index

t	Time index

B. Parameters

η^{fuel}	Efficiency of fossil fuel power generators
$\eta^{inv,BESS}$	Inverter efficiency of battery energy storage systems
$\eta^{inv,panel}$	Inverter efficiency of photovoltaic panel
η^{MH}	Micro-hydro efficiency
c^{BESS}	Cost per installed kW of battery energy storage systems [\$/kW]
c^{CO_2}	Cost of CO_2 emissions [\$/Ton]
c^{ENS}	Cost of energy not supplied [\$/kWh]
c^{fuel}	Fuel cost [\$/kg]
$c^{fuel,inst}$	Cost per installed kW of fossil fuel power generators [\$/kW]
$c^{MH,curt}$	Cost of active power curtailment from MH [\$/kWh]
$c^{MH,op}$	Operating cost from run-of-river micro-hydro [\$/kWh]
c^{MH}	Cost per installed kW of run-of-river micro-hydro [\$/kW]
$c^{PV,curt}$	Cost of active power curtailment from photovoltaic system [\$/kWh]
c^{PV}	Cost per installed kW of photovoltaic system [\$/kW]
c^{WT}	Cost per installed kW of wind turbine [\$/kW]
CRF	Capital recovery factor
$I_{s,t}$	Solar irradiance [W/m^2]

K^{CO_2}	Carbon footprint for the energy produced by GGS [Ton/kWh]
$P^{PV,rated}$	Power rated of PV [kW]
$P^{WT,rated}$	Power rated of WT [kW]
T	Estimated time horizon [Hours]
u^{fuel}	Energy density of the fossil fuel consumed [kWh/kg]
v_t^{wind}	Wind speed at hour t
v_{CI}	Cut-in wind speed of WT
v_R	Rated wind speed of WT
v_{CO}	Cut out wind speed of WT
$Level^{max}$	maximum capacity storage tank [l]
$Level^{min}$	minimum capacity storage tank [l]

C. Variables

A_{panel}	Area of PV panel $[m^2]$
$Demand_t^{water}$	water demand [l]
E_0	Initial energy of the BESS [kWh]
$E_{s,t}$	Energy of the BESS [kWh]
$E_{s,t}^{CO_2}$	Emissions of CO_2 [Ton]
$f_{s,t}^{gas}$	Consumed natural gas by gas generator set [kg]
IC	Investment cost [USD]
$Level_t^{water}$	water level at time t
N_{panels}	Number of PV panels
N_{WT}	Number of WT
OC	Operating cost [USD]
$P^{BESS,inst}$	Battery energy storage system installed capacity [kW]
$P^{fuel,inst}$	Fossil fuel generator set installed capacity [kW]
$P^{MH,inst}$	MH system installed capacity [kW]
$P^{PV,inst}$	PV system installed capacity [kW]
$P^{WT,inst}$	WT system installed capacity [kW]
$P_t^{BESS,char}$	Energy charge to BESS [kWh]
$P_t^{BESS,dis}$	Energy discharge to BESS [kWh]
P_t^{fuel}	Energy supplied by fossil fuel generator set [kWh]
$P_t^{MH,curt}$	Energy curtailment by run-of-river micro-hydro [kWh]
P_t^{MH}	Energy supplied by micro-hydro [kWh]
$P_t^{PV,curt}$	Energy curtailment by photovoltaic system [kWh]
P_t^{PV}	Energy supplied by photovoltaic system [kWh]
$P_t^{WT,curt}$	Energy curtailment by wind turbine [kWh]
P_t^{WT}	Energy supplied by wind turbine [kWh]
$Pumping^{water}$	capacity water pumping [l]
Q^{max}	Bypass channel maximum flow
Q_t	Bypass channel flow
T_t^{on}	Powering up and down of flexible loads [l]

References

1. Niez, A.: Comparative study on rural electrification policies in emerging economies: Keys to successful policies (2010)
2. Independent Evaluation Group. The welfare impact of rural electrification: A reassessment of the costs and benefits. Technical report (2008)
3. Jiménez-Estévez, R., Palma-Behnke, D., Ortiz-Villalba, O., Mata, N., Montes, C.S.: It takes a village: social scada and approaches to community engagement in isolated microgrids. IEEE Power Energy Maga. 12(4), 60–69 (2014)
4. Plan Maestro de Electricidad (2020). https://www.recursosyenergia.gob.ec/plan-maestro-de-electricidad/
5. Velásquez-Lozano, A., et al.: Practical framework for optimal planning of isolated rural microgrids. In: 2021 Conferencia Internacional de Tecnología (CIT) (2021)
6. Palma-Behnke, R., Ortiz, D., Reyes, L., Jimenez-Estevez, G., Garrido, N.: A social scada approach for a renewable based microgrid-the huatacondo project. In: 2011 IEEE Power and Energy Society General Meeting, pp. 1–7. IEEE (2011)
7. Palma-Behnke, R., Ortiz, D., Reyes, L., Jimenez-Estevez, G., Garrido, N.: Social scada and demand response for sustainable isolated microgrids. In: Innovative Smart Grid Technologies, IEEE PES. IEEE Computer Society (2012)
8. Schoonenberg, W., Farid, A.M.: A dynamic model for the energy management of microgrid-enabled production systems. J. Clean. Prod. 164, 816–830 (2017)
9. Fontanilla, S.: Estrategias de sustentabilidad de micro-redes/SMART-Farm en la comunidad Mapuche José Painecura de Hueñalihuen. PhD thesis, Universitat Politècnica de València (2020)
10. Photovoltaic geographical information system (pvgis) (2021). https://ec.europa.eu/jrc/en/pvgis
11. Sáez, D., et al.: Metodología participativa para el diseño y desarrollo de proyectos tecnológicos micro-red/smart-farm en comunidades rurales. In: Anales del Instituto de Ingenieros de Chile (2017)
12. Fico xpress optimization suite (2021). http://www.fico.com/en/products/
13. Bahramirad, S., Reder, W., Khodaei, A.: Reliability-constrained optimal sizing of energy storage system in a microgrid. IEEE Trans. Smart Grid 3(4), 2056–2062 (2012)
14. Mehrjerdi, H., Hemmati, R.: Modeling and optimal scheduling of battery energy storage systems in electric power distribution networks. J. Clean. Prod. 234, 810–821 (2019)
15. Aguirre-Velasco, M., Saltos-Rodríguez, M., Velásquez-Lozano, A., Ortiz-Villalba, D., Villamarín-Jácome, A.: Network allocation and optimal sizing of bess for resilience enhancement on power distribution systems against volcanic eruption. In: 2021 IEEE Power Energy Society General Meeting (PESGM), pp. 01–05 (2021)
16. Aguirre-Velasco, M., Saltos-Rodríguez, M., Velásquez-Lozano, A., Ortiz-Villalba, D.: Optimal sizing and placement of battery energy storage system for resilience enhancement in power distribution systems against volcanic eruptions. In: 2021 13th IEEE PES Asia Pacific Power Energy Engineering Conference (APPEEC), pp. 1–5 (2021)
17. Khan, M.R.B., Jidin, R., Pasupuleti, J., Shaaya, S.A.: Optimal combination of solar, wind, micro-hydro and diesel systems based on actual seasonal load profiles for a resort island in the south china sea. Energy 82, 80–97 (2015)
18. Zidan, A., Gabbar, H.A., Eldessouky, A.: Optimal planning of combined heat and power systems within microgrids. Energy 93, 235–244 (2015)

19. Saltos, M., Velásquez, A., Aguirre, M., Villamarín, A., Ortíz, D., Haro, R.: Planificación óptima de recursos energéticos distribuidos para mejorar la resiliencia de sistemas de distribución de energía eléctrica frente a desastres naturales: Caso en lahares volcánicos. Revista Técnica" energía 18(2), 13–24 (2022)
20. Rivadeneira, J., Anderson, E., Davila, S.: Peces de la cuenca del Pastaza. Ecuador, Fundación Natura (2010)
21. Winarko, T., Hariyanto, N., Rahman, F.S., Watanabe, M., Mitani, Y.: Cost-benefit analysis of pv penetration and its impact on the frequency stability: case study of the south-central kalimantan system. In: 2019 IEEE Innovative Smart Grid Technologies-Asia (ISGT Asia), pp. 1700–1705. IEEE (2019)
22. Rahmann, C., Mac-Clure, B., Vittal, V., Valencia, F.: Break-even points of battery energy storage systems for peak shaving applications. Energies 10(7), 833 (2017)
23. Bitar, Z., Khamis, I., Alsaka, Z., Al Jabi, S.: Pre-feasibility study for construction of mini hydro power plant. Energy Procedia 74, 404–413 (2015)
24. Zareipour, H., Bhattacharya, K., Canizares, C.: Distributed generation: current status and challenges. In: Annual North American Power Symposium (NAPS), pp. 1–8 (2004)

Knowledge Exploration in Life Sciences

Impact of the Association Quinoa (*Chenopodium quinoa* Willd) Bean (*Vicia faba* L.) on Agricultural Production, Biological Fixation and Recycling of Nitrogen

Emilio Basantes Morales[1,2(✉)], Margarita M. Alconada[3], Brenda L. Asimbaya[4], and José L. Pantoja[5]

[1] Department of Life Sciences and Agriculture, Soil, Water and Foliar Laboratory, IASA, University of the Armed Forces (ESPE), Sangolquí, Ecuador
erbasantes@espe.edu.ec, emiliobasantes@yahoo.es
[2] Faculty of Agricultural and Forestry Sciences, National University of La Plata, UNLP, La Plata, Argentina
[3] Agricultural Engineering, Faculty of Agricultural and Forestry Sciences, National University of La Plata, UNLP, La Plata, Argentina
[4] IASA, Sangolquí, Ecuador
[5] Consulting Company Agnlatam S.A., Ibarra, Ecuador

Abstract. The research was carried out in two Sites of Andean soils in the province of Pichincha at an altitude of 2800 masl. Two factors were used under a divided plot design in a DBCA arrangement with four repetitions, the main plot was the cultivation system (monoculture and association) and the subplot the N levels (0, 50, 100, 150, 200 and 250 kg ha^{-1}). Quinoa was continuously seeded, while the bean was interspersed 20 cm from the quinoa row and separated by site at 25 cm. Plant production varied according to the growth stage and cultivation system. The extraction of N was low in the initial stage of the crop (70 kg N) and was increasing to 206 and 479 kg N ha^{-1} in the panicle-flowering and beginning of the grain, respectively. The processes of rhizodeposition and fixation of N in an ecosystem: quinoa-bean, have a sustainable impact on crop nutrition, microbial activity and soil fertility, as demonstrated by the results cited by research carried out with traditional and isotopic techniques of N. Another verified impact is that there was no need to carry out phytosanitary controls. Quinoa productivity was significant ($p < 0.01$) for interactions between factors: culture, N levels, locality and between trials. The coefficient of variation was 14%. The highest grain productivity was obtained with the doses of 100 and 150 kg ha^{-1} of N and the content of N varied between 2.8 to 3.0% by effect of the bean on the levels of N.

Keywords: Biological N fixation · Nitrogen fertilization levels · Nutrient recycling · Quinoa-bean cultivation · Soil

1 Introduction

Associated cultivation has been done since times past in Latin America, although it is not a common practice today due to the intensity of monoculture and the need to produce food

M. Botto-Tobar et al. (Eds.): ICAT 2022, CCIS 1756, pp. 447–465, 2023.
https://doi.org/10.1007/978-3-031-24971-6_32

on a large scale. This planting system can be applied under various combinations of short-cycle crops, horticultural, N fixators (legumes) with non-fixative N (amaranths, grasses, nightshades, cucurbits and others), as in the case: quinoa-bean, and other arrangements with perennial crops, pastures and silvopastoral. The most frequent associations have been: corn-bean, corn-bean, potato-bean, uvillas (*Physalis peruviana*)-alfalfa and others, whose purpose in general has been to achieve contribution of the N set by the legume for the accompanying crop. This system is beneficial for the associative impact that allows to have economic benefit for the farmer, reduce erosive processes, compaction, salinization, soil infertility and less impact on the environment.

The origin of the bean (*Vicia faba* L.) as indicated by several authors is not very clear, some place it in the Near East, while others consider that its origin is in the African continent, however the important thing is that it is a crop that has now spread throughout the world being the seventh grain legume in world importance and the typical legume of double use (human and animal food), was brought to America by the Spanish in the sixteenth century [1]. The bean is a crop very sensitive to drought especially in the periods of flowering and setting. It is an annual dicotyledonous species (2n = 12 chromosomes), which is planted under temporary conditions, at altitudes between 1800 and 3000 m to the area of the paramos (3600 masl), being a traditional crop of the high mountains of Ecuador, among small producers from Carchi to Loja in Ecuador, as a monoculture and is also associated or interspersed with other species such as corn, pumpkin (*Cucurbita spp.*), potato (*Solanum tuberosum* L.) and in this study with quinoa (*Chenopodium quinoa* Willd). According to [2], the bean is important for the inhabitants of scarce resources that could be used in a genetic improvement program using them as an indirect selection criterion to increase productivity and its components in green.

It is an annual herbaceous plant, shrubby, radical system developed with pivoting root type axonomorph (thicker main root and other thinner secondary ones). Stems of quadrangular section, branched and hollow. Compound, alternate, paripinnate leaves with 2 to 4 pairs of glabrous leaflets. The sessile flowers occur in axillary clusters, in groups of 3 to 6, and are of white petals with dark spots on the wings. The fruits are inside a pod (legume) in number from 3 to 6, they are fleshy of intense green color when tender and at maturity they turn black without tendrils [3]. Legumes such as beans (Fig. 1) are covered with velvety tissue, although not all of them produce fruit because most abort even with embryos already formed, a fact that seems to be more related to problems caused by competition than by poor pollination. In the country there are improved varieties INIAP-440 Quitumbe (medium grain) and INIAP-441 Serrana (large grain) and local varieties: Sangre de Cristo and Chaucha. Productivity ranges from 1.0–2.5 t ha^{-1} and with a technical handling can reach productions of 4 t ha^{-1} [4].

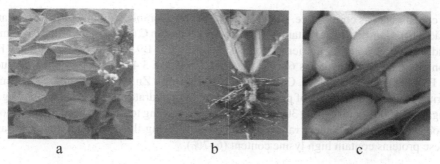

a   b   c

Fig. 1. Bean plant (a), root with bacterial nodules (b) and fruit-pod (c).

1.1 Climate and Soil

The ideal climate for the bean is between 8 and 14 °C, with annual rainfall between 600 and 1,000 mm. It withstands sudden changes in temperature, it is not very sensitive to frost, except at the time of flowering where the flowers fall due to low temperatures. High temperatures favor premature flowering. The pollination of the crop is autogamous, although with a high percentage of allogamy. Beans are sensitive to vernalization (response to cold periods required for flower opening) in early phenological states. Due to its ability to fix N in the soil it is undemanding, although it prefers deep soils with organic matter, medium texture, little clay with good water retention, rich in calcium and phosphorus, with a pH range of 5.5 to 7.5 and is tolerant to salinity 8.5. The application of compost can be used as a soil improvement strategy; however, the results of this in the productivity of the crop are observed after the second year of experimentation and that the immediate benefits correspond to the improvement of the structure and aggregates of the soil, which are not always reflected in the final productivity [5].

N is the most important nutrient in soil fertility and is a scarce and necessary element for agricultural production. Legumes increase N through a natural process called biological N fixation that can be used in plant nutrition and increased soil microbial life and restoration of degraded ecosystems [6, 7]. From the point of view of the inclusion of a legume such as beans, in a cultivation system, it reduces the C:N ratio of the residues incorporated into the soil, being able to affect the microbial activity, the transformations of N, the availability of nutrients and the growth of the plant; a C:N ratio (<25) contributes to a mineralization in the soil [8]. The N provided by legumes is distributed through the soil profile and can be recovered by the associated crop as if it were applied N-fertilizer. In practice it is not necessary that an inoculation be carried out in bean since its roots are nodulated by *Rhizobium leguminusarum* autochthonous present in the soil thanks to other legumes of the genus that are common in soils, hence, within a context of sustainable agriculture, beans are a resource to improve the production and fertility of soils.

1.2 Nutritional Value of the Bean

The bean is an important source of protein (9–11% in tender and 25–27% in dry), contains two main amino acids, lysine and arginine, which complement the low levels contained in cereals such as corn or rice. Vitamins contain considerable amounts of folic acid and niacin [9]. Contribution of vitamin B1 (0.35 mg), Vitamin C (12 mg), thiamine (0.45 mg) and folates. Among its nutrients are also vitamins B3, B9, A and K (Food, n.d.). Fat content 2.9%, carbohydrates 68.2%, fiber 9.4% and ash 3.4%, is rich in minerals such as P (420 mg), K (1190 mg), Ca (90 mg), Mg (110 mg), Zn (90 ppm) and Fe (74 ppm). Dried beans contain 26.1 g of protein, 33.3 g of carbohydrates, 2.1 g of fat and 33.3 g of sugar per 100 g, contributing 307 cal to the diet. According to [1], the bean is a nutritious food with a protein content ranging from 20–30% being this a varietal character, and these proteins contain high lysine content (6–7%).

1.3 Quinua

Quinoa var. Tunkahuan originated from a population of germplasm collected in Carchi Province, Ecuador in 1985. It is a variety of low saponin content with large triangular leaves and toothed edge typical of the Imbabura breed of the Andean zone [10]. According [11], quinoa is the only plant food that has all the essential amino acids, trace elements, vitamins and does not contain gluten. It is a crop of nutritional and functional value for its content of amino acids, proteins, vitamins, good quality oils, antioxidants and starch. In addition, it is an annual crop with a wide range of geographical distribution in the Andes, where the greatest diversity of crop forms, genotypes and wild progenitors is found. Quinoa has great capacity to adapt and grow in any type of soil, although it prefers soils rich in organic matter, good drainage, pH 6 to 8, is demanding in N and Ca, moderate in P and K. Farmers in the Ecuadorian Highlands in the high regions grow quinoa in small areas and/or plant in associations with two or more crops, for example, quinoa-potato (*Solanum tuberosum* L.), quinoa-chocho (*Lupinus mutabilis*) and interspersing or rotating with bean, goose (*Oxalis tuberosa*), melloco (*Ullucus tuberosus*) or potatoes intended for self-consumption. Under this system of association and crop rotation, the farmer has been trying to boost soil fertility, under manual production and with family participation. However, in the last two decades given the demand for quinoa some farmers have encouraged planting in larger areas and in the form of monoculture [12, 13].

1.4 Biological Nitrogen Fixation (FBN)

FBN is a process that involves the transformation of atmospheric N to inorganic or metabolized forms NH3 or NH4 + within the bacteroid or nodules [14, 15]. These ions combine with organic acids to form amino acids and then proteins. The nodules are the result of an adequate symbiosis relationship between the plant and the bacteria, that is, where both individuals help and benefit each other [16]. The bacteria fix the atmospheric N and incorporate into the protein base of the plant, while the plant gives lodging and favorable environment for the development of the microorganism inside [17]. FBN is a reduction reaction that requires energy (NADH, ATP and protons) and action of the enzyme nitrogenase, present in the fixing bacteria of the genus Rhizobium, Bradyrhizobium of legumes and other genera. FBN is a biochemical process that demands a large amount of metabolic energy (it is estimated between 14 to 24 ATP per mole of N_2 fixed), being therefore an alternative metabolic pathway for microorganisms. Nitrogenase is a reduction oxide enzyme that catalyzes the reduction reactions of several substrates, especially the reduction of atmospheric N (N_2), and is very versatile since in the absence of N_2, it acts as a hydrogenase to form H_2, useful in FBN reactions. Nitrogenase contains in its structure two proteins: one containing Fe (4Fe-4S) per 60,000, is of low molecular weight, called ferroprotein (Fe-protein). The other protein, Fe-Mo-protein is high molecular weight 220000 [18, 19]. The reaction that synthesizes the biological fixation of N is as follows:

$$N2 + 8H^+ + 8e^- \frac{nitrogenase}{16ATP(Fe - Mo)} > 2NH3^+ + H2 + 16Pi + 16ADP \quad (1)$$

The production of ammonium $NH4^+$ or ammonia NH_3 is a biological process carried out by prokaryotic organisms that possess the enzyme nitrogenase and in the case of the bean is produced by bacteria of the genus Rhizobium leguminusarum, forming nodules where atmospheric N is reduced to inorganic forms (NH_3, $NH4^+$) by nitrogenase that has the ability to break the triple chemical bond of N_2 (or other molecules such as acetylene) and produces ammonia NH_3 or $NH4^+$ ions that plants can harness to form proteins. This biochemical process is very active depending on the growth and development of the plant until flowering. The reduced N2 within the nodule is assimilated by the same plant, through the root to the aerial part or part can go out to the external environment, where it can be absorbed by other crops that grow next to the legume.

1.5 Rhizodeposition

The rhizodeposition of N in legumes is a mechanism that consists of the release of exudates from the root during plant growth, complementary to the decomposition and mineralization of the radical system, which contributes to the production of organic matter from soils. This process has an impact on the improvement and sustainability of soils, so the goal is for there to be more active roots curling the soil. According to [20], this curl in beans is 14–39% of the total N of the plant. Soil contains most of the terrestrial carbon, forming the basis for soil fertility and nutrient cycling, soil C is root-derived carbon or rhizodeposits, which underpin soil microorganisms that recycle nutrients such as N [21]. The interaction of the roots with the soil is linked in particular with the structure of the soil, affecting the productivity of agroecosystems, making them sustainable systems, since one of the factors that influences the functions of the soil is its structure and one of the most used indicators for its study is the stability of aggregates [22]. If microbial activity decreases, the formation of aggregates decreases and disturbances will be generated, so rhizodeposition is important in the role of roots, in the health of soils and ecosystems [23].

The root system has an extraordinary ability to secrete various compounds into the rhizosphere, in response to stress or biotic and abiotic fluctuations. The rhizosphere [24] it is the part of the soil closest to the roots of the plants (1–5 mm) and so it is influenced by them, which constitutes an ecosystem: soil-plant and microorganisms, which is very interrelated, that is, according to [25] is the soil, water, radical stools (exudates and mucilage) and microbiota (bacteria, fungi, algae). In the rhizosphere, the phenomenon of rhizodeposition is defined, referred to as the release of all forms of carbon from the roots. The products of rhizodeposition can be categorized as exudates, secretions and fats. However, legumes such as beans, although they take N from the atmosphere it is advisable to apply low doses of N (20–30 kg N. ha^{-1}) in planting, this helps root development and formation of nodules which develop from 30 dds and once formed the activity of the FBN is more efficient and as the vegetative cycle of the plant progresses, the roots of the bean increase the number of active nodules, visualized by their reddish color inside the nodule, from the protein leghemoglobin [26]. The bean is a legume that groups rhizobium leguminusarum bacteria, which have the property of taking N from the air and transforming it into assimilable N, by means of the nitrogenase enzyme (N_2 $\rightarrow$ NH4$^+$). The assimilable N is delivered to the plant and receives from it the nutrients necessary for its sustenance, this association is known as symbiosis and by this process the bean plant can fix between 30–60 kg of N ha^{-1}/year.

Studies carried out by [27] in other types of legumes such as beans and chickpeas (*Cicer arietinum*) indicate that the N fixed by the beans and chickpea was higher in the beans compared to the chickpea: 80 and 31 kg ha^{-1} year^{-1}, respectively, being able to affirm that the beans contribute more than the chickpea that was scarce in the economy of the N so the contribution to the N of the soil of the roots and the rhizodeposition of legumes should be taken into account for crop rotations [28]. As for the recovery of 15N by grain, straw and rhizodeposition, as well as the total of 15N recovered by beans were influenced by the year, the tillage system did not affect the recovery of 15N by beans, which captured an average of 65% of the 15N applied. The amount of N derived from the rhizodeposition (NdR) deposited in the soil by both crops was influenced by the year, the tillage system and soil depth. Overall, the NdR varied in the soil profile 0–90 cm from 33–162 kg N ha^{-1} in beans and chickpeas from 62–174 kg N ha^{-1}, likewise the amount of NdR was influenced by the tillage system in both legumes, being superior in non-tillage compared to conventional tillage. The results show that the amount of N derived from rhizodeposition is important for the balance of N and represents a key factor for soil fertility, although it is poorly known and has been poorly quantified due to the lack of use or knowledge of the isotopic dilution method with 15N *in situ*.

1.6   FBN Evaluated with ^{15}N and Traditional Techniques

The total N in an N-fixing legume plant such as the bean comes from 3 sources: N-soil (N-native to MO), N-fertilizer and N-FBN, while, in a non-N-fixing plant such as quinoa, the plant obtains it from two main sources: N-from the NPS soil and N-from NPF fertilizer [29–31]. This differentiation of N is only possible to quantify using isotopic techniques [32] such as the use of 15N, being the only method that quantifies N-from the soil, N-from fertilizer and N-from the FBN atmosphere, thus [33] using ammonium sulfate labeled with ^{15}N, obtained in tropical legumes that the values of dry matter and N-total were higher in the fixing legumes than in the controls (plants that do not nodulate), so for example in the Mucuna (*Mucuna pruriens*) 73% of absorbed N was from the atmospheric N, 26% of the soil and less than 1% of the fertilizer. Cowpea (*Vigna unguiculata*) obtained 60% of the biological fixation, 38% of the soil and 2% of the fertilizer. Non-N-fixing crops (control) absorbed amounts of about 95% of the soil and 5% of the fertilizer. This indicates that crops belonging to legumes cause less impact on the soil in relation to crops that do not correspond to legumes, which have as a source of N, soil and fertilizer.

Ranges of FBN cited by various authors indicate that the bean fixes around 100–300 kg N ha^{-1}; according to [34] the pea is the least efficient legume in fixing N 70–300 and the bacteria are characterized by their great capacity and efficiency in the recycling of nutrients and transfer of N; Lupine 40–300 and Bean 25–100 kg N fixed ha^{-1} year^{-1}, 200 kg of N ha^{-1} year^{-1} from the second year after sowing by multiannual clover [35]. By employing the method of natural abundance of ^{15}N and the difference of total N, [36] quantified the FBN of 59–72 kg ha^{-1} by *Canavalia ensiformis* (type of bean) in the rainy period. [37] using the technique of natural abundance of $\delta15$N in the soybean area of Argentina obtained average absorption values of 256 kg N ha^{-1}, with a slope of 13.6 kg of grain per kg of N absorbed, while the proportion of N derived from FBN in aerial biomass was 58% of the N absorbed. In this sense, the FBN was positively related to productivity (r2 = 0.55), with a slope of 52 kg of N fixed per ton produced. In soils in Brazil, Ndfa (fixed) percentage values higher than 75% were obtained. In North America, some estimates indicate a contribution of the order of 50–60% of FBN in soybeans. Additions of 600 mL ha^{-1} of Bradyrhizobium inoculant along with Ca + B stimulated soybean growth and the production variables [38].

1.7 Associated Crop System

Associated, intercropping or multiple crops are a practice in agriculture in which two or more crops coincide during most of their cycle two different plant species are developed in the same soil space and simultaneously. Arable crops, woody or arable crops can be associated with woody crops. This technique of interleaving or polyculture [39], despite being little used by farmers, it is very beneficial for poor soils of low fertility. In addition to promoting and optimizing nutrient uptake, pest control, pollination and improving production, some plants fix atmospheric N in the soil, making it available to other plants. These advantages include improving the dynamics of N as a nutrient, improving efficiency in water use, facilitating weed control, reducing attacks and damage by pests, increasing soil stability, aggregation and permeability, increasing biomass which has a positive impact on the activity and diversity of soil microorganisms.

The bean - corn association has been the most traditional and consists of planting these two species in the same place and at the same time. Its main feature is the higher production per unit area despite the competition between the two species that reduces the productivity of beans by more than 40% and corn by up to 22%. Higher production per unit of area indicates greater efficiency in land use, in the capture and use of light energy, water and nutrients. The characteristics of this productive arrangement allow the farmer to reduce his vulnerability to abiotic, biotic, economic and market factors; improve their sovereignty and food security, be efficient in the use of scarce resources such as land, labor and money, obtain higher productivity compared to monoculture of corn or beans, contribute to protection, improve biological efficiency compared to traditional monocultures and improve agrobiodiversity *in situ* [40, 41].

In Ecuador there is little information on the impact of the quinoa-bean association, contribution of biological fixation and recycling of N on the growth and productivity of quinoa, so the objective of this research was to evaluate the response of the contribution of N on the productivity of quinoa in association or interspersed with bean and its effect on the soil, in two areas of Sangolquí and Machachi, Pichincha Ecuador.

2   Materials and Method

2.1   Characteristics of the Localities

Table 1. Characteristics of climate and soil of the localities

Description	Hcda. El Prado, IASA 1 Sangolquí	Hcda Aychapicho. Machachi - Alóag
Altitude, masl	2780 m	2850 m
Latitude, longitude	Latitude 0°23'12" S; Longitude: 78°24'57" O	Latitude: 00°28' 27" S; Longitude: 78°34' 07" O
Temperature and relative humidity	14–17 °C	12 °C, HR 78%
Average annual rainfall, mm	800 mm año^{-1}	430 mm año^{-1}
Soil type Andisol	Soils derived from volcanic ash. Texture Silty clay loam	Soils Andosols derived from volcanic ashes. clayey sandy loam

The studies were conducted in 2016 and 2017 in Sangolquí and Machachi, belonging to the Province of Pichincha, Ecuador (Table 1). In Sangolquí due to the conditions and control for the handling were installed for two consecutive cycles while in Machachi a single test of the quinoa-bean production system was installed. Two factors were used under a divided plot design in a randomized complete block arrangement (DBCA) with four repetitions, where the main plot was the cultivation system (monoculture and association), and the subplot the N levels (0, 50, 100, 150, 200 y 250 kg ha^{-1}) [12]. Each experimental unit had 5 planting furrows (0.8 m between furrows) 7 m long (35 m^2) and the total area of the experiment occupied a total of 2500 m2 (Fig. 2). Quinoa was continuously seeded, while the bean was interspersed 20 cm from the quinoa line and separated by 25 cm sites.

2.2   Quinoa Plant Production

To determine plant production, samples were carried out around 40, 90 and 120 days after planting (dds). The measurement variables corresponded to the fresh weight, dry weight (g plant^{-1}), plant height (cm), NPK content and some micronutrients, to evaluate the growth and nutritional content of quinoa, in the treatments that received 0, 150 and 250 kg N ha^{-1}.

Fig. 2. Experimental plot of the quinoa test, var. Tunkahuan, during growth and flowering. Prado-IASA 1.

2.3 Total N Content in the Quinoa Plant

The percentage of total N in dry matter is measured by two methods, one called Dumas (1831) which is a dry combustion procedure and the other is the Kjeldahl method developed in 1883. Total Kjeldahl nitrogen is the sum of organic nitrogen, ammonia (NH_3) and ammonium ($NH4^+$) in the chemical analysis of soil, water and wastewater, and the method consists of three stages: digestion (organic N becomes $NH4^+$), distillation (NH_3 is distilled and collected in a receiving container) and titration or titration of N. There are several Kjeldahl systems including macro, micro and semimicro, which are based on the same principle, with the difference that, in the last two systems, less weight of the sample is used and the quantitate of reagents is reduced. In this research, the total N was determined in the dry matter of the plant by the micro Kjeldahl method. In general term and depending on the crop, the content of N varies from 1.5 to 6.0% dry weight, and in the plant, it is found in organic form: in amino acids, proteins, enzymes, chlorophyll and inorganic NH_4^+, NO_3^-. The content of N in quinoa seeds or grain is related to the dynamics of N from the soil to the plant where it is part of the structures of amino acids, proteins and other functional and nutritional molecules [42]. As well as the lignin content that is decisive in the palatability and digestibility of the grain [43]. The presence of carbohydrates such as amylase and amylopectin found in the perisperm are the main source of starch for human consumption [44].

The analysis of plant tissue was carried out in the soil, water and foliar analysis laboratory of INIAP and Agrocalidad, whose methodology includes drying the samples between 60 to 80 °C with continuous air circulation for at least 48 h and then grinding (particles smaller than 1 mm). For the determination of the total N, 2 g of plant sample is taken and determined by micro Kjeldahl. For the analysis of K, Ca, Mg and some micro Cu, Fe, Zn, a wet digestion of the tissue is carried out to obtain a mineral extract and quantify the P by colorimetry with ammonium molybdate and the Ca, K and Mg by atomic absorption spectrophotometry [45, 46].

With the results of the content of elements and knowing the dry weight per plant, the amount of nutrients per plant is determined and if multiplied by the total number of plants per hectare, the amount of any element is obtained, for example, the amount of total N per hectare, which represents the N that the crop extracts and that should be returned to the soil, as fertilizer or organic matter to maintain sustainable agriculture.

2.4 Grain Production

Prior to the manual harvesting, a sample was collected consisting of the three central furrows of each experimental unit. The harvested grain dried at room temperature up to 14% humidity.

2.5 Nutrient Content in the Grain

For the determination of this variable, a sample was formed that results from the taking of subsamples of harvested grain and the nutritional content was evaluated in the plots that received 0, 150 y 250 kg N ha^{-1}.

3 Results and Discussion

3.1 Fresh Weight Production

Plant production is the conversion of light energy into chemical energy that elevates simple substances such as water and CO_2 into organic compounds, which are necessary for plant growth and development. These metabolic processes also involve chemical elements and enzymes. There was a difference in the production of fresh weight, where it is observed that the fresh mass reached a 486.6 g plant^{-1}, being higher in the tests carried out in the Hcda. The Prado-IASA, where a clay F. soil predominates in front of the F. sandy soil of the Alóag-Machachi site (Table 2). As for the levels of N these had a greater effect when 150 kg N ha^{-1} was applied, doses of N higher and lower than this dose had lower productivity which indicates on the one hand that quinoa as a monoculture needs N, but should not exceed 150 kg ha^{-1}, the production in front of the control was almost double.

Quinoa reflected slow growth in the initial stage, then increases progressively until the stage of onset of maturation. The cultivation system used as monoculture (quinoa without bean) and associated (quinoa with bean), was of great impact since associated with bean decreases the amount of N to be incorporated as fertilizer to the soil, which causes less impact on expenditure for the farmer in addition to the impact on the soil and environment is less, for the protection of less soil exposure to evapotranspiration, less runoff in case of rain, less soil erosion, no use of herbicides and weed control work. Esto se debe al proceso de rizodeposición y fijación de N de la atmósfera que ocurre en las leguminosas y en un ecosistema implementado con un cultivo no fijador y un cultivo fijador de N, caso de quinua-haba, cuyos aportes de fijación de N obtenidos con técnicas tradicionales e isotópicas han sido antes descritas. Es importante señalar, que el abono verde de especies leguminosas aporta solo N, ya que los demás elementos fueron extraídos del suelo para su crecimiento [47].

Table 2. Fresh weight based on N levels, tests carried out, cultivation system (quinoa- without bean; quinoa with bean), locality or site carried out and sampling according to the growth stages.

Level	Cases	Fresh weight	Limit		
		g plant^{-1}	E.E	Lower	Upper
Overall mean	432	486,62			
Essays E1, E2 and E3					
2	144	528,0 a	8,92	497,9	558,2
1	144	505,6 a	8,92	475,5	535,8
3	144	426,2 b	8,92	396,1	456,3
N-levels					
150	72	645,4 a	12,61	605,4	685,4
100	72	527,5 b	12,61	487,5	567,5
200	72	521,9 b	12,61	481,9	561,9
250	72	503,2 b	12,61	463,2	543,2
50	72	390,2 c	12,61	350,2	430,2
0	72	331,5 c	12,61	291,5	371,5
Cultivation system					
Q with H	216	533,6 a	7,28	509,0	558,1
Q without H	216	439,7 b	7,28	415,2	464,2
Location					
Sangolquí-IASA	288	516,8 a	6,31	495,5	538,1
Machachi	144	426,2 b	8,92	396,1	456,3
Growth stages					
M3	144	759,5 a	8,92	740,8	778,2
M2	144	444,6 b	8,92	425,9	463,3
M1	144	255,7 c	8,92	237,0	274,5

The stockings with the same letter within each column are the same ($p = 0.05$).

3.2 Dry Weight Production

Dry weight is plant production discounted the percentage of water and is an important indicator to characterize crop growth and productivity. Dry mass is a measurement variable that describes the growth of a plant through its stages of development [48]. Studies of the distribution of dry matter in the different organ parts of the plant allow us to evaluate the growth and amount of nutrients it extracts, in order to determine the requirement of the crops at any stage of development and project ourselves through a mathematical regression model. Nutritional requirements based on the crop cycle are calculated by multiplying the dry mass by the nutritional content of any element and then by the total density of plants per hectare [49].

The accumulation of dry matter was low in the initial stages and increased to the phase of onset of physiological maturity of the grain (Fig. 3). This growth responds to the polynomial mathematical model of degree two, with an r2 = 95%. The treatment corresponding to the N dose of 150 kg ha^{-1}, was the best followed by N 100. The effect of the bean had an increasing impact on the vegetative phase, panojamiento and maturation, compared to the cultivation alone or monoculture. The greatest accumulation of dry mass occurs from 40 dds, so the management tasks must have special attention for greater productivity.

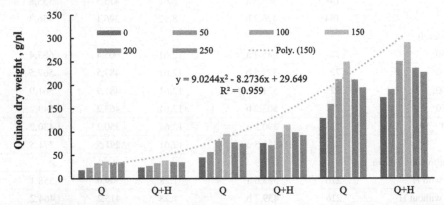

Fig. 3. Quinoa, dry mass averages (g plant-1) according to locality (Hcda. El Prado-IASA and Alóag-Machachi), Growth stages (M1, initial 0–40 dds; M2 panojamiento 60–90 and M3, beginning maturation of the grain 120 dds).

Dry mass (MS) results can be used to determine or perform nutrient extraction curves and make projections of crop requirements per plant or hectare using a regression [50, 51]. The concentration of the nutritional element is multiplied by the amount of dry matter in the respective organs or in the total plant. For the determination of the population, a density of 125000 ha^{-1} plants was estimated, which was obtained with planting density of 80 cm between rows and 10 plants per linear meter, meanwhile the plants per hectare of bean corresponded to 50000.

The amounts extracted from N according to the growth stage of quinoa as monoculture and interspersed with bean (Fig. 4), where the data indicate that the extraction is low in the initial stage of the crop (68 kg N ha^{-1}) and is increasing to considerable amounts, which fluctuated on average from 188–443 kg N ha^{-1} for quinoa in monoculture and from 72, 224 and 514 kg N ha^{-1} for associated quinoa, respectively. These amounts indicate that quinoa requires fertile soils so it must be supplied with organic fertilizers, chemical fertilizers or better an adequate organo-mineral supply, otherwise it can lead to soil impoverishment followed by soil erosion and degradation whose negative impact leads to problems of compaction and desertification of soils [52, 53].

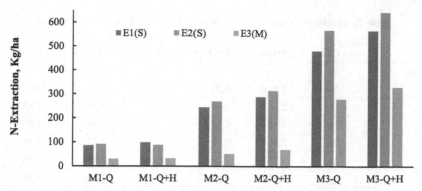

Fig. 4. Extraction of N by quinoa depending on the growth stages, locality of Sangolquí (S) and Machachi (M), under monoculture system and associated with bean. (M1, initial 0–40 dds; M2 panojamiento 60–90 and M3, beginning ripening of the grain 120 dds).

3.3 Quinoa Productivity

The productivity of quinoa presented a difference between the main plot that was the cultivation system (monoculture and association) and the subplot the levels of N (0, 50, 100, 150, 200 and 250 kg ha^{-1}) (Table 3). The same was true between the trials conducted and locality (P < 0.01). Differences were found (p < 0.01) for the interaction between factors: Levels of N*Trials*Locality. This behavior indicates that each factor acts dependent on each other on quinoa productivity. The coefficient of variation (CV) was 14%. The variation in average productivity of 3 trials in two locations due to the effect of N levels, where doses lower and greater than 100 and 150 kg N had lower quinoa productivity (Fig. 5), so it follows that quinoa requires adequate levels of N and that its excess or lack of N fertilizers, affect production and will also have impact on soil and salinity, which is negative for microbial activity at the rhizosphere level [25], mineralization of organic matter and therefore effects on physical properties such as structuring, compaction and deterioration of the soil in its physical, chemical and biological properties.

3.4 Nutritional Content of Quinoa Grain

Quinoa is a high-protein Andean grain that fluctuates from 14–18% or more [54, 55], but the most important thing is that it has excellent content of essential amino acids wider than in legumes and other cereals so it is called the "golden grain" and is very important for human and animal food [56], in addition to excellent aerodynamic properties which is important for the sizing of the machinery to be used for storage and harvesting and post-harvest operations [57]. The variation of the concentration of N of the grain by effect of the culture system and levels of N indicates that the associated culture system influenced the greater N, not so the levels of N since control was not different from the high doses of 150 and 250 kg N ha^{-1} (Fig. 6).

Table 3. Productivity (t ha^{-1}) by N levels, locality, cultivation and testing.

	Cases	Means	Est. Error (s grouped)	Lower L	Upper L
N-levels					
0	24	2,34 c	0,20	2,06	2,62
50	24	2,56 c	0,20	2,28	2,83
100	24	3,52 a	0,20	3,24	3,80
150	24	3,50 a	0,20	3,22	3,78
200	24	3,23 b	0,20	2,95	3,50
250	24	3,17 b	0,20	2,89	3,44
Total	144	3,05			
Location					
Sangolquí-IASA	96	2,48 b	0,07	2,38	2,58
Machachi-Alóag	48	4,19 a	0,10	4,04	4,32
Crop					
Q with H	72	3,18 a	0,12	3,00	3,35
Q without H	72	2,92 b	0,12	2,75	3,10
Total	144	3,05			
Essays					
1	48	2,72 b	0,10	2,58	2,86
2	48	2,24 c	0,10	2,11	2,38
3	48	4,19 a	0,10	4,05	4,32
Total	144	3,05			

Method: 95.0 percent LSD. Means with a common letter are no different (p = 0.05). Statistical program Statgraphics.

Quinoa grain is an excellent source of nutrients, especially N, hence its high protein content (Table 4). But foliage can also have up to 4.5% N, so young leaves can be a good source of protein in salads. This content as the plant matures goes down and is translocated to the storage organ that is the seed in this case the fruit that is the quinoa grain.

3.5 Impact of Crop Production, Soil and Society

The production of crops is an art oriented to the production of food for humanity and also for animals, during these agricultural practices can generate positive and negative effects on the soil-water-plant-atmosphere system, that is, on the environment as a whole, such as biodiversity losses [58], soil degradation, salinization, pollution, climatic effects, which can be attenuated through the use of methods of associated production systems, management of microorganisms [7], soil conservation practices and currently employing techniques associated with precision agriculture [59, 60], in order to optimize inputs, resources and increase yields for the economic benefit of the farmer, food security and minimize environmental impact.

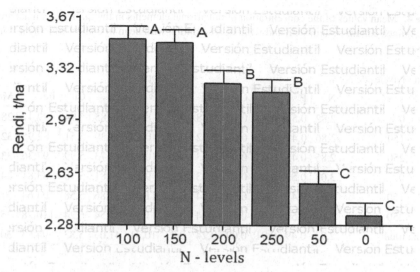

Fig. 5. Productivity of quinoa, var. Tunkahuan, with 6 levels of N as subplots, made in two localities Sangolquí-IASA and Machachi (Alóag).

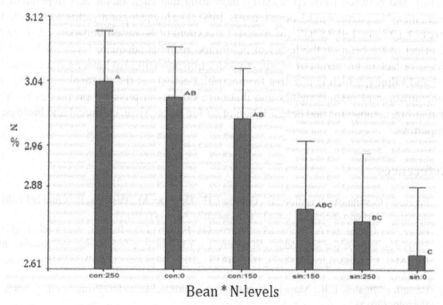

Fig. 6. Content of N in quinoa grain, var. Tunkahuan, under the effect of quinoa farming systems, with and without beans, and N levels as subplots. Sangolquí-IASA and Machachi (Alóag).

Table 4. Mean values of the concentration of nutritional elements in the quinoa grain according to the quinoa culture system with and without association with bean in control treatments and N levels.

Haba	Niveles de N	%						ppm				
		N	P	K	Ca	Mg	S	B	Zn	Cu	Fe	Mn
sin	0	2,82	0,51	0,83	0,10	0,28	0,22	8,18	45,85	5,94	99,47	28,24
sin	150	2,86	0,47	0,85	0,08	0,22	0,22	10,18	38,39	5,51	82,95	32,28
sin	250	2,85	0,48	0,95	0,09	0,23	0,26	10,86	43,73	5,99	97,36	33,32
con	0	3,03	0,53	0,87	0,07	0,23	0,21	9,58	38,81	5,70	83,81	24,50
con	150	3,01	0,47	0,97	0,09	0,24	0,23	11,28	37,86	5,58	94,64	31,05
con	250	3,04	0,50	1,02	0,10	0,24	0,27	11,83	41,54	6,24	110,78	35,89
Media total		2,93	0,49	0,91	0,09	0,24	0,23	10,31	41,03	5,83	94,83	30,88

4 Conclusions

Quinoa productivity differed for the interactions between factors: culture, N levels, locality and between trials (p < 0.01), indicating that each factor acts dependent on each other. The coefficient of variation was 14%. The highest grain yields were with the doses of 100 and 150 kg ha^{-1} of N and the content of N varied between 2.8 to 3.0% by effect of the bean on the levels of N. quinoa requires adequate levels of N and its excess or lack of fertilizers of N, affect production and will also have an impact on the soil and salinity, which is negative for microbial activity at the rhizosphere level [25], mineralization of organic matter and therefore effects on physical properties such as structuring, compaction and deterioration of soil in its physical, chemical and biological properties.

References

1. Perea, F., Castilla, A., Basallote, E., Canseco, E., Delgado, M., Pasadas, R.: Guía del cultivo de habas. Formato digital (e- book) - (Producción Agraria) (2015)
2. Pérez, D., González, A., Rubí, M., Franco, O., Franco, J.R., Padilla, A.: Análisis de 35 cultivares de haba por su producción de vaina verde y otros componentes del rendimiento. Rev. Mex. Ciencias Agrícolas **6**(7), 1601–1613 (2017). https://doi.org/10.29312/remexca.v6i 7.553
3. Basantes Morales, E.R.: Manejo de cultivos Andinos del Ecuador, Primera ed. Sangolquí, Ecuador (2015)
4. Guamba, A.: Evaluación de tres abonos orgánicos en la producción de dos variedades de haba (Vicia faba L) en el cantón Huaca (2021)
5. Estrada, C.R., Jarillo, J., Aragón, A., Juárez, D., Patrón, J.: Productividad forrajera de haba bajo diferentes condiciones de manejo. Agron. Costarric. **41**(1), 95–103 (2017). https://doi.org/10.15517/rac.v41i1.29755
6. Orchardson, E.: "El nitrógeno en la agricultura," CIMMYT (2020). https://www.cimmyt.org/es/noticias/el-nitrogeno-en-la-agricultura/

7. Bianco, L., Cenzano, A.M.: Leguminosas nativas: estrategias adaptativas y capacidad para la fijación biológica de nitrógeno. Implicancia ecológica. Idesia (Arica) (2018). https://doi.org/10.4067/s0718-34292018005002601

8. Castro, E., Mojica, J.E., Carulla, J.E., Lascano, C.: Abonos verdes de leguminosas: Integración en sistemas agrícolas y ganaderas del trópico. Agron. Mesoam. **29**(3), 711–729 (2018). https://doi.org/10.15517/ma.v29i3.31612

9. Espinosa, F. (2022). El haba - El Poder del Consumidor. Análisis de productos (2017). https://elpoderdelconsumidor.org/2017/05/el-poder-de-el-haba/. Accessed 23 Mar 2022

10. Peralta, E.: INIAP Tunkahuan. Variedad mejorada de quinua de bajo contenido de saponina (2010). https://repositorio.iniap.gob.ec/bitstream/41000/2639/1/iniapscpl345.pdf

11. FAO. La Quinua: Cultivo milenario para contribuir a la seguridad alimentaria mundial. In: Informe técnico elaborado por PROINPA, Cochabamba, Bolivia, p. 66 (2011)

12. Basantes, E.R., Alconada, M.M., Pantoja, J.L.: Producción de quinua (Chenopodium quinoa Willd) en monocultivo y en asociación con haba (Vicia faba) bajo las características físicas de un suelo andino del Ecuador. Brazil. J. Anim. Environ. Res. **5**(1), 596–613 (2022). https://doi.org/10.34188/BJAERV5N1-046

13. Basantes-Morales, E., Alconada, M.M., Pantoja, J.L.: Quinoa (chenopodium quinoa willd) production in the Andean Region: Challenges and potentials. J. Exp. Agric. Int. **36**(6), 1–18 (2019). https://doi.org/10.9734/jeai/2019/v36i630251

14. Smercina, D.N., Evans, S.E., Friesen, M.L., Tiemann, L.K.: To fix or not to fix: Controls on free-living nitrogen fixation in the rhizosphere. Appl. Environ. Microbiol. **85**(6), 1–14 (2019). https://doi.org/10.1128/AEM.02546-18

15. Basantes Morales, E.R.: Producción y Fisiología de Cultivos con énfasis en la Fertilidad del Suelo. Quito-Ecuador: Imprenta La Unión. Quito-Ecuador (2010). ISBN: 978-9942-02-336-0

16. Guzman, D., Montero, J.: Interacción de bacterias y plantas en la fijación del nitrógeno. Rev. Investig. e Innovación Agropecu. y Recur. Nat. **8**(2), 87–101 (2021)

17. López, J.P., Boronat Gil, R.: Aspectos básicos de la fijación de nitrógeno atmosférico por parte de bacterias. Estudio en el laboratorio de educación secundaria. Rev. eureka sobre enseñanza y Divulg. las ciencias **13**(1), 203–209 (2016). https://doi.org/10.25267/rev_eureka_ensen_divulg_cienc.2016.v13.i1.15

18. Salisbury, F.B., Ross, C.W.: Fisiología Vegetal. Grupo Editorial Iberoamericana S.A. México (1994)

19. Mengel, K., Kirkby, E.: Principios de Nutrición Vegetal. Traducido por Ricardo J. Melgar PhD. Instituto Internacional del Potasio, Basilea/Suiza (2000)

20. Jensen, E.S., Peoples, M.B., Hauggaard-Nielsen, H.: Faba bean in cropping systems. F. Crop. Res. **115**(3), 203–216 (2010). https://doi.org/10.1016/j.fcr.2009.10.008

21. Bowsher, A.W., Evans, S., Tiemann, L.K., Friesen, M.L.: Effects of soil nitrogen availability on rhizodeposition in plants: a review. Plant Soil **423**(1–2), 59–85 (2017). https://doi.org/10.1007/s11104-017-3497-1

22. Torres, C., Etchevers, J., Fuentes, M., Govaerts, B., De León, F., Herrera, J.: Influencia de las raíces sobre la agregación del suelo. Terra Latinoam. **31**(1), 71–84 (2013)

23. Roset, P.: Rizodeposición: el rol de las raíces en la salud de suelos y ecosistemas (2021). https://agribio.com.ar/noticias/rizodeposicion-el-rol-de-las-raices-en-la-salud-de-suelos-y-ecosistemas

24. Probanza, A.: La rizosfera: un 'criptoecosistema' vital. Aspectos básicos y aplicados. Conama 2012, Congr. Nac. del Medio Ambient., pp. 1–17 (2012). http://www.conama2012.conama.org/conama10/download/files/conama11/CT2010/1896700116.pdf

25. Márquez, A.: Rizosfera: qué es, para qué sirve, composición e importancia. Ecología verde (2021). https://www.ecologiaverde.com/rizosfera-que-es-para-que-sirve-composicion-e-importancia-3266.html

26. Aucancela, J., Basantes, E.: Efecto del ácido acetilsalicílico y silicio en la nutrición y sanidad del cultivo de haba (Vicia faba). Memorias VII Congr. REDU 2019. Univ. Yachay Tech. Libr. artículos científicos los Particip., pp. 608–615 (2020)

27. López Bellido, L., Benítez, J., Fernandes, P., López, R.J.: Influencia del sistema de laboreo en la rizodeposición de nitrógeno de habas y garbanzos. Vida Rural. Cereal. y Legum. Univ. Córdoba, pp. 44–48 (2010). https://dialnet.unirioja.es/servlet/articulo?codigo=3351526

28. Acosta, M.B.: Tipos de legumbres (2020). https://www.ecologiaverde.com/tipos-de-legumb res-2699.html#anchor_0

29. Basantes-Morales, E.R., Trivelin-Ocheuze, P.C.: Avaliação do Método da diluição isotópica com adição de fertilizante 15N ao solo, na quantificação da FBN de leguminosas. Tesis de Maestría - Escola Superior de Agricultura Luiz de Queiroz/USP, Piracicaba-Brasil (1990)

30. Basantes, M.E., Trivelín O.P.C., Tsai, M.S.: Cuantificación de la fijación biológica de nitrógeno por el método isotópico del 15N y evaluación del efecto de la micorriza en legu-minosas. Nucleociencias 4(4), 37–53 (1993). https://inis.iaea.org/search/searchsinglerecord. aspx?recordsFor=SingleRecord&RN=25000512

31. Lázzari, M.A., Videla, C.: El método del trazador isotópico. Uso del isótopo estable 15N en estudios de fertilidad de suelos y nutrición de plantas en el Cena – Brasil. Isot. Establ. en Agroecosistemas, pp. 1–20 (2018)

32. Fonseca-López, D., Vivas, N., Balaguera, H.: Técnicas aplicadas en la investigación agrícola para cuantificar la fijación de nitrógeno: una revisión sistemática. Cienc. Tecnol. Agropecuaria 21(1), 1–19 (2020). https://doi.org/10.21930/rcta.vol21_num1_art:1342

33. Basantes, E.: Metabolismo mineral del isótopo nitrógeno-15 en el suelo y planta. Nucleo-ciencias 2(2), 47–54 (1991). https://www.osti.gov/etdeweb/biblio/5309330

34. Brenes Rojas, P., Peña Cordero, W.: "Fijación Biológica De Nitrógeno En Arveja (Pisum Spp) Mediante Técnicas Isotópicas Del N15, En Un Suelo Andisol, Llano Grande Cartago. Repert. Científico 24(2), 1–7 (2022). https://doi.org/10.22458/rc.v24i2.3887

35. Pommeresche, Hansen: Examen de la actividad de los nódulos en raíces de leguminosas. Ficha Técnica (2017). https://orgprints.org/id/eprint/32468/1/pommeresche-hansen-2017-root-nod ules-spanish.pdf

36. Martín Alonso, G.M., Tamayo, Y., Hernández, I., Varela, M., da Silva, E.: Cuantificación de la fijación biológica de nitrógeno en Canavalia ensiformis crecida en un suelo pardo mullido carbonatado mediante los métodos de abundancia natural de 15N y diferencia de N total. Cultiv. Trop. 38(1), 122–130 (2017). http://ediciones.inca.edu.cu. Accessed 29 Mar 2022

37. Collino, D.J., et al.: Biological nitrogen fixation in soybean in Argentina: Relationships with crop, soil, and meteorological factors. Plant Soil 392(1–2), 239–252 (2015). https://doi.org/ 10.1007/s11104-015-2459-8

38. Pedrozo, A., João, N., De Oliveira, G., Alberton, O.: Fixação biológica de nitrogênio e aspectos agronômicos da soja (Glycine max (L.) Merr.) sob diferentes doses de inoculante. Acta Agron. 67(2), 297–302 (2018). https://doi.org/10.15446/acag.v67n2.56375

39. González, D., Álvarez, U., Lima, R.: Acumulación de biomasa fresca y materia seca por planta en el cultivo intercalado caupí – sorgo. Cent. Agrícola 45(2), 77–82 (2018). http://sci elo.sld.cu/scielo.php?script=sci_arttext&pid=S0253-57852018000200011

40. Vélez, L.D., Moya, A., Clavijo, L.: Relaciones de Competencia entre el Fríjol Trepador (Phase-olus vulgaris L.) y el Maíz (Zea mays L.) Sembrados en Asocio. Rev. Fac. Nal. Agr. Medellín. 64(2), 6065–6079 (2011). http://www.scielo.org.co/pdf/rfnam/v64n2/v64n2a04.pdf

41. Torres, S., Huaraca, J., Laura, D., Crisóstomo, R.: Asociación de cultivos, maíz y leguminosas para la conservación de la fertilidad del suelo. Rev. Investig. Ciencia, Tecnol. Desarro. 4(1) 2018. https://doi.org/10.17162/rictd.v4i1.1068

42. Garcia-Parra, M., García-Molano, J., Carvajal-Rodriguez, D.: Evaluación del efecto de la fertilización química y orgánica en la composición bromatológica de semillas de quinua (Chenopodium quinoa Willd) en Boyacá – Colombia. Rev. Investig. Agrar. y Ambient. **9**(6), 99–107 (2018). http://hemeroteca.unad.edu.co/index.php/riaa/article/view/2282

43. Bergesse, A., et al.: Aprovechamiento Integral del Grano de Quinoa, 262pp. Florencia Grasso Diseño. Córdoba-Argentina, Editora (2015)

44. Li, G., Zhu, F.: Amylopectin molecular structure in relation to physicochemical properties of quinoa starch. Carbohydr. Polym. **164**, 396–402 (2017). https://doi.org/10.1016/j.carbpol. 2017.02.014

45. INIAP. Análisis químico y físico en muestras de suelos, plantas y aguas. – Instituto Nacional de Investigaciones Agropecuarias. INIAP (2022)

46. CINCAE. Centro de investigación de la caña de azúcar del Ecuador. Laboratorio Químico (2022). https://cincae.org/laboratorio-quimico/

47. Cortez, J.: Producción de biomasa de Haba (Vicia faba L.) para abono verde bajo tres densidades de plantación en el Centro Experimental Cota Cota. Rev. la Carrera Ing. Agronómica – UMSA **3**(1), 39–49 (2017)

48. Rogelio, I., Chavarín, I., López, J., Rodríguez, E.: Acumulación de materia seca durante las etapas de desarrollo de variedades de frijol. Rev. Fitotec. Mex. **41**(3), 275–283 (2018)

49. Basantes, E.R., Sigüencia, D., Espinoza, P., Basantes-Aguas, S.X.: Requerimientos nutricionales de N y K en el cultivo de banano (Musa paradisiaca L.) en un suelo Entisol e Inceptisol. Las Ciencias Agropecu. Una mirada desde la Exp., pp. 115–127 (2019). https://www.researchgate.net/publication/337157615. Accessed 28 Feb 2022

50. Montemayor, J., Munguía, J, Segura, M., Yescas, P., Orozco, J., Woo Reza, J.: La regresión lineal en la evaluación de variables de ingeniería de riego agrícola y del cultivo de maíz forrajero. Acta Univ. **27**(1), 40–44 (2017). https://doi.org/10.15174/au.2017.1255

51. Di Benedetto, A., Tognetti, J.: Técnicas de análisis de crecimiento de plantas: su aplicación a cultivos intensivos. RIA. Rev. Investig. Agropecu. **42**(3), 258–282 (2016). https://www.red alyc.org/articulo.oa?id=86449712008

52. Argentina. Desertificación.Argentina.gob.ar (2022). https://www.argentina.gob.ar/ambiente/bosques/desertificacion

53. Selectra. Desertificación: definición, causas, consecuencias y retos. Climate Consulting. Selectra (2022). https://climate.selectra.com/es/que-es-desertificacion

54. Rojas, W., Vargas, A., Pinto, M.: La diversidad genética de la quinua: potenciales usos en el mejoramiento y agroindustria. Rev. Investig. e Iovación Agropecu. y Recur. Nat. **3**(2), 114–124 (2016). http://www.revistasbolivianas.org.bo/pdf/riiarn/v3n2/v3n2_a01.pdf

55. InfoQuinoa. Valor Nutricional. Quinua. Pozo al mar (2017). https://www.quinoareal.org/valor-nutricional

56. Huaraca, R., Kari, A., Tapia, F., Alvarez, C.: Contenido mineral y proteína en germinados de quinua (Chenopodium quinoa Willd). Rev. Alfa **5**(15), 516–522 (2021). https://doi.org/10. 33996/revistaalfa.v5i15.134

57. Caetano, J.M., Devilla, I.A., Melo, P.C., Sérvulo, A.C.O., Ferreira, R.B.: Propriedades aerodinâmicas dos grãos de quinoa (Chenopodium quinoa Willd.). Rev. Bras. Ciências Agrárias - Brazilian J. Agric. Sci. **17**(1), 1–8 (2022). https://doi.org/10.5039/agraria.v17i1a1143

58. Dieguez Santana, K., Zabala-Velin, A.A., Villarroel-Quijano, K.L., Sarduy-Pereira, L.B.: Evaluación del impacto ambiental del cultivo de la pitahaya, Cantón Palora, Ecuador. TecnoLógicas **2**(49), 113–128 (2020). https://doi.org/10.22430/22565337.1621

59. Ríos, R.: La Agricultura de Precisión. Una necesidad actual. Rev. Ing. Agrícola, **11**(1), 11 (2021). https://www.redalyc.org/journal/5862/586269368010/html/. Accessed 30 May 2022

60. Salas, W., Grueso, S., Bernal, D.: Agricultura sostenible como alternativa de control y mitigación de impactos ambientales. DTU Libr., p. 16 (2020). https://repository.usc.edu.co/han dle/20.500.12421/4954

Evaluation of the Environmental Impacts Generated by the Management of Urban Solid Waste in the Open Waste Dump in Loreto, Eastern Ecuador

Paulina Poma[1,2] (iD), Marco Usca[3] (iD), and Theofilos Toulkeridis[4(✉)] (iD)

[1] Universidad de Valladolid, Valladolid, Spain
[2] Escuela Superior Politécnica de Chimborazo, Sede Orellana, Francisco de Orellana, Ecuador
[3] Universidad de Salzburg, Salzburg, Austria
[4] Universidad de Las Fuerzas Armadas ESPE, Sangolquí, Ecuador
ttoulkeridis@espe.edu.ec

Abstract. Solid waste management is a subject that still represents enormous challenges worldwide and therefore also in Ecuador. In the current study, we evaluated the environmental impacts generated by the management of solid urban waste (SUW) and the disposal in the an open waste dump of in Loreto, eastern Ecuador, regulated by the local government in order to calculate the level of criticality and subsequently develop management strategies. The methodology applied for the evaluation of environmental Impacts is the Strengths-Weaknesses-Opportunities-Threats (SWOT), which allowed to better understand and to proceed in decisions making processes such as the implementation of measures that minimize environmental hazards as well as the identification of possible alterations of the environment by the actions of the SUW management. Furthermore, administrators and workers were surveyed, different factors were identified and evaluated and each of the parameters were assigned with impact values. Subsequently, we calculated the level of criticality, which may allow the local government to develop corresponding strategies. Among the most significant results has been the breach of current environmental regulations such as burning used tires at open air, and the discharge of leachate to a freshwater body without prior treatment. The application of the SWOT method indicated a lack of performance in the integral management of the SUW. Furthermore, there is the need for a plan for the municipal management of non-hazardous solid and sanitary waste and the absence of a department dedicated to the integral management SUW.

Keywords: Urban solid waste · Recycling · Leachate · SWOT · Integral management · Impact

1 Introduction

Global solid waste management is a subject that still represents enormous challenges worldwide [1–3]. Population growth, urbanization and climate change are factors to considerate into account for a suitable management of urban solid waste (USW). According

M. Botto-Tobar et al. (Eds.): ICAT 2022, CCIS 1756, pp. 466–481, 2023.
https://doi.org/10.1007/978-3-031-24971-6_33

to the World Bank (WB), urban population growth in Ecuador has had a further pro-liferation from 1.7% in 2013 to 2% in 2018 [1–4]. This fact brings along a significant increase in solid waste production. Furthermore, the Institute of statistics and census of Ecuador INEC) in 2015 and 2016 has claimed that each inhabitant generates on average 0,58 kg/hab/day of solid waste in the urban area INEC. Subsequently, in 2017 solid waste had a hefty growth to 0,86 (Kg/hab/day). In the same year, 1942,02 tons of solid waste were collected differentially daily, of which 66,5% corresponds to inorganic residues [5]. The Amazon region produces 71,3% of inorganic residues but missed the final provision on the basis of established rules [6]. The type of residues in 2017 was pinned down that houses in the urban area in the country produced 17, 54% of organic residues on the contrary of rural area with 48,97%[7, 8].

At the other end of the spectrum, throughout the country exist almost 5.705 com-panies which produce non-dangerous residues, such as organic residues, wood among others. To 92.72% of companies, the amount of residues produced is unknown, unlike 26.97% of the rest of the companies that bear it in mind [9, 10]. This causes an inadequate layout of urban solid waste (USW), which leads to environmental pollution of biotic, abiotic and social factors. In 2019 through the regulation to the environmental organic code (RCOA), the Ministry of the Environment (MAE) stated that urban solid waste must be arranged in a healthy way, by means of definitive isolation and lockdown pro-cesses in spaces that meet established technical provisions, such as landfills, focused on the waste that might not be reused amid previous stages of environmental management [10].

The Ecuadorian Amazon region is where inorganic solid waste is generated with far more quantity, with a percentage of 71,3% in accordance with the solid waste man-agement data from the Municipal Decentralized Autonomous Government (GAD) for 2017 reported by the Ecuadorian Standardization Service (INEN). The final provision of the USW has been conducted in dumping grounds (17,5%), emerging cells (10%) and landfills (72,5%) [11]. In Loreto canton, the final provision of the USW is executed in open dumping grounds where no checks are performed. Monitoring of residues gen-erated as leachates that are unloaded in the Suno River, gases that are released into the environment such as methane, burning special waste by the way of illustration vehicle tires. This activity is banned according to Environmental organic code (COA) [12, 13], due to the fact that this causes far-reaching effects in the physical components of the quality of Suno River's water and the quality of Loreto Canton's air [14].

The urban solid waste USW are those solid substances, semi-solid, liquid and gas, result of the daily activities in urban areas [7, 8]. Pending upon the activity in which they are produced, they are classified into agricultural (cattle sector) forestry, mining, industrial and urban [7]. In the Loreto Canton, one of the main environmental problems is the comprehensive management of urban solid waste USW and the residues gener-ated by the hydrocarbon activity. These pollute the Suno River, due to the discharge of leachates without prior treatment that parameters demand chemical oxygen (DQO) presents values of 7.5 and 25.0 mg/L. This indicates the presence of organic matter susceptible to oxidation [15], as well as total coliforms of 700mg/L and fecal coliforms of about 200 mg/L. Additionally, there is whether any analysis of the air quality of the canton, nor any treatment of the gases generated in the Garbage dump [11].

The open-pit dump in the canton of Loreto is located, some three km of the Cantonal head in the urban area belonging to the Municipal Estate, next to El Triunfo (Fig. 1). In the place aforementioned 5.76% is the native forest which can be found in the canton, it has been declared by the Ministry of the Environment as areas destined to the conservation of biodiversity as shown in Fig. 1, the canton's land use has a wooded area of 87,8%, agricultural 7,6%, pasture 1.9% and others 2.7% [10].

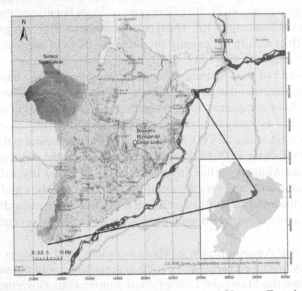

Fig. 1. Location of the landfill in the canton of Loreto-Ecuador

Currently, in the canton of Loreto, 12 ton/day of urban solid waste USW are generated, which are disposed of without inadequate control. Based on this preoccupying context, the current research aims to evaluate the environmental impacts that generate the lack of policies alongside with comprehensive management plans in the management and disposal of urban solid waste USW in the landfill. For the sake of evaluating environmental impacts, the SWOT method will be used, which may allow the analysis of the vulnerability in environmental performance of the local Government of Loreto GADML, as well as the possible alterations that the area of direct influence to the landfill in the canton might suffer.

2 Methodology

In order to evaluate the environmental impacts caused by open-pit dumps, due to the inadequate disposal of leachates where the chemical oxygen demand (COD) parameters present values of 7.5 and 25.0 mg/L [16], as well as total coliforms 700 mg/L and fecal coliforms 200 mg/L, all being outside the permissible limits of current environmental regulations, any sort of treatment or analysis of the gases generated in the garbage dump is performed [9, 17]. The methodology used to evaluate environmental impacts includes an initial diagnosis, which is based on the characterization of the abiotic (relief, geology, soil, water) and biotic (flora, fauna) factors, as well as the evaluation of social factors, the identification of environmental aspects and an environmental impact assessment [15].

2.1 Abiotic Factors

The Province of Orellana is located in the Amazon region where three main landscapes are distinguished being the Eastern Cordillera, the Sub-Andean zone and the Amazon Basin [18]. The relief has suffered severe erosive processes, resulting to a variety of reliefs being: abrupt 23.46%, weak flat or almost flat 12.57%, strong, hilly 30.25%, regular gently sloping 18.78%, irregular moderately hilly 4.67% and very strong steep 7.03% generated ArcGIS PRO 2.4 [19].

The canton of Loreto has formations of volcanic origin, as they are located in the foothills of the Andes mountain range and the nearby active Sumaco volcano, which has given rise to deep, clayey soils of the Miocene Arajuno Formation upon the Cretaceous Hollin and Napo formations as well as the Jurrasic Misahualli formation [20–22]. Such soils have a low fertility that are unsuitable for agriculture, therefore their use is with a focus on conservation and protection. There are a variety of geological types in the canton, with a predominance of clays and meteorized sandstones that generate deep, clayey, low-fertility soils currently occupied by native vegetation, crops and pastures [23].

The most representative soil type however is Inceptisol, which accounts for 82,80% of the canton's surface area and has suitable characteristics for perennial crops and forests, while Entisol 13,98%, Eriales or rocky outcrops 1,84% and natural water bodies 1,38%. It has a thin soil texture 34%, average 53%, moderately thick 10%, not applicable 4%. Nonetheless, 98.03% of the total area of the canton of Loreto has an adequate use, owing to the maintenance of the natural vegetation, 1.97% has been replaced by crops and pastures, the conflicts for the use of the soil correspond to 64.53% well used, overused 24.11% and underused 11.36%. This means that 64.53% of the canton's surface must be used for forests through the conservation and protection of natural vegetation where the largest extensions correspond to native forests [24].

The surrounding ot the study counts with more than 70 main water bodies. In the upper part of the canton, the rivers are less mighty and descend through waterfalls and waterfalls increasing their flow in the lower part. There are no specific water studies available, but the rivers are contaminated by urban solid waste, waste from oil activity and leachate discharge without previous treatment [25, 26]. There the parameters of the chemical oxygen demand (COD) present values of 7.5 and 25.0 mg/L, indicating the presence of organic matter susceptible to oxidation [12], as well as total coliforms 700 mg/L and fecal coliforms 200 mg/L. In January 2020, a visit was performed to the rubbish dump, where samples were taken of the leachate discharged into the Suno River where parameters of pH, electrical conductivity, turbidity, and dissolved oxygen (DO) were analyzed. Such data allowed to evaluate if the leachate being discharged is within the permissible limits to a freshwater body.

2.2 Biotic Factors

In the canton of Loreto there is the Napo Galeras National Park and the Hollin Protected Forest along with Original flora where no artificial cuts have occurred but natural processes in favour of the regeneration of the forest. There are families of giant Lobelias Siphocampilus, Asterácea, Solanácea, Poligalácea, Melastomatácea, Araliácea; Monocots such as Orchidiacea and Bromeliacea and in the higher areas are identified Pomacea, Rosacea, Gentianacea and Lycopodiacea [27].

There is no specific information about the classification and quantification of the fauna of the canton, but there is information over the most representative species. The biogeographical conditions of the Park, the extensive intermediate life zones and the Pre-Mountain and Low Mountain rainforests, make the fauna affluence very high. There are some 101 species of mammals, 36 of reptiles and 31 of amphibians in the southern zone. The birdlife is very rich including high Andean species, cloud forest, mesothermal and tropical zones. So far, 654 species of birds have been registered in the area, among which the families Emberizidae, Traupidae, Tyrannidae, Turdidae, Troglodytidae, Cotingidae, Formicariidae, Furnariidae, Ramphastidae and Trochilidae [28].

2.3 Social Factors

According to the 2010 census conducted by the INEC, there are 21,163 inhabitants, 10,124 of whom are women and 11,039 men. Some 98% of the rural population suffers from poverty and a high rate of unemployment, 9.57% is illiterate, and there is a lack of basic infrastructure and insufficient organizational structure among youth and women [10]. In order to identify existing problems in the administration of the GADML, 18 administrators and 2 workers were inquired regarding compliance with the responsibilities established in Article 57 of Ministerial Agreement 061 and the obligations established in Articles 228, 231, 232 and 239 of the Organic Code of the Environment to the GADML [29].

As a means to identify the environmental aspects in the urban solid waste USW management system carried out by GADML, activities that may cause impacts on the environment in terms of abiotic, biotic and social components will be analyzed for the transport and final disposal phase [30]. Table 1 describes the identification of the environmental aspects to be considered. Later, such environmental aspects will be considered as the evaluation parameters to be assessed with a value from 1 to 5 [30, 31].

The conducted process during the development of this study has been composed of five main stages, being obtaining geographic inputs, processing satellite images, generating layers of soil cover information for three different periods, generation of the predictive model and preparation of simulated products. These subprocesses are described in detail further below.

The SWOT method will be used in order to evaluate the environmental performance of the GADML (Hill & Westbrook, 1997; Houben et al., 1999; Kangas et al., 2003), as well as the possible changes that may occur in the area of a direct influence of the dump in all stages of the USW management system [33]. This may allow to perform the strategic planning that the GADML anticipates or minimizes the threats to the environment, as well as, the identification of possible alterations towards the environment by the actions

Table 1. Identification of environmental aspects

Environmental aspects	Environmental impacts
Emission of particulate matter	Effect on air quality
Increased sound pressure levels	Noise pollution
Discharge of liquids without previous treatment in the Suno River	Alteration of water quality
Lack of a landfill	Affecting the health of the community
Inadequate disposal of USW	Alteration of water and soil quality
Ignorance of the personnel in environmental issues	Water and soil contamination due to lack of knowledge for the development of activities
Collection, transport and final disposal of waste	Complaints and claims from users
Lack of technical feasibility of the control bodies Ministry of the Environment	Effect on the quality of water, soil and air
Open-air burning of used tyres	Affecting the quality of the air
Lack of classification of USW	Affecting the quality of water, soil and air
Monitoring of environmental factors	Air, water and soil pollution as well as non-compliance of regulations
Generation of environmental liabilities	Air, water and soil pollution

of the management of USW, with the intention of trying to strengthen the weaknesses, the empowering of the internal strengths and the real advantage of the opportunities that [30, 32]. The SWOT method consists of constructing a matrix based on the identification of a list of internal factors (strengths and weaknesses) and external factors (opportunities and threats) that influence the organization's performance [32, 34]. Subsequently, internal factors are contrasted with external factors to generate strategies rested on the strengths of the organization to correct its weaknesses, take advantage of opportunities and counteract threats, developing four types of strategies to obtain parameters to assess [31]. The parameters that back up the analysis are classified into strengths, opportunities, weaknesses and threats where the strengths and opportunities parameters are considered positive aspects and the weaknesses and threats parameters are negative aspects found in the internal and external environments of the GADML (Fig. 2).

Afterwards, it is necessary to assign to each of the listed parameters, impact and contingency measures in order to determine their level of criticality for the evaluation of strategies where criticality is assessed based on Eq. 1:

$$\text{Criticality} = (\text{Imapact level index}) \times (\text{Eventually level Index}) \tag{1.}$$

The level of criticality of the parameter gives either insight over the degree of importance or priority assigned to the type of strategies to be followed. For negative aspects, the level of criticality is stood on the fact that these are aspects that have far-reaching effects on the system and at the same time, a high probability of occurrence, in the case

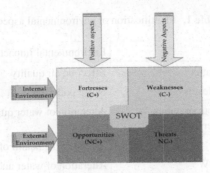

Fig. 2. SWOT method [35]

of threats, or a high-frequency rate, in the case of weaknesses [17]. For the analysis of negative and positive impact, the following nomenclature will be used for the internal environment: weakness (C-), which will be identified with the color light orange; strength (C+) with the color light green; and for the external environment: threats (NC-) with the color red and opportunity (NC+) with the color green, as demonstrated in Fig. 2. For the assignment of impact and probability levels, it is determined by the risk assessment applied to the external environment as internal to the GADML, as listed in table 2, impact levels and estimated contingencies are assigned [33]. In order to estimate values, an in-situ visit was performed, physical parameters of the leachate were analyzed, and finally, surveys were applied to GADML managers and workers. For the estimation of impact levels, indices with a range of 1 to 5 will be considered, and eventually an index with a range of 0.1 to 1.

Table 2. Assignment of impact levels and eventuality [30]

Impact level	Index	Eventuality	Index
Fundamental	5	Occurs always	1
High	4	Very probable	0.9
Moderate	3	Probable	0.5
Low	2	Not very probable	0.3
No impact	1	Never occurs	0.1

3 Results

3.1 Initial Diagnosis - Baseline

With the review of the biotic, abiotic and social factors, the present stage of the conditions and the use of soil of the canton of Loreto were identified. Hereby, some 3.76% of the area have been of extensive agricultural, while about 84.79% are used for conservation

Table 3. Land use of the Canton Loreto in km^2 and respective percentage

No	Types of soil use	Area in km^2 soil	%
1	Extensive farming	7024,23	3,76
2	Aquatic ecosystem	72,42	0,04
3	Conservation and protection	158524,60	84,79
4	Energy	31,14	0,02
5	Forest for wood	25,72	0,01
6	Residential	818,28	0,44
7	Unproductive	294,71	0,16
8	Industrial	1,10	0,00
9	Leisure	29,96	0,02
10	Other	112,04	0,06
11	Occasional grazing	728,46	0,39
12	Extensive cattle farming	16680,82	8,92
13	Irrigation energy consumption	2514,75	1,35
14	Leisure extractive irrigation	4,77	0,00
15	Unused	39,61	0,02
16	Social	20,29	0,01
17	Transport	24,23	0,01
18	Treatment and deposit of waste	4,84	0,00
	Grand total	186951,96	100,00

and protection as well as some extensive cattle ranching 8.92%, besides some other minor residual areas [7], as listed in Table 3.

From the in-situ visit of the landfill, the presence of ashes from vehicle tyres was seen around the pools, which, following Ministerial Agreement 142, are categorized as special waste with code ES-04 [14]. Not complying with the responsibilities and obligations stipulated in Ministerial Agreement 020 issued on February 20, 2013, wherein Art. 23, numeral 3 it mentions: "To follow up and control the activities related to the compliance with the Integral Management Plan for Used Tires in its jurisdiction and within the scope of its competencies to make the annual reports to the National Environmental Authority". Article 26 prohibits the burning of used tires in the open air [7, 36, 37]. The disposal of special wastes in pools where there was no technical confinement of special wastes established in the Organic Code of Territorial Organization, Autonomy and Decentralization (COOTAD), in Article 275 (see Fig. 3a and 3).

Fig. 3. Figure 3a (left) The Loreto open-pit dump area, with tire ashes Figure 3b (right) In the same site there is also sanitary waste.

We took three samples for the analysis to the leachate that is discharged into the Suno River, being P. 1 the leachate storage tank, P.2 the leachate discharge point and P.3 of the Suno River. Physical parameters of the leachate were analyzed with in situ pH, conductivity, DO, and turbidity. The analysis was conducted with the multiparameter measuring equipment brand HANNA HI 9829, (Table 4).

Table 4. Results of the leachate analysis of the landfill site

Points	pH	DO %	Conductivity μs/cm	Turbidity UNT
P. 1	9.5	68.5	780	35
P.2	7.64	78.8	320	22
P.3	7.2	89.7	677	15.8

At point P1, the pH value is out of the maximum permissible limits for discharge of freshwater body according state regulations, where the maximum permissible limit value is pH 6–9 [38–41]. In the P 3 Suno River, the DO value is also way above of the maximum permissible limits established [42, 43]. The criteria for the acceptable quality for the preservation of aquatic and wildlife in freshwaters are >80% saturation [39]. The total coliform parameters of 700 mg/L and the fecal coliform of some 200 mg/L, are outside the maximum permissible limits [44]. Along the lines of the survey of 16 questions applied to 18 administrators and 2 workers regarding compliance with the responsibilities outlined in Art. 57 of Ministerial Agreement 061 and the obligations established in Art. 228, 231, 232, 239 of the Organic Code of the Environment to the GADML Hereby, it resulted that 65% of those surveyed are aware of the responsibilities established in the COOTAD on the management of urban solid waste, while 35% are not. Some 81.25% are aware of the National Program for Integral Solid Waste Management (PNGIS). Based on the surveys of administrators and workers on the integrated management of on the integrated management of solid urban waste conducted by the GADML, it was possible to rate the impacts generated by the open-pit dump [45]. The discharge and dumping of either industrial sewage or water in dried streams or water sources are banned, as well as the use of the water supply system for the integral management of solid waste [12,

46, 47]. However, the current administration is presently carrying out an environmental consultancy in order to implement measures that will almost certainly minimize the environmental impacts that are currently being generated.

3.2 Evaluation of Environmental Impacts

Once the current state of the area of direct influence has been identified such as biotic, abiotic, social factors and the aspects that generate environmental effects (positive or negative), and the capacity for control based on the nomenclature described in Fig. 2, the parameters are evaluated according to the levels of impact and eventuality as detailed in Table 4 [9, 48, 49]. With these evaluated parameters, strategies were gained to reinforce, make alliances [50], modify, and prevent 4 based on the values laid bare by the GADML.

Table 5. SWOT matrix. Source [30]

Impact			Strengths		Opportunities	
	Positive	High Impact	Boost	Have an Integral Management Plan of RSU, including the treatment and use of solid waste.	Build alliances	Current environmental regulations that establish tax benefits for the development of activities of minimization, recycling and reuse of SUW.
		Low Impact	Accept	Explore	Accept	Adapt
			Weaknesses		Threats	
	Negative	High Impact	Modify	Establish awareness campaigns for the people in order to promote their environmental culture. This should include workshops in schools, colleges, communal houses and institutions as well as the promotion through media	Prevent	Administrative processes by the National Environmental Authority
		Low impact	Mitigate	Standardize	Mitigate	Outsource
Frequency			Low	High	Low probability	High probability
Controllable			Not controllable			

Table 6 below depicts the SWOT GADML. Employing the SWOT analysis, it has been possible to set up strategic lines through which it is possible to work to award the objective of implementing the Plan of Integral Management of USW [50], and the strengthening for the fulfillment of the goals planned by the GADML, such as, strengthening their administration awareness of the inhabitants to promote their environmental culture [8], recycling and recovery of waste, compliance with current environmental regulations and the creation of budget items in order to control and supervise the USW Integrated Management Plan. Finally it has been suggested to create an environmental

Table 6. Parameter evaluation COOTAD: organic code of territorial organization, autonomy and decentralization; SUW [46]

Parameters	Evaluation Criteria				Impact	Eventuality	Criticality
	NC-	C-	C+	NC+			
GADML aware of established competences in COOTAD.			X		5	0.3	1.5
They conduct educational programs in the area of their competence in order to promote the culture of minimization in the generation and integral management of SUW.			X		4	0.9	3.6
There is a schedule for scanning.			X		4	0.5	2
In the urban area, collection is performed in containers located in strategic sites.			X		3	1	3
Delivery of metal tanks to neighborhoods and districts.			X		2	0.9	1.8
Collection of hospital waste in health centers of the town.			X		5	0.3	1.5
There is a collection schedule from Monday to Sunday and defined routes.			X		2	1	2
Goals to improve the collection service.			X		1	1	1
Considerable level of knowledge of ministerial agreements 020 Tires, 021 Agrochemical Plastics, 022 Batteries and Batteries, 031 Technical Closure.			X		3	0.3	0.9
Knowledge of the general policies of the integral management of the SUW established in the Organic Environmental Code.			X		3	1	3
Development of policies, instructions, technical standards for comprehensive SUW management.			X		3	0.9	2.7
The cells (pools) are waterproofed.			X		4	1	4
Current environmental regulations that establish economic and fiscal benefits and incentives for organizations that promote the development of activities to minimize, recycle and reuse SUW.				x	3	1	3
Mitigation measures that demonstrate the effective reduction of greenhouse gas emissions.				x	4	0.9	3.6
Financial support from the National Program for the Integral Management of Solid Waste project for the study and implementation of the Urban solid waste Management Plan.				x	1	0.3	0.3
Lack of a comprehensive municipal management plan for non-hazardous solid waste, solid waste, sanitary and special waste.	x				5	1	5
Lack of a department dedicated to the management of integrated SUW management.	x				5	1	5
Lack of technicians for the control and monitoring of environmental management activities.	x				4	0.9	3.6
Lack of technical viability of the National Environmental Authority and the environmental administrative authorization of waste projects	x				4	1	4
Lack of policies (recycling and reuse) of SUW.	x				3	0.5	1.5
Burning used tires open air.	x				4	1	4
Discharge of sewage or industrial water in the Suno river.	x				4	1	4
There is no separation at source by the people that facilitates its subsequent temporary storage and use.	x				4	0.9	3.6
Administrative processes due to the lack of submission of an annual declaration on the generation and management of SUW, to the National Environmental Authority	x				5	0.5	2.5
Administrative processes for not presenting a report, environmental compliance audits.	x				5	0.9	4.5
Lack of continuity due to the change of municipal administrations. Failure to comply with current environmental regulations.	x				4	0.5	2
There is no Environmental Management Plan for the integral management of SUW.	x				5	0.3	1.5
No monitoring of leachates that are discharged into the Suno River.	x				5		0
No leachate treatment performance.	x				4	1	4

management department within the GADML, which will be responsible for planning, executing environmental projects and fulfilling the environmental control mechanisms.

4 Discussion

The lack of policies and integrated management plans to the final disposal of solid urban waste in the garbage dump has caused far-reaching effects on the suitable quality of the preservation of aquatic ecosystems and wildlife in the Suno River [38], As well as from the survey performed to the workers and administrators, it was evidenced that 65% of the surveyed people know about the competences set up in the COOTAD about the management of the urban solid waste, while some 35% do not know. Some 81.25% are aware of the PNGIS. While 75% do not know, 62.5% claims that the GADML classifies solid waste based on current regulations. Taking into account the weakness in the compliance with the environmental regulations prevailing for the integral management of solid waste USW, from the SWOT analysis [51], it has been possible to set up the strategic lines through which it is possible to work to achieve the objective of implementing the Plan of Integral Management of USW and the strengthening for the compliance of the goals planned by the GADML. The conditions under which it is found and the use of the soil of the canton of Loreto were identified where the 3.76 extensive agricultural, and 84.79% conservation and protection, extensive cattle raising 8.92%, irrigation energy consumption 1.35% among other minor parts [15, 26, 43, 52].

In the same way in the province of Orellana, within the canton of Francisco de Orellana appears a garbage dump alike the canton of Loreto. Nonetheless, the canton of Loreto lacked to perform a physical, chemical and biological characterization of the leachate that is discharged into the Suno River [53]. The canton of Francisco de Orellana (El Coca) has a characterization of the leachate that is discharged with these sedimentary solids being 2.55 ml/L, electrical conductivity 2581.97 uS/cm, turbidity 195.0 UFT, total hardness 36.25 mg/L, total solids 2697. 24 mg/l, BOD5 334.50 mg/L, COD 836.80 mg/L, total nitrogen 308.43, total phosphorus 5.91 mg/L, total hydrocarbons 10.60 mg/L, ammonium 161.48 mg/L, chlorides 439. 88 mg/L, OD 90%, total coliforms 1205000 col/100 ml and fecal coliforms 911500 NMP/100 [54]. In the province of Napo, the canton of Archidona has a garbage dump where there is a leachate catheterization where the parameters pH 8. 12, COD 3100 mg/L, BOD5, 820 mg/L, total solids 70.68 mg/L, total nitrogen 0.05%, total phosphorus 5.66mg/L [55], total hardness 975 mg/L, total alkalinity 2325 mg/L calcium 1. 34%, magnesium 0.19%, chlorides 1225 mg/L, sulfates <8 mg/L, iron 212.75 mg/L, sodium 0.73%, potassium 6.44%, lead 0.3 mg/L, total dissolved solids 7000 mg/L, mercury <0. 001 mg/L, OD 88%, cadmium < 0.04 mg/L, chromium 17.09 mg/L, cyanide <0.002 and phenols 0.018 mg/L, has projections of biogas generation and recovery for the years 2020 which is 2 m^3/min, year 2023 with 3.1 m^3/min until 2040 with a biogas value of 15.1 m^3/min [56, 57].

Comparing the analysis of the parameter DO and pH conducted in the Francisco de Orellana canton being 90% and in Archidona with 88% with a pH of 8.12 with the Loreto canton, where it reaches 89. 7 with a pH of 9.5, it appears that the pH of the Archidona canton is within the maximum permissible limits established [15]. Therefore, it is necessary to consider the aspects that generate environmental impacts on the quality of river water, generating greenhouse gases that contribute to the given climate change. As a result, there is a lack of policies and integrated management plans for the handling and final disposal of solid urban waste. Producing garbage dumps is a serious problem for municipal governments that do not have adequate environmental measures in order to implement an integrated management system for USW [1, 58].

The evaluation of environmental impacts has boundaries. First and foremost, the characterization of leachate and the correlation between variables to determine the age of young < 5 years, intermediate 5–10 years and mature > 10 years leachate were not conducted [57], and all the parameters of the Suno River established, admissible quality for the preservation of the aquatic ecosystem and fresh water wildlife were not analyzed. From the environmental impact assessment performed through the SWOT method [37], the parameters were evaluated according to the impact and contingency levels where strategies were obtained to strengthen 1, generate alliances 2, modify 3, prevent 4 based on the values calculated by the GADML.

This information may be useful for the GADML in order to establish the strategic lines through which it is able to work in order to achieve the objective of implementing the Integrated Management Plan for USW [35]. This may also support the strengthening of the administration in raising awareness among residents to encourage their environmental culture, recycling and recovery of waste, compliance with existing environmental regulations, create budget items for control and monitoring of the Integrated Management Plan for USW [5], by the creation of an environmental management directorate within the GADML. Future studies are necessary in order to obtain the age of the leachate, the physical, chemical and microbiological parameters and its toxicity as well as the amount of biogas generated. This may also serve for biological treatment of the leachate for organic matter degradation processes and for statistical analysis of solid waste generated in Loreto County [5, 59].

In the current research, the burning of used tires in the open air, the discharge of untreated leachate into the Suno River, and the physical analysis of the parameters of points 1, conductivity, pH, and point 3, the DO were found to be above the permissible limits according to the legal provisions. Based on various criteria, such as water quality for the preservation of aquatic life, determined that there is a lack of performance in the integrated management of USW due to the absence of a municipal integrated management plan for non-hazardous solid waste and sanitary as well as special waste.

5 Conclusions

We determined that the lack of policies, integrated management plans in the handling and final disposal of urban solid waste (MSW) in the garbage dump, has caused environmental impacts on water quality for the preservation of aquatic and wildlife in the Suno River presents parameters such as DO of 89,7%, a total coliforms 700 mg/L and fecal coliforms 200 mg/L as well as a pH 9.5, which all are above the maximum permissible limits.

From the surveys conducted to the workers and administrators, it was demonstrated that a majority of those surveyed know about the competencies established in the COOTAD as well as about the management of urban solid waste.

From the analysis with the SWOT method, the absence of a direction in charge of the management of urban solid waste was determined. Therefore, with the evaluation of the factors, those responsible for the GADML are forced to make decisions under the control of the decision makers in order to strengthen compliance with the goals set by the GADML and avoid administrative processes upon the control entities.

References

1. Allers, M.A., Hoeben, C.: Effects of unit-based garbage pricing: a differences-in-differences approach. Environ. Resour. Econ. **45**, 405–428 (2010)
2. Nawaz, S., et al.: Erratum: determination of heavy metals in fresh water fish species of the River Ravi, Pakistan compared to farmed fish varieties. Environ. Monit. Assess. **167**, 703 (2010)
3. Waheed, S., et al.: Assessing soil pollution from a municipal waste dump in Islamabad, Pakistan: a study by INAA and AAS. J. Radioanal. Nucl. Chem. **285**, 723–732 (2010)
4. Zulkarnain, M., et al.: The risk quotient of sulfide hydrogen toward lung vital capacity of people living around landfill area. Kesmas **12**, 142–147 (2018)
5. Wafi, T., Ben Othman, A., Besbes, M.: Qualitative and quantitative characterization of municipal solid waste and the unexploited potential of green energy in Tunisia. Bioresour. Bioprocess. **6**(1), 1–16 (2019). https://doi.org/10.1186/s40643-019-0274-4
6. Miranda, M.O.: Gestión integral de residuos sólidos en la empresa CYRGO SAS. Tendencias, XVIII, 103–121, (2018). https://doi.org/10.2307/j.ctv2tw04q
7. Pinheiro, N.C.A., Mochel, F.R.: Diagnosis of contaminated areas by final disposal of solid waste in the municipality of Paço do Lumiar (MA) Brazil. Eng. Sanit. e Ambient. **23**, 1173–1184 (2018)
8. Trang, P.T.T., et al.: The Effects of Socio-economic Factors on Household Solid Waste Generation and Composition: a Case Study in Thu Dau Mot. Vietnam. Energy Procedia **107**, 253–258 (2017)
9. Arrieta, F., Toro, W.: Afecciones respiratorias asociadas a factores ambientales y sanitarios en tres veredas de Guarne, Colombia, 2015. Rev. Salud Pública **21**, 217–223 (2019)
10. Pazmiño, J.P.W.; Arévalo, L.F.C. Análisis Estadístico De Los Residuos Sólidos Domésticos De La Parroquia San Sebastian Del Coca Del Cantón Joya De Los Sachas. Eur. Sci. J. ESJ, **14** 7, (2018).https://doi.org/10.19044/esj.2018.v14n24p7
11. Schweinle, J., et al.: Monitoring sustainability effects of the bioeconomy: a material flow based approach using the example of softwood lumber and its core product Epal 1 pallet. Sustain. **12**, 1–27 (2020). https://doi.org/10.3390/su12062444
12. Amrane, C., Bouhidel, K.E.: Analysis and speciation of heavy metals in the water, sediments, and drinking water plant sludge of a deep and sulfate-rich Algerian reservoir. Environ. Monit. Assess. **191**(2), 1–12 (2019). https://doi.org/10.1007/s10661-019-7222-9
13. Vågsholm, I., Arzoomand, N., Boqvist, S.: Food Security, Safety, and Sustainability—Getting the Trade-Offs Right. Front. Sustain. Food Syst. **4**, 1–14 (2020)
14. Ribeiro, N., Cantóia, S., O Lixão De Cuiabá, E.A.: Geração de Impactos the cuiabá dump and the generation of socio-environmental impacts, pp. 100–115 (2020)
15. Martínez, A., et al.: Characterization of environmental impact on resources, using strategic assessment of environmental impact and management of natural spaces of "Las Batuecas-Sierra de Francia" and "Quilamas" (Salamanca). Environ. Earth Sci. **71**, 39–51 (2014)
16. Jiao, F., et al.: On-site solid-phase extraction and application to in situ preconcentration of heavy metals in surface water. Environ. Monit. Assess. **185**, 39–44 (2013)

17. Loyo, G.A.: Métodos de Evaluación de Impacto Ambiental en Colombia Methods of Environmental Impact Métodos de avaliação de impacto ambiental na Colômbia. Rev. Investig. Agrar. y Ambient. UNAD **4**, 43–54 (2013)

18. Lozano, P., et al.: Plant diversity and composition changes along an altitudinal gradient in the isolated volcano sumaco in the ecuadorian amazon. Diversity **12**, 229 (2020)

19. Renzo, L.P.C.Y.J.: Di SpringerBriefs in Environmental Science. SpringerBriefs Environ. Sci. 103 (2012). https://doi.org/10.1007/978-3-319-96646-5

20. Wasson, T., et al.: American association of anatomists. Anat. Rec. **165**, 274–328 (1969)

21. Tschopp, H., Switzerland, B.: Oil explorations in the oriente of ecuador. Am. Assoc. **37**, 2303–2347 (1953)

22. Toulkeridis, T. et al: Wind directions of volcanic ash-charged clouds in Ecuador–implications for the public and flight. Geomatics, Nat. Hazards Risk. **8**, 242–256 (2017)

23. Bulot, L.G., Kennedy, W.J., Jaillard, E., Robert, E.: Late Middle-early Late Albian ammonites from Ecuador. Cretac. Res. **26**, 450–459 (2005)

24. Bravo, C., et al.: Evaluación de la Sustentabilidad Mediante Indicadores en Unidades de Producción de la Provincia de Napo. Amazonia Ecuatoriana. Bioagro **29**, 23–36 (2017)

25. Zhao, Y., et al.: Improvement of water quality in the Pearl River Estuary, China: a long-term case study of temporal-spatial variation, source identification and ecological risk of heavy metals in surface water of Guangzhou. Environ. Sci. Pollut. Res. **27**, 21084–21097 (2020)

26. Werth, C.J., et al.: A review of non-invasive imaging methods and applications in contaminant hydrogeology research. J. Contam. Hydrol. **113**, 1–24 (2010)

27. Hettiarachchi, H. et al.: Municipal Solid Waste Management in America and the Caribbean: Issues and Potential Solutions from the Governance Perspective. Recycling (2018)

28. Acurio, A., et al.: Description of a New Spotted-Thorax <I>Drosophila</I> (Diptera: Drosophilidae) species and its evolutionary relationships inferred by a cladistic analysis of morphological traits. Ann. Entomol. Soc. Am. **106**, 695–705 (2013)

29. Giraldo-Hurtado, T.M., Álvarez-Betancur, J.P., Parra-Henao, G.: Factores asociados a la infestación domiciliaria por Aedes aegypti en el corregimiento el Manzanillo, municipio de Itagüí (Antioquia) año 2015. Rev. Fac. Nac. Salud Pública **36**, 34–44 (2018)

30. Nikulin, C., et al.: Una metodología Sistémica y creativa para la gestión estratégica: Caso de Estudio Región de Atacama-Chile. Technol. Manag. y Innov. **10**, 127–144 (2017)

31. Kangas, J., Kurttila, M., Kajanusc, M., Kangas, A.: Evaluating the management strategies of a forestland estate - The S-O-S approach. J. Environ. Manage. **69**, 349–358 (2003)

32. Hill, T., et al.: SWOT Analysis. Long Range Plann. **30**, 46–52 (1997)

33. Houben, G., et al.: Knowledge-based SWOT-analysis system as an instrument for strategic planning in small and medium sized enterprises. Decis. Support Syst. **26**, 125–135 (1999)

34. Pitul'ko, V.M.; Dregulo, A.M.; Vitkovskaya, R.F. Ecological risks and problems of monitoring uncontrolled garbage gas emissions. Fibre Chem. **50**, 226–229 (2018)

35. Yang, X., et al.: Impact of food waste disposers on the generation rate and characteristics of municipal solid waste. J. Mater. Cycles Waste Manag. **12**, 17–24 (2010)

36. Bavusi, M., Rizzo, E., Lapenna, V.: Electromagnetic methods to characterize the Savoia di Lucania waste dump (Southern Italy). Environ. Geol. **51**, 301–308 (2006)

37. Starovoytova, D.: Solid Waste Management (SWM) at a University Campus (Part 1/10): Comprehensive-Review on Legal Framework and Background to Waste Management, at a Global Context. J. Environ. Earth Sci. **8**, 948–2225 (2018)

38. Liu, Q. et al.: Financial strategy optimization of municipal solid waste clean incineration power generation based on multi-agent evolutionary game model. IOP Conf. Ser. Earth Environ. Sci. 199 (2018)

39. Muñoz, H., et al.: Relación entre oxígeno disuelto, precipitación pluvial y temperatura: río Zahuapan, Tlaxcala. México. Tecnol. y Ciencias del Agua **6**, 59–74 (2015)

40. Oliver, J. Ensayos Toxicológicos y métodos de evaluación de calidad de aguas; Vol. 1; ISBN 9788578110796
41. Richmond, M.: Toxic chemicals: environmental impact, regulation, controversy, and education: editor's introduction. J. Environ. Stud. Sci. **6**(3), 541–542 (2016). https://doi.org/10.1007/s13412-016-0398-1
42. Gutiérrez-Fonseca, P.E., et al.: Evaluación de la calidad ecológica de los ríos en Puerto Rico: Principales amenazas y herramientas de evaluación. Hidrobiologica **26**, 433–441 (2016)
43. Özden, Ö., Erkan, N., Kaplan, M., Karakulak, F.: Toxic metals and omega-3 fatty acids of bluefin tuna from aquaculture: health risk and benefits. Exposure and Health **12**, 9–18 (2018). https://doi.org/10.1007/s12403-018-0279-9
44. Cifrian, E., Coz, A., Viguri, J., Andrés, A.: Indicators for valorisation of municipal solid waste and special waste. Waste Biomass Valorization **1**, 479–486 (2010)
45. Rachid, G., El Fadel, M.: Comparative SWOT analysis of strategic environmental assessment systems in the Middle East and North Africa region. J. Environ. Manage. **125**, 85–93 (2013). https://doi.org/10.1016/j.jenvman.2013.03.053
46. García, H., et al.: Percepción del manejo de residuos sólidos urbanos (fracción inorgánica) en una comunidad universitaria. Multiciencias **14**, 11 (2014)
47. Xie, X., et al.: Effects of soil reclamation on the oat cultivation in the newly reclaimed coastal land, eastern China. Ecol. Eng. **129**, 115–122 (2019)
48. Bau Satula, I., Ulloa Carcasés, M., Gola Cahimba, J.: Evaluación ambiental del depósito de residuos sólidos de Katenguenha. Angola. Minería y Geol. **33**, 350–362 (2017)
49. Mujica, V., Pérez, C.: Evaluación de impactos ambientales en el Laboratorio de Ingeniería Química de la Universidad de Carabobo. Rev. Ing. UC **12**, 23–31 (2005)
50. Pickton, D.W., et al.: What's swot in strategic analysis? Strateg. Chang. **7**, 101–109 (1998)
51. Muñoz, S., et al.: Metal concentrations in soil in the vicinity of a municipal solid waste landfill with a deactivated medical waste incineration plant, Ribeirão Preto Brazil. Bull. Environ. Contam. Toxicol. **73**, 575–582 (2004). https://doi.org/10.1007/s00128-004-0467-0
52. Akbulut, N.E., et al.: Accumulation of heavy metals with water quality parameters in KIzIlIk River Basin (Delice River) in Turkey. Environ. Monit. Assess. **173**, 387–395 (2011)
53. Marchenko, A.M., Pshinko, G.N., Demchenko, V.Y.: Erratum to: "ecological substantiation of invariably high concentrations of heavy metals in municipal wastewater sludges." J. Water Chem. Technol. **37**, 265 (2015)
54. Virha, R., et al.: Seasonal variation in physicochemical parameters and heavy metals in water of Upper Lake of Bhopal. Bull. Environ. Contam. Toxicol. **86**, 168–174 (2011)
55. Carrión, C.S., Mendoza, W.J.: Potential phytoremediator of native species in soils contaminated by heavy metals in the garbage dump quitasol-imponeda abancay. J. Sustain. Dev. Energy, Water Environ. Syst. **7**, 584–600, (2019). https://doi.org/10.13044/j.sdewes.d7.0261
56. Abedi Sarvestani, R., Aghasi, M.: Health risk assessment of heavy metals exposure (lead, cadmium, and copper) through drinking water consumption in Kerman city, Iran. Environ. Earth Sci. **78**(24), 1–11 (2019). https://doi.org/10.1007/s12665-019-8723-0
57. Torres Lozada, P.; et al. Influencia de la edad de lixiviados sobre su composición físico-química y su potencial de toxicidad. Rev. U.D.C.A Actual. Divulg. Científica. **17**, 245–256 (2014). https://doi.org/10.31910/rudca.v17.n1.2014.960
58. Kaza, S., Yao, L,, Bhada-Tata, P.: V.W.F. What a waste 2.0: a global snapshot of solid waste management to 2050 (2018) ISBN 9781464813290
59. Lider, A., et al.: Hydrogen accumulation and distribution in titanium coatings at gas-phase hydrogenation. Metals **10**(7), 880 (2020). https://doi.org/10.3390/met10070880

Spatial and Temporal Distribution of Salinity Levels and Macronutrients of Soils After the Construction of Dams on Tropical Dry Forest

David Carrera-Villacrés[1,2]([⊠]), Mishell Lara-Doicela[2], Fabián Rodríguez-Espinosa[1], and Theofilos Toulkeridis[1]

[1] Departamento de Ciencias de la Tierra y la Construcción. Carrera de Ingeniería Civil. Grupo de Investigación en Contaminación Ambiental (GICA), Universidad de las Fuerzas Armadas ESPE, Sangolquí, Ecuador
dvcarrera@espe.edu.ec

[2] Facultad de Ingeniería en Geología, Minas, Petróleos y Ambiental (FIGEMPA). Carrera de Ingeniería Ambiental, Universidad Central del Ecuador, Quito, Ecuador

Abstract. The excess of salinity in soils affects a number of environments, such as soils, where excess of salts damages its structure, it repels water, and it affects also crop production. In order to study such phenomenon, while trying to counteract such problems, we have chosen to study a variety of soil profiles between the Simbocal dam and the Chone Multiple Purpose Project (PPMCH) in western Ecuador. Therefore, the main objective of the current study has been to evaluate the quality of soils, where we measured the quantitative and quantitative salinity as well as the concentration of macronutrients in the soil at the surface and depth levels. Hereby, 27 out of 29 soil samples, appeared to have been non-saline soils with low levels of RASaj, while the two residual profiles were characterized as saline and saline-sodium soils, with high and very high RASaj. We encountered low concentrations of nutrients, which may also be accumulated due to the problems of salinity and sodicity derived from the presence of the nearby Simbocal dam. Within the probabilistic geostatistical analysis where we elaborated maps of spatial distribution it lacked to be the most suitable option, as these two saline samples had a regular correlation. Nonetheless, spatial distribution maps had to be elaborated applying the deterministic geostatistics, allowing an insight of fu-ture development of such soils.

Keywords: Salinity · Macronutrients · RAS · Geostatistics · Ecuador

1 Introduction

A high salinity in soils poses a fundamental problem with a variety of infrastructures in dry lands impacting them and reducing their lifespan, hereby causing enormous economic losses [1–3]. Among all ecosystems, tropical dry forests are more sensitive to anthropocentric perturbation due to human settlement and agricultural practices [4]. In Ecuador, tropical dry forests (Fig. 1) are located mainly on the pacific coastal region,

M. Botto-Tobar et al. (Eds.): ICAT 2022, CCIS 1756, pp. 482–494, 2023.
https://doi.org/10.1007/978-3-031-24971-6_34

right west of the Andes in a variety of provinces [5]. According to the World Wildlife Foundation (WWF) list of the most outstanding and representative areas of biodiversity, those aforementioned Ecuadorian tropical dry forests are in critical or endangered ecosystem status [6, 7].

The soil's salinity derives from natural sources such as geological and oceanic. Nevertheless, FAO indicated soils' salinity problems occur as a result of faulty tech-niques in large-scale irrigation projects [8, 9]. In addition, The World Commission on Dams (WCD) revealed that soils' salinity problem in eleven countries has reduced agricultural production by 25% [10]. Global income losses because of salinity reaches 11.4 billion US$/year and is able to erode small margins of agricultural crops contrib-uting to soils' erosion and rural poverty [11]. Furthermore, as the worlds Food and Agriculture Organization (FAO) stated that agriculture is the largest employer in the world, therefore, additional issues such as salinity increased even more rural areas poverty and affecting to United Nations Sustainable Development Goals [9]. However, the intensified use and bad practices have led to a significant loss of fertile soil, which is why agro-ecological production models must be strengthened to ensure food and the development of economic activities [12–14].

Salinity is measured quantitatively through Electrical Conductivity (EC) and qualitative form through the Sodium Adsorption Ratio (SAR) [15–19]. On the other hand, the contribution of nutrients in soils must be as a solution or ions available for the plants [20–22]. The elements consumed in moderate amounts also known as macro-nutrients are nitrogen (N), phosphorus (P) and potassium (K) [23–25].

The current study used geostatistical techniques in order to improve results interpretation. These techniques serve more adequately when the data present a regular and continuous distribution over time. Nevertheless, this is not an exclusive condition, as techniques may be used to understand the distribution and if there is any kind of relationship between the analyzed variables [26]. Therefore, the main aim of the present study has been to analyze the spatial and temporal distribution of salinity in representative soil profiles of a critical area between two dams in coastal Ecuador. Hereby, the main goal consisted to determine if the construction of the two dams are affected of the soil quality of the area whose main economic activity is agriculture.

2 Study Area

Dry forest are characterized by lowlands with elevations of less than 300 m above sea level (m.a.s.l.), although in southern part of Ecuador they may reach elevations above 800 m.a.s.l. [27]. Vegetation is characterized by a desert scrub, inter-montane thorn-forest, and deciduous and semi-deciduous forest [28]. Average precipitation ranges from 300 to 1500 mm per year, but there are great fluctuations between years. The elevation in the coastal Ecuadorian Province of Manabi is below 600 m.a.s.l. At low elevations the mean annual temperature varies between 24 and 26 °C with slight variations throughout the year, usually between 1–3 °C. Daily fluctuations are about 10–15 °C [29, 30].

The great fluctuation of precipitation in Manabi encouraged local and national governments to develop a regional plan in order to manage water resources [31]. Manabi province presents a very short rainy season from January to May and a longer dry season from June to December. Rain variation is very high between rainy (about 300 mm) and dry season (about 15 mm). As a result, between June and December there is a hydric deficit [32]. The consequence of a heavy rainy season and drought dry season is a high evapotranspiration [33, 34].

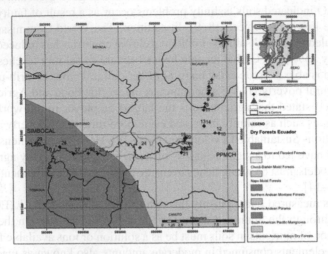

Fig. 1. Location map with setting of the sampling points

The result from this particular Manabi's weather characteristics from policy and technical point of view has been the construction of infrastructure to mitigate its hy-dric deficit (Fig. 1). There are three major dams in Manabi, being Poza Honda, La Esperanza and Daule Peripa. The latest is located between Manabi and Guayas provinces [36]. Additionally, Simbocal dam was built in order to regulate the annual river overflow of Chone River and to control the occasional high tides from the Pacific Ocean [37].

The Simbocal Dam has been in operation since 1982 to regulate high tides, protect the low salt-crusted areas and prevent shrimp farming from invading upstream lands [38, 39]. The Chone Multiple Purpose Project (PPMCH) began its execution in 2015, in order to mitigate the floods caused by the phenomenon of El Niño and to provide drinking water as well as irrigation to surrounding areas [40]. The economic activities of the study area are based on agriculture, livestock, forestry and fishing, while about 60% of the rural area is dedicated to agriculture [41]. The annual average precipitation registers 1113 mm/year [42].

3 Methodology

We evaluated some 29 soil profiles taken between the years 2014 and 2019 at surface level of 20 to 40 cm. The samples were integrated through the Analytic Hierarchy Process (AHP) and GIS [43]. The given data allowed to create map algebra, as it serves to evaluate a series of alternatives that facilitate decision making. Hereby, the analysis has been mainly of multicriteria [44]. The Mexican Standard NOM-021-RECNAT-2000 was taken as reference from which the sampling unit was delimited from 2 to 8 ha, and sampled in seven of profiles [45]. Simple and representative samples for and in-depth study were collected in the depths of 0 to 40, 60 to 80 and 100 to 120 cm. All 29 soil profiles were studied at surface level, while the in-depth soil profiles have been those of 23 to 29. The chemical determinations were determined in aqueous solutions of water-soil in relation of 1:1 (Table 1).

Table 1. Methods for chemical determination in a 1:1 ratio of the soil extract [46, 47, 71]

Parameters	Analytical method	Reference
pH	Potentiometer AS-02	NOM-021-RECNAT-2000 (2002)
Electric conductivity	Conductivity Meter AS-18	NOM-021-RECNAT-2000 (2002)
Sodium and potassium	Atomic absorption	3500-Na$^+$ y K$^+$, D (APHA 1995)
Calcium	Spectrophotometry	Adaptation of the Oxalate method (HI 2012)
Magnesium	Spectrophotometry	Adaptation of the Calmagita method (HI 2012)
Phosphates	Spectrophotometry	APHA 4500-NO3- E (APHA 2012)
Nitrates	Spectrophotometry	APHA 4500-P E (APHA 2012)

The interpretation of the quantitative and qualitative salinity results was per-formed in water-soil aqueous solutions in a ratio of 1: 1, because it has a high correlation (r: 0.93 a 0.99) with the saturation extract [18, 48]. The soil profiles from 1 to 22 were validated by APHA by analytical determination of the ion concentration [47]. Soil profiles from 23 to 29 were validated where they establish functional relation-ships between the concentration of salts and the EC, and the concentration of total dissolved solids (TDS) and the EC. The total elements of phosphorus (P) and nitrogen (N) were estimated using the method established by [49]. When the wash is increased, the element reaches the threshold and decreases, allowing to understand its behavior in the soil through a functional relationship of maximum and minimum. The results of N, P and K were subsequently interpreted [50–52].

The geostatistical analysis consisted in applying cokriging, which is a prediction method, for the non-sampled areas which occurs when the variable of interest is well correlated with the auxiliary variable [26]. The data were processed in free software R where the correlation with the Pearson Spearman coefficient between the EC and precipitation and ground level was executed.

4   Results

4.1   Ionic Composition of the Floors

Soils are composed of salts such as Na$^+$, Ca^{2+}, Mg^{2+} y K$^+$ ions, associated with Cl$^-$, SO$_4$$^{2-}$, HCO$_3$$^-$ anions, with which it has been possible to characterize salinity and its effects on the soil, while secondary salinization is due to the accumulation of these salts [53]. We yielded results of surface profile samples 1 to 22 and additional depth determinations of the profiles 23 to 29 (Table 2). CO_3^{2-} and HCO_3^- were not measured in the soil profiles 23 to 29. An average of the 22 profiles of CO_3^{2-} and HCO_3^- was calculated with which the Saturation Index (SI) and SARaj was determined according to the equations presented by [50]. We lacked to detect carbonates, as soils with pH less than 8 have been alkaline earth carbonate-free soils [54]. The macronutrients were evaluated considering the parameters for irrigation, in which it was shown that the irrigation water enters equilibrium with the soil solution in a saturation extract ratio that approaches in the ratio of 1:1 [48].

Table 2. Ionic composition of soil extract in the ratio of 1: 1, pH, EC, SI, SAR, SAR$_{aj}$ and macronutrients of given samples

N° sample	pH	EC dS/m	Ca^{2+} meq/L	Mg^{2+}	Na^+ meq/L	K^+	HCO_3^- meq/L	SI mg/L	SAR	SAR$_{aj}$	(NO_3-N)	P
	7,1	0,18	0,55	0,34	0,48	0,57	1,11	0	0,72	0,72	0,04	0,08
2	7,2	0,17	0,46	0,4	0,6	0,44	1,57	0,2	0,91	1,1	0,07	0,23
3	6,9	0,09	0,28	0,19	0,22	0,28	0,66	−0,4	0,45	0,27	0,09	0,05
4	6,9	0,34	0,13	0,05	0,11	0,05	0,14	−1,4	0,37	−0,15	< 0,1	< 0,05
5	7,2	0,63	0,18	0,14	0,19	0,13	0,25	−1,1	0,48	−0,05	< 0,1	< 0,05
6	7,1	0,19	0,5	0,53	0,46	0,5	1,19	0,1	0,64	0,71	0,2	0,3
7	6,6	0,66	0,2	0,11	0,25	0,11	0,23	−1,1	0,63	−0,06	< 0,1	< 0,05
8	7	0,1	0,34	0,22	0,29	0,39	0,98	−0,3	0,54	0,38	0,1	0,07
9	7,2	0,19	0,48	0,46	0,49	0,56	0,99	0	0,72	0,72	0,08	0,14
10	7,6	0,48	1,12	0,94	1,08	1,15	2,07	0,5	1,07	1,61	0,07	0,25
11	7,4	0,29	0,92	0,96	0,62	0,66	2,82	0,7	0,64	1,1	0,03	0,31
12	7,3	0,08	0,33	0,25	0,28	0,33	0,72	−0,4	0,51	0,31	0,12	0,05
13	6,8	0,31	0,12	0,06	0,09	0,05	0,13	−1,4	0,3	−0,12	< 0,1	< 0,05
14	6,9	0,26	0,09	0,05	0,08	0,04	0,11	−1,7	0,31	−0,22	< 0,1	< 0,05
15	7,4	0,15	0,55	0,45	0,39	0,26	0,82	−0,1	0,54	0,49	0,03	0,36
16	7,5	0,31	1,06	0,5	1,26	0,54	2,15	0,4	1,42	1,99	0,23	0,02
17	7,1	0,33	0,1	0,06	0,13	0,04	0,15	−1,5	0,47	−0,24	< 0,1	< 0,05
18	7,6	0,1	0,46	0,16	0,29	0,22	0,39	−0,7	0,53	0,16	0,01	0,12
19	6,6	0,25	0,1	0,03	0,09	0,03	0,13	−1,5	0,37	−0,19	< 0,1	< 0,05
20	7,1	0,26	0,67	0,51	0,92	0,76	1,36	0,2	1,2	1,44	0,04	< 0,05
21	6,6	0,54	0,14	0,08	0,26	0,07	0,28	−1,2	0,79	−0,16	< 0,1	< 0,05
22	6,6	0,3	0,16	0,04	0,07	0,04	0,13	−1,4	0,23	−0,09	< 0,1	< 0,05

(continued)

Table 2. (*continued*)

N° sample	pH	EC dS/m	Ca²⁺ meq/L	Mg²⁺	Na⁺ meq/L	K⁺	HCO₃⁻ meq/L	SI mg/L	SAR	SARaj	(NO₃-N)	P
23	6	0,16	1	0,39	0,4	0,11	0,76	0	0,48	0,48	< 0,1	3,95
	6,4	0,21	1,6	0,33	0,41	0,1	0,76	0,1	0,4	0,46	< 0,1	2,12
	6,9	0,19	1,4	0,33	0,41	0,1	0,76	0,1	0,4	0,48	< 0,1	0,29
24	6,8	1,38	10	0,82	3,7	0,09	0,76	0,7	1,59	2,7	0,5	1,8
	7,2	1,38	10	0,82	3,71	0,09	0,76	0,7	1,6	2,71	0,4	0,22
	7,4	1,48	10,6	1,23	3,8	0,16	0,76	0,7	1,6	2,66	0,5	0,26
25	7,9	0,4	1,9	0,82	1,5	0,31	0,76	0,2	1,29	1,54	0,3	0,34
	7,2	0,48	2,9	0,82	1,5	0,35	0,76	0,4	1,1	1,54	0,2	0,17
	7,4	0,49	3	0,82	1,5	0,31	0,76	0,4	1,1	1,52	0,6	0,34
26	7,2	0,54	5	0,7	0,77	0,35	0,76	0,5	0,46	0,68	2,4	0,39
	7,9	0,75	7	0,82	1,2	0,24	0,76	0,6	0,6	0,97	1,6	0,44
	7,6	1,39	10,8	1,4	3,5	0,27	0,76	0,8	1,4	2,55	0,4	0,67
27	7,7	0,84	5,5	1,4	2,4	0,3	0,76	0,5	1,29	1,94	2,2	0,56
	7,4	0,71	4,5	1,2	2,1	0,22	0,76	0,5	1,2	1,87	0,3	0,23
	7,9	0,94	6	1,8	3	0,25	0,76	0,6	1,5	2,43	0,6	0,48
28	7,4	7,45	30	19	22	2,82	0,76	1,2	4,44	9,78	0,5	0,25
	7,4	7,09	28	18,51	21,06	2,68	0,76	1,2	4,4	9,61	0,4	0,12
	8	7,28	36	11,52	22	2,47	0,76	1,2	4,5	9,93	0,3	0,09
29	7,5	3,54	15	5,76	19	2,24	0,76	0,9	5,9	11,2	0,2	0,75
	7,6	3,44	14	5,35	18	2,37	0,76	0,9	5,8	11	0,2	0,53
	7,7	6,03	27	6,99	31	2,84	0,76	1	7,5	15,04	0,4	2,09

4.2 Geostatistics

The application of the cokriging probabilistic method consisted in the execution of the correlation between the variable of interest EC with the auxiliary coordinates and precipitation, with values between 0.594 and −0.623, which indicated a positive and negative regular correlation [55]. Correspondingly, maps of spatial distribution were elaborated with the deterministic method IDW [56], of EC because a good correlation was not finding. RASaj and macronutrients were measured using the program ArcGis 10.3, with commercial license in the facilities of the laboratory computing of the Facultad de Ingeniería en Geología, Minas, Petróleos y Ambiental.

5 Discussion

5.1 Quantitative Salinity

All the profiles are classified as non-saline with values lower than 2 dS/m. The results show excess washing of the soils [57], as an effect of the high rainfall in the area.

Exception was for the entire profile 28 and the last depth of the 29. These pro-files were half saline with values greater than 4 dS/m. Latest profiles presented a secondary accumulation of salts causing their increase in the liquid phase of the soil product of the salt water intake in the tides [58]. It is indicated as an area with a high saline phreatic level and as a result its increase in depth [58]. The pH was in the range of 5.95 to 8.01, that is, they are slightly acidic to slightly alkaline soils [59].

5.2 Qualitative Salinity Based on SAR

The sodium salinity or sodification is determined through the Gapon equation, by calculating the SAR [18]. [60] explains that for the management of waters and sodic soils, the SARaj evaluates the most critical level of sodicity, by means of the calculation specified in [50]. The SARaj is related to the modified Langelier Saturation Index (SI), obtained from the pH calculated under conditions of equilibrium with $CaCO_3$ [61, 62]. The positive values of the saturation index indicate that the $CaCO_3$ tends to precipitate, and the negative values remain in the soil solution, these two conceptualizations show that the soil will lose the alkaline earth cations Ca^{2+} y Mg^{2+} y el Na^+ will appropriate the exchange sites [60].

Accordingly, no soil was classified as sodium or saline-sodium considering the SAR, however, the SI was positive in 55% of the samples. Less than half had a decrease in the concentration of Ca^{2+} because of $CaCO_3$, precipitation, and the Na^+ cation will appropriate the exchange sites [60]. The SARaj in profile 28 and depth 100 to 120 of profile 29 had high sodium S3 and very high S4 levels, due to the accumulation of sodium due to lack of drainage [58], and precipitation of Ca^{2+} y Mg^{2+} by the precipitation process indicated by the SI. Although the profiles 28 and 29 do not have the real values of SI and SARaj the existence of problems of alkalinity or sodicity can be inferred in the short term, due to the high concentration of calcium and sodium, respectively.

5.3 Qualitative Salinity Based on SAR

Soil fertility is affected by excess salts, as it affects the pH and solubility of the ions, factors that reduce the availability of nutrients [63]. Figure 2 shows the concentration of nutrients N, P and K at the surface level. The starting nutrient is N for vegetation growth. Nitrogen is part of the protein and chlorophyll and improves the absorption of phosphorus [59]. In this study N was evaluated in the form of nitrates. All of the samples indicated no degree of N restriction, as they had concentrations lower than 10 mg/L. The highest value was profile 25, and in 35% of the samples no nitrates were detected. This loss most likely appears to be the product of excess rainfall since nitrogen is washed in conjunction with K^+ and Mg^{2+} [64].

Phosphorus helps mature the plant and balance nitrogen, its excess hinders the absorption of other nutrients [59]. The concentration of P is within the range established by [50] except for profile 23 which has a value of 3.95 mg/L at the surface level. However, there is also an indication that the level of phosphorus is very low since all are below 5 mg/100g of soil [63]. Losses of P are associated with leaching, runoff, extraction by crops, among others [65]. The P is accumulated in the depth of point 29, because saline-sodium soils tend to release phosphorus [57].

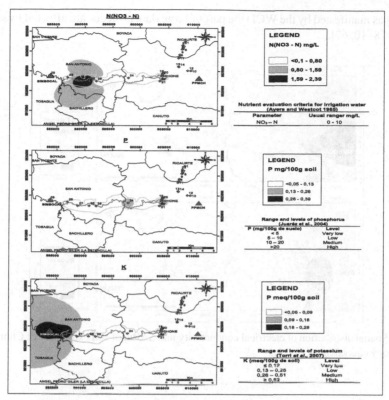

Fig. 2. Spatial distribution of the concentration of nutrients (N, P and K) in the soil extract 1:1 of soils in the Chone area. Symbology equivalent of Fig. 1.

The K acts to balance the effects of N, but its absorption in excess inhibits the absorption of magnesium, iron and zinc, generating deficiencies of these (Plaster, 2005). The 27 vertical and vertical surface soil profiles have a very low level, caused by leaching or extraction of crops [52, 65]. On the other hand, profiles 28 and 29 presented medium and low levels, respectively (Fig. 3). This may be possible, as the high percentage of base saturation, since less K is lost in leaching processes [65]. K concentration is regular when it comes to saline and saline-sodic soils, as is the case of such profiles.

5.4 Geostatistics

The evaluation and prediction of soil can be made using data from the hydrological properties of the basin, geographic information systems, topography or soil management, rainfall records [66], for this reason, the values of the cote and precipitation in the sampling points to relate them to the EC values determined are not associated, for the prediction with cokriging. However, maps of spatial distribution with Inverse Distance Weighting (IDW) have been performed, as it uses less data at long sampling distances [56]. Hereby, it is observed that profiles 28 and 29 are the more critical sites, due to the interception of drainage by the presence of obstacles, or mismanagement in large-scale projects as manifested by the WCD the part of large dam projects, are affected by salinity (Fig. 3) [8–10, 67].

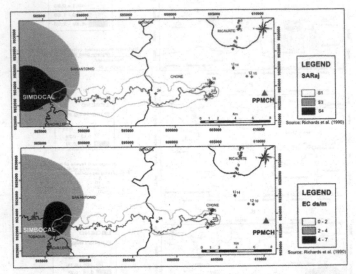

Fig. 3. Spatial distribution of electrical conductivity and SARaj of soil extract 1:1 of Chone soils. Symbology equivalent of Fig. 1.

5.5 Geostatistics

There is an accumulation of secondary salts which is generated by the presence of the Simbocal dam, similar to the Aswan High Dam in Egypt [68, 69]. This secondary salinization makes it difficult for the plant to absorb water, as it interferes with the growth of most crops [53]. Additionally, the processes of sodification would give rise to the loss of soil structure, limiting the number of crops [53]. The soils adjacent to the Simbocal dam are being affected by the presence of such processes, as there is a trend of accumulation at the surface level and depth of the N, P, and K nutrients, compromising agricultural production as also demonstrated by the Flumen-Monegros irrigation system in Spain [53].

The situation may worsen when adding fertilizer containing sodium or alkaline compounds and increase the salinity of the soil [57]. Likewise, if nutrients are added, it should be conducted in balanced proportions, otherwise it would lead to the contamination of groundwater and eutrophication of surface waters [70]. This counts also due to other external long-lasting circumstances like climate change [72].

6 Conclusions

In the spatial distribution we determined that the soil profiles 1 to 27 lacked of problems of quantitative and qualitative salinity, having low levels of nutrients, mainly as result of the wash-out of the components by precipitation.

However, the presence of the Simbocal dam generated problems of salinity and sodicity with a tendency to accumulate nutrients, derived from deficient drainage in profiles 28 and 29. These damage crops due to lack of availability and the quality of the structure ground. In addition, it can be inferred that the soils close to the PPMCH most likely will be compromised in the short or medium term, harming the agriculture and economy of the surrounding of Chone.

References

1. Pitman, M.G., Läuchli, A.: Global impact of salinity and agricultural ecosystems. In: Läuchli, A., Lüttge, U. (eds.) Salinity: Environment - Plants - Molecules, pp. 3–20. Kluwer Academic Publishers, Dordrecht (2004). https://doi.org/10.1007/0-306-48155-3_1
2. Yadav, S., Irfan, M., Ahmad, A., Hayat, S.: Causes of salinity and plant manifestations to salt stress: a review. J. Environ. Biol. 32(5), 667 (2011)
3. Vargas, R., Pankova, E., Balyuk, S., Krasilnikov, P., Khasankhanova, G.: Handbook for Saline Soil Management. Roma, Italia: FAO/LMSU, p.142 (2008).
4. Sánchez-Azofeita, G., et al.: Research priorities for noetropic dry forest. Biotropica 37(4), 477–485 (2005)
5. Aguirre, N., et al.: Potential impacts to dry forest species distribution under two climate change scenarios in southern Ecuador. Neotropical Biodivers. III(1), 18–29 (2017)
6. Olson, D.M., Dinerstein, E.: The Global 200: a representation approach to conserving the Earth's most biologically valuable ecoregions. Conserv. Biol. 12(3), 502–515 (1998)
7. Borchert, R., Meyer, S.A., Felger, R.S., Porter-Bolland, L.: Environmental control of flowering periodicity in Costa Rican and Mexican tropical dry forests. Glob. Ecol. Biogcogr. 13(5), 409–425 (2004)
8. Organización de las Naciones Unidas para la Alimentación y la Agricultura (FAO). La FAO y los 17 Objetivos de Desarrollo Sostenible. Roma, Italia, p. 8 (2015).
9. Organización de las Naciones Unidas para la Alimentación y la Agricultura (FAO) (Ed. Caon, L., Forlano, N., Keene, C., Sala, M., Sorokin, A., Verbeke, A., y Ward, C.). Estado Mundial del Recurso Suelo I Resumen Técnico. Roma, Italia, p. 82 (2016)
10. World Commission on Dams (WCD). (2000). Dams and development a new framework for decision-making: the report of the world commission on dams. London, England: WCD. 404p.
11. Ghassemi, F., Jakeman, A., Nix, H.: Salinisation of land and water resources: human causes, extent, management and case studies, p. 544p. University of New South Wales Press Ltd, Canberra, Autralia (1995)
12. Saifi, B., Drake, L.: A coevolutionary model for promoting agricultural sustainability. Ecol. Econ. 65(1), 24–34 (2008)
13. Horlings, L.G., Marsden, T.K.: Towards the real green revolution? exploring the conceptual dimensions of a new ecological modernisation of agriculture that could 'feed the world.' Glob. Environ. Chang. 21(2), 441–452 (2011)
14. Armah, F.A., Odoi, J.O., Yengoh, G.T., Obiri, S., Yawson, D.O., Afrifa, E.K.: Food security and climate change in drought-sensitive savanna zones of Ghana. Mitig. Adapt. Strat. Glob. Change 16(3), 291–306 (2011)
15. Seilsepour, M., Rashidi, M., Khabbaz, B.G.: Prediction of soil exchangeable sodium percentage based on soil sodium adsorption ratio. Am. Eurasian J. Agric. Environ. Sci. 5(1), 1–4 (2009)
16. Yao, R., Yang, J.: Quantitative evaluation of soil salinity and its spatial distribution using electromagnetic induction method. Agric. Water Manag. 97(12), 1961–1970 (2010)

17. Chi, C.-M., Zhao, C.-W., Sun, X.J., Wang, Z.C.: Estimating exchangeable sodium percentage from sodium adsorption ratio of salt-affected soil in the Songnen plain of northeast China. Pedosphere **21**(2), 271–276 (2011)

18. Carrera, D.: Salinidad en suelos y aguas superficiales y subterráneas de la cuenca evaporítica del río Verde-Matehuala, San Luis Potosí (Doctoral thesis). Colegio de Postgraduados Institución De Enseñanza E Investigación En Ciencias Agrícolas Campus Montecillo, México. p. 317. (2011)

19. Rahmati, M., Hamzehpour, N.: Quantitative remote sensing of soil electrical conductivity using ETM+ and ground measured data. Int. J. Remote Sens. **38**(1), 123–140 (2017)

20. Barber, S.A.: Soil-plant interactions in the phosphorus nutrition of plants. Role of Phosphor. Agricult. 591–615 (1980)

21. Comerford, N.B.: Soil factors affecting nutrient bioavailability. In: BassiriRad, H. (ed.) Nutrient acquisition by plants, pp. 1–14. Springer-Verlag, Berlin/Heidelberg (2005). https://doi.org/10.1007/3-540-27675-0_1

22. Acosta, C.: El suelo agrícola, un ser vivo. Inventio, la génesis de la cultura universitaria en Morelos **3**(5), 55–60 (2007)

23. Flores, J.: Agricultura Ecológica: Manual y guía didáctica. Madrid, España: Mundi-Prensa, p. 395 (2009)

24. Sinfield, J.V., Fagerman, D., Colic, O.: Evaluation of sensing technologies for on-the-go detection of macro-nutrients in cultivated soils. Comput. Electron. Agric. **70**(1), 1–18 (2010)

25. Hawkesford, M.: Functions of macronutrients. In Marschner's mineral nutrition of higher plants, pp. 135–189. Academic Press (2012)

26. Oliver, M.A.: Geostatistical Applications for Precision Agriculture. New York, USA: Springer Science+Business Media B.V. p. 348 (2010)

27. Renner, S.S., Balslev, H., Holm-Nielsen, L.B. (1990) Flowering plants of Amazonian Ecuador - a checklist. AAU Reports 24, 1-241

28. Sarmiento, G.: Ecological and floristic convergences between seasonal plant formations of tropical and subtropical South America. J. Ecol. 367–410 (1972)

29. Olson, D., Dinerstein, E.: The Global 200: priority ecoregions for global conservation. Ann. Mo. Bot. Gard. **89**(2), 199–224 (2002)

30. Echegaray-Aveiga, R.C., Masabanda, M., Rodríguez, F., Toulkeridis, T., Alegria, A., 2017: Solar energy potential in Ecuador. In: 2018 5th International Conference on eDemocracy and eGovernment, ICEDEG 2018 8372318 pp.46–51 (2017)

31. Cedeno, A.F.C., Alava, J.O.M., Sinichenko, E.K., Gritsuk, I.I.: Influence of the El Niño phenomena on the climate change of the Ecuadorian coast. RUDN J. Eng. Res. **19**(4), 513–523 (2018)

32. Manrique-Alba, À., et al.: Stem radial growth and water storage responses to heat and drought vary between conifers with differing hydraulic strategies. Plant, Cell Environ. **41**(8), 1926–1934 (2018)

33. Consejo Nacional de Recursos Hídricos (CNRH). (2002). Gestión de los recursos hídricos del Ecuador: políticas y estrategias. Quito, Ecuador: Consejo Nacional de Recursos

34. Yanez, L., Franco, P., Bastidas, W., Córdova, V.: Resumen del Plan Nacional de Gestión Integrada e Integral de los Recursos Hídricos y de las Cuencas y Microcuencas Hidrográficas del Ecuador. Aqua-LAC **9**(2), 124–132 (2017)

35. Toulkeridis, T.: Unexpected results of a seismic hazard evaluation applied to a modern hydroelectric plant in central Ecuador. J. Struct. Eng. **43**(4), 373–380 (2016)

36. Arriaga, L., Montaño, M., Vásconez, J.: Integrated management perspectives of the Bahía de Caráquez zone and Chone River estuary. Ecuador. Ocean Coastal Manage. **42**(2–4), 229–241 (1999)

37. Sandoval, W.: Diseño de Obras Hidrotécnicas. Quito, Ecuador: Universidad de las Fuerzas Armadas – ESPE, EDIESPE. p. 319 (2019).

38. Cedeño, R.: Mejoramiento de la calidad de vida de los habitantes de la zona 2 de la cabecera cantonal Calceta del cantón Bolívar-Manabí a través de la utilización adecuada del sistema de riego carrizal Chone primera etapa (Master tesis), Universidad Tecnologica Equinoccial. Facultad: Posgrados, Ecuador. p. 94. (2011)

39. Sacón, M.: Propuesta para reducir la cartera vencida del sistema de riego Carrizal Chone del cantón Bolívar a partir de un estudio socioeconómico (Bachelor's tesis), Escuela Superior Politécnica Agropecuaria de Manabí Manuel Félix López, Ecuador. p. 68. (2011)

40. Mato, F., Toulkeridis, T.: The missing Link in El Niño's phenomenon generation. Sci. Tsunami Haz. **36**, 128–144 (2017)

41. Gobierno Autónomo Descentralizado Municipal del cantón Chone (GADM Chone). Plan de Desarrollo y Ordenamiento Territorial del cantón Chone 2014–2019. Chone, Ecuador: GAD Municipal de Chone, p. 206 (2019).

42. Centro del Agua y Desarrollo Sustentable CADS y Escuela Superior Politécnica del Litoral (CADS – ESPOL) (2013). Análisis de vulnerabilidad del Cantón Chone. Perfil Territorial 2013. Quito, Ecuador: Programa de las Naciones Unidas para el Desarrollo. p. 63 (2013).

43. Patiño, H., León, A., Ávila. M.: Análisis de idoneidad del suelo para construcción de colegios públicos integrando SIG y PAJ en el área urbana de Bogotá. Redes De Ingeniería, 16–23 (2016). https://doi.org/10.14483/2248762X.11986

44. Escobar, J.: Metodología para la toma de decisiones de inversión en portafolio de acciones utilizando la técnica multicriterio AHP. Contaduría y Administración **60**(2), 346–366 (2015)

45. Secretaria del Medio Ambiente y Recursos Naturales (Semarnat).. Norma Oficial Mexicana NOM-021-SEMARNAT-2000. Establece los límites máximos permisibles de contaminantes en las descargas de aguas residuales en aguas y bienes nacionales. Ciudad de México D.F., México: Semarnat. p. 85 (2002)

46. American Public Health Association, American Water Works Association and Water Environment Federation (APHA) (edited by E. W. Rice, R. B. Baird, A. D. Eaton and L. S. Clesceri): Standard methods for the examination of water and wastewater. American Public Health Association, Washington, D.C., USA (2012)

47. American Public Health Association. American Water Works Association and Water Pollution Control Federation (APHA). (1995). Standard methods for the examination of water and wastewater. Washington, DC: USA: American Public Health Association

48. Carrera, D., Sánchez, V., Portilla, O., Bolaños, D.: Similarity index between irrigation water and soil saturation extract in the experimental field of Yachay University, Ecuador. IOP Conf. Series: Earth Environ.al Sci. **82**, 1–11 (2017)

49. Carrera, D., Merizalde, M., Viera, R.: New method to estimate total elements of chromium (VI), nickel and iron to analyze their mobility and spatial distribution from an open dump. IOP Conf. Ser. Earth Environ. Sci. **191**, 1–9 (2018)

50. Ayers, R.S., Westcot, D.W.: Water quality for agriculture. Rome, Italy: Food and Agriculture Organization of the United Nations, p. 186 (1985).

51. Juárez, M., Sánchez, Á., Jordà, J., Sánchez, J.: Diagnóstico potencial nutritivo del suelo. Alicante, España: Universidad de Alicante. p. 98 (2004)

52. Torri, S., Cabello, M., Lavado, R.: Diagnóstico de la calidad de los suelos y su fertilidad para el cultivo de Pecán. La Producción de Pecán en Argentina (p. 1.20). Buenos Aires, Argentina: INTA-FAUBA VI (2007).

53. Porta, J., López, M., Poch, R.. Edafología: Uso y protección de suelos. Madrid, España: Mundi-Prensa, p. 607 (2014)

54. Carrera, D., Guevara, P., Gualichicomin, G.: Caracterización físico-químico desde el punto de vista agrícola de los suelos en la zona de riego del proyecto multipropósito Chone. Congreso de Ciencia y Tecnología ESPE **9**(1), 71–80 (2014)

55. Martínez, R., Tuya, L., Martínez, M., Pérez, A., Ana, C.: El coeficiente de correlación de los rangos Spearman caracterización. Revista Habanera de Ciencias Médicas, VII I(2), 1–19 (2009)

56. Villatoro, M., Henríquez, C., Sancho, F.: Comparación de los interpoladores IDW kriging en la variación espacial de pH, CA. CICE del suelo. Agronomía Costarricense 332(1), 95–105 (2008)

57. García, A.: Manejo de suelos con acumulación de sales. VIII Congreso Ecuatoriano de la Ciencia del Suelo, pp.1–21 (2008)

58. Porta, J., Herrero, J., Latorre, S. : (Ed. Herrero, J.). Salinidad en los suelos: aspectos de su incidencia en regadios de Huesca Zaragoza: Diputación General de Aragón. Evaluación de suelos para riego: criterios problemática en los regadíos de Huesca. Zaragoza, España. 119–146 (1986).

59. Plaster, E.: La ciencia del suelo y su manejo. Madrid, España: Edit. Paraninfo, p. 419 (2000).

60. Carrera, D., et al.: Salinidad cuantitativa y cualitativa del sistema hidrográfico Santa María-Río Verde, México. Tecnología Ciencias del Agua I(2), 69–83 (2015)

61. Bower, A.: Prediction of the effects of irrigation waters on soils. In: Salinity Problems in the Arid Zones. Tehran, Iran: Proc. UNESCO Arid Zone Symposium, 215–222 (1961).

62. Hasheminejhad, Y., Ghane, F., Mazloom, N.: Teady-State Prediction of Sodium Adsorption Ratio (SAR) in Drainage Water Based on Irrigation Water Quality in a Lysimetric Study. Commun. Soil Sci. Plant Anal. 44(18), 2666–2677 (2013)

63. Juárez, M., Sánchez, J., Sánchez, A.: Química del suelo y medio ambiente. Alicante, España: Universidad de Alicante. p. 744 (2006)

64. Ochoa, R.: Consecuencias de la deposición de nitrógeno sobre la biodiversidad y el funcionamiento de los ecosistemas terrestres: Una aproximación general desde la ecología de ecosistemas. Ecosistemas 26(1), 25–36 (2017)

65. Navarro, G., Navarro, S.: Química agrícola. Madrid, España: Mundi-Prensa. p. 508 (2014).

66. Sentís, I.: Problemas de degradación de suelos en América Latina: Evaluación de causas y efectos. X Congreso Ecuatoriano de la Ciencia del Suelo. 1–10 (2012)

67. Badia, D.: Suelos afectados por sales. Boletín de las Sociedades Catalanas de Física, Química, Matemáticas Tecnología, XII I(12), 609–629 (1992)

68. Barrada, Y.: Empleo de humedímetros neutrónicos en Egipto para estudios sobre riegos. OIEA Boletín, VII I(3/4), 10–12 (1976)

69. Instituto Interamericano de Cooperación para la Agricultura (IICA). : Método para la Ejecución de Estudios Ambientales en la Formulación de Proyectos de Inversión para el Desarrollo Agrícola y Rural, Evaluación y Seguimiento del Impacto Ambiental en Proyectos de Inversión para el Desarrollo Agrícola y Rural (pp. 37–129). San José, Costa Rica: IICA (1996)

70. Masís, F., Piedra, G., Hernández, R.: Química Agrícola, p. 373p. Editorial Universidad Estatal a Distancia, San José, Costa Rica (2017)

71. Hanna Instruments Inc: Instruction Manual HI 83099 COD and Multiparameter Bench Photometer, p. 69, Hanna Instruments Inc, Woonsocket, USA (2012)

72. Toulkeridis, T.: Climate Change according to Ecuadorian academics–Perceptions versus facts. LA GRANJA. Revista de Ciencias de la Vida, 31(1), 21–46 (2020)

The Importance of Epigenetics in Leukemia

Milton Temistocles Andrade-Salazar[✉][iD], Verónica Martínez-Cepeda[iD],
Sandra Margoth Armijos-Hurtado[iD], Chenoa Katya Jarrín Barragan[iD],
Danna Thaiz Guilcamaigua Coronel[iD], and Erika Justine Gavilanez Lopez[iD]

Departamento de Ciencias de la Computación, Departamento de Ciencias Exactas,
Universidad de las Fuerzas Armadas ESPE, Sede Santo Domingo de los Tsáchilas,
Sangolquí, Ecuador
{mtandrade,vimartinez1,smarmijos1,ckjarrin,dtguilcamaigua,
ejgavilanez}@espe.edu.ec

Abstract. Leukemia is a blood cancer that begins when healthy blood
cells change and get out of control, this is one of the most common
types of cancer in children, and to a lesser extent it is also detected in
young people and adults; whereas epigenetics is responsible for studying the changes in gene function that are hereditary and cannot be
attributed to alterations in the DNA sequence; Epigenetics has become
an important part of the development and normal functioning of cells, by
means of which it is possible to arrive at exhaustive studies that allow
us to confront and understand some abnormalities that may occur in
human beings. There are several epigenetic mechanisms of gene regulation that were addressed such as: DNA methylation, histone modifications and microRNA expression. The objective of this research was to
determine the epigenetic methods that solve the control of leukemia and
to select the most efficient in terms of human health, especially children
and elderly adults, who are the most prone to suffer from it; and in
Ecuador it has been determined that there is a high mortality rate due
to leukemia. The type of research had a mixed approach, using content
analysis and reading record; likewise, the information was collected from
scientific articles specialized in the subject. Also, the survey technique
was used for data collection and analysis. Analyzing the different types
of epigenetic therapies, it was found that DNA methylation is one of the
optimal solutions.

Keywords: Epigenetics · Leukemia · Epigenetic methods ·
Methylation · Histones

1 Introduction

Epigenetics is an important part of normal cell development and function, including DNA methylation, histone modifications and microRNA expression. DNA

Supported by Universidad de las Fuerzas Armadas ESPE Sede Santo Domingo de los
Tsáchilas.

M. Botto-Tobar et al. (Eds.): ICAT 2022, CCIS 1756, pp. 495–506, 2023.
https://doi.org/10.1007/978-3-031-24971-6_35

methylation is the most studied epigenetic marker; it leads to repression of transcripts by either silencing the genome or blocking transcription factors that interact with DNA or recruiting co-repressor complexes [1]. Leukemia develops when the DNA of the blood cells that are being formed, mainly white blood cells, is damaged. This causes the blood cells to grow and divide uncontrollably; thus causing healthy blood cells to die and be replaced by abnormal blood cells that do not die, where they accumulate and take up more space.

Leukemia is a cancer of the blood, it begins when healthy blood cells change and get out of control, it is a cancer of the lymphocytes which are white blood cells that are part of the body's immune system; this is one of the most common types of cancer in children. Acute lymphoblastic leukemia is characterized by the uncontrolled proliferation of immature lymphocytes called lymphoblasts that dominate the bone marrow and interfere with normal hematopoiesis; it can also affect T or B cell lines, occurs in adults and children in the pediatric age, and is especially important because it is the most common type of cancer. The consequences arise as the bone marrow produces more cancer cells, as they begin to saturate the blood, thus preventing the healthy white blood cells that our body needs, to grow and fulfill their function. Likewise, genetics alone cannot explain phenotypic diversity in populations, and their members have different susceptibility to a range of diseases. Clearly when inherited it becomes a bridge between genetic and environmental interactions. In turn, it involves therapeutically reversible changes in gene expression levels without modification of the DNA (deoxyribonucleic acid) sequence. If we analyze the cellular evolution of cancer, epigenetics seems to play an important role. The natural history of human tumors is undergoing major changes; not only can the tumor metastasize to distant sites, creating new blood and lymphatic vessels to nourish and purge metabolites, but it can also change if chemotherapy, hormone therapy or radiation is used. The ability of cancer cells to undergo rapid genetic changes to adapt to a challenging microenvironment is limited.

With all the theory and practice that has been generated over the years, drugs have become more effective, and in turn various forms of application and different ways of counteracting the existing condition have been implemented. Thousands of diseases are present in the whole world, and not all of them can be cured with the same medicines, that is why treatments or methods were generated to intervene and eradicate these evils. These treatments help us to understand the behavior of the disease, in order to apply a better treatment to the patient who suffers from it. A treatment can be considered as a set of means used to alleviate or cure a disease, to get to the essence of that which is unknown or to transform something; this concept is common in the field of medicine. The success of epigenetic therapies for the treatment of leukemia and other cancers depends on the identification and implementation of rational combinations of drugs, including the combination of epigenetic therapies with chemotherapy, targeted therapy and immunotherapy. The applicability and use of this type of therapies, it is urgent that specialized personnel has enough knowledge in this regard, because in Ecuador for the year 2018 according to OMS there was an incidence of 157.2 cases per 100,000 population and rising, a fact that is of great concern both in health, economic and social aspects.

The identification of the most effective combination strategies will require time and careful evaluation, especially given that the specific genetic and/or epigenetic status of the tumor will undoubtedly influence the outcome. In this sense, with all the theory addressed, this study tried to determine the most effective procedures to be able to cope with leukemia; for which different epigenetic procedures were addressed, which is the most updated option and addressed by several researchers for the treatment of this disease. Making a comparison between the different methods exposed for the treatment of cancer and specifically leukemia, the application of DNA methylation is suggested, for being less invasive and more forceful.

2 Methodology

The present study was developed under a mixed paradigm, using the documentary analysis technique and the reading card instrument to organize the information, and a survey was used to collect quantitative information. The information was extracted from scientific articles indexed in different scientific databases, giving priority to those dealing with epigenetics and leukemia as the object of study of this research. Table 1 summarizes the epistemological configuration of this study:

Table 1. Epistemological configuration of the study [a]

Paradigm	Mixed
Epistemological Approach	Rationalist Empiricist Experientialist
Type of Research	Documentary Field
Method	Hermeneutic-Dialectical Phenomenological
Study Subjects	Scientific documents SOLCA physicians
Data Collection and Analysis Techniques	Survey, Criteria-Based Selection Theoretical Triangulation Methodological Triangulation
Instruments	Reading card Questionnaire

[a]Note: Source Andrade 2022

Humans have been acquiring diseases since their existence, whether genetic, hereditary or congenital, thus affecting every part of our body; therefore, thanks to science, several drugs have been developed to counteract these conditions or soothe their symptoms; however, there are diseases that do not have a totally effective treatment that helps to eliminate these pathologies, among them is cancer.

Cancer is a multifactorial disease in which genetic, epigenetic and environmental factors intervene in a complex interrelationship, which play a critical role in its onset and progression. The term epigenetics is associated with a phenotype inherited by chromosomal changes without alterations in the DNA sequence, epigenetic dyscontrol is common in cancer cells; therefore, these changes serve as diagnostic and prognostic markers for several types of cancer.

Leukemia is a type of cancer belonging to one of the diseases that most affects the blood, it develops when the DNA of the blood cells that are being formed, mainly the white blood cells, suffers damage; this is why the blood cells grow and divide uncontrollably, causing the same healthy cells to die and be replaced by abnormal blood cells that do not die. The body can be affected in different areas, as it depends on the type of leukemia the individual suffers from and how he/she may react to the behavior of the disease.

The term epigenetics has been approached by several scholars, but nevertheless, it is a term that causes controversy considering the different edges from which it can be approached. Thus, in the area of developmental genetics, it refers to the mechanisms of genetic regulation, in which DNA modification has nothing to do. If approached from the area of evolutionary biology, it is related to the mechanisms of inheritance, and does not respond to genetic heritability; and finally, if approached from the area of population genetics, it is related to physical variation influenced by environmental conditions.

Epigenetics, which does not affect the sequence of nitrogenous bases in DNA, is a promising field for the development of new therapies against leukemia, stimulating the immune system and potentially contributing to improved patient outcomes. The importance of epigenetics in leukemia aims to understand how epigenetics helps in treatments and medicines to counteract cancer. Among these are epigenetic therapies, which are among the most active areas of preclinical and clinical cancer research because of their potential to specifically target chromatin-mediated disease mechanisms and the expectation that these therapies will have fewer side effects than chemotherapies, i.e., which combinations of genes affect which diseases can be determined, and their silencing could be reversed.

Because epigenetic changes help determine whether genes are turned on or off, they influence the production of proteins in cells; this regulation helps ensure that each cell generates only what is necessary for its function. For example, proteins that promote bone growth are not produced in muscle cells; patterns of variation vary between individuals, within different tissues in individuals and even in different cells within tissue. Environmental influences, such as a person's diet and exposure to pollutants, can affect the epigenome; epigenetic modifications can be maintained from cell to cell as cells divide and in some cases can be inherited across generations.

The form and function of every cell in the human body is determined by the genes and proteins it expresses, as well as by the signals it receives from surrounding cells. Therefore, the regulation of gene transcription and translation are the main biological determinants of cell differentiation and function. Errors in epigenetic processes, such as modification of an incorrect gene or failure to add a chemical group to a particular gene or histone, can result in abnormal gene activity or inactivity, altered gene activity is included to the cause by epigenetic errors, is a common reason for genetic disorders such as cancer.

3   DNA Methylation

Methylation is a replication process that occurs in mammals when the DNA double helix is already formed. In general terms, it is a process that consists of the addition of methyl to one of the units that make up DNA, i.e. cytosine; several researchers have concluded that DNA methylation is essential in the organization of genes during the first stages of human life, such as gametogenesis and embryogenesis.

According to [2] DNA methylation is an epigenetic process that intervenes in the regulation of gene expression in two ways, directly by preventing the binding of transcription factors, and indirectly by promoting the "closed" structure of chromatin.

It is worth mentioning that DNA methylation is the most studied, since it allows silencing the genome and thus blocking both transcription and translation factors. In other words, this process changes the expression of a certain section without altering the sequence of the genome. This development occurs between CpG islands (rich in cytokine, phosphate and guanine). In this case, the DNA is exactly methylated in imprinting (genetic phenomena expressed directly related to the sex of its ancestor) also known as "genetic fingerprinting" [3].

There are two types of methylation; the first corresponds to maintenance methylation, which adds methyl groups to the DNA strand at the opposite position to the leading strand and causes the daughter DNA molecule to maintain a methylation pattern after cell division. The second corresponds to de novo methylation, which adds methyl groups in completely new positions and can alter methylation patterns in localized regions of the genome. In addition to this generating the ability to reactivate genes, including tumor suppressor genes, it induces the expression of thousands of transposable elements, including cancer antigens silenced by DNA methylation in most somatic cells, resulting in a state of viral mimicry in which the treated cells generate an immune response by activating viral defense genes and generating neoantigens (new protein produced when mutations appear in the DNA of a tumor).

The Fig. 1 shows the methylation of DNA with a methyl radical such as CH3.

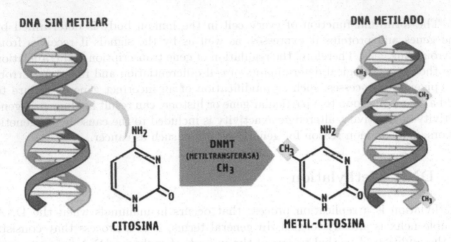

Fig. 1. Difference in structure between unmethylated and methylated DNA sequence

4   Histone Modifications

Histones are proteins involved in the regulation of DNA in the nucleus. There are five types of histones: H1/H5, H2A, H2B, H3 and H4. Histones H2A, H2B, H3 and H4 form the nucleosomes that encapsulate DNA, while histones H1 are found in the spaces between nucleosomes; Histone H5 is found in certain regions of DNA [4]

The state of chromosomes depends on post-translational histone modifications and affects the state of gene transcription. The main enzymes responsible for regulating histone changes are methyltransferases, demethylases, acetyltransferases, and deacetylases. The combined action of these enzymes results in a "histone code", which regulates chromatin topology and enhancer accessibility, thus regulating transcriptional activity and other processes such as DNA replication and repair.

Histone modifications are performed by enzymes that assist in the expression of a gene by repressing or silencing its expression. In addition to these there are kinases that both positively and negatively regulate gene expression. Histones can be modified post-translationally to alter their DNA-binding and nuclear protein binding properties. These heritable modifications affect gene expression and alter local chromatin structure. In general, histone acetylation by neutralizing the negatively charged DNA carboxyl groups that bind tightly to the positively charged lysine residues of histone tails leads to a more open chromatin structure that leads to the expression of genes involved in cell death.

Histone modifications produce two phenomena: First, a change occurs where the chromatin structure is altered by modifying non-covalent interactions in nucleosomes; and second, they then interact with effector or transducer proteins or protein complexes. Therefore, these modifications determine the general state of chromatin and regulate processes such as transcription, DNA repair and replication [5].

There is protein with lysine acetyl transferase activity in gene regulation. These proteins acetylate histone tails at the epsilonamino groups of lysine residues. This process leads to transcriptional activation of neutralization of the positive charge of lysine limiting to a decrease in affinity of histones for DNA. This will generate more weakly packed nucleosomes facilitating the access of regulatory proteins.

The compacted chromatin is associated with transcriptional silencing and is evidenced by histone modifications and DNA methylation, is maintained by the action of multi-protein complexes; the chromatin shows activating histone marks, absence of DNA methylation in the promoter region and allows the entry of transcription factors.

On the other hand, we have the less applied epigenetic method, which is RNA interference, which attempts to silence or stop the transcription of data that occurs in the messenger RNA, by using small double-stranded RNA molecules leading to the degradation of this, thus preventing its translation into proteins. But the major disadvantage of this mechanism is that by introducing small artificial RNA molecules to silence a disease-carrying gene, these pieces of RNA mimic cellular RNA, both of which use the cell's resources to perform their function, thus overtaxing the cell, causing the cell to succumb. In addition, micro-RNAs contribute to the formation of metastasis, i.e. cancer cells spread from the site of origin to other parts of the body.

Figure 2 shows the epigenetic impact of biochemical DNA modifications based on histone modification.

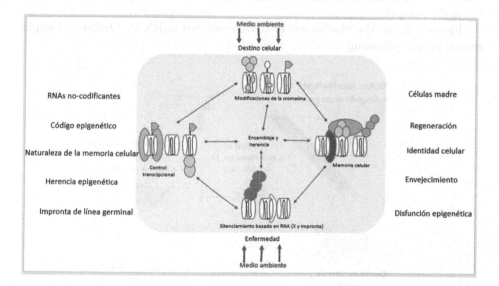

Fig. 2. Epigenetic impact of biochemical modifications of DNA based on histone modification.

5   RNA Interference

According to [6] RNA interference works by blocking the expression of certain genes, coupling to mature messenger RNAs in ribosomes, and preventing the translation process. It is a molecular mechanism that prevents deleterious effects on the transmission of genetic information in cells. The binding of the interfering RNA to a particular sequence of the corresponding RNA strand blocks the translation of that sequence. It is considered a protective mechanism against certain viral infections, based on the fact that only viruses possess a double helix RNA.

Certain small RNA molecules can silence gene expression by binding to DNA and interfering with transcription, or the process in which information is transferred from DNA to RNA. Double-stranded RNA molecules regulate gene expression. Several classes of small RNA molecules have been described that trigger the process of artificial silencing by interference. The most studied are small interfering RNAs and micro-RNAs, which attempt to silence or stop the transcription of data that occurs in messenger RNA by using small double-stranded RNA molecules leading to the degradation of RNA, thus preventing its translation into proteins.

To explain it in simpler terms, a person's genetic information is written in his DNA and organized into genes. In the nucleus, these genes transcribe the genetic information contained in its DNA into messenger RNA (mRNA). This mRNA leaves the nucleus and binds to the cell's ribosome, which translates the mRNA sequence into the corresponding protein/enzyme; this translation and protein synthesis can be blocked by acting on the mRNA, just as RNA interference does. Thus, in the last decade, RNA has become an invaluable experimental tool for the functional characterization of genes and especially in the areas of scientific research.

Figure 3 shows the Mechanism of RNA-mediated miRNAs. Origin and application in gene silencing.

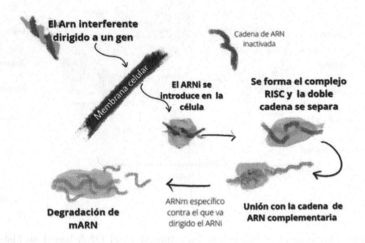

Fig. 3. RNA mechanism mediated by miRNAs

Gene silencing is a process of turning off or deactivating a gene, thus preventing it from producing any proteins or other forms of expression. This process occurs naturally in many cases with the intention of regulating gene expression and preventing potential damage caused by viruses. Gene silencing has become a very important laboratory technique, as turning off a gene is a very powerful way to determine the purpose of that gene.

6   Relationship Between Silencing Mechanisms

Condensed chromatin is associated with transcriptional silencing, is mediated by histone modifications and DNA methylation, and is maintained by protein complexes. Chromatin exhibits activating histone marks, no DNA methylation in promoter regions and allows entry of transcription factors.

The structure and degree of chromatin condensation are related to transcriptional activity. During differentiation of totipotent cells, a single DNA sequence produces multiple states in the chromatin (epigenome).

Methylation of cytosine residues in DNA reshapes chromatin structure by chemical modifications in histones, namely acetylations, methylations and regulatory processes mediated by non-coding or interfering RNA molecules.

Interpreting these results, [7] argue that "histone modifications act on chromatin by altering the ionic charges present in histone tails" (p. 9), acetylation is carried out by acetyltransferase enzymes, transferring an acetyl group to a lysine in the histone tail, this alters the positive charge contributed by the amino acid lysine so that the interaction of DNA with the histone is weakened.

mRNA-induced silencing occurs between proteins and RNA interference (RNAi) derived from non-protein-coding transcripts. Gene silencing impedes the flow of genetic information that prevents transcription, induces degradation or prevents translation. RNAs recognize specific nucleotide regions in the sequence of newly formed mRNAs by binding to them. This binding prevents translation of the mRNAs and causes their degradation.

As it could be observed, the application of the techniques and instruments of the present investigation, allows defining the epigenetic methods that play a fundamental role at the moment of controlling or preventing blood cancer, also called "leukemia". By explaining what each of them consists of, it will be possible to understand why one method is more effective than the others, thus providing the patient's safety and well-being.

The following table shows a comparison between the three methods most commonly used by scientists in relation to epigenetics.

Table 2. Comparison of epigenetic methods [a]

	Method	Additional benefits	Side effects
DNA methylation	Addition of a methyl group to the cytosine of the CpG dinucleotide	It has the function of providing stability in the genome, as well as transcriptional regulation, solving various types of cancer, as well as having the possibility of participating in the aging of people; dealing with the defective hormones present	Just as DNA methylation helps to counteract cancer, a misstep in the DNA methylation process can cause the reverse, i.e., it would be capable of initiating genome modification and instability, leading to a new cancer
RNA interference	Gene silencing using small siRNA fragments	Prevent viral infections by aggressive viruses. Speculates the possible use of siRNA fragments as antiviral vaccines. RNAi studies the pathogenesis of metabolic diseases, investigates insulin signaling pathways	Difficulty in delivering RNAi into cells, because they are designed for nanomolar doses and must be introduced at a site close to the tissue. They could alter the regulatory functions of some cellular microRNAs
Histone modification	Histone deacetylase inhibitors	A substance that produces a chemical change that prevents tumor cells from multiplying. Histone deacetylase inhibitors are being studied for the treatment of cancer. Also called HDAC inhibitor	These inhibitors are based on the fact that HDACs are involved in DNA replication and repair: if inhibited, cancer cells will not be able to properly repair their DNA, making them more sensitive to chemotherapy based on damage to the genetic material

[a]Note: Source Andrade 2022

7   Results

In order to have a general idea of the methods that are established as a solution towards the control of leukemia, a data survey was carried out; by means of information gathered after a systematic literature review study, which allowed us to select relevant documents for the research, with authors specialized in the area of both genetics and cancer diseases, specifically in the healing methods involved in epigenetics and leukemia; as well as the development of surveys carried out with specialized personnel of the SOLCA oncology unit.

Table 3 shows the degree of knowledge that the physicians of the SOLCA oncology unit have regarding the use and practice of epigenetic therapies for the treatment of leukemia; where it is evident that a high percentage do not know what consists of the treatment of epigenetics.

Table 3. Physicians with knowledge of epigenetic therapy[a]

Knowledge	Quantity	Percentage
Yes	4	44%
No	5	56%
Total	9	100%

[a]Note: Source Andrade 2022

Table 4 shows that doctors identify DNA methylation as the best epigenetic method at the time of eradicating leukemia; since this treatment is less laborious and painful, thus replacing oncological treatments that have health consequences, such as chemotherapy.

Table 4. Epigenetic method considered relevant when treating leukemia[a]

	Quantity	Percentage
DNA Meditation	5	56%
Histone modifications	3	33%
RNA interference	1	11%
Total	9	100%

[a] Note: Source Andrade 2022

Based on the results acquired in the previously carried out survey, it is determined that a large part of the doctors of the SOLCA oncology unit say they know what epigenetics is; however, most are unaware of epigenetic therapies. Taking into account that treatment should be started between the fifth and fourteenth day; since, by extending the start of therapy, it could cause the leukemia to progress, and the treatment would run the risk of not giving results, in turn, the treatment must be carried out in the hospital or clinic within the first 10 months after diagnosis. In addition, it is verified that leukemia affects a large part of the population in Ecuador, mainly affecting children from 1 to 10 years old and the elderly. It is also evident that the SOLCA Oncology Unit does not implement epigenetic therapies in treatment, with an emphasis on leukemia.

The application of epigenetic methods based on DNA methylation and histone modification to prevent the progression of leukemia is considered as a proposal. Describing these mechanisms as the addition of a methyl group at specific points of the DNA, generating a silencing of it, thus obtaining immune cells. It is worth mentioning that the use of these strategies leads to the elimination of epigenetic marks, that is, it increases the genetic variability of populations, since they generate more flexible individuals capable of adapting to changing environmental conditions.

So, once this process of obtaining results has been developed, it is said that leukemia is diagnosed more in infants; therefore, the epigenetic molecular mechanisms involved in the development of cancer have great potential to be used as preventive strategies and thus be able to counteract the adverse effects of the disease, as well as requiring studies that project the improvement of the quality of life of these patients and their families.

8   Conclusions

The process for the success of epigenetic therapies in the treatment of leukemia depends on the identification and implementation of the rational combination of drugs and includes the combination of epigenetic therapies with chemotherapy.

The most beneficial epigenetic method was determined to be DNA methylation, due to its various effects in terms of leukemia control.

The second alternative to solve the causes that interfere in the leukemia patient is the histone modification method.

The second alternative to solve the causes that interfere in the patient with leukemia is the histone modification method. of transcription and binding.

It is known that at the molecular level, epigenetic inheritance is defined as a series of changes in the genetic material that do not alter the DNA sequence, causing changes in the final transcription and union products.

Epigenetic therapy can target chromatin-mediated pathological mechanisms in which double-stranded RNA molecules regulate gene expression.

Lymphoblastic leukemia is a cancer of the blood and bone marrow that, in most cases, grows quickly and gets worse if not treated early.

Cancer is a multifactorial disease in which a complex interdependence of genetic, epigenetic and environmental factors interferes and plays an important role in its pathogenesis and progression.

References

1. Jaqueline Carvalho de Oliveira. Epigenética e doenças humanas. Semina: Ciëncias Biológicas e da Saúde **33**(1), 21–34 (2012)
2. Salozhin, S.V., Prokhorchuk, E.B., Georgiev, G.P.: Methylation of DNA-one of the major epigenetic markers. Biochemistry (Moscow) **70**(5), 525–532 (2005)
3. Camara, M.S., Martín Bujanda, M., Mendioroz Iriarte, M.: Epigenetic changes in headache. Neurología (English Edition) **36**(5), 369–376 (2021)
4. del Pilar Navarrete-Meneses, M., Pérez-Vera, P.: Alteraciones epigenéticas en leucemia linfoblástica aguda. Boletín médico del Hospital Infantil de México **74**(4), 243–264 (2017)
5. Díaz-Rivavelarde, A., Soledad, M., et al.: Avances sobre epigenética en cáncer (2016)
6. López Tricas, J.M.: Las posibilidades terapéuticas del arn de interferencia. Farmacia Hospitalaria **36**(3) (2012)
7. León, M.D.: Desarrollo de un sistema de detección para analizar mecanismos de silenciamiento génico (2018)

Author Index

510   Author Index

Printed in the United States
by Baker & Taylor Publisher Services

Printed in the United States
by Baker & Taylor Publisher Services